Business
A Changing World

First Canadian Edition

O.C. Ferrell
Colorado State University

Geoffrey Hirt
DePaul University

Rick Bates
University of Guelph

Elliott Currie
University of Guelph

**McGraw-Hill
Ryerson**

Toronto Montréal Boston Burr Ridge, IL Dubuque, IA Madison, WI New York
San Francisco St. Louis Bangkok Bogotá Caracas Kuala Lumpur Lisbon London
Madrid Mexico City Milan New Delhi Santiago Seoul Singapore Sydney Taipei

McGraw-Hill
Ryerson Limited
A Subsidiary of The **McGraw·Hill** Companies

Dedicated to:

The young ladies who always keep me charmed in no particular order:
Riannon, Kayleigh, Janessa, Rebecca, Emma, and Cara.   *E.J.C.*

To my parents for their years of support and encouragement.   *M.R.B.*

Business: A Changing World, First Canadian Edition

Copyright © 2003 by McGraw-Hill Ryerson Limited, a Subsidiary of The McGraw-Hill Companies, Inc. Copyright © 2000, 1996, 1993 by The McGraw-Hill Companies, Inc. All rights reserved. No part of this publication may be reproduced or transmitted in any form or by any means, or stored in a data base or retrieval system, without the prior written permission of McGraw-Hill Ryerson Limited, or in the case of photocopying or other reprographic copying, a licence from CANCOPY (the Canadian Copyright Licensing Agency), 6 Adelaide Street East, Suite 900, Toronto, Ontario, M5C 1H6

Statistics Canada information is used with the permission of the Minister of Industry, as Minister responsible for Statistics Canada. Information on the availability of the wide range of data from Statistics Canada can be obtained from Statistics Canada's Regional Offices, its World Wide Web site at http://www.stat.can.ca, and its toll-free access number 1-800-263-1136.

ISBN: 0-07-089837-5

1 2 3 4 5 6 7 8 9 10   TCP   0 9 8 7 6 5 4 3

Printed and bound in Canada

Care has been taken to trace ownership of copyright material contained in this text; however, the publisher will welcome any information that enables them to rectify any reference or credit for subsequent editions.

Vice President and Editorial Director: Pat Ferrier
Sponsoring Editor: Lenore Gray Spence
Managing Editor, Development: Kim Brewster
Director of Marketing: Jeff MacLean
Supervising Editor: Anne Macdonald
Copy Editor: Valerie Adams
Production Coordinator: Madeleine Harrington
Composition: Bookman Typesetting Co.
Cover Design: Dianna Little
Cover Image Credits: © Firefly Productions/Firstlight.ca
Photos and Permissions: Alison Derry, Permissions Plus
Printer: Transcontinental Printing

National Library of Canada Cataloguing in Publication Data

Main entry under title:
   Business: a changing world

1st Canadian ed.
Earlier eds. by O.C. Ferrell and Geoffrey A. Hirt.
Includes bibliographical references and indexes.

ISBN 0-07-089837-5

1. Business. 2. Management.   I. Ferrell, O.C.   II. Ferrell, O.C. Business.

HF1008.B88 2002   650   C2002-900833-6

Authors

O.C. FERRELL is Professor of Marketing at Colorado State University. He also has held faculty positions at the University of Memphis, University of Tampa, Texas A&M University, Illinois State University, and Southern Illinois University, as well as visiting positions at Queen's University (Ontario, Canada), University of Michigan (Ann Arbor), University of Wisconsin (Madison), and University of Hannover (Germany). He has served as a faculty member for the Masters Degree Program in Marketing at Thammasat University (Bangkok, Thailand). Dr. Ferrell received his B.A. and M.B.A. from Florida State University and his Ph.D. from Louisiana State University. His teaching and research interests include business ethics, corporate citizenship, and marketing.

Dr. Ferrell is widely recognized as a leading teacher and scholar in business. His articles have appeared in the *Journal of Marketing Research, Journal of Business Ethics, Journal of Marketing, Journal of Business Research, Journal of Macromarketing, Journal of the Academy of Marketing Science,* and others. His textbook entitled *Business Ethics: Ethical Decision Making and Cases* is the leading text in this field. He has also coauthored numerous textbooks for marketing, management, and other business courses, as well as a trade book on business ethics. He chaired the American Marketing Association (AMA) ethics committee that developed its current code of ethics. He was the vice-president of Marketing Education and president of the Academic Council for the AMA.

Dr. Ferrell's major focus is teaching and preparing learning material for students. He has traveled extensively to work with students and understands the needs of instructors of introductory business courses. He lives in Fort Collins, Colorado and enjoys skiing, golf, and international travel.

GEOFFREY A. HIRT is currently Professor of Finance at DePaul University and Director of Equity Research at Mesirow Financial. He received his Ph.D. in Finance from the University of Illinois at Champaign-Urbana, his MBA from Miami University of Ohio and his B.A. from Ohio-Wesleyan University. Geoff has directed the Chartered Financial Analysts Study program for the Investment Analysts Society of Chicago since 1987.

From 1987 to 1997 he was Chairman of the Finance Department at DePaul University and taught investments, corporate finance, and strategic planning. He developed and was director of DePaul's MBA in Hong Kong and has taught in Poland, Germany, Thailand, and Hong Kong.

Geoff has published several books. The sixth edition of *Fundamentals of Investment Management* was released in July 1998 and is published by Irwin/McGraw-Hill. Additionally, Geoff is well known for his book *Fundamentals of Financial Management* published by Irwin/McGraw-Hill. Now in its eighth edition, this book is used at over 600 colleges and universities worldwide, and it has been translated into Chinese, Japanese, and Spanish.

Geoff plays tennis and golf, is a music lover, and enjoys traveling with his wife, Linda.

ELLIOTT CURRIE is currently an Assistant Professor at the University of Guelph, where he teaches accounting, finance, human resource management, and business policy and strategy. His career achievements include working as an Outdoor Venture Instructor (with the Ministry of Corrections), as a commercial pilot and flying instructor, and as a corporate pilot and manager in the construction-aggregate industry. Prior to joining the academic world he also worked in finance with Petro-Canada, in marketing in the foundry industry, and as a corporate banker and controller in the insurance industry.

Professor Currie received a BA in Psychology from McMaster University and an MBA in finance (also from McMaster) and is a designated Certified Management Accountant. In 1992, Professor

Currie joined Wilfrid Laurier University where he taught business policy, management controls, organizational behaviour, small business management, and new venture creation. Elliott has been teaching at the University of Guelph since 1998 where he has published in the area of personal finance. Currently he is researching small business control systems and succession planning of small businesses.

Elliott hikes and canoes, and enjoys cooking and traveling with his wife Ann.

RICK BATES is currently an Associate Professor of accounting and finance in the Department of Agricultural Economics and Business at the University of Guelph. He received his BA in Economics from the U. of G. in 1971, an MBA from York University in 1978, and his CA designation in 1978.

From 1971 to 1979 Rick held a variety of positions with financial institutions including Household Finance Corporation, Imperial Life Assurance Company, and Sterling Trust (now Laurentian Bank). He completed his CA training with Peat, Marwick, Mitchel & Co in Toronto.

Professor Bates brought a broad background in accounting, taxation, finance, auditing, and management to his faculty position in 1980. Since then he has been actively involved in the design and delivery of undergraduate, graduate, and diploma courses in the areas of accounting, finance, and taxation.

Rick and his wife, Wanda, have two grown children, and reside in the Village of Hillsburgh, Ontario. In his spare time, Rick is a motorcycle enthusiast. He is also involved in the local community where he is currently vice-president of the Erin Agricultural Society and an active volunteer at the local Fall Fair.

Contents

v

Chapter 9
Production and Operations Management   208

Part Four
Creating the Human Resource Advantage   237

Chapter 10
Motivating the Work Force   238

Chapter 11
Managing Human Resources   262

Preface

With the success of the third edition of *Business: A Changing World* in the United States, we were excited with the opportunity to provide the Canadian edition of this award-winning text. The compact format helps instructors move away from rushing through the material, and allows them to cover everything in a single semester or quarter. Technology, specifically the Internet, makes it possible to expand the subject matter, content, and learning devices beyond the textbook—while, at the same time, helping students learn to compete in a world where businesses use virtual components.

After extensive research and suggestions from our reviewers, the 1st Canadian edition of *Business: A Changing World* reflects the exciting challenges presented by business in the twenty-first century. This text provides 16 chapters on topics that instructors view as essential for the highly competitive introduction to business market.

The **Ferrell Online Learning Centre (www.mcgrawhill.ca/college/ferrell)** provides the first introduction to a business teaching package that has a web site fully integrated with chapter content. This interactive web site for students and instructors provides a learning module for each chapter in the text. The content of the text and Online Learning Centre (OLC) focus on maintaining the currency and integration of important concepts. We have used the latest technology and business terms to make traditional concepts more practical and applicable to students' daily lives and work.

Each chapter has the following study aids online: a **Cybersummary, "Test Your Understanding"** quiz, **e-Learning Sessions**, and **Internet Exercises.** The online **Cybersummary** allows students to review the chapter and then link to key terms that they cannot understand. The **e-Learning Sessions** include multiple choice and true/false quizzes so that students can check their knowledge online. The **Internet Exercises** are extra exercises for the student that can be assigned or done independently. Each exercise directs the student to a web site and asks questions related to chapter concepts.

Six perspectives that are changing the world of business are emphasized throughout the complete teaching package—the globalization of business, quality, ethics and social responsibility, diversity, technology, and productivity. These current business challenges are integrated into the text and also appear in boxes in each chapter.

 Think Globally   Value Diversity

 Strive for Quality   Embrace Technology

 Consider Ethics & Social Responsibility   Enhance Productivity

All six parts have a **Cyberzone part-ending feature** that provide insights on how the Internet is changing the business arena. These features provide an up-to-date report while also linking to sites that focus on the Internet's use in different areas of business. Each Cyberzone can also be found at the Ferrell OLC in its entirety with links to more information on the web about what is discussed in the Cyberzone.

In the text, the use of real-world examples, boxed features, and new video cases (written only months before the book was printed) create excitement about business and stimulate students' thought processes, judgement, and communications skills. To assist in cognitive processes related to decision skills, the text provides a dilemma and a skill-building exercise in each chapter. We wanted this book to encourage students to think, communicate, and make their own decisions—invaluable critical skills that can always be used in the changing world of business.

Based on feedback from reviewers, **a complete chapter on the legal and regulatory environment is included.** We were told that this critical area of business is too important to be an appendix. Of course, legal and regulatory issues are also integrated throughout the text, but this chapter provides many real-world examples and will enable students to gain insights into the legal and regulatory issues that they may see in the business press. We found that instructors want students to understand appropriate professional conduct; therefore, we considered coverage of the legal and regulatory environment important to complement the business ethics and social responsibility chapter that follows this chapter.

Our mission was to develop a book that prepares students for today's rapidly changing business environment. We wanted to prepare them to understand how businesses use the Internet. It was important that they recognize how global competition, economic fluctuations in different parts of the world, and a push for more customer-focused and people-friendly organizations make business decision-making more challenging. By promoting a greater understanding of essential technological issues and instilling a higher sense of self-development, this new Canadian edition prepares students for a variety of opportunities and challenges. With that kind of preparation, we believe that any student will be ready to succeed—in business and beyond.

ORGANIZATION

Business: A Changing World is divided into six parts. Part One introduces the fundamentals of contemporary business and economics and discusses legal, regulatory, social responsibility, ethics, and global business concerns. Part Two deals with forms of business organization and small business and entrepreneurship. Part Three explores management principles, structuring the organization, teamwork, communication, and production and operations management. Part Four focuses on human relations and human resources management. Part Five covers customer-driven marketing. Part Six addresses financial management. In addition, the book includes appendices on preparing a business plan and a personal career plan.

Pedagogy

Business: A Changing World provides numerous features to facilitate student learning:

- **Maps** are provided immediately before Chapter One for student reference in their study of business and globalization. The maps we've supplied include: a map of Canada (with 2001 census statistics), a map of the world, and a map of the European Union.
- **Learning objectives** at the beginning of each chapter inform students about what should be achieved after reading and studying the chapter.
- A **chapter-opening vignette** sets the scene for issues discussed in each chapter.

- **Value Diversity, Consider Ethics and Social Responsibility, Think Globally, Enhance Productivity, Strive for Quality,** and **Embrace Technology** boxes highlight real, familiar companies or business issues to help students gain practical experience about business and focus on the issues of concern in business today.

- Because of the prevalence of small business in the Canadian economy, many small businesses are featured in boxes and examples within the text.

- A **Solve the Dilemma** box in each chapter gives students an opportunity to think creatively in applying chapter concepts to hypothetical situations that could occur in the real world.

- An **Explore Your Career Options** box in each chapter provides information about career planning and business career opportunities.

- End-of-chapter learning devices include a **summary** that repeats chapter learning objectives, a list of **key terms, Check Your Progress** questions to test and reinforce understanding, and **Get Involved** exercises to challenge students to apply and expand on concepts learned in the chapter.

- A comprehensive, challenging **CBC video case** at the end of each chapter tests students' judgement and decision-making skills.

- A **Build Your Skills** exercise at the end of each chapter provides an opportunity to build critical skills through a variety of self-tests and other exercises.

- Application-oriented **appendices** at the end of the book focus on preparing a business plan and a career plan.

- An end-of-book **glossary** is included featuring all of the margin terms and concepts boldfaced in the text.

- **Name, subject, and URL indexes** at the end of the book aid in finding topics, key companies, individuals, and web sites featured throughout the book.

- A full and robust **Online Learning Centre** at *www.mcgrawhill.ca/college/ferrell.*

Support Materials for the Student

- **Study Guide.** Each chapter of the *Study Guide* includes a chapter summary; learning objectives; and true/false, multiple-choice, matching, and skill-building questions.

- **Online Learning Centre.** A comprehensive student Web site at *www.mcgrawhill.ca/college/ferrell* contains the following:

  1. "Cyberzones" at the end of each of the six parts of the text provide a comprehensive overview of how the Internet is being used in business today. Part One introduces the Internet and examines its five basic characteristics. Part Two examines the wealth of information available to small business owners. Part Three focuses on management's use of the Internet, while Part Four specifically addresses Internet use in human resource management. Part Five covers e-commerce, and Part Six examines Internet use in the areas of accounting and finance.

  2. "Cybersummary" provides a short chapter summary in which key terms are hyperlinks that can be viewed when students are not sure of a

definition. This feature permits students to quickly review all key terms in an overview that presents key term integration.

3. "e-Learning Sessions" include true/false and multiple-choice questions from each chapter.

4. "Internet Exercises" provide an opportunity to reinforce chapter concepts by guiding students through specific Web sites that ask them to assess information on the site and answer questions that apply chapter concepts.

Support Materials for the Instructor

The following supplements are available on the Instructor's CD-ROM, and can also be downloaded from the Online Learning Centre.

- **Instructor CD-ROM**. This CD-ROM collects all of the text's visually oriented supplement items in one presentation management system. By combining features of the Instructor's Manual, video notes, PowerPoint slides, Computerized Test Bank, and lecture material into an electronic format, this CD offers a comprehensive and convenient tool that allows you to customize your lectures and presentations.

- **Instructor's Manual**. The *Instructor's Manual* includes: a list of chapter learning objectives; key terms and their definitions; a lecture outline and notes; a supplemental lecture; a short discussion of a controversial issue; answers to the "Check Your Progress" questions; questions pertaining to the "Solve the Dilemma" and "Explore Your Career Options" boxes; additional discussion questions and exercises; a chapter quiz; teaching suggestions; and answers to the end-of-chapter case and exercise.

- **Computerized Test Bank**. Test your class with this easy-to-use Brownstone *Computerized Test Bank* software which contains true/false, multiple-choice, and essay questions. Questions are linked to chapter learning objectives so that instructors can tailor exams to their classes' needs. This enhanced-feature test generator allows you to add and edit questions, save and reload multiple tests, select questions based on type, difficulty or keyword, and more.

- **PowerPoint Presentations**. Over 300 electronic slides keyed to the text are available. These slides can be modified with PowerPoint.

- **CBC Videos**. A complete set of CBC videos is available. Video cases for the student can be found in the text. And for instructors there is a video guide in the Instructor's Manual that is also downloadable from the Online Learning Centre.

- **"PageOut" - create your own course Web site**. McGraw-Hill's new web site development tool allows you to create a customized web site for your course. By utilizing material located in the text, you can include features such as: Instructor information, Interactive Course Syllabus, Web Links, Discussion Area, Assignments/Quizzing, Gradebook, and Student web pages. Ask your local representative for a quick consultation.

- **WebCT/BlackBoard**. This textbook is available in two of the most popular course-delivery platforms—WebCT and BlackBoard—for more user-friendliness and enhanced features.

ACKNOWLEDGEMENTS

Many people have assisted us with their helpful comments, recommendations, and support throughout this first Canadian edition. We extend special appreciation to the following instructors who provided valuable feedback during the writing process:

Barbara Smith
Niagara College

Walter Isenor
Acadia University

Ron Shay
Kwantlen University College

Chuck Lamantia
Centennial College

Keith Hebblewhite
Humber College

June Nagy
Seneca College

Valerie Miceli
Seneca College

Michelle Dejak
Seneca College

Alex Bouthbee
Seneca College

Tom Lawrence
University of Victoria

Diane Gauvin
McGill University

Laurel Donaldson
Douglas College

Steve Jonas
Seneca College

Jenny Yang
Seneca College

Patricia Draves
Seneca College

We would be remiss if we did not include our excellent task masters and guides at McGraw-Hill Ryerson: Lenore Gray Spence, Sponsoring Editor; Anne Macdonald, Supervising Editor; Valerie Adams, Copy Editor; Alison Derry, Photo and Permissions Editor, and especially;

Kim Brewster, Managing Editor, Development, who was always available day or night, weekday or weekends whenever we needed assistance and encouragement.

Thanks also to Joy Armitage Taylor, Senior *i*-Learning Sales Specialist, who is very effective at selling both books and authors.

Map of Canada

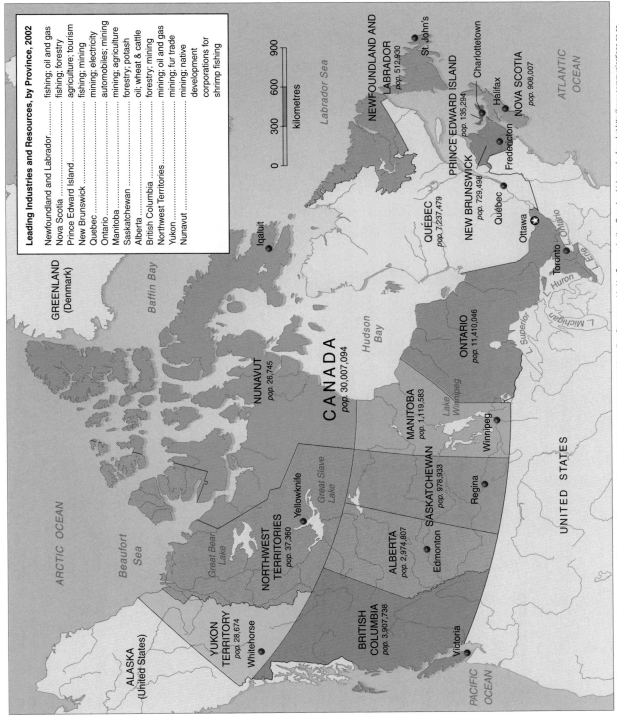

Leading Industries and Resources, by Province, 2002

Newfoundland and Labrador	fishing; oil and gas
Nova Scotia	fishing; forestry
Prince Edward Island	agriculture; tourism
New Brunswick	fishing; mining
Quebec	mining; electricity
Ontario	automobiles; mining
Manitoba	mining; agriculture
Saskatchewan	forestry; potash
Alberta	oil; wheat & cattle
British Columbia	forestry; mining
Northwest Territories	mining; oil and gas
Yukon	mining; fur trade
Nunavut	mining; native development corporations for shrimp fishing

ALASKA (United States)

YUKON TERRITORY
pop. 28,674
Whitehorse

BRITISH COLUMBIA
pop. 3,907,738
Victoria

NORTHWEST TERRITORIES
pop. 37,360
Yellowknife

ALBERTA
pop. 2,974,807
Edmonton

SASKATCHEWAN
pop. 978,933
Regina

MANITOBA
pop. 1,119,583
Winnipeg

NUNAVUT
pop. 26,745
Iqaluit

GREENLAND (Denmark)

CANADA
pop. 30,007,094

Hudson Bay

ONTARIO
pop. 11,410,046

QUÉBEC
pop. 7,237,479

NEWFOUNDLAND AND LABRADOR
pop. 512,930
St. John's

PRINCE EDWARD ISLAND
pop. 135,294
Charlottetown

NOVA SCOTIA
pop. 908,007
Halifax

NEW BRUNSWICK
pop. 729,498
Fredericton
Québec

Ottawa
Toronto

UNITED STATES

ARCTIC OCEAN
Beaufort Sea
Great Bear Lake
Great Slave Lake
Lake Winnipeg
Baffin Bay
Labrador Sea
ATLANTIC OCEAN
PACIFIC OCEAN
L. Superior
L. Michigan
L. Huron
L. Erie
L. Ontario

kilometres
0   300   600   900

Source: Population data from Statistics Canada, 2001 Census Release 1, March 12, 2002. Information compiled from Fact Sheets provided by Communication Canada which can be found at http://www.communications.gc.ca.

Map of the World

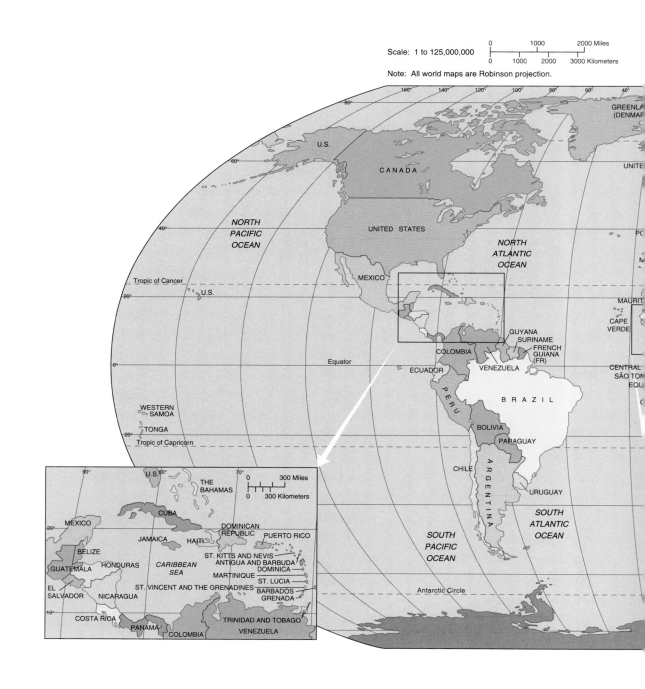

Scale: 1 to 125,000,000

0   1000   2000 Miles
0   1000   2000   3000 Kilometers

Note: All world maps are Robinson projection.

Map of the European Union

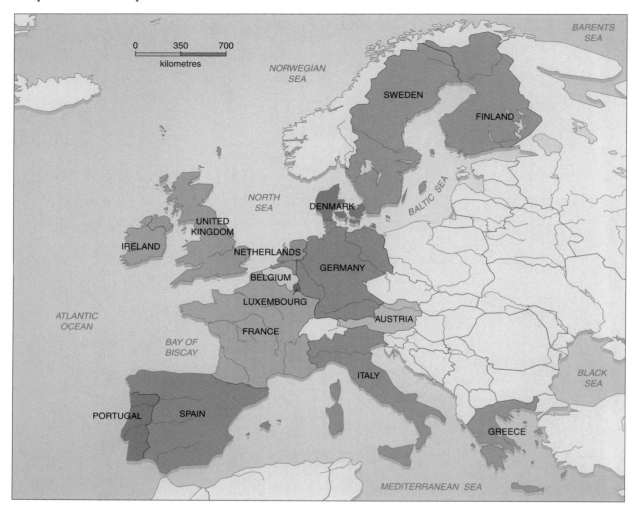

McGraw-Hill Ryerson
Online Learning Centre

McGraw-Hill Ryerson offers you an online resource that combines the best content with the flexibility and power of the Internet. Organized by chapter, the FERRELL Online Learning Centre (OLC) offers the following features to enhance your learning and understanding of Business:

- Online Quizzes
- CBC Video Streaming
- E-Learning Sessions and Web Links
- Internet Essay Questions
- Cyber Summary

By connecting to the "real world" through the OLC, you will enjoy a dynamic and rich source of current information that will help you get more from your course and improve your chances for success, both in this course and in the future.

For the Instructor

Downloadable Supplements

All key supplements are available, password-protected for instant access!

PageOut   PageOut
Create a custom course Website with PageOut, free with every McGraw-Hill Ryerson textbook.

Create your own course Web page for free, quickly and easily. Your professionally designed Web site links directly to OLC material, allows you to post a class syllabus, offers an online gradebook, and much more! Visit www.pageout.net

Online CBC Cases and Video Streaming   CBC

New to this edition, view the CBC segments online as chosen by the author to illustrate key concepts and demonstrate how these concepts work in the world of business. The video notes and discussion questions are also available for downloading.

Online Resources

McGraw-Hill Ryerson offers various online resource tools such as CBC video streaming and web links to help you get the latest information for immediate use in class.

For the Student

Online Quizzes

Do you understand the material? You'll know after taking an Online Quiz! Try the Multiple Choice questions to help you review the material you've learned in each chapter. They're auto-graded with feedback and the option to send results directly to faculty.

CBC Video Streaming   CBC

View selected CBC segments discussed in the text. Great for pre-class preparation and post-class review.

E-Learning Sessions

A unique integrated multimedia online study guide helps you prepare for tests with chapter summary materials, PowerPoint® Presentations, figures, tables and more.

Internet Essay Questions and Web Links

Go online to learn how companies use the Internet in their day-to-day activities. Answer theoretical and analytical questions based on current organization Web sites and strategies. In addition, all company Web sites are linked from the text.

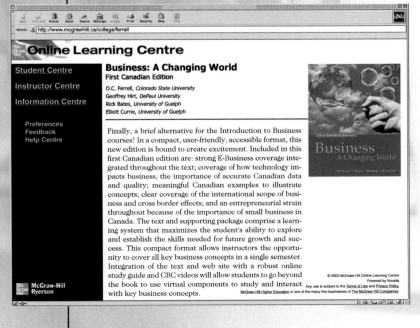

Your Internet companion to the most exciting educational tools on the Web!

The Online Learning Centre can be found at:

www.mcgrawhill.ca/college/ferrell

Part One

Business in a Changing World

Chapter 1

The Dynamics of Business and Economics

Chapter Outline

Objectives

After reading this chapter, you will be able to:

- Define basic concepts such as business, product, and profit, and explain why studying business is important.
- Identify the main participants and activities of business.
- Define economics and compare the four types of economic systems.
- Describe the role of supply, demand, and competition in a free-enterprise system.
- Specify why and how the health of the economy is measured.
- Trace the evolution of the Canadian economy and discuss the role of the entrepreneur in the economy.
- Evaluate a small-business owner's situation and propose a course of action.

The Fat Guy BBQ—Small Business Success Through the SEED Loan Fund

Canada is a nation of small businesses. In recent years the majority of employment growth has been generated by the 99 percent of Canadian businesses having fewer than five employees. The success of a new small business is a majority contributor to economic growth, but it is the effect on the life of the individual entrepreneur that can be most important.

Gary Zuber of Guelph, Ontario, is just such a success story. For almost a decade Gary was unable to retain steady employment because of his health. During those years he contributed to the community by volunteering his time from one to three days a month as the operator of a sausage BBQ cart for a local charity. In 1999, the charity decided to no longer operate this fundraiser. Gary, with financing from the SEED Loan Fund, purchased the cart and began his full-time business. Two years later, Gary, who addresses most of his customers by name and engages all in friendly conversation, is a successful entrepreneur.

You are unlikely to read of the success of such small, micro-businesses in the financial press and he has not become a millionaire. In two years Gary's life has changed dramatically as a result of his business. Gary's lifestyle has greatly improved, and he has purchased his first car and one for his son. Gary is now looking for a second location, which of course will require the hiring of his first full-time employee, providing more of the employment growth the economy needs.

The SEED Loan Fund

Many successful businesses in the Waterloo region and Wellington County in Ontario have grown from ideas germinated with the assistance of the SEED Loan Fund, an independent community agency formed by a group of concerned residents to provide start-up financing for micro-businesses.

**Photo Sources: (top) Rick Bates;
(bottom) © Alan Levenson**

The candidates are not simply granted funding on request. Funding is the culmination of a four-step process:

1. Applicants must complete an education program on starting and managing a business. The founding member of the fund, Lutherwood-CODA, or the local college or university presents the training program.
2. Candidates must write a formal business plan incorporating primary market research. To ensure commitment and understanding, the research must be carried out by the client rather than purchased.
3. Community members, business managers, professors, and previous candidates review the business plan and interview the candidate. The goal is to assess the viability of the business proposal and the commitment and ability of the candidate.
4. Only after passing the interview process does the candidate reach the fourth level, access to funding in the form of a loan guarantee.

This process has provided initial financing to over 50 businesses between 1997 and 2001, with total funding of $700,000. These dedicated people are justly proud of the almost 80 percent success rate of the new businesses started with the fund's assistance.

The fund began operations with initial capital of $380,000 provided by local business, private foundations, and individuals. Fund-raising efforts in 2001 have the objective of increasing the loan fund to $1,500,000.

Why do the local credit unions, MacNeil Products, Pricewaterhouse-Coopers, and the other supporters make this investment? The new businesses started help create a vital and successful community in which to operate and live.

INTRODUCTION

SEED Loan Fund
www.seedloanfund.org

The business and management knowledge gained by SEED Loan Fund clients serves them well in the operation of their businesses. This is one of the critical factors in allowing the high success rate of Fund clients, almost double the average for new small businesses.

We begin our study of business by examining the fundamentals of business and economics in this chapter. First, we introduce the nature of business, including its goals, activities, and participants. Next, we describe the basics of economics and apply them to the Canadian economy. Finally, we establish a framework for studying business in this text.

business

individuals or organizations who try to earn a profit by providing products that satisfy people's needs

THE NATURE OF BUSINESS

The SEED Loan Fund is not itself a **business** since its fundamental purpose is not the earning of profits. The SEED Loan Fund is incorporated under the Ontario Corporations Act as a not-for-profit organization.

The purpose of the corporation is to use its capital base to provide financing and mentoring for small entrepreneurial business start-ups. Thus, like a business, the Fund provides a **product**, in this case an intangible product or service.

In order to achieve this goal, not-for-profit organizations have a strong need to follow good business practices just as for-profit businesses do.

Most people associate the word *product* with tangible goods—an automobile, computer, loaf of bread, coat, or some other tangible item. However, a product can also be a service, which results when people or machines provide or process something of value to customers. Dry cleaning, photo processing, a checkup by a doctor, a performance by a movie star or basketball player—these are examples of services. A product can also be an idea. Consultants and lawyers, for example, generate ideas for solving problems.

The Goal of Business

The primary goal of all businesses is to earn a **profit,** the difference between what it costs to make and sell a product and what a customer pays for it. If a company spends $2.00 to manufacture, finance, promote, and distribute a product that it sells for $2.75, the business earns a profit of 75 cents on each product sold. Businesses have the right to keep and use their profits as they choose—within legal limits—because profit is the reward for the risks they take in providing products. Not all organizations are businesses. **Nonprofit organizations,** such as Greenpeace, Special Olympics, SEED Loan Fund, and other charities and social causes, do not have the fundamental purpose of earning profits, although they may provide goods or services.

To earn a profit, a person or organization needs management skills to plan, organize, and control the activities of the business and to find and develop employees so that it can make products consumers will buy. A business also needs marketing expertise to learn what products consumers need and want and to develop, manufacture, price, promote, and distribute those products. Additionally, a business needs financial resources and skills to fund, maintain, and expand its operations. Other challenges for businesspeople include abiding by laws and government regulations, acting in a socially responsible manner, and adapting to economic, technological, and social changes. Even nonprofit organizations engage in management, marketing, and finance activities to help reach their goals.

The goal of a business is not just to earn a profit. To be successful, businesses need to be socially responsible and ethical in dealing with customers, employees, investors, the community, and society. Many businesses, for example, are concerned about how the production and distribution of their products impact the environment. Johnson & Johnson is committed to reducing the packaging material for its products. It exceeded its goal of 10 percent cumulative reduction in packaging material use worldwide two years earlier than planned. A higher goal of a 25 percent cumulative reduction by 2000 was then set. Johnson & Johnson reported a 27 percent reduction in their 2000 Annual Report.[1] Other businesses are concerned about the quality of life in the communities in which they operate. IBM and Kodak, for example, have contributed funds and equipment to local schools to help educate the next generation. Still other businesses are concerned with social responsibility in times of natural disasters.

For example, the Canadian Tire Corporation through its Foundation for Families, together with Canadian Tire employees, supports several community initiatives across Canada. During the 1999 holiday season, $5 from the sale of each artificial tree and an additional $5 from tree purchases made with a Canadian Tire credit card raised $700,000 to help families across Canada.

product
a good or service with tangible and intangible characteristics that provide satisfaction and benefits

profit
the excess of revenues (the proceeds from the sale of goods and services) over expenses (the costs incurred to earn the revenues) for a period

nonprofit organizations
organizations that may provide goods or services but do not have the fundamental purpose of earning profits

Canadian Tire Foundation for Families
www2.canadiantire.ca/ CTenglish/foundation. html

Figure 1.1

*Overview of the
Business World*

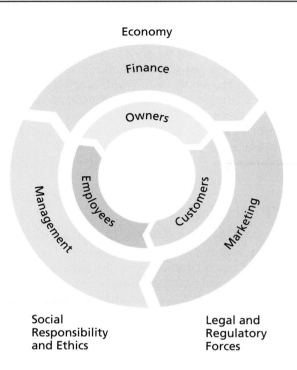

Economy

Finance

Owners

Management

Employees

Customers

Marketing

Social
Responsibility
and Ethics

Legal and
Regulatory
Forces

The Foundation also responded in 1998 with 65 emergency trailer shipments during the Quebec ice storm and by transporting via Canadian Tire trailers over 40,000 kilograms of clothing, sleeping bags, water, and nonperishable food items to affected areas in the Winnipeg flood.[2]

The People and Activities of Business

Figure 1.1 shows the people and activities involved in business. At the centre of the figure are owners, employees, and customers; the outer circle includes the primary business activities—management, marketing, and finance. Owners have to put up resources—money or credit—to start a business. Employees are responsible for the work that goes on within a business. Owners can manage the business themselves or hire employees to accomplish this task. The president of General Motors, for example, does not own GM but is an employee who is responsible for managing all the other employees in a way that earns a profit for investors, who are the real owners. Finally, and most importantly, a business's major role is to satisfy the customers who buy its goods or services. Note also that people and forces beyond an organization's control—such as government and legal forces, the economy, competition, and ethical and social concerns—all have an impact on the daily operations of businesses. You will learn more about these participants in business activities throughout this book. Next, we will examine the major activities of business.

Management. Notice that in Figure 1.1 management and employees are in the same segment of the circle. This is because management involves coordinating employees' actions to achieve the firm's goals, organizing people to work efficiently, and motivating them to achieve the business's goals. A survey of almost 1,300 workers and supervisors showed that while money is a motivator for some, it is not the most important aspect of staying with a company. In fact, 56 percent of these employees did not include money among the top three reasons for leaving a position. The most important reasons to remain with a firm, according to the survey results, were advancement opportunities, the feeling of being valued by the employer, and a conflict-free relationship with supervisors.[3] At Procter & Gamble, for example, employees are motivated through mentoring, networking, and flexible-scheduling programs that have resulted in higher productivity and lower turnover.[4] Management is also concerned with acquiring, developing, and using resources (including people) effectively and efficiently. Production and manufacturing is another element of management. Management at Johnson & Johnson reconfigured its worldwide network of manufacturing and operating facilities in order to gain efficiencies, increase productivity, and invest in new opportunities. The number of manufacturing facilities was reduced from 158 to 122—a change expected to result in annual savings of US$250–300 million.[5] In essence, managers plan, organize, staff, and control the tasks required to carry out the work of the company. We will take a closer look at management activities in Parts Three and Four of this text.

To illustrate the importance of management, consider any small local business such as a hardware store or lumber yard. Until recently, such businesses faced competition only within their own communities. The entrance into the Canadian market of the US-based Home Depot and now the Canadian-owned Building Box is a major market change. Many of the local business customers are willing to travel to obtain lower prices and a wider selection of products offered by these "big box" stores.

If the small local businesses, usually owner managed, are to survive, they must adapt to these new competitive threats. They may, for example, unite to form buying groups such as Timbr-mart in an effort to take advantage of volume discounts to lower their costs and thus their prices. They may also find ways to succeed by offering better service such as quicker more conveniently scheduled deliveries.

The Building Box
www.thebuildingbox.com

Marketing. Marketing and consumers are in the same segment of Figure 1.1 because the focus of all marketing activities is satisfying customers. Marketing includes all the activities designed to provide goods and services that satisfy consumers' needs and wants. Marketers gather information and conduct research to determine what customers want. Saturn, for example, discovered that current owners who had outgrown their small Saturns were buying Toyotas and Hondas because they offer larger models. Consequently, Saturn introduced the LS, a midsize car, and plans to introduce a sport utility vehicle to appeal to these consumers. Using information gathered from marketing research, marketers plan and develop products and make decisions about how much to charge for their products and where to make them available. NCR, the computer and cash-register maker, developed Micro Web, a microwave oven that also functions as a PC. It looks like a microwave but comes with a liquid-crystal screen built into the door. While microwaving your dinner, you can also do your banking, search for a recipe on the Internet, make an online purchase, send e-mail, or even watch TV. Micro Web accepts verbal commands and comes with a conventional keyboard and modem. The projected price is US$700.[6] Marketers use promotion—advertising, personal selling, sales promotion (coupons, games, sweepstakes, movie tie-ins), and publicity—to communicate the benefits and advantages of their products to consumers and increase sales. For example, Burger King's promotional tie-ins with children's movies over the past few years have significantly boosted sales and increased store traffic in its restaurants to record levels. The tie-in with Disney's *Toy Story* film resulted in the distribution of 45 million toys and 15 million puppets over a four and one-half week period.[7] In 2001, Burger King is hoping for similar success with its use of *The Lord of the Rings* in its advertising. We will examine marketing activities in Part Five of this text.

Finance. Owners and finance are in the same part of Figure 1.1 because, although management and marketing have to deal with financial considerations, it is the primary responsibility of the owners to provide financial resources for the operation of the business. Moreover, the owners have the most to lose if the business fails to make a profit. Finance refers to all activities concerned with obtaining money and using it effectively. Owners sometimes have to borrow money to get started or attract additional owners who become partners or shareholders. For instance, the founders of California Pizza Kitchen began their chain with US$500,000 in capital and then raised an additional US$6.5 million to finance the opening of 25 stores. Then, PepsiCo paid US$100 million for a 67 percent stake in the chain and spent US$100 million more to expand the business.[8] Owners of small businesses in particular often rely on bank loans for funding. Part Six of this text discusses financial management.

Why Study Business?

Business is important because it provides both employment for most people and the vast majority of products consumers need to survive and enjoy life. In addition, most business activities and skills occur in nonprofit organizations as well. Consequently, studying business will help you prepare for your future career and become a better-informed consumer. Learning about business also helps you become a well-informed member of society. Most of our social, political, and economic developments are closely linked to business. Understanding how our free-enterprise economic system allocates resources and provides incentives for industry and work is important to everyone.

THE ECONOMIC FOUNDATIONS OF BUSINESS

To continue our introduction to business, it is useful to explore the economic environment in which business is conducted. In this section, we examine economic systems, the free-enterprise system, the concepts of supply and demand, and the role of competition. These concepts play important roles in determining how businesses operate in a particular society.

Economics is the study of how resources are distributed for the production of goods and services within a social system. You are already familiar with the types of resources available. Land, forests, minerals, water, and other things that are not made by people are **natural resources. Human resources,** or labour, refers to the physical and mental abilities that people use to produce goods and services. **Financial resources,** or capital, are the funds used to acquire the natural and human resources needed to provide products. Because natural, human, and financial resources are used to produce goods and services, they are sometimes called *factors of production.*

Economic Systems

An **economic system** describes how a particular society distributes its resources to produce goods and services. A central issue of economics is how to fulfill an unlimited demand for goods and services in a world with a limited supply of resources. Different economic systems attempt to resolve this central issue in numerous ways, as we shall see.

economics
the study of how resources are distributed for the production of goods and services within a social system

natural resources
land, forests, minerals, water, and other things that are not made by people

human resources
the physical and mental abilities that people use to produce goods and services; also called labour

financial resources
the funds used to acquire the natural and human resources needed to provide products; also called capital

economic system
a description of how a particular society distributes its resources to produce goods and services

Although economic systems handle the distribution of resources in different ways, all economic systems must address three important issues:

1. What goods and services, and how much of each, will satisfy consumers' needs?
2. How will goods and services be produced, who will produce them, and with what resources will they be produced?
3. How are the goods and services to be distributed to consumers?

Communism, socialism, and capitalism, the basic economic systems found in the world today (Table 1.1), have fundamental differences in the way they address these issues.

Communism. Karl Marx (1818–1883) first described **communism** as a society in which the people, without regard to class, own all the nation's resources. In his ideal political-economic system, everyone contributes according to ability and receives benefits according to need. In a communist economy, the people (through the government) own and operate all businesses and factors of production. Central government planning determines what goods and services satisfy citizens' needs, how the goods and services are produced, and how they are distributed. However, no true communist economy exists today that satisfies Marx's ideal.

communism
first described by Karl Marx as a society in which the people, without regard to class, own all the nation's resources

Table 1.1 *Comparison of Communism, Socialism, and Capitalism*

	Communism	**Socialism**	**Capitalism**
Business ownership	Most businesses are owned and operated by the government.	The government owns and operates major industries; individuals own small businesses.	Individuals own and operate all businesses.
Competition	None. The government owns and operates everything.	Restricted in major industries; encouraged in small business.	Encouraged by market forces and government regulations.
Profits	Excess income goes to the government.	Profits earned by small businesses may be reinvested in the business; profits from government-owned industries go to the government.	Individuals are free to keep profits and use them as they wish.
Product availability and price	Consumers have a limited choice of goods and services; prices are usually high.	Consumers have some choice of goods and services; prices are determined by supply and demand.	Consumers have a wide choice of goods and services; prices are determined by supply and demand.
Employment options	Little choice in choosing a career; most people work for government-owned industries or farms.	Some choice of careers; many people work in government jobs.	Unlimited choice of careers.

On paper, communism appears to be efficient and equitable, producing less of a gap between rich and poor. In practice, however, communist economies have been marked by low standards of living, critical shortages of consumer goods, high prices, and little freedom. In recent years, the Commonwealth of Independent States (previously known as the Soviet Union), Poland, Hungary, and other Eastern European nations have turned away from communism and toward economic systems governed by supply and demand rather than by central planning. However, their experiments with alternative economic systems have been fraught with difficulty and hardship. China, North Korea, and Cuba continue to apply communist principles to their economies, but these countries are also enduring economic and political change. Consequently, communism is declining and its future as an economic system is uncertain.

socialism

an economic system in which the government owns and operates basic industries but individuals own most businesses

Socialism. Closely related to communism is **socialism,** an economic system in which the government owns and operates basic industries—postal service, telephone, utilities, transportation, health care, banking, and some manufacturing—but individuals own most businesses. Central planning determines what basic goods and services are produced, how they are produced, and how they are distributed. Individuals and small businesses provide other goods and services based on consumer demand and the availability of resources. As with communism, citizens are dependent on the government for many goods and services.

Most socialist nations, such as Sweden, India, France, and Israel, are democratic and recognize basic individual freedoms. Citizens can vote for political offices, but central government planners usually make decisions about what is best for the nation. People are free to go into the occupation of their choice, but they often work in government-operated organizations. Socialists believe their system permits a higher standard of living than other economic systems, but the difference often applies to the nation as a whole rather than to its individual citizens. Socialist economies profess egalitarianism—equal distribution of income and social services. They believe their economies are more stable than those of other nations. Although this may be true, taxes and unemployment are generally higher in socialist countries. Perhaps as a result, many socialist countries are also experiencing economic turmoil.

capitalism, or free enterprise

an economic system in which individuals own and operate the majority of businesses that provide goods and services

free-market system

pure capitalism, in which all economic decisions are made without government intervention

Capitalism. **Capitalism,** or **free enterprise,** is an economic system in which individuals own and operate the majority of businesses that provide goods and services. Competition, supply, and demand determine which goods and services are produced, how they are produced, and how they are distributed. Canada, the United States, Japan, and Australia are examples of economic systems based on capitalism.

There are two forms of capitalism: pure capitalism and modified capitalism. In pure capitalism, also called a **free-market system,** all economic decisions are made without government intervention. This economic system was first described by Adam Smith in *The Wealth of Nations* (1776). Smith, often called the father of capitalism, believed that the "invisible hand of competition" best regulates the economy. He argued that competition should determine what goods and services people need. Smith's system is also called *laissez-faire* ("to leave alone") *capitalism* because the government does not interfere in business.

Modified capitalism differs from pure capitalism in that the government intervenes and regulates business to some extent. One of the ways in which the United States and Canadian governments regulate business is through laws. The Workplace Hazardous Materials Information System (WHMIS) is the legislation covering hazardous materials used in Canadian workplaces. The legislation is the mandate of

Health Canada and was implemented by the federal, provincial, and territorial governments, effective October 31, 1988. This requires the labelling of potentially harmful household products and illustrates the importance of the government's role in the economy.

Mixed Economies. No country practices a pure form of communism, socialism, or capitalism, although most tend to favour one system over the others. Most nations operate as **mixed economies,** which have elements from more than one economic system. In socialist Sweden, most businesses are owned and operated by private individuals. In capitalist United States, the federal government owns and operates the postal service and the Tennessee Valley Authority, an electric utility.

mixed economies
economies made up of elements from more than one economic system

The US system is more capitalistic than Canada's, where the federal and provincial governments are more involved in the economy. Our federal government lists 42 parent Crown corporations. Each of these may have numerous subsidiaries exerting influence and carrying out government policy in all sectors of the economy. Examples include the Farm Credit Corporation in the agriculture and agri-food area to Via Rail Canada Inc. in the transportation sector.[9]

Provincial governments are similarly involved in our mixed economy, although some, notably Ontario and Alberta are moving towards privatization in many areas. In 1998 Ontario passed the Energy Competition Act to deregulate the electricity industry. The intent of the deregulation is to increase competition in the marketplace, with the hoped-for result being improved service and lower costs for consumers.

Under the Act, Ontario Hydro became two separate companies: Ontario Power Generation Company and Ontario Hydro Services Company. The reorganization continued with the May 1, 2000, launch of Hydro One, which through its subsidiaries services the retail residential electricity market. These corporations are still owned by the Province of Ontario. The move to a competitive market has seen the leasing of the Bruce nuclear generation facility to Bruce Power. The major shareholder of Bruce Power, British Energy, reported a $90 million operating profit on the facility for the six months ended September 30, 2001.

Ontario Power Generation Company has been ordered by the province to reduce to 35 percent its current 80 percent share of the electricity market in anticipation of opening the market to competition in May 2002. In once-communist Russia, Hungary, Poland, and other Eastern European nations, capitalist ideas have been implemented, including private ownership of businesses.

The Free-Enterprise System

Many economies—including those of Canada, the United States, and Japan—are based on free enterprise, and many communist and socialist countries, such as China and Russia, are applying more principles of free enterprise to their own economic systems. Free enterprise provides an opportunity for a business to succeed or fail on the basis of market demand. In a free-enterprise system, companies that can efficiently manufacture and sell products that consumers desire will probably succeed. Inefficient businesses and those that sell products that do not offer needed benefits will likely fail as consumers take their business to firms that have more competitive products.

A number of basic individual and business rights must exist for free enterprise to work. These rights are the goals of many countries that have recently embraced free enterprise.

demand

the number of goods and services that consumers are willing to buy at different prices at a specific time

supply

the number of products —goods and services— that businesses are willing to sell at different prices at a specific time

equilibrium price

the price at which the number of products that businesses are willing to supply equals the amount of products that consumers are willing to buy at a specific point in time

1. Individuals must have the right to own property and to pass this property on to their heirs. This right motivates people to work hard and save to buy property.

2. Individuals and businesses must have the right to earn profits and to use the profits as they wish, within the constraints of their society's laws and values.

3. Individuals and businesses must have the right to make decisions that determine the way the business operates. Although there is government regulation, the philosophy in countries like Canada, the United States, and Australia is to permit maximum freedom within a set of rules of fairness.

4. Individuals must have the right to choose what career to pursue, where to live, what goods and services to purchase, and more. Businesses must have the right to choose where to locate, what goods and services to produce, what resources to use in the production process, and so on.

Without these rights, businesses cannot function effectively because they are not motivated to succeed. Thus, these rights make possible the open exchange of goods and services.

The Forces of Supply and Demand

In Canada and in other free-enterprise systems, the distribution of resources and products is determined by supply and demand. **Demand** is the number of goods and services that consumers are willing to buy at different prices at a specific time. From your own experience, you probably recognize that consumers are usually willing to buy more of an item as its price falls because they want to save money. Consider soft drinks, for example. Consumers may be willing to buy six cans at $0.70 each, four at $1.00 each, but only two at $1.30 each. The relationship between the price and the amount of soda consumers are willing to buy can be shown graphically, with a *demand curve* (see Figure 1.2).

Supply is the number of products that businesses are willing to sell at different prices at a specific time. In general, because the potential for profits is higher, businesses are willing to supply more of a good or service at higher prices. For example, a company that sells soft drinks may be willing to sell six cans at $1.30 each, four cans at $1.00 each, but just two cans at $0.70 each. The relationship between the price of soft drinks and the quantity the company is willing to supply can be shown graphically with a *supply curve* (see Figure 1.2).

In Figure 1.2, the supply and demand curves intersect at the point where supply and demand are equal. The price at which the number of products that businesses are willing to supply equals the amount of products that consumers are willing to buy at a specific point in time is the **equilibrium price.** In our soft drink example, the company is willing to supply four cans at $1.00 each, and consumers are willing to buy four cans

Severe weather that reduces crop output may affect supply.

© 1999 PhotoDisc, Inc.

Shelly Acres, whose grandmother gave her a family recipe for making pies, loved to cook so she decided to start a business she called Mrs. Acres Homemade Pies. The company produces specialty pies and sells them in local supermarkets and select family restaurants. In each of the first six months, Shelly and three part-time employees sold 2,000 pies for $4.50 each, netting $1.50 profit per pie. The pies were quite successful and Shelly could not keep up with demand. The company's success results from a quality product and productive employees who are motivated by incentives and who enjoy being part of a successful new business.

To meet demand, Shelly expanded operations, borrowing money and increasing staff to four full-time employees. Production and sales increased to 8,000 pies per month, and profits

soared to $12,000 per month. However, demand for Mrs. Acres Homemade Pies continues to accelerate beyond what Shelly can supply. She has several options: (1) maintain current production levels and raise prices; (2) expand the facility and staff while maintaining the current price; or (3) contract the production of the pies to a national restaurant chain, giving Shelly a percentage of profits with minimal involvement.

1. Explain and demonstrate the relationship between supply and demand for Mrs. Acres Homemade Pies.
2. What challenges does Shelly face as she considers the three options?
3. What would you do in Shelly's position?

Solve the Dilemma

Mrs. Acres Homemade Pies

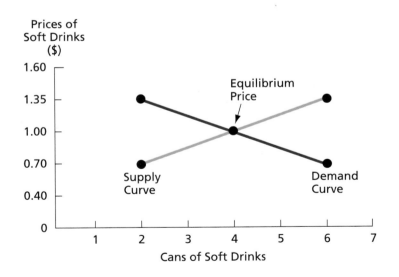

Figure 1.2

Equilibrium Price of Soft Drinks

at $1.00 each. Therefore, $1.00 is the equilibrium price for a can of soda at that point in time, and most soft drink companies will price their soft drinks at $1.00. As you might imagine, a business that charges more than $1.00 (or whatever the current equilibrium price is) for its soft drinks will not sell many and might not earn a profit. On the other hand, a business that charges less than $1.00 accepts a lower profit per can than could be made at the equilibrium price.

If the cost of making soft drinks goes up, businesses will not offer as many cans of soda at the old price. Changing the price alters the supply curve, and a new equilibrium price results. This is an ongoing process, with supply and demand constantly changing in response to changes in economic conditions, availability of resources, and degree of competition. For example, many computer manufacturers offer powerful personal computers for much less than the typical $2,000 or more of several years ago. About 70 percent of all PCs sold in the US cost about US$1,200, but the average price is predicted to drop to US$600 in 2002.[10] Prices for goods and services vary according to these changes in supply and demand. This concept is the force that drives the distribution of resources (goods and services, labour, money) in a free-enterprise economy.

Critics of supply and demand say the system does not distribute resources equally. The forces of supply and demand prevent sellers who have to sell at higher prices (because their costs are high) and buyers who cannot afford to buy goods at the equilibrium price from participating in the market. According to critics, the wealthy can afford to buy more than they need, but the poor are unable to buy enough of what they need to survive.

The Nature of Competition

competition
the rivalry among businesses for consumers' dollars

Competition, the rivalry among businesses for consumers' dollars, is another vital element in free enterprise. According to Adam Smith, competition fosters efficiency and low prices by forcing producers to offer the best products at the most reasonable price; those who fail to do so are not able to stay in business. Thus, competition should improve the quality of the goods and services available. For example, competition in the personal computer market has allowed PC manufacturers to offer high-quality, custom-built products in a very short time. Compaq's Prosignia line ships as quickly as the next day after an order is received.[11]

Within a free-enterprise system, there are four types of competitive environments: pure competition, monopolistic competition, oligopoly, and monopoly.

pure competition
the market structure that exists when there are many small businesses selling one standardized product

Pure competition exists when there are many small businesses selling one standardized product, such as agricultural commodities like wheat, corn, and cotton. No one business sells enough of the product to influence the product's price. And, because there is no difference in the products, prices are determined solely by the forces of supply and demand.

monopolistic competition
the market structure that exists when there are fewer businesses than in a pure-competition environment and the differences among the goods they sell are small

Monopolistic competition exists when there are fewer businesses than in a pure-competition environment and the differences among the goods they sell is small. Aspirin, soft drinks, and vacuum cleaners are examples of such goods. These products differ slightly in packaging, warranty, name, and other characteristics, but all satisfy the same consumer need. Businesses have some power over the price they charge in monopolistic competition because they can make consumers aware of product differences through advertising. Consumers value some features more than others and are often willing to pay higher prices for a product with the features they want. For example, Advil, a nonprescription pain reliever, contains ibuprofen instead of aspirin. Consumers who cannot take aspirin or who believe ibuprofen is a more effective pain reliever may not mind paying a little extra for the ibuprofen in Advil.

oligopoly
the market structure that exists when there are very few businesses selling a product

An **oligopoly** exists when there are very few businesses selling a product. In an oligopoly, individual businesses have control over their products' price because each business supplies a large portion of the products sold in the marketplace.

Nonetheless, the prices charged by different firms stay fairly close because a price cut or increase by one company will trigger a similar response from another company. In the airline industry, for example, when one airline cuts fares to boost sales, other airlines quickly follow with rate decreases to remain competitive. Oligopolies exist when it is expensive for new firms to enter the marketplace. Not just anyone can acquire enough financial capital to build an automobile production facility or purchase enough airplanes and related resources to build an airline.

When there is one business providing a product in a given market, a **monopoly** exists. Utility companies that supply electricity, natural gas, cable, and water are monopolies. The government permits such monopolies because the cost of creating the good or supplying the service is so great that new producers cannot compete for sales. Government-granted monopolies are subject to government-regulated prices. Some monopolies exist because of technological developments that are protected by patent laws. Patent laws grant the developer of new technology a period of time (usually a maximum of 20 years) during which no other producer can use the same technology without the agreement of the original developer. This monopoly allows the developer to recover research, development, and production expenses and to earn a reasonable profit. Examples of this type of monopoly are the dry-copier process developed by Xerox and the self-developing photographic technology created by Polaroid. Both companies operated for years without competition and could charge premium prices because no alternative products existed to compete with their products. Through continuous development, Polaroid maintains market dominance. Xerox's patents have expired, however, and many imitators have forced market prices to decline.

Economic Cycles and Productivity

Expansion and Contraction. Economies are not stagnant; they expand and contract. **Economic expansion** occurs when an economy is growing and people are spending more money. Their purchases stimulate the production of goods and services, which in turn stimulates employment. The standard of living rises because more people are employed and have money to spend. Rapid expansions of the economy, however, may result in **inflation,** a continuing rise in prices. Inflation can be harmful if individuals' income does not increase at the same pace as rising prices, reducing their buying power.

Economic contraction occurs when spending declines. Businesses cut back on production and lay off workers, and the economy as a whole slows down. Contractions of the economy lead to **recession**—a decline in production, employment, and income. Recessions are often characterized by rising levels of **unemployment,** which is measured as the percentage of the population that wants to work but is unable to find jobs. Table 1.2 shows the unemployment rates for different segments of the Canadian population over a five-year period. The close ties between the Canadian and US economies are evidenced by the similarity in timing of such economic events as the recessions of 1981–1982 and 1990–1991. A severe recession may turn into a **depression,** in which unemployment is very high, consumer spending is low, and business output is sharply reduced, such as occurred in the early 1930s.

Economies expand and contract in response to changes in consumer, business, and government spending. War, too, can affect an economy, sometimes stimulating it (as in the United States during World Wars I and II) and sometimes stifling it (as during the Vietnam and Persian Gulf wars). Although fluctuations in the economy

monopoly
the market structure that exists when there is only one business providing a product in a given market

economic expansion
the situation that occurs when an economy is growing and people are spending more money; their purchases stimulate the production of goods and services, which in turn stimulates employment

inflation
a condition characterized by a continuing rise in prices

economic contraction
a slowdown of the economy characterized by a decline in spending and during which businesses cut back on production and lay off workers

recession
a decline in production, employment, and income

unemployment
the condition in which a percentage of the population wants to work but is unable to find jobs

depression
a condition of the economy in which unemployment is very high, consumer spending is low, and business output is sharply reduced

Table 1.2

Labour Force and Participation Rates 1996–2000

Source: Adapted from the Statistics Canada CANSIM database <http://www.cansima.statcan.ca/CANSIMME.HTM>, Matrix 3472.

	1996	1997	1998	1999	2000
	(thousands)				
Labour force	**14,899.5**	**15,153.0**	**15,417.7**	**15,721.2**	**15,999.2**
Men	8,157.4	8,277.5	8,380.2	8,534.0	8,649.2
Women	6,742.1	6,875.5	7,037.5	7,187.2	7,350.0
Participation rates			%		
15 years and over	64.7	64.9	65.1	65.6	65.9
Men	72.2	72.2	72.1	72.5	72.5
Women	57.5	57.8	58.4	58.9	59.5
15–24 years	62.3	61.5	61.9	63.5	64.4
Men	64.0	63.5	63.5	65.3	65.9
Women	60.5	59.3	60.2	61.7	62.9
25–44 years	84.7	85.2	85.6	85.8	86.0
Men	91.6	91.8	92.2	92.1	92.1
Women	77.8	78.5	79.0	79.6	80.0
45–64 years	66.9	67.8	68.4	69.3	70.0
Men	76.7	77.2	76.8	77.8	78.1
Women	57.3	58.6	60.1	60.9	62.1
65 years and over	6.1	6.3	6.4	6.2	6.0
Men	9.7	9.8	10.2	9.8	9.5
Women	3.4	3.6	3.5	3.4	3.3

are inevitable and to a certain extent predictable, their effects—inflation and unemployment—disrupt lives and thus governments try to minimize them.

Measuring the Economy. Countries measure the state of their economies to determine whether they are expanding or contracting and whether corrective action is necessary to minimize the fluctuations. One commonly used measure is **gross domestic product (GDP)**—the sum of all goods and services produced in a country during a year. GDP measures only those goods and services made within a country and therefore does not include profits from companies' overseas operations; it does include profits earned by foreign companies within the country being measured. Table 1.3 shows the increase in Canada's GDP over five years.

Another important indicator of a nation's economic health is the relationship between its spending and income (from taxes). When a nation spends more than it takes in from taxes, it has a **budget deficit.** Throughout the last three decades of the twentieth century, beginning in 1969 the federal government spent more money

gross domestic product (GDP)
the sum of all goods and services produced in a country during a year

budget deficit
the condition in which a nation spends more than it takes in from taxes

	1995	1996	1997	1998	1999
			($ millions)		
Newfoundland	10,649	10,403	10,462	11,232	12,110
Prince Edward Island	2,663	2,814	2,763	2,851	2,994
Nova Scotia	19,263	19,436	20,195	21,110	22,407
New Brunswick	16,349	16,580	16,779	17,457	18,390
Quebec	177,107	180,199	187,862	193,695	204,062
Ontario	327,246	335,843	357,300	372,630	396,775
Manitoba	26,837	28,319	29,407	29,966	30,995
Saskatchewan	26,334	28,927	29,046	28,828	30,143
Alberta	91,634	98,197	106,518	106,174	116,990
British Columbia	105,319	108,454	113,596	113,945	118,783
Yukon	1,049	1,126	1,096	1,054	1,080
Northwest Territories including Nunavut	2,396	2,516	2,641	2,577	—
Northwest Territories	—	—	—	—	2,167
Nunavut	—	—	—	—	731
Total	806,846	832,814	877,665	901,519	957,627

Table 1.3

Gross Domestic Product by Province

Source: Adapted from Statistics Canada CANSIM database <http://www.cansima.statcan.ca/CANSIMME.HTM>, Matrix 9015–9026 and 8996–8997, and publication "Provincial economic accounts, annual estimates, tables and analytical document," Catalogue No. 13-213, June 2001.

each year on social, defence, and other programs than it collected from taxes. This annual excess of expenditures over revenues is called a deficit. Because people do not want their taxes to increase but are usually unwilling to accept cutbacks in government services, it is difficult for governments to reduce the deficit. Like consumers and businesses, when the government needs money, it borrows from the public, banks, and other institutions, both domestic and foreign.

In fiscal 1997–98, for the first time in 27 years, the government recorded a financial surplus—revenues exceeded expenditures for the year. By this time the accumulated gross federal debt, the sum of the unpaid annual deficits, had reached $652 billion. With four years of financial surpluses the debt was reduced to $651 billion by March 31, 2001.

THE CANADIAN ECONOMY

As we said previously, Canada is a mixed economy based on free enterprise. The answers to the three basic economic issues are determined primarily by competition and the forces of supply and demand, although the federal government does intervene in economic decisions to a significant extent. To understand the current state of the economy and its effect on business practices, it is helpful to examine its history and the roles of the entrepreneur and the government.

A Brief History of the Canadian Economy

The Early Economy. Before the colonization of North America, the First Nations peoples lived as hunter/gatherers and farmers with some trade among tribes. The first European settlements on the east coast of what was to become Canada came about as a result of the fishing industry.

The fur trade began in the early 1500s and remained a major industry for almost three centuries. The first major business competitors in Canada were the North West Company and the Hudson's Bay Company, which remained active in the fur trade until the 1980s. The Atlantic fisheries and the fur trade were the dominant commercial activities into the late 1700s.

During the late 18th century and the first half of the 19th century, forestry developed as a major industry. This led to the establishment of several shipyards in Atlantic Canada.

It was during this period that financial services began to appear to meet the needs of the expanding population and new commercial enterprises. The Bank of Montreal was established in 1817, the Bank of Nova Scotia in 1832, and the Merchants Bank of Halifax in 1864. The Merchants Bank of Halifax was renamed the Royal Bank in 1901.

The Industrial Revolution. The 19th century and the Industrial Revolution brought the development of new technology and factories. The factory brought together all the resources needed to make a product—materials, machines, and workers. Work in factories became specialized as workers focused on one or two tasks. As work became more efficient, productivity increased, making more goods available at lower prices. Railroads brought major changes, allowing farmers to send crops and goods to the urban areas of the nation for barter or sale.

From the mid-19th century the development of the railways moved settlement westward, leading to major growth in agriculture. The government of the day established what has become traditional in Canada by being heavily involved in the construction of transportation systems, both canals and railways. The Canadian Pacific Railway was completed in 1885.

Industrialization in Canada was not as widespread as in the United States and was predominantly in central Canada. A manufacturing sector developed, producing such products as iron and steel, farm equipment, sugar, and alcohol. Although industrialization continued, Canada remained a primarily agrarian economy as the 19th century drew to a close.

The Manufacturing and Marketing Economies. Industrialization brought increased prosperity and Canada moved towards becoming a manufacturing economy—one devoted to manufacturing goods and providing services rather than producing agricultural products. Agriculture and resource-based industries such as forestry and mining remained a much more significant proportion of the Canadian economy than was the case in the United States.

As production capabilities increased, companies became more focused on the needs of the consumer and entered the marketing economy. Expensive goods such as cars and appliances could be purchased on credit. Companies conducted research to find out what products customers needed and wanted. Advertising made consumers aware of the differences in products and prices.

Because these developments occurred in a free-enterprise system, consumers determined what goods and services were produced. They did this by purchasing the products they liked at prices they were willing to pay. Canada, like the United States, prospered, and Canadian citizens had one of the highest standards of living in the world.

Cyberspace's biggest consumer merchant is Amazon.com Inc.—with 4.5 million customers and sales that increased from US$148 million to US$540 million in just one year. With the number of people going online expected to jump to 320 million in the next few years, Amazon's potential is vast.

Choosing a market with no big online or dominant traditional competitors, Jeffrey Bezos launched Amazon in mid-1995 as an Internet bookseller. Amazon offers an easily searchable store of 3.1 million titles—15 times more than any bookstore. Bezos set out to make shopping on the Amazon site a friendly, frictionless, fun experience. In addition to the huge selection and simple, quickly loaded Web pages, Bezos wanted to create a sense of online community. Site users are encouraged to post their own reviews of books, and authors are brought in for online chats with readers.

Its effective use of technology has skyrocketed Amazon to the top in online retailing. It was one of the first sites to take advantage of the Internet's computing power to allow consumers to search easily for any book in print, read thousands of reviews, and make purchases with a few clicks of a mouse.

Customers' shipping and credit card information are stored securely after their first purchase. Subsequent purchases require only a single click to send the requested titles on their way. E-mail confirmations are sent to purchasers, and shipping is often upgraded for free. Amazon was also the first commercial site to incorporate the technology necessary to analyze a customer's purchases and make recommendations for other books. The technology also allows Amazon to gather instant feedback on customer preferences and other items they might want to buy online.

Targeting the areas customers have requested, Amazon now sells CDs, videos, and an expanded gift line that includes everything from games and toys to Sony Walkman cassette and CD players and watches. Future opportunities include software, health supplies, apparel, flowers, magazine subscriptions, and travel arrangements. Bezos wants to make Amazon the Internet's premier shopping destination, but some market analysts say that straying too far from its core business of selling books and trying to compete against established rivals in other areas may turn Amazon.com into "Amazon.toast." Only time will tell.[12]

Embrace Technology

Amazon.com

The Service and Internet-based Economy. After World War II, with the increased standard of living, Canadians had more money and more time. They began to pay others to perform services that made their lives easier. Beginning in the 1960s, more and more women entered the work force. The profile of the family changed: Today there are more single-parent families and individuals living alone, and in two-parent families, both parents often work. These trends are gradually changing Canada to a *service economy*—one devoted to the production of services that make life easier for busy consumers. Service industries such as banking, medicine, utilities, child care, leisure-related industries, and education are growing rapidly. This trend continues with advanced technology contributing to new service products such as overnight mail, electronic banking, and shopping through computer, cable, and satellite television networks. Service industries—trade, communications, transportation, food and lodging, financial, medical, education, and technical services—account for over half of Canadian employment. Table 1.4 provides a summary of employment by sector.

There are new initiatives from government agencies to speed up the Internet, help small businesses get online, monitor the economic

Did you know? *12.3 percent of Canadian households made purchases over the Internet totalling $1.1 billion in 2000.*

Table 1.4

Employment by Sector, 2000

Source: Statistics Canada, www.statcan.ca/english/ Pgdb/economy/ communications/ trade03.htm.

Sector	Employment (thousands)	Percentage
Logging and forestry	68.0	0.56
Mining, quarrying, and oil wells	140.9	1.15
Transportation, communication, and other utilities	908.9	7.45
Trade (wholesale and retail)	2,273.8	18.64
Manufacturing	2,005.7	16.44
Construction	557.7	4.57
Finance, insurance, and real estate	734.5	6.02
Education and related services	931.7	7.64
Health and social services	1,226.2	10.05
Accommodation, food, and beverage services	884.4	7.25
Miscellaneous services	730.9	5.99
Public administration	680.6	5.58
Other	1,056.3	8.66
Total	12,199.6	100.00

effects of the digital economy, and promote electronic commerce. Sometimes called "e-tailers" rather than retailers, online businesses include Internet-only companies such as Amazon.com, cataloguers such as Land's End, and traditional firms such as Canadian Tire. Forecasters predict that 16 million shoppers in the US alone will buy through the Internet in 2000, and that figure is expected to reach 61 million by 2002.[13] Online business is the fastest growing segment of the economy and may significantly change the way business is conducted in the future.

The Better Business Bureau provides resources for sound Internet commerce and establishes online privacy policies. BBBOnline allows site users to search the Bureau's database to see if a particular online business has met the Bureau's high standards of reliability. Companies that have shown a commitment to honest advertising and customer satisfaction post the BBBOnline Reliability Seal on their web sites.

The Role of the Entrepreneur

entrepreneur
an individual who risks his or her wealth, time, and effort to develop for profit an innovative product or way of doing something

An **entrepreneur** is an individual who risks his or her wealth, time, and effort to develop for profit an innovative product or way of doing something. For example, in 1984 Mike Llazaridis, with a loan from his parents and a contract to produce a display system for General Motors, dropped out of fourth-year engineering at the University of Waterloo. Although he attempted to return to complete his degree, business demands were too great. Seventeen years later the company he founded, Research In Motion, employs 1,400 people and is worth $7 billion.[14] The free-enterprise system provides the conditions necessary for entrepreneurs to succeed. In the past, entrepreneurs were often inventors who brought all the factors of production together to produce a new product. Thomas Edison, whose inventions include the record player and light bulb, was an early American entrepreneur. Henry Ford was one of the first persons to develop mass assembly methods in the automobile industry.

In 1942 J. Armand Bombardier founded a business to manufacture tracked vehicles for transportation on snow-covered terrain. The corporation, which still bears his name, is now a major competitor in aerospace, rail transportation, and recreational vehicles. Revenues for the year ended January 31, 2001, were in excess of US$16 billion.

John W. Billes and Alfred Billes, with combined savings of $1,800, bought Hamilton Tire and Garage Ltd. in 1922. Five years later the business became Canadian Tire Corporation. This business, described as the only truly unique Canadian business, now has stores within a 15-minute drive of 85 percent of the population. Today nine out of ten Canadians shop at Canadian Tire at least twice a year, and 40 percent of us shop there each week.

Other well-known Canadian entrepreneurs include Paul Demarais of Power Corporation, Frank Stronach of Magna Corporation, Frank J. Hasenfratz of Linamar, and K.C. Irving of Irving.

Research In Motion's co-CEOs, Jim Balsillie (right) and Mike Lazaridis, pioneered the popular wireless digital assistants (think BlackBerry) and doubled their number of employees while producing five times more of the popular devices over the next year.

The Kitchener-Waterloo Record. Used with permission.

Research In Motion
www.rim.net

Entrepreneurs are constantly changing North American business practices with new technology and innovative management techniques. Bill Gates, for example, built Microsoft, a software company whose products include MS-DOS (a disk operating system), Word, and Windows, into a multibillion-dollar enterprise. Frederick Smith had an idea to deliver packages overnight, and now his FedEx Company plays an important role in getting documents and packages delivered all over the world for businesses and individuals. Entrepreneurs have been associated with such unique concepts as Dell Computers, Ben & Jerry's, Levi's, Holiday Inns, McDonald's, Dr Pepper, and Wal-Mart. Wal-Mart was the first retailer to reach US$100 billion in sales in one year and now routinely passes that mark. Sales in 1999 were expected to top US$135 billion. With its 2,400 discount stores, 450 wholesale Sam's Clubs, and 600 stores outside the US, Wal-Mart serves over 90 million customers each week.[15] We will examine the importance of entrepreneurship further in Chapter 6.

The Role of Government in the Canadian Economy

The Canadian economic system is best described as modified capitalism because the government regulates business to preserve competition and protect consumers and employees. Federal, provincial, and local governments intervene in the economy with laws and regulations designed to promote competition and to protect consumers, employees, and the environment. Many of these laws are discussed in Chapter 2.

Additionally, government agencies such as the Department of Finance and the Bank of Canada, with input from Statistics Canada, measure the health of the economy (GDP, productivity, etc.) and, when necessary, take steps to minimize the disruptive effects of economic fluctuations and reduce unemployment. When the economy is contracting and unemployment is rising, the federal government tries to spur growth so that consumers will spend more money and businesses will hire more employees. To accomplish this, it may reduce interest rates or increase its own spending for goods and services. The slowdown in the economy throughout 2001 was exacerbated by the events of September 11. In response to this, the Canadian government took steps to inject liquidity, cash, into the system to prevent or at least slow the decline. In the two months following September 11, the Bank of Canada reduced interest rates to their lowest levels in 40 years. When the economy expands so fast that inflation results, the government may intervene to reduce inflation by slowing down economic growth. This can be accomplished by raising interest rates to discourage spending by businesses and consumers. In extreme circumstances, the federal government can introduce wage and price controls, as was done in the 1970s. The specific techniques used to control the economy will be discussed later in this book.

CAN YOU LEARN BUSINESS IN A CLASSROOM?

Obviously, the answer is yes, or there would be no purpose for this textbook! To be successful in business, you need knowledge, skills, experience, and good judgment. The topics covered in this chapter and throughout this book provide some of the knowledge you need to understand the world of business. The opening vignette at the beginning of each chapter, boxes, examples within each chapter, and the case at

---

Figure 1.3

The Organization of This Book

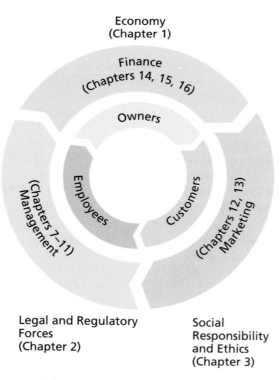

Economy
(Chapter 1)

Finance
(Chapters 14, 15, 16)

Owners

Employees

Customers

(Chapters 12, 13)
Marketing

(Chapters 7–11)
Management

Legal and Regulatory
Forces
(Chapter 2)

Social
Responsibility
and Ethics
(Chapter 3)

Special Topics:
Global Business (Chapter 4)
Forms of Ownership (Chapter 5)
Small Business, Entrepreneurship, and Franchising (Chapter 6)
Part-ending CyberZones

the end of each chapter describe experiences to help you develop good business judgment. The "Build Your Skills" exercise at the end of each chapter and the "Solve the Dilemma" box will help you develop skills that may be useful in your future career. However, good judgment is based on knowledge and experience plus personal insight and understanding. Therefore, you need more courses in business, along with some practical experience in the business world, to help you develop the special insight necessary to put your personal stamp on knowledge as you apply it. The challenge in business is in the area of judgment, and judgment does not develop from memorizing an introductory business textbook. If you are observant in your daily experiences as an employee, as a student, and as a consumer, you will improve your ability to make good business judgments.

Figure 1.3 is an overview of how the chapters in this book are linked together and how the chapters relate to the participants, the activities, and the environmental factors found in the business world. The topics presented in the chapters that follow are those that will give you the best opportunity to begin the process of understanding the world of business.

The only thing certain anymore is that the world is constantly changing, and this applies to future career options for you and your classmates. The traditional career track that earlier generations followed, in which a person started working at one company upon graduation and worked his or her way up until retirement, is passé. In fact, the average large corporation replaces the equivalent of its entire work force every four years. Moreover, constantly evolving technology means today's graduates and workers need to be computer literate and able to adapt to new technologies. The globalization of business suggests that you be fluent in a second or even third language, for there is a good chance that you'll be working with people from around the world, and you may even do a stint overseas yourself. Changes in the makeup of the work force mean more doors opening for women and minorities as companies recognize the need to understand and cater to the desires of a diverse customer base. Changes in organizational structure may require you to work in teams, where communication is a crucial skill, or they may leave you out of the corporate hierarchy altogether, and instead put you in an entrepreneurial

role as a self-employed contractor or small-business owner.

Because of these and other changes taking place in the business world that we will discuss throughout this book, when you enter the work force full time, you are far more likely to define yourself by what you do ("I design RISC chips") than by your employer ("I work for Motorola"). And, you're more likely to think in terms of short-term projects, such as launching a product or reengineering a process, rather than a long-term career track like the one your grandfather may have followed.

This business course and textbook, including the boxes, cases, and skills-building exercises, will help you learn the basic knowledge, skills, and trends that you can use whether you work for a corporation or run your own small business, whether you work in upper management or on the shop floor. Along the way, we'll introduce you to some specific careers and offer advice on developing your own job opportunities in career boxes in each chapter. Throughout, the best advice we can offer is that students today need to be flexible to adapt to and survive the changing business world.[16]

Explore Your Career Options

Changes

Review Your Understanding

Define basic concepts such as business, product, and profit, and explain why studying business is important.

A business is an organization or individual that seeks a profit by providing products that satisfy people's needs. A product is a good, service, or idea that has both tangible and intangible characteristics that provide satisfaction and benefits. Profit, the basic goal of business, is the difference between what it costs to make and sell a product and what a customer pays for it. Studying business can help you prepare for a career and become a better consumer.

Identify the main participants and activities of business.

The three main participants in business are owners, employees, and customers, but others—government regulators, suppliers, social groups, etc.—are also important. Management involves planning, organizing, and controlling the tasks required to carry out the work of the company. Marketing refers to those activities—research, product development, promotion, pricing, and distribution—designed to provide goods and services that satisfy customers. Finance refers to activities concerned with funding a business and using its funds effectively.

Define economics and compare the four types of economic systems.

Economics is the study of how resources are distributed for the production of goods and services within a social system; an economic system describes how a particular society distributes its resources. Communism is an economic system in which the people, without regard to class, own all the nation's resources. In a socialist system, the government owns and operates basic industries, but individuals own most businesses. Under capitalism, individuals own and operate the majority of businesses that provide goods and services. Mixed economies have elements from more than one economic system; most countries have mixed economies.

Describe the role of supply, demand, and competition in a free-enterprise system.

In a free-enterprise system, individuals own and operate the majority of businesses, and the distribu-

tion of resources is determined by competition, supply, and demand. Demand is the number of goods and services that consumers are willing to buy at different prices at a specific time. Supply is the number of goods or services that businesses are willing to sell at different prices at a specific time. The price at which the supply of a product equals demand at a specific point in time is the equilibrium price. Competition is the rivalry among businesses to convince consumers to buy goods or services. Four types of competitive environments are pure competition, monopolistic competition, oligopoly, and monopoly. These economic concepts determine how businesses may operate in a particular society and, often, how much they can charge for their products.

Specify why and how the health of the economy is measured.

A country measures the state of its economy to determine whether it is expanding or contracting and whether the country needs to take steps to minimize fluctuations. One commonly used measure is gross domestic product (GDP), the sum of all goods and services produced in a country during a year. A budget deficit occurs when a nation spends more than it takes in from taxes.

Trace the evolution of the Canadian economy and discuss the role of the entrepreneur in the economy.

The Canadian economy has evolved through several stages: the early economy, the Industrial Revolution, the manufacturing economy, the marketing economy, and the service and Internet-based economy of today. Entrepreneurs play an important role because they risk their time, wealth, and efforts to develop new goods, services, and ideas that fuel the growth of the Canadian economy.

Evaluate a small-business owner's situation and propose a course of action.

The "Solve the Dilemma" box presents a problem for the owner of the firm. Should you, as the owner, raise prices, expand operations, or form a venture with a larger company to deal with demand? You should be able to apply your new-found understanding of the relationship between supply and demand to assess the situation and reach a decision about how to proceed.

Learn the Terms

budget deficit 16

business 4

capitalism, or free enterprise 10

communism 9

competition 14

demand 12

depression 15

economic contraction 15

economic expansion 15

economic system 8

economics 8

entrepreneur 20

equilibrium price 12

financial resources 8

free-market system 10

gross domestic product (GDP) 16

human resources 8

inflation 15

mixed economies 11

monopolistic competition 14

monopoly 15

natural resources 8

nonprofit organizations 5

oligopoly 14

product 4

profit 5

pure competition 14

recession 15

socialism 10

supply 12

unemployment 15

Check Your Progress

1. What is the fundamental goal of business? Do all organizations share this goal?
2. Name the three forms a product may take, and give some examples of each.
3. Who are the main participants of business? What are the main activities? What other factors have an impact on the conduct of business in Canada?
4. What are four types of economic systems? Can you provide an example of a country using each type?
5. Explain the terms *supply, demand, equilibrium price,* and *competition.* How do these forces interact in the Canadian economy?

6. List the four types of competitive environments and provide an example of a product of each environment.
7. List and define the various measures governments may use to gauge the state of their economies. If unemployment is high, will the growth of GDP be great or small?
8. Why are fluctuations in the economy harmful?
9. How did the Industrial Revolution influence the growth of the Canadian economy? As Canada moves towards a service economy, what will be the effect on the types of employment opportunities for Canadians and the activities of Canadian business?
10. Explain the federal government's role in the Canadian economy.

Get Involved

1. Discuss the economic changes occurring in the Commonwealth of Independent States and Eastern European countries, which once operated as communist economic systems. Why are these changes occurring? What do you think the result will be?
2. Why is it important for the government to measure the economy? What kinds of actions might it take to control the economy's growth?

3. Is the Canadian economy currently expanding or contracting? Defend your answer with the latest statistics on GDP, inflation, unemployment, and so on. How is the federal government responding? (Begin your information search at Statistics Canada's website: www.statscan.ca.)

Build Your Skills

The Forces of Supply and Demand

Background: WagWumps are a new children's toy with the potential to be a highly successful product. WagWumps are cute, furry, and their eyes glow in the dark. Each family set consists of a mother, a father, and two children. Wee-Toys' manufacturing costs are about $6 per set, with $3 representing marketing and distribution costs. The wholesale price of a Wag-Wump family for a retailer is $15.75, and the toy carries a suggested retail price of $26.99.

Task: Assume you are a decision maker at a retailer, such as Zellers or Wal-Mart, that must determine the price the stores in your district should charge customers for the WagWump family set. From the information provided above, you know that the SRP (suggested retail price) is $26.99 per set and that your company can purchase the toy set from your wholesaler for $15.75 each. Based on the following assumptions, plot your company's supply curve on the graph provided in Figure 1.4 and label it "supply curve."

Quantity	Price
3,000	$16.99
5,000	21.99
7,000	26.99

Using the following assumptions, plot your customers' demand curve on Figure 1.4, and label it "demand curve."

Quantity	Price
10,000	$16.99
6,000	21.99
2,000	26.99

For this specific time, determine the point at which the quantity of toys your company is willing to supply equals the quantity of toys the customers in your sales district are willing to buy, and label that point "equilibrium price."

Figure 1.4

Equilibrium Price of WagWumps

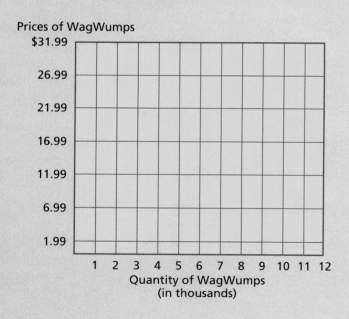

 **See for Yourself Videocase**   **www.cbc.ca**

Classic Cheesecake Industry

Small businesses, family businesses, large businesses —any business faces growing pains. Brad Miller and his wife are facing many hurdles in their attempt to grow their business Classic Cheesecake in Sydney, Nova Scotia. They have come across a niche for cheesecakes, the diabetic market, the gluten-free clients, and Sobey's grocery chain. Individuals and businesses are buying from them if they can deliver, and they need to get bigger just to service their current customers. They want to grow and expand sales even more by selling into Ontario, Quebec, Boston, and New York.

The cheesecake business needs larger facilities than their former garage to service the anticipated orders. Sales had been $140,000 the year before but now there is a need to finance the new factory and the new equipment, and as with most plans of any business there are delays. Family and friends and a silent partner have all bought shares. Equipment and construction delays all add up to needing more time and hence more money.

Government funding played a large role in the initial expansion and now further needs require more government money to assist in covering the loss of a large sale, carrying costs of the previous loans, and a new grant for the marketing program.

The roles of government in Canada are many in fledgling businesses like this. They assist in financing some start-ups, especially in areas that require economic development such as Cape Breton.

Questions

1. What different roles and tasks does the owner, Brad Miller, face in his vocation as entrepreneur?

2. What role does the accountant play for Brad Miller and for his financiers?

3. At the stage the video leaves us in the progress of the Classic Cheesecake Company, what major functions has Brad Miller been focusing on and what roles are needed to be addressed if his family will see the promising future he is planning for?

Source: *Venture*, show numbers 755/726, "A Cottage Cheesecake Industry," August 22, 2000, running time 9:04.

Remember to check out our Online Learning Centre at **www.mcgrawhill.ca/college/ferrell**.

Chapter 2

The Legal and Regulatory Environment

Chapter Outline

Objectives

After reading this chapter, you will be able to:

- Identify the sources of law.
- Summarize the court system and the methods of conflict resolution.
- Gain an appreciation of the framework for regulating business through administrative agencies.
- Review important elements of business law, including the Sale of Goods Act, the law of torts and fraud, the law of contracts, the law of agency, the law of property, and the law of bankruptcy.
- Review the legal and regulatory implications of electronic business.
- Provide an overview of the legal pressure for responsible business conduct.
- Identify the legal issues in a business dispute.

Insurance against Lawsuits

Did you ever think that providing insurance to protect people against lawsuits would be a viable business? Well, today, companies like Pre-Paid Legal Services, Inc., are helping individuals—including law enforcement professionals, commercial drivers, and small business owners—to protect themselves and obtain needed legal services for both routine legal requirements and potential lawsuits related to business relationships.

For $25 a month, anyone can buy a package that will provide legal services when needed—services that include telephone consultations with an attorney, preparation of a will, defence against a tax audit, basic trial defence, and a discount on any legal service not covered under the plan. In today's lawsuit environment, buying such insurance provides peace of mind to many people.

Pre-Paid Legal Services, Inc., founded by Harland Stonecipher, began by collecting data that allowed it to predict how much it would cost to handle simple legal matters. Then, Pre-Paid approached law firms about providing its customers with the legal services they needed. In return for the large volume of business being offered, the law firms were able to offer low prices. Today, Pre-Paid has US$250 million in revenues.

Professionals in many businesses, such as medicine, law, engineering, and others that require extensive education, are obtaining liability insurance to protect themselves against potential lawsuits in situations where the professional has rendered an opinion or decision that could result in damage to another. Insurance to reduce the financial burden of such lawsuits is important in these areas.[1] In Canada as of January 2001, the service provided is considered a buyer's group, as the sales associates are not licensed insurance agents.

Enter the World of Business

Ray Nig

INTRODUCTION

Every day you read in the newspaper or hear news reports about businesses that are experiencing legal problems because they have violated a law or regulation, failed to honour a contract, acted carelessly, or caused potential damage to a competitor. For example, recent headlines reveal that Microsoft, Visa, and Mastercard have been sued by the US government for limiting customer choice and inhibiting competition. Pepsico has sued archrival Coca-Cola, accusing its competitor of unfairly controlling beverages served by restaurants.[2] Most highly respected corporations have a number of legal issues to resolve on a continuous basis. Many of these issues could be avoided if managers had more knowledge of business law and the regulatory environment.

business law

the rules and regulations that govern the conduct of business

Business law refers to the rules and regulations that govern the conduct of business. Problems in this area come from the failure to keep promises, misunderstandings, disagreements about expectations, or, in some cases, attempts to take advantage of others. The regulatory environment offers a framework and enforcement system in order to provide a fair playing field for all businesses. The regulatory environment is created based on inputs from competitors, customers, employees, special interest groups, and the public's elected representatives. Lobbying by pressure groups who try to influence legislation often shapes the legal and regulatory environment.

An examination of business law and the regulatory environment will not only help you appreciate this important area of the business environment, but it will also make you aware of your rights in the event that you are wronged in the course of doing business. In this chapter, we will look at the various sources of business law and discuss how disputes may be resolved. Next, we review the administrative agencies that enforce the regulatory environment. We will also examine a number of aspects of the law that affect business, including sales, contracts, agents, property, bankruptcy, and competition. Next, we provide a brief overview of regulatory issues related to electronic business. Finally, we examine the legal pressure for responsible business conduct and organizational compliance programs.

SOURCES OF LAW

Laws are classified as either criminal or civil. *Criminal law* not only prohibits a specific kind of action, such as unfair competition or mail fraud, but also imposes a fine or imprisonment as punishment for violating the law. A violation of a criminal law is thus called a crime. *Civil law* defines all the laws not classified as criminal, and it specifies the rights and duties of individuals and organizations (including businesses). Violations of civil law may result in fines but not imprisonment. The primary difference between criminal and civil law is that criminal laws are enforced by the country or province, whereas civil laws are enforced through the court system by individuals or organizations.

Criminal and civil laws are derived from four sources: the Constitution (the Canadian Charter of Rights and Freedoms), precedents established by judges (common law) where traditional laws stem from England, provincial and federal statutes (statute law), and federal and provincial administrative agencies (administrative law). Quebec has codified much of the laws for that province in the Civil Code. The Civil Code acts similarly to the common law of the other provinces. Common law is encountered throughout the English-speaking world, whereas most of the rest of the world uses some form of codified law for establishing rights and freedoms. Administrative commissions and boards have expanded significantly since World

War II and regulate many activities such as the sale of securities in publicly traded companies, broadcasting and telecommunications, employment standards, labour relations, aeronautics, the sale and consumption of alcohol, and many other commercial activities. Ultimately, the Supreme Court of Canada is the final authority on the legal and regulatory decisions for the conduct of business. For example, the Supreme Court ruled in 1995 that the Tobacco Products Control Act impinged on the right of RJR-MacDonald Inc. and Imperial Tobacco Ltd.'s right of freedom of expression by denying them the right to post signs at sporting and cultural events. The government then had to demonstrate that the tobacco law was justified and reasonable in infringing on the right of freedom of expression of the tobacco industry.

Supreme Court of Canada
www.scc.csc.gc.ca

COURTS AND THE RESOLUTION OF DISPUTES

The primary method of resolving conflicts and business disputes is through **lawsuits,** where one individual or organization takes another to court using civil laws. For example, in June of 2000, Glen Clark, the former premier of British Columbia, was ordered to pay a critic of his fast ferry project $150,000. Bob Ward, the plaintiff, claimed that Mr. Clark slandered him with false statements that caused his clients to take their business elsewhere, and yet his claims about the catamaran ferry project were all found to be true in the end. Despite Mr. Clark's defence that he was acting as the minister responsible for the ferries, his comments extended beyond the truth and he was found liable. The legal system, therefore, provides a forum for people to resolve disputes based on our legal foundations. The courts may decide when harm or damage results from the actions of others.

lawsuits
dispute resolution procedures in which one individual or organization takes another to court

Because lawsuits are so frequent in the world of business, it is important to understand more about the court system where such disputes are resolved. In almost any newspaper or business magazine, lawsuits are reported as frequently as almost any other event that occurs in business. For example, AT&T sued Business Discount Plan (BDP), accusing it of using fraud and deception to routinely slam customers to its telecommunication service. *Slamming* refers to changing a customer's phone service without the customer's authorization. AT&T charged that BDP gave the impression it was affiliated with AT&T. As a part of the settlement, BDP had to send letters to consumers telling them they were not affiliated with AT&T.[3] This example illustrates that both financial restitution and specific actions to undo wrongdoing can result from going before a court to resolve a conflict. All decisions made in the courts are based on criminal and civil laws derived from the legal and regulatory system.

Thousands of lawsuits have already been filed over alleged losses related to the chaos that was predicted to occur on January 1, 2000, due to computer problems caused by systems not programmed to recognize dates after 1999. Targeted in the lawsuits were some top high-tech companies and consulting firms. Intuit, Inc., maker of the popular Quicken software, has faced six class-action suits, including one by customers who demanded millions in software upgrades to avoid potential problems.[4]

A businessperson may win a lawsuit in court and receive a judgment, or court order, requiring the loser of the suit to pay monetary damages. However, this does not guarantee the victor will be able to collect those damages. If the loser of the suit lacks the financial resources to pay the judgment—for example, if the loser is a bankrupt business—the winner of the suit may not be able to collect the award. Most business lawsuits involve a request for a sum of money, but some lawsuits request that a court specifically order a person or organization to do or to refrain from doing a certain act, such as slamming telephone customers.

The Court System

jurisdiction
the legal power of a court, through a judge, to interpret and apply the law and make a binding decision in a particular case

Jurisdiction is the legal power of a court, through a judge, to interpret and apply the law and make a binding decision in a particular case. In some instances, other courts will not enforce the decision of a prior court because it lacked jurisdiction. There are, in general, two kinds of courts—the **courts of original jurisdiction**, sometimes referred to as trial courts, and **courts of appeal**. In the court of original jurisdiction, a judge first hears the facts of the case so that he or she may render a decision on the civil dispute or criminal case. The second court, as the name states, hears appeals of the decisions of the trial court. Their primary function is to review decisions of the lower court when one of the parties believes that the original judge made an erroneous decision. They hear factual arguments but do not normally hear evidence, and base their decisions on the transcripts of the trial and the arguments presented. The appeals court may overturn the lower court decision, revise the amount of damages in a civil case, or alter the severity of the penalty in a criminal case.

court of original jurisdiction
a court that determines the facts of a case, decides which laws pertain, and applies those laws to resolve the dispute

Federal courts are primarily focused on federal cases that involve the exclusive jurisdiction of the federal government or disputes between the federal and provincial governments. Disputes between taxpayers and Canada Customs and Revenue Agency are heard in a special tax court with the opportunity to appeal decisions to the federal trial courts. Provinces have two court systems, criminal and civil. The criminal cases that are very serious are heard in the various provincial Supreme or Superior Courts, while most are heard in Provincial Court or Magistrate's Court (or Court of Sessions of the Peace in Quebec). Young offenders have their cases heard in youth courts, and family matters are heard in family court. In civil cases, disputes under $10,000 are dealt with in small claims court and there is no jury. Larger disputes go to a magistrate or provincial court and both have some limited rights of appeal. Some provinces have surrogate or probate courts to deal with wills and the administration of the estates of deceased persons. All court decisions may ultimately be brought to the final court of appeal the Supreme Court of Canada if it grants leave to appeal the lower case decision. Usually the decision it would be requested to make must be of national importance.

court of appeal
a court that deals solely with appeals relating to the interpretation of law

Alternative Dispute Resolution Methods

Although many disputes are resolved via a lawsuit, other dispute resolution methods are becoming popular. The schedules of trial courts are often crowded; long delays between the filing of a case and the trial date are common. Further, complex cases can become quite expensive to pursue. As a result, many businesspeople are turning to alternative methods of resolving business arguments: mediation and arbitration, the mini-trial, and litigation in a private court.

mediation
a form of negotiation to resolve a dispute by bringing in one or more third-party mediators to help reach a settlement

Mediation is a form of negotiation to resolve a dispute by bringing in one or more third-party mediators, usually chosen by the disputing parties, to help reach a settlement. The mediator suggests different ways to resolve a dispute between the parties. The mediator's resolution is nonbinding—that is, the parties do not have to accept the mediator's suggestions; they are strictly voluntary. Should the parties accept the settlement recommended by the mediator, they can reduce legal and court costs by up to 75 percent. In Ontario it is estimated that 80 to 90 percent of all cases submitted to mediation are resolved out of court, and 40 percent are resolved even before they reach mediation. This is faster than the average five-year time frame for a legal case where up to 70 percent of the amount of money awarded may be used up in legal fees. This process is so well accepted that in Quebec the legal profession, chartered accountants, engineers, and others involved in the dispute resolution process have established a free multidisciplinary civil and commercial mediation service. Hydro-Quebec and Telebec, a BCE subsidiary, resolved a 20-year dispute in less than two months. With the complex human issues involved in disputes and the ever-changing business environment, especially with e-commerce, the need for quick resolution of disputes underscores the need to increase the use of mediation and arbitration.[5]

Arbitration involves submission of a dispute to one or more third-party arbitrators, usually chosen by the disputing parties, whose decision usually is final. Arbitration differs from mediation in that an arbitrator's decision must be followed, whereas a mediator merely offers suggestions and facilitates negotiations. Cases may be submitted to arbitration because a contract—such as a labour contract—requires it or because the parties agree to do so.

Some consumers are barred from taking claims to court by agreements drafted by banks, brokers, insurance plans, and others. Instead, they are required to take complaints to mandatory arbitration.

Arbitration can be an attractive alternative to a lawsuit because it is often cheaper and quicker, and the parties frequently can choose arbitrators who are knowledgeable about the particular area of business at issue. Merrill Lynch, recognized by *Fortune, Business Week,* and *Working Mother* for its progressive employee programs, settled a discrimination lawsuit with eight current and former employees through arbitration. The company has established a program that utilizes arbitration options to resolve employee disputes. Merrill Lynch is very concerned about the quality of work life for its employees and strives to be sensitive to employee concerns.[6] Using arbitration allows Merrill Lynch to be fair and open by using a third party to settle conflicts and quickly find solutions to disputes.

arbitration
settlement of a labour/management dispute by a third party whose solution is legally binding and enforceable

Merrill Lynch
www.ml.com/

ADMINISTRATIVE TRIBUNALS

Federal and provincial administrative tribunals also have some judicial powers. Many administrative tribunals, such as the Competition Tribunal, decide issues and disputes that involve their regulations. Usually the hearings are before a panel of both lay persons and judges who decide the issues presented to them.

For example, the federal Competition Act and the Competition Tribunal Act of 1986 have established our Competition Tribunal. Its purpose is to "maintain and encourage competition in Canada in order to promote the efficiency and adaptability of the Canadian Economy." The three persons sitting on the panel do not have powers that include collective bargaining regulation. That falls under the labour acts either federally or provincially. Should a party that has been heard by the Competition Tribunal wish to appeal the decision, they must then proceed to the federal court system. In provincial cases, tribunal decisions may proceed through the court system or they must be appealed to the provincial cabinet in question.

Competition Tribunal
www.ct-tc.gc.ca/

IMPORTANT ELEMENTS OF BUSINESS LAW

To avoid violating criminal and civil laws, as well as discouraging lawsuits from consumers, employees, suppliers, and others, businesspeople need to be familiar with laws that address business practices. In this section, we'll examine some laws with which businesses must be concerned: laws relating to sales, contracts, agents, property, and competition.

The Sale of Goods Act

Most provinces have enacted a form of the Sale of Goods Act based on the English Sale of Goods Act of 1893. Even the United States has incorporated the same concepts in its Uniform Commercial Code (UCC) regulating the sale and limits of transactions regarding the sale of goods. The term goods, excludes such things as real property (such as land or buildings) and monetary items (such as bonds, stocks, and cash). Goods also exclude "work" (such as the contract to paint a house) or rights (such as patents and copyrights). The act does require that for a sale to occur there must be a payment of money for the goods, so in the case of a barter where no money changes hands, the act does not apply. There are many provincial laws covering the other sales procedures, but the sale of goods are governed by similar laws, including Quebec, which has incorporated portions of the laws into its Civil Code.

In most cases where the sale price is above a certain value, most provinces require a written contract to lay out the conditions of the sale. The values are usually in the realm of $40–$50. This requirement is waived, however, where the buyer accepts part of the goods sold, makes partial payment for the goods, or gives something in earnest to bind the contract.

To protect secured creditors in this age of high mobility of people and property, most provinces have enacted a Personal Property Security Act (PPSA), which establishes a registry of the property interests of secured creditors on a computer-based system. This process was based in part on Article 9 of the UCC of the United States. Ontario was the first province to establish the system in the 1970s, with Manitoba second. Quebec has incorporated similar procedures in its Civil Code. As expected, the provinces have similar laws but the laws are again not uniform across the country.

The Competition Act, as mentioned earlier, encourages competition and penalizes actions that may limit competition, so society may benefit from the continuous improvements in quality, service, and innovation that competition generates. In 1999 the federal government ruled that the bank mergers proposed were not in the nation's interests and disallowed the mergers of the Royal Bank and Bank of Montreal,

The Sale of Goods Act requires that for a sale to occur, there must be a payment of money for the goods. Most provinces also require a written contract to lay out the conditions of the sale.

© 1999 PhotoDisc, Inc.

and the CIBC and the TD Bank. Later though, the tribunal permitted the merger of Air Canada and Canadian Airlines, providing the new merged company did not stifle competition, as it would possess more than 50 percent of the airline traffic in Canada. The end result of the merger is yet to be determined, as it is further confused by the fallout from the September 11th attack on the World Trade Center in New York. Travel declined significantly and the already marginally profitable company faced large financial losses.

The Law of Torts and Fraud

A **tort** is a wrong to another or their property or their reputation. For example, a tort can result if the driver of a Domino's Pizza delivery car loses control of the vehicle and damages property or injures a person. In the case of the delivery car accident, the injured persons might sue the driver and the company—Domino's in this case—for damages resulting from the accident.

Fraudulent misrepresentation is a purposeful unlawful act to deceive or manipulate another. This kind of act may even include criminal acts such as fraudulent claims for Employment Insurance or Workers Compensation. **Deceit** is the tort that the lawsuit may be acted under, and an example was mentioned earlier regarding the former premier of British Columbia. Fraudulent conversion of goods occurs when a person obtains goods under false pretenses. This is not theft, as the wronged party willingly delivered the goods to the person committing the fraud. This kind of act is also a criminal offence. It is estimated that there are fraudulent auto insurance claims totalling $1.3 billion annually in Canada.[7]

tort
a wrong to another or their property or their reputation

fraudulent misrepresentation
A false statement of fact by a person who knows, or should know, that it is false, and is made with the intention of deceiving another

deceit
A tort that arises where a party suffers damage by acting upon a false representation made by a party with the intention of deceiving the other

---

R.E.M., a popular alternative rock band, has a policy of neither endorsing products nor allowing commercial use of its name because band members feel that such commercialism detracts from their artistic integrity. The group has publicized this policy in magazine, radio, and newspaper interviews.

Hershey Foods Corporation used R.E.M.'s name in a contest to promote its Kit Kat candy bar. The promotion included national radio advertising that aired on stations that play R.E.M.'s music and thus represent its target market. The radio ad used generic rock music as background rather than an actual R.E.M. song. R.E.M. quickly filed a civil suit against Hershey Foods charging Hershey with exploiting the R.E.M. name for crass commercial purposes. In R.E.M.'s view, the background music was vastly inferior to its music, and the group's members believed radio listeners would likely believe the music was R.E.M.'s.

The two sides settled their dispute out of court. Hershey's advertising agency agreed to make a US$50,000 contribution to charities specified by R.E.M. The agency also agreed not to use R.E.M.'s name in connection with any commercial endorsement or promotion without R.E.M.'s prior written approval.

1. What were some of the legal issues between R.E.M. and Hershey Foods?
2. How do you think this dispute should have been resolved?
3. What could Hershey Foods do in the future to avoid legal problems like the R.E.M. dispute?

Solve the Dilemma

R.E.M. Goes to Court Over Dispute

product liability
businesses' legal responsibility for any negligence in the design, production, sale, and consumption of products

An important aspect of tort law involves **product liability**—businesses' legal responsibility for any negligence in the manufacture of goods, or for failure to adequately warn consumers of any dangers associated with those goods. This duty of care extends not only to the purchaser but the consumer of the good. In the United States, the liability of the manufacturer is not limited to cases where negligence may be proven but to strict liability. For some goods, no matter how much effort the manufacturer makes to warn consumers of the risks, they may be held liable for any injury resulting from the consumption of the good.

For example, in a much-publicized case, a McDonald's customer was awarded US$2.9 million after she spilled hot McDonald's coffee in her lap and was scalded. Although that award eventually was reduced, McDonald's restaurants now display warning signs that their coffee is hot in order to eliminate both further injury and liability.

The Law of Contracts

contract
a mutual agreement between two or more parties that can be enforced in a court if one party chooses not to comply with the terms

Virtually every business transaction is carried out by means of a **contract,** a mutual agreement between two or more parties that can be enforced in a court if one party chooses not to comply with the terms of the contract. If you rent an apartment or house, for example, your lease is a contract. If you have borrowed money under a student loan program, you have a contractual agreement to repay the money.

A "handshake deal" is in most cases as fully and completely binding as a written, signed contract agreement. Indeed, many construction contractors have for years agreed to take on projects on the basis of such handshake deals. However, individual jurisdictions require that some contracts be in writing to be enforceable. Most provinces require that at least some of the following contracts be in writing:

- Contracts involving the sale of land or an interest in land.
- Contracts to pay somebody else's debt.
- Contracts that cannot be fulfilled within one year.
- Contracts for the sale of goods that cost more than $50 or so (value depends on province in question).

Only those contracts that meet certain requirements—called *elements*—are enforceable by the courts. A person or business seeking to enforce a contract must show that it contains the following elements: intention to create a legal relationship, an offer, acceptance of the offer, consideration, contractual capacity of the parties, and legality.

For any agreement to be considered a legal contract, all persons involved must agree to be bound by the terms of the contract. The intention to create the legal relationship is for the parties to promise to do something (or refrain from doing something) and have the intent of being bound by the agreement. The offer must be made, but the contract is not binding until the other party accepts the offer. The offer is not valid until received by the offeree, and the contract is binding upon acceptance in either writing or action taken to fulfill the contract. The agreement typically comes about when one party makes an offer and the other accepts. If both the offer and the acceptance are freely, voluntarily, and knowingly made, the acceptance forms the basis for the contract. If, however, either the offer or the acceptance are the result of fraud or force, the individual or organization subject to the fraud or force can void, or invalidate, the resulting agreement or receive compensation for damages.

The next requirement for enforcement of a contract is that it must be supported by *consideration*—that is, money or something of value must be given in return for fulfilling a contract. As a general rule, a person cannot be forced to abide by the terms of a promise unless that person receives a consideration. The something-of-value could be money, goods, services, or even a promise to do or not to do something. Generally, the courts are not concerned with the adequacy of the consideration— only that there is some.

Contractual capacity is the legal ability to enter into a contract. As a general rule, a court cannot enforce a contract if either party to the agreement lacks contractual capacity. A person's contractual capacity may be limited or nonexistent if he or she is an infant (usually under the age of 18), insane, intoxicated, or suffering from some mental impairment.

Legality is the state or condition of being lawful. For an otherwise binding contract to be enforceable, both the purpose of and the consideration for the contract must be legal. A contract in which a bank loans money at a rate of interest prohibited by law, a practice known as usury, would be an illegal contract, for example. The fact that one of the parties may commit an illegal act while performing a contract does not render the contract itself illegal, however.

Breach of contract is the failure or refusal of a party to a contract to live up to his or her promises. In the case of an apartment lease, failure to pay rent would be considered breach of contract. The breaching party—the one who fails to comply—may be liable for monetary damages that he or she causes the other person, or the courts may order that the contract be fulfilled. For example, firms that hire research and development personnel from competitors must examine written employment agreements for noncompetition clauses. Disregarding an employment contract with such a clause is usually a willful tort.[8]

> **breach of contract**
> the failure or refusal of a party to a contract to live up to his or her promises

The Law of Agency

An **agency** is a common business relationship created when one person acts on behalf of another and under that person's control. Two parties are involved in an agency relationship: The **principal** is the one who wishes to have a specific task accomplished; the **agent** is the one who acts on behalf of the principal to accomplish the task. Authors, movie stars, and athletes often employ agents to help them obtain the best contract terms.

An agency relationship is created by the mutual agreement of the principal and the agent. It is usually not necessary that such an agreement be in writing, although putting it in writing is certainly advisable. An agency relationship continues as long as both the principal and the agent so desire. It can be terminated by mutual agreement, by fulfillment of the purpose of the agency, by the refusal of either party to continue in the relationship, or by the death of either the principal or the agent. In most cases, a principal grants authority to the agent through a formal *power of attorney,* which is a legal document authorizing a person to act as someone else's agent. The power of attorney can be used for any agency relationship, and its use is not limited to lawyers. For instance, in real estate transactions, often a lawyer or real estate agent is given power of attorney with the authority to purchase real estate for the buyer. Accounting firms often give employees agency relationships in making financial transactions. Price Waterhouse was charged with exchanging drug money on a

> **agency**
> a common business relationship created when one person acts on behalf of another and under that person's control
>
> **principal**
> in an agency relationship, the party who wishes to have a specific task accomplished
>
> **agent**
> acts on behalf of the principal to accomplish the task

currency black market in Colombia. According to the seizure affidavit, "in electing for an exchange of Colombian pesos for US dollars on the black market, the officials of Price Waterhouse S.A., who were agents of the firm, knew they were breaking Colombian law and had reason to believe the US dollars they received were likely proceeds from drug sales in the United States."[9] This agency relationship created a legal problem for the firm and its employees.

The Law of Property

real property
real estate and everything permanently attached to it

personal property
all property other than real property

intellectual property
property that is generated by a person's creative activities

Property law is extremely broad in scope because it covers the ownership and transfer of all kinds of real, personal, and intellectual property. **Real property** consists of real estate and everything permanently attached to it; **personal property** basically is everything else. Personal property can be further subdivided into tangible and intangible property. *Tangible property* refers to items that have a physical existence, such as automobiles, business inventory, and clothing. *Intangible property* consists of rights and duties; its existence may be represented by a document or by some other tangible item. For example, accounts receivable, stock in a corporation, goodwill, and trademarks are all examples of intangible personal property. **Intellectual property** refers to property, such as musical works, artwork, books, and computer software, that is generated by a person's creative activities. A picture taken by a commercial photographer of the Simon family was supposed to be only for the family's private use, but somehow a copy of the photo was put into a collection of stock photos for commercial use. The photo collection was digitized and widely distributed on a CD-ROM published by PhotoDisc. The Simon family photo appeared in a calendar, a Costco ad, two trade magazines, and other places as well. The ensuing lawsuit probably cost PhotoDisc more than US$1 million. There have been at least half a dozen lawsuits involving PhotoDisc's products. Most have been settled for a few thousand dollars, but one involving a part-time model whose "wholesome" pose on a tennis court ended up in breast-implant and dating-service ads cost the defendants or their insurers a total of US$175,000.[10]

Copyrights, patents, and trademarks provide protection to the owners of property by giving them the exclusive right to use it. *Copyrights* protect the ownership rights on material (often intellectual property) such as books, music, videos, photos, and computer software. The creators of such works, or their heirs, generally have exclusive rights to the published or unpublished works for the creator's lifetime, plus 50 years. *Patents* give inventors exclusive rights to their invention for 20 years. The most intense competition for patents is in the pharmaceutical industry.

A *trademark* is a brand (name, mark, or symbol) that is registered with the Trade Marks Office in Ottawa. Protection is not immediate. The Mark holder must go to court to protect the trademark by obtaining an injunction forcing the offending party to stop using the Mark. Sometimes if unauthorized goods have been sold under the registered mark, an accounting may be undertaken to determine the lost profits of the holder. Forgery of a trademark is a criminal offence as is the attempt to pass off a product under another trademark. Among the symbols that have been so protected are McDonald's golden arches and Coca-Cola's distinctive bottle shape. It is estimated that large multinational firms may have as many as 15,000 conflicts related to trademarks.[11] Companies are diligent about protecting their trademarks both to avoid confusion in consumers' minds and because a term that becomes part of everyday language can no longer be trademarked. The name *aspirin*, for example, was once the exclusive property of its creator but became so widely used as a product

After declaring bankruptcy, this store's assets were sold to pay off as much debt as possible.

Dion Ogust/The Image Works

name (rather than a brand name) that now anyone can use it in the United States. The name, however, is still registered in Canada.

As the trend toward globalization of trade continues, and more and more businesses trade across national boundaries, protecting property rights, particularly intellectual property such as computer software, has become an increasing challenge. While a company may be able to register as a trademark a brand name or symbol in its home country, it may not be able to secure that protection abroad. Some countries have copyright and patent laws that are less strict than those of Canada; some countries will not enforce foreign laws. China, for example, has often been criticized for permitting foreign goods to be counterfeited there. Such counterfeiting harms not only the sales of foreign companies but also their reputations if the knockoffs are of poor quality. Thus, businesses engaging in foreign trade may have to take extra steps to protect their property because local laws may be insufficient to protect them.

The Law of Bankruptcy

Although few businesses and individuals intentionally fail to repay (or default on) their debts, sometimes they cannot fulfill their financial obligations. Individuals may charge goods and services beyond their ability to pay for them. Businesses may take on too much debt in order to finance growth. An option of last resort in these cases is **bankruptcy**. For example, Eaton's, once one of Canada's leading retailers, filed for bankruptcy in 1999.

Under the Canadian Bankruptcy and Insolvency Act, a person or company may be insolvent because they essentially are not able to pay their creditors. This in turn may be the result of a lack of cash flow to meet their obligations. **Insolvency** does not immediately mean the debtor is bankrupt, though it frequently precedes bankruptcy. Bankruptcy is defined under the law requiring any one of 10 conditions to be met. Ultimately, bankruptcy reflects the condition where the debtor has assets of less value than their debts, and an attempt is made to settle the debts and, in particular, for consumers get a fresh start.

bankruptcy
legal insolvency

insolvency
the inability to pay debts as they become due under the normal course of business

Figure 2.1

*Bankruptcy
Proceedings*

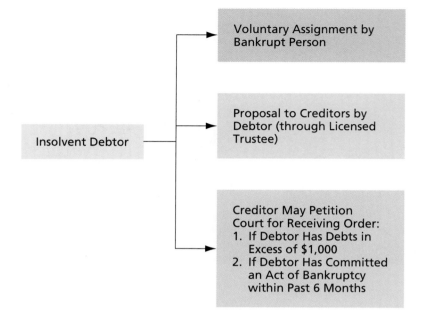

Debtors may voluntarily assign themselves into bankruptcy, be petitioned into bankruptcy by their creditors or, in the case of corporation, seek protection from the Official Receiver while they develop a proposal for the creditors to restructure the debt repayment. The business in question then has 30 days to present a proposal to the creditors. The time period may be extended for up to a maximum of five months, but all creditors, secured and unsecured, vote on the acceptability of the plan. Primarily though, the law is focused on the unsecured creditors who possess fewer assets to claim or lack a specific claim on any assets. The corporation must pay the total debt or the creditors must accept the proposal; otherwise, the company can no longer operate and is wound up, and the assets are sold to satisfy the creditors. Generally, the law is set up to speed the return of the consumer back into gainful activity in the community, while businesses are to repay their creditors as much as can be realized on the assets. Bankruptcy proceedings are outlined in Figure 2.1.

Provincial statutes limit the assets that may be seized and sold for personal bankruptcy. It is the intent of the law to assist individuals to not only repay their creditors but also to get a new start on their lives. Still, the law has some teeth that enable criminal proceedings if the debtor has used fraud or some other means to take advantage of the creditors.

THE INTERNET: LEGAL AND REGULATORY ISSUES

Our use and dependence on the Internet is increasingly creating a potential legal problem for businesses. With this growing use come questions of maintaining an acceptable level of privacy for consumers and proper competitive use of the medium. Some might consider that tracking individuals who visit or "hit" their web site by

Law clerks/legal assistants work for lawyers and are trained to do independent legal work under the direction of a lawyer. They perform routine legal and administrative duties, including filing legal documents, maintaining corporate documents, searching titles, interviewing clients or witnesses, managing correspondence, preparing for legal proceedings, and in some circumstances may appear before administrative tribunals and certain courts. Most provinces require graduation from an accredited program, usually of two years in length, from a community college, as well as appropriate work experience within the last two years.

Law clerks are employed in law offices, corporate offices of large firms, real estate offices, and government offices (including municipal, provincial and federal government departments). Salaries may start in the mid-$20,000s per year, but may top out in the corporate world and large law offices at $75,000 or more. Information on finding a job in the area of law is available from the law society of your province, your local college career office, or the provincial body representing law clerks/legal assistants.[12]

Explore Your Career Options

Legal and Regulatory Career Options

attaching a "cookie" (identifying you as a web site visitor for potential recontact and tracking your movement throughout the site) is an improper use of the Internet for business purposes. Others may find such practices acceptable and similar to the practices of non-Internet retailers who copy information from cheques or ask customers for their name, address, or phone number before they will process a transaction. There are few specific laws that regulate business on the Internet but the standards for acceptable behaviour that are reflected in the basic laws and regulations designed for traditional businesses can be applied to business on the Internet, as well.

The major questions that arise are in the area of who regulates the transaction and where it takes place. When an individual goes online and clicks to buy something, has that person entered into a contract? The federal government has enacted a few laws limiting the extent of sharing of Internet users' data. Ontario and Saskatchewan have conformed to the federal laws and extended the rules to include how contracts are to take place and what is included in the transaction. In Ontario, when the user clicks on the box that states "I Agree," that person is deemed to have entered into a contract.

The European Union (EU) was the first in regulating Internet commerce. The key message of this initiative is that online services that are not restricted by geographic boundaries should be regulated by country of origin, not the country where the individual connects to the service.[13] As a result of these standards, no company will be able to deliver personal information about EU citizens to countries whose privacy laws do not meet the EU standards. Developing these standards took more than six years, and their goal is to protect and control the use of data related to European citizens. Companies will have to make customer data files available upon request, much as Canadian consumers have access to their personal credit histories in order to ensure accuracy. Web site operators will not be able to use data tags or cookies to track consumers' movements and preferences without obtaining their permission first. Selling e-mail addresses will also not be allowed without customer permission.[14]

The Institute of Law Clerks of Ontario
www.ilco.on.ca

The Ministry of Training, Colleges and Universities, Province of Ontario
www.edu.gov.on.ca/ eng/general/college/ progstan/humserv/ lawclerk.html

Pre-Paid Legal Services®, Inc.
www.prepaidlegal.com

The Internet has also created a copyright dilemma for some organizations that have found that the web addresses of other online firms either match or are very similar to their company trademark. "Cyber-squatters" attempt to sell back the registration of these matching sites to the trademark owner. Companies such as Taco Bell, MTC, and KFC have paid thousands of dollars to gain control of domain names that match or parallel company trademarks.[15]

The reduction of geographic barriers, speed of response, and memory capability of the Internet will continue to create new challenges for the legal and regulatory environment in the future.

Review Your Understanding

Identify the sources of law.

Business law refers to the rules and regulations that govern the conduct of business. Laws are classified as either criminal or civil. Criminal law prohibits specific kinds of actions and imposes fines or imprisonment for violations. Civil law specifies the rights and duties of individuals and organizations and may result in fines but not imprisonment. Criminal and civil laws are derived from four sources: the Constitution (Constitutional law), precedents established by judges (common law), federal and provincial statutes (statute law), and federal and provincial administrative agencies (administrative law).

Gain an appreciation of the framework for regulating business through administrative agencies.

Federal and provincial administrative agencies have some judicial power and many decide disputes that involve their regulations.

Review important elements of business law, including the Sale of Goods Act, the law of torts and fraud, the law of contracts, the law of agency, the law of property, and the law of bankruptcy.

The Sale of Goods Act requires that money must be paid for the goods received. A tort is a civil wrong that may be intentional or result from negligence. Fraud is a purposeful unlawful act to deceive or manipulate in order to damage others. Contracts are mutual agreements between two or more parties that can be enforced in a court if one party chooses not to comply with the terms. Breach of contract is the failure or refusal of a party to a contract to live up to his or her promises. An agency is a common business relationship in which one person acts on behalf of another and under that person's control. Property law is extremely broad in scope because it covers the ownership and transfer of all kinds of real, personal, and intellectual property. Bankruptcy results when individuals or businesses cannot fulfill their financial obligations.

Review the legal and regulatory implications of electronic business.

Increasing use of the Internet is creating potential legal problems for businesses. Few regulations exist today, but, just as other forms of communications media have required different standards of regulation, the Internet also will have a unique set of regulations developed over time.

Provide an overview of the legal pressure for responsible business conduct.

To ensure greater compliance with society's desires, federal and provincial governments are moving toward increased organizational accountability for misconduct. The government places responsibility for controlling and preventing misconduct on top management.

Identify the legal issues in a business dispute.

The "Solve the Dilemma" box provides information on a legal dispute. Based on the material presented in this chapter, you should be able to identify the legal issues and make recommendations for avoiding such disputes in the future.

Learn the Terms

agency 37	court of original jurisdiction 32	mediation 32
agent 37	deceit 35	personal property 38
arbitration 35	fraudulent misrepresentation 35	principal 37
bankruptcy 39	insolvency 39	product liability 36
breach of contract 37	intellectual property 38	real property 38
business law 30	jurisdiction 32	tort 35
contract 36	lawsuits 31	
court of appeal 32		

Check Your Progress

1. List four sources of law and differentiate among them. Which have the greatest impact on business?
2. What is the purpose of a lawsuit?
3. Discuss the role of the court system in the legal and regulatory environment of business.
4. What are the advantages and disadvantages of choosing arbitration as a method to resolve disputes?
5. What does a businessperson need to know about the Competition Tribunal and its impact on business relationships?
6. What areas of business are most affected by the Sale of Goods Act?
7. What is a tort? Discuss how tort law has affected business in Canada.
8. List the elements required to have an enforceable contract. If one party to a contract breaches it, what can the other party do?
9. Define bankruptcy. If a business or individual can no longer pay its debts but wants to find a way to work out its financial problems and continue to operate, what are their options?
10. What are the legal and regulatory issues associated with using the Internet to conduct business?

Get Involved

1. If you rent an apartment, bring your lease to class. What does the owner/manager of the apartment promise to do? What is the consideration? Where do both parties show voluntary agreement? Is the lease legal? On what legal grounds might one or both of the parties terminate the agreement? Discuss what happens if one of the parties "breaks the lease."
2. In recent years, Microsoft Corporation (which markets Windows 2000, Windows 98, Microsoft Word, and Internet Explorer) has come under fire from competitors and customers for its business tactics, and the US Justice Department has prosecuted the software giant for antitrust and anticompetitive activities. Research these developments and write a paper analyzing what happened in this case. What laws were at stake, and what were the specific charges levied against Microsoft? Do you believe Microsoft committed any wrongdoing? Defend your answer. What (if any) differences would a Canadian company face?

Build Your Skills

Examining Legal Issues in the Health Care Industry

Background: In 1997, Fawcett Memorial Hospital in Port Charlotte, Florida, was named as the focal point of the biggest case of fraud ever in the US health care industry. A government probe resulted in the indictment of three mid-level Columbia/HCA Healthcare Corporation executives, who were charged with filing false cost reports for Fawcett that resulted in losses of more than US$4.4 million from government programs. Federal investigators seized hospital documents relating to its home health care services and its close relationships with doctors, and also charged the hospital with defrauding the federal Medicare and military health care programs by inflating reimbursement requests. The government declared a criminal investigation, meaning that there was evidence not only to indict individual Columbia executives but also potentially to prove that the company was involved in systematic organizational efforts to defraud the government. The government alleged that at least part of the profit obtained by Columbia was gained by overcharging for Medicare and other federal health programs by unscrupulous executives who billed the government for nonreimbursable interest expenses. Other concerns involved illegal incentives offered to physicians and the possible overuse of home health care services.

Task:

1. Break into groups of three to five students.

2. Each team member should provide, in his or her own words, a definition of fraud in the context of business relationships.

3. Each team member should provide possible explanations that Columbia/HCA executives might use to justify filing false cost reports to the federal Medicare program.

4. The team as a group should develop an explanation of the various organizational pressures that might have caused employees at Columbia/HCA to engage in overbilling the government.

5. The team should determine if knowledge of laws or regulatory forces discussed in this chapter could have helped Columbia/HCA executives avoid their legal problems. Identify specific laws or regulations.

6. Could Canadian hospitals or doctors also be encouraged to undertake this same action?

7. What factors discourage this kind of action taking place in Canada, if at all?

 **See for Yourself Videocase** www.cbc.ca

Employee Fraud

Most companies and other organizations concern themselves with theft and the passing of bad cheques and counterfeit bills. But the largest losses of companies are due to employees, four times the annual losses to outsiders, totalling $4 billion per year in Canada. To a large company the loss is at least a nuisance, but for a small company it can lead to bankruptcy. Many of the losses are to trusted employees and result when there are few, if any, controls on the items of value, usually money. The pictures are rather shocking in many ways and apparently more common than most people think.

But are the police any help? They are, but only after the owners or managers have spent the time to develop the paper trail to prove the theft or fraud has occurred. This documentation may require the use of a forensic audit, which can cost thousands of dollars to conduct. At this time, the police get involved, but they do not investigate; the company does. The police lay charges. Ernst & Young, one of Canada's largest accounting firms, attributes much of the cause of fraud and employee theft to simple human nature. People have the opportunity and take advantage of trusting employers, and their colleagues frequently turn a blind eye to the practice.

Still, an ounce of prevention is worth a pound of cure. A company should decrease the opportunities. Highly ranked persons, usually the owners, should reconcile the bank statements to ensure that no inappropriate cheques have been issued and that all deposits have made it to the bank, especially if the company handles large amounts of cash. Watch for telltale signs of persons skimming from the company, such as a lifestyle that exceeds the salary earned. Is the new car more expensive than that person should be able to afford? Does the person take holidays? If not, that may be because he or she must remain on site to ensure the books are managed to cover up the theft. This is why in some industries mandatory holidays must take place. It would then take more than one person to be involved and that is sometimes hard to manage. Can the parties trust one another?

Questions

1. Have you ever taken something from work without paying for it? Be honest.

2. At what amount should an employee be fired for theft from an employer? And does this amount vary by size of company?

3. Why would so few companies attend the police workshop in Edmonton?

4. What kinds of persons steal from their employer?

5. Considering the discussion in the chapter regarding the justice system, do you think the police should be more involved?

6. Do you think the time being served by the former employee is adequate? What is the likelihood of this individual ever paying back the money stolen?

Source: *Venture*, show number 767, "Employee Fraud," December 5, 2000, running time 6:03.

Remember to check out our Online Learning Centre at **www.mcgrawhill.ca/college/ferrell.**

Chapter 3

Business Ethics and Social Responsibility

Chapter Outline

Introduction

Business Ethics and Social Responsibility

The Role of Ethics in Business

Recognizing Ethical Issues in Business

Improving Ethical Behaviour in Business

The Nature of Social Responsibility

Social Responsibility Issues

Objectives

After reading this chapter, you will be able to:

- Define business ethics and examine its importance.
- Detect some of the ethical issues that may arise in business.
- Specify how businesses can promote ethical behaviour.
- Define social responsibility and explain its relevance to business.
- Debate an organization's social responsibilities to owners, employees, consumers, the environment, and the community.
- Evaluate the ethics of a business's decision.

Starbucks

Starbucks is the number-one specialty coffee retailer in the United States and has grown to extremely popular status in Canada. Founded in 1971, the gourmet coffee-bar chain has grown from a local business with six stores into an international retail enterprise with more than 1,400 stores and 25,000 employees. The company's sales and profits have grown by more than 50 percent a year for the last six years. It also has won a number of ethics awards and been recognized as a role model for social responsibility.

Starbucks's first priority is to take care of the people who work in its retail stores because they are responsible for communicating with and serving customers. Executives believe that by taking care of its employees, the company will provide long-term value to shareholders. To encourage employees to support the company's commitment to quality, Starbucks provides a stock option program worth 12 percent of each employee's annual base pay. Probably no other company has attempted a stock option plan as widespread and ambitious. Additionally, the company provides health care benefits to *all* employees, even part-time ones. These employee-focused benefits have resulted in an annual employee turnover rate that is one-fourth that of the competition.

Starbucks's commitment to its people extends beyond its coffee-bar counters. Building on its concern for quality of life, Starbucks has become the first importer of an agricultural commodity to develop a framework for a code of conduct designed to improve working conditions in the countries that grow coffee. By paying a premium, above-market price for coffee, Starbucks hopes to increase the supply of high-quality coffee while, at the same time, improving workers' lives. The company also makes payments to farms and mills in Guatemala and Costa Rica to cofund health care centres, farm schools, and scholarships for farm workers' children.

Starbucks is also the leading North American sponsor of CARE, an international relief and development organization, giving an annual corporate contribution plus $2 per CARE coffee sampler product sold. Starbucks further contributes to a variety of organizations benefiting AIDS research, child welfare, environmental awareness, and the arts. The company also empowers its employees to take an active role in their own neighbourhoods.[1]

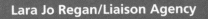

Lara Jo Regan/Liaison Agency

INTRODUCTION

As the opening vignette illustrates, determining how to conduct business appropriately can be challenging. Wrongdoing by businesses has focused public attention and government involvement to encourage more acceptable business conduct. Any business decision may be judged as right or wrong, ethical or unethical, legal or illegal.

In this chapter, we will take a look at the role of ethics and social responsibility in business decision making. First we define business ethics and examine why it is important to understand ethics' role in business. Next we explore a number of business ethics issues to help you learn to recognize such issues when they arise. Finally, we consider steps businesses can take to improve ethical behaviour in their organizations. The second half of the chapter focuses on social responsibility. We define social responsibility and then survey some important responsibility issues and how companies have responded to them.

BUSINESS ETHICS AND SOCIAL RESPONSIBILITY

business ethics

principles and standards that determine acceptable conduct in business

In this chapter, we define **business ethics** as the principles and standards that determine acceptable conduct in business organizations. The acceptability of behaviour in business is determined by customers, competitors, government regulators, interest groups, and the public, as well as each individual's personal moral principles and values. For example, Honda Motor Co. was sued by its dealers in a class action lawsuit, which was finally settled for US$316 million. The suit alleged that executives in Honda's US division demanded cash, cars, and other gifts in exchange for larger inventories of the popular Accord and Accura models. More than 1,800 US car dealers were given a portion of the cash settlement, auto parts, and signs.[2]

Many consumers and social advocates believe that businesses should not only make a profit but also consider the social implications of their activities. We define social responsibility as a business's obligation to maximize its positive impact and minimize its negative impact on society. Although many people use the terms *social responsibility* and *ethics* interchangeably, they do not mean the same thing. Business ethics relates to an *individual's* or a *work group's* decisions that society evaluates as right or wrong, whereas social responsibility is a broader concept that concerns the impact of the *entire business's* activities on society. From an ethical perspective, for example, we may be concerned about a health care organization or practitioner overcharging the provincial government for medical services. From a social responsibility perspective, we might be concerned about the impact that this overcharging will have on the ability of the health care system to provide adequate services for all citizens.

As discussed in Chapter 2, the most basic ethical and social responsibility concerns have been codified as laws and regulations that encourage businesses to conform to society's standards, values, and attitudes. At a minimum, managers are expected to obey these laws and regulations. Most legal issues arise as choices that society deems unethical, irresponsible, or otherwise unacceptable. However, all actions deemed unethical by society are not necessarily illegal, and both legal and ethical concerns change over time. As we said in Chapter 2, business law refers to the laws and regulations that govern the conduct of business. Many problems and conflicts in business can be avoided if owners, managers, and employees know more about business law and the legal system. Business ethics, social responsibility, and laws together act as a compliance system requiring that businesses and employees act responsibly in society.

THE ROLE OF ETHICS IN BUSINESS

Although we will not tell you in this chapter what you ought to do, others—your superiors, coworkers, and family—will make judgments about the ethics of your actions and decisions. Learning how to recognize and resolve ethical issues is an important step in evaluating ethical decisions in business.

You have only to pick up *The National Post* or the *Globe and Mail Report on Business* to see how truly difficult it is to deal with legal and ethical issues. In an Ethics Officer Association survey, 48 percent of employees surveyed indicated they had done something unethical or illegal in the past year. The costs of unethical and fraudulent acts committed by US employees total US$400 billion annually.[3] Such losses are significant, but the impact of a single environmental error on a corporation can be staggering. It is reported that the total cost to Exxon to settle claims related to the *Valdez* oil spill off the coast of Alaska was US$3.2 billion. During the period between the spill in 1989 and the settlement in 1995, Exxon's reported profits totalled US$5.8 billion.[4]

It is not just altruism that motivates corporations to operate in a socially responsible manner, but also consideration of the "bottom line." There are good business reasons for a strong commitment to ethical values:

1. Ethical companies have been shown to be more profitable.
2. Making ethical choices results in lower stress for corporate managers and other employees.
3. Our reputation, good or bad, endures.
4. Ethical behaviour enhances leadership.
5. The alternative to voluntary ethical behaviour is demanding and costly regulation.

Regular readers of the news will have seen reports of unethical or aggressive sales tactics used to prey upon vulnerable consumers, most often seniors. Examples include persons claiming to be inspectors, citing roof and chimney repairs as being needed or even required by law. Others, while not resorting to such subterfuge, utilize sales techniques that are confusing or hard to resist for the vulnerable. In the past, persons falling prey to such tactics and signing purchase contracts in their homes had, in Ontario, only 24 hours to rescind the contract. Such direct sales contracts had to be cancelled in writing. As of May 18, 2001, the Ontario Consumer Protection Act provides a ten-day "cooling-off" period in which to cancel a direct sales contract worth $50 or more. This is just one example of the ongoing efforts of both the federal and provincial governments in Canada to respond to unethical business practices.

It is important to understand that business ethics goes beyond legal issues. Ethical conduct builds trust among individuals and in business relationships, which validates and promotes confidence in business relationships. Establishing trust and confidence is much more difficult in organizations that have established reputations for acting unethically. If you were to discover, for example, that a manager had misled you about company benefits when you were hired, your trust and confidence in the company would probably diminish. And, if you learned that a colleague had lied to you about something, you probably would not trust or rely on that person in the future. KPMG, a leading accounting and consulting firm, provides assistance to firms that want to develop ethics programs to avoid ethical problems and build trust and integrity in business relationships.

Well-publicized incidents of unethical activity—ranging from health care fraud to using the Internet to gain personal information from young children to charges of deceptive advertising of food and diet products to unfair competitive practices in the computer software industry—strengthen the public's perception that ethical standards and the level of trust in business need to be raised. Two African-American health groups filed a lawsuit against 12 tobacco companies alleging that menthol cigarettes were specifically marketed to African-American communities, thereby violating their civil rights. The suit charges that menthol cigarettes are more dangerous than regular cigarettes. This is the first litigation against tobacco manufacturers that does not use personal injury or product liability laws.[5] This represents only a portion of the ongoing ethical and legal concerns with respect to cigarette marketing and distribution. Often, such charges start as ethical conflicts but turn into legal disputes when cooperative conflict resolution cannot be accomplished.

RECOGNIZING ETHICAL ISSUES IN BUSINESS

ethical issue

an identifiable problem, situation, or opportunity that requires a person to choose from among several actions that may be evaluated as right or wrong, ethical or unethical

Learning to recognize ethical issues is the most important step in understanding business ethics. An **ethical issue** is an identifiable problem, situation, or opportunity that requires a person to choose from among several actions that may be evaluated as right or wrong, ethical or unethical. In business, such a choice often involves weighing monetary profit against what a person considers appropriate conduct. The best way to judge the ethics of a decision is to look at a situation from a customer's or competitor's viewpoint: Should liquid-diet manufacturers make unsubstantiated claims about their products? Should an engineer agree to divulge her former employer's trade secrets to ensure that she gets a better job with a competitor? Should a salesperson omit facts about a product's poor safety record in his presentation to a customer? Such questions require the decision maker to evaluate the ethics of his or her choice.

Many business issues may seem straightforward and easy to resolve, but in reality, a person often needs several years of experience in business to understand what is acceptable or ethical. For example, if you are a salesperson, when does offering a gift—such as season basketball tickets—to a customer become a bribe rather than just a sales practice? Clearly, there are no easy answers to such a question. But the size of the transaction, the history of personal relationships within the particular company, as well as many other factors may determine whether an action will be judged as right or wrong by others. When Wal-Mart began selling sandals that strongly resembled the popular Teva brand, Mark Thatcher, founder of the Teva Sports Sandal, took notice. Sales of Teva sandals fell from US$69 million to US$42 million, and company executives believed this was because Wal-Mart was selling copies (or "knock-offs") for 25 percent less. This ethical issue of right or wrong was resolved in court. Teva won the lawsuit, and Wal-Mart agreed to stop selling the shoes.[6]

> Did you know? *A 1999 survey by KPMG found that 72.7 percent of companies have some sort of program focused on promoting ethical values and principles.*

Ethics is also related to the culture in which a business operates. In Canada or the United States, for example, it would be inappropriate for a businessperson to bring an elaborately wrapped gift to a prospective client on their first meeting—the gift could be viewed as a bribe. In Japan, however, it is considered impolite *not* to bring a gift. Experience with the culture in which a business operates is critical to understanding what is ethical or unethical.

KPMG
www.kpmg.ca

Ethical Issues

To help you understand ethical issues that perplex businesspeople today, we will take a brief look at some of them in this section. The vast number of news-format investigative programs has increased consumer and employee awareness of organizational misconduct. In addition, the multitude of cable channels and Internet resources has improved the awareness of ethical problems among the general public.

An Ethics Resource Center/Society for Human Resource Management survey of US employees indicates that workers witness many instances of ethical misconduct in their organizations. The specific percentages are noted in Table 3.1. Note that workers report multiple observations of ethical misconduct; therefore, each category is an independent question of observed misconduct. When employees were asked the principal causes of unethical behaviour in their organizations, the key factor reported was overly aggressive financial or business objectives. Many of these issues relate to decisions and concerns that managers have to deal with daily. It is not possible to discuss every issue, of course. However, a discussion of a few issues can help you begin to recognize the ethical problems with which businesspersons must deal. Many ethical issues in business can be categorized in the context of their relation with conflicts of interest, fairness and honesty, communications, and business associations.

Conflict of Interest. A conflict of interest exists when a person must choose whether to advance his or her own personal interests or those of others. For example, a manager in a corporation is supposed to ensure that the company is profitable so that its stockholder-owners receive a return on their investment. In other words, the manager has a responsibility to investors. If she instead makes decisions that give her more power or money but do not help the company, then she has a conflict of interest—she is acting to benefit herself at the expense of her company and is not fulfilling her responsibilities. To avoid conflicts of interest, employees must be able to separate their personal financial interests from their business dealings. Sunbeam Corporation has lost tremendous market value (falling from $55 a share to under $5 a share) and damaged its reputation as a result of decisions made while Al Dunlap was CEO. Shareholders are suing the company for inflated earnings figures during Dunlap's tenure. Some believe that Dunlap was manipulating organizational profitability statements for his own gain.

As mentioned earlier, it is considered improper to give or accept **bribes**— payments, gifts, or special favours intended to influence the outcome of a decision. A bribe is a conflict of interest because it benefits an individual at the expense of an organization or society. Wal-Mart Stores, Inc., may have the toughest policy against conflict of interest in the retail industry. Sam Walton, the late founder of Wal-Mart,

bribes
payments, gifts, or special favours intended to influence the outcome of a decision

Table 3.1

Percentage of Workers Who Say These Ethical Infractions Are Committed by Coworkers

Source: Ethics Resource Center/Society for Human Resource Management, 1997 Business Ethics Survey Report, p. 20.

Lying to supervisors	45%
Falsifying records	36
Alcohol and drug abuse	36
Conflict of interest	34
Stealing or theft	27
Gift receipt/entertainment in violation of company policy	26

prohibited company buyers from accepting so much as a cup of coffee from suppliers. The Wal-Mart policy is black and white and leaves no room for interpretation, and it is probably a factor in helping Wal-Mart reduce costs. Other retailers typically allow buyers to accept meals, small gifts, and outings such as golf, fishing, or hunting trips. Defence contractors, such as Lockheed Martin and Texas Instruments, have strict gift policies, as does the Royal Bank of Canada.

Fairness and Honesty. Fairness and honesty are at the heart of business ethics and relate to the general values of decision makers. At a minimum, businesspersons are expected to follow all applicable laws and regulations. But beyond obeying the law, they are expected not to harm customers, employees, clients, or competitors knowingly through deception, misrepresentation, coercion, or discrimination. A recent survey showed that nearly one-fourth of workers have been asked to engage in an unethical act at work, and 41 percent carried out the act.[8]

One aspect of fairness relates to competition. Although numerous laws have been passed to foster competition and make monopolistic practices illegal, companies sometimes gain control over markets by using questionable practices that harm competition. Rivals of Microsoft, for example, have accused the software giant of using unfair and monopolistic practices to maintain market dominance with its Microsoft Network web browser. Competitors such as Netscape feel at a competitive disadvantage since the Microsoft Network is coupled with the Windows operating system and is readily available to 90 percent of the PC market. The US Justice Department has claimed that "Microsoft wanted to hurt rival Netscape at all costs." The initial court judgment found in favour of the Justice Department. This ruling is under appeal by Microsoft.[9]

Another aspect of fairness and honesty relates to disclosure of potential harm caused by product use. When Procter & Gamble introduced Olestra, the low-cholesterol fat substitute, products in which it was used had labels warning consumers of potential problems with abdominal cramping.

Dishonesty has become a significant problem in North America. In a study conducted by the Josephson Institute, 92 percent of older teenagers admitted to lying and 70 percent admitted to cheating on tests. However, 97 percent of those surveyed say that good character is important, while 69 percent believe that the ethics of this generation are satisfactory.[10]

Communications. Communications is another area in which ethical concerns may arise. False and misleading advertising, as well as deceptive personal-selling tactics, anger consumers and can lead to the failure of a business. Truthfulness about product safety and quality are also important to consumers. In the pharmaceutical industry, for example, dietary supplements, such as herbs, are sold with limited regulation and testing, and many supplements are sold by small, independent marketers. Some tests show that herbs, such as ginseng, may be sold without enough of the active ingredients to be effective. Now, large pharmaceutical firms, such as Warner-Lambert, are entering the US$4 billion herb market and communicating the quality control and credibility associated with their names.[11] However, ample opportunities remain for unethical firms to mislead consumers about herbal products.

Some manufacturers fail to provide enough information for consumers about differences between products. In the contact-lens-solution market, a number of manufacturers are marketing identical products with different prices. Bausch & Lomb, for example, priced its one-ounce bottle of Sensitive Eyes Drops at about $5.65. But a 12-ounce bottle of its Sensitive Eyes Saline Solution, which had the same ingredients and formulation but a different label, was priced at $2.79. Other manufacturers do the same thing. Says consultant Jack Trout, "It's not only a sneaky way to make money, but it's lousy marketing, the type of thing that backfires . . . when it's made public."[12]

Another important aspect of communications that may raise ethical concerns relates to product labelling. Health warnings on cigarette packages were first imposed by federal law in 1989. In 1994 a new set of eight messages were required that covered the top 35 percent of each main display surface of a cigarette package. The Canadian system was adopted by Australia, Thailand, and Poland. The 1994 warnings also led to legislative proposals in both the United States and the European Union.

In 1995 the Supreme Court of Canada ruled large parts of the Tobacco Products Control Act unconstitutional, removing the legal basis for imposing the warnings.

New regulations were passed on June 26, 2000. The new act, requiring even more graphic warnings on 50 percent of the package panels, combined with inside package messages about health damage caused by tobacco and information about quitting, has also been challenged in court. The Quebec Superior Court ruled in

Managers have the responsibility to create a work environment to help an organization maintain ethical business relationships while achieving its objectives.

© 1999 PhotoDisc, Inc.

Checkers Pizza was one of the first to offer home delivery service, with overwhelming success. However, the major pizza chains soon followed suit, taking away Checkers's competitive edge. Jon Barnard, Checkers's founder and co-owner, needed a new gimmick to beat the competition. He decided to develop a computerized information database that would make Checkers the most efficient competitor and provide insight into consumer buying behaviour at the same time. Under the system, telephone customers were asked their phone number; if they had ordered from Checkers before, their address and previous order information came up on the computer screen.

After successfully testing the new system, Barnard put the computerized order network in place in all Checkers outlets. After three months of success, he decided to give an award to the family that ate the most Checkers pizza. Through the tracking system, the company identified the biggest customer, who had ordered a pizza every weekday for the past three months (63 pizzas). The company put together a program to surprise the family with an award, free-food certificates, and a news story announcing the award. As Barnard began to plan for the event, however, he began to think that maybe the family might not want all the attention and publicity.

1. What are some of the ethical issues in giving customers an award for consumption behaviour without notifying them first?
2. Do you see this as a potential violation of privacy? Explain.
3. How would you handle the situation if you were Barnard?

favour of the government. Canadians are more willing to accept the guidance of government censors, and we have an almost complete ban on tobacco advertising under the Federal Tobacco Act of 1998.

Business Relationships. The behaviour of businesspersons toward customers, suppliers, and others in their workplace may also generate ethical concerns. Ethical behaviour within a business involves keeping company secrets, meeting obligations and responsibilities, and avoiding undue pressure that may force others to act unethically.

Managers, in particular, because of the authority of their position, have the opportunity to influence employees' actions. For example, a manager can influence employees to use pirated computer software to save costs. The use of illegal software puts the employee and the company at legal risk, but employees may feel pressured to do so by their superior's authority. On the other hand, new network management programs enable managers to try to control when and where software programs can be used. This could introduce an issue of personal privacy: Should your company be able to monitor your computer? Unauthorized copying of games and other programs has exposed companies to copyright-infringement suits, computer viruses, and system overload as well as the loss of productivity from employees spending time playing games.[13]

It is the responsibility of managers to create a work environment that helps the company achieve its objectives and fulfill its responsibilities. However, the methods that managers use to enforce these responsibilities should not compromise employee rights. Organizational pressures may encourage a person to engage in activities that he or she might otherwise view as unethical, such as invading others' privacy or stealing a competitor's secrets. Or the firm may provide only vague or lax supervision on ethical issues, providing the opportunity for misconduct. Managers who offer no ethical direction to employees create many opportunities for manipulation, dishonesty, and conflicts of interest.

Plagiarism—taking someone else's work and presenting it as your own without mentioning the source—is another ethical issue. As a student, you may be familiar with plagiarism in school, for example, copying someone else's term paper or quoting from a published work without acknowledging it. In business, an ethical issue arises when an employee copies reports or takes the work or ideas of others and presents it as his or her own. A manager attempting to take credit for a subordinate's ideas is engaging in another type of plagiarism. Several well-known musicians, including Michael Jackson, George Harrison, and Michael Bolton, have been accused of taking credit for the work of others.

plagiarism
the act of taking someone else's work and presenting it as your own without mentioning the source

Making Decisions about Ethical Issues

Although we've presented a variety of ethical issues that may arise in business, it can be difficult to recognize specific ethical issues in practice. Whether a decision maker recognizes an issue as an ethical one often depends on the issue itself. Managers, for example, tend to be more concerned about issues that affect those close to them, as well as issues that have immediate rather than long-term consequences. Thus, the perceived importance of an ethical issue substantially affects choices, and only a few issues receive scrutiny, while most receive no attention at all.[14]

Table 3.2 lists some questions you may want to ask yourself and others when trying to determine whether an action is ethical. Open discussion of ethical issues does not eliminate ethical problems, but it does promote both trust and learning in an organization.[15] When people feel that they cannot discuss what they are doing with their coworkers or superiors, there is a good chance that an ethical issue exists. Once a person has recognized an ethical issue and can openly discuss it with others, he or she has begun the process of resolving an ethical issue. Companies subcontracting manufacturing operations abroad are now aware of the ethical issues associated with supporting facilities that abuse and/or underpay their work forces. Such facilities have been termed "sweatshops." Maximizing profits is often the motivation behind a company's decision to utilize sweatshops. For each $14.99 pair of J.C. Penney Arizona jeans, workers earn 11 cents. For each $12 Victoria's Secret garment made, employees earn 3 cents. Wal-Mart, Kmart, and Nike also have been accused by the US National Labor Committee of outsourcing production to countries with low wages to boost profitability.[16] New codes of conduct have been established to assist companies in identifying and addressing these ethical issues.

Are there any potential legal restrictions or violations that could result from the action?
Does your company have a specific code of ethics or policy on the action?
Is this activity customary in your industry? Are there any industry trade groups that provide guidelines or codes of conduct that address this issue?
Would this activity be accepted by your coworkers? Will your decision or action withstand open discussion with coworkers and managers and survive untarnished?
How does this activity fit with your own beliefs and values?
How would you feel if your actions were published in the newspaper?

Table 3.2

Questions to Consider in Determining Whether an Action Is Ethical

Ethical decisions involve questions about how we ought to behave. The decision process must consider cultural and religious background. A review of the literature will reveal many possible frameworks for making ethical and moral decisions, but all will consider the matter relative to those standards held important by the decision maker. Such traits as honesty, compassion, and fairness, as well as the individual's sense of right and wrong, will play an important part.

One five-step framework published by the Markkula Center for Applied Ethics is:

1. Recognize a moral issue.
2. Get the facts.
3. Evaluate the alternative actions from various moral perspectives.
4. Make a decision.
5. Act, then reflect on the decision later.

IMPROVING ETHICAL BEHAVIOUR IN BUSINESS

Understanding how people make ethical choices and what prompts a person to act unethically may reverse the current trend toward unethical behaviour in business. Ethical decisions in an organization are influenced by three key factors: individual moral standards, the influence of managers and coworkers, and the opportunity to engage in misconduct (Figure 3.1). While you have great control over your personal ethics outside the workplace, your coworkers and management team exert significant control over your choices at work through authority and example. In fact, the activities and examples set by coworkers, along with rules and policies established by the firm, are critical in gaining consistent ethical compliance in an organization. If the company fails to provide good examples and direction for appropriate conduct, confusion and conflict will develop and result in the opportunity for misconduct. If your boss or coworkers leave work early, you may be tempted to do so as well. If you see coworkers making personal long-distance phone calls at work and charging them to the company, then you may be more likely to do so also. In addition, having sound personal values contributes to an ethical workplace.

It is difficult for employees to determine what conduct is acceptable within a company if the firm does not have ethics policies and standards. And without such policies and standards, employees may base decisions on how their peers and superiors behave. Professional **codes of ethics** are formalized rules and standards that describe what the company expects of its employees. The Ethics Officer Association is a professional association of top managers in 500 companies who have responsibility for developing ethical policies and programs for their organizations, with members based in Australia, Canada, France, Germany, Great Britain, India, Japan, Switzerland, and the United States.

codes of ethics
formalized rules and standards that describe what a company expects of its employees

---

Figure 3.1   *Three Factors that Influence Business Ethics*

Individual Standards and Values		Managers' and Coworkers' Influence		Opportunity: Codes and Compliance Requirements		Ethical/Unethical Choices in Business
	+		+		=	

Codes of ethics, policies on ethics, and ethics training programs advance ethical behaviour because they prescribe which activities are acceptable and which are not, and they limit the opportunity for misconduct by providing punishments for violations of the rules and standards. The enforcement of such codes and policies through rewards and punishments increases the acceptance of ethical standards by employees.

Enforcement of ethics policies is a common way of dealing with ethical problems. A survey by the US Ethics Resource Center on attitudes toward and knowledge of ethics and ethics programs indicated that employees' personal ethics improve when their organization has a comprehensive ethics training program. In addition, the study found that individuals in companies that have ethics training programs believe that their business ethics have improved during the course of their career.[17] These findings suggest that people do bring a set of personal values into an organization, and, further, that organizational pressures affect not only how individuals conduct themselves within the organization but also can improve their personal ethics outside of work.

The Conference Board of Canada points out that having an ethics program is not only part of being a socially responsible corporation but is also likely to increase profitability. Lost sales, legal fees, and fines, and the demoralization of the work force resulting from unethical behaviour can be very costly. In an effort to avoid such costs, many Canadian organizations are implementing ethics programs to ensure that employee behaviour is in accordance with corporate values and relevant legislation.[18]

Because ethical issues often emerge from conflict, it is useful to examine the causes of ethical conflict. Business managers and employees often experience some tension between their own ethical beliefs and their obligations to the organizations in which they work.

Many employees utilize different ethical standards at work than they do at home. This conflict increases when employees feel that their company is encouraging unethical conduct or exerting pressure on them to engage in it. Figure 3.2 shows that over 25 percent of employees believe that this pressure is real.

Individuals also play a key role in promoting ethical decisions in the workplace. **Whistleblowing** occurs when an employee exposes an employer's wrongdoing to outsiders, such as the media or government regulatory agencies. However, more companies are establishing programs to encourage employees to report illegal or unethical practices internally so that they can take steps to remedy problems before they

Conference Board
of Canada
www.conferenceboard.ca/

whistleblowing
the act of an employee exposing an employer's wrongdoing to outsiders, such as the media or government regulatory agencies

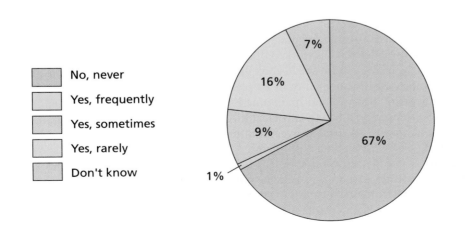

Figure 3.2

Percentage of Employees Who Believe that Their Company Encourages Unethical Conduct

Source: Ethics Resource Center/Society for Human Resource Management, 1997 Business Ethics Survey Report, p. 19.

No, never
Yes, frequently
Yes, sometimes
Yes, rarely
Don't know

7%
16%
9%
67%
1%

result in legal action or generate negative publicity. Unfortunately, whistleblowers are often treated negatively in organizations.

Dr. Nancy Olivieri, a faculty member at the University of Toronto, was carrying out research at the Hospital for Sick Children on a drug for treating the blood disease thalassaemia. Preliminary results were hopeful, but later work raised concerns about toxicity. Dr. Olivieri alleged that Apotex, the company sponsoring the research, made great efforts to prevent her from publishing the results of her research.

While Dr. Olivieri has reached a settlement agreement with all the parties involved and continues her research career, the agreement came about only after a protracted and acrimonious process during which her employment was temporarily terminated more than once.

The current trend is to move away from legally based ethical initiatives in organizations to cultural- or integrity-based initiatives that make ethics a part of core organizational values. Organizations recognize that effective business ethics programs are good for business performance. Firms that develop higher levels of trust function more efficiently and effectively and avoid damaged company reputations and product images. Organizational ethics initiatives have been supportive of many positive and diverse organizational objectives, such as profitability, hiring, employee satisfaction, and customer loyalty.[19]

THE NATURE OF SOCIAL RESPONSIBILITY

There are four dimensions of social responsibility: economic, legal, ethical, and voluntary (including philanthropic) (Figure 3.3).[20] Earning profits is the economic foundation of the pyramid in Figure 3.3, and complying with the law is the next step. A business whose *sole* objective is to maximize profits is not likely to consider its social responsibility, although its activities will probably be legal. (We looked at ethical responsibilities in the first half of this chapter.) Finally, voluntary responsibilities are additional activities that may not be required but which promote human welfare or goodwill. Legal and economic concerns have long been acknowledged in business, but voluntary and ethical issues are more recent concerns.

A business that is concerned about society as well as earning profits is likely to invest voluntarily in socially responsible activities. For example, some companies, such as Canadian Tire through the Foundation for Families and Honda Motors Canada, support numerous social initiatives. Such businesses win the trust and respect of their employees, customers, and society by implementing socially responsible programs and, in the long run, increase profits. Irresponsible companies risk losing consumers as well as encouraging the public and government to take action to constrict their activities. Reebok has worked diligently to improve the conditions in its factories over the past several years. Reebok has removed organic solvents that pose health risks, improved the air quality in its plants, explored nontoxic alternatives in the manufacturing process, and maintained stricter safety standards than required by the US Occupational Safety and Health Administration (OSHA). Reebok has also increased wages (20 percent over minimum wage), reduced overtime, and eliminated fines for disciplinary problems.[21] All of this has been done to show that Reebok is socially responsible in its world manufacturing of athletic shoes. In one particular study, 48 percent of the respondents cited business practices as a reason for switching from one business to another; other reasons included treatment of employees, the environment, stability, and community.[22] Most companies today consider being socially responsible a cost of doing business.

**Voluntary
Responsibilities**
being a
"good corporate citizen";
contributing to the
community and quality of life

Ethical Responsibilities
being ethical;
doing what is right, just, and fair;
avoiding harm

Legal Responsibilities
obeying the law (society's codification of
right and wrong);
playing by the rules of the game

Economic Responsibilities
being profitable

Figure 3.3

*The Pyramid of Social
Responsibility*

Source: Adapted from
Archie B. Carroll, "The
Pyramid of Corporate
Social Responsibility:
Toward the Moral Manage-
ment of Organizational
Stakeholders." Reprinted
from *Business Horizons* 34
(July/August 1991), p. 42.
Copyright 1991 by the
Foundation for the School
of Business at Indiana
University. Used with
permission.

Although the concept of social responsibility is receiving more and more attention, it is still not universally accepted. Table 3.3 lists some of the arguments for and
against social responsibility.

SOCIAL RESPONSIBILITY ISSUES

As with ethics, managers consider social responsibility on a daily basis as they deal
with real issues. Among the many social issues that managers must consider are their
firms' relations with employees, government regulators, owners, suppliers, customers, and the community.

Table 3.4 shows companies currently held in a socially responsible stock fund. The
criteria for inclusion: quality goods and services, equitable employee and community relations, and care for the environment. The ten-year return on these funds
ranged from 4 percent to 14 percent. Nike was under consideration for inclusion in
the Friends Stewardship Trust Portfolio in the US, but due to a labour controversy
with subcontractors in Asia, it was excluded.[23] At its annual meeting, Nike unveiled
plans to address the issues plaguing the company. Nike announced a wage increase
for Asian workers and, beginning in 2002, it will no longer do business with factories that do not have educational programs for workers. Currently, education programs are available in 15 of Nike's 43 factories in four countries. Workers who graduate from these programs receive wage increases.[24]

Social responsibility is a dynamic area with issues changing constantly in response
to society's desires. On the other hand, there is much evidence that social responsibility is associated with improved business performance. Consumers are refusing to
buy from businesses that receive publicity about misconduct. A number of studies

Ethical Funds Inc.
**www.ethicalfunds.com/
content**

Table 3.3

The Arguments for and against Social Responsibility

For:
1. Business helped to create many of the social problems that exist today, so it should play a significant role in solving them, especially in the areas of pollution reduction and cleanup.
2. Businesses should be more responsible because they have the financial and technical resources to help solve social problems.
3. As members of society, businesses should do their fair share to help others.
4. Socially responsible decision making by businesses can prevent increased government regulation.
5. Social responsibility is necessary to ensure economic survival: If businesses want educated and healthy employees, customers with money to spend, and suppliers with quality goods and services in years to come, they must take steps to help solve the social and environmental problems that exist today.
Against:
1. It sidetracks managers from the primary goal of business—earning profits. Every dollar donated to social causes or otherwise spent on society's problems is a dollar less for owners and investors.
2. Participation in social programs gives businesses greater power, perhaps at the expense of particular segments of society.
3. Some people question whether business has the expertise needed to assess and make decisions about social problems.
4. Many people believe that social problems are the responsibility of government agencies and officials, who can be held accountable by voters.

have found a direct relationship between social responsibility and profitability, as well as that social responsibility is linked to employee commitment and customer loyalty—major concerns of any firm trying to increase profits.[25] This section highlights a few of the many social responsibility issues that managers face; as managers become aware of and work toward the solution of current social problems, new ones will certainly emerge.

Relations with Owners and Shareholders

Businesses must first be responsible to their owners, who are primarily concerned with earning a profit or a return on their investment in a company. In a small

Table 3.4

Funds Managed by Companies Held in Ethical Funds Incorporated Mutual Funds

Royal Bank of Canada	Nortel Networks Corp.
DuPont Canada	Placer Dome
Petro-Canada Ltd.	Magna International
Aliant Inc.	Canadian National Railway
Noranda	BCE Inc.

business, this responsibility is fairly easy to fulfill because the owner(s) personally manages the business or knows the managers well. In larger businesses, particularly corporations owned by thousands of stockholders, assuring responsibility to the owners becomes a more difficult task.

A business's responsibilities to its owners and investors, as well as to the financial community at large, include maintaining proper accounting procedures, providing all relevant information to investors about the current and projected performance of the firm, and protecting the owners' rights and investments. In short, the business must maximize the owners' investment in the firm. Ben & Jerry's settled a class action lawsuit for US$1.1 million that alleged it had misrepresented its financial condition. Thirteen hundred investors claimed that they purchased stock at inflated prices. The CEO of Ben & Jerry's stated that the suit was settled because a trial would have been costly.[26] In Canada, legal proceedings against Bre-X in gold-mining and Livent in the entertainment business continue.

Employee Relations

Another issue of importance to a business is its responsibilities to employees, for without employees a business cannot carry out its goals. Employees expect businesses to provide a safe workplace, pay them adequately for their work, and tell them what is happening in their company. They want employers to listen to their grievances and treat them fairly.

Each of the ten provinces, three territories, and the federal government has its own Occupational Health and Safety Regulations enacted to protect workers. Labour unions have also made significant contributions to achieving safety in the workplace and improving wages and benefits. Most organizations now recognize that the safety and satisfaction of their employees are a critical ingredient in their success, and many strive to go beyond what is expected of them by the law. Healthy, satisfied employees supply more than just labour to their employers, however. Employers are beginning to realize the importance of obtaining input from even the lowest-level employees to help the company reach its objectives.

A major social responsibility for business is providing equal opportunities for all employees regardless of their sex, age, race, religion, or nationality. Women and minorities have been slighted in the past in terms of education, employment, and advancement opportunities; additionally, many of their needs have not been addressed by business. For example, women, who continue to bear most child-rearing responsibilities, often experience conflict between those responsibilities and their duties as employees. Consequently, day care has become a major employment issue for women, and more companies are providing day-care facilities as part of their effort to recruit and advance women in the work force. In addition, companies are considering alternative scheduling such as flex-time and job sharing to accommodate employee concerns. Telecommuting has grown significantly over the past 5 to 10 years, as well. Many Canadians and Americans today believe business has a social obligation to provide special opportunities for women and minorities to improve their standing in society.

Consumer Relations

A critical issue in business today is business's responsibility to customers, who look to business to provide them with satisfying, safe products and to respect their rights

Consider Ethics and Social Responsibility

"Chainsaw Al's" Mean Business at Sunbeam

In July 1996, Sunbeam hired Albert Dunlap (known as "Chainsaw Al") as chairman and CEO to try to save the company and increase declining stock values and profits. Dunlap is known for making extreme cuts in all areas of operations, including massive layoffs, to streamline business. The concepts of teamwork and group dynamics are unknown to Dunlap. He even authored a book, *Mean Business,* that states that making money for shareholders is the most important goal of any business. Increasing shareholder wealth, at any cost, is his objective. Clearly, his philosophy is deficient in regard to ethical responsibility.

The day Dunlap was hired, Sunbeam's stock jumped 49 percent. True to his reputation, "Chainsaw Al" fired thousands of employees, shut down factories and warehouses, and streamlined the company by eliminating products and selling businesses unrelated to its core products. He even attained his objective and made money for shareholders. However, the wealth did not last. In April 1998, Sunbeam announced a first-quarter loss, and stock prices fell by 25 percent.

Dunlap realized his reputation and "Rambo"-style cuts were not going to maintain the high stock prices or profits at Sunbeam. His solution was to shift sales from future quarters to the current one by using a "bill and hold" strategy, which involves selling products to retailers for large discounts and holding them in third-party warehouses to be delivered at a later date. By booking sales months prior to the actual shipment or billing, Sunbeam was able to report higher revenues in the form of accounts receivable. The strategy helped Dunlap boost Sunbeam's revenues by 18 percent in 1997.

Although what Dunlap had done was not illegal, shareholders filed lawsuits alleging that the company made misleading statements about its finances and deceived them so that they would purchase Sunbeam's artificially inflated stock. In 1998, second-quarter sales were considerably below Dunlap's forecasted increase and, in fact, the company was in crisis with projections of a US$60 million loss for the quarter. On June 13, 1998, Sunbeam's board of directors unanimously agreed that their confidence in Dunlap was lost. Dunlap was told that same day via a one-minute conference call that he was the next person to be cut from Sunbeam's payroll.

Sunbeam is again facing the need to revitalize the organization, but this time the challenges have a different focus. Along with the shareholder lawsuits, Sunbeam is in litigation with the American Medical Association, and the US Securities and Exchange Commission is scrutinizing Sunbeam's accounting practices. Also, Sunbeam's Audit Committee has determined that it will be required to restate its audited financial statements for the first quarter of 1998, 1997, and possibly 1996. Jerry W. Levin, Dunlap's replacement, now must outline a strategy to revitalize the company and restore investor confidence.[27]

consumerism
the activities that independent individuals, groups, and organizations undertake to protect their rights as consumers

as consumers. The activities that independent individuals, groups, and organizations undertake to protect their rights as consumers are known as **consumerism.** To achieve their objectives, consumers and their advocates write letters to companies, lobby government agencies, make public service announcements, and boycott companies whose activities they deem irresponsible. Some consumers have aggressively boycotted Home Depot for selling "old growth" ancient redwoods and other old-forest products. As the largest home improvement retailer, Home Depot is also the largest reseller of such products, even though it manufactures none of the products it sells in its stores.[28] Other companies, such as 3M and Mitsubishi, have stringent policies on the purchase of such materials.

Many of the desires of those involved in the consumer movement have a foundation in US president John F. Kennedy's 1962 consumer bill of rights, which highlighted four rights. The *right to safety* means that a business must not knowingly sell anything that could result in personal injury or harm to consumers. Defective or dangerous products erode public confidence in the ability of business to serve society. They also result in expensive litigation that ultimately increases the cost of products for all consumers. The *right to be informed* gives consumers the freedom to review complete information about a product before they buy. This means that detailed information about ingredients, risks, and instructions for use are to be printed on labels and packages. The *right to choose* ensures that consumers have access to a variety of products and services at competitive prices. The assurance of both satisfactory quality and service at a fair price is also a part of the consumer's right to choose. The *right to be heard* assures consumers that their interests will receive full and sympathetic consideration when the government formulates policy. It also assures the fair treatment of consumers who voice complaints about a purchased product.

Some countries have adopted these rights as government policy while others, like Canada, use them informally as a framework to develop policy.

Environmental Issues

Environmental responsibility has become a leading issue in the last decade as both business and the public acknowledge the damage done to the environment in the past. Today's consumers are increasingly demanding that businesses take a greater responsibility for their actions and how they impact the environment.

Animal Rights. One area of environmental concern in society today is animal rights. Probably the most controversial business practice in this area is the testing of cosmetics and drugs on animals who may be injured or killed as a result. Animal-rights activists, such as People for the Ethical Treatment of Animals, say such research is morally wrong because it harms living creatures. Consumers who share this sentiment may boycott companies that test products on animals and take their business instead to companies such as The Body Shop and John Paul Mitchell Systems, which do not use animal testing. However, researchers in the cosmetics and pharmaceutical industries argue that animal testing is necessary to prevent harm to human beings who will eventually use the products.

Business practices that harm endangered wildlife and their habitats are another environmental issue. The use of fur for luxury coats has been controversial for many years. In Canada, the Hudson Bay Company sold their Northern stores and fur auction business in 1985, 313 years after their first public fur auction. In New York, the Animal Defense League (ADL) has protested Macy's sale of fur coats. The ADL claims that more than 40 million animals are killed each year for their fur.[29]

Pollution. Another major issue in the area of environmental responsibility is pollution. In Oregon, the US government is working jointly with state and local officials to protect the habitat of eight different species of endangered salmon and two species of endangered trout. Farmers will be paid an annual rental fee to take crop land

People for the Ethical Treatment of Animals
www.peta-online.org/

around streams and rivers out of production and plant trees and grasses to minimize pesticide and herbicide runoff.[30]

Water pollution results from dumping toxic chemicals and raw sewage into rivers and oceans, oil spills, and the burial of industrial waste in the ground where it may filter into underground water supplies. Fertilizers and insecticides used in farming and grounds maintenance also run off into water supplies with each rainfall. Water pollution problems are especially notable in heavily industrialized areas.

In May of 2000 the water supply of Walkerton, Ontario, was contaminated with E. coli bacteria. The result was the death of seven people and 2,300 were made ill. The suspected cause of the contamination was untreated manure from a dairy farm being carried into a municipal well by spring runoff. It should be noted that while a judicial inquiry is being held in an effort to assess responsibility, no regulations were broken by the farmer, who has the reputation of being environmentally responsible. As a result of such occurrences, society is demanding that regulations be enacted and enforced to safeguard clean, healthful water supplies.

Air pollution is usually the result of smoke and other pollutants emitted by manufacturing facilities, as well as carbon monoxide and hydrocarbons emitted by motor vehicles. In addition to the health risks posed by air pollution, when some chemical compounds emitted by manufacturing facilities react with air and rain, acid rain results. Acid rain has contributed to the deaths of many valuable forests and lakes in North America as well as in Europe. Air pollution may also contribute to the so-called greenhouse effect, in which carbon dioxide collects in the earth's atmosphere, trapping the sun's heat and preventing the earth's surface from cooling. Chlorofluorocarbons also harm the earth's ozone layer, which filters out the sun's harmful ultraviolet light; this too may be a cause of the greenhouse effect. The greenhouse effect is highly controversial, however, and some scientists doubt its existence. Royal Dutch/Shell Group, parent company of Shell Oil, plans to cut greenhouse gas emissions by 10 percent over the next three years. Shell plans to spend US$500 million over the next five years to develop renewable energy sources such as solar and wind power.[31]

Land pollution is tied directly to water pollution because many of the chemicals and toxic wastes that are dumped on the land eventually work their way into the water supply. Land pollution results from the dumping of residential and industrial waste, strip mining, forest fires, and poor forest conservation. Manufacturers in the United States produce approximately 45 million tonnes of contaminants each year. The dumping of toxic wastes in Love Canal (near Niagara Falls, New York) caused later residents to experience high rates of birth defects and cancer before they were forced by the US government to abandon their homes in the late 1970s and early 1980s. In Brazil and other South American countries, rain forests are being destroyed—at a rate of nearly half a hectare per minute—to make way for farms and ranches, at a cost of the extinction of the many animals and plants (some endangered species) that call the rain forest home. Large-scale deforestation also depletes the oxygen supply available to humans and other animals.

In Sydney, Nova Scotia, 80 years of coke-oven operation in the area known as Muggah Creek have left ground and surface water seriously contaminated with arsenic, lead, and other toxins. It has left an accumulation, in an area the size of three city blocks now called the "Tar Ponds," of some 70,000 tonnes of chemical waste and raw sewage, 40,000 tonnes of which are carcinogenic PCBs. Residents of the area reported that an orange goo would seep into their basements and that puddles would turn fluorescent green after a rainfall. They have also complained of numerous health problems, including massive headaches, nosebleeds, and respiratory problems. Today the area has one of the highest rates of cancer, birth defects, and miscarriages in Canada.

Efforts at cleaning up the Sydney Tar Ponds were initiated with $34.4 million in government funding in 1986. After 15 years, the problem remains unsolved, as 13 mllion litres of untreated waste continues to enter the site daily, and bio-remediation efforts are expected to take centuries to rehabilitate the area.

Related to the problem of land pollution is the larger issue of how to dispose of waste in an environmentally responsible manner. Consumers contribute approximately 680 kilograms of garbage per person each year to landfills. Compounding the waste-disposal problem is the fact that more than 50 percent of all garbage is made out of plastic, which does not decompose. Some communities have passed laws that prohibit the use of plastics such as Styrofoam for this reason.

Response to Environmental Issues. Partly in response to federal legislation such as the Canadian Environmental Protection Act and partly due to consumer concerns, businesses are responding to environmental issues. Many small and large companies, including Walt Disney Company, Chevron, and Scott Paper, have created a new executive position—a vice president of environmental affairs—to help them achieve their business goals in an environmentally responsible manner.

Many firms are trying to eliminate wasteful practices, the emission of pollutants, and/or the use of harmful chemicals from their manufacturing processes. Other companies are seeking ways to improve their products. Auto makers, such as General Motors and Honda, are developing automobiles that run on alternative fuels—electricity, solar power, natural gas, and methanol. Many businesses have turned to *recycling,* the reprocessing of materials—aluminum, paper, glass, and some plastic—for re-use. Procter & Gamble uses recycled materials in some of its packaging and markets refills for some of its products, which creates less packaging waste. In the United States, roughly 40 percent of paper and paperboard, 36.5 percent of iron and steel, and 34.5 percent of aluminum is recycled out of roughly 190 tonnes of trash created each year.[32] Such efforts to make products, packaging, and processes more environmentally friendly have been labelled "green" business or marketing by the public and media.

It is important to recognize that, with current technology, environmental responsibility requires trade-offs. Society must weigh the huge costs of limiting or eliminating pollution against the health threat posed by the pollution. Environmental responsibility imposes costs on both business and the public. Although people certainly do not want oil fouling beautiful waterways and killing wildlife, they insist on low-cost, readily available gasoline and heating oil. People do not want to contribute to the growing garbage-disposal problem, but they often refuse to pay more for "green" products packaged in an environmentally friendly manner, to recycle as much of their own waste as possible, or to permit the building of additional waste-disposal facilities (the "not in my backyard" or NIMBY syndrome). Thus, managers must coordinate environmental goals with other social and economic ones.

Community Relations

A final, yet very significant, issue for businesses concerns their responsibilities to the general welfare of the communities and societies in which they operate. Many businesses simply want to make their communities better places for everyone to live and

Many career opportunities are emerging today in the field of business ethics and social responsibility. Approximately one-third of *Fortune* 1,000 firms have an ethics officer, a position that most companies have created only in the last several years. The ethics officer is typically responsible for (1) meeting with employees, the board of directors, and top management to discuss and provide advice about ethics issues; (2) distributing a code of ethics; (3) creating and maintaining an anonymous, confidential service to answer questions about ethical issues; (4) taking actions on possible ethics code violations; and (5) reviewing and modifying the code of ethics. Entry-level jobs in ethics involve assisting with communications programs or training.

If you are interested in a career in the area of business ethics and social responsibility, take courses in business ethics, legal environment, and business and society. Many ethics officers have law degrees due to the interrelationship of many legal and ethical issues. Some elective courses in moral philosophy or sociology may also be useful. Subscribe to a magazine such as *Business Ethics*, a popular trade journal that provides information about companies that have ethics programs or are involved with socially responsible activities. By learning more about how real companies are carrying out the ethics/social responsibility function, you will be better prepared to apply for a job and be knowledgeable in matching your interests with a company's needs. Although there are only a small number of jobs available today in this emerging area, you could be in the forefront of a developing concern that has much potential for career advancement. If you prepare yourself properly through education and possibly a part-time job or internship in a large firm with an ethics department, you will greatly enhance the probability of developing a successful career in business ethics and social responsibility.[33]

work. Although such efforts cover many diverse areas, some actions are especially noteworthy. As one example, Smith Kline Beecham has formed a partnership with the World Health Organization to develop and donate drugs to eradicate lymphatic filariasis, a disease that affects 120 million people worldwide.[34] The most common way that businesses exercise their community responsibility is through donations to local and national charitable organizations. Microsoft's goal for charitable donations is US$10.4 million (US$5.2 million from employees and a matching US$5.2 million from the company). This represents a 20 percent increase over the previous year's giving. Including cash contributions, software donations, and other charitable acts, Microsoft gives over US$106 million each year to nonprofit agencies and educational organizations.[35]

Home Depot excels at strategic philanthropy. It has a close relationship with Habitat for Humanity, donating products and employee time to assist in the organization's building efforts. Minute Maid Company, a division of Coca-Cola, produces 2,000 cases of Hi-C drink for Second Harvest, a charitable hunger relief organization.[36] Northwest Airlines encourages passengers to donate frequent flyer miles to charitable causes. With this program, St. Jude Children's Research Hospital in Memphis, Tennessee, earned 120 free tickets in the first month. The mileage is used to fly sick children and their families to Memphis for treatment. Other charities that Northwest supports through AirCares include the American Red Cross, The

The Ethics in Action Awards recognize businesses, and individuals in business, whose actions and decisions have made a positive impact on our communities.

Source: 2001 Ethics in Action Awards.

Ethics in Action
www.ethicsinaction.com

Salvation Army, Junior Achievement, the Make-A-Wish Foundation of America, and Toys for Tots. More than 13 million Worldperk miles were donated in the first month of this program.[37]

Average contributions by Canadian corporations grew by 20 percent from 1995 to 1997. The largest proportion of these contributions was received by education, followed by social services and health care. Table 3.5 shows the complete breakdown of support by area.

That education is viewed as important by corporate Canada is evidenced by the fact that in 2000 over 15,000 Canadian organizations applied for Conference Board of Canada Awards for:

- business education partnerships;
- youth employment;
- workplace literacy/business skills upgrading; and
- corporate leadership.

Table 3.5

Corporate Philanthropy by Area of Support

Source: Based on 1997 Corporate Community Investment in Canada, conducted by the Canadian Centre for Business in the Community, as reported in Taking Action on Trends in Corporate Social Responsibility, at **www2.conferenceboard.ca/ ccbc/knowledge-areas/csr/ csroct98.htm.**

Education	26%	Civic causes	8%
Social services	23%	Environment	4%
Health	22%	Sports	1%
Arts & culture	11%	Other	4%

Council on Corporate-Aboriginal Relations **www.conferenceboard. ca/ccbc/aboriginal/ aboriginal_council.htm**

Caux Round Table **www.cauxroundtable. org**

The winning projects benefit both the organization investing in education and the community. By developing employability skills, entrepreneurship, and literacy, a more productive work force is created. This results in higher productivity and greater economic welfare for all Canadians. Many of the winners of these awards are ranked among Canada's most productive companies.[38]

Business is also beginning to take more responsibility for the hard-core unemployed. Some are mentally or physically handicapped; some are homeless. Others are members of traditionally disadvantaged social or racial groups.

Over 20,000 North American Indians, Metis, and Inuit in Canada operate their own businesses. While the majority are profitable, they lag behind the Canadian average. The corporate members of the Council on Corporate-Aboriginal Relations established by the Conference Board of Canada work with Aboriginal business to improve capacity, management skills, and technical training, and to provide greater opportunity for expansion.

This is accomplished through mentoring programs such as that provided by Syncrude Canada. Syncrude executives have built successful relationships by communicating their business requirements to Aboriginal firms and by making their executives available as business mentors, providing management expertise and training.[39]

To promote ethics and social responsibility around the globe, the Caux Round Table, a group of business, political, and civic leaders in Europe, Japan, and the United States, created international principles related to responsible corporate citizenship. The role of business in the lives of customers, employees, owners, competitors, suppliers, and communities was communicated in clear terms. International codes allow businesses to confidently adjust their practices to accommodate cultural, social, and ethical differences in international business.

Review Your Understanding

Define business ethics and examine its importance.

Business ethics refers to principles and standards that define acceptable business conduct. Acceptable business behaviour is defined by customers, competitors, government regulators, interest groups, the public, and each individual's personal moral principles and values. Ethics is important in business because it builds trust and confidence in business relationships. Unethical actions may result in negative publicity, declining sales, and even legal action.

Detect some of the ethical issues that may arise in business.

An ethical issue is an identifiable problem, situation, or opportunity requiring a person or organization to choose from among several actions that must be evaluated as right or wrong. Ethical issues can be categorized in the context of their relation with conflicts of interest, fairness and honesty, communications, and business associations.

Specify how businesses can promote ethical behaviour by employees.

Businesses can promote ethical behaviour by employees by limiting their opportunity to engage in misconduct. Formal codes of ethics, ethical policies, and ethics training programs reduce the incidence of unethical behaviour by informing employees what is expected of them and providing punishments for those who fail to comply.

Define social responsibility and explain its relevance to business.

Social responsibility is the obligation an organization assumes to maximize its positive impact and minimize its negative impact on society. Socially responsible businesses win the trust and respect of their employees, customers, and society and, in the long run, increase profits.

Debate an organization's social responsibilities to owners, employees, consumers, the environment, and the community.

Businesses must maintain proper accounting procedures, provide all relevant information about the performance of the firm to investors, and protect the owners' rights and investments. In relations with employees, businesses are expected to provide a safe workplace, pay employees adequately for their work, and treat them fairly. Consumerism refers to the activities undertaken by independent individuals, groups, and organizations to protect their rights as consumers. Increasingly, society expects business to take greater responsibility for the environment, especially with regard to animal rights, as well as water, air, land, and noise pollution. Many businesses engage in activities to make the communities in which they operate better places for everyone to live and work.

Evaluate the ethics of a business's decision.

The "Solve the Dilemma" box presents an ethical dilemma at Checkers Pizza. Using the material presented in this chapter, you should be able to analyze the ethical issues present in the dilemma, evaluate Barnard's plan, and develop a course of action for the firm.

Learn the Terms

bribes 51	consumerism 62	plagiarism 55
business ethics 48	ethical issue 50	whistleblowing 57
codes of ethics 56		

Check Your Progress

1. Define business ethics. Who determines whether a business activity is ethical? Is unethical conduct always illegal? What factors influence business ethics?
2. Distinguish between ethics and social responsibility.
3. Why has ethics become so important in business?
4. What is an ethical issue? What are some of the ethical issues named in your text? Why are they ethical issues?
5. What is a code of ethics? How can one reduce unethical behaviour in business?
6. List and discuss the arguments for and against social responsibility by business (Table 3.3). Can you think of any additional arguments (for or against)?
7. What responsibilities does a business have toward its employees?
8. What responsibilities does business have with regard to the environment? What steps have been taken by some responsible businesses to minimize the negative impact of their activities on the environment?
9. What are a business's responsibilities toward the community in which it operates?

Get Involved

1. Discuss some recent examples of businesses engaging in unethical practices. Classify these practices as issues of conflict of interest, fairness and honesty, communications, or business relationships. Why do you think the businesses chose to behave unethically? What actions might the businesses have taken?
2. Discuss with your class some possible methods of improving ethical standards in business. Do you think that business should regulate its own activities or that the federal government should establish and enforce ethical standards? How do you think businesspeople feel?
3. Find some examples of socially responsible businesses in newspapers or business journals. Explain why you believe their actions are socially responsible. Why do you think the companies chose to act as they did?

Build Your Skills

Making Decisions about Ethical Issues

Background: The fictional merger of Laurent Inc. and Western Ltd. created Western Laurent, the number-one company in the farming industry.

You and the rest of the class are managers at Western Laurent Corporation, Winnipeg, Manitoba. You are getting ready to do the group exercise in an ethics training session. The training instructor announces you will be playing *Gray Matters: The Ethics Game.* You are told that *Gray Matters,* which was prepared for your company's employees, is also played at 41 universities and at 65 other companies. Although there are 55 scenarios in *Gray Matters,* you will have time during this session to complete only the four scenarios that your group draws from the stack of cards.[40]

Task: Form into groups of four to six managers and appoint a group leader who will lead a discussion of the case, obtain a consensus answer to the case, and be the one to report the group's answers to the instructor. You will have five minutes to reach each decision, after which time, the instructor will give the point values and rationale for each choice. Then you will have five minutes for the next case, etc., until all four cases have been completed. Keep track of your group's score for each case; the winning team will be the group scoring the most points.

Since this game is designed to reflect life, you may believe that some cases lack clarity or that some of your choices are not as precise as you would have liked. Also, some cases have only one solution, while others have more than one solution. Each choice is assessed points to reflect which answer is the most correct. **Your group's task is to select only one option in each case.**

Your group draws cards 4, 7, 36, and 40.

4

Mini-Case

For several months now, one of your colleagues has been slacking off, and you are getting stuck doing the work. You think it is unfair. What do you do?

Potential Answers

A. Recognize this as an opportunity for you to demonstrate how capable you are.

B. Go to your supervisor and complain about this unfair workload.

C. Discuss the problem with your colleague in an attempt to solve the problem without involving others.

D. Discuss the problem with the human resources department.

7

Mini-Case

You are aware that a fellow employee uses drugs on the job. Another friend encourages you to confront the person instead of informing the supervisor. What do you do?

Potential Answers

A. You speak to the alleged user and encourage him to get help.

B. You elect to tell your supervisor that you suspect an employee is using drugs on the job.

C. You confront the alleged user and tell him either to quit using drugs or you will "turn him in."

D. Report the matter to employee assistance.

36

Mini-Case

You work for a company that has implemented a policy of a smoke-free environment. You discover employees smoking in the restrooms of the building. You also smoke and don't like having to go outside to do it. What do you do?

Potential Answers

A. You ignore the situation.

B. You confront the employees and ask them to stop.

C. You join them, but only occasionally.

D. You contact your ethics or human resources representative and ask him or her to handle the situation.

40

Mini-Case

Your coworker is copying company-purchased software and taking it home. You know a certain program costs $400, and you have been saving for a while to buy it. What do you do?

Potential Answers

A. You figure you can copy it too since nothing has ever happened to your coworker.

B. You tell your coworker he can't legally do this.

C. You report the matter to the ethics office.

D. You mention this to your supervisor.

Wake Up and Smell the Coffee

Every day Canadians consume over 3.5 million cups of coffee. Many people couldn't imagine starting the day without it. Canadians can be found drinking coffee at home, at work, and while they commute. For many the coffee shop fulfills an important social need as we meet friends and acquaintances for conversation over coffee. So pervasive is our thirst for coffee that cup holders have even featured prominently as a sales point in the advertisements for new cars. Coffee consumption is a part of our culture.

Worldwide, coffee represents a US$55 billion a year industry, employing 25 million people. Of those employed in the industry, over 20 million are small farmers, typically producing less than 1,500 kilograms of beans per year on one- to two-hectare properties. These growers, who struggle to survive on incomes averaging less than US$1.00 per day, receive less than 10 percent of the retail value of their product.

The low prices, lower now than during the 1930s Depression, are only part of what many perceive as the unfair treatment of these farmers. As with many North American farmers, their income is received only after harvest; therefore, they must often borrow to acquire inputs such as fertilizer. For the small producers in the less developed economies, the only source of credit is often the intermediary who purchases their crop, and interests rates are often as high as 20 percent per annum. Such costs further reduce the incomes of these poorest members of society, who face the prospect of losing their land if they default on the loans.

One group attempting to improve the situation for the small growers of coffee and other commodities such as tea, cocoa, and sugar is TransFair Canada (TFC), the Canadian affiliate of Fairtrade Labeling Organization (FLO). Through its procedures, TransFair ensures that coffee bearing its Fair Trade certification has met the requirements of the FLO. Fair Trade-certified coffee is purchased from over 300 cooperatives representing 550,000 small growers. The cooperative receives a minimum of US$1.26 per pound, more than double the current world price of less than US$0.60 per pound. A premium is paid if the beans are certified as organically grown. Since the members of the cooperatives are small growers who follow traditional methods of growing coffee, few chemical inputs are used. The price of chemical fertilizers is also prohibitive. Therefore, almost 40 percent of the cooperatives on the FLO register were either certified organic or in the process of becoming certified as of February 2001.

Only about 22 percent of the 78.7 million kilograms of coffee produced by the FLO-registered cooperatives in 1999 was sold though Fair Trade. However, the small growers also benefit from the more direct access to world markets that the cooperatives provide. This marginal increase in income when combined with the more profitable Fair Trade sales has a disproportionate economic impact on the growers. The cooperative also lowers production costs by recycling wastes into low-cost organic fertilizers, which in turn produces higher incomes for the growers and at the same time improves environmental stewardship.

Higher incomes allow the small growers to reinvest in their farms, to provide better nutrition and housing for their families, and through cooperative-funded schools, to provide more educational opportunities for their children.

These benefits accrue even though Fair Trade-certified sales in Canada, as in other countries, represent only a small but growing proportion of the total coffee market.

Questions

1. Is it the responsibility of coffee consumers to ensure that the small producers receive a fair price for their product? Why or why not?

2. If the price paid to the grower represents only 10 percent of the retail price of coffee, why is the retail price of Fair Trade coffee approximately double the regular price?

3. Who benefits the most from the higher price paid by consumers for Fair Trade labelled coffee?

4. What alternative approach to the problem of poverty among small producers can you suggest?

Source: *Marketplace*, show number 612–2185–9077, "Coffee," February 15, 2000, running time 13:36.

Remember to check out our Online Learning Centre at **www.mcgrawhill.ca/college/ferrell.**

Chapter 4

Business in a Borderless World

Chapter Outline

Objectives

After reading this chapter, you will be able to:

- Explore some of the factors within the international trade environment that influence business.
- Investigate some of the economic, legal-political, social, cultural, and technological barriers to international business.
- Specify some of the agreements, alliances, and organizations that may encourage trade across international boundaries.
- Summarize the different levels of organizational involvement in international trade.
- Contrast two basic strategies used in international business.
- Assess the opportunities and problems facing a small business considering expanding into international markets.

Foreign Retailers in Japan

Foreign retailers have been opening many stores in Japan, and plans call for many more over the next few years. Japanese real estate prices have plunged, and the laws and regulations involved with opening stores have diminished considerably. Firms in many industries are stampeding into Japan, but fast food, office supplies, toys, and clothing are the hottest.

McDonald's expects to have 10,000 outlets in Japan by 2006. Office Depot plans 350 stores by 2007. Toys "R" Us has moved into Japan in a big way with sales exceeding US$1.2 billion in 2001. L.L. Bean will have 150 stores by 2008.

Many of these stores will open in one of eight new malls planned over the next decade. American Malls International Japan has plans for opening these malls—with over 200,000 square metres each—in sites around Tokyo, Osaka, and Nagoya. The sites are within reach of 75 percent of Japan's 125 million consumers.

Of course, some changes must be made in items offered by foreign retailers in Japan. At Office Depot, for instance, Japanese consumers can find computers, pens, and paper clips, just as in any Office Depot location in Canada. However, they can also find three kinds of green tea, six flavours of instant *ramen*, decorative *noshi bukuro* envelopes for cash gifts, and large crystal ashtrays—items definitely not offered in Canada. Sales at Office Depot stores in Japan are expected to reach US$2.1 billion annually and generated over US$1.5 billion from international sales in 2001. Some of those sales come from the e-commerce ventures.

Foreign retailers in Japan are expected to drive inefficient operators out of business, lower costs, and streamline industries in many ways. As a result, Japan's economy should become more efficient—good news for Japanese consumers.[1]

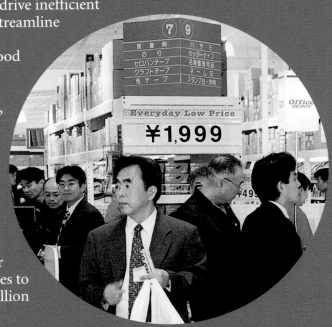

Canada has few international retailers to compete with either Japanese or US retailers, as we primarily export commodities to Japan in the form of coal, grain, and foodstuffs. We do, however, export such products as houses. Our designs are significantly stronger in earthquakes, and such producers as Viceroy Homes are successfully exporting modular homes into Japan, possessing 7 percent of the Japanese market in 1997. This growth represents over 65 percent of the total value of company sales to Japan in 2001 in six months, or US$32.5 million out of US$49.9 million.[2]

Courtesy of Office Max

INTRODUCTION

Consumers around the world can drink Coca-Cola and Pepsi; eat at McDonald's and Pizza Hut; see movies from Mexico, England, France, Australia, and China; and watch CNN and MTV on Toshiba and Sony televisions. The products you consume today are just as likely to have been made in Korea or Germany as in North America. Likewise, consumers in other countries buy Western electrical equipment, clothing, rock music, cosmetics, and toiletries, as well as computers, robots, and earth-moving equipment.

Many firms are finding that international markets provide tremendous opportunities for growth. The consulting firm Deloitte and Touche estimates that about 95 percent of the world's population and two-thirds of its total purchasing power are outside the United States.[3] Accessing these markets can promote innovation, while intensifying global competition spurs companies to market better and less expensive products.[4]

In this chapter, we explore business in this exciting global marketplace. First, we'll look at the nature of international business, including barriers and promoters of trade across international boundaries. Next, we consider the levels of organizational involvement in international business. Finally, we briefly discuss strategies for trading across national borders.

THE ROLE OF INTERNATIONAL BUSINESS

international business
the buying, selling, and trading of goods and services across national boundaries

International business refers to the buying, selling, and trading of goods and services across national boundaries. Falling political barriers and new technology are making it possible for more and more companies to sell their products overseas as well as at home. And, as differences among nations continue to narrow, the trend toward the globalization of business is becoming increasingly important. Colgate-Palmolive markets its oral care, household, personal care, fabric care, and pet nutrition goods to more than 200 countries and territories, earning 70 percent of its revenues from countries other than the United States.[5]

When Bombardier sells an airplane in the US, Sony sells a stereo in Vancouver, or a small Swiss medical supply company sells a shipment of orthopedic devices to a hospital in Monterrey, Mexico, the sale affects the economies of the countries involved. To begin our study of international business, we must first consider some economic issues: why nations trade, exporting and importing, and the balance of trade.

Why Nations Trade

absolute advantage
a monopoly that exists when a country is the only source of an item, the only producer of an item, or the most efficient producer of an item

Nations and businesses engage in international trade to obtain raw materials and goods that are otherwise unavailable to them or are available elsewhere at a lower price than that at which they themselves can produce. A nation, or individuals and organizations from a nation, sells surplus materials and goods to acquire funds to buy the goods, services, and ideas its people need. Poland and Hungary, for example, want to trade with Western nations so that they can acquire new technology and techniques to revitalize their economies. Which goods and services a nation sells depends on what resources it has available.

Some nations have a monopoly on the production of a particular resource or product. Such a monopoly, or **absolute advantage,** exists when a country is the only source of an item, the only producer of an item, or the most efficient producer of an item. Because South Africa has the largest deposits of diamonds in the world, one company, De Beers Consolidated Mines, Ltd., virtually controls the world's diamond trade and uses its control to maintain high prices for gem-quality diamonds. The United States, until recently, held an absolute advantage in oil-drilling equipment. But an absolute advantage not based on the availability of natural resources rarely lasts, and Japan and the former Soviet Union are now challenging the United States in the production of oil-drilling equipment.

Most international trade is based on **comparative advantage,** which occurs when a country specializes in products that it can supply more efficiently or at a lower cost than it can produce other items. Until recently, the United States had a comparative advantage in manufacturing automobiles, heavy machinery, airplanes, and weapons; other countries now hold the comparative advantage for many of these products (Canada, in particular, for automotive goods versus the United States).

Trade between Countries

To obtain needed goods and services and the funds to pay for them, nations trade by exporting and importing. **Exporting** is the sale of goods and services to foreign markets. If current trends continue, world exports of goods and services will reach $16 trillion by 2005.[6] Canadian businesses export many goods and services. Table 4.1 shows where Canadian exports went in 2000. **Importing** is the purchase of goods and services from foreign sources. Many of the goods you buy in Canada are likely to be imports or to have some imported components. Sometimes, you may not even realize they're imports.

Balance of Trade

A nation's **balance of trade** is the difference in value between its exports and imports. Because Canada exports more products and services than it imports, it has a positive balance of trade, or **trade surplus.** The Canadian trade surplus was $55 billion in 2000 because Canada exported $412 billion in goods and services and imported $356 billion. Canada's economy depends significantly on exports, as the $412 billion exported in 2000 represents over 37 percent of the value of all goods and services produced in that year. Japan also currently has a trade surplus with many of the countries with whom it trades.

The opposite of a trade surplus is a trade deficit. Trade deficits are harmful because they can mean the failure of businesses, the loss of jobs, and a lowered standard of living.

comparative advantage
the basis of most international trade, when a country specializes in products that it can supply more efficiently or at a lower cost than it can produce other items

exporting
the sale of goods and services to foreign markets

importing
the purchase of goods and services from foreign sources

balance of trade
the difference in value between a nation's exports and its imports

trade surplus
a nation's positive balance of trade, which exists when that country imports less than it exports

United States	87.1%
Japan	2.2%
United Kingdom	1.4%
China	0.9%
Germany	0.8%

Table 4.1

Where Canadian Exports Went in 2000

Source: "Trade by Products (HS)—HS Codes," adapted from the Statistics Canada Web site at, **www.statcan.ca/english/ads/trade/index/htm.**

Table 4.2

*The Top 5 Countries
Canada Traded with
in 2000*

Source: Statistics Canada
and US Census Bureau,
**www.strategis.ic.gc.ca/sc_
mrkti/tdst/tdo/tdo.php.**

	Exports ($ billions)	%	Imports ($ billions)	%	Trade Balance ($ billions)
United States	$359.2	87.1	$229.5	64.4	$129.0 Surplus
Japan	$ 9.1	2.2	$ 16.6	4.7	$ 7.5 Deficit
United Kingdom	$ 5.7	1.4	$ 13.0	3.6	$ 7.3 Deficit
China	$ 3.6	0.9	$ 11.3	3.2	$ 7.7 Deficit
Mexico	$ 2.0	0.5	$ 12.1	3.4	$ 10.1 Deficit

Japan currently has a trade surplus with many of the countries with whom it trades. Of course, when a nation exports more goods than it imports, it has a favourable balance of trade, or trade surplus. Table 4.2 shows the top five countries Canada traded with in 2000, and indicates whether there was a trade surplus or a trade deficit.

**balance of
payments**

the difference between
the flow of money into
and out of a country

The difference between the flow of money into and out of a country is called its **balance of payments.** A country's balance of trade, foreign investments, foreign aid, loans, military expenditures, and money spent by tourists comprise its balance of payments. As you might expect, a country with a trade surplus generally has a favourable balance of payments because it is receiving more money from trade with foreign countries than it is paying out. When a country has a trade deficit, more money flows out of the country than into it. If more money flows out of the country than into it from tourism and other sources, the country may experience declining production and higher unemployment, because there is less money available for spending.

When the Canadian dollar drops in relation to other currencies, such as the US dollar, it costs more to import from the US, especially fresh fruit and vegetables in the winter. Conversely, Canadian products become less expensive to US consumers and businesses. This increases exports for Canadians and creates many jobs, helping our economy, boosting productivity, and increasing our competitiveness on the global stage. At the same time as foreign products become more expensive, we buy fewer foreign goods, and combined it all improves our balance of trade, thus increasing jobs, keeping our cost of living in check, and ultimately providing a better economic environment in Canada. In 1999, Canada recorded a positive balance of payments of $1.7 billion, and it jumped to $4.2 billion in just the first quarter of 2001, primarily due to energy exports to the United States.

INTERNATIONAL TRADE BARRIERS

Completely free trade seldom exists. When a company decides to do business outside its own country, it will encounter a number of barriers to international trade. Any firm considering international business must research the other country's economic, legal, political, social, cultural, and technological background. Such research will help the company choose an appropriate level of involvement and operating strategies, as we will see later in this chapter.

Economic Barriers

When looking at doing business in another country, managers must consider a number of basic economic factors, such as economic development, infrastructure, and exchange rates.

Economic Development. When considering doing business abroad, business-people need to recognize that they cannot take for granted that other countries offer the same things as are found in *industrialized nations*—economically advanced countries such as the United States, Japan, Great Britain, and Canada. Many countries in Africa, Asia, and South America, for example, are in general poorer and less economically advanced than those in North America and Europe; they are often called *less-developed countries* (LDCs). LDCs are characterized by low per capita income (income generated by the nation's production of goods and services divided by the population), which means that consumers are not likely to purchase nonessential products. Nonetheless, LDCs represent a potentially huge and profitable market for many businesses because they may be buying technology to improve their infrastructures, and much of the population may desire consumer products—such as personal care products and soft drinks. The erosion of Kodak's domestic market share is being more than offset by the firm's expansion into emerging markets such as China, India, and Latin America. Kodak now holds 45 percent of the world market.[7]

A country's level of development is determined in part by its **infrastructure,** the physical facilities that support its economic activities, such as railroads, highways, ports, airfields, utilities and power plants, schools, hospitals, communication systems, and commercial distribution systems. When doing business in LDCs, for example, a business may need to compensate for rudimentary distribution and communication systems, or even a lack of technology.

Exchange Rates. The ratio at which one nation's currency can be exchanged for another nation's currency or for gold is the **exchange rate.** Exchange rates vary daily and can be found in newspapers and through many sites on the Internet. One such site, XE.com, asks the user to enter the amount desired to convert and the two types of currency involved in the exchange. For example, you could find out how many euros you would receive for $500 Canadian. The site also offers a table of rates. Familiarity with exchange rates is important because they affect the cost of imports and exports. Current exchange rates provide an opportunity for Canada to export cheaper products to the US. Tourists find that the US dollar goes a lot further in Canada, as the advertisement for Canadian ski resorts shows.

Occasionally, a government may alter the value of its national currency. Devaluation decreases the value of currency in relation to other currencies. If the US government were to devalue its dollar, it would lower the cost of American goods abroad and make trips to the United States less expensive for foreign tourists. Thus, devaluation encourages the sale of domestic goods and tourism. Mexico has repeatedly devalued the peso for this reason. Revaluation, which increases the value of a currency in relation to other currencies, occurs rarely.

Legal and Political Barriers

A company that decides to enter the international marketplace must contend with potentially complex relationships among the different laws of its own nation, international laws, and the laws of the nation with which it will be trading; various trade restrictions imposed on international trade; and changing political climates.

Laws and Regulations. Canada has a number of laws and regulations that govern the activities of Canadian firms engaged in international trade. Generally though, Canada adheres to the many agreements that have evolved from the United Nations, the World Trade Organization, and other trading groups such as NAFTA, of

infrastructure
the physical facilities that support a country's economic activities, such as railroads, highways, ports, airfields, utilities and power plants, schools, hospitals, communication systems, and commercial distribution systems

exchange rate
the ratio at which one nation's currency can be exchanged for another nation's currency or for gold

XE.com
www.xe.com
This website permits conversion calculations of most major currencies, but a caution: the rates are updated every minute and the rate may not be available to consumers depending upon the actual dollar value being used.

Canadian ski resorts advertise the benefits of the current exchange rate between Canada and the US to American ski enthusiasts.

Courtesy of IntraWest

which we are members. These rules govern how documents are to be recognized; the minimum age for workers (child labour laws); the trade in ivory; and the movement of people, goods, and intellectual rights, such as patents, trademarks, and copyrights. As a normal process, we have international negotiators participate in the drafting of such treaties and accords, and these are then ratified by Parliament. Still, Canadians doing business outside our borders or with visitors from other countries need to be careful.

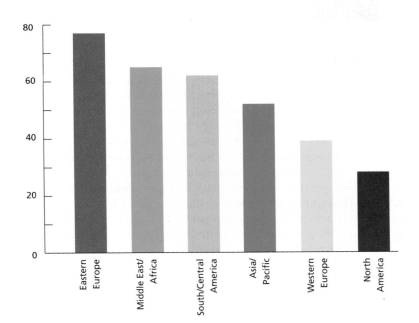

Figure 4.1

Software Piracy Rate by Region

Source: "Software Piracy Flourishing," *USA Today Snapshots,* August 13, 1998, p. B1.

Once outside Canadian borders, businesspeople are likely to find that the laws of other nations differ from those of Canada. Many of the legal rights that Canadians take for granted do not exist in other countries, and a firm doing business abroad must understand and obey the laws of the host country. Many countries forbid foreigners from owning real property outright; others have strict laws limiting the amount of local currency that can be taken out of the country and the amount of foreign currency that can be brought in.

Some countries have copyright and patent laws that are less strict than those of Canada, and some countries fail to honour Canadian laws. China, for example, has recently been threatened with severe trade sanctions by the US because of a history of allowing US goods to be copied or counterfeited there. Such unauthorized Chinese goods cost US providers of software, movies, books, and music recordings billions of dollars in lost sales and the problem extends to other industries as well. Of the 574 million business software applications installed worldwide in 1997, 40 percent were stolen.[8] Figure 4.1 shows the piracy rates by regions of the world. North American companies are angry because the fakes harm not only their sales, but also their reputations if the knockoffs are of poor quality. Such counterfeiting is not limited to China, and in countries where these activities occur, laws against them may not be sufficiently enforced, if counterfeiting is in fact deemed illegal. Thus, businesses engaging in foreign trade may have to take extra steps to protect their products because local laws may be insufficient to do so. Transparency International provides a listing of the most corrupt countries in the world. Its Corruption Perceptions Index has triggered meaningful reform in many countries by raising public awareness of the problem.

Transparency International
www.transparency.org/

Tariffs and Trade Restrictions. Tariffs and other trade restrictions are part of a country's legal structure but may be established or removed for political reasons. An

import tariff
a tax levied by a nation on goods imported into the country

import tariff is a tax levied by a nation on goods imported into the country. A *fixed tariff* is a specific amount of money levied on each unit of a product brought into the country, while an *ad valorem tariff* is based on the value of the item. Most countries allow citizens travelling abroad to bring home a certain amount of merchandise without paying an import tariff. A Canadian citizen may bring $50 worth of merchandise into Canada duty free after 24 hours outside of Canada, $200 worth of merchandise after 48 hours, and $750 after seven days. After that, Canadian citizens must pay a duty based on the cost of the item and the country of origin. Thus, identical items purchased in different countries might have different tariffs.

Countries sometimes levy tariffs for political reasons, as when they impose sanctions against other countries to protest their actions. However, import tariffs are more commonly imposed to protect domestic products by raising the price of imported ones. Such protective tariffs have become controversial, especially for Americans as they become concerned over the US trade deficit. Protective tariffs allow more expensive domestic goods to compete with foreign ones. For example, many advocate the imposition of tariffs on products imported from Japan, particularly luxury automobiles, audio components, and computers. However, governments fear economic reprisals from Japan if the tariffs are levied on Japanese products.

Critics of protective tariffs argue that their use inhibits free trade and competition. Supporters of protective tariffs say they insulate domestic industries, particularly new ones, against well-established foreign competitors. Once an industry matures, however, its advocates may be reluctant to let go of the tariff that protected it. Tariffs also help when, because of low labour costs and other advantages, foreign competitors can afford to sell their products at prices lower than those charged by domestic companies. Some protectionists argue that tariffs should be used to keep domestic wages high and unemployment low.

exchange controls
regulations that restrict the amount of currency that can be bought or sold

Exchange controls restrict the amount of currency that can be bought or sold. Some countries control their foreign trade by forcing businesspeople to buy and sell foreign products through a central bank. If John Deere, for example, receives payments for its tractors in a foreign currency, it may be required to sell the currency to that nation's central bank. When foreign currency is in short supply, as it is in many Third World and Eastern European countries, the government uses foreign currency to purchase necessities and capital goods and produces other products locally, thus limiting its need for foreign imports.

quota
a restriction on the number of units of a particular product that can be imported into a country

A **quota** limits the number of units of a particular product that can be imported into a country. A quota may be established by voluntary agreement or by government decree. The United States has imposed an import quota on some Japanese economy cars in an effort to reduce the amount of US dollars leaving the country.

embargo
a prohibition on trade in a particular product

An **embargo** prohibits trade in a particular product. Embargoes are generally directed at specific goods or countries and may be established for political, economic, health, or religious reasons. The US forbids the importation of cigars from Cuba for political reasons. However, demand for Cuban cigars is so strong that corporate pressure to end such sanctions is increasing.[9] Health embargoes prevent the importing of various pharmaceuticals, animals, plants, and agricultural products. Muslim nations forbid the importation of alcoholic beverages on religious grounds.

dumping
the act of a country or business selling products at less than what it costs to produce them

One common reason for setting quotas is to prohibit **dumping,** which occurs when a country or business sells products at less than what it costs to produce them. Canadian and US steelmakers have accused firms in South Korea, Japan, and Russia of dumping steel in North America for less than what it cost to be produced in their home countries. This in turn would cause domestic producers to lose business and jobs.

A company may dump its products for several reasons. Dumping permits quick entry into a market. Sometimes dumping occurs when the domestic market for a firm's product is too small to support an efficient level of production. In other cases, technologically obsolete products that are no longer salable in the country of origin are dumped overseas. Dumping is relatively difficult to prove, but even the suspicion of dumping can lead to the imposition of quotas.

Political Barriers. Unlike legal issues, political considerations are seldom written down and often change rapidly. Nations that have been subject to economic sanctions for political reasons in recent years include China, Iraq, Iran, Syria, and South Africa. While these were dramatic events, political considerations affect international business daily as governments enact tariffs, embargoes, or other types of trade restrictions in response to political events.

Businesses engaged in international trade must consider the relative instability of countries such as Iraq, South Africa, and Honduras. Political unrest in countries such as Peru, Haiti, Somalia, and Russia may create a hostile or even dangerous environment for foreign businesses. Civil war, as in Sudan and Sri Lanka, may disrupt business activities and place lives in danger. And, a sudden change in power can result in a regime that is hostile to foreign investment. Some businesses have been forced out of a country altogether, as they were when Fidel Castro closed Cuba to American business. Whether they like it or not, companies are often involved directly or indirectly in international politics. Many Canadian companies have replaced the US firms that left Cuba, despite US pressure to cease doing business with Cuba.

Political concerns may lead a group of nations to form a **cartel,** a group of firms or nations that agrees to act as a monopoly and not compete with each other, to generate a competitive advantage in world markets. Probably the most famous cartel is OPEC, the Organization of Petroleum Exporting Countries, founded in the 1960s to increase the price of petroleum throughout the world and to maintain high prices. By working to ensure stable oil prices, OPEC hopes to enhance the economies of its member nations. At the same time, they do not try to stifle the economies of their client nations.

cartel
a group of firms or nations that agrees to act as a monopoly and not compete with each other, in order to generate a competitive advantage in world markets

OPEC
www.opec.org

Social and Cultural Barriers

Most businesspeople engaged in international trade underestimate the importance of social and cultural differences; but these differences can derail an important transaction. Australians spend only one-third of their food budget on food prepared outside the home, whereas Americans spend over one-half. Anticipating growth in Australians' consumption of fast food, however, Burger King has opened a restaurant in Sydney.[10] Unfortunately, cultural norms are rarely written down, and what is written down may well be inaccurate.

Cultural differences include differences in spoken and body language. Although it is certainly possible to translate words from one language to another, the true meaning is sometimes misinterpreted or lost. In Italy, an advertising campaign for Schweppes Tonic Water translated the name into "Schweppes Toilet Water." An ad in Mexico for Parker ballpoint pens was supposed to say "It won't leak in your pocket and embarrass you." Parker assumed that *embarazar* means "to embarrass," but it actually means "to impregnate." So, the ad read, "It won't leak in your pocket and make you pregnant."[11] While such examples make us laugh, they also illustrate the difficulty of conducting business in other languages and cultures.

Value Diversity

Cultural Awareness in Global Marketing

Coors's slogan "Turn it loose" was translated into Spanish where it was read as "Suffer from diarrhea." Colgate introduced Cue toothpaste in France, only to discover that *Cue* is a French pornographic magazine. Translated into Chinese, Pepsi's "Come alive with the Pepsi generation" became "Pepsi brings back your ancestors from the grave." Clairol introduced the Mist Stick curling iron in Germany where "mist" is German slang for manure.

These examples underscore that firms that want to market a product globally and reach consumers of varying cultures need to become thoroughly acquainted with the language, customs, prejudices, and tastes of the intended market. Failing to do so can be costly in terms of unproductive advertising, lost sales, and lost goodwill. Words, images, gestures, and even colours and numbers have different meanings in different countries.

Marketers should avoid using the number four when addressing Chinese, Korean, and Japanese consumers. Although advertising that says "four times the savings" would probably appeal to North American consumers, it would not appeal to an Asian audience because four is the number for death in Asian numerology. Korean and Japanese consumers will recognize a promotion that uses red and gold colours as one that was created for Chinese consumers. Not only are they less likely to respond to the ad, but they may feel insulted.

Marketers must find out what is important or relevant in a particular market and recognize that North American icons, holidays, and heroes are often meaningless in other cultures. For example, there are few beauty magazines in Latin America, so the idea of a "cover girl" or supermodel like Cindy Crawford is unknown. However, beauty pageants are common. Therefore, when Cover Girl cosmetics entered the Latin American market, it selected a former Venezuelan Miss Universe to become the product spokesperson.

Global marketers should never assume they know who the audience is or what it desires. Such an assumption may be based on inaccurate or even offensive stereotypes. Successful marketing must include the creation of messages that appeal to the sensitivities of the intended audience. Products and promotions must be culturally relevant and understanding of a group's values and customs. Successful marketing demands a commitment to a community, as well as a specific advertising campaign. For instance, understanding the importance of soccer to the Hispanic culture, Budweiser sponsored Major League Soccer, the US and Mexican national soccer teams, and three World Cups. As the popularity of this sport continues to increase among all groups, the investment is paying off for Budweiser.

Companies that are successful in global marketing realize that it requires a long-term commitment. Coca-Cola, McDonald's, and Procter & Gamble support the communities to which they try to sell their products. They are involved in community events, provide good places for minorities to work, and are good corporate citizens.[12]

Differences in body language and personal space also affect international trade. Body language is nonverbal, usually unconscious communication through gestures, posture, and facial expression. Personal space is the distance at which one person feels comfortable talking to another. North Americans tend to stand a moderate distance away from the person with whom they are speaking. Arab businessmen tend to stand face to face with the object of their conversation. Additionally, gestures vary from culture to culture, and gestures considered acceptable in North American society—pointing, for example—may be considered rude in others. Such cultural differences may generate uncomfortable feelings or misunderstandings when business-people of different countries negotiate with each other.

Family roles also influence marketing activities. Many countries do not allow children to be used in advertising, for example. Advertising that features people in non-traditional social roles may not be successful, either. Procter & Gamble has been experimenting with ads in India that depict men doing housework, a nontraditional role. Although some Indian men do help with housework, ads that show men performing such chores may not appeal to Asian women. However, two firms, Korea's LG Electronics and Kuala Lumpur's National Panasonic, have successfully used such advertising.[13]

The people of other nations quite often have a different perception of time as well. North Americans value promptness; a business meeting scheduled for a specific time seldom starts more than a few minutes late. In Mexico and Spain, however, it is not unusual for a meeting to be delayed half an hour or more. Such a late start might produce resentment in a North American negotiating in Spain for the first time.

Companies engaged in foreign trade must observe the national and religious holidays and local customs of the host country. In many Islamic countries, for example, workers expect to take a break at certain times of the day to observe religious rites. Companies also must monitor their advertising to guard against offending customers. In Thailand and many other countries, public displays of affection between the sexes are unacceptable in advertising messages; in many Middle Eastern nations, it is unacceptable to show the soles of one's feet.

With the exception of the United States, most nations use the metric system. This lack of uniformity creates problems for both buyers and sellers in the international marketplace. American sellers, for instance, must package goods destined for foreign markets in litres or metres, and Japanese sellers must convert to the English system if they plan to sell a product in the United States. Tools also must be calibrated in the correct system if they are to function correctly. Hyundai and Honda service technicians need metric tools to make repairs on those cars. This provides Canada with an advantage compared to US competitors as we don't have to convert our packaging.

The literature dealing with international business is filled with accounts of sometimes humorous but often costly mistakes that occurred because of a lack of understanding of the social and cultural differences between buyers and sellers. Such problems cannot always be avoided, but they can be minimized through research on the cultural and social differences of the host country.

Technological Barriers

Many countries lack the technological infrastructure found in North America, and some marketers are viewing such barriers as opportunities. For example, cellular and wireless phone technology is actually less expensive in some countries than traditional telephone systems. With installation costs of US$440 and months on waiting lists, few households in China have private phone lines. Many Chinese consumers are bypassing these expensive private lines and turning instead to wireless communications, doubling the mobile phone market in China to 13 million units. With the market expected to increase to 50 million units, many firms, including Motorola, Nokia, and Ericsson, have started marketing wireless communications in China.[14] Nortel, of course, has been operating in China since the 1980s.

General Agreement on Tariffs and Trade (GATT)

a trade agreement, originally signed by 23 nations in 1947, that provides a forum for tariff negotiations and a place where international trade problems can be discussed and resolved

World Trade Organization (WTO)

international organization that deals with the global rules of trade between nations

World Trade Organization **www.wto.org/wto/ about/about/htm**

TRADE ALLIANCES, SPECIFIC MARKETS, AND TRADE SUPPORTERS

Although these economic, political, legal, and sociocultural issues may seem like daunting barriers to international trade, there are also organizations and agreements—such as the General Agreement on Tariffs and Trade, the World Bank, and the International Monetary Fund—that foster international trade and can help managers get involved in and succeed in global markets. Various regional trade agreements, such as the North American Free Trade Agreement and the European Union, also promote trade among member nations by eliminating tariffs and trade restrictions. In this section, we'll look briefly at these agreements and organizations, as well as the specific market in the Pacific Rim.

General Agreement on Tariffs and Trade (GATT)

During the Great Depression of the 1930s, nations established so many protective tariffs covering so many products that international trade became virtually impossible. By the end of World War II, there was considerable international momentum to liberalize trade and minimize the effects of tariffs. The **General Agreement on Tariffs and Trade (GATT),** originally signed by 23 nations in 1947, provides a forum for tariff negotiations and a place where international trade problems can be discussed and resolved. Currently, more than 140 nations abide by its rules, managed by the **World Trade Organization (WTO).**

WTO sponsors rounds of negotiations aimed at reducing trade restrictions. Two of the most successful of these sessions were the Kennedy and Tokyo rounds. The Kennedy Round, named for US President John F. Kennedy, reduced tariffs on more than 60,000 items by an average of 40 percent among 50 members of GATT. The Tokyo Round (1973–1979) involved 100 nations. It reduced many tariffs by 30 percent, and the negotiators were able to eliminate or ease nontariff trade restrictions such as import quotas, red tape in customs procedures, and "buy national" agreements. The Tokyo Round also worked to increase the availability of foreign currency. The Uruguay Round (1988–1994) further reduced trade barriers for most products and provided new rules to prevent dumping. The Qatar round of negotiations was established in November 2001 to further reduce trade barriers and encourage global economic growth for more than 140 nations.

Each of the previous GATT rounds has reduced trade barriers and has been followed by a period of strong economic growth. By the year 2002, falling trade barriers are

Barriers to international trade were significantly reduced by the General Agreement on Tariffs and Trade, resulting in an increase in international cargo ship traffic.

© 1999 PhotoDisc, Inc.

expected to add US$250 billion to the value of goods and services worldwide, which translates into an 8 percent boost in the global domestic product.[15] It is hoped that, by reducing trade barriers, nations will develop closer relationships. As this happens, global markets should become more efficient, and possibly political strife will decrease.

The North American Free Trade Agreement (NAFTA)

The **North American Free Trade Agreement (NAFTA),** which went into effect on January 1, 1994, effectively merged Canada, the United States, and Mexico into one market of about 400 million consumers. NAFTA eliminates most tariffs (import taxes) and trade restrictions on agricultural and manufactured products among the three countries over a period of 15 years. It is estimated that output for this trade alliance is US$7 trillion.

For the United States, NAFTA makes it easier for businesses to invest in Mexico and Canada, provides protection for intellectual property (of special interest to high-technology industries), and expands trade by requiring equal treatment of US firms in both countries. Although most tariffs on products going to the United States will be eliminated, duties on products such as household glassware, footwear, and some fruits and vegetables will be phased out over the 15-year period. South Dakota farmers have recently protested what they say is the dumping of agricultural commodities by Canada. The farmers have staged blockades, halting Canadian trucks carrying grain and livestock into the US. The farmers claim that Canadian agricultural imports are depressing US prices, and, as one farmer said, "We want fair trade, not just free trade."[16]

Although NAFTA has been controversial, it has become a positive factor for North American firms wishing to engage in international business. US retailers such as Wal-Mart and AutoZone are opening stores in Mexico and Canada. Canada's Research In Motion exports its BlackBerry throughout the US and Mexico. And because licensing requirements have been relaxed under the pact, smaller businesses that previously could not afford to invest in the US and Mexico are able to do business in those markets without having to locate there. NAFTA's long phase-in period provides ample time for adjustment by those firms affected by reduced tariffs on imports. Furthermore, increased competition should lead to a more efficient market, and the long-term prospects of including most countries in the Western Hemisphere in the alliance promise additional opportunities for Canadian marketers.

Specifically, NAFTA has increased trade for Canadian businesses affording access to the world's largest market, the United States. At the same time, Canada has become a prime location for foreign companies to access the North American market by locating in Canada and exporting to the United States. For example, Honda has located in Alliston, Ontario, and Toyota in Cambridge, Ontario. Food is transferred quickly across the border for the benefit of both countries, providing Canadian hothouse vegetables to the US and field-grown vegetables to Canadians. Still, the relationship is not all smooth sailing. In the 1990s and again in 2001, the United States placed tariffs and duties on Canadian softwood lumber, accusing federal and provincial governments of providing unfair subsidies to the lumber industry in BC and the Maritimes, and thus hurting the US lumber industry. This dispute, and others like it, can then be resolved through either negotiation, a tribunal hearing under NAFTA rules, or ultimately by the WTO.

The European Union (EU)

The **European Union (EU),** also called the European Community or Common Market, was established in 1958 to promote trade among its members, which initially

North American Free Trade Agreement (NAFTA) agreement that eliminates most tariffs and trade restrictions on agricultural and manufactured products to encourage trade among Canada, the US, and Mexico

The NAFTA Secretariat **www.nafta-sec-alena. org/**

The European Union's Official Website **www.userpage.chemie. fu-berlin.de/adressen/ eu.html**

European Union (EU) a union of European nations established in 1958 to promote trade among its members; one of the largest single markets today

Solve the Dilemma

Global Expansion or Business as Usual?

?

Audiotech Electronics, founded in 1959 by a father and son, currently operates a 3,200-square-metre factory with 75 employees. The company produces control consoles for television and radio stations and recording studios. It is involved in every facet of production—designing the systems, installing the circuits in its computer boards, and even manufacturing and painting the metal cases housing the consoles. The company's products are used by all the major broadcast and cable networks. The firm's newest products allow television correspondents to simultaneously hear and communicate with their counterparts in different geographic locations. Audiotech has been very successful meeting its customers' needs efficiently.

Audiotech sales have historically been strong in Canada, but recently growth is stagnating. Even though Audiotech is a small, family-owned firm, it believes it should evaluate and consider global expansion.

1. What are the key issues that need to be considered in determining global expansion?
2. What are some of the unique problems that a small business might face in global expansion that larger firms would not?
3. Should Audiotech consider a joint venture? Should it hire a sales force of people native to the countries it enters?

included Belgium, France, Italy, West Germany, Luxembourg, and The Netherlands. In 1991, East and West Germany united, and by 1993, the United Kingdom, Spain, Denmark, Greece, Portugal, and Ireland had joined as well. Cyprus, Poland, Hungary, the Czech Republic, Slovenia, and Estonia have begun formal negotiations to join the EU; Latvia, Lithuania, Slovakia, Romania, and Bulgaria have requested membership as well.[17] Until 1993, each nation functioned as a separate market, but at that time, they officially united into one of the largest single world markets, with nearly 340 million consumers. Should the other nations join, their total population will exceed North America's.

To facilitate free trade among its members, the EU is working toward the standardization of business regulations and requirements, import duties, and value-added taxes; the elimination of customs checks; and the creation of a standardized currency for use by all members. Many European nations (Austria, Belgium, Finland, France, Germany, Ireland, Italy, Luxembourg, The Netherlands, Portugal, and Spain) have already begun linking their exchange rates together in preparation for a common currency, the *euro,* which debuted on January 1, 1999. Greece entered in 2001, and the UK, Denmark, and Sweden have decided to delay entry.[18] In January 2002, the euro was launched for individuals to use and each country's notes and coins were eliminated.

The common currency may require many marketers to modify their pricing strategies and will subject them to increased competition. However, the use of a single currency will free those companies that sell goods among European countries from the nuisance of dealing with complex exchange rates.[19] The long-term goals are to eliminate all barriers for trade within the EU, improve the economic efficiency of the EU nations, and stimulate economic growth—thus making the union economy more competitive in global markets, particularly against Japan, the rest of the Pacific Rim, and North America. However, several disputes and debates still divide the member nations, and many barriers to completely free trade remain. Consequently, it may take many years before the EU is truly one deregulated market.

The Pacific Rim Nations

Despite economic turmoil and a recession in Asia in recent years, companies of the Pacific Rim nations—Japan, China, South Korea, Taiwan, Singapore, Hong Kong, the Philippines, Malaysia, Indonesia, Australia, and Indochina—have become increasingly competitive and sophisticated in global business over the last three decades. They represent tremendous opportunities for marketers who understand these markets.

The Japanese in particular have made inroads into the world consumer markets for automobiles, motorcycles, watches, cameras, and audio and video equipment. Products from Sony, Sanyo, Toyota, Mitsubishi, Canon, Suzuki, and Toshiba are sold all over the world. Despite the high volume of trade between the US and Japan, the two economies are less integrated than is the US economy with Canada and Western Europe. Economists estimate that if Japan imported goods at the same rate as other major nations, the US would sell US$50 billion more annually to Japan.[20] The US and Japan continually struggle with cultural and political differences and are, in general, at odds over how to do business with each other.[21] Among the Japanese markets opening for the US are telecommunications products, such as cell phones and personal computers.

The People's Republic of China, a country of 1.4 billion people, has launched a program of economic reform designed to stimulate its economy by privatizing many industries, restructuring its banking system, and increasing public spending on infrastructure (including railways and telecommunications).[22] The potential of China's consumer market is so vast that it is almost impossible to measure, but there are risks associated with doing business in China. Political and economic instability, especially inflation, combined with corruption and erratic policy shifts have undercut marketers' efforts to stake a claim in what could become the world's largest market.[23]

Despite an economic crisis in the late 1990s, South Korea has been quite successful in global markets with familiar brand names such as Samsung, Daewoo, and Hyundai. Korean companies are grabbing market share from Japanese companies in global markets for videocassette recorders, colour televisions, and computers.

Less visible and sometimes less stable Pacific Rim regions, such as Thailand, Malaysia, Singapore, Taiwan, and Hong Kong, have become major manufacturing and financial centres. Singapore boasts huge global markets for rubber goods and pharmaceuticals. Taiwan may have the most promising future of all the Pacific Rim nations, with a strong local economy and low import barriers that are drawing increasing imports. Firms from Thailand and Malaysia are carving out niches in world markets for a variety of products, from toys to automobile parts.[24] And Vietnam is becoming one of Asia's fastest growing markets for North American businesses.

World Bank

The **World Bank,** more formally known as the International Bank for Reconstruction and Development, was established by the industrialized nations, including Canada, in 1946 to loan money to underdeveloped and developing countries. It loans its own funds or borrows funds from member countries to finance projects ranging from road and factory construction to the building of medical and educational facilities. The World Bank and other multilateral development banks (banks with international support that provide loans to developing countries) are the largest source of advice and assistance for developing nations. The International Development Association and the International Finance Corporation are associated with the World Bank and provide loans to private businesses and member countries.

World Bank
an organization established by the industrialized nations in 1946 to loan money to underdeveloped and developing countries; formally known as the International Bank for Reconstruction and Development

International Monetary Fund

International Monetary Fund
www.imf.org/

The **International Monetary Fund (IMF)** was established in 1947 to promote trade among member nations by eliminating trade barriers and fostering financial cooperation. It also makes short-term loans to member countries that have balance-of-payment deficits and provides foreign currencies to member nations. For example, the IMF approved US$56 million for the Dominican Republic after Hurricane Georges left an estimated US$1.3 billion in damages.[25] The International Monetary Fund also tries to avoid financial crises and panics by alerting the international community about countries that will not be able to repay their debts.[26] The IMF's Internet site provides additional information about the organization, including news releases, frequently asked questions, and members.

GETTING INVOLVED IN INTERNATIONAL BUSINESS

Businesses may get involved in international trade at many levels—from a small Kenyan firm that occasionally exports African crafts to a huge multinational corporation such as Shell Oil that sells products around the globe. The degree of commitment of resources and effort required increases according to the level at which a business involves itself in international trade. This section examines exporting and importing, trading companies, licensing and franchising, contract manufacturing, joint ventures, direct investment, and multinational corporations.

Statistics Canada's Web Site for General Information and Research
www.statcan.ca

Strategis Canada (Statistics Canada's Web Site of Business Information)
www.strategis.ic.gc.ca

Exporting and Importing

Many companies first get involved in international trade when they import goods from other countries for resale in their own businesses. For example, a grocery store chain may import bananas from Honduras and coffee from Colombia. A business may get involved in exporting when it is called upon to supply a foreign company with a particular product. Such exporting enables enterprises of all sizes to participate in international business. According to *The Daily*, Statistics Canada's report on March 28, 2001, exporters of less than $1,000,000 per year represented 62 percent of all exporters and 65 percent of all exports. Still, from 1993 to 1999, the number of exporters has doubled as exports increased by 84 percent.

Exporting sometimes takes place through **countertrade agreements,** which involve bartering products for other products instead of for currency. Such arrangements are fairly common in international trade, especially between Western companies and Eastern European nations. An estimated 40 percent or more of all international trade agreements contain countertrade provisions.

Although a company may export its wares overseas directly or import goods directly from their manufacturer, many choose to deal with an intermediary, commonly called an *export agent*. Export agents seldom produce goods themselves; instead, they usually handle international transactions for other firms. Export agents either purchase products outright or take them on consignment. If they purchase them outright, they generally mark up the price they have paid and attempt to sell the product in the international marketplace. They are also responsible for storage and transportation.

An advantage of trading through an agent instead of directly is that the company does not have to deal with foreign currencies or the red tape (paying tariffs and handling paperwork) of international business. A major disadvantage is that, because the export agent must make a profit, either the price of the product must be increased or the domestic company must provide a larger discount than it would in a domestic transaction.

Trading Companies

A **trading company** buys goods in one country and sells them to buyers in another country. Trading companies handle all activities required to move products from one country to another, including consulting, marketing research, advertising, insurance, product research and design, warehousing, and foreign exchange services to companies interested in selling their products in foreign markets. Trading companies are similar to export agents, but their role in international trade is larger. By linking sellers and buyers of goods in different countries, trading companies promote international trade.

Canada has few trading companies but one of the oldest is the Canadian Commercial Corporation (CCC), a Crown corporation in existence since 1942, with a primary goal of assisting Canadian companies involved in producing military products for our allies. The CCC may assist in the negotiating or financing of the receivable for the producing company. The Export Development Company (EDC), another Crown corporation, and some private companies get involved in financing commercial transactions that may be too large for a Canadian company to finance through normal methods or that require waiting long periods to receive payment.

Licensing and Franchising

Licensing is a trade arrangement in which one company—the *licensor*—allows another company—the *licensee*—to use its company name, products, patents, brands, trademarks, raw materials, and/or production processes in exchange for a fee or royalty. The Coca-Cola Company and PepsiCo frequently use licensing as a means to market their soft drinks in other countries. Yoplait is a French yogurt that is licensed for production in North America to General Mills.

Franchising is a form of licensing in which a company—the *franchiser*—agrees to provide a *franchisee* a name, logo, methods of operation, advertising, products, and other elements associated with the franchiser's business, in return for a financial commitment and the agreement to conduct business in accordance with the franchiser's standard of operations. Wendy's, McDonald's, Pizza Hut, and Holiday Inn are well-known franchisers with international visibility.

Licensing and franchising enable a company to enter the international marketplace without spending large sums of money abroad or hiring or transferring personnel to handle overseas affairs. They also minimize problems associated with shipping costs, tariffs, and trade restrictions. And, they allow the firm to establish goodwill for its products in a foreign market, which will help the company if it decides to produce or market its products directly in the foreign country at some future date. However, if the licensee (or franchisee) does not maintain high standards of quality, the product's image may be hurt; therefore, it is important for the licensor to monitor its products overseas and to enforce its quality standards.

Contract Manufacturing

Contract manufacturing occurs when a company hires a foreign company to produce a specified volume of the firm's product to specification; the final product carries the domestic firm's name. Spalding, for example, relies on contract manufacturing for its sports equipment; Reebok uses Korean contract manufacturers to manufacture many of its athletic shoes.

trading company
a firm that buys goods in one country and sells them to buyers in another country

licensing
a trade agreement in which one company—the licensor—allows another company—the licensee—to use its company name, products, patents, brands, trademarks, raw materials, and/or production processes in exchange for a fee or royalty

franchising
a form of licensing in which a company—the franchiser—agrees to provide a franchisee a name, logo, methods of operation, advertising, products, and other elements associated with a franchiser's business, in return for a financial commitment and the agreement to conduct business in accordance with the franchiser's standard of operations

contract manufacturing
the hiring of a foreign company to produce a specified volume of the initiating company's product to specification; the final product carries the domestic firm's name

Joint Ventures and Alliances

joint venture
the sharing of the costs and operation of a business between a foreign company and a local partner

Many countries, particularly LDCs, do not permit direct investment by foreign companies or individuals. Or, a company may lack sufficient resources or expertise to operate in another country. In such cases, a company that wants to do business in another country may set up a **joint venture** by finding a local partner (occasionally, the host nation itself) to share the costs and operation of the business. For example, the Campbell Soup Company markets and distributes soup in Japan through a joint venture with Nakano Vinegar Company.[27]

strategic alliance
a partnership formed to create competitive advantage on a worldwide basis

In some industries, such as automobiles and computers, strategic alliances are becoming the predominant means of competing. A **strategic alliance** is a partnership formed to create competitive advantage on a worldwide basis. In such industries, international competition is so fierce and the costs of competing on a global basis are so high that few firms have the resources to go it alone, so they collaborate with other companies. One such collaboration is Star Alliance, including Air Canada, Lufthansa, SAS, United Airlines, All Nippon Airways, and others, which was formed to improve service and reduce costs.[28]

Direct Investment

direct investment
the ownership of overseas facilities

Companies that want more control and are willing to invest considerable resources in international business may consider **direct investment,** the ownership of overseas facilities. The business may control the facilities outright, or it may hold the majority ownership interest in the company that controls the facilities. For example, Motorola, Inc., the world's largest cellular phone maker, owns 51 percent of Appeal Telecom Co., a small Korean competitor. Steelcase, Inc., owns 25 percent of Thailand's largest furniture maker. And Wal-Mart paid US$179 million for a majority interest in four stores and six store sites in Korea.[29]

outsourcing
a form of direct investment that involves the transferring of manufacturing or other tasks— such as data processing —to countries where labour and supplies are less expensive

Outsourcing, a form of direct investment, involves transferring manufacturing or other tasks (such as data processing) to countries where labour and supplies are less expensive. When Sears decided to outsource its Craftsman brand bench and stationary tools overseas, Home Depot formed a partnership with the Emerson Tool Company in Paris, Tennessee. The employees of Emerson had been building the Craftsman tools for Sears for 30 years, and the 400 current employees would have lost their jobs if Home Depot had not intervened.[30] Many North American computer, apparel, and shoe makers, for example, have transferred production to Asian countries, where labour costs are lower than in North America. Some companies have transferred selected operations to Mexican plants under the *maquiladora* system. Under this system, US and Canadian companies supply labour-intensive assembly plants, called *maquilas,* with components for assembly, processing, or repair. The Mexican plant returns the finished products to the United States or Canada for further processing or shipment to customers. The company pays a tariff or duty only on the value added to the product in Mexico. Canadian and US businesses benefit from Mexico's proximity, low labour rates, and relatively cheap peso, while Mexico benefits from the increased economic development and the creation of new jobs. *Maquilas* are not limited to North American firms; increasingly, firms from Japan and other countries are outsourcing to Mexico.

Multinational Corporations

multinational corporation (MNC)
a corporation that operates on a worldwide scale, without significant ties to any one nation or region

The highest level of international business involvement is the **multinational corporation (MNC),** a corporation, such as IBM and Exxon, that operates on a worldwide scale, without significant ties to any one nation or region. MNCs are more than simple corporations. They often have greater assets than some of the countries in which

Many North American companies are expanding their Internet marketing overseas. There is great opportunity for savvy firms to capitalize on the growth of the Internet throughout Europe, Asia, and the rest of the world. Research indicates that the number of overseas web surfers will continue to increase, outpacing growth in North America. To utilize the web as a global marketing tool, however, companies must take a number of issues into consideration, including language, culture, regulations and laws, differing standards for telecommunication infrastructures, and privacy concerns.

The most dominant language on the Internet is English, but 44 percent of users (56 million people worldwide) use a language other than English. The most popular non-English languages on the Net are Spanish (24 percent), Japanese (22 percent), German (13 percent), and French (10 percent). Other languages, including Chinese, Swedish, Italian, and Dutch, make up the remainder. Problems can occur when web sites try to adapt to a foreign country. For example, when MSNBC launched its first European site, it had to completely rewrite the code to accommodate the German language. Also, since NBC is not a recognized name in Germany, the company partnered with a German news organization to develop content locally.

MSNBC is planning additional overseas ventures and will probably follow the same format that it did in Germany.

Content also must be changed to reflect cultural differences. For instance, baseball is not widely followed in Great Britain, so a web site catering to baseball enthusiasts would be unsuccessful there. However, cricket is very popular, and a site incorporating the sport would probably do well. In addition to sports, other cultural and social concerns to be addressed include buying and eating habits, entertainment, family values and roles, and other lifestyle issues. To be successful, web content must take into account local, regional, and country tastes.

Privacy is another key issue in online global marketing. Many web publishers in some European and Latin American countries do not share data about site visits. Advertising deals are often made in these areas because of personal relationships rather than potential revenue. North American companies that want to develop a web presence must understand local laws, regulations, and even customs to be successful. Many struggle with other countries' commercial policies.

Creating customized content to fit local tastes is essential to successful online global marketing. Based on the potential growth of Internet users abroad, many firms are doing just that.[31]

Embrace Technology

Online Global Marketing

they do business. General Motors, Ford Motors, and General Electric, for example, have sales higher than the GDP of many of the countries in which they operate. Nestlé, with headquarters in Switzerland, operates more than 300 plants around the world and receives revenues from Europe; North, Central, and South America; Africa; and Asia. The Royal Dutch/Shell Group, one of the world's major oil producers, is another MNC. Its main offices are located in The Hague and London. Other MNCs include BASF, British Petroleum, Cadbury Schweppes, Matsushita, Mitsubishi, Siemens, Texaco, Toyota, and Unilever.

INTERNATIONAL BUSINESS STRATEGIES

Planning in a global economy requires businesspeople to understand the economic, legal, political, and sociocultural realities of the countries in which they will operate. These factors will affect the strategy a business chooses to use outside its own borders.

Developing Strategies

multinational strategy

a plan, used by international companies, that involves customizing products, promotion, and distribution according to cultural, technological, regional, and national differences

Companies doing business internationally have traditionally used a **multinational strategy,** customizing their products, promotion, and distribution according to cultural, technological, regional, and national differences. Campbell Soup Company divides its world product advertising between two separate advertising agencies to accommodate customized ad messages. BBDO Worldwide handles most of Campbell's soup business in the US, Canada, Mexico, and Australia, and Young and Rubicam handles the soup and sauce business in Europe, Asia, and the UK. Young and Rubicam also has the "chunky" soup brand in North America, as well as the Pepperidge Farm and V-8 brands and the Prego, Pace, and Franco American lines.[33] As another example of a multinational strategy, many soap and detergent manufacturers have adapted their products to local water conditions, washing equipment, and washing habits. For customers in some less-developed countries, Colgate-Palmolive Co. has developed an inexpensive, plastic, hand-powered washing machine for use in households that have no electricity. The Campbell Soup Company tailors its soups to suit local tastes by selling cream of pumpkin soup in Australia, watercress-and-duck-gizzard soup in Hong Kong, and corn potage and *tap-puri yasai* in Japan.[34] Even when products are standardized, advertising often has to be modified to adapt to language and cultural differences. Celebrities used in advertising in North America, for example, may be unfamiliar to foreign consumers and thus would not be effective in advertising products in other countries.

More and more companies are moving from this customization strategy to a **global strategy (globalization),** which involves standardizing products (and, as much as possible, their promotion and distribution) for the whole world, as if it were a single entity. Examples of globalized products are North American clothing, movies, music, and cosmetics. Sony televisions, Levi jeans, and American cigarette brands seem to make year-to-year gains in the world market.

Before moving outside their own borders, companies must conduct environmental analyses to evaluate the potential of and problems associated with various markets and to determine what strategy is best for doing business in those markets. Failure to do so may result in losses and even negative publicity. Schlotzsky's, the Texas-based sandwich chain, experienced slower than expected sales when it opened a new restaurant in Beijing. The Chinese are less accustomed to eating foods with their hands, and they often like to share meals with a companion. Schlotzsky's hopes that, by training staff and placing pictures on restaurant tables that demonstrate how to hold and eat sandwiches, Chinese customers will learn to appreciate the large sandwiches—and, hopefully, sales will increase.[35] Some companies rely on local managers to gain greater insights and faster response to changes within a country. Astute businesspeople today "think globally, act locally"; that is, while constantly being aware of the total picture, they adjust their firms' strategies to conform to local needs and tastes.

global strategy (globalization)

a strategy that involves standardizing products (and, as much as possible, their promotion and distribution) for the whole world, as if it were a single entity

Managing the Challenges of Global Business

As we've pointed out in this chapter, many past political barriers to trade have fallen or been minimized, expanding and opening new market opportunities. Managers who can meet the challenges of creating and implementing effective and sensitive business strategies for the global marketplace can help lead their companies to success. Multinational corporations such as General Electric and Ford, which derive a substantial portion of their revenues from international business, depend on savvy managers who can adapt to different cultures. Lucent Technologies is investing more than US$24 million in a design centre in China in an effort to aid in China's modernization of its infrastructure and telecommunications technology. The income potential from Lucent, which manufactures, designs, and delivers products for networking, communications systems, software, data networking systems, business telephone systems, and microelectronic components, is enormous.[36] Small businesses, too, can succeed in foreign markets when their managers have carefully studied those markets and prepared and implemented appropriate strategies. Being globally aware is therefore an important quality for today's managers and will become a critical attribute for managers of the 21st century.

Review Your Understanding

Explore some of the factors within the international trade environment that influence business.

International business is the buying, selling, and trading of goods and services across national boundaries. Importing is the purchase of products and raw materials from another nation; exporting is the sale of domestic goods and materials to another nation. A nation's balance of trade is the difference in value between its exports and imports; a positive balance of trade is a trade surplus, and a negative balance is a trade deficit. The difference between the flow of money into a country and the flow of money out of it is called the balance of payments. An absolute or comparative advantage in trade may determine what products a company from a particular nation will export.

Investigate some of the economic, legal-political, social, cultural, and technological barriers to international business.

Companies engaged in international trade must consider the effects of economic, legal, political, social, and cultural differences between nations. Economic barriers are a country's level of development (infrastructure) and exchange rates. Wide-ranging legal and political barriers include differing laws (and enforcement), tariffs, exchange controls, quotas, embargoes, political instability, and war. Ambiguous cultural and social barriers involve differences in spoken and body language, time, holidays and other observances, and customs.

Specify some of the agreements, alliances, and organizations that may encourage trade across international boundaries.

Among the most important promoters of international business are the World Trade Organization, the North American Free Trade Agreement, the European Union, the World Bank, and the International Monetary Fund.

Summarize the different levels of organizational involvement in international trade.

A company may be involved in international trade at several levels, each requiring a greater commitment of resources and effort, ranging from importing/exporting to multinational corporations. Countertrade agreements occur at the import/export level and involve bartering products for other products instead of currency. At the next level, a trading company links buyers and sellers in different countries to foster trade. In licensing and franchising, one company agrees to allow a foreign company the use of its company name, products, patents, brands, trade-marks, raw materials, and production processes, in exchange for a flat fee or royalty. Contract manufacturing occurs when a company hires a foreign company to produce a specified volume of the firm's product to specification; the final product carries the domestic firm's name. A joint venture is a partnership in which companies from different countries agree to share the costs and operation of the business. The purchase of overseas production and marketing facilities is direct investment. Outsourcing, a form of direct investment, involves transferring manufacturing to countries where labour and supplies are cheap. A multinational corporation is one that operates on a worldwide scale, without significant ties to any one nation or region.

Contrast two basic strategies used in international business.

Companies typically use one of two basic strategies in international business. A multinational strategy customizes products, promotion, and distribution according to cultural, technological, regional, and national differences. A global strategy (globalization) standardizes products (and, as much as possible, their promotion and distribution) for the whole world, as if it were a single entity.

Assess the opportunities and problems facing a small business considering expanding into international markets.

The "Solve the Dilemma" box presents a small business considering expansion into international markets. Based on the material provided in the chapter, analyze the business's position, evaluating specific markets, anticipating problems, and exploring methods of international involvement.

Learn the Terms

Check Your Progress

1. Distinguish between an absolute advantage and a comparative advantage. Cite an example of a country that has an absolute advantage and one with a comparative advantage.
2. What effect does devaluation have on a nation's currency? Can you think of a country that has devaluated or revaluated its currency? What have been the results?
3. What effect does a country's economic development have on international business?
4. How do political issues affect international business?
5. What is an import tariff? A quota? Dumping? How might a country use import tariffs and quotas to control its balance of trade and payments? Why can dumping result in the imposition of tariffs and quotas?
6. How do social and cultural differences create barriers to international trade? Can you think of any additional social or cultural barriers (other than those mentioned in this chapter) that might inhibit international business?
7. Explain how a countertrade agreement can be considered a trade promoter. How does the General Agreement on Tariffs and Trade (GATT) encourage trade?
8. At what levels might a firm get involved in international business? What level requires the least commitment of resources? What level requires the most?
9. Compare and contrast licensing, franchising, contract manufacturing, and outsourcing.
10. Compare multinational and global strategies. Which is best? Under what circumstances might each be used?

Get Involved

1. If the United States were to impose additional tariffs on cars imported from Japan, what would happen to the price of Japanese cars sold in the United States? What would happen to the price of American cars? What action might Japan take to continue to compete in the US automobile market?
2. Although NAFTA has been controversial, it has been a positive factor for Canadian firms desiring to engage in international business. What industries and specific companies have the greatest potential for opening stores in the US and Mexico? What opportunities exist for small businesses that cannot afford direct investment in the US and Mexico?
3. Identify a local company that is active in international trade. What is its level of international business involvement and why? Analyze the threats and opportunities it faces in foreign markets, as well as its strengths and weaknesses in meeting those challenges. Based on your analysis, make some recommendations for the business's future involvement in international trade. (Your instructor may ask you to share your report with the business.)

Build Your Skills

Global Awareness

Background: As businesspeople travel the globe, they encounter and must quickly adapt to a variety of cultural norms quite different from North America. When encountering individuals from other parts of the world, the best attitude to adopt is "Here is my way. Now what is yours?" The more you see that you are part of a complex world and that your culture is different from, not better than, others, the better you will communicate and the more effective you will be in a variety of situations. It takes time, energy, understanding, and tolerance to learn about and appreciate other cultures. Naturally you're more comfortable doing things the way you've always done them. Remember, however, that this fact will also be true of the people from other cultures with whom you are doing business.

Task: You will "travel the globe" by answering questions related to some of the cultural norms that are found in other countries. Form groups of four to six class members and determine the answers to the following questions. Your instructor has the answer key, which will allow you to determine your group's Global Awareness IQ, which is based on a maximum score of 100 points (10 points per question).

Match the country with the cultural descriptor provided.

A.   Saudi Arabia
B.   Japan
C.   Great Britain
D.   Germany
E.   Venezuela

_____ 1.   When people in this country table a motion, they want to discuss it. In the US, "to table a motion" means to put off discussion.

_____ 2.   In this country, special forms of speech called *keigo* convey status among speakers. When talking with a person in this country, one should know the person's rank. People from this country will not initiate a conversation without a formal introduction.

_____ 3.   People from this country pride themselves on enhancing their image by keeping others waiting.

_____ 4.   When writing a business letter, people in this country like to provide a great deal of background information and detail before presenting their main points.

_____ 5.   For a man to inquire about another man's wife (even a general question about how she is doing) is considered very offensive in this country.

Match the country with the cultural descriptor provided.

F.   China
G.   Greece
H.   Korea
I.   India
J.   Mexico

_____ 6.   When in this country, you are expected to negotiate the price on goods you wish to purchase.

_____ 7.   While North Americans want to decide the main points at a business meeting and leave the details for later, people in this country need to have all details decided before the meeting ends, to avoid suspicion and distrust.

_____ 8.   Children in this country learn from a very early age to look down respectfully when talking to those of higher status.

_____ 9.   In this country the husband is the ruler of the household, and the custom is to keep the women hidden.

_____ 10.   Many businesspeople from Canada experience frustration because *yes* does not always mean the same thing in other cultures. For example, the word *yes* in this country means, "OK, I want to respect you and not offend you." It does not necessarily show agreement.

 **See for Yourself Videocase**　　　www.cbc.ca

Going Global

International customers are the lifeblood of the Canadian economy, but what do you do when your customers are not buying? Find new customers. Dynamotive Technologies of Vancouver is facing the task of replacing customers that are no longer buying their automotive products. The new market is Europe, but Dynamotive is not focused on this new market. This market of almost 300 million people is second only to the United States in economic power. Europe is almost as accessible as North America and, from a consumer perspective, is an environment full of potential customers for any exporter. Still, Dynamotive needs to overcome significant hurdles to enter the European automotive market and has turned to an English investment banker for assistance.

Newbridge Technologies has been in Europe for some time, entering through its own offices. They have built their customer base on their own. The president of Newbridge views the large market as a sophisticated environment, with new opportunities as a result of the common currency, the euro, being fully implemented in many European countries as of January 2002.

Unicam Security Systems Ltd. of Montreal has entered the European market another way, by acquiring many competing firms to expand its markets. Its acquisitions are varied in size and are expensive. Still, this method reduces the number of competitors from the playing field and rapidly provides customers and production opportunities. Unicam, however, must adjust its production for a new market and face larger and energetic competitors. Even the way business is conducted in Europe varies from North America—decisions take longer, changes are encountered in product design, and there is a need to be ready for constant change.

Questions

1. What are the benefits of using the three different methods displayed to enter the European market?

2. What would motivate a company to use each of the methods to enter a new market?

3. What are the benefits of having customers in more than one country or region to a company?

4. What are the benefits to Canadian exporters of Europe's adoption of a single currency?

5. For what must every businessperson be on the constant look out to catch? What does this mean to the businessperson?

Source: *Venture*, show number 709, "Top Seller (Europe)," January 19, 1999, running time 6:47.

Remember to check out our Online Learning Centre at **www.mcgrawhill.ca/college/ferrell.**

Cyberzone

Introduction to the Internet

The Internet (or the "Net") is a collection of connected computers; it is a network of business, university, government, and Internet-access providers that enables users to share information across the globe. Many people describe the Internet as a highway system (it is often referred to as the "information superhighway"). However, the highway analogy implies a system that is well planned, organized, and heavily regulated, which the Internet is not. It might be more constructive to think of the Internet as a river of data with thousands of tributaries (representing the networks linked to the Net) feeding into and out of it, with many of the tributaries having tributaries of their own. Of course, you'll have to imagine a river that flows in multiple directions because information on the Net flows in all directions. Like a river system, the Net is constantly changing, with new tributaries feeding into the river, channels deepening with greater use and new technology, channel routes changing to take advantage of new technology and access points, and so on.

To go online, you need a computer, a modem (typically an internal device that connects the computer to a phone line), and access to the Internet through an Internet-service provider, which is a local or national business that connects customers to the Internet with basic services, or through a national online service, such as America Online. These services provide access to discussion groups, downloadable files, chat rooms, news, entertainment, shopping, and much more.

One of the most common uses of the Internet is e-mail, electronic messages that are transmitted—usually in a matter of seconds—from one user to another via the Internet. People use e-mail to keep in touch with out-of-town friends and relatives; have private conversations with people they "meet" online; communicate and share information with coworkers, suppliers, and customers across the globe, country, or within the office; and find information about products, companies, and ideas. A recent survey showed that one-fourth of CEOs use the Internet for one hour or more each day, and 84 percent use it to send and receive e-mail.[1]

The World Wide Web (WWW) organizes much of the vast information available on the Internet into a series of interconnected "pages" or "sites" that may include text, graphics, sound, and video. Web search engines and directories such as Yahoo!, Excite, Google, Alta Vista, and Infoseek keep track of and index the information available on the WWW. Finding useful information without the aid of one of the search engines or directories can be difficult and slow. However, using the search capabilities provided by them allows users to access a wealth of information on hundreds of thousands of topics. It is easy to see why these are some of the most heavily visited sites on the Internet.

In order to access a particular web site, you will need the address or uniform resource locator (URL). Typically, the URL for a site is the name of the company, magazine, newspaper, or government office. For example, the URL for *Canadian Business* is **http://www.canadianbusiness.com,** and the address for Saturn is **http://www.saturn.com.** However, the first firm to register a particular URL with the Inter-Networking Information Center has the exclusive right to use that URL as its site address. So, in some cases, your first thought on a company's URL may be incorrect. The web site for Coca-Cola is not **http://www.coke.com,** as you might expect, because that URL was registered first by another firm.

The Internet is useful to both individuals and businesses. Individual uses include accessing news on

both local and international levels, conducting research on products, companies, and various topics of interest, making online purchases of everything from toys to stocks to airline tickets, and for entertainment purposes. Businesses initially used the Net to facilitate communications between widespread operations and suppliers, but over time it has become an increasing source of revenue.

The Internet environment has five basic characteristics: addressability, interactivity, control, memory, and accessibility.[2] Each is discussed below.

Addressability refers to the ability to identify users. Internet technology makes it possible for visitors to a web site to identify themselves and provide information about their wants and needs. Many sites encourage, or even require, visitors to register in order to maximize their use of the site or to gain access to certain areas of the site. Registration forms typically ask for name, e-mail address, age, occupation, and sometimes preferences. Some web sites offer contests or prizes to encourage registration by users.

Interactivity allows Net users to express their needs and wants in real time or nearly real time. Users can communicate with other users. Community sites on the Net provide a sense of group membership or a feeling of belonging among individual members of a group. One such community is Tripod, a site where Generation Xers can chat, exchange messages on virtual bulletin boards, and share information on various topics.

Control refers to the user's ability to control the type, rate, and sequence of the information he or she views. Users who encounter an offensive site or one accessed in error can simply click to close that site and move on to another. Most web sites use hyperlinks that offer users the ability to move from one point in a site to others or even to different sites depending on their preferences.

Memory is the ability to access databases or data warehouses that contain individual user profiles and to use this information in real time. Current technology allows instantaneous access to the identity of a site visitor; if a profile for a particular visitor exists, a company can display past purchases or suggest new products based on past purchases while the user is visiting the site. Bluefly, for example, is an online clothing retailer that asks visitors to provide their e-mail address, clothing preferences, and sizes. It then offers "My Catalog" which is an online catalog of clothing that matches that particular visitor's preferences. When new items that match a user's preferences are added to the firm's inventory, the individual is alerted via e-mail.

Accessibility refers to the wealth of information available to Internet users. A vast amount of information on products, including features, prices, and reviews, allows users to make informed decisions on purchases without ever leaving the privacy and comfort of their home or office. Access to other types of information, including financial, medical, and educational material, is quick and generally very easy. The survey of CEOs found that 81 percent use the Internet for general research, and 80 percent search for data on other companies.[3]

Because of the increasing importance of the Internet in the world of business today, each of the remaining Cyberzone features in this text cover Internet applications to specific concepts and ideas. Part Two (Starting and Growing a Business) addresses Internet uses for small businesses and entrepreneurs. The application of the Internet to general managerial decision making is covered in Part Three (Managing for Quality and Competitiveness), and Part Four (Creating the Human Resource Advantage) covers Internet use for human resource managers. Electronic commerce is addressed in Part Five (Marketing: Developing Relationships), and online finance is examined in Part Six (Financing the Enterprise).

Part Two

Starting and Growing a Business

Chapter 5

Options for Organizing Business

Chapter Outline

Introduction

Sole Proprietorships

Partnerships

Corporations

Cooperatives

Trends in Business Ownership:
Mergers and Acquisitions

Objectives

After reading this chapter, you will be able to:

- Define and examine the advantages and disadvantages of the sole proprietorship form of organization.
- Identify three types of partnership and evaluate the advantages and disadvantages of the partnership form of organization.
- Describe the corporate form of organization and cite the advantages and disadvantages of corporations.
- Define and debate the advantages and disadvantages of mergers, acquisitions, and leveraged buyouts.
- Propose an appropriate organizational form for a start-up business.

Deciding the Ownership Form

As you will see in this chapter, there are advantages and disadvantages to all forms of business ownership. There is no universal right choice for deciding whether the legal structure of a business venture should be a sole proprietorship, a partnership, or a corporation. One of the biggest concerns is liability for financial obligations incurred by the business. Other issues include ease and cost of formation, distribution of profits, taxation, control of the business, and government regulation. To give you an idea of how the ownership decision is made, we will briefly profile three firms and present the decision factors of each.

Proudfoot Wearable Art is a sole proprietorship operated by Judy Proudfoot. She designs and sells handpainted clothing items at shops and craft shows. Her decision to operate as a sole proprietor was largely based on the issues of affordability, simplicity, and control.

Initial decisions on business ownership form do not have to be permanent. The legal structure can change as a business changes. Marian Fletcher launched Let's Go Party as a sole proprietorship but changed the structure to a corporation to formally bring her daughter into the business as a partner. Fletcher changed the ownership of the profitable party planning and catering service to protect her personal assets while still retaining the tax benefits of a traditional partnership.[1]

Johanne Dion started her first business with a partner in 1987 to gain access to business experience, but this partnership did not work out, and after five years she left and started Trans-Herb e Inc. on her own. Now incorporated with a new $4.1 million plant, she has the experience, sales of $6.6 million per year, and over 70 employees producing and selling herbal teas from St-Bruno, Quebec.[2]

The choice of an appropriate form of business ownership depends on the number and capacity of owners as well as their individual circumstances, preferences, goals, and needs. Owners must learn how each form of ownership works and then consider which will best suit their needs.

Courtesy of Sondra Biggs, Papel

Enter the World of Business

INTRODUCTION

The legal form of ownership taken by business is seldom of great concern to you as a customer. When you eat at a restaurant, you probably don't care whether the restaurant is owned by one person (a sole proprietorship), has two or more owners who share the business (a partnership), or is an entity owned by many stockholders (a corporation); all you want is good food. If you buy a foreign car, you probably don't care whether the company that made it has laws governing its form of organization that are different from those for businesses in Canada. You are buying the car because it is well made, fits your price range, or appeals to your sense of style. Nonetheless, a business's legal form of ownership affects how it operates, how much tax it pays, and how much control its owners have.

This chapter examines three primary forms of business ownership—sole proprietorship, partnership, and corporation—and weighs the advantages and disadvantages of each. We also take a look at cooperatives, and discuss some trends in business ownership.

SOLE PROPRIETORSHIPS

sole proprietorships
businesses owned and operated by one individual; the most common form of business organization in Canada

Sole proprietorships, businesses owned and operated by one individual, are the most common form of business organization in Canada. Common examples include many restaurants, barber shops, flower shops, dog kennels, and independent grocery stores. Sondra Noffel Biggs opened her own stationery store called Papel (Spanish for "paper") in a high-traffic shopping centre. Biggs operates the store as a sole proprietorship. Indeed, many sole proprietors focus on services—small retail stores, financial counselling, appliance repair, child care, and the like—rather than on the manufacture of goods, which often requires large amounts of money not available to small businesses.

Sole proprietorships are typically small businesses employing fewer than 50 people. (We'll look at small businesses in greater detail in Chapter 6.)

Advantages of Sole Proprietorships

Sole proprietorships are generally managed by their owners. Because of this simple management structure, the owner/manager can make decisions quickly. This is just one of many advantages of the sole proprietorship form of business.

Ease and Cost of Formation. Forming a sole proprietorship is relatively easy and inexpensive. In some provinces, creating a sole proprietorship involves merely announcing the new business in the local newspaper. Other proprietorships, such as barber shops and restaurants, may require provincial and local licences and permits because of the nature of the business. The cost of these permits may run from $25 to $100. No lawyer is needed to create such enterprises, and the owner can usually take care of the required paperwork.

Of course, an entrepreneur starting a new sole proprietorship must find a suitable site from which to operate the business. Some sole proprietors look no farther than their garage or a spare bedroom that they can convert into a workshop or office. Computers, personal copiers, fax machines, and other high-tech gadgets have been a boon for home-based businesses, permitting them to interact quickly with customers, suppliers, and others. Many independent salespersons and contractors can perform their work using a notebook computer as they travel. E-mail and cell phones have made it possible for many proprietorships to develop in the services area.

Secrecy. Sole proprietorships make possible the greatest degree of secrecy. The proprietor, unlike the owners of a partnership or corporation, does not have to discuss publicly his or her operating plans, minimizing the possibility that competitors can obtain trade secrets. Financial reports need not be disclosed, as do the financial reports of publicly owned corporations.

Distribution and Use of Profits. All profits from a sole proprietorship belong exclusively to the owner. He or she does not have to share them with any partners or stockholders. The owner decides how to use the profits—for expansion of the business, for salary increases, or for travel to purchase additional inventory or find new customers.

Flexibility and Control of the Business. The sole proprietor has complete control over the business and can make decisions on the spot without anyone else's approval. This control allows the owner to respond quickly to competitive business conditions or to changes in the economy.

Government Regulation. Sole proprietorships have the most freedom from government regulation. Many government regulations—federal, provincial, and local— apply only to businesses that have a certain number of employees, and securities laws apply only to corporations that issue stock. Nonetheless, sole proprietors must ensure that they follow all laws that do apply to their business.

Taxation. Profits from the business are considered personal income to the sole proprietor and are taxed at individual tax rates. The owner pays one income tax. Another tax benefit is that a small business owner, or former, who sells the business, can receive up to $500,000 of the gain on the sale of the business tax-free. Any amount above that is taxed at 50 percent of the applicable federal tax rate.

Closing the Business. A sole proprietorship can be dissolved easily. No approval of co-owners or partners is necessary. The only legal condition is that all loans must be paid off.

Disadvantages of Sole Proprietorships

What may be seen as an advantage by one person may turn out to be a disadvantage to another. The goals and talents of the individual owner are the deciding factors. For profitable businesses managed by capable owners, many of the following factors do not cause problems. On the other hand, proprietors starting out with little management experience and little money are likely to encounter many of the disadvantages.

Unlimited Liability. The sole proprietor has unlimited liability in meeting the debts of the business. In other words, if the business cannot pay its creditors, the owner may be forced to use personal, nonbusiness holdings such as a car or a home to pay off the debts. The more wealth an individual has, the greater is the disadvantage of unlimited liability.

Limited Sources of Funds. Among the relatively few sources of money available to the sole proprietorship are a bank, friends, family, or his or her own funds. The owner's personal financial condition, then, determines his or her credit standing.

Often the only way a sole proprietor can borrow for business purposes is to pledge a car, a house, other real estate, or other personal assets to guarantee the loan. And if the business fails, the owner may lose the personal assets as well as the business. Publicly owned corporations, in contrast, can not only obtain funds from commercial banks but can sell stocks and bonds to the public to raise money. If a public company goes out of business, the owners do not lose personal assets.

Limited Skills. The sole proprietor must be able to perform many functions and possess skills in diverse fields such as management, marketing, finance, accounting, bookkeeping, and personnel. Although the owner can rely on specialized professionals to provide advice, he or she must make the final decision in each of these areas.

Lack of Continuity. The life expectancy of a sole proprietorship is directly related to that of the owner and his or her ability to work. The serious illness of the owner could result in failure if competent help cannot be found.

It is difficult to arrange for the sale of a proprietorship and at the same time assure customers that the business will continue to meet their needs. For instance, how does one sell a veterinary practice? A veterinarian's major asset is patients. If the vet dies suddenly, the equipment can be sold but the patients will not necessarily remain loyal to the office. On the other hand, a veterinarian who wants to retire could take in a younger partner and sell the practice to the partner over time. And one advantage to the partnership is that not all the patients are likely to look for a new vet.

Lack of Qualified Employees. It is usually difficult for a small sole proprietorship to match the wages and benefits offered by a large competing corporation because the proprietorship's level of profits may not be as high. In addition, there is little room for advancement within a sole proprietorship, so the owner may have difficulty attracting and retaining qualified employees.

Taxation. Although we listed taxation as an advantage for sole proprietorships, it can also be a disadvantage, depending on the proprietor's income. Under current tax rates, sole proprietors pay a higher marginal tax rate than do small corporations on income of less than $200,000. The tax effect often determines whether a sole proprietor chooses to incorporate his or her business. One point to keep in mind is that a proprietor who incorporates receives a salary taxable at individual rates, in addition to the taxes paid by the corporation. This double taxation of dividends makes the total tax on corporate income higher than it may appear, if you look just at the tax tables.

PARTNERSHIPS

partnership
an association of two or more persons who carry on as co-owners of a business for profit

general partnership
a partnership that involves a complete sharing in both the management and the liability of the business

One way to minimize the disadvantages of a sole proprietorship and maximize its advantages is to have more than one owner. A **partnership** is an association of two or more persons who carry on as co-owners of a business for profit. Partnerships are the least used form of business organization. Moreover, partnerships account for only 5 percent of sales and 10 percent of income. They are typically larger than sole proprietorships but smaller than corporations.

Types of Partnership

There are three basic types of partnership: general partnership, limited partnership, and joint venture. A **general partnership** involves a complete sharing in the management of a business. In a general partnership, each partner has unlimited liability for the debts of the business. Professionals such as lawyers, accountants, and architects often join together in general partnerships.

A **limited partnership** has at least one general partner, who assumes unlimited liability, and at least one limited partner, whose liability is limited to his or her investment in the business. Limited partnerships exist for risky investment projects where the chance of loss is great. The general partners accept the risk of loss; the limited partners' losses are limited to their initial investment. Limited partners do not participate in the management of the business but share in the profits in accordance with the terms of a partnership agreement. Usually the general partner receives a larger share of the profits after the limited partners have received their initial investment back. Popular examples are oil-drilling partnerships and real-estate partnerships.

A **joint venture** is a partnership established for a specific project or for a limited time. The partners in a joint venture may be individuals or organizations, as in the case of the international joint ventures discussed in Chapter 4. Control of a joint venture may be shared equally, or one partner may control decision making. Joint ventures are especially popular in situations that call for large investments, such as extraction of natural resources and the development of new products.

Partnership Agreements

Partnership agreements are legal documents that set forth the basic agreement between partners. Most jurisdictions do not require partnership agreements, but even so, it makes good sense for partners to draw them up. Partnership agreements usually list the money or assets that each partner has contributed (called *partnership capital*), state each partner's individual management role or duty, specify how the profits and losses of the partnership will be divided among the partners, and describe how a partner may leave the partnership as well as any other restrictions that might apply to the agreement.

Advantages of Partnerships

Law firms, accounting firms, and investment firms with several hundred partners have partnership agreements that are quite complicated in comparison with the partnership agreement among two or three people owning a computer repair shop. The advantages must be compared with those offered by other forms of business organization, and not all apply to every partnership.

Ease of Organization. Starting a partnership requires little more than drawing up articles of partnership. No legal charters have to be granted, but the name of the business should be registered with the province.

Availability of Capital and Credit. When a business has several partners, it has the benefit of a combination of talents and skills and pooled financial resources. Partnerships tend to be larger than sole proprietorships and therefore have greater earning power and better credit ratings. Because many limited partnerships have been formed for tax purposes rather than for economic profits, the combined income of all partnerships is quite low. Nevertheless, the professional partnerships of many lawyers, accountants, and doctors do make large profits. Goldman Sachs, a

limited partnership
a business organization that has at least one general partner, who assumes unlimited liability, and at least one limited partner, whose liability is limited to his or her investment in the business

joint venture
a partnership established for a specific project or for a limited time

partnership agreements
legal documents that set forth the basic agreement between partners

large New York investment banking partnership, earns several hundred million dollars in an average year.

Combined Knowledge and Skills. Partners in the most successful partnerships acknowledge each other's talents and avoid confusion and conflict by specializing in a particular area of expertise such as marketing, production, accounting, or service. The diversity of skills in a partnership makes it possible for the business to be run by a management team of specialists instead of by a generalist sole proprietor. Service-oriented partnerships in fields such as law, financial planning, and accounting may attract customers because clients may think that the service offered by a diverse team is of higher quality than that provided by one person. Larger law firms, for example, often have individual partners who specialize in certain areas of the law—such as family, bankruptcy, corporate, entertainment, and criminal law.

Decision Making. Small partnerships can react more quickly to changes in the business environment than can large partnerships and corporations. Such fast reactions are possible because the partners are involved in day-to-day operations and can make decisions quickly after consultation. Large partnerships with hundreds of partners in many provinces are not common. In those that do exist, decision making is likely to be slow.

Regulatory Controls. Like a sole proprietorship, a partnership has fewer regulatory controls affecting its activities than does a corporation. A partnership does not have to file public financial statements with government agencies or send out quarterly financial statements to several thousand owners, as do corporations such as BCE or the CIBC. A partnership does, however, have to abide by all laws relevant to the industry or profession in which it operates as well as provincial and federal laws relating to hiring and firing, food handling, and so on, just as the sole proprietorship does.

Disadvantages of Partnerships

Partnerships have many advantages compared to sole proprietorships and corporations, but they also have some disadvantages. Limited partners have no voice in the management of the partnership, and they may bear most of the risk of the business while the general partner reaps a larger share of the benefits. There may be a change in the goals and objectives of one partner but not the other, particularly when the partners are multinational organizations. This can cause friction, giving rise to an enterprise that fails to satisfy both parties or even forcing an end to the partnership. Major disadvantages of partnerships include the following.

Unlimited Liability. In general partnerships, the general partners have unlimited liability for the debts incurred by the business, just as the sole proprietor has unlimited liability for his or her business. Such unlimited liability can be a distinct disadvantage to one partner if his or her personal financial resources are greater than those of the others. A potential partner should check to make sure that all partners have comparable resources to help the business in time of trouble. This disadvantage is eliminated for limited partners, who can lose only their initial investment.

Business Responsibility. All partners are responsible for the business actions of all others. Partners may have the ability to commit the partnership to a contract without approval of the other partners. A bad decision by one partner may put the other partners' personal resources in jeopardy. Personal problems such as a divorce can eliminate a significant portion of one partner's financial resources and weaken the financial structure of the whole partnership.

Life of the Partnership. A partnership is terminated when a partner dies or withdraws. In a two-person partnership, if one partner withdraws, the firm's liabilities would be paid off and the assets divided between the partners. Obviously, the partner who wishes to continue in the business would be at a serious disadvantage. The business could be disrupted, financing would be reduced, and the management skills of the departing partner might be lost. The remaining partner would have to find another or reorganize the business as a sole proprietorship. In very large partnerships such as those found in law firms and investment banks, the continuation of the partnership may be provided for in the articles of partnership. The provision may simply state the terms for a new partnership agreement among the remaining partners. In such cases, the disadvantage to the other partners is minimal.

Selling a partnership interest has the same effect as the death or withdrawal of a partner. It is difficult to place a value on a partner's share of the partnership. No public value is placed on the partnership, as there is on publicly owned corporations. What is a law firm worth? What is the local hardware store worth? Coming up with a fair value that all partners can agree to is not easy. Selling a partnership interest is easier if the articles of partnership specify a method of valuation. Even if there is not a procedure for selling one partner's interest, the old partnership must still be dissolved and a new one created. In contrast, in the corporate form of business, the departure of owners has little effect on the financial resources of the business, and the loss of managers does not cause long-term changes in the structure of the organization.

Distribution of Profits. Profits earned by the partnership are distributed to the partners in the proportions specified in the articles of partnership. This may be a disadvantage if the division of the profits does not reflect the work each partner puts into the business. You may have encountered this disadvantage working on a student group project. You may have felt that you did most of the work and that the other students in the group received grades based on your efforts. Even the perception of an unfair profit-sharing agreement may cause tension between the partners, and unhappy partners can have a negative effect on the profitability of the business.

Limited Sources of Funds. As with a sole proprietorship, the sources of funds available to a partnership are limited. Because no public value is placed on the business (such as the current trading price of a corporation's stock), potential partners do not know what one partnership share is worth. Moreover, because partnership shares cannot be bought and sold easily in public markets, potential owners may not want to tie up their money in assets that cannot be readily sold on short notice. Accumulating enough funds to operate a national business, especially a business requiring intensive investments in facilities and equipment, can be difficult. Partnerships also may have to pay higher interest rates on funds borrowed from banks than do large corporations because partnerships may be considered greater risks.

Taxation of Partnerships

Partnerships are not taxable organizations. Partners must report their share of profits on their individual tax returns and pay taxes at the income tax rate for individuals.

CORPORATIONS

corporation
a legal entity, created by the state, whose assets and liabilities are separate from its owners

When you think of a business, you probably think of a huge corporation such as General Electric, Procter & Gamble, or Nortel because most of your consumer dollars go to such corporations. A **corporation** is a legal entity, created by the state, whose assets and liabilities are separate from its owners. As a legal entity, a corporation has many of the rights, duties, and powers of a person, such as the right to receive, own, and transfer property. Corporations can enter into contracts with individuals or with other legal entities, and they can sue and be sued in court.

Corporations account for over 90 percent of all Canadian sales. Thus, most of the dollars you spend as a consumer probably go to incorporated businesses.

stock
shares of a corporation that may be bought or sold

dividends
profits of a corporation that are distributed in the form of cash payments to stockholders

Corporations are typically owned by many individuals and organizations who own shares of the business, called **stock** (thus, corporate owners are often called *shareholders* or *stockholders*). Shareholders can buy, sell, give or receive as gifts, or inherit their shares of stock. As owners, the shareholders are entitled to all profits that are left after all the corporation's other obligations have been paid. These profits are distributed in the form of cash payments called **dividends.** For example, if a corporation earns $100 million after expenses and taxes and decides to pay the owners $40 million in dividends, the shareholders receive 40 percent of the profits in cash dividends. However, not all after-tax profits are paid to shareholders in dividends. In this example, the corporation retained $60 million of profits to finance expansion.

Creating a Corporation

A corporation is created, or incorporated, under the laws of the province or federal government depending on the industry and location. The individuals creating the corporation are known as *incorporators.* Each government has a specific procedure, sometimes called *chartering the corporation,* for incorporating a business. Most jurisdictions require a minimum of one incorporator; thus, many small businesses can be and are incorporated. Another requirement is that the new corporation's name cannot be similar to that of another business. In most jurisdictions, a corporation's name must end in "company," "corporation," "incorporated," or "limited" to show that the owners have limited liability. (In this text, however, the word *company* means any organization engaged in a commercial enterprise and can refer to a sole proprietorship, a partnership, or a corporation.)

The incorporators must file legal documents generally referred to as *articles of incorporation* with the appropriate government office. The articles of incorporation contain basic information about the business. The following items are required by most jurisdictions:

1. Name and address of the corporation and principal place of business.
2. Objectives of the corporation.
3. Classes of stock (common, preferred, voting, nonvoting) and the number of shares for each class of stock to be issued.
4. Whether the company will be a publicly traded or private company.
5. Provisions for transferring shares of stock between owners if private. (Public companies may not have restrictions.)
6. Provisions for the regulation of internal corporate affairs.

7. Names and addresses of the initial board of directors.
8. Names and addresses of the incorporators.

Based on the information in the articles of incorporation, the province or federal government issues a **certificate of incorporation** (or, in some provinces, a *memorandum of association*) to the company. After securing this charter, the owners hold an organizational meeting at which they establish the corporation's bylaws and elect a board of directors. The bylaws might set up committees of the board of directors and describe the rules and procedures for their operation.

Types of Corporations

If the corporation does business in the country in which it is chartered, it is known as a *domestic corporation*. In other countries where the corporation does business, it is known as a *foreign corporation*. A corporation may be privately or publicly owned.

A **private corporation** is owned by just one or a few people who are closely involved in managing the business. These people, often a family, own all the corporation's stock, and no stock is sold to the public. Many corporations are quite large, yet remain private, including Cargill, the largest private corporation, Hallmark, and Levi Strauss & Co. Privately owned corporations are not required to disclose financial information publicly, but they must, of course, pay taxes.

A **public corporation** is one whose stock anyone may buy or sell or trade. Table 5.1 lists the largest Canadian corporations by revenues. Thousands of smaller public corporations in Canada have sales under $10 million. In large public corporations such as BCE, the shareholders are often far removed from the management of the company. In other public corporations, the managers are often the founders and the major shareholders, as with Sleeman's or Transalta. Another example, Nordstrom, the Seattle-based specialty retailer of fashion apparel, was founded by a Nordstrom and currently has six fourth-generation Nordstroms serving as copresidents of the company. Nordstrom is a public company, but approximately 35 percent of its stock is held by

certificate of incorporation
a legal document that the province or federal government issues to a company based on information the company provides in the articles of incorporation

private corporation
a corporation owned by just one or a few people who are closely involved in managing the business

public corporation
a corporation whose stock anyone may buy, sell, or trade

Rank	Company	Revenues ($ millions)
1.	Nortel Networks Corp.	$46,509
2.	Onex Corp.	24,531
3.	George Weston Ltd.	22,344
4.	Trans Canada Pipelines Ltd.	21,156
5.	Loblaws Cos. Ltd.	21,121
6.	BCE Inc.	18,094
7.	Imperial Oil Ltd.	18,053
8.	Power Corp. of Canada	16,906
9.	Power Financial Corp.	16,531
10.	Sun Life Financial Services of Canada Inc.	16,206

Table 5.1

The Largest Canadian Corporations Ranked by Revenues

Source: *Canadian Business*, July 9, 2001, Investor 500, page 84, based on 2000 revenue.

Canadian Business magazine
www.canadian business.com/index.asp

Horizon Organic Dairy
**www.horizonorganic.
com/**

**subsidiary
corporation**

a corporation the
majority of whose stock
is owned by another
corporation (known as
the parent company)

holding company

a corporation that
controls one or more
other corporations
through ownership of
their common stock

*Horizon Organic Dairy
became a public
corporation by offering
stock in order to take
advantage of
opportunities presented
by the increase in interest
and sales of organic
products. Pictured here is
the CEO Barnett
Feinblum and cofounder
Paul Repetto, with some
of their organic dairy
products.*

Jon Hatch

family members.[3] Publicly owned corporations must disclose financial information to the public under specific laws that regulate the trade of stocks and other securities.

A private corporation that needs more money to expand or take advantage of opportunities may have to obtain financing by "going public," that is, becoming a public corporation. As interest and sales of organic products increased, Horizon Organic Dairy, operator of the world's largest dairy farm, went public with an initial stock price of US$11 per share.[4] Also, privately owned firms are occasionally forced to go public with stock offerings when a major owner dies and the estate has enormous income taxes to pay. The tax payment becomes possible only with the proceeds of the sale of stock. This happened to the brewer Adolph Coors, Inc. When Adolph Coors died, his business went public and his family sold shares of stock to the public to pay the taxes.

On the other hand, public corporations can be "taken private" when one or a few individuals (perhaps the management of the firm) purchase all the firm's stock so that it can no longer be sold publicly. Levi Strauss & Co., for example, went private when the Haas and Koshland families—descendants of Levi Strauss's nephews—purchased all the company's stock. Taking a corporation private may be desirable when new owners want to exert more control over the firm or they want to avoid the necessity of public disclosure of future activities for competitive reasons. Taking a corporation private is also one technique for avoiding a takeover by another corporation.

A **subsidiary corporation** is one that has the majority of its stock owned by another corporation known as the parent company. The subsidiary company has its own corporate structure, with a president and other senior officers. Usually the officers of a subsidiary are selected by the officers of the parent company with the approval of the parent company.

A **holding company** is a special type of corporation because it controls one or more other corporations through ownership of their common stock. The other corporations remain separate entities, legally responsible for their own operations. They

Sole proprietorships, partnerships, and corporations can use the Internet successfully in many ways. A small business or partnership might use the Net for market research and e-mail communications only. It might also set up a web site to advertise its products or services and sell them online. The web site for Fresh Samantha, a fresh juice company with sales of US$7 million, tells its history, offers products for sale online, and requests feedback from site users. Large corporations may use the Net for all these purposes.

However business owners choose to use the Internet, their online strategy should be tied to the company's core mission. A poor effort probably will not reach the desired audience and will result in wasted time and money. Employees should support Internet efforts, and launching a "mycompany.com" web page should not distract from the business at hand.

The starting point for any Internet strategy should be the answer to "What is the core of the business?" If a business has a special character or "great feel," designers should try to create a web site that captures that character or feel through graphics, sound, and text.

The second question to ask before launching an Internet strategy is "Are we ready?" Owners and employees must be able to handle inquiries and/or orders from around the world. If a business is local or regional, one alternative to a stand-alone web site would be to advertise or rent space on a city-based web site or regional guide site.

Some Internet strategies focus on building relationships with clients rather than on end customers. It is possible to buy supplies, check specifications, or get a copy of a user manual via the Net. Using the Net for such tasks reduces the time normally needed and allows that saved time to be directed to more productive uses.

Many sites allow for customer feedback, which can be highly valuable information if used properly. Internet strategies also should include plans for adapting to and handling change and providing fast answers to users of the site.

As the Net matures and the number of web users grows, business owners, regardless of the form of ownership, need to consider this medium. Many will need help to plan and execute a successful Internet strategy. There are many web design firms that can do just that.

One such firm is Agency.com Ltd. Agency.com is one of the hottest web-design shops in New York City. Begun in 1995, it now has 1000 employees in over 15 offices in 8 countries. Its client list includes 3M, British Airways and Compaq. No matter how an Internet strategy is designed, careful consideration should be given to the vast technological opportunities available on the web.[5]

have other shareholders in addition to the holding company and are not wholly owned subsidiary companies.

Two other types of corporations are Crown corporations and nonprofit corporations. **Crown corporations** are owned and operated by a federal, provincial, or local government. The focus of these corporations is providing a service to citizens, such as mail delivery, and earn a profit. Indeed, many Crown corporations operate at a loss. Examples of Crown corporations include Via Rail, Canada Post, Quebec Hydro, GO Transit in Ontario, and the CBC. Crown corporations operate in areas where a public company cannot because of scarce profits or the difficulty in providing the service (such as mail delivery in Toronto and Cornerbrook for the same price).

Crown corporations corporations owned and operated by the federal, provincial, or local government

Atomic Energy Canada
www.aecl.ca/

Business Development
Bank
www.bdc.ca/

nonprofit corporations

corporations that focus on providing a service rather than earning a profit but are not owned by a government entity

board of directors

a group of individuals, elected by the stockholders to oversee the general operation of the corporation, who set the corporation's long-range objectives

Mark's Work Wearhouse
www.marks.com

preferred stock

a special type of stock whose owners, though not generally having a say in running the company, have a claim to profits before other stockholders do

Atomic Energy Canada has the responsibility of developing the market for selling Candu reactors, a long process, which is unprofitable in the short term. However, when a reactor is sold, the value to Canadian businesses is measured in the tens or hundreds of millions of dollars. The Business Development Bank provides both consulting and financing to growing businesses.

Like Crown corporations, **nonprofit corporations** focus on providing a service rather than earning a profit, but they are not owned by a government entity. Organizations like the Children's Television Workshop, the Lions Clubs, the Canadian Red Cross, museums, and private schools provide services without a profit motive. To fund their operations and services, nonprofit organizations solicit donations from individuals and companies and grants from the government and other charitable foundations.

Elements of a Corporation

The Board of Directors. A **board of directors,** elected by the shareholders to oversee the general operation of the corporation, sets the long-range objectives of the corporation. It is the board's responsibility to ensure that the objectives are achieved on schedule. Board members are legally liable for the mismanagement of the firm or for any misuse of funds. An important duty of the board of directors is to hire corporate officers, such as the president and the chief executive officer (CEO), who are responsible to the directors for the management and daily operations of the firm.

Directors can be employees of the company (*inside directors*) or people unaffiliated with the company (*outside directors*). Inside directors are usually the officers responsible for running the company. Outside directors are often top executives from other companies, lawyers, bankers, even professors. They are not part of management and are not involved in the day-to-day operations of the firm. One of the chief responsibilities of outside directors is to hold the corporate officers responsible for meeting the goals and objectives of the firm. Because the board of directors consists of both the officers and the outside directors, the outside directors must maintain objectivity in their appraisal of the company's performance. Most boards have outside directors because it is assumed that inside directors are likely to have a narrow and biased view of the company's progress. Table 5.2 lists the inside and outside directors of Mark's Work Wearhouse Ltd.

Stock Ownership. Corporations issue two types of stock: preferred and common. Owners of **preferred stock** are a special class of owners because, although they generally do not have any say in running the company, they have a claim to any profits before any other shareholders do. Other shareholders do not receive any dividends unless the preferred shareholders have already been paid. Dividend payments on preferred stock are usually a fixed percentage of the initial issuing price (set by the board of directors). For example, if a share of preferred stock originally cost $100 and the dividend rate was stated at 7.5 percent, the dividend payment will be $7.50 per share per year. Dividends are usually paid quarterly.

Most preferred stock carries a cumulative claim to dividends. This means that if the company does not pay preferred-stock dividends in one year because of losses, the dividends accumulate to the next year. Such dividends unpaid from previous years must also be paid to preferred shareholders before other shareholders can receive any dividends.

Art Berliner	Partner of Walden Group, a venture capital firm
Michael Fox	Private consultant and non-management Chairman of the Board
William Hardstaff	Retired president of American Eagle Petroleums Ltd.
Michael Lambert*	Chief Financial Officer of the company
Bruce R. Libin, Q.C.	President of B.R. Libin Capital Corp.
Garth Mitchell*	President and C.E.O. of the company
Wallace Murray	Former Senior Vice President of the company
Jake Scudamore	President of Scudamore and Associates Inc. corporate consultants

Table 5.2

Directors of Mark's Work Wearhouse Ltd.

*Inside director

Source: 2000 Annual Report of Mark's Work Wearhouse Ltd., page 76.

Although owners of **common stock** do not get such preferential treatment with regard to dividends, they do get some say in the operation of the corporation. Their ownership gives them the right to vote for members of the board of directors and on other important issues. Common stock dividends may vary according to the profitability of the business, and some corporations do not issue dividends at all, but instead plow their profits back into the company to fund expansion.

Common shareholders are the voting owners of a corporation. They are usually entitled to one vote per share of common stock. During an annual shareholders' meeting, common shareholders elect a board of directors. Because they can choose the board of directors, common shareholders have some say in how the company will operate. Common shareholders may vote by *proxy,* which is a written authorization by which shareholders assign their voting privilege to someone else, who then votes for his or her choice at the shareholders' meeting. It is a normal practice for management to request proxy statements from shareholders who are not planning to attend the annual meeting. Most owners do not attend annual meetings of the very large companies, such as Westinghouse or Bombardier, unless they live in the city where the meeting is held.

Common shareholders have another advantage over preferred shareholders. When the corporation decides to sell new shares of common stock in the marketplace, common shareholders may have the first right, called a *preemptive right,* to purchase new shares of the stock from the corporation. A preemptive right is often included in the articles of incorporation. This right is important because it allows shareholders to purchase new shares to maintain their original positions. For example, if a shareholder owns 10 percent of a corporation that decides to issue new shares, that shareholder has the right to buy enough of the new shares to retain the 10 percent ownership.

common stock

stock whose owners have voting rights in the corporation, yet do not receive preferential treatment regarding dividends

Advantages of Corporations

Because a corporation is a separate legal entity, it has some very specific advantages over other forms of ownership. The biggest advantage may be the limited liability of the owners.

Limited Liability. Because the corporation's assets (money and resources) and liabilities (debts and other obligations) are separate from its owners', in most cases the shareholders are not held responsible for the firm's debts if it fails. Their liability or potential loss is limited to the amount of their original investment. Although a creditor can sue a corporation for not paying its debts, even forcing the corporation into bankruptcy, it cannot make the shareholders pay the corporation's debts out of their personal assets. Occasionally, the owners of a private corporation may pledge personal assets to secure a loan for the corporation; this would be most unusual for a public corporation.

Ease of Transfer of Ownership. Shareholders can sell or trade shares of stock to other people without causing the termination of the corporation, and they can do this without the prior approval of other shareholders. The transfer of ownership (unless it is a majority position) does not affect the daily or long-term operations of the corporation.

Perpetual Life. A corporation usually is chartered to last forever unless its articles of incorporation stipulate otherwise. The existence of the corporation is unaffected by the death or withdrawal of any of its shareholders. It survives until the owners sell it or liquidate its assets. However, in some cases, bankruptcy ends a corporation's life. Bankruptcies occur when companies are unable to compete and earn profits. Eventually, uncompetitive businesses must close or seek protection from creditors in bankruptcy court while the business tries to reorganize. The oldest corporation in the world is the Hudson Bay Company, which is over 330 years old.

External Sources of Funds. Of all the forms of business organization, the public corporation finds it easiest to raise money. When a corporation needs to raise more money, it can sell more stock shares or issue bonds (corporate "IOUs," which pledge to repay debt), attracting funds from anywhere in Canada and even overseas. The larger a corporation becomes, the more sources of financing are available to it.

Expansion Potential. Because large public corporations can find long-term financing readily, they can easily expand into national and international markets. And, as a legal entity, a corporation can enter into contracts without as much difficulty as a partnership.

Disadvantages of Corporations

Corporations have some distinct disadvantages resulting from tax laws and government regulation.

Double Taxation. As a legal entity, the corporation must pay taxes on its income just like you do. When after-tax corporate profits are paid out as dividends to the shareholders, the dividends are taxed a second time as part of the individual owner's income. This process creates double taxation for the shareholders of dividend-paying corporations.

For holding companies, taxation is even more complex. The holding company (let's call it Firm A) receives dividends from the companies whose stock it owns (Firm X, Firm Y, and Firm Z). The dividends provide income but may give rise to triple taxation: Firms X, Y, and Z pay taxes on their incomes, and the holding company may pay taxes on the dividends. If the holding company pays out dividends to

Think Globally

Kinko's, Inc., Plans for a Global Network

Kinko's, Inc., began in 1970 with one store equipped with one copy machine. Over the years, Kinko's grew and mushroomed into 128 joint ventures, small companies, and partnerships. The company was reshaped in 1997 into a single corporate structure. Founder and chairman Paul Orfalea owns 34 percent of the closely held private corporation, with the remaining shares owned by employees and former partners. However, there was some discussion at the end of the decade of Kinko's going public.

Kinko's has expanded from just copying and printing to providing office services. Orfalea wants to create a global network of outlets where businesses can send and receive information and meet through videoconferencing, as well as access fax machines, ultra-fast colour printers, and computers linked to the Internet.

Kinko's currently has more than 900 locations in the US and Canada and 43 other countries, including Japan, Korea, China, and the UK. Annual revenues are close to US$1 billion. Plans call for aggressive expansion in Japan, Australia, and England. To attain its global expansion, Kinko's is forming alliances with other firms. One such alliance formed in 1998 allowed for the opening of its first European store, a 550-square metre store in London.

As part of Kinko's effort to create a global network, its home page on the web has been translated into many languages, including Arabic, Chinese, Dutch, French, German, Hebrew, Japanese, Korean, Russian, Spanish, Thai, and Vietnamese. These translations allow access to a broad range of culturally diverse customers and employees.

Another key focus in Kinko's global plans is its videoconferencing capabilities. Videoconferencing provides a forum for users at two or more sites to talk with each other, discuss project details, and show charts, graphics, and videotapes. Videoconferencing benefits include reduced travel expenses and increased productivity by cutting down on travel time. According to Kinko's web site, "Videoconferencing lets you do everything you normally would during a meeting, except shake hands." More than 155 videoconferencing sites are available worldwide, including sites in Japan, Korea, and The Netherlands.

Kinko's future looks bright. Its long-term strategy of creating a global network can only strengthen its position as the world leader in copying and office services. Kinko's remains committed to providing the latest in technological advances to its ever-widening base of global consumers.[6]

its own shareholders, they pay a tax on the dividends. Dividends received from a taxable Canadian company are tax-free.

Forming a Corporation. The formation of a corporation can be costly. A certificate of incorporation must be obtained, and this usually requires the services of a lawyer and payment of legal fees. Filing fees ranging from $75 to $150 must be paid to the province or federal government that awards the certificate of incorporation.

Disclosure of Information. Corporations must make information available to their owners, usually through an annual report to shareholders. The annual report contains financial infor-

Did you know?

The first corporation with a net income of more than $1 billion in one year was General Motors, with a net income in 1955 of US$1,189,477,082.

Thomas O'Grady and Bryan Rossisky have decided to start a small business buying flowers, shrubs, and trees wholesale and reselling them to the general public. They plan to contribute $5,000 each in start-up capital and lease a one-hectare tract of land with a small, portable sales office.

Thomas and Bryan are trying to decide what form of organization would be appropriate. Bryan thinks they should create a corporation because they would have limited liability and the image of a large organization. Thomas thinks a partnership would be easier to start and would allow them to

rely on the combination of their talents and financial resources. In addition, there might be fewer reports and regulatory controls to cope with.

1. What are some of the advantages and disadvantages of Thomas and Bryan forming a corporation?

2. What are the advantages and disadvantages of their forming a partnership?

3. Which organizational form do you think would be best for Thomas and Bryan's company and why?

mation about the firm's profits, sales, facilities and equipment, and debts, as well as descriptions of the company's operations, products, and plans for the future. Public corporations must also file reports with the provincial securities commissions such as the Ontario Securities Commission or the Quebec Securities Commission. These reports are public and, hence, competitors can access them. Filing these reports also consumes time and resources.

Employee-Owner Separation. Many employees are not shareholders of the company for which they work. This separation of owners and employees may cause employees to feel that their work benefits only the owners. Employees without an ownership stake do not always see how they fit into the corporate picture and may not understand the importance of profits to the health of the organization. If managers are part owners but other employees are not, management–labour relations take on a different, sometimes difficult, aspect from those in partnerships and sole proprietorships. However, this situation is changing as more corporations establish employee stock ownership plans (ESOPs), which give shares of the company's stock to its employees. Such plans build a partnership between employee and employer and can boost productivity because they motivate employees to work harder so that they can earn dividends from their hard work as well as from their regular wages.

COOPERATIVES

cooperative (or co-op)

an organization composed of individuals or small businesses that have banded together to reap the benefits of belonging to a larger organization

Another form of organization in business is the **cooperative** or **co-op,** an organization composed of individuals or small businesses that have banded together to reap the benefits of belonging to a larger organization. Gay Lea, for example, is a cooperative of Ontario dairy farmers; Ocean Spray is a cooperative of cranberry farmers. A co-op is set up not to make money as an entity but so that its members can become more profitable or save money. Co-ops are generally expected to operate without profit or to create only enough profit to maintain the co-op organization.

A co-op can purchase supplies in large quantities and pass the savings on to its members. It also can help distribute the products of its members more efficiently than each could on an individual basis. A cooperative can advertise its members' products and thus generate demand. Home Hardware, a cooperative of independent hardware store owners, allows its members to share in the savings that result from buying supplies in large quantities; it also provides advertising, which individual members might not be able to afford on their own.

Many cooperatives exist in small farming communities. The co-op stores and markets grain; orders large quantities of fertilizer, seed, and other supplies at discounted prices; and reduces costs and increases efficiency with good management.

TRENDS IN BUSINESS OWNERSHIP: MERGERS AND ACQUISITIONS

Companies large and small achieve growth and improve profitability by expanding their operations, often by developing and selling new products or selling current products to new groups of customers in different geographic areas. Such growth, when carefully planned and controlled, is usually beneficial to the firm and ultimately helps it reach its goal of enhanced profitability. But companies also grow by merging with or purchasing other companies.

A **merger** occurs when two companies (usually corporations) combine to form a new company. An **acquisition** occurs when one company purchases another, generally by buying most of its stock. The acquired company may become a subsidiary of the buyer, or its operations and assets may be merged with those of the buyer. The buying company gains control of the property and assets of the other firm but also assumes its obligations. Acquisitions sometimes involve the purchase of a division or some other part of a company rather than the entire company. A merger and acquisition frenzy in the late 1990s saw a record 10,401 worldwide deals with a US$1.3 trillion price tag in one year alone.[7] The previous record set in the late 1980s was US$667 billion.[8] Nine of the 11 largest deals in US history were announced in 1998, including the Travelers Group merger with Citicorp, Daimler-Benz's merger with Chrysler, and Exxon's purchase of Mobil.[9] In Canada we have recently seen the acquisition of Canada Trust by the Toronto Dominion Bank, Indigo's purchase of Chapters, and a merger of Seagram and Vivendi of France.

When firms that make and sell similar products to the same customers merge, it is known as a *horizontal merger,* as when Martin Marietta and Lockheed, both defence contractors, merged to form Martin Lockheed. Horizontal mergers, however, reduce the number of corporations competing within an industry, and for this reason they are usually reviewed carefully by federal regulators before the merger is allowed to proceed.

When companies operating at different but related levels of an industry merge, it is known as a *vertical merger.* In many instances, a vertical merger results when one corporation merges with one of its customers or suppliers. For example, if Burger King were to purchase a large PEI potato farm—to ensure a ready supply of potatoes for its french fries—a vertical merger would result.

A *conglomerate merger* results when two firms in unrelated industries merge. For example, the purchase of Sterling Drug, a pharmaceutical firm, by Eastman Kodak, best-known for its films and

merger
the combination of two companies (usually corporations) to form a new company

acquisition
the purchase of one company by another, usually by buying its stock

Edgar Bronfman Jr., left, president and chief executive officer of Seagram, Jean-Marie Messier, centre, chairman and chief executive officer of Vivendi, and Pierre Lescure, chairman of French pay-television Canal Plus, pose after the official announcement of their merger, Tuesday, June 20, 2000, in Paris. The $34 billion merger will combine Seagram's film production and music interests with Vivendi's European cable TV, satellite, and Internet distribution systems to create a new group to be called Vivendi Universal, which will be based in Paris.

Associated Press AP. Photograph by Laurent Rebours.

cameras, represents a conglomerate merger because the two companies are of different industries.

When a company (or an individual), sometimes called a *corporate raider*, wants to acquire or take over another company, it first offers to buy some or all of the other company's stock at a premium over its current price in a *tender offer*. Most such offers are "friendly," with both groups agreeing to the proposed deal, but some are "hostile," when the second company does not want to be taken over. For example, Claire's Stores Inc., the fast-growing accessories retailer that targets girls aged 12 to 19, amassed an 11.8 percent stake in Gadzooks, Inc., a trendy teen clothing store. Gadzooks was not interested in being acquired by Claire's or anyone else and adopted a shareholder rights plan to block unwanted advances.[10]

To head off a hostile takeover attempt, a threatened company's managers may use one or more of several techniques. They may ask shareholders not to sell to the raider; file a lawsuit in an effort to abort the takeover; institute a *poison pill* (in which the firm allows shareholders to buy more shares of stock at prices lower than the current market value) or *shark repellant* (in which management requires a large majority of shareholders to approve the takeover); or seek a *white knight* (a more acceptable firm that is willing to acquire the threatened company). In some cases, management may take the company private or even take on more debt so that the heavy debt obligation will "scare off" the raider. To persuade shareholders to reject a hostile takeover bid by Allied Signal, Inc., AMP Inc. considered buying back a large number of shares at above-market prices and paying an extraordinary cash dividend, as well as other less traditional means.[11]

In a **leveraged buyout (LBO),** a group of investors borrows money from banks and other institutions to acquire a company (or a division of one), using the assets of the purchased company to guarantee repayment of the loan. In some LBOs, as much as 95 percent of the buyout price is paid with borrowed money, which eventually must be repaid.

With the explosion of mergers, acquisitions, and leveraged buyouts in the 1980s and 1990s, some financial journalists coined the term *merger mania*. Many companies joined the merger mania simply to enhance their own operations by consolidating them with the operations of other firms. Mergers and acquisitions enabled these companies to gain a larger market share in their industries, acquire valuable assets, such as new products or plants and equipment, and lower their costs. Mergers also represent a means of making profits quickly, as was the case during the 1980s when many companies' stock was undervalued. Quite simply, such companies represent a bargain to other companies that can afford to buy them. Additionally, deregulation of some industries has permitted consolidation of firms within those industries for the first time, as is the case in the banking and airline industries. The number of credit unions has dropped from almost 5,000 in 1965 to just over 2,000 today.[12]

Some people view mergers and acquisitions favourably, pointing out that they boost corporations' stock prices and market value, to the benefit of their shareholders. In many instances, mergers enhance a company's ability to meet foreign competition in an increasingly global marketplace. To gain technological competence among interactive ad agencies, US Web, an Internet services firm, acquired 27 companies in one and one-half years.[13] And, companies that are victims of hostile takeovers generally streamline their operations, reduce unnecessary staff, cut costs, and otherwise become more efficient operations, which benefits their shareholders whether or not the takeover succeeds.

leveraged buyout (LBO)

a purchase in which a group of investors borrows money from banks and other institutions to acquire a company (or a division of one), using the assets of the purchased company to guarantee repayment of the loan

Critics, however, argue that mergers hurt companies because they force managers to focus their efforts on avoiding takeovers rather than managing effectively and profitably. Some companies have taken on a heavy debt burden to stave off a takeover, later to be forced into bankruptcy when economic downturns left them unable to handle the debt. Mergers and acquisitions also can damage employee morale and productivity, as well as the quality of the companies' products.

Many mergers have been beneficial for all involved; others have had damaging effects for the companies, their employees, and customers. No one can say how and when the merger boom will end, but many experts say the boom is just getting started in utilities, telecommunications, financial services, natural resources, computer hardware and software, gaming, managed health care, and technology.[14]

Explore Your Career Options

Evaluating a Job Offer

Before you choose to accept or reject any job offer, whether it comes from a sole proprietorship, a partnership, or a corporation, it needs to be properly evaluated. Most organizations will not expect an immediate decision, so you will have time to consider issues regarding the organization, the job, compensation, and benefits.

Obtaining background information on the organization is important and doing so is generally easy. Factors to consider include the organization's business or activity, as well as its financial condition, age, size, and location. A public company's annual report contains this information and is usually available through the company's public relations office. Press releases and company brochures or newsletters also can be helpful. Background information on many organizations is available at public libraries through reference directories such as *Dun & Bradstreet's Million Dollar Directory* and *Standard and Poor's Register of Corporations*. Also, ask yourself whether the organization's business or activity coincides with your interest and values and whether the organization is in an industry with favourable long-term prospects.

Consider the nature of the job offered. Does the work match your interests and make good use of your skills and abilities? Are you comfortable with the hours? Are there opportunities to learn new skills, increase your earnings, and rise to positions of greater responsibility and authority? Ask for an explanation of where the offered job fits into the organization and how you will contribute to overall organizational objectives.

In considering the salary offered, you should have a rough estimate of what the particular type of job should pay. Start with family or friends who may have similar jobs. Ask your college placement director about starting salaries in different industries and for applicants with qualifications such as yours. Consider cost-of-living differences if the job requires relocation to another city. Factor in the offered benefits as they add to base pay.

Review Your Understanding

Define and examine the advantages and disadvantages of the sole proprietorship form of organization.

Sole proprietorships—businesses owned and managed by one person—are the most common form of organization. Their major advantages are the following: (1) They are easy and inexpensive to form; (2) they allow a high level of secrecy; (3) all profits belong to the owner; (4) the owner has complete control over the business; (5) government regulation is minimal; (6) taxes are paid only once; and (7) the business can be closed easily. The disadvantages include: (1) The owner may have to use personal assets to borrow money; (2) sources of external funds are more difficult to find; (3) the owner must have many diverse skills; (4) the survival of the business is tied to the life of the owner and his or her ability to work; (5) qualified employees are hard to find; and (6) sole proprietors may pay a higher tax than they would under the corporate form of business.

Identify three types of partnership and evaluate the advantages and disadvantages of the partnership form of organization.

A partnership is a business formed by several individuals; a partnership may be general, limited, or a joint venture. Partnerships offer the following advantages: (1) They are easy to organize; (2) they may have higher credit ratings because the partners possibly have more combined wealth; (3) partners can specialize; (4) partnerships can make decisions faster than larger businesses; and (5) government regulations are few. Partnerships also have several disadvantages: (1) General partners have unlimited liability for the debts of the partnership; (2) partners are responsible for each others' decisions; (3) the death or termination of one partner requires a new partnership agreement to be drawn up; (4) it is difficult to sell a partnership interest at a fair price; (5) the distribution of profits may not correctly reflect the amount of work done by each partner; and (6) partnerships cannot find external sources of funds as easily as can large corporations.

Describe the corporate form of organization and cite the advantages and disadvantages of corporations.

A corporation is a legal entity created by the state, whose assets and liabilities are separate from those of its owners. Corporations are chartered by a province through certificates of incorporation. They have a board of directors made up of corporate officers or people from outside the company. Corporations, whether private or public, are owned by shareholders (or stockholders). Common shareholders have the right to elect the board of directors. Preferred shareholders do not have a vote but get preferential dividend treatment over common shareholders.

Advantages of the corporate form of business include: (1) The owners have limited liability; (2) ownership (stock) can be easily transferred; (3) corporations usually last forever; (4) raising money is easier than for other forms of business; and (5) expansion into new businesses is simpler because of the ability of the company to enter into contracts. Corporations also have disadvantages: (1) The company is taxed on its income, and owners pay a second tax on any profits received as dividends; (2) forming a corporation can be expensive; (3) keeping trade secrets is difficult because so much information must be made available to the public and to government agencies; and (4) owners and managers are not always the same and can have different goals.

Define and debate the advantages and disadvantages of mergers, acquisitions, and leveraged buyouts.

A merger occurs when two companies (usually corporations) combine to form a new company. An acquisition occurs when one company buys most of another company's stock. In a leveraged buyout, a group of investors borrows money to acquire a company, using the assets of the purchased company to guarantee the loan. They can help merging firms to gain a larger market share in their industries, acquire valuable assets such as new products or plants and equipment, and lower their costs. Consequently, they can benefit stockholders by improving the companies' market value and stock prices. However, they also can hurt companies if they force managers to focus on avoiding takeovers at the expense of productivity and profits. They may lead a company to take on too much debt and can harm employee morale and productivity.

Propose an appropriate organizational form for a start-up business.

After reading the facts in the "Solve the Dilemma" box and considering the advantages and disadvantages of the various forms of business organization described in this chapter, you should be able to suggest an appropriate form for the start-up nursery.

Learn the Terms

Check Your Progress

1. Name five advantages of a sole proprietorship.
2. List the three different types of partnerships and describe each.
3. Differentiate among the different types of corporations. Can you supply an example of each type?
4. Would you rather own preferred stock or common stock? Why?
5. Contrast how profits are distributed in sole proprietorships, partnerships, and corporations.
6. Which form of business organization has the least government regulation? Which has the most?
7. Compare the liability of the owners of partnerships, sole proprietorships, and corporations.
8. Why would secrecy in operating a business be important to an owner? What form of organization would be most appropriate for a business requiring great secrecy?
9. Which form of business requires the most specialization of skills? Which requires the least? Why?
10. The most common example of a cooperative is a farm co-op. Explain the reasons for this and the benefits that result for members of cooperatives.

Get Involved

1. Select a publicly owned corporation and bring to class a list of its subsidiaries. These data should be available in the firm's corporate annual report, *Standard and Poor's Corporate Records,* or *Moody Corporate Manuals.* Ask your librarian for help in finding these resources.
2. Select a publicly owned corporation and make a list of its outside directors. Information of this nature can be found in several places in your library: the company's annual report, its list of corporate directors, and various financial sources. If possible, include each director's title and the name of the company that employs him or her on a full-time basis.
3. List five companies that you have done business with or worked for recently. Determine what kind of ownership structure each uses and whether there is any particular regulation limiting their ownership structure.

Build Your Skills

Selecting a Form of Business Opportunity

Background: Alison Bush sees an opportunity to start her own web-site development business. Alison has just graduated from the University of Waterloo with a master's degree in computer science. Although she has many job opportunities outside the Waterloo area, she wishes to remain there to care for her aging parents. She already has most of the computer equipment necessary to start the business, but she needs additional software. She is considering the purchase of a server to maintain web sites for small businesses. Alison feels she has the ability to take this start-up firm and create a long-term career opportunity for herself and others. She knows she can hire University of Waterloo students to work on a part-time basis to support her business. For now, as she starts the business, she can work out of the extra bedroom of her apartment. As the business grows, she'll hire the additional full and/or part-time help needed and reassess the location of the business.

Task:

1. Using what you've learned in this chapter, decide which form of business ownership is most appropriate for Alison. Use the tables to the right to assist you in evaluating the advantages and disadvantages of each decision.

Sole Proprietorship

Advantages	Disadvantages
•	•
•	•
•	•
•	•
•	•
•	•
•	•

Corporation

Advantages	Disadvantages
•	•
•	•
•	•
•	•
•	•
•	•

 **See for Yourself Videocase** www.cbc.ca

Jimmy Pattison

Jimmy Pattison has built an economic empire from small beginnings as a used-car salesman. Quietly he has amassed a group of businesses worth over $3 billion. Here is a man always on the move—travelling in his private jet, surveying his businesses at least quarterly, and asking the tough questions of his managers. His 17,000 employees are in over 12 countries and he is familiar with all the major salespeople.

This man is serious about being on time. He does not respond to the writings of analysts—his empire is all private. There are no outside investors and, hence, he has the ability to make quick decisions. But this does not mean he makes rash decisions. They are made in the context of a long-term view of the world, with an eye on growth and what is best for the business. His strategy is basic and focuses on those businesses that he can relate to, and this is a reflection of his sales background. The business needs to grow and help in the diversification of the empire. The focuses of his acquisitions are those companies that he can turn around from losses to success. A favourite method of improving performance in these companies is firing the lowest-performing salesperson each month. Perform or get out.

Jimmy Pattison runs a tight ship. It is disciplined and fast. He acquired 21 companies in one year and was involved in 50 deals. That means buying a company every two-and-a-half weeks and making a deal every week. Everything is on time, as he sees speed as essential to success: his decisions, hiring, and firing, but not his changes. These he considers to be more of evolution and not revolution.

Today his empire includes over 50 companies generating $5 billion in sales. According to *Canadian Business*, in December 2001, Jimmy Pattison was worth $2.75 billion himself.

Questions

1. What are the advantages of Pattison owning 50 corporations and not merging the companies?

2. What are the advantages and disadvantages of keeping the business private?

3. Why would Pattison not operate as a sole proprietorship?

4. What do you think the impact of Pattison's salesforce management techniques are on the salesforce and firms?

Source: *Venture*, show number 687, "Jimmy Pattison," June 30, 1998, running time 10:27.

Remember to check out our Online Learning Centre at **www.mcgrawhill.ca/college/ferrell.**

Chapter 6

Small Business, Entrepreneurship, and Franchising

Chapter Outline

Objectives

After reading this chapter, you will be able to:

- Define entrepreneurship and small business.
- Investigate the importance of small business in the Canadian economy and why certain fields attract small business.
- Specify the advantages of small-business ownership.
- Summarize the disadvantages of small-business ownership and analyze why many small businesses fail.
- Describe how you go about starting a small business and what resources are needed.
- Explain why many large businesses are trying to "think small."
- Assess two entrepreneurs' plans for starting a small business.

Are You Ready to Be An Entrepreneur?

Enter the World of Business

Do you, like one in three Canadians, want to start your own business? Perhaps like many others you have the desire, or even a dream, but are unsure how or where to begin. Help is available, but caution and effort are needed on your part.

Your first challenge is a critical self-evaluation to determine if self-employment or entrepreneurship is right for you. An interesting starting point is the Entrepreneur Questionnaire by the Hay Group at www.haygroup.co.uk. This is a short questionnaire with immediate feedback. A search on the web will reveal numerous such questionnaires. Use them to assist you in your self-evaluation.

If you are certain you want to join the more than 1,000,000 Canadians who are currently self-employed but lack experience or business knowledge, perhaps you should consider acquiring a franchise. The Canadian Franchise Association is a good place to begin your search for information about franchising and the franchises available. There are a number of other sites offering information about franchising. The information they provide can be very useful in directing your search for the ideal franchise for you, but remember it is critical that you do careful and complete research. When acquiring a franchise, despite the usual training and procedures available, you are purchasing a business. It is you who risk your time, effort, and invested capital. It is you who must understand all the details of the franchise agreement and the commitment you are making to the business venture.

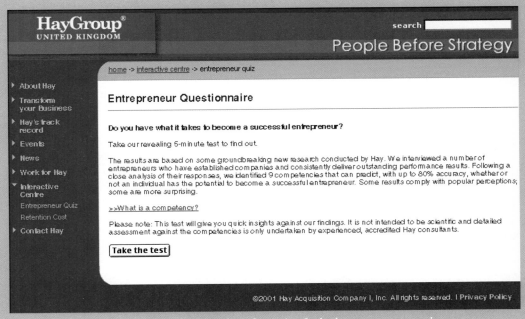

The HayGroup UK Interactive Centre provides information for both entrepreneurs and managers.

INTRODUCTION

Although many business students go to work for large corporations upon graduation, others may choose to start their own business or find employment opportunities in small businesses with 500 or fewer employees. There are approximately 2 million businesses operating in Canada today; with small businesses having fewer than 50 employees accounting for 97.3 percent of the total. In Canada small businesses are a significant part of the economy. Employer deduction records for 1993 show that the number of firms with paid employees increased by nearly 1,500 to 922,182. This growth came solely from increases in very small firms with fewer than five employees. By 2000, there were 1,687,000 such firms representing over 78 percent of all firms.[1] This is a compound annual growth rate of 8 percent. During 1996–97 small businesses generated over 80 percent of all new jobs.[2] By 1999 small- and medium-sized entities (SMEs) accounted for 50 percent of GDP and over half of the total employment in Canada.[3] Table 6.1 lists some statistics about small businesses in Canada. According to Canadian Federation of Independent Business research, SMEs needed between 250,000 and 300,000 employees to fill job vacancies in 2001. Each small business represents the vision of its entrepreneurial owners to succeed by providing new or better products. Small businesses are the heart of the Canadian economic and social system because they offer opportunities and express the freedom of people to make their own destinies. Today, the entrepreneurial spirit is growing around the world, from Russia and China to Germany, Brazil, Mexico, and the US.

This chapter surveys the world of entrepreneurship and small business. First we define entrepreneurship and small business and examine the role of small business in the Canadian economy. Then we explore the advantages and disadvantages of small-business ownership and analyze why small businesses succeed or fail. Next, we discuss how an entrepreneur goes about starting a small business. Finally, we look at entrepreneurship in larger businesses.

THE NATURE OF ENTREPRENEURSHIP AND SMALL BUSINESS

entrepreneurship
the process of creating and managing a business to achieve desired objectives

In Chapter 1, we defined an entrepreneur as a person who risks his or her wealth, time, and effort to develop for profit an innovative product or way of doing something. **Entrepreneurship** is the process of creating and managing a business to achieve desired objectives, and there are about 2 million Canadians engaged in some entrepreneurial activity, and one in three people want to start their own business.[4] Many large businesses you may recognize, including Magna International, Linamar, Canadian Tire, and Tim Hortons, all began as small businesses based on the entrepreneurial visions of their founders. Some entrepreneurs who start small businesses have the ability to see emerging trends; in response, they create a company to provide a product that serves customer needs. James Clark is a Silicon Valley entrepreneur

Table 6.1

Facts about Small Businesses in Canada

Sources: Statistics Canada, Establishments by Industry, December 2000; "Venturing Out: How HDRC Can Help in Small Business," *Canada Magazine*, January 1999; "Moving Forward: Small Business is the Key to Economic Recovery," CFIB, October 29, 2001.

- Represent 97.3% of business establishments.
- Created more than 80% of all new jobs in fiscal 1996–97.
- Accounted for 50% of GDP in 1999.
- Provided over half of the employment in Canada in 1999.

who founded Silicon Graphics, Inc., which brought 3-D computing to engineers. He then founded the Internet pioneer, Netscape Communications Corp. More recently, Clark founded Healtheon Corp. to provide online medical data to physicians.[5]

Of course, smaller businesses do not have to evolve into such highly visible companies to be successful, but those entrepreneurial efforts that result in rapidly growing businesses become more visible with their success. Entrepreneurs who have achieved success, like Mike Lazaridis (Research In Motion) and Frank Stronach (Magna), are the most visible.

The entrepreneurship movement is accelerating with many new, smaller businesses emerging. Technology once available only to the largest firms can now be acquired by a small business. Printers, fax machines, copiers, voice mail, computer bulletin boards and networks, cellular phones, and even overnight delivery services enable small businesses to be more competitive with today's giant corporations. Small businesses can also form alliances with other companies to produce and sell products in domestic and global markets.

What Is a Small Business?

This question is difficult to answer because smallness is relative. In this book, we will define a **small business** as any independently owned and operated business that is not dominant in its competitive area and does not employ more than 500 people. A local Mexican restaurant may be the most patronized Mexican restaurant in your community, but because it does not dominate the restaurant industry as a whole, the restaurant can be considered a small business. The definition of small and medium-sized entities (SMEs) varies between government programs. Industry Canada's Canadian Small Business Financing Program defines small business as having gross revenue of less than $5,000,000. The Federal Program for Export Development defines small business as having less than $10,000,000 in annual sales and fewer than 100 employees.

Small business owners, such as the landscaping contractor shown here, play a vital role in the Canadian economy.

© 1999 PhotoDisc, Inc.

small business
any independently owned and operated business that is not dominant in its competitive area and does not employ more than 500 people

The Role of Small Business in the Canadian Economy

No matter how you define small business, one fact is clear: Small businesses are vital to the soundness of the Canadian economy. Over 97 percent of all Canadian firms are classified as small businesses, and they employ almost 60 percent of private workers. In addition, small businesses are largely responsible for fuelling job creation and innovation.

Job Creation. The energy, creativity, and innovative abilities of small-business owners have resulted in jobs for other people. Table 6.2 indicates that businesses employing fewer than five people account for more than three-quarters of all firms in Canada. Table 6.3 shows the breakdown by industry.

During the 1980s small and new businesses were the major source of net new jobs across Canada. Small firms accounted for 85 percent of the 2.5 million new jobs in the private sector.

Table 6.2

*Number of Firms by
Employment Size,
December 31, 2000*

Source: From the Statistics
Canada Web site at
**www.statcan.ca/English/
Pgdb/Economy/
Economic/econ18.htm**.

Firm Size	Number of Firms (thousands)	Percentage of all Firms
0–4	1,587	78.4
5–49	383	18.9
50–99	31	1.5
100+	24	1.2
All size firms	2,025	100

With the onset of recession in 1990, small business still led the way in job creation. In 1990 increases in employment by small business more than offset the cutbacks by large firms. In 1993 small business generated 1.23 million jobs. In the same year 1.44 million jobs were lost as a result of cutbacks and closures.[6]

While larger firms with more than three hundred employees created the majority of new jobs between the fourth quarter of 1999 and the fourth quarter of 2000, small business was still an important factor creating almost 10,000 new jobs during the period.[7]

Many small businesses today are being started because of encouragement from larger ones. Many jobs are being created by big company/small company alliances. For example, giants such as Nike, Williams-Sonoma, and Brother Industries have led to the creation of many small ventures in Memphis, Tennessee, which was recently recognized as one of the top 20 cities in the United States for small business. Whether through formal joint ventures, supplier relationships, or product or marketing cooperative projects, the rewards of collaborative relationships are creating many jobs for small-business owners and their employees. Some publishing companies, for example,

Table 6.3

*Establishments by
Industry as at
December 31, 2000*

Source: Statistics Canada,
www.statcan.ca/english/
Pgdb/Economy/Economic/
econ18.htm.

		Number of Establishments			
	TOTAL	0–4 Employees	5–49 Employees	50–99 Employees	100+ Employees
All industries	2,024,508	1,586,749	383,062	31,081	23,616
Goods-producing sector	545,600	447,881	82,320	8,234	7,165
Service-producing sector	1,478,908	1,138,868	300,742	22,847	16,451
Primary industries	209,644	191,573	16,600	865	606
Construction	225,821	186,946	35,477	2,218	1,180
Manufacturing	105,209	66,080	28,893	5,028	5,208
Wholesale trade	132,640	93,384	35,096	2,716	1,444
Retail trade	242,852	167,138	68,951	4,162	2,601
Finance, insurance, and real estate	301,519	267,137	30,349	2,431	1,602
Business and personal services	541,065	420,683	107,006	8,662	4,714

contract out almost all their editing and production to small businesses. Elm Street Publishing Services is a small editing/production house in Hinsdale, Illinois, that provides most services required to turn a manuscript into a bound book.

Innovation. Small businesses are able to overcome the inertia of larger, longer established firms to capitalize on new technology. They develop new products in the early stages of an industry's life cycle when new features and responsiveness to customer demands are the basis of competition. In a study based on Statistics Canada's Survey of Innovation 1996, Guy Gellatly reports that 40 percent of small businesses identify themselves as innovators. These firms report the introduction of new or improved products (81 percent of innovators), process innovation (46 percent of innovators), and organizational innovation (33 percent of innovators). Almost half of all innovators reported multiple forms of innovation activity. Research has shown that innovation and success are complementary.[8]

Among notable 20th century innovations by Canadians or in Canada are the AC Radio Tube, the telephone, the IMAX Movie System, the paint roller, the Robertson screw, and, no doubt in response to our climate, the snowblower and the snowmobile.[9]

The innovation of successful firms takes many forms. For example, when California beefed up its environmental standards, Marcella Oster, a dental assistant in northern California, realized there might be a profitable business in the treatment and disposal of dental office toxic waste. She founded Eco-Solutions, one of the only women-owned toxic-disposal companies in the US. Today, Eco-Solutions has 10 employees and nearly 1,000 customers.[10] Small businessman Ray Kroc found a new way to sell hamburgers and turned his ideas into one of the most successful fast-food franchises in the world—McDonald's. Not all new businesses deliver a new product. For some the innovation is in the new approach to the delivery of an existing product. In 1964, the first Tim Hortons store opened. Ron Joyce, the first successful franchisee, became full partners with Tim Horton in 1967. The concept was a hit with Canadians and by February 2002, there were almost 2,000 Tim Hortons stores in Canada and 130 in the US, employing a total of 55,000[11] people. Small businesses have become an integral part of our lives. They provide fresh ideas and usually have greater flexibility to change than do large companies.

Innovation in Canada lags behind that in the United States. Canadians are typically more averse to risk than Americans. This lessens our capacity to innovate, making Canadian business less competitive. Eighty percent of Canadian manufacturers do innovate, but over 60 percent of these innovators are adaptors. Innovators develop new products, processes, and organizational forms. Adaptors make innovations that are new to their firms but are not new to the market.[12]

Exporting. Small firms are also important as exporters, representing 95.7 percent of US exporters of goods and contributing 29.5 percent of the value of exported goods. Interestingly, 30 percent of women-owned firms export 50 percent or more of their product compared to 21.9 percent of those owned by men.[13]

As firm size increases, so does the tendency of the firm to export their product. Almost 45 percent of Canadian firms with more than 50 employees export to the United States or abroad. Only 18 percent of firms with fewer than five employees do so.[14]

Industries That Attract Small Business

Small businesses are found in nearly every industry, but retailing and wholesaling, services, manufacturing, and high technology are especially attractive to entrepreneurs

**Consider
Ethics and
Social
Responsibility**

*The Manchester
Craftsmen's
Guild and
Bidwell
Training
Center, Inc.*

In September 1963, Bill Strickland, then a 16-year-old African American bored by school and life in his decaying Pittsburgh neighbourhood of Manchester, made a discovery that led him to college and a way out. What Strickland saw that afternoon was a lump of clay being shaped by a teacher on a potter's wheel. The people who now work with him and attend his programs say that day Strickland began reinventing this country's approach to social entrepreneurship.

During his remaining two years of high school, Strickland learned as much as he could from the teacher. Strickland went on to the University of Pittsburgh, made the dean's list by the end of his first year, and wound up on the university's board of trustees 32 years later.

In the meantime, social upheaval and rioting were rocking the United States. Strickland decided in 1968 that it was time for him to do something that would bring hope to the inhabitants of his old neighbourhood. He opened an after-school program to teach pottery skills to neighbourhood children and named the program the Manchester Craftsmen's Guild (MCG). A local church donated space for the program. After college, Strickland built a staff of volunteers and ran the program on an annual budget of US$50,000, mostly from grants and contributions from community leaders.

Three years later, Strickland was asked to take over the Bidwell Training Center (BTC), a neighbourhood vocational training program. By combining MCG and BTC, Strickland approached community rebuilding from two directions—by saving troubled kids and motivating them to go to college and helping adults by giving them an opportunity at a second start in life. For the next 10 years, Strickland worked at both programs, forming a vision of social change and attracting people to help.

In just three years, he raised enough money to build a showplace that would serve as a centre for social innovation and allow him to demonstrate how his ideas worked and what they could do. Strickland's programs reach about 400 kids and 475 adults each year. For the past five years, 75–80 percent of the at-risk high school kids who have attended MCG have gone on to college, and 78 percent of the adults who have graduated from his vocational program have found jobs. Just as impressive as Strickland's record are Strickland's supporters. George Bush named Strickland to a six-year term on the board of the National Endowment for the Arts. The Harvard Business School described him as a "social entrepreneur" and invited him to share his lessons on teaching with Harvard students.

Strickland has secured funds of US$3.5 million a year in the state budget for BTC. A new 5,600 square metre building will be used for expanded training programs and will also turn Strickland into a commercial landlord with a commitment by the UPMC Health Systems to lease 2,800 square metres of space. The food services company that was a spin-off of BTC's culinary training program has revenues of US$1.5 million. A deal currently in the works for a food services contract is worth US$250 million a year. The mayor of San Francisco and jazz musician Herbie Hancock have teamed up with Strickland to replicate his Pittsburgh program in San Francisco. Strickland envisions this undertaking as the first of 100 "franchises" he will set up over the next 30 years.

Strickland says, "Nonprofits have to recognize that they're businesses, not just causes. There's a way to combine the very best of the not-for-profit, philanthropic world with the very best of the for-profit, enterprising world. This hybrid is the wave of the future for both profit and nonprofit companies."[15]

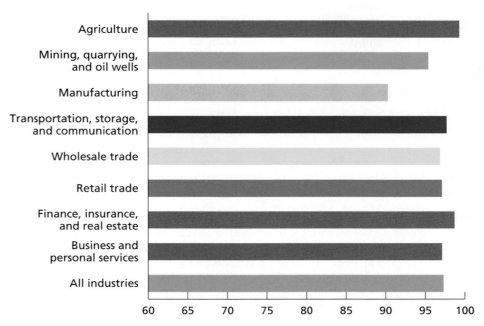

Figure 6.1

Small Business Percentage of Establishments by Industry

Source: From the Statistics Canada Web site at **www.statcan.ca/English/Pgdb/Economy/Economic/econ18.htm**.

because they are relatively easy to enter and require low initial financing. Small-business owners also find it easier to focus on a specific group of consumers in these fields than in others, and new firms in these industries suffer less from heavy competition, at least in the early stages, than do established firms. Figure 6.1 shows the relative proportion of small businesses in Canada by industry, and Table 6.4 shows the top five small business industries in the US, based on employment.

Retailing and Wholesaling. Retailers acquire goods from producers or whole-salers and sell them to consumers. Main streets, shopping strips, and shopping malls are lined with independent record stores, sporting-goods shops, dry cleaners, boutiques, drugstores, restaurants, caterers, service stations, and hardware stores that sell directly to consumers. Retailing attracts entrepreneurs because gaining experience and exposure in retailing is relatively easy. Additionally, an entrepreneur opening a new retailing store does not have to spend the large sums of money for the equipment and distribution systems that a manufacturing business requires. All that a new retailer needs is a lease on store space, merchandise, enough money to sustain the business, a knowledge about prospective customers' needs and desires, the ability to use promotion to generate awareness, and basic management skills.

Wholesalers supply products to industrial, retail, and institutional users for resale or for use in making other products. Wholesaling activities range from planning and negotiating for supplies, promoting, and distributing (warehousing and transporting) to providing management and merchandising assistance to clients. Wholesalers are extremely important for many products, especially consumer goods, because of the marketing activities they perform. Although it is true that wholesalers themselves can be eliminated, their functions must be passed on to some other organization such as the producer, or another intermediary, often a small business. Frequently, small businesses are closer to the final customers and know what it takes to keep

Table 6.4

Top Five Small Business Industries by Employment

Source: 1997 Small Business Profile, Small Business Administration Office of Advocacy, "Small Business: Backbone of the United States Economy," **http://www.sba.gov/ADVO /stats/profiles/97us.html,** September 30, 1998.

Industry	Employment in Firms with 0–499 Employees	Small Businesses (%)
Eating and drinking places	4,625,040	65.9%
Health services	4,385,299	40.8
Business services	3,191,279	50.1
Special trade contractors	2,682,009	93.2
Wholesale trade—durable goods	2,643,265	71.4

them satisfied. Some smaller businesses start out manufacturing but find their real niche as a supplier or distributor of larger firms' products.

Services. Services include businesses that work for others but do not actually produce tangible goods. In Canada almost three-quarters of the nearly 15 million people employed work in the service-producing sector. While manufacturing dominated employment growth in 1999, the service sector dominated in 2000. Employment in the services producing sector grew 2.7 percent in 2000, representing almost 293,000 jobs, more than 90 percent of the new jobs created that year. Employment in the goods producing sector grew by only 0.7 percent, or 27,000 jobs, during the same period.[16] Real estate, insurance, and personnel agencies, barbershops, banks, television and computer repair shops, copy centres, dry cleaners, and accounting firms are all service businesses. Services also attract individuals—such as beauticians, morticians, jewellers, doctors, and veterinarians—whose skills are not usually required by large firms. Many of these service providers are also retailers because they provide their services to ultimate consumers.

Manufacturing. Manufacturing goods can provide unique opportunities for small businesses. The National Quality Institute annually confers the Canada Awards for Excellence to Canada's best run companies and public sector organizations. Among the winners since the award's inception in 1983 are some of Canada's best-known success stories including Skyjack, Linda Lundstrom, and Research In Motion. According to NQI media releases, the annual awards are intended to recognize "Canadian organizations that have effectively transformed themselves to become more efficient, expand market share, provide employment opportunities and enhance international competitiveness."[17] Small businesses can often customize products to meet specific customer needs and wants. Such products include custom artwork, jewellery, clothing, furniture, and computer software.

High Technology. High technology is a broad term used to describe businesses that depend heavily on advanced scientific and engineering knowledge. Personify Inc. is a small business created to sell interactive marketing software and services that enable businesses of all sizes to analyze and anticipate web site audience preferences and convert site visitors into loyal customers. Its point-and-click web marketing software models visitors' behaviours, identifies key market segments, and enables real-time targeting of promotions, content, and internet purchase transactions.[18] People who have been able to innovate or identify new markets in the fields of computers, biotechnology, genetic engineering, robotics, and other markets have become today's high-tech giants. Michael Dell, for example, started building personal computers in his University of Texas dorm room at age 19. His Dell Computer is now one of the

Jody Steinhauer, the 2001 Innovation Award recipient from the Rotman Canadian Woman Entrepreneur of the Year Awards, is described in the award profile as "one part entrepreneur and one part innovator."

Jody is a 1986 graduate of the International Academy of Fashion, Merchandising & Design in Toronto, where she earned the President's Pin for academic excellence and the Retail Council of Canada's Award for the most promising student. Jody entered the job market even before graduation. She started her career selling luxurious clothing lines to such high-end retailers as Holt Renfrew.

Tiring of her first job, which she describes as "too superficial," Jody started her own business. With $1,000 initial capital and a strong interest in the discount retail market, the Bargains Group was founded in 1988.

Initially operating from Jody's apartment dining room, the now multi-million dollar business is headquartered in a facility near the Yorkdale Shopping Centre in Toronto, with an office, warehouse, and showroom space.

The Bargains Group is now a large wholesaler of children's, women's, and men's clothing and accessories to such retailers as Winners, Fields, and Stedmans. Included among the over 4,000 items in the showroom and ready for immediate delivery are gloves, mitts, scarves, sweatpants, underwear, sleeping bags, and of course the $0.50 socks for which the Bargains Group has become famous.

The Bargains Group is a profitable, well-managed business but the bottom line is not Jody's only passion. Her strong desire to give something back to the community and to help those in need is evident from even the briefest of conversations.

The large volume of sales allows the Bargains Group to sell at very low prices and still earn a good profit. Unlike many businesses, however, the Bargains Group provides the same low price service to small nonprofit organizations as to their high-volume customers.

The processing, invoicing, and delivery costs to service a customer are almost the same for those who order in the smallest lots of 24 items as for those purchasing 24,000 items. This severely reduces the profitability of small customers, which is why many vendors provide volume discounts. By extending this service and including delivery anywhere in Canada, Jody and the Bargains Group increase the purchasing power of charitable groups by up to 400 percent.

The Bargains Group's clients in the not-for-profit sector include such widely known organizations as the Red Cross, the Salvation Army, the Canadian Mental Health Association, and Habitat for Humanity, as well as numerous small local groups throughout the country.

Jody is quick to point that while the profits are sparse in dealing with such organizations, the rewards are great in terms of personal satisfaction. One could hear the pride in her voice as she told of receiving a half dozen thank-you cards from charitable groups in the corporate mail the day we spoke.

Low prices are not the Bargains Group's only efforts to assist charitable groups and the community. The company actively recruits the clients of their not-for-profit customers when seeking new employees. While hiring the disadvantaged is not without problems, Jody speaks with pride of those who have benefited from the opportunity for employment and the training they have received at the Bargains Group.

The Bargains Group also provides training in management and operations for charitable groups as well as assistance in seeking sources of funding. Future plans include using the company's new web site to provide such groups with a one-stop reference and resource centre.

The Bargains Group is an excellent example of how business success and social responsibility benefit the community as a whole.[19]

Consider Ethics and Social Responsibility

The Bargains Group

leading PC companies in the world, with annual revenues over US$15 billion.[20] Apple Computers began in a garage. The Apple prototype was financed by the proceeds Steven Wozniak received from selling his Hewlett-Packard calculator and Steven Jobs got from selling his van. In general, high technology businesses require greater capital and have higher initial start-up costs than do other small businesses. Many of them, nonetheless, started out in garages, basements, kitchens, and dorm rooms.

ADVANTAGES OF SMALL-BUSINESS OWNERSHIP

There are many advantages to establishing and running a small business. These can be categorized as personal advantages and business advantages.

Personal Advantages

Independence is probably one of the leading reasons that entrepreneurs choose to go into business for themselves. Being a small-business owner means being your own boss. Many people start their own businesses because they believe they will do better for themselves than they could do by remaining with their current employer or by changing jobs. They may feel stuck on the corporate ladder and that no business would take them seriously enough to fund their ideas. Sometimes people who venture forth to start their own small business are those who simply cannot work for someone else. Such people may say that they just do not fit the "corporate mould."

More often, small-business owners just want the freedom to choose whom they work with, the flexibility to pick where and when to work, and the option of working in a family setting. The availability of the computer, copy machine, business telephone, and fax machine has permitted many people to work at home. Only a few years ago, most of them would have needed the support that an office provides.

Business Advantages

Costs. As already mentioned, small businesses often require less money to start and maintain than do large ones. Obviously, a firm with just 25 people in a small factory spends less money on wages and salaries, rent, utilities, and other expenses than does a firm employing tens of thousands of people in several large facilities. And, rather than maintain the expense and staff of keeping separate departments for accounting, advertising, and legal counselling, small businesses can hire other firms (often small businesses themselves) to supply these services as they are needed. Additionally, small-business owners can sometimes rely on friends and family members who volunteer to work to get out a difficult project in order to save money.

Flexibility. With small size comes the flexibility to adapt to changing market demands. Small businesses usually have only one layer of management—the owners. Decisions therefore can be made and carried out quickly. In larger firms, decisions about even routine matters can take weeks because they must pass through two or more levels of management before action is authorized. When McDonald's introduces a new product, for example, it must first research what consumers want, then develop the product and test it carefully before introducing it in all of its restaurants, a process that sometimes takes years. An independent snack shop, however, can develop and introduce a new product (perhaps to meet a customer's request) in a much shorter time.

Focus. Small firms can focus their efforts on a few key customers or on a precisely defined market niche—that is, a specific group of customers. Many large corporations must compete in the mass market or for large market segments. Smaller firms can develop products for particular groups of customers or to satisfy a need that other companies have not addressed. For example, Tracey Campbell stumbled onto an unmet need with Innseekers, an online listing service for bed and breakfast establishments. Campbell asked members of an Internet discussion group for disabled people what they would prefer to be called in her listings. An online contact led to mention of her service in a magazine for the disabled. Within days of the article's appearance, inns listed with her service received bookings from wheelchair-bound travellers for more than 400 room nights. Turning her discovery into a strategy, Campbell now writes a column in a newsletter for disabled travellers and caters to the disabled through her web site.[21] By targeting small niches or product needs, small businesses can sometimes avoid fierce competition from larger firms, helping them to grow into stronger companies.

Reputation. Small firms, because of their capacity to focus on narrow niches, can develop enviable reputations for quality and service. A good example of such a business is the Dominion Seed House of Georgetown, Ontario. The company has specialized in mail order gardening products since 1928. Their guarantee states, "If after 4–6 weeks of planting the results are not satisfactory … We will replace or credit." Such guarantees demonstrate a strong commitment to customer satisfaction.

Dominion Seed House
www.dominion-seed-house.com

DISADVANTAGES OF SMALL-BUSINESS OWNERSHIP

The rewards associated with running a small business are so enticing that it's no wonder many people dream of it. However, as with any undertaking, small-business ownership has its disadvantages.

High Stress Level

A small business is likely to provide a living for its owner, but not much more (although there are exceptions as some examples in this chapter have shown). There are always worries about competition, employee problems, new equipment, expanding inventory, rent increases, or changing market demand. In addition to other stresses, small-business owners tend to be victims of physical and psychological stress. The small-business person is often the owner, manager, sales force, shipping and receiving clerk, bookkeeper, and custodian. A poll of 300 small-business owners in the US found that 22 percent of the respondents spend most of their time in sales/customer contact or with accounting/bookkeeping activities (21 percent). Only 35 percent of those surveyed use financial or accounting software for bill paying, and 21 percent report they do not use a computer at all.[22] Many creative persons succeed or fail, not because of their business concepts, but rather because of difficulties in managing their business.

High Failure Rate

Despite the importance of small businesses to our economy, there is no guarantee of small-business success. Many enterprises that fail do not formally declare bankruptcy; they simply close up shop. Table 6.5 shows the number of bankruptcies for

Table 6.5

Commercial Bankruptcies, 1995–1999

Source: From the Statistics Canada Web site at **www.statcan.ca/english/ Pgdb/Economy/ Economic/econ11.htm**.

	1995	1996	1997	1998	1999
All industries	13,258	14,229	12,200	10,791	10,026
Agriculture and related services	307	315	276	272	287
Manufacturing	966	1,070	862	802	750
Construction	2,146	1,965	1,680	1,510	1,445
Retail trade	2,930	3,097	2,579	2,266	1,964
Real estate and insurance agencies	442	415	272	233	175
Accommodation, food and beverage services	1,976	2,069	1,805	1,586	1,396
Other service industries	1,445	1,640	1,506	1,461	1,469

businesses of all sizes from 1995 to 1999. Remember when studying this table that only 0.2 percent of all businesses in Canada are large and that small businesses have a higher failure rate than do large ones. Neighbourhood restaurants are a case in point. Look around your own neighbourhood, and you can probably spot the locations of several restaurants that are no longer in business.

Small businesses fail for many reasons. A poor business concept—such as insecticides for garbage cans (research found that consumers are not concerned with insects in their garbage)—will produce disaster nearly every time. Expanding a hobby into a business may work if a genuine market niche exists, but all too often people start such a business without identifying a real need for the goods or services. Other notable causes of small-business failure include the burdens imposed by government regulation, insufficient funds to withstand slow sales, and vulnerability to competition from larger companies. However, three major causes of small-business failure deserve a close look: undercapitalization, managerial inexperience or incompetence, and inability to cope with growth.

undercapitalization
the lack of funds to operate a business normally

Canadian Federation of Independent Business **www.cfib.ca/**

Undercapitalization. The shortest path to failure in business is **undercapitalization,** the lack of funds to operate a business normally. Too many entrepreneurs think that all they need is enough money to get started, that the business can survive on cash generated from sales soon thereafter. But almost all businesses suffer from seasonal variations in sales, which make cash tight, and few businesses make money from the start. The Canadian Federation of Independent Business reported the results of their banking survey in March 2001. The survey showed that the banking sector does a satisfactory job of servicing the more established small firms, those that have been in business for at least 11 years. The same survey reveals financing difficulties for less established firms. Those small enterprises in business less than 10 years reported loan refusals by their main lending institutions at twice the rate (16 percent) as that of the more established firms. When loans were granted, the small firms paid an average rate of 0.39 percent higher than the established firms. Well-established firms gained financing at an average interest rate of prime plus 1.39 percent, while the newer firms paid an average of prime plus 1.78 percent.[23]

Managerial Inexperience or Incompetence. Poor management is the cause of many business failures. Just because an entrepreneur has a brilliant vision for a small business does not mean he or she has the knowledge or experience to manage a growing business effectively. A person who is good at creating great product ideas and marketing them may lack the skills and experience to make good management decisions in hiring, negotiating, finance, and control. Moreover, entrepreneurs may neglect those areas of management they know little about or find tedious, at the expense of the business's success.

Inability to Cope with Growth. Sometimes, the very factors that are advantages turn into serious disadvantages when the time comes for a small business to grow. Growth often requires the owner to give up a certain amount of direct authority, and it is frequently hard for someone who has called all the shots to give up control. Similarly, growth requires specialized management skills in areas such as credit analysis and promotion—skills that the founder may lack or not have time to apply. The founders of many small businesses, including those of Gateway and Dell Computers, found that they needed to bring in more experienced managers to help manage their companies through intense growing pains.

Poorly managed growth probably affects a company's reputation more than anything else, at least initially. And products that do not arrive on time or goods that are poorly made can quickly reverse a company's success.

STARTING A SMALL BUSINESS

We've told you how important small businesses are, and why they succeed and fail, but *how do you go about* starting your own business? To start any business, large or small, you must first have an idea. Sam Walton, founder of Wal-Mart stores, had an idea for a discount retailing enterprise and spawned a global retailing empire that changed the way traditional companies look at their business. Next, you need to devise a business plan to guide planning and development in the business. Finally, you must make decisions about form of ownership, the financial resources needed, and whether to buy an existing business, start a new one, or buy a franchise.

The Business Plan

A key element of business success is a **business plan**—a precise statement of the rationale for the business and a step-by-step explanation of how it will achieve its goals. The business plan should include an explanation of the business, an analysis of the competition, estimates of income and expenses, and other information. It should establish a strategy for acquiring sufficient funds to keep the business going. Indeed, many financial institutions decide whether to loan a small business money based on its business plan. However, the business plan should act as a guide and reference document—not a shackle to limit the business's flexibility and decision making. The Government of Canada web site at www.BusinessGateway.ca provides excellent background material, format suggestions, and advice on the preparation of a small business plan. This site also provides many links to other valuable information for small business.

Several other sites provide models of business plans and assistance in their preparation. One such site is for the Canada Business Services Centres at www.cbsc.org. This interactive business planner is intended to guide the user in what to include in

business plan
a precise statement of the rationale for a business and a step-by-step explanation of how it will achieve its goals

the business plan, to assist in determining what information is needed and in obtaining it, and finally to help in writing the plan.

Most lending institutions will provide prospective borrowers with loan application packages that include a recommended business plan format.

Forms of Business Ownership

After developing a business plan, the entrepreneur has to decide on an appropriate legal form of business ownership—whether it is best to operate as a sole proprietorship, partnership, or corporation—and examine the many factors that affect that decision, which we explored in Chapter 5.

Financial Resources

The old adage "it takes money to make money" holds true in developing a business enterprise. To make money from a small business, the owner must first provide or obtain money (capital) to start the business and keep it running smoothly. Even a small retail store will probably need at least $50,000 in initial financing to rent space, purchase or lease necessary equipment and furnishings, buy the initial inventory of merchandise, and provide working capital. Often, the small-business owner has to put up a significant percentage of the necessary capital. Few new business owners have the entire amount, however, and must look to other sources for additional financing.

Equity Financing. The most important source of funds for any new business is the owner. Many owners include among their personal resources ownership of a home or the accumulated value in a life-insurance policy or a savings account. A new business owner may sell or borrow against the value of such assets to obtain funds to operate a business. Additionally, the owner may bring useful personal assets—such as a computer, desks and other furniture, a car or truck—as part of his or her ownership interest in the firm. Such financing is referred to as *equity financing* because the owner uses real personal assets rather than borrowing funds from outside sources to get started in a new business. The owner can also provide working capital by reinvesting profits into the business or simply by not drawing a full salary.

venture capitalists
persons or organizations that agree to provide some funds for a new business in exchange for an ownership interest or stock

Small businesses can also obtain equity financing by finding investors for their operations. They may sell stock in the business to family members, friends, employees, or other investors. **Venture capitalists** are persons or organizations that agree to provide some funds for a new business in exchange for an ownership interest or stock. Venture capitalists hope to purchase the stock of a small business at a low price and then sell the stock for a profit after the business has grown successful. Although these forms of equity financing have helped many small businesses, they require that the small-business owner share the profits of the business—and sometimes control, as well—with the investors.

Debt Financing. New businesses sometimes borrow over half of their financial resources. Banks are the main suppliers of external financing to small businesses, with a 75 percent market share. They can also look to family and friends as sources for loans of long-term funds or other assets, such as a computer or an automobile, that are exchanged for an ownership interest in a business. In such cases, the business owner can usually structure a favourable repayment schedule and sometimes negotiate an interest rate below current bank rates. If the business goes bad, however, the emotional losses for all concerned may greatly exceed the money involved. Anyone lending a friend or family member money for a venture should state the agreement clearly in writing.

The amount a bank or other institution is willing to loan depends on its assessment of the venture's likelihood of success and of the entrepreneur's ability to repay the loan. The bank will often require the entrepreneur to put up *collateral*, a financial interest in the property or fixtures of the business, to guarantee payment of the debt. Additionally, the small-business owner may have to offer some personal property as collateral, such as his or her home, in which case the loan is called a *mortgage*. If the small business fails to repay the loan, the lending institution may eventually claim and sell the collateral (or the owner's home, in the case of a mortgage) to recover its loss.

Banks and other financial institutions can also grant a small business a *line of credit*—an agreement by which a financial institution promises to lend a business a predetermined sum on demand. A line of credit permits an entrepreneur to take quick advantage of opportunities that require a bank loan. Small businesses may obtain funding from their suppliers in the form of a *trade credit*—that is, suppliers allow the business to take possession of the needed goods and services and pay for them at a later date or in installments. Occasionally, small businesses engage in *bartering*—trading their own products for the goods and services offered by other businesses. For example, an accountant may offer accounting services to an office supply firm in exchange for computer paper and diskettes.

Additionally some community groups such as the Seed Loan Fund, discussed in Chapter 1, sponsor loan funds to encourage the development of small businesses. The federal and provincial governments provide numerous programs to foster new business growth. These programs often take the form of loan guarantees. One such program is established under the Canada Small Business Financing Program delivered through a network of community groups called community business development corporations. Extensive detailed information on this and other government and private-sector sources of financing is available at www.BusinessGateway.ca, a site maintained by the Government of Canada.

Approaches to Starting a Small Business

Starting from Scratch versus Buying an Existing Business. Although entrepreneurs often start new small businesses from scratch much the way we have discussed in this section, they may elect instead to buy an already existing business. This has the advantage of providing a network of existing customers, suppliers, and distributors and reducing some of the guesswork inherent in starting a new business from scratch. However, an entrepreneur buying an existing business must also deal with whatever problems the business already has.

Extensive government and private-sector programs exist to assist small businesses in Canada. The Canada Business Service Centres lists 23 federal government departments or agencies providing financial and management assistance to small businesses. These include departments such as Agriculture and Agrifood Canada, Transport Canada, and the Department of Foreign Affairs and International Trade. Agencies listed include Atlantic Canada Opportunities Agency, Farm Credit, and the Business Development Bank. Table 6.6 lists a sample of the available programs offered by the Business Development Bank.

Franchising. Many small-business owners find entry into the business world through franchising. A licence to sell another's products or to use another's name in

Canada Business
Services Centres
www.cbsc.org

Business Development
Bank of Canada
www.bdc.ca/

Table 6.6

A Sample of the Business Development Bank of Canada's Programs

Source: www.cbsc.org/ english.

Program	Description
Innovation Financing	Available to any company with growth potential, a solid business plan and a viable strategy. The purpose is to provide working capital, pay for R & D costs, and explore new markets and methods. Provides financing of up to $250,000 with flexible repayment terms over up to eight years.
Visa Global Line of Credit	Available to small and medium-sized enterprises. Provides a no-fee line of credit of $2,000 to $50,000.
Cultural Industries Development Fund	Suitable for Canadian owned and controlled cultural industry firms, such as book editors, film and video producers, and multimedia producers meeting specified criteria. Provides loans of up to $250,000 per 12-month period, with a total commitment of $1,000,000 over time. The funds are to be used for working capital needs, capital expenditures, and certain ownership changes.
Student Business Loans Program	Available to full-time students in most provinces. The program offers loans of up to $3,000 for student entrepreneurs to operate their own businesses during the summer months.

franchise

a licence to sell another's products or to use another's name in business, or both

franchisor

the company that sells a franchise

franchisee

the purchaser of a franchise

business, or both, is a **franchise.** The company that sells the franchise is the **franchisor.** Tim Hortons, McDonald's, and Swiss Chalet are well-known franchisors with national visibility. The purchaser of a franchise is called a **franchisee.**

The franchisee acquires the rights to a name, logo, methods of operation, national advertising, products, and other elements associated with the franchiser's business in return for a financial commitment and the agreement to conduct business in accordance with the franchiser's standard of operations. Depending on the franchise, the initial fee to join a system varies. In addition, franchisees buy equipment, pay for training, and obtain a mortgage or lease. The franchisee also pays the franchiser a monthly or annual fee based on a percentage of sales or profits. In return, the franchisee often receives building specifications and designs, site recommendations, management and accounting support, and perhaps most importantly, immediate name recognition.

The practice of franchising first began in the United States when Singer used it to sell sewing machines in the nineteenth century. It soon became commonplace in the distribution of goods in the automobile, gasoline, soft drink, and hotel industries. The concept of franchising grew especially rapidly during the 1960s, when it expanded to more diverse industries. Table 6.7 shows the franchise fee and capital requirements for some well-known Canadian franchises. Table 6.8 lists the top franchises in the United States, Table 6.9 lists the fastest-growing franchises worldwide, and Table 6.10 shows the latest in franchising trends.

Franchisor	Franchise Fees	Capital Requirement
A & W Food Services of Canada	$50,000	$125,000 to $250,000
Baskin Robbins	$30,000	$200,000 to $625,000
McDonalds Restaurants of Canada	$45,000	$600,000 to $800,000
Pizza Hut	US$35,000	US$320,000 to US$1 million
Subway	$10,000	$82,100 to $181,200
Dairy Queen Canada	$45,000	$200,000

Table 6.7

Franchise Fees and Capital Requirements of Canadian Franchises

Source: Based on material from the Canadian Franchise Association, 2001.

Franchise	Number of Units (2001)
1. Subway	15,248
2. Jackson Hewitt Tax Service	3,344
3. Curves for Women	2,412
4. 7-Eleven Inc.	21,142
5. Yogen Früz Worldwide	5,228
6. Quizno's Franchise Co.	1,270
7. McDonald's	28,236
8. Management Recruiters/Sales Consult. MRI Worldwide	1,360
9. Holiday Inn Worldwide	3,176
10. Jani-King	8,685

Table 6.8

Top 10 US Franchises for 2002

Source: Based on material from Entrepreneur's Franchise 500 for 2002 as reported February 25, 2002, at **www.entrepreneurmag. com/Franchise_Zone**

Franchise	Growth during 2001
Kumon Math & Reading Centres	2,259
7-Eleven Inc.	1,654
Curves for Women	555
Coverall North America Inc.	1,675
Subway	1,356
Jani-King	681
Jackson Hewitt Tax Service	483
KFC Corp.	996
McDonald's	895
Budget Rent a Car Corp.	97

Table 6.9

Top 10 Fastest-Growing Global Franchises for 2002

Source: Based on material from **www.entrepreneurmag.com/ Franchise_Zone**

Table 6.10

Franchising Trends

Source: Janean Chun, "Get A Clue," *Entrepreneur*, January 1998. Reprinted with permission from *Entrepreneur Magazine*.

In	Out
Wraps	Rotisserie chicken
Frozen desserts	Bagels
Health care businesses	Cosmetics companies
Video game franchises	Video rental stores
Soup bars	
Hot	**Hotter**
Golf	Women's golf

Help for Small-Business Managers

Because of the crucial role that small business and entrepreneurs play in the Canadian economy, a number of organizations offer programs to improve the small-business owner's ability to compete. These include entrepreneurial training programs and programs sponsored by both government and private sector groups. Such programs provide small-business owners with invaluable assistance in managing their businesses, often at little or no cost to the owner.

Entrepreneurs can learn critical marketing, management, and finance skills in seminars and college courses. In addition, knowledge, experience, and judgment are necessary for success in a new business. While knowledge can be communicated and some experiences can be simulated in the classroom, good judgment must be developed by the entrepreneur.

The federal government provides a wealth of information and guidance for small business through its web sites, including Strategis, BusinessGateway, and Canada Business Services Centres. The Canadian Federation of Independent Business and the Canadian Franchise Association are reliable sources of information and guidance. Publications including *Profit Magazine*, *The Journal of Small Business and Entrepreneurship*, and *Canadian Small Business Magazine*, as well as US publications such as *Inc.* and *Entrepreneur*, share statistics, advice, tips, and success and failure stories. The Association of Collegiate Entrepreneurs (ACE), the Canadian Technology Network, and Community Business Development Corporations all provide low- or no-cost advice to small businesses.

Finally, the small-business owner can obtain advice from other small-business owners, suppliers, and even customers. A customer may approach a small business it frequents with a request for a new product, for example, or a supplier may offer suggestions for improving a manufacturing process. Networking—building relationships and sharing information with colleagues—

Founded by Aaron, Michael, and Simon Serruya, Yogen Früz Worldwide, Inc. is one of the fastest growing franchises today, with almost 4,000 outlets.

Courtesy of Yogen Früz. Inc.

In October 1998, Jack Gray and his best friend, Bruce McVay, decided to start their own small business. Jack had developed recipes for fat-free and low-fat cookies and muffins in an effort to satisfy his personal health needs. Bruce had extensive experience in managing food-service establishments. They knew that a start-up company needs a quality product, adequate funds, a written business plan, some outside financial support, and a good promotion program. Jack and Bruce felt they had all of this and more and were ready to embark on their new low-fat cookie/muffin store. Each had $35,000 to invest and with their homes and other resources they had borrowing power of an additional $125,000.

However, they still have many decisions to make, including what form or organization to use, how to market their product, and how to determine exactly what products to sell—whether just cookies and muffins or additional products.

1. Evaluate the idea of a low-fat cookie and muffin retail store.

2. Are there any concerns in connection with starting a small business that Jack and Bruce have not considered?

3. What advice would you give Jack and Bruce as they start up their business?

Solve the Dilemma

The Small-Business Challenge

is vital for any businessperson, whether you work for a huge corporation or run your own small business. Communicating with other business owners is a great way to find ideas for dealing with employees and government regulation, improving processes, or solving problems. New technology is making it easier to network. For example, some places are setting up computer bulletin boards for the use of their businesses to network and share ideas.

Business success is an outgrowth of knowledge and experience. All kinds of life experiences—as a family member, friend, student, employee, or consumer, or in sports or art—are valuable. "The things you know and love and see opportunities in—you ought to pick your business based on that," says Bill Gates, founder of Microsoft.

Because of financial constraints and the lack of experience, most college students cannot start a business immediately after graduation. However, the challenge in starting and running a successful business is to demonstrate good judgment. Someone with a BS degree, a $50,000 inheritance, and poor judgment will not succeed as an entrepreneur. On the other hand, a person with $2,000 in savings may end up wealthy because of good business judgment. Steve Jobs and Steve Wozniak started Apple Computer in a garage with only a few thousand dollars. Another high-tech entrepreneur, Michael Dell, started Dell Computers in his University of Texas dorm room. So great was the success of both Apple and Dell that IBM and other large corporations rushed to create new products to compete with them.

It is estimated that 80 percent of new jobs for college graduates will be found in small business. Therefore, knowing about successful small businesses may be the first step in assessing job opportunities. Along with this chapter, reading magazines such as *Inc., Entrepreneur* or *Profit Magazine* can provide a good start in learning more about small business opportunities.[24]

Explore Your Career Options

Look to Small Business

MAKING BIG BUSINESSES ACT "SMALL"

The continuing success and competitiveness of small businesses through rapidly changing conditions in the business world have led many large corporations to take a closer look at what makes their smaller rivals tick. More and more firms are emulating small businesses in an effort to improve their own bottom line. Beginning in the 1980s and continuing through the present, the buzzword in business has been to *downsize,* to reduce management layers, corporate staff, and work tasks in order to make the firm more flexible, resourceful, and innovative like a smaller business. Many well-known US companies, including IBM, Gillette, Apple Computer, General Electric, Xerox, and 3M, have downsized to improve their competitiveness, as have German, British, and Japanese firms. Since there are so few large businesses in Canada, there are fewer opportunities for such activities. Nortel Networks is one notable Canadian example of corporate downsizing. Other firms have sought to make their businesses "smaller" by making their operating units function more like independent small businesses, each responsible for its profits, losses, and resources. Of course, some large corporations, such as Southwest Airlines, have acted like small businesses from their inception, with great success.

intrapreneurs
individuals in large firms who take responsibility for the development of innovations within the organizations

Trying to capitalize on small-business success in introducing innovative new products, more and more companies are attempting to instill a spirit of entrepreneurship into even the largest firms. In major corporations, **intrapreneurs,** like entrepreneurs, take responsibility for, or "champion," the development of innovations of any kind *within* the larger organization.[25] Often, they use company resources and time to develop a new product for the company.

Review Your Understanding

Define entrepreneurship and small business.

An entrepreneur is a person who creates a business or product and manages his or her resources and takes risks to gain a profit; entrepreneurship is the process of creating and managing a business to achieve desired objectives. A small business is one that is not dominant in its competitive area and does not employ more than 500 people.

Investigate the importance of small business in the Canadian economy and why certain fields attract small business.

Small businesses are vital to the Canadian economy because they provide products, jobs, innovation, and opportunities. Retailing, wholesaling, services, manufacturing, and high technology attract small businesses because these industries are relatively easy to enter, require relatively low initial financing, and may experience less heavy competition.

Specify the advantages of small-business ownership.

Small-business ownership offers some personal advantages, including independence, freedom of choice, and the option of working at home. Business advantages include flexibility, the ability to focus on a few key customers, and the chance to develop a reputation for quality and service.

Summarize the disadvantages of small-business ownership and analyze why many small businesses fail.

Small businesses have many disadvantages for their owners such as expense, physical and psychological stress, and a high failure rate. Small businesses fail for many reasons: undercapitalization, management inexperience or incompetence, neglect, disproportionate burdens imposed by government regulation, and vulnerability to competition from larger companies.

Describe how you go about starting a small business and what resources are needed.

First, you must have an idea for developing a small business. Next, you need to devise a business plan to guide planning and development of the business. Then you must decide what form of business ownership to use: sole proprietorship, partnership, or corporation. Small-business owners are expected to provide some of the funds required to start their businesses, but funds also can be obtained from friends and family, financial institutions, other businesses in the form of trade credit, investors (venture capitalists), federal and provincial governments, local organizations, and the Business Development Bank. In addition to loans, the Business Development Bank and other organizations offer counselling, consulting, and training services. Finally, you must decide whether to start a new business from scratch, buy an existing one, or buy a franchise operation.

Explain why many large businesses are trying to "think small."

More large companies are copying small businesses in an effort to make their firms more flexible, resourceful, and innovative, and generally to improve their bottom line. This effort often involves downsizing (reducing management layers, laying off employees, and reducing work tasks) and intrapreneurship, where an employee takes responsibility for (champions) developing innovations of any kind within the larger organization.

Assess two entrepreneurs' plans for starting a small business.

Based on the facts given in the "Solve the Dilemma" box and the material presented in this chapter, you should be able to assess the feasibility and potential success of Gray and McVay's idea for starting a small business.

Learn the Terms

business plan   141

entrepreneurship   130

franchise   144

franchisee   144

franchisor   144

intrapreneurs   148

small business   131

undercapitalization   140

venture capitalists   142

Check Your Progress

1. Why are small businesses so important to the Canadian economy?
2. Which fields tend to attract entrepreneurs the most? Why?
3. What are the advantages of starting a small business? The disadvantages?
4. What are the principal reasons for the high failure rate among small businesses?
5. What decisions must an entrepreneur make when starting a small business?
6. What types of financing do small entrepreneurs typically use? What are some of the pros and cons of each?
7. List 10 programs offered by the federal government to assist small businesses financially. (Hint: Start your search at cbsc.org/english/finance.)
8. Describe the franchising relationship.
9. Why do large corporations want to become more like small businesses?

Get Involved

1. Interview a local small-business owner. Why did he or she start the business? What factors have led to the business's success? What problems has the owner experienced? What advice would he or she offer a potential entrepreneur?
2. Using business journals, find an example of a company that is trying to emulate the factors that make small businesses flexible and more responsive. Describe and evaluate the company's activities. Have they been successful? Why or why not?
3. Using the business plan outline in Appendix A, create a business plan for a business idea that you have. (A man named Frederic Smith once did a similar project for a business class at Yale. His paper became the basis for the business he later founded: Federal Express!)

Build Your Skills

Creativity

Background: The entrepreneurial success stories in this chapter are about people who used their creative abilities to develop innovative products or ways of doing something that became the basis of a new business. Of course, being creative is not just for entrepreneurs or inventors; creativity is an important tool to help you find the optimal solutions to the problems you face on a daily basis. Employees rely heavily on their creativity skills to help them solve daily workplace problems.

According to brain experts, the right-brain hemisphere is the source of creative thinking; and the cre-ative part of the brain can "atrophy" from lack of use. Let's see how much "exercise" you're giving your right-brain hemisphere.

Task:

1. Take the self-test below to check your Creativity Quotient.[26]

2. Write the appropriate number in the box next to each statement according to whether the statement describes your behaviour always (3), sometimes (2), once in a while (1), or never (0).

	Always 3	Sometimes 2	Once in a While 1	Never 0
1. I am a curious person who is interested in other people's opinions.				
2. I look for opportunities to solve problems.				
3. I respond to changes in my life creatively by using them to redefine my goals and revising plans to reach them.				
4. I am willing to develop and experiment with ideas of my own.				
5. I rely on my hunches and insights.				
6. I can reduce complex decisions to a few simple questions by seeing the "big picture."				
7. I am good at promoting and gathering support for my ideas.				
8. I think farther ahead than most people I associate with by thinking long term and sharing my vision with others.				
9. I dig out research and information to support my ideas.				
10. I am supportive of the creative ideas from my peers and subordinates and welcome "better ideas" from others.				
11. I read books and magazine articles to stay on the "cutting edge" in my areas of interest. I am fascinated by the future.				
12. I believe I am creative and have faith in my good ideas.				
Subtotal for each column				
Grand Total				

3. Check your score using the following scale:

   30–36 High creativity. You are giving your right-brain hemisphere a regular workout.

   20–29 Average creativity. You could use your creativity capacity more regularly to ensure against "creativity atrophy."

   10–19 Low creativity. You could benefit by reviewing the questions you answered "never" in the above assessment and selecting one or two of the behaviours that you could start practising.

   0–9 Undiscovered creativity. You have yet to uncover your creative potential.

CBC **See for Yourself Videocase** **www.cbc.ca**

Reading the Fine Print

Purchasing a franchise is a major investment. As with any investment you must carry out due diligence; that is, you must exercise appropriate care to ensure your understanding of the contract you are making.

Many people are led to consider a franchise opportunity when thinking of self-employment because they lack experience or business training. The franchise system appears to offer the chance to own your own business while providing some assurance of success.

Not all franchise chains are successful and not all units within successful chains survive. Also not every franchise is a perfect match for the individual investor.

Like most small business owners, franchisees work long hours and commit most if not all of their financial resources to the business. Facing these conditions, you should only make the acquisition when you undertstand the details completely. The Canadian Franchise Association identifies eight areas you should research before signing the franchise agreement:

1. *Investigate the franchisor.* You should know who the principals are and their business history. How long has the franchisor been in operation and how many units are operating?

2. *What are the franchisor's relations with the franchisees?* How are franchisees selected and how does the franchisor monitor franchise operations? Do franchisees have any input into operating decisions, such as advertising, product development, and pricing?

3. *What is the total financial commitment of the franchisee?* The franchise fee is only the first cost. You should determine the total investment required to set up the franchise, including initial capital, inventory, leasehold improvements, and working capital requirements. Ongoing costs such as royalties and advertising levees must also be considered.

4. *Understand the product or service.* How long has the product or service been on the market and what makes it unique? What products must be purchased from the franchisor and what price protection are franchisees provided?

5. *Know your territorial rights.* Is the franchise granted exclusive rights in an area or can more units be opened nearby? Does the franchisor sell the product through competing distribution channels?

6. *How satisfied are existing franchisees?* Do current franchisees feel they received adequate training? Are they earning a satisfactory return for their labour and investment? What is their relationship with the franchisor?

7. *The contract.* You should understand every detail of the contract before you sign.

8. *Franchisor support.* What does the franchisor do for you? Do they assist with site selection, building design, and construction? What ongoing management assistance do franchisees receive?

Carrying out due diligence requires professional knowledge, time, and care. Even if you feel qualified, it is wise to seek independent legal, financial, and business advice to avoid any errors or omissions that may cause difficulties or financial losses later.

Questions

1. What is the importance of the information gained from the investigation in each of the CFA's eight recommended areas?

2. What advantages do franchises offer the investor relative to an independent operation?

3. What disadvantages of owning a franchise might the entrepreneurial individual perceive?

4. Which of the eight areas discussed above gave rise to the problems encountered by Paul Dollan and Dale Hunt? How might they have become aware of the potential for these problems and avoided them?

Source: *Venture*, show number 740, "Reading the Fine Print," February 22, 2000, running time 8:52.

Remember to check out our Online Learning Centre at **www.mcgrawhill.ca/college/ferrell**.

Cyberzone

Small Business and the Internet

In today's increasingly service- and information-oriented economy, millions of small businesses, entrepreneurs, and home-based workers are emerging as the real engines of long-term growth. Technology typically plays a deciding role in the competitiveness and viability of these ventures. As prices for computers, software, and Internet access fall, many small businesses are able to compete with much larger companies by using technology to manage customer calls, maintain financial records, build databases of clients and prospects, conduct research on competitors, produce reports, publications, and marketing materials, and even create web-based sales and marketing services.[1]

Small businesses not connected to the Internet are in a minority. A recent survey shows that 78 percent of Canadian SMEs use the Internet. The total value of online activity by SMEs in 2001 was $2 billion.[2] Basic Internet service allows instant access to people and information from all around the globe and is very inexpensive. E-mail is fast and costs just a fraction of regular mail or overnight courier rates. Internet-connected small business owners shopping for supplies or services are not restricted to nearby suppliers, and it is equally easy for prospective clients and customers to contact web-based firms. Also, the costs involved in banking transactions, purchase orders, invoices, and payments can be reduced significantly for the small business owner and its customers by using the Internet.

Perhaps the best place to begin a search for available information on the Internet on small business, entrepreneurship, and franchising is the comprehensive site maintained by Industry Canada, strategis.gc.ca. This site offers information on starting a business, financing, exporting, market research, human resource management, and using electronic commerce. This site is also linked to another federal government site, BusinessGateway.ca, which provides further information on the same topics, as well as links to regulatory sites, taxation information, business statistics and resources for analysis and innovation.

The Strategis.ca site provides a strategic planning tool in the section Nine Steps to Competitiveness. The fourth step, Technology, includes a Technology Diagnostic Tool consisting of 23 questions. After answering the questions an almost immediate response provides a customized report on areas of strength, areas of concern, and areas for further study.

Many print publications offer web sites devoted almost entirely to small business owners. Small Business Canada offers a catalogue of low-cost online courses for the small business owner, as well as interesting and informative articles. *Profit Magazine*'s Profitguide has informative articles, a calendar of small business-oriented events, and an extensive list of award-winning Canadian companies with profiles of each.

Business is becoming more global in outlook, at least in part because of the Internet. Do not limit yourself to Canadian sites. Many excellent non-Canadian sites offer relevant material for Canadian business. Just remember when using foreign-sourced information that taxation, regulations, and government programs are inapplicable, and allow for cultural and market differences when using the information obtained.

Many US sites are very useful. Business Week Enterprises is a comprehensive resource that offers current and archival stories on finance, technology, market research, and human resources. The *Entrepreneur Magazine* site is similarly broad in scope, and provides some sections especially for the home business operator, and a franchising guide giving extensive information on franchise trends and opportunities.

Small businesses can use the Internet as a networking tool (e-mail) to keep in constant contact with customers and suppliers. A second purpose is as an advertising medium. A properly designed web page can be a cost-effective means of advertising. A third and possibly as yet the broadest use is as a research tool to find information, products, suppliers, and business opportunities.

Use the search engines of your choice to begin. GDSourcing research and Retrieval maintains the Canada Site Search, a collection of search engines and directories for Canadian information. Yahoo.ca allows you to limit your search to Canadian sites only.

The American search engine Yahoo!'s Small Business site is extensive and provides search and link capabilities in areas that include business opportunities, financing, employment law, government agencies, publications, taxes, and women-owned businesses, as well as many others. It also provides links to recent articles on small business in publications such as *Fast Company, Inc.,* and *Entrepreneur* magazine. Information on building an e-commerce site, expanding a business globally, identifying target markets, analyzing competition, and conducting sales forecasts is also provided.

Part Three

Managing for Quality and Competitiveness

Chapter 7

Managerial Decision Making

Chapter Outline

Introduction

Nature of Management

Management Functions

Types of Management

Skills Needed by Managers

Where Do Managers Come From?

Decision Making

The Reality of Management

Objectives

After reading this chapter, you will be able to:

- Define management and explain its role in the achievement of organizational objectives.
- Describe the major functions of management.
- Distinguish among three levels of management and the concerns of managers at each level.
- Specify the skills managers need in order to be successful.
- Summarize the systematic approach to decision making used by many business managers.
- Recommend a new strategy to revive a struggling business.

The Art of Power:

Micheline Bouchard, P. Eng, President and Chief Executive Officer, Motorola Canada

As a six-year-old child growing up in Montreal, Micheline Bouchard's parents presented her with a Meccano set, a gift that sparked her interest in industrial design and resulted in her becoming a leading Canadian engineer and the first woman president of the of the Academy of Engineering. Ms Bouchard attributes this gift, the support she received at a young age, and a visit to l'École Polytechnique engineering department at age 14 as the deciding factors in her decision to pursue a career in engineering.

Joining Hydro Quebec after graduation in 1969, Ms Bouchard's dedication to excellence and leadership has resulted in many honours, awards, and achievements. Her corporate résumé includes vice president, business development, Canada, for Hewlett-Packard (Canada) Ltd.; vice president, business development, and vice president, marketing, for DMR Group; and vice president, management consulting services, at CGI Group. Ms Bouchard joined Motorola Canada Ltd. in 1998 where she served as president and chief executive officer, as well as corporate vice president of Motorola Inc. Her role at Motorola Canada was to build on Motorola's renewal in the country, to develop new joint business opportunities, and to enhance Motorola's presence in Canada.[1]

On October 22, 2001, Ms Bouchard addressed the Chatelaine Women of Influence Luncheon in Ottawa on "The Art of Power." She opened with this cautionary note for all would-be leaders, "Don't set any limits to your potential." Her address set out four steps to developing your personal "Art of Power." These steps are:

1. *Developing self-confidence.* Always look forward to future success and deal with rejection. Always preserve your enthusiasm and don't be afraid to make changes.

2. *Seeking situations where you can be a leader.* Remember that to increase your reputation as a leader your actions must be highly visible. Seek out leadership opportunities in both volunteer and paid positions.

3. *Having a vision.* Create a vision that others can buy into; this will help your organization achieve its goals.

4. *Developing a network.* No one has ever succeeded alone, so always build a network.[2]

Her extensive list of awards includes honorary degrees and the Order of Canada, and her outstanding business career are evidence of the value of Ms Bouchard's advice.

In March of 2001, Ms Bouchard left Motorola Canada to join Motorola US as corporate vice president and general manager of enterprise services organization.

Courtesy of Micheline Bouchard

INTRODUCTION

For any business—small or large—to achieve its objectives, it must have equipment and raw materials to turn into products to sell, employees to make and sell the products, and financial resources to purchase additional goods and services, pay employees, and generally operate the business. To accomplish this, it must also have one or more managers to plan, organize, staff, direct, and control the work that goes on.

This chapter introduces the field of management. It examines and surveys the various functions, levels, and areas of management in business. The skills that managers need for success and the steps that lead to effective decision making are also discussed.

NATURE OF MANAGEMENT

management

a process designed to achieve an organization's objectives by using its resources effectively and efficiently in a changing environment

managers

those individuals in organizations who make decisions about the use of resources and who are concerned with planning, organizing, leading, and controlling the organization's activities to reach its objectives

Management is a process designed to achieve an organization's objectives by using its resources effectively and efficiently in a changing environment. *Effectively* means having the intended result; *efficiently* means accomplishing the objectives with a minimum of resources. **Managers** make decisions about the use of the organization's resources and are concerned with planning, organizing, leading, and controlling the organization's activities so as to reach its objectives. Ann Moore, president of *People* magazine, has helped *People* become the world's most successful magazine, with annual revenues of US$1 billion. Similarly, Judy McGrath, president, has been instrumental in propelling MTV and M2 into 85 countries.[3] Management is universal. It takes place not only in businesses of all sizes, but also in government, the military, labour unions, hospitals, schools, and religious groups—any organization requiring the coordination of resources.

Every organization, in the pursuit of its objectives, must acquire resources (people, raw materials and equipment, money, and information) and coordinate their use to turn out a final good or service. The manager of a local movie theatre, for example, must make decisions about seating, projectors, sound equipment, screens, concession stands, and ticket booths. All this equipment must be in proper working condition. The manager must also make decisions about materials. There must be films to show, popcorn and candy to sell, and so on. To transform the physical resources into final products, the manager must also have human resources—employees to sell the tickets, run the concession stand, run the projector, and maintain the facilities. Finally, the manager needs adequate financial resources to pay for the essential activities; the primary source of funding is the money generated from sales of tickets and snacks. All these resources and activities must be coordinated and controlled if the theatre is to earn a profit. Organizations must have adequate resources of all types, and managers must carefully coordinate the use of these resources if they are to achieve the organization's objectives.

MANAGEMENT FUNCTIONS

To coordinate the use of resources so that the business can develop, make, and sell products, managers engage in a series of activities: planning, organizing, staffing, directing, and controlling (Figure 7.1). Although we describe each separately, these five functions are interrelated, and managers may perform two or more of them at the same time.

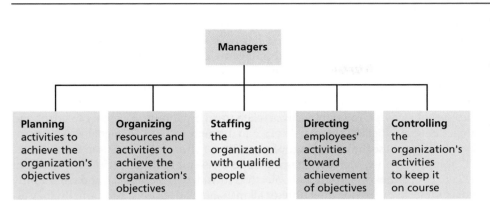

Figure 7.1

The Functions of Management

Planning

Planning, the process of determining the organization's objectives and deciding how to accomplish them is the first function of management. Planning is a crucial activity, for it designs the map that lays the groundwork for the other functions. It involves forecasting events and determining the best course of action from a set of options or choices. When Mercedes decided to build a manufacturing plant in the US, it engaged in extensive research and planning (assessing 150 sites in 30 states) to find the optimal location. The firm selected Birmingham, Alabama, based on the city's good infrastructure, quality of life, educated and motivated work force, strong business climate, and proximity to ports, a metropolitan area, and a university, as well as the state's efforts to attract Mercedes.[4] The plan itself specifies what should be done, by whom, where, when, and how. All businesses—from the smallest restaurant to the largest multinational corporation—need to develop plans for achieving success. But before an organization can plan a course of action, it must first determine what it wants to achieve.

Objectives. Objectives, the ends or results desired by the organization, derive from the organization's **mission,** which describes its fundamental purpose and basic philosophy. A photo lab, for example, might say that its mission is to provide customers with memories. To carry out its mission, the photo lab sets specific objectives relating to its mission, such as reducing development defects to less than 2 percent, introducing a selection of photo albums and frames for customers' use in displaying their photos, providing customers' proofs or negatives over the Internet, providing technical assistance, and so on. Cara Operations' vision statement is "To be the acknowledged leader in Canadian food services." This leads to their mission statement, "To build shareholder value through leadership in our business—achieving sustainable profitable growth with responsible use of capital." Canadian Tire expresses its vision simply: "To be the best at what our customers value most." The mission statement derived from this vision is "To be the first choice among Canadians in automotive, sports and leisure, and home products, providing total customer value through customer-driven service, focused assortments and competitive operations." Saturn's mission is "To market vehicles developed and manufactured in the United States that are world leaders in quality, cost, and customer satisfaction through the interaction of people, technology, and business systems and to transfer knowledge, technology, and experience through General Motors."[5]

planning
the process of determining the organization's objectives and deciding how to accomplish them; the first function of management

mission
the statement of an organization's fundamental purpose and basic philosophy

Cara Operations Ltd.
www.cara.com/

A business's objectives may be elaborate or simple. Common objectives relate to profit, competitive advantage, efficiency, and growth. Organizations with profit as a goal want to have money and assets left over after paying off business expenses. Objectives regarding competitive advantage are generally stated in terms of percentage of sales increase and market share, with the goal of increasing those figures. Efficiency objectives involve making the best use of the organization's resources. The photo lab's objective of holding defects to less than 2 percent is an example of an efficiency objective. Growth objectives relate to an organization's ability to adapt and to get new products to the marketplace in a timely fashion. The goal at Mercedes-Benz is to decrease the average age of its customers from the mid-50s to the mid-40s. To accomplish this, Mercedes has introduced several models that sell for less than US$40,000. Other organizational objectives include service, ethical, and community goals. Objectives provide direction for all managerial decisions; additionally, they establish criteria by which performance can be evaluated.

strategic plans

those plans that establish the long-range objectives and overall strategy or course of action by which a firm fulfills its mission

Plans.   There are three general types of plans for meeting objectives—strategic, tactical, and operational. A firm's highest managers develop its **strategic plans,** which establish the long-range objectives and overall strategy or course of action by which the firm fulfills its mission. Strategic plans generally cover periods ranging from 2 to 10 years or even longer. They include plans to add products, purchase companies, sell unprofitable segments of the business, issue stock, and move into international markets. For example, to support its goal to double oral health care sales by 2001, Gillette has introduced two new products, the CrossAction Toothbrush (priced at $4.99) and the SATINfloss dental floss line (priced at $2.99).[6] Strategic plans must take into account the organization's capabilities and resources, the changing business environment, and organizational objectives. Procter & Gamble's strategic plan, for example, calls for sales to double by the year 2005.[7]

tactical plans

short-range plans designed to implement the activities and objectives specified in the strategic plan

Tactical plans are short-range plans designed to implement the activities and objectives specified in the strategic plan. These plans, which usually cover a period of one year or less, help keep the organization on the course established in the strategic plan. In order to meet the objectives of its strategic plan to double sales by 2005, Procter & Gamble sales must increase by 7 percent annually.[8] Because tactical plans permit the organization to react to changes in the environment while continuing to focus on the company's overall strategy, management must periodically review and update them.

A retailing organization with a five-year strategic plan to invest $5 billion in 750 new retail stores may develop five tactical plans (each covering one year) specifying how much to spend to set up each new store, where to locate each new store, and when to open each new store. Tactical plans are designed to execute the overall strategic plan. Because of their short-term nature, they are easier to adjust or abandon if changes in the environment or the company's performance so warrant. Pizza Hut had to adjust its plans when the ailing Russian economy adversely affected sales. Pizza Hut, the first fast-food business to enter Russia over 10 years ago, closed its two Moscow locations.[9]

operational plans

very short-term plans that specify what actions individuals, work groups, or departments need to accomplish in order to achieve the tactical plan and ultimately the strategic plan

Operational plans are very short term and specify what actions specific individuals, work groups, or departments need to accomplish in order to achieve the tactical plan and ultimately the strategic plan. They may apply to just one month, week, or even day. For example, a work group may be assigned a weekly production quota in order to ensure there are sufficient products available to elevate market share (tactical goal) and ultimately help the firm be number one in its product category (strategic goal). Returning to our retail store example, operational plans may specify the schedule for opening one new store, hiring new employees, obtaining merchandise, training new employees, and opening for actual business.

Another element in planning is the idea of **crisis management** or **contingency planning,** which deals with potential disasters such as product tampering, oil spills, fire, earthquake, computer virus, or airplane crash. Many companies had to have plans to avoid computer problems caused by the year 2000. The crisis was termed the millennium bug or Y2K. More recently, the events of September 11, 2001, made it necessary for many companies to move into crisis management mode, both in the US and Canada. Sister companies and head offices of hundreds of companies located in the World Trade Center were closed permanently or damaged beyond repair. Of course, all companies hope such problems never happen, but businesses that have contingency plans tend to respond more effectively when problems occur than do businesses who lack such planning. Fisher Price agreed to make repairs on up to 10 million Barbie Jeeps, Big Jakes, and Extreme Machine cars sold over the past 14 years due to a Consumer Product Safety Commission recall. The product recall was the result of over 150 fires that burned nine children and caused US$300,000 in property damage to 22 homes. Crisis plans allowed Fisher Price to ready repair centres and communicate directly with consumers through an 800 number.[10]

Managers will often hold a meeting to form or to delegate tasks to an already existing team. Organizing the team in a flow chart or diagram can be the first step in recognizing who will be responsible for certain objectives.

©1999 PhotoDisc, Inc.

Many companies, including Ashland Oil, H.J. Heinz, and Johnson & Johnson, have crisis management teams to deal specifically with problems, permitting other managers to continue to focus on their regular duties. Some companies even hold regular disaster drills to ensure that their employees know how to respond when a crisis does occur. Crisis management plans generally cover maintaining business operations throughout a crisis and communicating with the public, employees, and officials about the nature of and the company's response to the problem. Communication is especially important to minimize panic and damaging rumours; it also demonstrates that the company is aware of the problem and plans to respond. In Nigeria, over 500 people were killed when a petroleum pipeline exploded. Pipeline and Products Marketing Company was quick to communicate with the public its belief that the explosion was caused by sabotage, not company or employee negligence. Sabotage of pipelines has occurred in this region in the past.[11] Incidents such as this highlight the importance of tactical planning for crises and the need to respond publicly and quickly when a disaster occurs.

crisis management or contingency planning
An element in planning that deals with potential disasters such as product tampering, oil spills, fire, earthquake, computer virus, or airplane crash

Organizing

Rarely are individuals in an organization able to achieve common goals without some form of structure. **Organizing** is the structuring of resources and activities to accomplish objectives in an efficient and effective manner. Managers organize by reviewing plans and determining what activities are necessary to implement them; then, they divide the work into small units and assign it to specific individuals, groups, or departments. As companies reorganize for greater efficiency, more often than not, they are organizing work into teams to handle core processes such as new product development instead of organizing around traditional departments such as marketing and production.

Organizing is important for several reasons. It helps create synergy, whereby the effect of a whole system equals more than that of its parts. It also establishes lines of authority, improves communication, helps avoid the duplication of resources, and can improve competitiveness by speeding up decision making. In an effort to boost sales and bring new products to market faster, Procter & Gamble has changed its corporate

organizing
the structuring of resources and activities to accomplish objectives in an efficient and effective manner

structure, shifting from regional business units to product-based global business units. Rather than overseeing a region, such as North America, senior executives now have global responsibility for a product category, such as laundry and cleaning.[12] Because organizing is so important, we'll take a closer look at it in Chapter 8.

Staffing

staffing
the hiring of people to carry out the work of the organization

Once managers have determined what work is to be done and how it is to be organized, they must ensure that the organization has enough employees with appropriate skills to do the work. Hiring people to carry out the work of the organization is known as **staffing.** Beyond recruiting people for positions within the firm, managers must determine what skills are needed for specific jobs, how to motivate and train employees to do their assigned jobs, how much to pay employees, what benefits to provide, and how to prepare employees for higher-level jobs in the firm at a later date. These elements of staffing will be explored in detail in Chapters 10 and 11.

Directing

directing
motivating and leading employees to achieve organizational objectives

Once the organization has been staffed, management must direct the employees. **Directing** is motivating and leading employees to achieve organizational objectives. All managers are involved in directing, but it is especially important for lower-level managers who interact daily with the employees operating the organization. For example, an assembly-line supervisor for Frito-Lay must ensure that her workers know how to use their equipment properly and have the resources needed to carry out their jobs, and she must motivate her workers to achieve their expected output of packaged snacks.

Managers motivate employees by providing incentives—such as the promise of a raise or promotion—for them to do a good job. But most workers want more than money from their jobs: They need to know that their employer values their ideas and input. Xerox understands the importance of recognizing its employee contributions and has created a program called "Chairman's Forum"—a three-day off-site retreat with the company chairman, Paul Allaire. The purpose of the program is to help employees become better problem solvers and to polish their executive skills. By providing this program for high-potential employees, Xerox has increased both satisfaction and retention.[13] Smart managers, therefore, ask workers to contribute ideas for reducing costs, making equipment more efficient, or even developing new products. This participation makes workers feel important, and the company benefits from new ideas. Magna International Inc., based in Aurora, Ontario, states that its Employee's Charter, introduced in 1988, "is the foundation of Magna's operating principles." The charter sets out the following principles:

- Job security
- A safe and healthful workplace
- Fair treatment
- Competitive wages and benefits
- Employee equity and profit participation
- Communication and information
- The Hotline

Under these principles, employees are provided a suggestion award program, open access to management and the right to express their views and concerns, 10 percent of corporate before-tax profits allocated to employees, wage and benefit surveys that allow employees to compare their total compensation package to competitors and other local firms, and a scholarship fund.[14] Recognition and appreciation are often the best motivators for employees. Employees who understand more about their impact on the financial success of the company may be motivated to work harder for that success, and managers who understand the needs and desires of workers can motivate their employees to work harder and more productively. The motivation of employees is discussed in detail in Chapter 10.

Controlling

Planning, organizing, staffing, and directing are all important to the success of an organization, whether its objective is earning a profit or something else. But what happens when a firm fails to reach its goals despite a strong planning effort? **Controlling** is the process of evaluating and correcting activities to keep the organization on course. Control involves five activities: (1) measuring performance, (2) comparing present performance with standards or objectives, (3) identifying deviations from the standards, (4) investigating the causes of deviations, and (5) taking corrective action when necessary.

Controlling and planning are closely linked. Planning establishes goals and standards for performance. By monitoring performance and comparing it with standards, managers can determine whether performance is on target. When performance is substandard, management must determine why and take appropriate actions to get the firm back on course. In short, the control function helps managers assess the success of their plans. When plans have not been successful, the control process facilitates revision of the plans. For example, John Roth, former president and CEO of Nortel Networks Corporation, was once the hero of high-tech investors. During that period, many were profiting from the rise in value of the shares of Canada's premier technology company. After the dot-com market crash and the loss of over 95 percent of the market value of Nortel shares (dropping to a low of $7.50 from a high of $211.35), Mr. Roth became the focal point for investors who felt they had been misled. Legal actions were launched against the corporation, also naming Mr. Roth. Many shareholders called for his resignation. In October 2001 Mr. Roth retired as president and chief executive officer, moving to the newly created position of vice chairman.[15]

The control process also helps managers deal with problems arising outside the firm. For example, if a firm is the subject of negative publicity, management should use the control process to determine why and to guide the firm's response.

controlling
the process of evaluating and correcting activities to keep the organization on course

TYPES OF MANAGEMENT

All managers—whether the sole proprietor of a small video store or the hundreds of managers of a large company such as Paramount Pictures—perform the five functions just discussed. In the case of the video store, the owner handles all the functions, but in a large company with more than one manager, responsibilities must be divided and delegated. This division of responsibility is generally achieved by establishing levels of management and areas of specialization—finance, marketing, and so on.

Levels of Management

As we have hinted, many organizations have multiple levels of management—top management, middle management, and first-line, or supervisory management. These levels form a pyramid, as shown in Figure 7.2. As the pyramid shape implies, there are generally more middle managers than top managers, and still more

Figure 7.2

Levels of Management

first-line managers. Very small organizations may have only one manager (typically, the owner), who assumes the responsibilities of all three levels. Large businesses have many managers at each level to coordinate the use of the organization's resources. Managers at all three levels perform all five management functions, but the amount of time they spend on each function varies, as we shall see (Figure 7.3).

Top Management. In businesses, **top managers** include the president and other top executives, such as the chief executive officer (CEO), chief financial officer (CFO), and chief operations officer (COO), who have overall responsibility for the organization. In government, top management refers to the prime minister, a premier, or a mayor; in education, a chancellor of a university or a county superintendent of education.

Top-level managers spend most of their time planning. They make the organization's strategic decisions, decisions that focus on an overall scheme or key idea for using resources to take advantage of opportunities. They decide whether to add products, acquire companies, sell unprofitable business segments, and move into foreign markets. Top managers also represent their company to the public and to government regulators. Richard Branson, the high-profile CEO of the Virgin company (transportation and entertainment), spoke on innovation at a United Kingdom conference. Branson spoke to 7,000 people through a satellite connection and highlighted the importance of people at every level in an organization. He noted, "It's the individual efforts that make the difference."[16] Given the importance and range of top management's decisions, top managers generally have many years of varied experience and command top salaries. Table 7.1 lists the 10 highest paid executives in Canada.

Some people question the pay disparity between top executives and average workers. The average CEO makes 728 times more than a minimum-wage worker in the US. If the minimum wage had risen at the same rate as executive pay, today's wage would be almost $41 an hour rather than $5.15.[17] In Canada companies are not required to disclose such information but indications are that a similar disparity

top managers

the president and other top executives of a business, such as the chief executive officer (CEO), chief financial officer (CFO), and chief operations officer (COO), who have overall responsibility for the organization

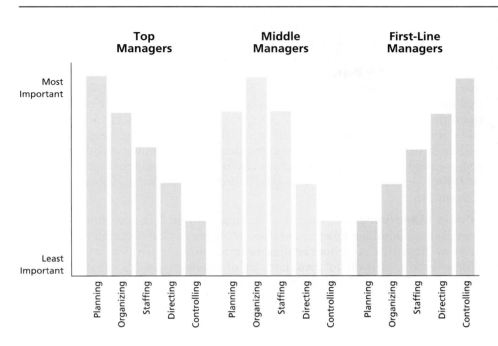

Figure 7.3

Importance of Management Functions to Managers in Each Level

exists. Some CEOs, however, limit the level of compensation that they and other top managers can receive to minimize the disparity between the levels of employees and to show social responsibility with respect to their compensation. Ben & Jerry's limits the ratio between the highest paid person in the company (the CEO) and the lowest paid employee in the company (an ice-cream server). Magna International Inc. sets out in its corporate constitution minimum percentages of before-tax profits to be distributed to employees, management, shareholders, research and development,

Magna International Inc.
www.magnaint.com/

Table 7.1

The 10 Highest Paid Executives in Canada

Source: "50 Best Paid Executives," *Report on Business Magazine,* July 2001.

Company	Executive	Total Compensation ($ in millions)
Nortel Networks Corporation	John A. Roth	$70.754
Nortel Networks Corporation	Clarence J. Chandran	59.303
Magna International Corporation	Frank Stronach	48.529
Nortel Networks Corporation	Frank A. Dunn	26.749
Alcan Aluminium Ltd.	Jacques Bougie	23.863
Biovail	Eugene Melnyk	21.073
CIBC, World Markets	David Cassie	18.732
Ballard Power Systems Inc.	Firoz Rasul	18.039
Ballard Power Systems Inc.	L.K. Smith	18.039
Manulife Financial Corp.	Dominic D'Alessandro	17.833

In 2000 women represented 35.4% of those employed in management, an increase of more than 20% since 1987.

and social responsibility (charitable, cultural, educational, and political purposes).

Work force diversity is an important issue in today's corporations. CEOs at 54 percent of the fastest growing firms in the US say that the presence of women and minority executives on their management teams is important in fuelling business growth. Over the past five years, firms that have more diversified senior management teams have grown 22 percent faster than other fast-track corporations.[18] After an aggressive effort that included internal advertising campaigns, surveys of current and former female employees, and female-friendly benefits, women now account for almost 33 percent of vice presidents and general managers in Procter & Gamble's advertising and brand management teams, up from 5 percent just a few years ago.[19] Diversity is explored in greater detail in Chapter 11.

Middle Management. Rather than making strategic decisions about the whole organization, **middle managers** are responsible for tactical planning that will implement the general guidelines established by top management. Thus, their responsibility is more narrowly focused than that of top managers. Middle managers are involved in the specific operations of the organization and spend more time organizing than other managers. In business, plant managers, division managers, and department managers make up middle management. The product manager for Tide laundry detergent at Procter & Gamble and the department chairperson in a university are middle managers. The ranks of middle managers have been shrinking as more and more companies downsize to be more productive.

middle managers
those members of an organization responsible for the tactical planning that implements the general guidelines established by top management

First-Line Management. Most people get their first managerial experience as **first-line managers,** who supervise workers and the daily operations of the organization. They are responsible for implementing the plans established by middle management and directing workers' daily performance on the job. They spend most of their time directing and controlling. Common titles for first-line managers are forepersons, supervisor, and office manager.

first-line managers
those who supervise both workers and the daily operations of an organization

Areas of Management

At each level, there are managers who specialize in the basic functional areas of business: finance, production and operations, human resources (personnel), marketing, and administration.

financial managers
those who deal with an organization's financial resources

Financial Management. **Financial managers,** as you might guess, deal with the organization's financial resources. Their focus is obtaining the money needed for the successful operation of the organization and using that money in accordance with organizational goals. Among the responsibilities of financial managers are projecting income and expenses over a specified period, determining short- and long-term financing needs and finding sources of financing to fill those needs, identifying and selecting appropriate ways to invest extra funds, monitoring the flow of financial resources, and protecting the financial resources of the organization. A financial manager at Subway, for example, may be asked to analyze the costs and revenues of a new sandwich product to determine its contribution to Subway's profitability. All organizations must have adequate financial resources to acquire the physical and human resources that are necessary to create goods and services. Consequently, financial resource management is of the utmost importance.

Electronic commerce offers numerous advantages to both consumers and business. E-commerce allows small and medium-sized enterprises to reach a wider market than traditional business models, and there can be significant overhead cost reductions and improved customer service. For the consumer, e-commerce facilitates research on both competing products and prices, it provides convenience, and in many instances it offers broader access to good deals.

Despite these advantages, the growth of e-commerce has not been as rapid as was widely forecast. The most apparent reason is the concern of both businesses and consumers with the confidentiality of information transferred on the Internet. Security of personal information has always been important, but the growth of electronic media has made users more aware of the dangers of poor security. People are now concerned with just what the government, banks, and businesses do with the information they collect.

In an effort to address concerns about trust and to further the growth of e-commerce in Canada, the federal government announced Canada's Electronic Commerce Strategy in 1998. The strategy focused on building trust in electronic markets through cryptography, authentification, privacy, and consumer confidence. An integral part of the strategy is enabling legislation. The first step in bringing Canada into line with international standards was passage of the Personal Information Protection and Electronic Documents Act in April 2000. Its provisions are being phased in from January 2001 to January 2004. This act complements the 1983 Privacy Act.

Attached to the act are the principles of fair information developed by the Canadian Standards Association. Briefly, the ten principles are:

- Accountability of organizations
- Identifying the purpose of information collected
- Consent of the information provider
- Limiting collection of information
- Limiting the use, retention, and disclosure of information collected
- Accuracy
- Safeguards
- Openness
- Individual access
- Challenging compliance

Individuals can complain to the Privacy Commissioner of Canada about violations of the Personal Information Act, and the commissioner may institute investigations without a complaint being filed.

If you are concerned about the accuracy of information the federal government has about you, you may seek information with a formal request under the Privacy Act. If you believe any of the information on file is inaccurate, you can send a letter to the Privacy Coordinator requesting that it be corrected. Even if the government does not alter the information, a note of your request must be attached to the file.

Legislation and voluntary codes of conduct will help develop the trust needed to resolve the concerns of potential e-commerce users. However, individuals must be knowledgeable of their rights and responsibilities and the remedies available to them. Caution and common sense will always be necessary.

Consider Ethics and Social Responsibility

The Need for Privacy

production and operations managers
those who develop and administer the activities involved in transforming resources into goods, services, and ideas ready for the marketplace

Production and Operations Management. **Production and operations managers** develop and administer the activities involved in transforming resources into goods, services, and ideas ready for the marketplace. Production and operations managers are typically involved in planning and designing production facilities, purchasing raw materials and supplies, managing inventory, scheduling processes to meet demand, and ensuring that products meet quality standards. Because no business can exist without the production of goods and services, production and operations managers are vital to an organization's success. Production and operations managers at Federal Express, for example, engage in the activities just mentioned to ensure that all customers' overnight packages are delivered on schedule.

human resources managers
those who handle the staffing function and deal with employees in a formalized manner

Human Resources Management. **Human resources managers** handle the staffing function and deal with employees in a formalized manner. Once known as personnel managers, they determine an organization's human resource needs; recruit and hire new employees; develop and administer employee benefits, training, and performance appraisal programs; and deal with government regulations concerning employment practices. For example, some companies recognize that their employees' health affects their health care costs. Therefore, more progressive companies provide health care facilities and outside health club memberships, encourage proper nutrition, and discourage smoking in an effort to improve employee health and lower the costs of providing health care benefits. DaimlerChrysler's human resources managers may develop educational programs to improve employees' health and thereby decrease DaimlerChrysler's cost of providing benefits.

marketing managers
those who are responsible for planning, pricing, and promoting products and making them available to customers

Marketing Management. **Marketing managers** are responsible for planning, pricing, and promoting products and making them available to customers. The marketing manager who oversees Sony televisions, for example, must make decisions regarding a new television's size, features, name, price, and packaging, as well as plan what type of stores to distribute the television through and the advertising campaign that will introduce the new television to consumers. Within the realm of marketing, there are several areas of specialization: product development and management, pricing, promotion, and distribution.

administrative managers
those who manage an entire business or a major segment of a business; they are not specialists but coordinate the activities of specialized managers

Administrative Management. **Administrative managers** are not specialists; rather they manage an entire business or a major segment of a business, such as the Cadillac Division of General Motors. Such managers coordinate the activities of specialized managers, which in the GM Cadillac Division would include marketing managers, production managers, and financial managers. Because of the broad nature of their responsibilities, administrative managers are often called general managers. However, this does not mean that administrative managers lack expertise in any particular area. Many top executives have risen through the ranks of financial management, production and operations management, or marketing management; but most top managers are actually administrative managers, employing skills in all areas of management.

SKILLS NEEDED BY MANAGERS

Managers are typically evaluated as to how effective and efficient they are. Managing effectively and efficiently requires certain skills—leadership, technical expertise, conceptual skills, analytical skills, and human relations skills.

Leadership

Leadership is the ability to influence employees to work toward organizational goals. A leader can stir people's emotions, raise their expectations, and take them in new directions.[20] The key traits of a successful leader include emotional stability, dominance, enthusiasm, conscientiousness, social boldness, tough-mindedness, self-assurance, and compulsiveness.[21] Figure 7.4 shows the personality traits that leaders of the future must have. Strong leaders manage and pay attention to the culture of their organizations and the needs of their customers. Table 7.2 lists the world's 10 most admired companies and their CEOs.

Managers can often be classified into three types based on their leadership style. *Autocratic leaders* make all the decisions and then tell employees what must be done and how to do it. They generally use their authority and economic rewards to get employees to comply with their directions. *Democratic leaders* involve their employees in decisions. The manager presents a situation and encourages his or her subordinates to express opinions and contribute ideas. The manager then considers the employees' points of view and makes the decision. *Free-rein leaders* let their employees work without much interference. The manager sets performance standards and allows employees to find their own ways to meet them. For this style to be effective, employees must know what the standards are, and they must be motivated to attain the standards. The free-rein style of leadership can be a powerful motivator because it demonstrates a great deal of trust and confidence in the employee.

The effectiveness of the autocratic, democratic, and free-rein styles depends on several factors. One consideration is the type of employees. An autocratic style of leadership is generally needed to stimulate unskilled, unmotivated employees; highly skilled, trained, and motivated employees may respond better to democratic or free-rein leaders. On the other hand, employees who have been involved in decision making generally require less supervision than those not similarly involved. Other considerations are the manager's abilities and the situation itself. When a situation requires quick decisions, an autocratic style of leadership may be best because the manager does not have to consider input from a lot of people. If a special task force must be set up to solve a quality-control problem, a normally democratic manager may give free rein to the task force. Many managers, however, are unable to use more than one style of

leadership
the ability to influence employees to work toward organizational goals

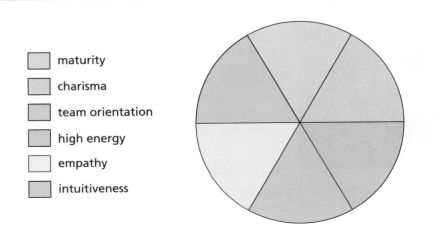

Figure 7.4

Personality Traits of Successful Leaders of the Future

Source: "Key Traits of Successful Leaders," **www. onlinewbc.org/docs/ manage/traits.html**, October 19, 1998.

- maturity
- charisma
- team orientation
- high energy
- empathy
- intuitiveness

Table 7.2

World's Most Admired Companies and Their CEOs

Source: Jeremy Kahn, "The World's Most Admired Companies," *Fortune,* October 26, 1998, pp. 207–226. Reprinted by special permission; copyright 1998, Time Inc.

Company	CEO
General Electric	Jack Welch
Coca-Cola	Doug Ivester
Microsoft	Bill Gates
Walt Disney	Michael Eisner
Intel	Craig Barrett
Hewlett-Packard	Lew Platt
Berkshire Hathaway	Warren Buffet
Pfizer	William C. Steere, Jr.
Sony	Norio Ohga
Dell Computer	Michael Dell

technical expertise
the specialized knowledge and training needed to perform jobs that are related to particular areas of management

conceptual skills
the ability to think in abstract terms and to see how parts fit together to form the whole

leadership. Some are unable to allow their subordinates to participate in decision making, let alone make any decisions. Thus, what leadership style is "best" depends on specific circumstances, and effective managers strive to adapt their leadership style as circumstances warrant. According to Noel Tichy, a professor at the University of Michigan, "Leadership is about change . . . The best way to get people to venture into unknown terrain is to make it desirable by taking them there in their imaginations.[22]

Technical Expertise

Managers need **technical expertise,** the specialized knowledge and training needed to perform jobs that are related to their area of management. Accounting managers need to be able to perform accounting jobs, and production managers need to be able to perform production jobs. Although a production manager may not actually perform a job, he or she needs technical expertise to train employees, answer questions, provide guidance, and solve problems. Technical skills are most needed by first-line managers and least critical to top-level managers.

Today, most organizations rely on computers to perform routine data processing, simplify complex calculations, organize and maintain vast amounts of information, and help managers make sound decisions. For this reason, many managers have found computer expertise to be a valuable skill. For the manager of the twenty-first century, such expertise will be critical.

Managers effectively organize and lead a young, diverse group at City Year, a nonprofit service organization.

Mary Crawford Samuelson

Conceptual Skills

Conceptual skills, the ability to think in abstract terms and to see how parts fit together to form the whole, are needed by all managers, but particularly top-level managers. Top management must be able to evaluate continually where the company will be in the future. Conceptual skills also involve the ability to think creatively. Recent scientific research has revealed that creative thinking, which is behind the development of many innovative products and ideas, including fibre optics and compact disks, can be learned. As a result, IBM, AT&T, GE, Hewlett-Packard, Intel, and other top firms are hiring creative consultants to teach their managers how to think creatively.

Analytical Skills

Analytical skills refer to the ability to identify relevant issues and recognize their importance, understand the relationships between them, and perceive the underlying causes of a situation. When managers have identified critical factors and causes, they can take appropriate action. All managers need to think logically, but this skill is probably most important to the success of top-level managers. Steve Jobs, the cofounder of Apple Computer, Inc., displayed well-honed analytical skills in recognizing the need for personal computers and then producing an inexpensive product to meet that need. He resurrected Apple again in the late 1990s as he instigated the introduction of the revolutionary iMac computer. Jobs recognized there was a large market for an easy-to-use and assemble computer predominantly designed for Internet use.[23]

Human Relations Skills

People skills, or **human relations skills,** are the ability to deal with people, both inside and outside the organization. Those who can relate to others, communicate well with others, understand the needs of others, and show a true appreciation for others are generally more successful than managers who lack human relations skills. People skills are especially important in hospitals, airline companies, banks, and other organizations that provide services. For example, at Southwest Airlines, every new employee attends "You, Southwest and Success," a day-long class designed to teach employees about the airline and its reputation for impeccable customer service. All employees in management positions at Southwest take mandatory leadership classes that address skills related to listening, staying in touch with employees, and handling change without compromising values. According to Libby Sartain, vice president for people, "We always tell our people to do what it takes to get the job done, and we always give them the tools."[24]

WHERE DO MANAGERS COME FROM?

Good managers are not born; they are made. An organization acquires managers in three ways: promoting employees from within, hiring managers from other organizations, and hiring managers graduating from universities.

Promoting people within the organization into management positions tends to increase motivation by showing employees that those who work hard and are competent can advance in the company. Internal promotion also provides managers who are already familiar with the company's goals and problems. Procter & Gamble prefers to promote managers from within, which creates managers who are familiar with the company's products and policies and builds company loyalty. Promoting from within, however, can lead to problems: It may limit innovation. The new manager may continue the practices and policies of previous managers. Thus it is vital

analytical skills
the ability to identify relevant issues, recognize their importance, understand the relationships between them, and perceive the underlying causes of a situation

Apple Computer, Inc.
www.apple.com/

human relations skills
the ability to deal with people, both inside and outside the organization

Enhance Productivity

Successful Meeting Styles

In the fast-paced business world, effective managers should be able to plan and run successful meetings. As the following examples show, different ideas and styles are effective in different companies.

At 9 AM every weekday morning, 80 of the Ritz-Carlton chain's top executives gather for a 10-minute, stand-up meeting in the hall outside the office of Horst Schulze, president and chief operating officer. Ten-minute daily shift meetings are held at each of the chain's hotels, as well. Each meeting addresses only one issue. Topics are scheduled on a monthly calendar and e-mailed to all participants. For those few minutes every day, the entire organization is focused on the same concern. The meetings are divided into three parts: topic introduction, customer service basics, and operational issues specific to each department. The fast-focus, part training, part operations, part philosophy meetings are effective. The Ritz-Carlton has been the only hotel company to receive the coveted Malcolm Baldrige National Quality Award.

Meetings at City Year, a nonprofit service organization of 1,200, begin with the simple phrase, "OK, hands up." One by one, hands are raised, conversation stops, and all is quiet. This start-up technique is particularly effective in large groups but works well in smaller ones, too. To keep any one person from dominating meetings, City Year employs "NOSTUESO"—which stands for "No One Speaks Twice Until Everybody Speaks Once." Meetings end with an assessment of the meeting itself, using "$+\Delta$." Effective points are recorded under the plus sign, and needed changes are written under the delta symbol.

Many other effective meeting styles have been developed, including using only one person as a note-taker, employing networked computers to aid in brainstorming sessions, and limiting session lengths. Successful meetings need prepared leaders and a standardized format so that participants know what to expect and are at ease. A suggested format includes:

1. Meeting start-up—Introduce topic.
2. Meeting body—Follow agenda.
3. Meeting wrap-up—Summarize decisions and required action.
4. Follow-up and preparation for next meeting—Prepare/distribute meeting minutes.[25]

for companies—even companies committed to promotion from within—to hire outside people from time to time to bring new ideas into the organization.

Finding managers with the skills, knowledge, and experience required to run an organization or department is sometimes difficult. Specialized executive employment agencies—sometimes called headhunters, recruiting managers, or executive search firms—can help locate candidates from other companies. The downside is that even though outside people can bring fresh ideas to a company, hiring them may cause resentment among existing employees as well as involve greater expense in relocating an individual to another city or province.

Schools and universities provide a large pool of potential managers, and entry-level applicants can be screened for their developmental potential. People with specialized management skills, such as those with an MBA (Master of Business Administration) degree, are especially good candidates. Some companies—including Telus and Sears Canada—provide special training programs for potential managers just graduating from college or university. McNeil Pharmaceuticals offers numerous experiential learning opportunities for secondary and post-secondary students through cooperative education placements and internships. McNeil also offers work placement programs for adult workers returning to the work force after a lengthy absence.

DECISION MAKING

Managers make many different kinds of decisions, such as hours of work, what employees to hire, what products to introduce, and what price to charge for a product. Decision making is important in all management functions and levels, whether the decisions are on a strategic, tactical, or operational level. A systematic approach using these six steps usually leads to more effective decision making: (1) recognizing and defining the decision situation; (2) developing options to resolve the situation; (3) analyzing the options; (4) selecting the best option; (5) implementing the decision; and (6) monitoring the consequences of the decision (Figure 7.5).

Recognizing and Defining the Decision Situation

The first step in decision making is recognizing and defining the situation. The situation may be negative—for example, huge losses on a particular product—or positive—for example, an opportunity to increase sales. In an effort to increase sales of Coke products in a grocery store in Texas, Henry Schimberg, chief executive of Coca-Cola Enterprises, planned 34 places where Coke products would be displayed, including the ice-cream aisle (Coke floats), the pizza freezer, frozen dinner display cases, the produce section, and even next to the live lobster tank.[26]

Situations calling for small-scale decisions often occur without warning. Situations requiring large-scale decisions, however, generally occur after some warning signals. Effective managers pay attention to such signals. Declining profits, small-scale losses in previous years, inventory buildup, and retailers' unwillingness to stock a product are signals that may warn of huge losses to come. Procter & Gamble found that shampoo buyers in Asia like to try different shampoos—which helped explain why the large containers of P&G shampoos did not sell. By shifting to single-use packets, P&G was better able to meet Asian consumers' needs.[27] If managers pay attention to such signals, problems can be contained.

Once a situation has been recognized, management must define it. Huge losses reveal a problem—for example, a failing product. One manager may define the situation

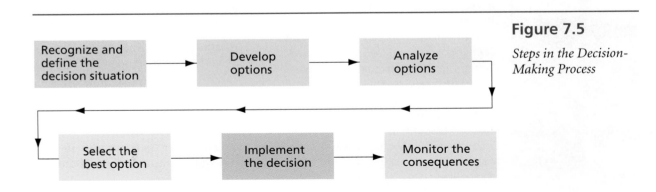

Figure 7.5

Steps in the Decision-Making Process

as a product quality problem; another may define it as a change in consumer preference. These two definitions may lead to vastly different solutions to the problem. The first manager, for example, may seek new sources of raw materials of better quality. The second manager may believe that the product has reached the end of its lifespan and decide to discontinue it. This example emphasizes the importance of carefully defining the problem rather than jumping to conclusions.

Developing Options

Once the decision situation has been recognized and defined, the next step is to develop a list of possible courses of action. The best lists include both standard courses of action and creative ones. As a general rule, more time and expertise are devoted to the development stage of decision making when the decision is of major importance. When the decision is of lesser importance, less time and expertise will be spent on this stage.

Analyzing Options

After developing a list of possible courses of action, management should analyze the practicality and appropriateness of each option. An option may be deemed impractical because of a lack of financial resources to implement it, legal restrictions, ethical and social responsibility considerations, authority constraints, technological constraints, economic limitations, or simply a lack of information and expertise to implement the option. For example, a small computer manufacturer may recognize an opportunity to introduce a new type of computer but lack the financial resources to do so. Other op-

---

Solve the Dilemma

Making Infinity Computers Competitive

?

Infinity Computers, Inc., produces notebook computers, which it sells through direct-mail catalog companies under the Infinity name and in some retail computer stores under their private brand names. Infinity's products are not significantly different from competitors', nor do they have extra product-enhancing features, although they are very price competitive. The strength of the company has been its CEO and president, George Anderson, and a highly motivated, loyal work force. The firm's weakness is having too many employees and too great a reliance on one product. The firm switched from the Intel 486 chip to the Pentium chip only after it saw a significant decline in 486 notebook computer sales.

Recognizing that the strategies that initially made the firm successful are no longer working effectively, Anderson wants to reorganize the company to make it more responsive and competitive and to cut costs. The threat of new technological developments and current competitive conditions could eliminate Infinity.

1. Evaluate Infinity's current situation and analyze its strengths and weaknesses.

2. Evaluate the opportunities for Infinity, including using its current strategy, and propose alternative strategies.

3. Suggest a plan for Infinity to compete successfully over the next 10 years.

If you've been reading business news over the last several years, you may be a bit skeptical about a career in management. Many companies have sharply reduced their management layers, especially at the middle level. However, management is, and will continue to be, one of the most crucial functions in the survival and growth of every business. Human Resources Development Canada (HRDC) in *Job Futures 2000* reports that labour market conditions for management occupations are rated as good and are expected to remain good through 2004. HRDC defines a good rating as indicating that the chances of finding work are relatively good, the chances of losing employment are relatively weak, and that earnings are relatively attractive. HRDC further reports that 17 percent of new jobs created between 1999 and 2004 are expected to be in management positions. Executive, administrative, and managerial workers make up one of the fastest growing job segments, and it is likely that many of these jobs will be services oriented.

Examples of industries projected to continue to employ managers at higher than average rates include hotels and restaurants, health care, public relations, and employment training. In the health care industry, for example, job growth will be driven by an aging population, insistence on better care, and breakthroughs in medical technology.

The TD Bank reports that industrial sectors expected to have growth rates greater than that of the economy as a whole in the decade ending 2010 are communications, business services, wholesale and retail trade, and mining. New jobs are usually generated in the fastest-growing industries in the economy. Some industries, because of productivity increases, can grow without generating a lot of new jobs.

The fastest-growing area of economic activity is expected to be private-sector services. By 2010 overall service-sector activity (including both private and public sectors) is expected to account for 70 percent of GDP. At that time, private-sector service activities are expected to account for 55 percent of GDP, up from 50 percent in 2000.[28] The government of Ontario confirms this outlook with the forecast that 50 percent of job creation in the province in the period from 2000 to 2005 will be in community, business, and personal services.[29]

Companies will continue to recruit and offer positions to candidates with training and experience in how to manage capital and human resources. In order to secure a good job once you graduate, you must have realistic expectations and be adequately prepared to join the working world. This preparation means that you must set realistic goals, adopt positive attitudes, and learn to communicate your skills effectively.[30]

Explore Your Career Options

Management Is Alive and Well

tions may be more practical for the computer company: It may consider selling its technology to another computer company that has adequate resources or it may allow itself to be purchased by a larger company that can introduce the new technology.

When assessing appropriateness, the decision maker should consider whether the proposed option adequately addresses the situation. When analyzing the consequences of an option, managers should consider the impact the option will have on the situation and on the organization as a whole. For example, when considering a price cut to boost sales, management must consider the consequences of the action on the organization's cash flow and consumers' reaction to the price change.

Selecting the Best Option

When all courses of action have been analyzed, management must select the best one. Selection is often a subjective procedure because many situations do not lend themselves to mathematical analysis. Of course, it is not always necessary to select only one option and reject all others; it may be possible to select and use several options.

Implementing the Decision

To deal with the situation at hand, the selected option or options must be put into action. Implementation can be fairly simple or very complex, depending on the nature of the decision. Effective implementation of a decision to abandon a product, close a plant, purchase a new business, or something similar requires planning. For example, when a product is dropped, managers must decide how to handle distributors and customers and what to do with the idle production facility. Additionally, they should anticipate resistance from people within the organization (people tend to resist change because they fear the unknown). Finally, management should be ready to deal with the unexpected consequences. No matter how well planned implementation is, unforseen problems will arise. Management must be ready to address these situations when they occur.

Monitoring the Consequences

After managers have implemented the decision, they must determine whether the decision has accomplished the desired result. Without proper monitoring, the consequences of decisions may not be known quickly enough to make efficient changes. If the desired result is achieved, management can reasonably conclude that it made a good decision. If the desired result is not achieved, further analysis is warranted. Was the decision simply wrong, or did the situation change? Should some other option have been implemented?

If the desired result is not achieved, management may discover that the situation was incorrectly defined from the beginning. That may require starting the decision-making process all over again. Finally, management may determine that the decision was good even though the desired results have not yet shown up or it may determine a flaw in the decision's implementation. In the latter case, management would not change the decision but would change the way in which it was implemented.

THE REALITY OF MANAGEMENT

Management is not a cut-and-dried process. There is no mathematical formula for managing an organization, although many managers passionately wish for one! Management is a widely varying process for achieving organizational goals. Managers plan, organize, staff, direct, and control, but management expert John P. Kotter says even these functions can be boiled down to two basic activities:

1. Figuring out what to do despite uncertainty, great diversity, and an enormous amount of potentially relevant information, and

2. Getting things done through a large and diverse set of people despite having little direct control over most of them.[31]

Managers spend as much as 75 percent of their time working with others—not only with subordinates but with bosses, people outside their hierarchy at work, and people outside the organization itself. In these interactions they discuss anything and everything remotely connected with their business. Henry Schimberg, CEO of Coca-Cola Enterprises, averages 100 store visits each week, covering vast territories in his Gulfstream-3.[32]

Managers spend a lot of time establishing and updating an agenda of goals and plans for carrying out their responsibilities. An **agenda** contains both specific and vague items, covering short-term goals and long-term objectives. Like a calendar, an agenda helps the manager figure out what must be done and how to get it done to meet the objectives set by the organization. Software tools, such as personal information managers (PIMs), can help managers manage their agendas, contacts, and time.

Managers also spend a lot of time **networking**—building relationships and sharing information with colleagues who can help them achieve the items on their agendas. Managers spend much of their time communicating with a variety of people and participating in activities that on the surface do not seem to have much to do with the goals of their organization. Nevertheless, these activities are crucial to getting the job done. Networks are not limited to immediate subordinates and bosses; they include other people in the company as well as customers, suppliers, and friends. These contacts provide managers with information and advice on diverse topics. Managers ask, persuade, and even intimidate members of their network in order to get information and to get things done. Networking helps managers carry out their responsibilities.

Finally, managers spend a great deal of time confronting the complex and difficult challenges of the business world today. Some of these challenges relate to rapidly changing technology (especially in production and information processing), increased scrutiny of individual and corporate ethics and social responsibility, the changing nature of the work force, new laws and regulations, increased global competition and more challenging foreign markets, declining educational standards (which may limit the skills and knowledge of the future labour and customer pool), and time itself—that is, making the best use of it. But such diverse issues cannot simply be plugged into a computer program that supplies correct, easy-to-apply solutions. It is only through creativity and imagination that managers can make effective decisions that benefit their organizations.

agenda
a calendar, containing both specific and vague items, that covers short-term goals and long-term objectives

networking
the building of relationships and sharing of information with colleagues who can help managers achieve the items on their agendas

Review Your Understanding

Define management and explain its role in the achievement of organizational objectives.

Management is a process designed to achieve an organization's objectives by using its resources effectively and efficiently in a changing environment. Managers make decisions about the use of the organization's resources and are concerned with planning, organizing, leading, and controlling the organization's activities so as to reach its objectives.

Describe the major functions of management.

Planning is the process of determining the organization's objectives and deciding how to accomplish them. Organizing is the structuring of resources and activities to accomplish those objectives efficiently and effectively. Staffing obtains people with the necessary skills to carry out the work of the company. Directing is motivating and leading employees to achieve organizational objectives. Controlling is the process of evaluating and correcting activities to keep the organization on course.

Distinguish among three levels of management and the concerns of managers at each level.

Top management is responsible for the whole organization and focuses primarily on strategic planning. Middle management develops plans for specific operating areas and carries out the general guidelines set by top management. First-line, or supervisory, management supervises the workers and day-to-day operations. Managers can also be categorized as to their area of responsibility: finance, production and operations, human resources, marketing, or administration.

Specify the skills managers need in order to be successful.

To be successful, managers need leadership skills (the ability to influence employees to work toward organizational goals), technical expertise (the specialized knowledge and training needed to perform a job), conceptual skills (the ability to think in abstract terms and see how parts fit together to form the whole), analytical skills (the ability to identify relevant issues and recognize their importance, understand the relationships between issues, and perceive the underlying causes of a situation), and human relations (people) skills.

Summarize the systematic approach to decision making used by many business managers.

A systematic approach to decision making follows these steps: recognizing and defining the situation, developing options, analyzing options, selecting the best option, implementing the decision, and monitoring the consequences.

Recommend a new strategy to revive a struggling business.

Using the decision-making process described in this chapter, analyze the struggling company's problems described in "Solve the Dilemma" and formulate a strategy to turn the company around and aim it toward future success.

Learn the Terms

administrative managers 168	human relations skills 171	organizing 161
agenda 177	human resources managers 168	planning 159
analytical skills 171	leadership 168	production and operations
conceptual skills 170	management 158	managers 168
controlling 163	managers 158	staffing 162
crisis management or	marketing managers 168	strategic plans 160
contingency planning 161	middle managers 166	tactical plans 160
directing 162	mission 159	technical expertise 170
financial managers 166	networking 177	top managers 164
first-line managers 166	operational plans 160	

Check Your Progress

1. Why is management so important, and what is its purpose?
2. Explain why the Canadian Cancer Society would need management, even though its goal is not profit related.
3. Why must a company have financial resources before it can use human and physical resources?
4. Name the five functions of management, and briefly describe each function.
5. Identify the three levels of management. What is the focus of managers at each level?
6. In what areas can managers specialize? From what area do top managers typically come?

7. What skills do managers need? Give examples of how managers use these skills to do their jobs.

8. What are three styles of leadership? Describe situations in which each style would be appropriate.

9. Explain the steps in the decision-making process.

10. What is the mathematical formula for perfect management? What do managers spend most of their time doing?

Get Involved

1. Give examples of the activities that each of the following managers might be involved in if he or she worked for the Coca-Cola Company:
   Financial manager
   Production and operations manager
   Personnel manager
   Marketing manager
   Administrative manager
   Foreperson

2. Interview a small sample of managers, attempting to include representatives from all three levels and all areas of management. Discuss their daily activities and relate these activities to the management functions of planning, organizing, staffing, directing, and controlling. What skills do the managers say they need to carry out their tasks?

3. You are a manager of a firm that manufactures conventional ovens. Over the past several years, sales of many of your products have declined; this year, your losses may be quite large. Using the steps of the decision-making process, briefly describe how you arrive at a strategy for correcting the situation.

Build Your Skills

Functions of Management

Background: Although the text describes each of the five management functions separately, you learned that these five functions are interrelated, and managers sometimes perform two or more of them at the same time. Here you will broaden your perspective of how these functions occur simultaneously in management activities.

Task:

1. Imagine that you are the manager in each scenario described in the table on the next page and you have to decide which management function(s) to use in each.

2. Mark your answers using the following codes:

Codes	Management Functions
P	Planning
O	Organizing
S	Staffing
D	Directing
C	Controlling

No.	Scenario	Answer(s)
1	Your group's work is centred around a project that is due in two months. Although everyone is working on the project, you have observed your employees involved in what you believe is excessive socializing and other time-filling behaviours. You decide to meet with the group to have them help you break down the project into smaller subprojects with mini-deadlines. You believe this will help keep the group members focused on the project and that the quality of the finished project will then reflect the true capabilities of your group.	
2	Your first impression of the new group you'll be managing is not too great. You tell your friend at dinner after your first day on the job: "Looks like I got a babysitting job instead of a management job."	
3	You call a meeting of your work group and begin it by letting them know that a major procedure used by the work group for the past two years is being significantly revamped, and your department will have to phase in the change during the next six weeks. You proceed by explaining to them the reasoning your boss gave you for this change. You then say, "Let's take the next 5 to 10 minutes to let you voice your reactions to this change." After 10 minutes elapse with the majority of comments being critical of the change, you say: "I appreciate each of you sharing your reactions; and I, too, recognize that *all* change creates problems. The way I see it, however, is that we can spend the remaining 45 minutes of our meeting focusing on why we don't want the change and why we don't think it's necessary; or we can work together to come up with viable solutions to solve the problems that implementing this change will most likely create." After about five more minutes of comments being exchanged, the consensus of the group is that the remainder of the meeting needs to be focused on how to deal with the potential problems the group anticipates having to deal with as the new procedure is implemented.	
4	You are preparing for the annual budget allocation meetings to be held in the plant manager's office next week. You determine to present a strong case to support your department getting money for some high-tech equipment that will help your employees do their jobs better. You will stand firm against any suggestions of budget cuts in your area.	
5	Early in your career you learned an important lesson about employee selection. One of the nurses on your floor unexpectedly quits. The other nurses were putting pressure on you to fill the position quickly because they were overworked even before the nurse left, and now things were really bad. After a hasty recruitment effort, you made a decision based on insufficient information. You ended up regretting your quick decision during the three months of problems that followed until you finally had to discharge the new hire. Since then, you have never let anybody pressure you into making a quick hiring decision.	

 **See for Yourself Videocase** **www.cbc.ca**

She-EO

"I'm road kill on the information highway,"[33] was Melanie Marshall's insightful comment about her experience in building her dot-com dream with NRG Group's She-EO Award.

"NRG and Hipikat have determined that it is in the mutual best interests of both companies to dissolve the incubation arrangement, which arose from the initial She-EO competition."[34] With this announcement in the NRG Group report of third quarter results at September 30, 2000, the dream of Melanie Marshall to build a new venue for the presentation of the international news with $250,000 of venture capital and expert guidance came to an end.

As of January 2002, the flash page for Melanie's idea is at www.hipikat.com but no news, international, interactive, or otherwise, is available.

This CBC Venture program outlines the beginning with much fanfare at the NRG 2000 She-EO Gala, celebrating what appeared to be a prize of $250,000 and the use of a new car to help bring the Hipikat concept to profitable reality. Melanie's winning proposal included a business plan, a revenue model, and presentations to venture capitalists. Despite this, little progress was made throughout the summer, during which Melanie spent much of her time being inter-viewed by various media about NRG and the She-EO concept. By fall, Internet-related businesses suffered a rapid decline in the stock market. NRG Group's shares had plummeted and revenue generation became the focus of the incubator group.

After termination of the incubation agreement, Melanie remained in the employ of NRG for a short period. By the end of 2000 one NRG founder, John Rae Grant, had resigned and the remaining founders, including Vicki Saunders, left in early 2001.

Questions

1. Based on your earlier study of business plans and the events described in the video, what areas of the business plan seem likely to have been lacking in detail.

2. The chapter lists three general types of plans. Evaluate the performance of Melanie Marshall and NRG in each of these areas.

3. In addition to planning, Figure 7.1 outlines four other areas of management. Evaluate the performance of the Hipikat team in each of those areas.

Source: *Venture*, show number 770, "She-EO," January 16, 2001, running time 14:26.

Remember to check out our Online Learning Centre at **www.mcgrawhill.ca/college/ferrell**.

Chapter 8

Organization, Teamwork, and Communication

Chapter Outline

Objectives

After reading this chapter, you will be able to:

- Define organizational structure and relate how organizational structures develop.
- Describe how specialization and departmentalization help an organization achieve its goals.
- Distinguish between groups and teams and identify the types of groups that exist in organizations.
- Determine how organizations assign responsibility for tasks and delegate authority.
- Compare and contrast some common forms of organizational structure.
- Describe how communication occurs in organizations.
- Analyze a business's use of teams.

Breakfast Communication at Cisco

Enter the World of Business

During their birthday month, each of the more than 7,000 employees at the headquarters of Cisco Systems receives an e-mail invitation to a birthday breakfast with CEO John Chambers. The US$22 billion networking giant has reinvented the power breakfast, giving everyone in the company a chance to offer candid feedback on any subject. No question or comment is off-limits, and Chambers admits there have been some difficult queries.

Chambers hosts up to 100 employees at the monthly, hour-and-a-half long breakfasts and fields between 20 and 50 questions during that time. He says the meetings are effective for discovering potential problems and possible opportunities. Chambers strives for an informal atmosphere by not using a podium and discouraging directors and vice presidents from attending since their presence might inhibit some employees' participation. Chambers views the breakfast sessions, as well as quarterly meetings with employees, as essential to his philosophy of open and direct communication.[1]

It is this management style that has helped propel a company of only US$70 million in sales when it went public in 1990, to the multi-billion dollar giant it is today. The creativity and commitment of the thousands of employees is critical to the success of the Internet hardware developer.

Courtesy of Cisco Corporation

INTRODUCTION

A business's structure determines how well it makes decisions and responds to problems, and it influences employees' attitudes toward their work. A suitable structure can minimize a business's costs and maximize its efficiency. For these reasons, many businesses, such as Motorola, Apple Computer, and Hewlett-Packard, have changed their organizational structures in recent years in an effort to enhance their profits and competitive edge.

Because a business's structure can so profoundly affect its success, this chapter will examine organizational structure in detail. First, we discuss the development of structure, including how tasks and responsibilities are organized through specialization and departmentalization. Next, we explore some of the forms organizational structure may take. Finally, we consider how an organization's culture affects its operations.

DEVELOPING ORGANIZATIONAL STRUCTURE

structure

the arrangement or relationship of positions within an organization

Structure is the arrangement or relationship of positions within an organization. Rarely is an organization, or any group of individuals working together, able to achieve common objectives without some form of structure, whether that structure is explicitly defined or only implied. A professional baseball team such as the Toronto Blue Jays is a business organization with an explicit formal structure that guides the team's activities so that it can increase game attendance, win games, and sell souvenirs such as T-shirts. But even an informal group playing softball for fun has an organization that specifies who will pitch, catch, coach, and so on. Getting people to work together efficiently and coordinating the skills of diverse individuals require careful planning. Developing appropriate organizational structures is therefore a major challenge for managers in both large and small organizations.

An organization's structure develops when managers assign work tasks and activities to specific individuals or work groups and coordinate the diverse activities required to reach the firm's objectives. When the Hudson's Bay Co., for example, has a sale, the store manager must work with the advertising department to make the public aware of the sale, with department managers to ensure that extra salespeople are scheduled to handle the increased customer traffic, and with merchandise buyers to ensure that enough sale merchandise is available to meet expected consumer demand. All the people occupying these positions must work together to achieve the store's objectives.

The best way to begin to understand how organizational structure develops is to consider the evolution of a new business such as a clothing store. At first, the business is a sole proprietorship in which the owner does everything—buys, prices, and displays the merchandise; does the accounting and tax records; and assists customers. As the business grows, the owner hires a salesperson and perhaps a merchandise buyer to help run the store. As the business continues to grow, the owner hires more salespeople. The growth and success of the business now require the owner to be away from the store frequently, meeting with suppliers, engaging in public relations, and attending trade shows. Thus, the owner must designate someone to manage the salespeople and maintain the accounting, payroll, and tax functions. If the owner decides to expand by opening more stores, still more managers will be needed. Figure 8.1 shows these stages of growth.

Growth requires organizing—the structuring of human, physical, and financial resources to achieve objectives in an effective and efficient manner. Growth necessitates hiring people who have specialized skills. With more people and greater spe-

Figure 8.1

The Evolution of a Clothing Store, Phases 1, 2 and 3

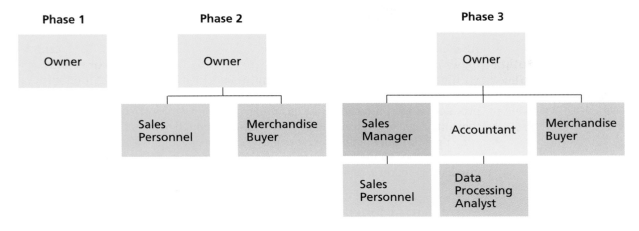

cialization, the organization needs to develop a formal structure to function efficiently. As we shall see, structuring an organization requires that management assign work tasks to specific individuals and departments and assign responsibility for the achievement of specific organizational objectives.

SPECIALIZATION

For a business to earn profits, its managers must first determine what activities are necessary to achieve the organization's objectives. Managers then break these activities down into specific tasks that can be handled by individual employees. This division of labour into small, specific tasks and the assignment of employees to do a single task is called **specialization.**

The rationale for specialization is efficiency. People can perform more efficiently if they master just one task rather than all tasks. In *Wealth of Nations*, eighteenth-century economist Adam Smith discussed specialization, using the manufacture of straight pins as an example. Individually, workers could produce 20 pins a day when each employee produced complete pins. Thus, 10 employees working independently of each other could produce 200 pins a day. However, when one worker drew the wire, another straightened it, a third cut it, and a fourth ground the point, 10 workers could produce 48,000 pins per day.[2]

Specialization means workers don't waste time shifting from one job to another, and training is easier. However, efficiency is not the only motivation for specialization. Specialization also occurs when the activities that must be performed within an organization are too numerous for one person to handle. Recall the example of the clothing store. When the business was young and small, the owner could do everything; but when the business grew, the owner needed help waiting on customers, keeping the books, and managing other business activities.

Overspecialization can have negative consequences. Employees may become bored and dissatisfied with their jobs, and the result of their unhappiness is likely to be poor quality work, more injuries, and high employee turnover. This has led

specialization

the division of labour into small, specific tasks and the assignment of employees to do a single task

Japanese automobile manufacturers to employ robots for many repetitive tasks. Although some degree of specialization is necessary for efficiency, because of differences in skills, abilities, and interests, all people are not equally suited for all jobs.

DEPARTMENTALIZATION

departmentalization
the grouping of jobs into working units usually called departments, units, groups, or divisions

After assigning specialized tasks to individuals, managers next organize workers doing similar jobs into groups to make them easier to manage. **Departmentalization** is the grouping of jobs into working units usually called departments, units, groups, or divisions. As we shall see, departments are commonly organized by function, product, geographic region, or customer (Figure 8.2). Most companies use more than one departmentalization plan to enhance productivity. For instance, many consumer goods manufacturers have departments for specific product lines (beverages, frozen dinners, canned goods, and so on) as well as departments dealing with legal, purchasing, finance, human resources, and other business functions.

Functional Departmentalization

functional departmentalization
the grouping of jobs that perform similar functional activities, such as finance, manufacturing, marketing, and human resources

Functional departmentalization groups jobs that perform similar functional activities, such as finance, manufacturing, marketing, and human resources. Each of these functions is managed by an expert in the work done by the department—an engineer supervises the production department; a financial executive supervises the finance department. A weakness of functional departmentalization is that, because it tends to emphasize departmental units rather than the organization as a whole, decision making that involves more than one department may be slow, and it requires greater coordination.

Product Departmentalization

product departmentalization
the organization of jobs in relation to the products of the firm

Product departmentalization, as you might guess, organizes jobs around the products of the firm. Procter & Gamble has global units, such as laundry and cleaning products, paper products, and health care products. Each division develops and implements its own product plans, monitors the results, and takes corrective action as necessary. Functional activities—production, finance, marketing, and others—are located within each product division. Consequently, organizing by products duplicates functions and resources and emphasizes the product rather than achievement of the organization's overall objectives. However, it simplifies decision making and helps coordinate all activities related to a product or product group.

Geographical Departmentalization

geographical departmentalization
the grouping of jobs according to geographic location, such as province, region, country, or continent

Geographical departmentalization groups jobs according to geographic location, such as a province, region, country, or continent. FritoLay, for example, is organized into four regional divisions, allowing the company to get closer to its customers and respond more quickly and efficiently to regional competitors. Multinational corporations often use a geographical approach because of vast differences between different regions. Coca-Cola, General Motors, and Caterpillar are organized by region. However, organizing by region requires a large administrative staff and control system to coordinate operations, and tasks are duplicated among the different regions.

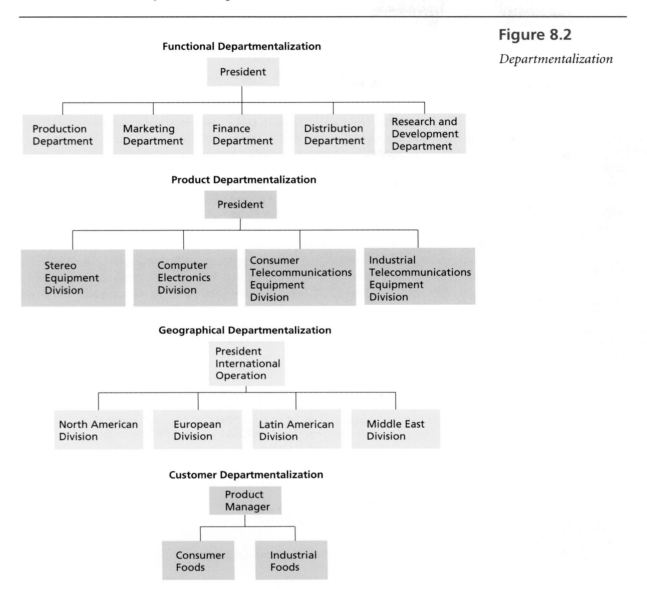

Figure 8.2

Departmentalization

Customer Departmentalization

Customer departmentalization arranges jobs around the needs of various types of customers. Banks, for example, typically have separate departments for commercial banking activities and for consumer or retail banking. This permits the bank to address the unique requirements of each group. Airlines, such as Air Canada and Lufthansa, provide prices and services customized for either business/frequent travellers or infrequent/vacationing customers. Customer departmentalization, like geographical departmentalization, does not focus on the organization as a whole and therefore requires a large administrative staff to coordinate the operations of the various groups.

customer departmentalization
the arrangement of jobs around the needs of various types of customers, such as commercial banking versus consumer banking services

THE ROLE OF GROUPS AND TEAMS IN ORGANIZATIONS

Regardless of how they are organized, most of the essential work of business occurs in individual work groups and teams, so we'll take a closer look at them now. Although some experts do not make a distinction between groups and teams, in recent years there has been a gradual shift toward an emphasis on teams and managing them to enhance individual and organizational success. Some experts now believe that highest productivity results only when groups become teams.[3]

Traditionally, a **group** has been defined as two or more individuals who communicate with one another, share a common identity, and have a common goal. A **team** is a small group whose members have complementary skills; have a common purpose, goals, and approach; and hold themselves mutually accountable.[4] All teams are groups, but not all groups are teams. Table 8.1 points out some important differences between them. Work groups emphasize individual work products, individual accountability, and even individual leadership. Salespeople working independently for the same company could be a work group. In contrast, work teams share leadership roles, have both individual and mutual accountability, and create collective work products. In other words, a work group's performance depends on what its members do as individuals, while a team's performance is based on creating a knowledge centre and a competency to work together to accomplish a goal.

group

two or more individuals who communicate with one another, share a common identity, and have a common goal

team

a small group whose members have complementary skills; have a common purpose, goals, and approach; and hold themselves mutually accountable

Benefits of Teams

Teams are becoming far more common in the Canadian workplace as businesses strive to enhance productivity and global competitiveness. In general, teams have the benefit of being able to pool members' knowledge and skills and make greater use of them than can individuals working alone. Teams can also create more solutions to problems than can individuals. Furthermore, team participation enhances employee

Table 8.1 *Differences between Groups and Teams*

Working Group	Team
Has strong, clearly focused leader	Has shared leadership roles
Has individual accountability	Has individual and group accountability
Has the same purpose as the broader organizational mission	Has a specific purpose that the team itself delivers
Creates individual work products	Creates collective work products
Runs efficient meetings	Encourages open-ended discussion and active problem-solving meetings
Measures its effectiveness indirectly by its effects on others (e.g., financial performance of the business)	Measures performance directly by assessing collective work products
Discusses, decides, and delegates	Discusses, decides, and does real work together

Source: Robert Gatewood, Robert Taylor, and O. C. Ferrell, *Management: Comprehension, Analysis, and Application,* 1995, p. 427. Copyright © 1995 Richard D. Irwin, a Times Mirror Higher Education Group, Inc., company. Reproduced with permission of the McGraw-Hill Companies.

acceptance of, understanding of, and commitment to team goals. Teams motivate workers by providing internal rewards in the form of an enhanced sense of accomplishment for employees as they achieve more, and external rewards in the form of praise and certain perks. Consequently, they can help get workers more involved. They can help companies be more innovative, and they can boost productivity and cut costs. Research In Motion (RIM) builds wireless systems for Internet access, among other digital offerings, based out of its Kitchener-Waterloo head offices. Founded in 1984, RIM has grown to 1,400 employees from 200 in 1998. The co-CEOs, Mike Lazaridis and Jim Balsillie, rely heavily on the different highly expert teams to develop the products and software. At the same time, they also turn to their strong marketing

Research In Motion's co-CEOs, Mike Lazaridis (right) and Jim Balsillie, ensure that their expert teams remain well motivated, boosting creativity and innovation in the company.

Courtesy of Research In Motion Limited.

and sales teams to promote current products around the world while developing new opportunities. The creativity of the teams is crucial.[5]

Types of Groups

The type of groups an organization establishes depends on the tasks it needs to accomplish and the situation it faces. Some specific kinds of groups and teams include committees, task forces, project teams, product-development teams, quality-assurance teams, and self-directed work teams.

Committees. A **committee** is usually a permanent, formal group that does some specific task. For example, many firms have a compensation or finance committee to examine the effectiveness of these areas of operation as well as the need for possible changes. Ethics committees are formed to develop and revise codes of ethics, suggest methods for implementing ethical standards, and review specific issues and concerns.

Task Forces. A **task force** is a temporary group of employees responsible for bringing about a particular change. They typically come from across all departments and levels of an organization. Task force membership is usually based on expertise rather than organizational position. A task force was formed at Deloitte & Touche, a provider of accounting, auditing, tax, and management consulting services, to investigate why women were not represented at the partner level and why women left the firm at a higher rate than men. Based on the findings and recommendations of the task force, an initiative was launched that resulted in a dramatic increase in the number of women in key leadership positions (tripling in four years) and a reduction in the turnover rate. A savings of US$10 million was associated with lowering the turnover rate.[6]

Project Teams. Project teams are similar to task forces, but normally they run their operation and have total control of a specific work project. Like task forces, their membership is likely to cut across the firm's hierarchy and be composed of people from different functional areas. They are almost always temporary, although a large project, such as designing and building a new airplane at Boeing Corporation, may last for years. Mervyn's, a department store chain with 32,000 employees and 270 locations in the United States, uses a project team to help with crises that occur in the

committee
a permanent, formal group that performs a specific task

task force
a temporary group of employees responsible for bringing about a particular change

Deloitte & Touche
www.deloitte.ca/

project teams
groups similar to task forces which normally run their operation and have total control of a specific work project

**Enhance
Productivity**

*War Games to
Learn TLC*

Teamwork, leadership, and communication skills (or TLC) are especially important in maintaining coordination and commitment to an organization's goals. To help employees become more involved and to boost productivity, many firms, including Domino's Pizza, are sending their managers to Leading Concepts Boot Camp, a military style camp run by former US Army Rangers. The purpose of the camp is to help managers improve their TLC. Approximately 18 Domino's managers attend the camp at a time, with days beginning at the crack of dawn and ending around 2 a.m. Much of the intervening time is spent running through the woods and jumping on the ground to avoid being hit by "enemy" paint balls. Camp participants wear army fatigues and combat boots and eat army rations. Leading Concepts believes that the war games will help participants develop superior TLC by forcing them to work together to "survive."

The camp teaches "soldiers" to step into a new role at a moment's notice. Most Domino's managers who complete the program promise to cross-train their employees as soon as they return to work, and most believe the camp makes them better communicators. Many Domino's managers who attend the boot camp have been promoted to high-level supervisory positions. The company is hard-pressed to find anyone who doesn't give the experience a positive assessment. The experience motivates managers to work harder, listen more, and be judged as part of a team rather than an individual. In general, managers link their boot camp experience with increased teamwork and improved productivity.[7]

**product-
development
teams**
a specific type of project team formed to devise, design, and implement a new product

high-pressure retail environment. The project team consists of 19 managers who each have expertise in at least one specific area—buying, merchandising, or advertising. The group is highly trained and can be sent anywhere, anytime it is needed. Assignments can be as short as one week or as long as six months.[8]

Product-development teams are a special type of project team formed to devise, design, and implement a new product. Sometimes product-development teams exist within a functional area—research and development—but now they more frequently include people from numerous functional areas and may even include customers to help ensure that the end product meets the customers' needs.

**quality-assurance
teams (or quality
circles)**
small groups of workers brought together from throughout the organization to solve specific quality, productivity, or service problems

Quality-Assurance Teams. **Quality-assurance teams,** sometimes called **quality circles,** are fairly small groups of workers brought together from throughout the organization to solve specific quality, productivity, or service problems. Although the "quality circle" term is not as popular as it once was, the concern about quality is stronger than ever. The use of teams to address quality issues will no doubt continue to increase throughout the business world. Quality circles are addressed in more detail in Chapter 10.

**self-directed work
team (SDWT)**
a group of employees responsible for an entire work process or segment that delivers a product to an internal or external customer

Self-Directed Work Teams. A **self-directed work team (SDWT)** is a group of employees responsible for an entire work process or segment that delivers a product to an internal or external customer.[9] Sometimes called self-managed teams or autonomous work groups, SDWTs reduce the need for extra layers of management and thus can help control costs. SDWTs also permit the flexibility to change rapidly to meet the competition or respond to customer needs. The defining characteristic of an SDWT is the extent to which it is empowered or given authority to make and implement work decisions. Thus, SDWTs are designed to give employees a feeling of "ownership" of a whole job. With shared team responsibility for work outcomes, team members often have broader job assignments and cross-train to master other jobs, thus permitting greater team flexibility.

ASSIGNING RESPONSIBILITY AND DELEGATING AUTHORITY

After all workers and work groups have been assigned their tasks, they must be given the responsibility to carry out their assigned activities. This requires that management determine the extent to which responsibility will be delegated throughout the organization, the chain of command of authority, and how many employees will report to each manager.

Delegation of Authority

Delegation of authority means not only giving tasks to employees but also empowering them to make commitments, use resources, and take whatever actions are necessary to carry out those tasks. Let's say a marketing manager at Campbell Soup Company has assigned an employee to design a new package that is less wasteful (more environmentally responsible) than the current package for one of the company's frozen dinner lines. To carry out the assignment, the employee needs access to information and the authority to make certain decisions on packaging materials, costs, and so on. Without the authority to carry out the assigned task, the employee would have to get the approval of others for every decision and every request for materials. As a business grows, so do the number and complexity of decisions that must be made; no one manager can handle them all. Hotels such as Westin Hotels and Resorts and the Ritz-Carlton give authority to service providers, including front desk personnel, to make service decisions such as moving a guest to another room or providing a discount to guests who experience a problem at the hotel. Delegation of authority frees a manager to concentrate on larger issues, such as planning or dealing with problems and opportunities.

Delegation also gives a **responsibility,** or obligation, to employees to carry out assigned tasks satisfactorily and holds them accountable for the proper execution of their assigned work. The principle of **accountability** means that employees who accept an assignment and the authority to carry it out are answerable to a superior for the outcome. Returning to the Campbell Soup example, if the packaging design prepared by the employee is unacceptable or late, the employee must accept the blame. If the new design is innovative, attractive, and cost-efficient, as well as environmentally responsible, or is completed ahead of schedule, the employee will accept the credit.

The process of delegating authority establishes a pattern of relationships and accountability between a superior and his or her subordinates. The president of a firm delegates responsibility for all marketing activities to the vice president of marketing. The vice president accepts this responsibility and has the authority to obtain all relevant information, make certain decisions, and delegate any or all activities to his or her subordinates. The vice president, in turn, delegates all advertising activities to the advertising manager, all sales activities to the sales manager, and so on. These managers then delegate specific tasks to their subordinates. However, the act of delegating authority to a subordinate does not relieve the superior of accountability for the delegated job. Even though the vice president of marketing delegates work to

delegation of authority
giving employees not only tasks, but also the power to make commitments, use resources, and take whatever actions are necessary to carry out those tasks

responsibility
the obligation, placed on employees through delegation, to perform assigned tasks satisfactorily and be held accountable for the proper execution of work

accountability
the principle that employees who accept an assignment and the authority to carry it out are answerable to a superior for the outcome

organizational chart

a visual display of the organizational structure, lines of authority (chain of command), staff relationships, permanent committee arrangements, and lines of communication

centralized organization

a structure in which authority is concentrated at the top, and very little decision-making authority is delegated to lower levels

subordinates, he or she is still ultimately accountable to the president for all marketing activities.

These authority and responsibility relationships are often depicted graphically in an **organizational chart** showing organizational structure, lines of authority (chain of command), staff relationships, permanent committee arrangements, and lines of communication. Figure 8.2 (page 187) shows partial organizational charts that illustrate departmentalization.

Degree of Centralization

The extent to which authority is delegated throughout an organization determines its degree of centralization.

Centralized Organizations. In a **centralized organization,** authority is concentrated at the top, and very little decision-making authority is delegated to lower levels. Although decision-making authority in centralized organizations rests with top levels of management, a vast amount of responsibility for carrying out daily and routine procedures is delegated to even the lowest levels of the organization. Many government organizations, including the Canadian Armed Forces, Canada Post, and the Canada Customs and Revenue Agency, are centralized.

Businesses tend to be more centralized when the decisions to be made are risky and when low-level managers are not highly skilled in decision making. In the banking industry, for example, authority to make routine car loans is given to all loan managers, while the authority to make high-risk loans, such as for a large residential development, may be restricted to upper-level loan officers.

Overcentralization can cause serious problems for a company, in part because it may take longer for the organization as a whole to implement decisions and to respond to changes and problems on a regional scale. McDonald's, for example, was one of the last chains to introduce a chicken sandwich because of the amount of research, development, test marketing, and layers of approval the product had to go through. In the area of toys, most highly centralized organizations, such as Toys "R" Us, have been very successful. Increasing competition from more decentralized competitors such as Wal-Mart and other toy chains could change their status, however.

decentralized organization

an organization in which decision-making authority is delegated as far down the chain of command as possible

Decentralized Organizations. A **decentralized organization** is one in which decision-making authority is delegated as far down the chain of command as possible. Decentralization is characteristic of organizations that operate in complex, unpredictable environments. Businesses that face intense competition often decentralize to improve responsiveness and enhance creativity. Lower-level managers who interact with the external environment often develop a good understanding of it and thus are able to react quickly to changes.

Delegating authority to lower levels of managers may increase the organization's productivity. Decentralization requires that lower-level managers have strong decision-making skills. In recent years the trend has been toward more decentralized organizations, and some of the largest and most successful companies, including GE, Sears, and IBM, have decentralized decision-making authority. Nonprofit organizations benefit from decentralization as well. The Salvation Army, a charitable global organization with locations in 103 countries, is highly decentralized. Each country is divided into basic units, and each is expected to finance all its activities through local fund-raising efforts. The Salvation Army is successful in meeting its goal to help people, with 86 cents of every $1 spent actually going toward this purpose.[10]

Salvation Army
www.salvationarmy.org/

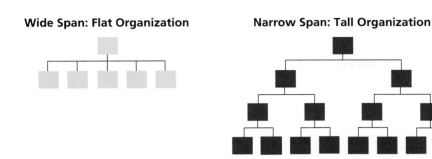

Wide Span: Flat Organization   **Narrow Span: Tall Organization**

Figure 8.3

Span of Management: Wide Span and Narrow Span

Span of Management

How many subordinates should a manager manage? There is no simple answer. Experts generally agree, however, that top managers should not directly supervise more than four to eight people, while lower-level managers who supervise routine tasks are capable of managing a much larger number of subordinates. For example, the manager of the finance department may supervise 25 employees, whereas the vice president of finance may supervise only five managers. **Span of management** refers to the number of subordinates who report to a particular manager. A *wide span of management* exists when a manager directly supervises a very large number of employees. A *narrow span of management* exists when a manager directly supervises only a few subordinates (Figure 8.3).

span of management
the number of subordinates who report to a particular manager

Should the span of management be wide or narrow? To answer this question, several factors need to be considered. A narrow span of management is appropriate when superiors and subordinates are not in close proximity, the manager has many responsibilities in addition to the supervision, the interaction between superiors and subordinates is frequent, and problems are common. However, when superiors and subordinates are located close to one another, the manager has few responsibilities other than supervision, the level of interaction between superiors and subordinates is low, few problems arise, subordinates are highly competent, and a set of specific operating procedures governs the activities of managers and their subordinates, a wide span of management will be more appropriate. Narrow spans of management are typical in centralized organizations, while wide spans of management are more common in decentralized firms.

Organizational Layers. Complementing the concept of span of management is **organizational layers,** the levels of management in an organization.

A company with many layers of managers is considered tall; in a tall organization, the span of management is narrow (see Figure 8.3). Because each manager supervises only a few subordinates, many layers of management are necessary to carry out the operations of the business. McDonald's, for example, has a tall organization with many layers, including store managers, district managers, regional managers, and functional managers (finance, marketing, and so on), as well as a chief executive officer and many vice presidents. Because there are more managers in tall organizations than in flat organizations, administrative costs are usually higher. Communication is slower because information must pass through many layers.

organizational layers
the levels of management in an organization

Organizations with few layers are flat and have wide spans of management. When managers supervise a large number of employees, fewer management layers are needed to conduct the organization's activities. Managers in flat organizations typically perform more administrative duties than managers in tall organizations because there are fewer of them. They also spend more time supervising and working with subordinates.

Many of the companies that decentralized during the 1980s and 1990s also flattened their structures and widened their spans of management, often by eliminating layers of middle management. Many corporations, including Avon, AT&T, and Ford Motor Company, did so to reduce costs, speed decision making, and boost overall productivity.

Downsizing Organizations

downsizing

the elimination of significant numbers of employees from an organization in order to reduce costs

Downsizing, the elimination of significant numbers of employees from an organization, has been a pervasive and much-talked-about trend. In a three-year period, 8 million US workers, or 1 out of every 15 adult job holders, were pushed out of their jobs involuntarily.[11]

Downsizing makes tall organizations flatter as companies lay off large numbers of employees, widen spans of management, and decentralize to reduce costs and increase responsiveness and creativity in the face of increasing global competition. Whether it is called downsizing, rightsizing, trimming the fat, or the new reality in business, the implications of downsizing have been dramatic. Downsizing has helped numerous firms become more profitable (or become profitable after lengthy losses) in a short period of time. Gillette has cut 11 percent of its work force (4,700 jobs) and closed 14 factories, 12 warehouses, and 30 offices worldwide. Annual savings of US$200 million are expected.[12]

Downsizing, however, also has painful consequences. Obviously, the biggest casualty is those who lose their jobs, along with their incomes, insurance, and pensions. Some find new jobs quickly; others do not. Another victim is the morale of the employees at downsized firms who get to keep their jobs.

Some firms attempt to deal with downsizing in a positive manner. For example, Cisco Systems offered six months pay to those affected by the downsizing in April 2001, regardless of their work history. The employees left behind in a downsizing often feel more insecure, angry, and sad, and their productivity may decline as a result, the opposite of the effect sought. As a result, downsizing as a method for increasing profits is a controversial topic.

Nortel and JDS Uniphase have laid off thousands of workers worldwide in an attempt to reduce losses and trim off losing divisions, and the damage can be significant to affected communities as well. In Ottawa, where both companies shed over 5,000 jobs in 2000–2001, this could have been a major blow to the remaining people, but the other employers are actually benefiting. The federal government had been downsizing itself and is now facing a labour shortage, finding itself looking for young energetic people to either work as consultants or as direct employees to replace retirees or facilitate the need for more services for a growing and aging nation. Other small technology companies that could not previously compete with the Nortels for high-priced talent are now able to attract those persons they need to grow their businesses and consulting firms.

FORMS OF ORGANIZATIONAL STRUCTURE

Along with assigning tasks and the responsibility for carrying them out, managers must consider how to structure their authority relationships—that is, what structure the organization itself will have and how it will appear on the organizational chart.

Quest Star (QS), which manufactures quality stereo loudspeakers, wants to improve its ability to compete against Japanese firms. Accordingly, the company has launched a comprehensive quality-improvement program for its Montreal plant. The QS Intracommunication Leadership Initiative (ILI) has flattened the layers of management. The program uses teams and peer pressure to accomplish the plant's goals instead of multiple management layers with their limited opportunities for communication. Under the initiative, employees make all decisions within the boundaries of their responsibilities, and they elect team representatives to coordinate with other teams. Teams are also assigned tasks ranging from establishing policies to evaluating on-the-job safety.

However, employees who are not self-motivated team players are having difficulty getting used to their peers' authority within this system. Upper-level managers face stress and frustration because they must train workers to supervise themselves.

1. What techniques or skills should an employee have to assume a leadership role within a work group?

2. If each work group has a team representative, what problems will be faced in supervising these representatives?

3. Evaluate the pros and cons of the system developed by QS.

Common forms of organization include line structure, line-and-staff structure, multidivisional structure, and matrix structure.

Line Structure

The simplest organizational structure, **line structure,** has direct lines of authority that extend from the top manager to employees at the lowest level of the organization. For example, a convenience store employee may report to an assistant manager, who reports to the store manager, who reports to a regional manager, or, in an independent store, directly to the owner (Figure 8.4). This structure has a clear chain of command, which enables managers to make decisions quickly. A mid-level manager facing a decision must consult only one person, his or her immediate supervisor. However, this structure requires that managers possess a wide range of knowledge and skills. They are responsible for a variety of activities and must be knowledgeable about them all. Line structures are most common in small businesses.

line structure
the simplest organizational structure in which direct lines of authority extend from the top manager to the lowest level of the organization

Figure 8.4

Line Structure

Convenience Store

| Owner | — | Manager | — | Assistant Manager | — | Hourly Employee |

Line-and-Staff Structure

line-and-staff structure

a structure having a traditional line relationship between superiors and subordinates and also specialized managers—called staff managers—who are available to assist line managers

The **line-and-staff structure** has a traditional line relationship between superiors and subordinates, and specialized managers—called staff managers—are available to assist line managers (Figure 8.5). Line managers can focus on their area of expertise in the operation of the business, while staff managers provide advice and support to line departments on specialized matters such as finance, engineering, human resources, and the law. Staff managers do not have direct authority over line managers or over the line manager's subordinates, but they do have direct authority over subordinates in their own departments. However, line-and-staff organizations may experience problems with overstaffing and ambiguous lines of communication. Additionally, employees may become frustrated because they lack the authority to carry out certain decisions.

Multidivisional Structure

multidivisional structure

a structure that organizes departments into larger groups called divisions

As companies grow and diversify, traditional line structures become difficult to coordinate, making communication difficult and decision making slow.[13] When the weaknesses of the structure—the "turf wars," miscommunication, and working at cross-purposes—exceed the benefits, growing firms tend to restructure, often into the divisionalized form. A **multidivisional structure** organizes departments into larger groups called divisions. Just as departments might be formed on the basis of

Figure 8.5

Line-and-Staff Structure

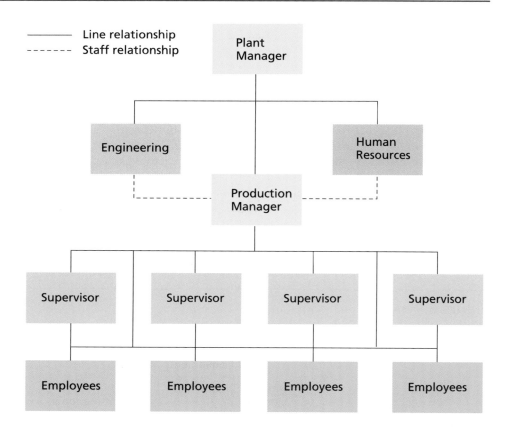

geography, customer, product, or a combination of these, so divisions can be formed based on any of these methods of organizing. For example, the Walt Disney Company, whose organizational chart is shown in Figure 8.6, has divisions for its theme parks, movie and television studios, and consumer products. Within each of these divisions, departments may be organized by product, geographic region, function, or some combination of all three.

Multidivisional structures permit delegation of decision-making authority, allowing divisional and department managers to specialize. They allow those closest to the action to make the decisions that will affect them. Delegation of authority and divisionalized work also mean that better decisions are made faster, and they tend to be more innovative. Most importantly, by focusing each division on a common region, product, or customer, each is more likely to provide products that meet the needs of its particular customers. However, the divisional structure inevitably creates work duplication, which makes it more difficult to realize the economies of scale that result from grouping functions together.

Disney Online
www.disney.go.com

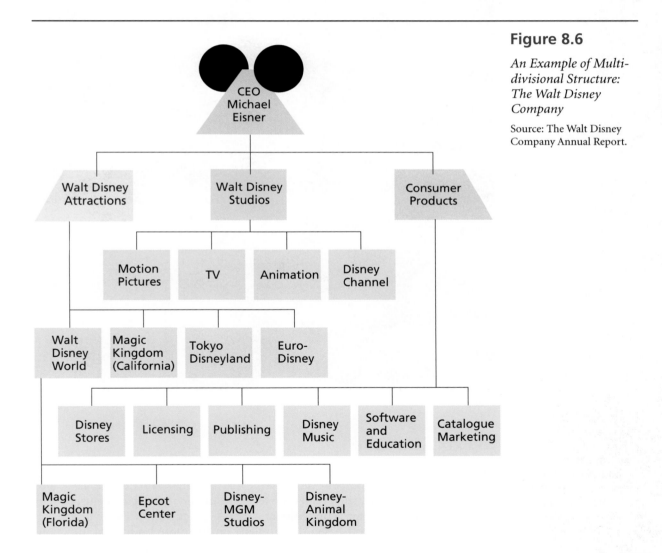

Figure 8.6

An Example of Multidivisional Structure: The Walt Disney Company

Source: The Walt Disney Company Annual Report.

matrix structure
a structure that sets up teams from different departments, thereby creating two or more intersecting lines of authority; also called a project-management structure

Matrix Structure

Another structure that attempts to address issues that arise with growth, diversification, productivity, and competitiveness, is the matrix. A **matrix structure,** also called a project-management structure, sets up teams from different departments, thereby creating two or more intersecting lines of authority (Figure 8.7). The matrix structure superimposes project-based departments on the more traditional, function-

Figure 8.7

Matrix Structure

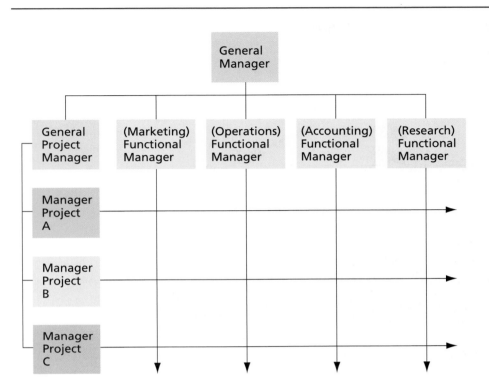

based departments. Project teams bring together specialists from a variety of areas to work together on a single project, such as developing a new fighter jet. In this arrangement, employees are responsible to two managers—functional managers and project managers. Matrix structures are usually temporary: Team members typically go back to their functional or line department after a project is finished. However, more firms are becoming permanent matrix structures, creating and dissolving project teams as needed to meet customer needs. The aerospace industry was one of the first to apply the matrix structure, but today it is used by universities and schools, accounting firms, banks, and organizations in other industries.

Matrix structures provide flexibility, enhanced cooperation, and creativity, and they enable the company to respond quickly to changes in the environment by giving special attention to specific projects or problems. However, they are generally expensive and quite complex, and employees may be confused as to whose authority has priority—the project manager's or the immediate supervisor's.

COMMUNICATING IN ORGANIZATIONS

Communication within an organization can flow in a variety of directions and from a number of sources, each using both oral and written forms of communication. The success of communication systems within the organization has a tremendous effect on the overall success of the firm. Communication mistakes can lower productivity and morale. A survey by OfficeTeam found that 14 percent of each 40-hour work week is wasted because of poor communication between managers and staffers. That totals seven weeks

Did you know?

Corporate employees receive an average of 83 messages per day—most of them electronic.

Figure 8.8

The Flow of Communication in an Organizational Hierarchy

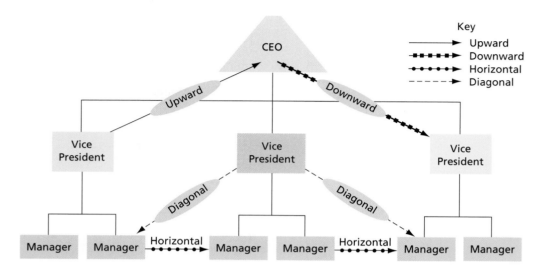

of lost productivity per year.[14] As alternatives to face-to-face communication such as voice mail, e-mail, and online company newsletters increase, management is experiencing more problems. Experts say that managers must (1) plan how they will share important news, (2) repeat important information, and (3) rehearse key presentations. Communication is vital, especially during times of widespread change. According to one executive, "People don't resist change, they resist the unknown."[15] There are both formal and informal communication flows within organizations.

Formal Communication

Formal channels of communication are intentionally defined and designed by the organization. They represent the flow of communication within the formal organizational structure, as shown on organizational charts. Traditionally, formal communication patterns were classified as vertical and horizontal, but with the increased use of teams and matrix structures, formal communication may occur in a number of patterns (Figure 8.8).

Upward communication flows from lower to higher levels of the organization and includes information such as progress reports, suggestions for improvement, inquiries, and grievances. *Downward communication* refers to the traditional flow of information from upper organizational levels to lower levels. This type of communication typically involves directions, the assignment of tasks and responsibilities, performance feedback, and certain details about the organization's strategies and goals. Speeches, policy and procedures manuals, employee handbooks, company leaflets, telecommunications, and job descriptions are examples of downward communication.

Horizontal communication involves the exchange of information among colleagues and peers on the same organizational level, such as across or within departments. Horizontal information informs, supports, and coordinates activities both within the department and with other departments. At times, the business will for-

Enhance Productivity

BSG Creates an Organizational Culture to Reduce Cycle Time

The flow of communication and the structure of an organization provide part of the corporate culture infrastructure that enhances productivity. Cycle time is the time it takes to complete a process or series of tasks. Cycle time management is driven by information technology to improve the performance of employees, reduce costs, and improve service to customers. Many firms are reducing cycle time through improved information access systems that empower employees to make decisions faster and create a corporate culture that focuses on speed and efficiency.

BSG Corporation, a computer services company, believes the only way to beat its much larger competitors is to move faster in a corporate culture that accelerates time. The firm has developed a culture where speed and change are at the core of everything the company does. BSG holds annual meetings every three months in the belief that a year's worth of change occurs every quarter. The meetings reinforce the firm's culture and values as well as address current issues. Other symbolic activities that highlight the culture include the Monday dress code that forbids white or blue shirts (IBM's culture in reverse). Each regional location is divided into neighbourhoods with street signs and mileage markers that indicate the distance to other BSG locations to create a sense of togetherness and time awareness to complete a task.

However, fast is not fast enough for BSG. Fearing that quarterly meetings may be too slow, the firm convenes a monthly meeting over the company's high-speed, wide-area network. The meetings work like a chatroom on the Internet—interactive electronic discussions in which people can exchange ideas and information in real time. Employees who want to join the meeting log onto the system and participate in discussions. The monthly cyberchats do not replace the quarterly annual meetings.

BSG recognizes that cycle time reduction begins with employees. Creating a corporate culture where employees are connected and flourish provides an atmosphere that promotes teamwork and shared values through ongoing training and particpation in group problem solving.[16]

mally require horizontal communication among particular organizational members, as is the case with task forces or project teams.

With more and more companies downsizing and increasing the use of self-managed work teams, many workers are being required to communicate with others in different departments and on different levels to solve problems and coordinate work. When these individuals from different units and organizational levels communicate, it is *diagonal communication*. At 3M, for instance, a team might be formed of workers from all functional areas (accounting, marketing, operations, and human resources) to work on a specific product project to ensure that all points of view are considered. Whenever meetings are held, they should accomplish one of the following: (1) resolve a customer problem or need, (2) create a new way for an organization to do its work, or (3) solve a problem in the business.[17]

Informal Communication Channels

Along with the formal channels of communication shown on an organizational chart, all firms communicate informally as well. Communication between friends, for instance, cuts across department, division, and even management-subordinate boundaries. Such friendships and other nonwork social relationships comprise the *informal organization* of a firm, and their impact can be great.

A two-year study by the US Center for Workforce Development analyzed informal communication and learning in seven companies. The study found that informal learning occurs during shift changes, chance hallway meetings, coffee breaks, and interactions with customers; through mentors and supervisors; and just by doing one's job. Such learning makes up 70 percent of all workplace education.[18] At Sprint, for example, employees meet for 30 minutes at the beginning of each shift to share information on what to expect during the day, new products, and customer reactions. Sprint installers and technicians have daily "tailgate" meetings—actually standing around the back of a truck—to talk about weather, safety issues, and other factors critical to their job performance.[19]

grapevine

an informal channel of communication, separate from management's formal, official communication channels

The most significant informal communication occurs through the **grapevine,** an informal channel of communication, separate from management's formal, official communication channels. Grapevines exist in all organizations. Information passed along the grapevine may relate to the job or organization, or it may be gossip and rumours unrelated to either. The accuracy of grapevine information has been of great concern to managers.

Additionally, managers can turn the grapevine to their advantage. Using it as a "sounding device" for possible new policies is one example. Managers can obtain valuable information from the grapevine that could improve decision making. Some organizations use the grapevine to their advantage by floating ideas, soliciting feedback, and reacting accordingly. Patricia Kane, a teamwork consultant, says that savvy organizations "know that the more you communicate, the more people understand how what they do relates to business goals, and the better off they are."[20] People love to gossip, and managers need to be aware that grapevines exist in every organization. Managers who understand how the grapevine works can also use it to their advantage by feeding it facts to squelch rumours and incorrect information.

ORGANIZATIONAL CULTURE

organizational culture

the firm's shared values, beliefs, traditions, philosophies, rules, and heroes

One notable aspect that should not be overlooked in the development of an organization is its **organizational culture,** the firm's shared values, beliefs, traditions, philosophies, rules, and heroes. Also called *corporate culture,* organizational culture gives the members of an organization meaning and suggests rules for how to behave and deal with problems within the organization. A firm's culture may be expressed formally through codes of ethics, memos, manuals, and ceremonies, but it is more often expressed informally through dress codes, work habits, extracurricular activities, and stories.

At Southwest Airlines, for example, CEO Herb Kelleher tries to call each of his employees by name; they call him Herb. New employees watch videotapes and attend training sessions that extol the company's policies, philosophies, and culture. Employees are encouraged to have fun and make flying exciting for their passengers (Herb has even been seen in various costumes on Southwest flights). Such activities mark Southwest's culture as fun, casual, and friendly. Disneyland/Disneyworld and McDonald's have organizational cultures that focus on cleanliness, value, and service. When such values and philosophies are shared by all members of the organization, they will be expressed in the organization's relationships with outsiders, especially customers. However, organizational cultures that lack such positive values may

Most business school students major in marketing, finance, accounting, management information systems, general management, or sales. Upon graduation, they generally expect to be hired by a company to do more of whatever it is they were trained to do as a student. For example, an accounting major expects to be an accountant. However, depending upon the way the company is organized, the roles played by the employees will differ.

If you are hired by a large, divisionalized company, you might expect to practice your profession among many others doing the same or similar tasks. You are likely to learn one part of the business fairly well but be completely uninformed about other departments or divisions. A wise employee in this situation will learn to request occasional transfers to other divisions to learn all aspects of the corporation, thereby improving his or her usefulness to the company and promotion chances.

On the other hand, if you gain employment in a very small company or in one that is heavily decentralized, you may find that you are expected to do more than the tasks for which you were trained. In many small organizations, employees are often expected to wear many hats in order to make the organization more efficient. For example, it can come as a shock to an accounting graduate to discover that, in addition to accounting, he or she will also be doing bookkeeping, secretarial work, and public relations.

Likewise, employees in larger organizations that make heavy use of teams and decentralized decision making may find that the company expects more of them than the skills learned in school. To be an effective team member, you may find that you will not only contribute your skills and expertise, but you will also be expected to learn some engineering, computer science, and marketing to be able to understand the needs and constraints of the other members of the team. Organizational flexibility requires individual flexibility, and those employees willing to take on new domains and challenges will be the employees who survive and prosper in the future.[21]

Explore Your Career Options

Flexibility First!

result in employees who are unproductive and indifferent and have poor attitudes, which will be reflected externally to customers.

WestJet's culture encourages employees to make decisions without seeking the many levels of permission. WestJet has started on the Southwest Airlines model of running a low-cost operation, but Clive Beddoe, CEO of WestJet, insists it is the culture of the people that generates success. He has attempted to align the employees' interests with the company by matching employee contributions to share ownership plans and a profit-sharing plan where up to 20 percent of the pretax profits are shared among the employees. WestJet has also developed the Pro-Active Communication Team (PACT) to facilitate the same services that union employees would receive and provide channels for up and down communication. Despite the wages being lower than Air Canada's, the profit sharing and share ownership generally leave the employees better off. The employees even set the pay scale at 95 percent of the industry median, but together, the company experiences lower expenses by having only 59 people per aircraft versus the industry average of 140 people per aircraft.[22] The key to success in any organization is satisfying customers. An efficient organizational structure and matching culture should help an organization do just that.

Review Your Understanding

Define organizational structure and relate how organizational structures develop.

Structure is the arrangement or relationship of positions within an organization; it develops when managers assign work activities to work groups and specific individuals and coordinate the diverse activities required to attain organizational objectives. Organizational structure evolves to accommodate growth, which requires people with specialized skills.

Describe how specialization and departmentalization help an organization achieve its goals.

Structuring an organization requires that management assign work tasks to specific individuals and groups. Under specialization, managers break labour into small, specialized tasks and assign employees to do a single task, fostering efficiency. Departmentalization is the grouping of jobs into working units (departments, units, groups, or divisions). Businesses may departmentalize by function, product, geographic region, or customer, or they may combine two or more of these.

Distinguish between groups and teams and identify the types of groups that exist in organizations.

A group is two or more persons who communicate, share a common identity, and have a common goal. A team is a small group whose members have complementary skills, a common purpose, goals, and approach; and who hold themselves mutually accountable. The major distinction is that individual performance is most important in groups, while collective work group performance counts most in teams. Special kinds of groups include task forces, committees, project teams, product-development teams, quality-assurance teams, and self-directed work teams.

Determine how organizations assign responsibility for tasks and delegate authority.

Delegation of authority means assigning tasks to employees and giving them the power to make commitments, use resources, and take whatever actions are necessary to accomplish the tasks. It lays responsibility on employees to carry out assigned tasks satisfactorily and holds them accountable to a superior for the proper execution of their assigned work. The extent to which authority is delegated throughout an organization determines its degree of centralization. Span of management refers to the number of subordinates who report to a particular manager. A wide span of management occurs in flat organizations; a narrow one exists in tall organizations.

Compare and contrast some common forms of organizational structure.

Line structures have direct lines of authority that extend from the top manager to employees at the lowest level of the organization. The line-and-staff structure has a traditional line relationship between superiors and subordinates, and specialized staff managers are available to assist line managers. A multidivisional structure gathers departments into larger groups called divisions. A matrix, or project-management, structure sets up teams from different departments, thereby creating two or more intersecting lines of authority.

Describe how communication occurs in organizations.

Communication occurs both formally and informally in organizations. Formal communication may be downward, upward, horizontal, and even diagonal. Informal communication takes place through friendships and the grapevine.

Analyze a business's use of teams.

The "Solve the Dilemma" box introduced a firm attempting to restructure to a team environment. Based on the material presented in this chapter, you should be able to evaluate the firm's efforts and make recommendations for resolving the problems that have developed.

Learn the Terms

accountability 191
centralized organization 192
committee 189

customer departmentalization 187
decentralized organization 192

delegation of authority 191
departmentalization 186
downsizing 194

Check Your Progress

1. Identify four types of departmentalization and give an example of each type.
2. Explain the difference between groups and teams.
3. What are self-managed work teams and what tasks might they perform that traditionally are performed by managers?
4. Explain how delegating authority, responsibility, and accountability are related.
5. Distinguish between centralization and decentralization. Under what circumstances is each appropriate?
6. Define span of management. Why do some organizations have narrow spans and others wide spans?
7. What is downsizing? Why have so many companies downsized in recent years?
8. Discuss the different forms of organizational structure. What are the primary advantages and disadvantages of each form?
9. Discuss the role of the grapevine within organizations. How can managers use it to further the goals of the firm?
10. Discuss how an organization's culture might influence its ability to achieve its objectives. Do you think that managers can "manage" the organization's culture?

Get Involved

1. Explain, using a specific example (perhaps your own future business), how an organizational structure might evolve. How would you handle the issues of specialization, delegation of authority, and centralization? Which structure would you use? Explain your answers.
2. Interview the department chairperson in charge of one of the academic departments in your college or university. Using Table 8.1 as a guideline, explore whether the professors function more like a group or a team. Contrast what you find here with what you see on your school's basketball, football, or hockey team.
3. Find a current example of a company that has downsized. What reasons did the company give for its restructuring? How has the company helped displaced employees? Debate the pros and cons of downsizing with your classmates.

Build Your Skills

Teamwork

Background: Think about all the different kinds of groups and teams you have been a member of or been involved with. Here's a checklist to help you remember them—with "Other" spaces to fill in ones not listed. Check all that apply.

School Groups/Teams

- [ ] Sports teams
- [ ] Cheerleading squads
- [ ] Musical groups
- [ ] Hobby clubs
- [ ] Foreign language clubs
- [ ] Study groups
- [ ] Other _____

Community Groups/Teams

- [ ] Fund-raising groups
- [ ] Religious groups
- [ ] Sports teams
- [ ] Political groups
- [ ] Boy Scout/Girl Guide groups
- [ ] Volunteer organizations
- [ ] Other _____

Employment Groups/Teams

- [ ] Problem-solving teams
- [ ] Work committees
- [ ] Project teams
- [ ] Labour union groups
- [ ] Work crews
- [ ] Other _____

Task:

1. Of those you checked, circle those that you would categorize as a "really great team."

2. Examine the following table[23] and circle those characteristics from columns two and three that were represented in your "really great" team experiences.

Indicator	Good Team Experience	Not-So-Good Team Experience
Members arrive on time?	Members are prompt because they know others will be.	Members drift in sporadically, and some leave early.
Members prepared?	Members are prepared and know what to expect.	Members are unclear what the agenda is.
Meeting organized?	Members follow a planned agenda.	The agenda is tossed aside, and freewheeling discussion ensues.
Members contribute equally?	Members give each other a chance to speak; quiet members are encouraged.	Some members always dominate the discussion; some are reluctant to speak their minds.
Discussions help members make decisions?	Members learn from others' points of view, new facts are discussed, creative ideas evolve, and alternatives emerge.	Members reinforce their belief in their own points of view, or their decisions were made long before the meeting.
Any disagreement?	Members follow a conflict-resolution process established as part of the team's policies.	Conflict turns to argument, angry words, emotion, blaming.
More cooperation or more conflict?	Cooperation is clearly an important ingredient.	Conflict flares openly, as well as simmering below the surface.
Commitment to decisions?	Members reach consensus before leaving.	Compromise is the best outcome possible; some members don't care about the result.
Member feelings after team decision?	Members are satisfied and are valued for their ideas.	Members are glad it's over, not sure of results or outcome.
Members support decision afterward?	Members are committed to implementation.	Some members second-guess or undermine the team's decision.

3. What can you take with you from your positive team experiences and apply to a work-related group or team situation in which you might be involved? _____

_____

_____

_____

_____

 **See for Yourself Videocase**   **www.cbc.ca**

The Trouble with Teams

Teams are all the rage, or so we all thought. But what about leadership?

Our initial five partners performed well when they started out with five dedicated individuals and a shared dream. Yes, the process was slower, but they built consensus. But now even Peter Drucker says leaders are key to success.

Historically, when new companies were being formed in automobiles and manufacturing, control and direction were key. But management schools have gone through fads and adopted the team approach after spying the large successes of Japanese businesses in the 70s, 80s, and into the 90s. Quaker Oats in Peterborough adopted the system and reduced their management expenses by two thirds. But the whole process took time and a lot of learning by all people involved. This learning takes place continually and consumes a lot of company time. Organizations must keep in mind that though the workers are more knowledgeable, the time taken for meetings and learning reduces productivity. When people are talking, they are usually not producing.

Ford and Taylor may be right for the Western culture, where we focus on stars and not the success of the team. Perhaps this is a major cultural difference between the Japanese model and Western organizations.

Questions

1. What are the driving forces that you see for the adoption of teams in the workplace?

2. In the jobs and organizations that you have worked in, were teams used to make decisions? If so, were they successful?

3. When is it better to use teams instead of a strong leader?

4. Why would a manufacturing business like Ford not be successful with teams, but the five partners in the technical business were when they started out?

Source: *Venture*, show number 703, "The Trouble with Teams," November 10, 1998, running time 6:16.

Remember to check out our Online Learning Centre at **www.mcgrawhill.ca/college/ferrell**.

Chapter 9

Production and Operations Management

Chapter Outline

Objectives

After reading this chapter, you will be able to:

- Define operations management and differentiate between operations and manufacturing.
- Explain how operations management differs in manufacturing and service firms.
- Describe the elements involved in planning and designing an operations system.
- Specify some techniques managers may use to manage the logistics of transforming inputs into finished products.
- Assess the importance of quality in operations management.
- Evaluate a business's dilemma and propose a solution.

Operations Management at Schlitterbahn

Schlitterbahn is a summertime waterpark that sits on more than 26 hectares, has more than 40 water attractions, and a staff of 1,500. Managing and maintaining the park is a year-round process. The season opens in late April, and the park closes in late September, but opening preparations and training begin in March and winterizing the park takes most of October, making the work season about seven months. Management spends the other five months developing new attractions, building onto the park, and attending conferences and trade shows, and marketing Schlitterbahn's concepts to other parks.

Schlitterbahn is best known for its innovative water rides and family-fun image, and it is the park's behind-the-scenes management that makes it all work. Members of its efficient and organized staff are well trained and serious about their work. When asked why they work there, most employees answer "because it's fun." Having fun is serious business at Schlitterbahn. A. T. Hill is the admissions director and is responsible for keeping the staff motivated. Employees are given a season-end bonus of $1 for every hour worked during the summer. The park offers numerous staff parties and encourages employees to participate in charitable activities such as an annual food drive. There is an incentive program to encourage employees to turn in items lost by park customers, including everything from keys and wallets to CD players and even a drawer full of money. Schlitterbahn management rewards "Bahn Bones" (certificates worth $5, $10, and $20) for any money found in the park and turned in to its Lost and Found. Employees then exchange the Bahn Bones for certificates for movies, CDs, and restaurant meals. Or employees can use Bahn Bones to purchase unclaimed items from Lost and Found at the end of each season. All of these incentive programs appear to be working; the park retains up to 50 percent of its staff from one year to the next.

Operations management also includes managing the vast amounts of water used daily in the park. The Comal River flows through the main park, and the remainder of the park is supplied by a 1 million-litre reservoir. More than a dozen massive pumps power this water to the rides. The reservoir uses 4,500 litres of liquid chlorine and 275 kilograms of chlorine pellets each week. The pumps are turned on each day at 7 AM. Then 8 to 10 operations inspectors spend two hours each day checking every part of every slide for water levels and making any needed repairs.

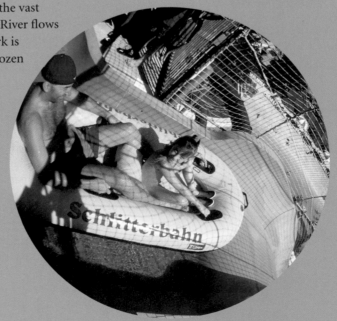

The operations management at Schlitterbahn is effective. It is the most popular summertime waterpark in the United States, and its annual attendance is over 800,000.[1]

Courtesy of Schlitterbahn

INTRODUCTION

All organizations create products—goods, services, or ideas—for customers. Thus, organizations as diverse as Dell Computer, Kraft Canada Inc., UPS, and a hospital share a number of similarities relating to how they transform resources into the products we consume. Most hospitals use similar admission procedures, while Burger King and Dairy Queen use similar food preparation methods to make hamburgers. Such similarities are to be expected. But even organizations in unrelated industries take similar steps in creating goods or services. The check-in procedures of hotels and commercial airlines are comparable, for example. The way Subway assembles a sandwich and the way General Motors assembles a truck are similar (both use automation and an assembly line). These similarities are the result of operations management, the focus of this chapter.

Here, we discuss the role of production or operations management in acquiring and managing the resources necessary to create goods and services. Production and operations management involves planning and designing the processes that will transform those resources into finished products, managing the movement of those resources through the transformation process, and ensuring that the products are of the quality expected by customers.

THE NATURE OF OPERATIONS MANAGEMENT

operations management (OM)
the development and administration of the activities involved in transforming resources into goods and services

As we have said before, the three primary functions within a business are finance, marketing, and operations. Thus, **operations management (OM),** the development and administration of the activities involved in transforming resources into goods and services, is of critical importance. Operations managers oversee the transformation process and the planning and designing of operations systems, managing logistics, quality, and productivity. Quality and productivity have become fundamental aspects of operations management because a company that cannot make products of the quality desired by consumers, using resources efficiently and effectively, will not be able to remain in business. OM is the "core" of most organizations because it is responsible for the creation of the organization's products.

All types of organizations must design systems to create goods and services. For example, auto manufacturers are designing better ways to integrate features and build major automobile components—such as traction control, leather interior, or a Blaupunkt radio—as plug-in modules that can make the assembly process flexible and customer driven.[2] Grocery Gateway is an online grocery store serving Toronto and surrounding areas that provides customers an opportunity to select available items. Grocery Gateway has integrated picking the order, checkout, and delivery of groceries into a seamless process that provides goods and services to satisfy customers.

Grocery Gateway
www.grocerygateway.com

Historically, operations management has been called "production" or "manufacturing" primarily because of the view that it was limited to the manufacture of physical goods. Its focus was on methods and techniques required to operate a factory efficiently. The change from "production" to "operations" recognizes the increasing importance of organizations that provide services and ideas. Additionally, the term *operations* represents an interest in viewing the operations function as a whole rather than simply as an analysis of inputs and outputs.

Today, OM includes a wide range of organizational activities and situations outside of manufacturing, such as health care, food service, banking, entertainment, education, transportation, and charity. Thus, we use the terms **manufacturing** and **production** interchangeably to represent the activities and processes used in making *tangible* products, whereas we use the broader term **operations** to describe those processes used in the making of *both tangible and intangible products*. Manufacturing provides tangible products such as Hewlett-Packard's latest printer, and operations provides intangibles such as a stay at the Banff Springs Hotel.

The Transformation Process

At the heart of operations management is the transformation process through which **inputs** (resources such as labour, money, materials, and energy) are converted into **outputs** (goods, services, and ideas). The transformation process combines inputs in predetermined ways using different equipment, administrative procedures, and technology to create a product (Figure 9.1). To ensure that this process generates quality products efficiently, operations managers control the process by taking measurements (feedback) at various points in the transformation process and comparing them to previously established standards. If there is any deviation between the actual and desired outputs, the manager may take some sort of corrective action.

Dell Computers has achieved transformational excellence that has resulted in US$10 million in sales per day over the Internet. Dell is considered the benchmark among the direct build-to-order computer manufacturers. Dell is able to build and ship customized personal computers in about seven days. Companies such as Gateway, Dell, Compaq, and Micron are positioning themselves not as manufacturers of a box (PC), but as total solution providers. Compaq, traditionally sold through retailers, now provides computers via the Internet and direct telephone sales and customizes products to fit exact customer requirements.[3] All adjustments made to create a satisfying product are a part of the transformation process.

Transformation may take place through one or more processes. In a business that manufactures oak furniture, for example, inputs pass through several processes before being turned into the final outputs—furniture that has been designed to meet the desires of customers (Figure 9.2). The furniture maker must first strip the oak

manufacturing
the activities and processes used in making tangible products; also called production

production
the activities and processes used in making tangible products; also called manufacturing

operations
the activities and processes used in making both tangible and intangible products

inputs
the resources—such as labour, money, materials, and energy—that are converted into outputs

outputs
the goods, services, and ideas that result from the conversion of inputs

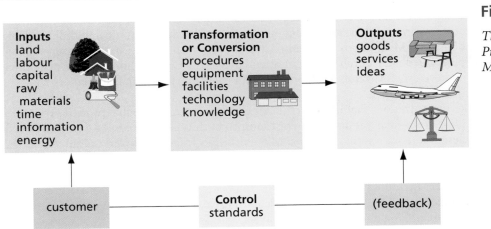

Figure 9.1

The Transformation Process of Operations Management

Figure 9.2

*Inputs, Outputs, and
Transformation
Processes in the
Manufacture of Oak
Furniture*

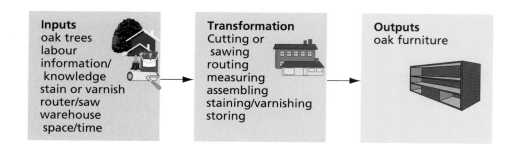

trees of their bark and saw them into appropriate sizes—one step in the transformation process. Next, the firm dries the strips of oak lumber, a second form of transformation. Third, the dried wood is routed into its appropriate shape and made smooth. Fourth, workers assemble and treat the wood pieces, then stain or varnish the piece of assembled furniture. Finally, the completed piece of furniture is stored until it can be shipped to customers at the appropriate time.

Operations Management in Service Businesses

Different types of transformation processes take place in organizations that provide services, such as airlines, colleges, and most nonprofit organizations. An airline transforms inputs such as employees, time, money, and equipment through processes such as booking flights, flying airplanes, maintaining equipment, and training crews. The output of these processes is flying passengers and/or packages to their destinations. In a nonprofit organization like Habitat for Humanity, inputs such as money, materials, information, and volunteer time and labour are used to transform raw materials into homes for needy families. In this setting, transformation processes include fund-raising and promoting the cause in order to gain new volunteers and donations of supplies, as well as pouring concrete, raising walls, and setting roofs. Transformation processes occur in all organizations, regardless of what they produce or their objectives. For most organizations, the ultimate objective is for the produced outputs to be worth more than the combined costs of the inputs.

Service organizations must build their operations around good execution, which comes from hiring and training excellent employees, developing flexible systems, customizing services, and maintaining adjustable capacity to deal with fluctuating demand.[4] Most goods are manufactured prior to purchase, but most services are performed after purchase. Flight attendants at Air Canada, hotel service personnel, and even the BC Lions CFL football team engage in performances that are a part of the total product.[5]

Organizations that manufacture tangible goods and those that provide services or ideas are similar yet different. For example, both types of organizations must make design and operating decisions. Mitsubishi Electric designs and manufactures the equipment that makes true high-definition TV signals possible. On the other hand, an online brokerage (Scotia Discount Brokerage Inc.) provides a range of online services including real-time and delayed quotes, historical charting, order entry for Canadian and US equities and mutual funds, account inquiry, transfer of funds between banking and brokerage accounts, and access to in-depth financial research. Though manufacturers and service providers often perform similar activities, they also differ in several respects. We can classify these differences in five basic ways.

Habitat for Humanity
www.habitat.org/

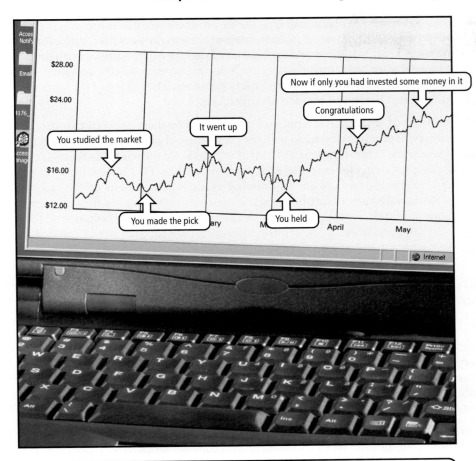

Design and operating decisions are made by Scotia Discount Brokerage, an online service organization, much like such decisions would be made by a manufacturing organization.

Courtesy of Bensimon-Byrne D'Arcy, Toronto.

Okay, you've been reading the financial pages. You're watching all the trading shows. So now that you have a pretty good sense of the market's trends, it's time to start trading. With Scotia Discount Brokerage you can take advantage of market opportunities on your terms. You'll get in-depth professional market commentary, online portfolio tracking and the ability to transfer cash between your banking and brokerage accounts - in real time. You can even research companies you're interested in right from our website. Why not visit us at www.sdbi.com and try our demo. You can sign up online, or call us at 1-800-263-3430. Your account will be opened within 24 hours.*

Scotia Discount Brokerage®

™Trademark of The Bank of Nova Scotia. ® Registered trademark of The Bank of Nova Scotia. Trademark used under authorization and control of The Bank of Nova Scotia. Brokerage services are offered by Scotia Discount Brokerage Inc. Member CIPF. No advice or recommendations are provided on Scotia Discount Brokerage accounts. * For personal cash and RSP accounts opened online.

Nature and Consumption of Output. First, manufacturers and service providers differ in the nature and consumption of their output. For example, the term *manufacturer* implies a firm that makes tangible products. A service provider, on the other hand, produces more intangible outputs such as Canada Post's delivery of priority mail or a business stay in a Delta hotel. The very nature of the service provider's product requires a higher degree of customer contact. Moreover, the actual performance of the service typically occurs at the point of consumption. At Delta, the business traveller may evaluate in-room communications and the restaurant. Toyota and other automakers, on the other hand, can separate the production of a car from its actual use. Manufacturing, then, can occur in an isolated environment, away from the customer. On the other hand, service providers, because of their need for customer contact, are often more limited than manufacturers in selecting work methods, assigning jobs, scheduling work, and exercising control over operations. The quality of the service experience is often controlled by a service contact employee.

Uniformity of Inputs. A second way to classify differences between manufacturers and service providers has to do with the uniformity of inputs. Manufacturers typically have more control over the amount of variability of the resources they use than do service providers. For example, each customer calling TD Canada Trust is likely to require different services due to differing needs, whereas many of the tasks required to manufacture a Lincoln Navigator sport utility vehicle are the same across each unit of output. Consequently, the products of service organizations tend to be more "customized" than those of their manufacturing counterparts. Consider, for example, a haircut versus a bottle of shampoo. The haircut is much more likely to incorporate your specific desires (customization) than is the bottle of shampoo.

Uniformity of Output. Manufacturers and service providers also differ in the uniformity of their output, the final product. Because of the human element inherent in providing services, each service tends to be performed differently. Not all grocery checkers, for example, wait on customers in the same way. If a barber or stylist performs 15 haircuts in a day, it is unlikely that any two of them will be exactly the same. In manufacturing, the high degree of automation available allows manufacturers to generate uniform outputs and, thus, the operations are more effective and efficient. For example, we would expect every Movado or Rolex watch to maintain very high standards of quality and performance.

Labour Required. A fourth point of difference is the amount of labour required to produce an output. Service providers are generally more labour-intensive (require more labour) because of the high level of customer contact, perishability of the output (must be consumed immediately), and high degree of variation of inputs and outputs (customization). For example, Accountemps, a Robert Half International Company, provides temporary support personnel. Each temporary worker's performance determines Accountemps' product quality. A manufacturer, on the other hand, is likely to be more capital-intensive because of the machinery and technology used in the mass production of highly similar goods. For instance, it would take a considerable investment for Nokia to make a digital phone that has a battery with longer life.

Measurement of Productivity. The final distinction between service providers and manufacturers involves the measurement of productivity for each output produced. For manufacturers, measuring productivity is fairly straightforward because of the tangibility of the output and its high degree of uniformity. For the service provider, variations in demand (for example, higher demand for air travel in some seasons than in others), variations in service requirements from job to job, and the intangibility of the product make productivity measurement more difficult. Consider, for example, how much easier it is to measure the productivity of employees involved in the production of Intel computer processors as opposed to serving the needs of Prudential Securities' clients.

It is convenient and simple to think of organizations as being either manufacturers or service providers as in the preceding discussion. In reality, however, most organizations are a combination of the two, with both **tangible components** and **intangible components** embodied in what they produce. For example, Porsche provides customer services such as toll-free hotlines and warranty protection, while banks may sell cheques and other tangible products that complement their primarily intangible product offering. Thus, we consider "products" to include both tangible physical goods as well as intangible service offerings. It is the level of tangibility of its principal product that tends to classify a company as either a manufacturer or a service provider. From an OM standpoint, this level of tangibility greatly influences the nature of the company's operational processes and procedures.

PLANNING AND DESIGNING OPERATIONS SYSTEMS

Before a company can produce any product, it must first decide what it will produce and for what group of customers. It must then determine what processes it will use to make these products as well as the facilities it needs to produce them. These decisions comprise operations planning. Although planning was once the sole realm of the production and operations department, today's successful companies involve all departments within an organization, particularly marketing and research and development, in these decisions.

Planning the Product

Before making any product, a company first must determine what consumers want and then design a product to satisfy that want. Most companies use marketing research (discussed in Chapter 12) to determine the kinds of goods and services to provide and the features they must possess. For example, in response to consumers' desires for thinner televisions and computers that take up less space in homes and on desks, Sony has introduced two new products—Trinitron TV sets that have flat-screen picture tubes and the 505 SuperSlim Notebook computer that weighs less than two kilograms and is less than three centimetres thick.[5] Marketing research can also help gauge the demand for a product and how much consumers are willing to pay for it.

Developing a product can be a lengthy, expensive process. For example, in the automobile industry, developing the new technology for night vision, bumper-mounted sonar systems that make parking easier, and a satellite service that locates and analyzes car problems has been a lengthy, expensive process. Most companies work to reduce development time and costs. For instance, Black & Decker, the "Michael Jordan of power tools," has cut its development time for new products from 36 months to 20 months.[6] Once management has developed an idea for a product that customers will buy, it must then plan how to produce the product.

Within a company, the engineering or research and development department is charged with turning a product idea into a workable design that can be produced economically. In smaller companies, a single individual (perhaps the owner) may be solely responsible for this crucial activity. Regardless of who is responsible for product design, planning does not stop with a blueprint for a product or a description of a service; it must also work out efficient production of the product to ensure that enough is available to satisfy consumer demand. How does a lawn mower company transform steel, aluminum, and other materials into a mower design that satisfies

tangible component
that part of the product having physical existence; it can be felt

intangible component
that part of the product lacking physical existence; often a service component or contractual obligation such as a warranty

consumer and environmental requirements? Operations managers must plan for the types and quantities of materials needed to produce the product, the skills and quantity of people needed to make the product, and the actual processes through which the inputs must pass in their transformation to outputs.

Designing the Operations Processes

Before a firm can begin production, it must first determine the appropriate method of transforming resources into the desired product. Often, consumers' specific needs and desires dictate a process. Customer needs, for example, require that all 2 cm bolts have the same basic thread size, function, and quality; if they did not, engineers and builders could not rely on 2 cm bolts in their construction projects. A bolt manufacturer, then, will likely use a standardized process so that every 2 cm bolt produced is like every other one. On the other hand, often a bridge must be customized so that it is appropriate for the site and expected load; furthermore, the bridge must be constructed on site rather than in a factory. Typically, products are designed to be manufactured by one of three processes: standardization, modular design, or customization.

standardization
the making of identical, interchangeable components or products

Standardization. Most firms that manufacture products in large quantities for many customers have found that they can make them cheaper and faster by standardizing designs. **Standardization** is making identical, interchangeable components or even complete products. With standardization, a customer may not get exactly what he or she wants, but the product generally costs less than a custom-designed product. Television sets, ballpoint pens, and tortilla chips are standardized products; most are manufactured on an assembly line. Standardization speeds up production and quality control and reduces production costs. And, as in the example of the 2 cm bolts, standardization provides consistency so that customers who need certain products to function uniformly all the time will get a product that meets their expectations.

modular design
the creation of an item in self-contained units, or modules, that can be combined or interchanged to create different products

Modular Design. **Modular design** involves building an item in self-contained units, or modules, that can be combined or interchanged to create different products. Personal computers, for example, are generally composed of a number of components—CPU case, motherboard, RAM chips, hard drives, floppy drives, graphics card, etc.—that can be installed in different configurations to meet the customer's needs. Because many modular components are produced as integrated units, the failure of any portion of a modular component usually means replacing the entire component. Modular design allows products to be repaired quickly, thus reducing the cost of labour, but the component itself is expensive, raising the cost of repair materials. Many automobile manufacturers use modular design in the production process.

customization
making products to meet a particular customer's needs or wants

Customization. **Customization** is making products to meet a particular customer's needs or wants. Products produced in this way are generally unique. Such products include repair services, photocopy services, custom artwork, jewellery, and furniture, as well as large-scale products such as bridges, ships, and computer software. Although there may be similarities among ships, for example, builders generally design and build each ship to meet the needs of the customer who will use it. Likewise, when you go to a printing shop to order business cards, the company must customize the cards with your name, address, and title. The "Personal Pair" jeans program at Levi Strauss & Co. provides an opportunity for customers to be measured and fitted for a pair of customized jeans. The jeans are made and delivered in a few weeks, and an online system allows for future orders.

Levi Strauss & Co.
www.levistrauss.com/

Strive for Quality

Modular Vehicle Assembly

The Mercedes-Benz M-Class sport utility vehicle (SUV) and the Dodge Dakota pickup are examples of the hottest trend in automaking today—modular assembly. In this manufacturing process, suppliers design and build major portions of the vehicles before they ever reach the automaker's assembly line. Many North American and European automakers, including General Motors, Mercedes, BMW, Chrysler, Ford, and Volkswagen, are using modular assembly. Components, especially seats and dashboards, are preassembled by suppliers and shipped to the automaker for assembly.

Mercedes manufactures the engine for the M-Class SUV, but much of the rest of the vehicle is made by other companies. Budd Co. makes the frame, and the dashboard is produced by Delphi Automotive Systems. The seats are made by Johnson Controls, the wheel assembly by T&WA, and the door panels by Becker Group. Another example is the Dodge Dakota pickup, one-third of which is made by outside suppliers.

Supporters of modular assembly say there are benefits for everyone. Automakers spend less on design, engineering, inventory, and labour and manufacturing costs. Suppliers of components gain long-term contracts and opportunities for growth. But the biggest benefactors of modular assembly may be consumers—not just in terms of lower prices but in terms of better quality products, as well.

Automakers say that modular assembly improves quality because suppliers use fewer parts in a module, thereby decreasing the chances of a component breaking down. Ford says that panel repair work decreased 95 percent when it began modular assembly of instrument panels for its Lincoln Navigator and Ford Expedition SUVs. Suppliers take responsibility for testing and certifying parts.

Opponents of modular assembly, including Japanese automakers, argue that automakers have less control over quality, but proponents say they maintain strict quality control over their vehicles. Automakers' engineers have the expertise to ensure that all modules work together and give the vehicle the proper ride and feel. With expected savings for automakers reaching millions of dollars and fewer quality complaints from consumers, modular assembly is here to stay.[7]

Planning Capacity

Planning the operational processes for the organization involves two important areas: capacity planning and facilities planning. The term **capacity** basically refers to the maximum load that an organizational unit can carry or operate. The unit of measurement may be a worker or machine, a department, a branch, or even an entire plant. Maximum capacity can be stated in terms of the inputs or outputs provided. For example, an electric plant might state plant capacity in terms of the maximum number of kilowatt hours that can be produced without causing a power outage, while a restaurant might state capacity in terms of the maximum number of customers who can be effectively—comfortably and courteously—served at any one particular time. The Ball Corp. produces aluminum soft drink can bodies and beer and soft drink can ends. Ball's production capacity is 35 billion cans.[8]

Efficiently planning the organization's capacity needs is an important process for the operations manager. Capacity levels that fall short can result in unmet demand, and consequently, lost customers. On the other hand, when there is more capacity available than needed, operating costs are driven up needlessly due to unused and

capacity
the maximum load that an organizational unit can carry or operate

often expensive resources. To avoid such situations, organizations must accurately forecast demand and then plan capacity based on these forecasts. Another reason for the importance of efficient capacity planning has to do with long-term commitment of resources. Often, once a capacity decision—such as factory size—has been implemented, it is very difficult to change the decision without incurring substantial costs.

Planning Facilities

Once a company knows what process it will use to create its products, it then can design and build an appropriate facility in which to make them. Many products are manufactured in factories, but others are produced in stores, at home, or where the product ultimately will be used. Companies must decide where to locate their operations facilities, what layout is best for producing their particular product, and even what technology to apply to the transformation process.

Many firms are developing both a traditional organization for customer contact as well as a virtual organization. RBC Financial Group (formerly the Royal Bank) maintains traditional branches and has developed complete telephone and Internet services for customers. Through its web site, investors can obtain personal investment information and trade securities over the Internet without leaving their home or office.

RBC Financial Group
www.royalbank.com/

Facility Location. Where to locate a firm's facilities is a significant question because, once the decision has been made and implemented, the firm must live with it due to the high costs involved. When a company decides to relocate or open a facility at a new location, it must pay careful attention to factors such as proximity to market, availability of raw materials, availability of transportation, availability of power, climatic influences, availability of labour, community characteristics (quality of life), and taxes and inducements. Inducements and tax reductions have become an increasingly important criterion in recent years. When Mercedes decided to build a manufacturing plant in the US, it engaged in extensive research and planning (assessing 150 sites in 30 states) to find the best location. Birmingham, Alabama, was selected because of its good infrastructure, quality of life, educated and motivated work force, strong business climate, and closeness to ports, a metropolitan area, and a university, as well as the state's efforts to attract Mercedes.[9] The facility-location decision is complex because it involves the evaluation of many factors, some of which cannot be measured with precision. Because of the long-term impact of the decision, however, it is one that cannot be taken lightly.

fixed-position layout
a layout that brings all resources required to create the product to a central location

project organization
a company using a fixed-position layout because it is typically involved in large, complex projects such as construction or exploration

process layout
a layout that organizes the transformation process into departments that group related processes

Facility Layout. Arranging the physical layout of a facility is a complex, highly technical task. Some industrial architects specialize in the design and layout of certain types of businesses. There are three basic layouts: fixed-position, process, and product.

A company using a **fixed-position layout** brings all resources required to create the product to a central location. The product—perhaps an office building, house, hydroelectric plant, or bridge—does not move. A company using a fixed-position layout may be called a **project organization** because it is typically involved in large, complex projects such as construction or exploration. Project organizations generally make a unique product, rely on highly skilled labour, produce very few units, and have high production costs per unit.

Firms that use a **process layout** organize the transformation process into departments that group related processes. A metal fabrication plant, for example, may have a cutting department, a drilling department, and a polishing department. A hospital may have an X-ray unit, an obstetrics unit, and so on. These types of organizations are sometimes called **intermittent organizations,** which deal with products of a lesser magnitude than do project organizations, and their products are not necessarily unique but possess a significant number of differences. Doctors, makers of custom-made cabinets, commercial printers, and advertising agencies are intermittent organizations because they tend to create products to customers' specifications and produce relatively few units of each product. Because of the low level of output, the cost per unit of product is generally high.

The **product layout** requires that production be broken down into relatively simple tasks assigned to workers, who are usually positioned along an assembly line. Workers remain in one location, and the product moves from one worker to another. Each person in turn performs his or her required tasks or activities. Companies that use assembly lines are usually known as **continuous manufacturing organizations,** so named because once they are set up, they run continuously, creating products with many similar characteristics. Examples of products produced on assembly lines are automobiles, television sets, vacuum cleaners, toothpaste, and meals from a cafeteria. Continuous manufacturing organizations using a product layout are characterized by the standardized product they produce, the large number of units produced, and the relatively low unit cost of production.

Many companies actually use a combination of layout designs. For example, an automobile manufacturer may rely on an assembly line (product layout) but may also use a process layout to manufacture parts. Dana Corp. collects components from 70 subsuppliers and bolts together a "rolling chassis" for delivery to a Chrysler Dodge Dakota pickup truck plant located a few kilometres away. Resembling a ladder on wheels, the chassis—complete with tires, suspension, fuel tank, wiring, and more—represents about one-third of the cost of the entire truck. Dana supplies 17 different versions of the chassis and says it could add even more components.[10]

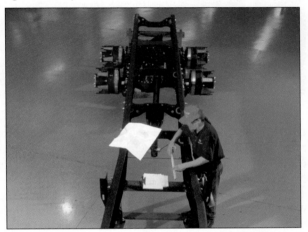

This photo illustrates the "rolling chassis" that Dana Corp. supplies to its customers.

Courtesy of Dana Corporation

Technology. Every industry has a basic, underlying technology that dictates the nature of its transformation process. The steel industry continually tries to improve steelmaking techniques. The health care industry performs research into medical technologies and pharmaceuticals to improve the quality of health-care service. Two developments that have strongly influenced the operations of many businesses are computers and robotics.

Computers have been used for decades and on a relatively large scale since IBM introduced its 650 series in the late 1950s. The operations function makes great use of computers in all phases of the transformation process. **Computer-assisted design (CAD),** for example, helps engineers design components, products, and processes on the computer instead of on paper. AeroHydro of Southwest Harbor, Maine, has developed CAD software for use in the marine industry. The software, MultiSurf, was utilized by Team New Zealand to design its yacht, *Black Magic,* winner of an America's

intermittent organizations
organizations that deal with products of a lesser magnitude than do project organizations; their products are not necessarily unique but possess a significant number of differences

product layout
a layout requiring that production be broken down into relatively simple tasks assigned to workers, who are usually positioned along an assembly line

continuous manufacturing organizations
companies that use continuously running assembly lines, creating products with many similar characteristics

computer-assisted design (CAD)
the design of components, products, and processes on computers instead of on paper

McKing Corporation operates fast-food restaurants in six provinces, selling hamburgers, roast beef and chicken sandwiches, french fries, and salads. The company wants to diversify into the growing pizza business. Six months of tests revealed that the ideal pizza to sell was a 40 cm pizza in three varieties: cheese, pepperoni, and deluxe (multiple toppings). Research found the size and toppings acceptable to families as well as to individuals (single buyers could freeze the leftovers), and the price was acceptable for a fast-food restaurant ($14.99 for cheese, $16.49 for pepperoni, and $18.99 for deluxe).

Marketing and human resources personnel prepared training manuals for employees, advertising materials, and the rationale to present to the restaurant managers (many stores are franchised). Store managers, franchisees, and employees are excited about the new plan. There is just one problem: The drive-through windows in current restaurants are too small for a 40 cm pizza to pass through. The largest size the present windows can accommodate is a 30 cm pizza. The managers and franchisees are concerned that if this aspect of operations has been overlooked perhaps the product is not ready to be launched. Maybe there are other problems yet to be uncovered.

1. What mistake did McKing make in approaching the introduction of pizza?

2. How could this product introduction have been coordinated to avoid the problems that were encountered?

3. If you were an executive at McKing, how would you proceed with the introduction of pizza into the restaurants?

computer-assisted manufacturing (CAM)
manufacturing that employs specialized computer systems to actually guide and control the transformation processes

flexible manufacturing
the direction of machinery by computers to adapt to different versions of similar operations

Cup.[11] **Computer-assisted manufacturing (CAM)** goes a step further, employing specialized computer systems to actually guide and control the transformation processes. Such systems can monitor the transformation process, gathering information about the equipment used to produce the products and about the product itself as it goes from one stage of the transformation process to the next. The computer provides information to an operator who may, if necessary, take corrective action. In some highly automated systems, the computer itself can take corrective action.

Using **flexible manufacturing,** computers can direct machinery to adapt to different versions of similar operations. For example, with instructions from a computer, one machine can be programmed to carry out its function for several different versions of an engine without shutting down the production line for refitting.

Robots are also becoming increasingly useful in the transformation process. These "steel-collar" workers have become particularly important in industries such as nuclear power, hazardous-waste disposal, ocean research, and space construction and maintenance, in which human lives would otherwise be at risk. Robots are used in numerous applications by companies around the world. Many assembly operations—cars, television sets, telephones, stereo equipment, and numerous other products—depend on industrial robots. TechniStar Corporation, one of the leading robotics-based packaging systems integrators in the US, designs, manufactures, and markets flexible automation systems to the consumer goods packaging market. One such system is designed for use in large bakeries. The robot automatically de-pans and transfers muffins directly to trays or cases in a single step and requires minimal space. Another robot automatically loads wrapped products into standard bakery baskets or trays at speeds of up to 130 products per minute. Using robotics results in a reduction in direct labour costs and improvements in productivity.[12] Researchers continue to make more sophisticated robots, and some speculate that in the future robots will not be limited to space programs and production and operations, but will also be able to engage in farming, laboratory research, and even household activities. Moreover, robotics are increasingly being used in the medical field. Voice-activated robotic arms operate video cameras for surgeons. Similar technology assists with biopsies, as well as heart, spine, and nervous system procedures. Robotic devices are also being studied to assist in joint replacement surgeries, laparoscopic procedures, and closed-chest heart bypass surgery. Robotic assistance allows surgeons to execute more complex procedures and reduce pain, trauma, and patient hospital stays.[13]

When all these technologies—CAD/CAM, flexible manufacturing, robotics, computer systems, and more—are integrated, the result is **computer-integrated manufacturing (CIM),** a complete system that designs products, manages machines and materials, and controls the operations function. Companies adopt CIM to boost productivity and quality and reduce costs. Such technology, and computers in particular, will continue to make strong inroads into operations on two fronts—one dealing with the technology involved in manufacturing and one dealing with the administrative functions and processes used by operations managers. The operations manager must be willing to work with computers and other forms of technology and to develop a high degree of computer literacy.

computer-integrated manufacturing (CIM)
a complete system that designs products, manages machines and materials, and controls the operations function

MANAGING LOGISTICS

Logistics, a major function of operations, refers to all the activities involved in obtaining and managing raw materials and component parts, managing finished products, packaging them, and getting them to customers. Some aspects of logistics (warehousing, packaging, distributing) are so closely linked with marketing that we will discuss them in Chapter 13. In this section, we will look at purchasing, managing inventory, and scheduling, which are vital tasks in the transformation of raw materials into finished goods. To illustrate logistics, consider a hypothetical small business—we'll call it Rushing Water Canoes, Inc.—that manufactures aluminum canoes, which it sells primarily to sporting goods stores and river-rafting expeditions. Our company also makes paddles and helmets, but the focus of the following discussion is the manufacture of the company's quality canoes as they proceed through the logistics process.

logistics
all activities involved in obtaining and managing raw materials and component parts, managing finished products, packaging them, and getting them to customers

Purchasing

Purchasing, also known as procurement, is the buying of all the materials needed by the organization. The purchasing department aims to obtain items of the desired quality in the right quantities at the lowest possible cost. Rushing Water Canoes, for example, must procure not only aluminum and other raw materials, and various canoe parts and components, but also machines and equipment, manufacturing supplies (oil, electricity, and so on), and office supplies in order to make its canoes. People in the purchasing department locate and evaluate suppliers of these items. They must constantly be on the lookout for new materials or parts that will do a better job or cost less than those currently being used.

The purchasing function can be quite complex. Chrys Barnes, head of procurement for Los Angeles County, oversees an organization that purchased US$650 million in goods and services in 2000 using paper forms. Buyers used more than 25,000 suppliers to stock the county's hospitals, offices, and jails. With no unified purchasing system,

purchasing
the buying of all the materials needed by the organization; also called procurement

one buyer might order pencils, not knowing that thousands of unused pencils could be found in a county warehouse. To solve the problem, a US$2 million Internet-based procurement program was constructed. Buyers now use desktop computers to comparison shop among approved suppliers that are linked over the Net—a process expected to add up to tens of millions of dollars in savings each year. Routine purchases are approved using rules built into the program, and special orders are routed to managers for approval. Orders and payments are all electronic. The program will result in better inventory management and allow the county to close its central warehouse, resulting in a US$38 million savings over the next five years.[14]

Not all companies purchase all the materials needed to create their products. Oftentimes, they can make some components more economically and efficiently than can an outside supplier. Coors, for example, manufactures its own cans at a subsidiary plant. On the other hand, firms sometimes find that it is uneconomical to make or purchase an item, and instead arrange to lease it from another organization. Some airlines, for example, lease airplanes rather than buy them. Whether to purchase, make, or lease a needed item generally depends on cost, as well as on product availability and supplier reliability.

Managing Inventory

inventory
all raw materials, components, completed or partially completed products, and pieces of equipment a firm uses

Once the items needed to create a product have been procured, some provision has to be made for storing them until they are needed. Every raw material, component, completed or partially completed product, and piece of equipment a firm uses—its **inventory**—must be accounted for, or controlled. There are three basic types of inventory. *Finished-goods inventory* includes those products that are ready for sale, such as a fully assembled automobile ready to ship to a dealer. *Work-in-process inventory* consists of those products that are partly completed or are in some stage of the transformation process. At McDonald's, a cooking hamburger represents work-in-process inventory because it must go through several more stages before it can be sold to a customer. *Raw materials inventory* includes all the materials that have been purchased to be used as inputs for making other products. Nuts and bolts are raw materials for an automobile manufacturer, while hamburger patties, vegetables, and buns are raw materials for the fast-food restaurant. Our fictional Rushing Water Canoes has an inventory of materials for making canoes, paddles, and helmets, as well as its inventory of finished products for sale to consumers. **Inventory control** is the process of determining how many supplies and goods are needed and keeping track of quantities on hand, where each item is, and who is responsible for it.

inventory control
the process of determining how many supplies and goods are needed and keeping track of quantities on hand, where each item is, and who is responsible for it

Operations management must be closely coordinated with inventory control. The production of televisions, for example, cannot be planned without some knowledge of the availability of all the necessary materials—the chassis, picture tubes, colour guns, and so forth. Also, each item held in inventory—any type of inventory—carries with it a cost. For example, storing fully assembled televisions in a warehouse to sell to a dealer at a future date requires not only the use of space, but also the purchase of insurance to cover any losses that might occur due to fire or other unforeseen events. Tigre, the leading PVC manufacturer in Brazil and one of the five largest PVC manufacturers worldwide, processes approximately 20,000 orders every month. Using a fleet of about 300 vehicles, the company delivers each order from its production plants to more than 16,000 direct clients throughout Brazil. Tigre's decentralized sales force uses notebook computers hooked into the main network to service clients, use the direct order system, and communicate via e-mail. The company has two toll-free direct telephone services designed to enhance customer service—Tigre TeleServices, which provides complete commercial information on prices, orders, and delivery, and Tele-Tigre, which provides technical support.[15]

Inventory managers spend a great deal of time trying to determine the proper inventory level for each item. The answer to the question of how many units to hold in inventory depends on variables such as the usage rate of the item, the cost of maintaining the item in inventory, the cost of paperwork and other procedures associated with ordering or making the item, and the cost of the item itself. Several approaches may be used to determine how many units of a given item should be procured at one time and when that procurement should take place.

The Economic Order Quantity Model. To control the number of items maintained in inventory, managers need to determine how much of any given item they should order. One popular approach is the **economic order quantity (EOQ) model,** which identifies the optimum number of items to order to minimize the costs of managing (ordering, storing, and using) them.

Just-in-Time Inventory Management. An increasingly popular technique is **just-in-time (JIT) inventory management,** which eliminates waste by using smaller quantities of materials that arrive "just in time" for use in the transformation process and therefore require less storage space and other inventory management expense. JIT minimizes inventory by providing an almost continuous flow of items from suppliers to the production facility. Many North American companies, including General Motors, Hewlett-Packard, IBM, and Honda Motors Canada, have adopted JIT to reduce costs and boost efficiency. Ford estimates that just-in-time parts delivery from suppliers (which it calls in-sequence delivery), along with modular assembly, has resulted in annual savings of US$9 million at its Wixon, Michigan, factory.[16]

Let's say that Rushing Water Canoes uses 20 units of aluminum from a supplier per day. Traditionally, its inventory manager might order enough for one month at a time: 440 units per order (20 units per day times 22 workdays per month). The expense of such a large inventory could be considerable because of the cost of insurance coverage, recordkeeping, rented storage space, and so on. The just-in-time approach would reduce these costs because aluminum would be purchased in smaller quantities, perhaps in lot sizes of 20, which the supplier would deliver once a day. Of course, for such an approach to be effective, the supplier must be extremely reliable and relatively close to the production facility.

Material-Requirements Planning. Another inventory management technique is **material-requirements planning (MRP),** a planning system that schedules the precise quantity of materials needed to make the product. The basic components of MRP are a master production schedule, a bill of materials, and an inventory status file. At Rushing Water Canoes, for example, the inventory-control manager will look at the production schedule to determine how many canoes the company plans to make. He or she will then prepare a bill of materials—a list of all the materials needed to make that quantity of canoes. Next, the manager will determine the quantity of these items that RWC already holds in inventory (to avoid ordering excess materials) and then develop a schedule for ordering and accepting delivery of the right quantity of materials to satisfy the firm's needs. Because of the large number of parts and materials that go into a typical production process, MRP must be done on a computer. It can be, and often is, used in conjunction with just-in-time inventory management.

economic order quantity (EOQ) model
a model that identifies the optimum number of items to order to minimize the costs of managing (ordering, storing, and using) them

just-in-time (JIT) inventory management
a technique using smaller quantities of materials that arrive "just in time" for use in the transformation process and therefore require less storage space and other inventory management expense

material-requirements planning (MRP)
a planning system that schedules the precise quantity of materials needed to make the product

Routing and Scheduling

routing

the sequence of operations through which the product must pass

After all materials have been procured and their use determined, managers must then consider the **routing,** or sequence of operations through which the product must pass. For example, before employees at Rushing Water Canoes can form aluminum sheets into a canoe, the aluminum must be cut to size. Likewise, the canoe's flotation material must be installed before workers can secure the wood seats. The sequence depends on the product specifications developed by the engineering department of the company.

scheduling

the assignment of required tasks that is given to departments or even specific machines, workers, or teams

Once management knows the routing, the actual work can be scheduled. **Scheduling** assigns the tasks to be done to departments or even specific machines, workers, or teams. At Rushing Water, cutting aluminum for the company's canoes might be scheduled to be done by the "cutting and finishing" department on machines designed especially for that purpose.

Many approaches to scheduling have been developed, ranging from simple trial and error to highly sophisticated computer programs. One popular method is the *Program Evaluation and Review Technique (PERT),* which identifies all the major activities or events required to complete a project, arranges them in a sequence or path, determines the critical path, and estimates the time required for each event. Producing a McDonald's Big Mac, for example, involves removing meat, cheese, sauce, and vegetables from the refrigerator; grilling the hamburger patties; assembling the ingredients; placing the completed Big Mac in its package; and serving it to the customer (Figure 9.3). The cheese, pickles, onions, and sauce cannot be put on before the hamburger patty is completely grilled and placed on the bun. The path that requires the longest time from start to finish is called the *critical path* because it determines the minimum amount of time in which the process can be completed. If any of the activities on the critical path for production of the Big Mac fall behind

Figure 9.3

A Hypothetical PERT Diagram for a McDonald's Big Mac

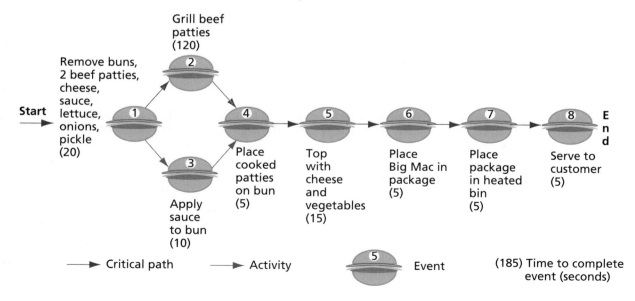

schedule, the sandwich will not be completed on time, causing customers to wait longer than they usually would.

Another approach to scheduling is the Gant chart (Figure 9.4). A Gant chart plots the tasks, the personnel responsible for each task, and a timeline for task and project completion. The chart provides a visualization of the project, allowing each team member to identify his or her responsibilities and to see how tasks interrelate. The basic format of the chart consists of listing the tasks, followed by the start date (or time), time allowed for task completion, and planned completion date (or time). Each task should be assigned an "owner," the individual responsible for completion of the task. The right-hand side of the chart is a graphical presentation of the project timeline.

MANAGING QUALITY

Quality, like cost and efficiency, is a critical element of operations management, for defective products can quickly ruin a firm. At Boeing's Everett, Washington, plant, this issue is being addressed. It takes millions of parts to build a Boeing jet, but sometimes, a few too many parts have been included. Items such as stray bolts, trash, wrenches, and flashlights (known as FOD, or foreign-object debris) have been finding their way into finished planes. One plane was grounded after a flashlight was found sealed inside its wing. The flashlight's corroded batteries caused a landing light to short out. In addition to the safety factor, there is a financial concern as well. FOD costs Boeing and its clients up to US$4 billion a year in repair costs. To help control this problem, plant mechanics now must check out their tools at the beginning of their shift and check them back in after the shift is over. Boeing is also offering noncash prizes for the most FOD retrieved. One employee at Everett has found so much debris, she's now known as "Fodzilla."[14]

Quality reflects the degree to which a good or service meets the demands and requirements of customers. Determining quality can be difficult because it depends on customers' perceptions of how well the product meets or exceeds their expectations. For example, the fuel economy of an automobile or its reliability (defined in terms of frequency of repairs) can be measured with some degree of precision. However, it is more difficult to measure psychological characteristics such as design, colour, or status. It is especially difficult to measure these characteristics when the product is a service. A company has to decide exactly which quality characteristics it considers important and then define those characteristics in terms that can be measured. The Canada Awards for Excellence are given each year by the National Quality Institute to companies that meet rigorous standards. Over 300 Canadian organizations have been honoured with Excellence Awards since their inception in 1983. Recent winners include Delta Hotels and Honeywell Ltd. in 2000 and Telus–BC Operator Services in 1999. The National Quality Institute lists eight "Principles of Business Excellence" on which the candidates are judged:

National Quality Institute
www.nqi.ca/

1. Leadership through involvement
2. Primary focus on stakeholders/customers and the marketplace
3. Cooperation and team work
4. Prevention based on process management
5. Factual approach to decision making
6. Continuous learning and people involvement
7. Focus on continuous improvement
8. Fulfillment of obligations to all stakeholders and society

Figure 9.4

A Hypothetical Gant Chart for a McDonald's Big Mac

#	Task	Start Time	Time Allowed	Finish Time	Staff	0–10	10–20	20–30	30–40	40–50	50–60	60–70	70–80	80–90	90–100	100–110	110–120	120–130	130–140	140–150	150–160	160–170	170–180
1	Remove ingredients	0	20 sec	20	Cook	▓	▓																
2	Grill patties	20	120 sec	140	Cook			▓	▓	▓	▓	▓	▓	▓	▓	▓	▓	▓	▓				
3	Apply sauce	40	10 sec	50	Cook					▓													
4	Place on bun	140	5 sec	145	Cook															▓			
5	Add toppings	145	15 sec	160	Cook																▓		
6	Package	160	5 sec	165	Cook																	▓	
7	Place in bin	165	5 sec	170	Cook																	▓	
8	Serve to customer	170	5 sec	175	Server																		▓

Time Elapsed (seconds)

Quality is so important that we need to examine it in the context of operations management. **Quality control** refers to the processes an organization uses to maintain its established quality standards. Wireless mobile computers are helping Chrysler monitor quality control at its Detroit Jefferson North Plant where the Jeep Grand Cherokee is produced. The mobile computer is placed on a test track that simulates inclines, hills, and other actual road conditions. If a problem occurs, a technician stops the car, identifies the problem, and touches that part of the vehicle illustrated on the mobile computer screen. The information is immediately transmitted to the main computer that is accessible to everyone involved. Repairs are then made, and the vehicle is returned to the track for another test before passing inspection. If the problem persists in a number of vehicles, technicians search the assembly line to find the cause and correct it. Additional applications of this wireless mobile computer technology are expected when Chrysler expands the production line at the plant.[18]

The areas of planning, management, and control discussed thus far should not be thought of as independent functions but rather as components of a unified process. Planning, management, and control must be an ongoing process in seeking continual improvement if a business is to thrive in today's competitive environment.

Two approaches to continual improvement are total quality management and enterprise resource planning. **Total quality management (TQM)** is both a philosophy and a set of guiding principles that provide a foundation for the continuous improvement of an enterprise. TQM is based on the leadership of top management and the involvement of all employees and all departments of the organization. The methodology integrates fundamental management techniques, existing improvement efforts, and technical tools using a disciplined approach to focus on quality assurance. The goal is to achieve those qualities that satisfy customers.

Companies employing TQM programs know that quality control should be incorporated throughout the transformation process, from the initial plans to develop a specific product through the product and production-facility design processes to the actual manufacture of the product. In other words, they view quality control as an element of the product itself, rather than as simply a function of the operations process. When a company makes the product correctly from the outset, it eliminates the need to rework defective products, expedites the transformation process itself, and allows employees to make better use of their time and materials. One method through which many companies have tried to improve quality is **statistical process control**, a system in which management collects and analyzes information about the production process to pinpoint quality problems in the production system.

Enterprise resource planning (ERP) is the integration of all departments and functions of a company into one computer system. In integrating applications, databases, interfaces, and tools, ERP attempts to meet the unique needs of people in diverse areas such as accounting, warehousing, and production. With a company-wide integrated system, a customer order, for example, can be more easily tracked from receipt to delivery than with a paper-based system. Since all personnel have access to the same database and view the same ERP screens, communication throughout the enterprise is improved and customer service is heightened. The system can be applied to all business processes such as financial reporting and human resource records.

quality control
the processes an organization uses to maintain its established quality standards

total quality management (TQM)
philosophy and set of guiding principles that provide a foundation for the continuous improvement of an enterprise

statistical process control
a system in which management collects and analyzes information about the production process to pinpoint quality problems in the production system

enterprise resource planning (ERP)
the inegration of all departments and functions of a company into one computer system

Consider Ethics and Social Responsibility

Zero Emissions Manufacturing

Gunter Pauli is an innovative social entrepreneur. His philosophy is that companies not only have to be financially sustainable but socially sustainable, as well. Pauli's vision is to create manufacturing facilities that completely eliminate waste by reusing or recycling all the raw materials used in the manufacturing process. He calls it zero emissions manufacturing.

Pauli's idea is that zero emissions result in increased business productivity through faster growth; additional revenue is generated and new jobs are created by finding uses for waste products or employing seasonally used equipment and factories to produce other products. The beer brewing and sugar processing industries are two good examples.

The brewing process for beer wastes massive amounts of water. Japanese brewers use 10 litres of water to brew one litre of beer. Brewing also requires huge supplies of grain, but the fermentation process uses only 8 percent of the nutrients in the grain. Of the unused nutrients, 26 percent is pure protein. Pauli argues that it does not make sense morally, environmentally, or economically to waste these resources. The world's most unconventional brewery, located in Namibia, Africa, is putting Pauli's zero emissions philosophy into practice. Water from the brewery flows into ponds which have been designed for fish farming and support eight different types of fish. Mushrooms grow on piles of grain left over from the fermentation process. Chickens feed on earthworms set loose in the grain. The chickens create waste, which is collected and put in a machine called a digester. The digester generates methane gas, which produces steam for the fermentation process. Waste from the digester is used as feed in fish farming. Although it seems part science experiment and part environmental theme park, Pauli maintains it is serious business. The brewery uses 40 different biochemical processes to reuse everything, and these processes create 12 different products in addition to the beer, including mushrooms, chicken feed, chickens, and fish. Pauli estimates that the brewery will produce seven times more food, fuel, and fertilizer than a conventional operation and create four times as many jobs.

The core technology isn't biology, chemistry, or engineering—it's the Internet. Using the Internet, over 4,600 scientists participate in 60 different discussion groups that have very specific subjects. There is one discussion group for each field of expertise—mushrooms, earthworms, methane gas, and so on. This global team of experts exchange ideas, brainstorm about problems, and conduct experiments.

Pauli says that zero emissions manufacturing is the next breakthrough in business. Total quality management meant zero defects. Just-in-time manufacturing meant zero inventories. Zero emissions manufacturing means zero waste.[19]

Establishing Standards—ISO 9000

Regardless of whether a company has a TQM and/or ERP program, it must first determine what standard of quality it desires and then assess whether its products meet that standard. Product specifications and quality standards must be set so the company can create a product that will compete in the marketplace. Rushing Water Canoes, for example, may specify that each of its canoes has aluminum walls of a

In an increasingly competitive global marketplace, quality becomes a key attribute on which companies can differentiate their products from competitors' in the minds and wallets of consumers. Quality has therefore become ever more important in all aspects of business, but particularly in production and operations management. More and more firms are adopting total quality management (TQM) programs to ensure that quality pervades all aspects of their businesses. Many firms are working to satisfy universal quality standards, such as ISO 9000, so that they can compete globally. This has created new career opportunities for students interested in working in TQM and other quality programs.

Included among the almost 13,000 ISO 9000 certified sites in Canada are many large organizations such as Linamar Inc., with 21 certified sites, and Euclid-Hitachi Heavy Equipment Ltd.

Even public sector organizations such as Public Works and Government Services Canada have obtained ISO 9000 series certification and now require many of their suppliers to meet ISO 9000 quality standards as well. As a result, companies are experiencing difficulty recruiting graduates who understand the design and implementation of quality-improvement programs.

For these reasons, all students are encouraged to "think quality" when preparing for a business career. Even quality-oriented candidates in fields such as sales, finance, and human resources have the potential to play key roles in the integration of quality throughout their companies. For those who pursue advanced study in TQM in either an undergraduate or graduate program, the prospects for employment and career advancement in the field are promising.[20]

specified uniform thickness, that the front and back of each canoe be reinforced with a specified level of steel, and that each canoe contain a specified amount of flotation material for safety. Production facilities must be designed that can produce products with the desired specifications.

Quality standards can be incorporated into service businesses as well. A hamburger chain, for example, may establish standards relating to how long it takes to cook an order and serve it to customers, how many fries are in each order, how thick the burgers are, or how many customer complaints might be acceptable. Once the desired quality characteristics, specifications, and standards have been stated in measurable terms, the next step is inspection.

The International Organization for Standardization (ISO) has created a series of quality assurance standards—**ISO 9000**—designed to ensure consistent product quality under many conditions. The standards provide a framework for documenting how a certified business keeps records, trains employees, tests products, and fixes defects. To obtain ISO 9000 certification, an independent auditor must verify that a business's factory, laboratory, or office meets the quality standards spelled out by the International Organization for Standardization. The certification process can be complex, difficult, and expensive, but for many companies, the process is essential to being able to compete. Over 40,000 sites are certified in the US and almost 13,000 are certified in Canada, representing almost 16 percent of the over 340,000 certifications issued worldwide. Menlo Logistics, a full-service, global logistics provider, uses advanced management systems to cost-effectively integrate and simplify complex logistics operations. Menlo recently received ISO certification for its work with NCR, a

ISO 9000

a series of quality assurance standards designed by the International Organization for Standardization (ISO) to ensure consistent product quality under many conditions leading provider of information technology solutions.[21] Certification has become a virtual necessity for doing business in Europe in some high-technology businesses.

ISO 9002 certification has also been established for service providers. Rainier Corporation recently became the first public relations and advertising agency in North America to receive ISO 9002 certification. In working toward the certification, Rainier achieved higher efficiency, better internal and external communications, less rework, and the near elimination of the mistakes and oversights found in many agencies.[22]

Inspection

Inspection reveals whether a product meets quality standards. Some product characteristics may be discerned by fairly simple inspection techniques—weighing the contents of cereal boxes or measuring the time it takes for a customer to receive his or her hamburger. Other inspection techniques are more elaborate. Automobile manufacturers use automated machines to open and close car doors to test the durability of latches and hinges. The food-processing and pharmaceutical industries use various chemical tests to determine the quality of their output. Rushing Water Canoes might use a special device that can precisely measure the thickness of each canoe wall to ensure that it meets the company's specifications.

Organizations normally inspect purchased items, work-in-process, and finished items. The inspection of purchased items and finished items takes place after the fact; the inspection of work-in-process is preventive. In other words, the purpose of inspection of purchased items and finished items is to determine what the quality level is. For items that are being worked on—an automobile moving down the assembly line or a canoe being assembled—the purpose of the inspection is to find defects before the product is completed so that necessary corrections can be made.

Sampling

An important question relating to inspection is how many items should be inspected. If Rushing Water Canoes produces more than 20 canoes a day, should they all be inspected or just some of them? Whether to inspect 100 percent of the output or only part of it is related to the cost of the inspection process, the destructiveness of the inspection process (some tests last until the product fails), and the potential cost of product flaws in terms of human lives and safety.

Some inspection procedures are quite expensive, use elaborate testing equipment, destroy products, and/or require a significant number of hours to complete. In such cases, it is usually desirable to test only a sample of the output. If the sample passes inspection, the inspector may assume that all the items in the lot from which the sample was drawn would also pass inspection. By using principles of statistical inference, management can employ sampling techniques that assure a relatively high probability of reaching the right conclusion—that is, rejecting a lot that does not meet standards and accepting a lot that does. Nevertheless, there will always be a risk of making an incorrect conclusion—accepting a population that *does not* meet standards (because the sample was satisfactory) or rejecting a population that *does* meet standards (because the sample contained too many defective items).

Sampling is likely to be used when inspection tests are destructive. Determining the life expectancy of light bulbs by turning them on and recording how long they last would be foolish: There is virtually no market for burned-out light bulbs. Instead, a generalization based on the quality of a sample would be applied to the entire population of light bulbs from which the sample was drawn. However, human life and safety often depend on the proper functioning of specific items, such as the navigational systems installed in commercial airliners. For such items, even though the inspection process is costly, the potential cost of flawed systems—in human lives and safety—is too great not to inspect 100 percent of the output.

Review Your Understanding

Define operations management and differentiate between operations and manufacturing.

Operations management (OM) is the development and administration of the activities involved in transforming resources into goods and services. Operations managers oversee the transformation process and the planning and designing of operations systems, managing logistics, quality, and productivity. The terms *manufacturing* and *production* are used interchangeably to describe the activities and processes used in making tangible products, whereas *operations* is a broader term used to describe the process of making both tangible and intangible products.

Explain how operations management differs in manufacturing and service firms.

Manufacturers and service firms both transform inputs into outputs, but service providers differ from manufacturers in several ways: They have greater customer contact because the service typically occurs at the point of consumption; their inputs and outputs are more variable than manufacturers', largely because of the human element; service providers are generally more labour-intensive; and their productivity measurement is more complex.

Describe the elements involved in planning and designing an operations system.

Operations planning relates to decisions about what product(s) to make, for whom, and what processes and facilities are needed to produce them. OM is often joined by marketing and research and development in these decisions. Common facility layouts include fixed-position layouts, process layouts, or product layouts. Where to locate operations facilities is a crucial decision that depends on proximity to the market, availability of raw materials, availability of transportation, availability of power, climatic influences, availability of labour, and community characteristics. Technology is also vital to operations, particularly computer-assisted design, computer-assisted manufacturing, flexible manufacturing, robotics, and computer-integrated manufacturing.

Specify some techniques managers may use to manage the logistics of transforming inputs into finished products.

Logistics includes all the activities involved in obtaining and managing raw materials and component parts, managing finished products, packaging them, and getting them to customers. The organization must first make or purchase (procure) all the materials it needs. Next, it must control its inventory by determining how many supplies and goods it needs and keeping track of every raw material, component, completed or partially completed product, and piece of equipment, how many of each are on hand, where they are, and who has responsibility for them. Common approaches to inventory control include the economic order quantity (EOQ) model, the just-in-time (JIT) inventory concept, and material-requirements planning (MRP). Logistics also includes routing and scheduling processes and activities to complete products.

Assess the importance of quality in operations management.

Quality is a critical element of OM because low-quality products can hurt people and harm the business. Quality control refers to the processes an organization uses to maintain its established quality standards. To control quality, a company must establish what standard of quality it desires and then determine whether its products meet that standard through inspection.

Evaluate a business's dilemma and propose a solution.

Based on this chapter and the facts presented in the "Solve the Dilemma" box, you should be able to evaluate the business's problem and propose one or more solutions for resolving it.

Learn the Terms

capacity 217

computer-assisted design (CAD) 219

computer-assisted manufacturing (CAM) 220

computer-integrated manufacturing (CIM) 221

continuous manufacturing organizations 219

customization 216

economic order quantity (EOQ) model 223

enterprise resource planning (ERP) 227

fixed-position layout 218

flexible manufacturing 220

inputs 211

intangible component 215

intermittent organizations 219

inventory 222

inventory control 222

ISO 9000 229

just-in-time (JIT) inventory management 223

logistics 221

manufacturing 211

material-requirements planning (MRP) 224

modular design 216

operations 211

operations management (OM) 210

outputs 211

process layout 218

product layout 219

production 211

project organization 218

purchasing 221

quality control 227

routing 224

scheduling 227

standardization 216

statistical process control 227

tangible component 215

total quality management (TQM) 227

Check Your Progress

1. What is operations management and why is it important?
2. Differentiate among the terms *operations*, *production*, and *manufacturing*.
3. Compare and contrast a manufacturer versus a service provider in terms of operations management.
4. Who is involved in planning products?
5. In what industry would the fixed-position layout be most efficient? The process layout? The product layout? Use real examples.
6. What criteria do businesses use when deciding where to locate a plant?
7. What is flexible manufacturing? How can it help firms improve quality?
8. Define logistics and summarize the activities it involves.
9. Describe some of the methods a firm may use to control inventory.
10. When might a firm decide to inspect a sample of its products rather than test every product for quality?

Get Involved

1. Compare and contrast OM at McDonald's with that of Honda Motors Canada. Compare and contrast OM at McDonald's with that of RBC Financial Group (formerly the Royal Bank).
2. Find a real company that uses JIT, either in your local community or in a business journal. Why did the company decide to use JIT? What have been the advantages and disadvantages of using JIT for that particular company? What has been the overall effect on the quality of the company's products or services? What has been the overall effect on the company's bottom line?
3. Interview someone from your local Chamber of Commerce and ask him or her what incentives the community offers to encourage organizations to locate there. (See if these incentives relate to the criteria firms use to make location decisions.)

Build Your Skills

Reducing Cycle Time

Background: An important goal of production and operations management is reducing cycle time—the time it takes to complete a task or process. The goal in cycle time reduction is to reduce costs and/or increase customer service.[23] Many experts believe that the rate of change in our society is so fast that a firm must master speed and connectivity.[24] Connectivity refers to a seamless integration of customers, suppliers, employees, and organizational, production, and operations management. The use of the Internet and other telecommunications systems helps many organizations connect and reduce cycle time.

Task: Break up into pairs throughout the class. Select two businesses (local restaurants, retail stores, etc.) that both of you frequent, are employed by, and/or are fairly well acquainted with. For the first business, one of you will role play the "manager" and the other will role play the "customer." Reverse roles for the second business you have selected. As managers at your respective businesses, you are to prepare a list of five questions you will ask the customer during the role play. The questions you prepare should be designed to get the customer's viewpoint on how good the cycle time is at your business. If one of the responses leads to a problem area, you may need to ask a follow-up question to determine the nature of the dissatisfaction. Prepare one main question and a follow-up, if necessary, for each of the five dimensions of cycle time:

1. **Speed**—the delivery of goods and services in the minimum time; efficient communications; the elimination of wasted time.

2. **Connectivity**—all operations and systems in the business appear connected with the customer.

3. **Interactive relationships**—a continual dialogue exists between operations units, service providers, and customers that permits the exchange of feedback on concerns or needs.

4. **Customization**—each product is tailored to the needs of the customer.

5. **Responsiveness**—the willingness to make adjustments and be flexible to help customers and to provide prompt service when a problem develops.

Begin the two role plays. When it is your turn to be the manager, listen carefully when your partner answers your prepared questions. You need to elicit information on how to improve the cycle time at your business. You will achieve this by identifying the problem areas (weaknesses) that need attention.

After completing both role play situations, fill out the form below for the role play where you were the manager. You may not have gathered enough information to fill in all the boxes. For example, for some categories, the customer may have had only good things to say; for others, the comments may all be negative. Be prepared to share the information you gain with the rest of the class.

I role played the manager at _____ (business). After listening carefully to the customer's responses to my five questions, I determined the following strengths and weaknesses as they relate to the cycle time at my business.

Dimension	Strength	Weakness
Speed		
Connectivity		
Interactive relationships		
Customization		
Responsiveness		

 **See for Yourself Videocase**   **www.cbc.ca**

Diamonds on Ice

The video ends with the project having received the go ahead from Rio Tinto and Bob Gannicott but still seeking the remaining financing to cover Aber Diamond Corporation's 40 percent share of the capital needed to bring the mine into production.

On January 29, 2002, Aber Diamond Corporation announced the closing of its US$230 million loan facility. Underwritten on November 2, 2001, by a lead group made up of the Bank of Montreal, CIBC, Deutsche Bank AG, Export Development Canada, and the Royal Bank of Canada, with the Bank of Tokyo-Mitsubishi joining later. The successfully syndicated loan facility now involves a banking group of 14 lenders. This loan facility will fund Aber's remaining financial requirements through the beginning of project operations in 2003. The facility is scheduled to be repaid in eight equal semi-annual installments following project completion.

The project costs remain within budget projections. It is expected that the Diavik mine will produce about 5 percent of the world's current diamond output over an estimated 20 year life.

Aber's overall capital commitment to the Diavik diamond project represents the largest financial undertaking by an independent, single-asset Canadian mining company in history.

The project, as seen in the video, has required significant planning and effort to coordinate transportation and construction. The project involves identification of key tasks to be performed, estimating time needed to complete the tasks and the timing of windows of opportunity to carry out the tasks, the determination of material and human resource requirements, budgeting, and the organization of financing. The entire process requires careful management oversight and appropriate revision of plans when delays occur.

Questions

1. Discuss the planning considerations that were required in the building of the Diavik diamond mine.

2. Discuss how the PERT diagram and the Gant chart approaches could be applied to this project.

3. What ethical questions and social responsibility considerations did you find in the Diavik diamond project as reported in the video?

Source: *Venture*, show number 768, "Diamonds on Ice," January 2, 2001, Pt. I 8:47, Pt. II 8:34.

Remember to check out our Online Learning Centre at **www.mcgrawhill.ca/college/ferrell**.

Cyberzone

The Internet and Managerial Decision Making

Managing for quality and competitiveness has been greatly facilitated by the use of the Internet. The skills that managers need to be successful are becoming even more important in keeping up with the pace of change. In a world of virtual decision making, Internet time is much shorter than traditional time. The Internet permits a new start-up company to enter the market and change the fundamental rules of how business is conducted within an industry. For example, eBay has changed the rules by creating a company which enables customers to make transactions through public auctions, a service that could not exist without the Internet. Amazon.com has changed the way books are made available by providing an opportunity to purchase almost any book over the Internet. Amazon is also working to maintain a longer-term customer relationship in the face of emerging competition from stores such as Barnes and Noble by providing recommendations on books which the reader might find enjoyable based on a profile of previous purchases. These advances in how business is conducted place even greater pressure on leaders and decision makers in most companies. Keeping up with the information technology needed to be successful in a new business is required of all managers.

Decision making is important in all management functions and levels, whether decisions are strategic or at the operational level. Since the most important part of a manager's job is working with other employees and customers, the Internet can provide the information that is needed at the point at which a decision needs to be made. At People Soft, Inc., a designer of human resources software for managers, the philosophy is that eliminating the clutter that prevents people from making good decisions is necessary because the Internet can provide too much information. Doing a search on a topic of interest can result in 5,000 to 10,000 pieces of information. Therefore, combining information from outside of the organization—from customers, suppliers, and service providers—with internal information about employees, products, and processes makes decisions more effective.

The ability to facilitate teamwork and communication is an important contribution that the Internet can provide. Computer Language Research Inc. tries to eliminate every piece of paper possible. Employees submit expense reports and purchase orders, reserve meeting rooms, and conduct salary reviews online. Salespersons use notebook computers to place orders and establish lines of credit for customers.

Computer Language Research Inc. develops tax-compliance and accounting software for its customers. The firm analyzes 25,000 government forms for companies, accounting firms, and bank trust departments. Its planning and development of operating systems occurs online, with 75 percent of the paper traffic eliminated and the cycle time for product development shortened significantly. Quality is maintained through a database built to track recurring product problems.

The development, transformation, and administration of activities involved in operations management have been enhanced by the Internet and the online linking of processes. VF Corporation, maker of Lee, Wrangler, Britannia, and Rustler jeans, Healthtex clothes for children, and Jantzen bathing suits, as well as other apparel, has developed an information process to eliminate redundancies, coordinate manufacturing, and maximize efficiency and output. The company has connected product development, forecasting demand, manufacturing control, raw materials planning, and warehouse control with the marketing system. In the near future, the firm will be able to predict that a Wal-Mart store will sell a given number of Wrangler jeans in a particular size during a specific selling season. VF will then be able to ensure that those jeans are available and scheduled to ship synchronously with demand.

VF's warehouse data system calculates the most efficient way to store, retrieve, and ship products. Every subsystem, such as production or planning, is integrated around enterprise resource planning. Managers at VF can establish and maintain quality standards that can be incorporated throughout the planning, manufacturing, and operations process. Custom-designed software and Internet accessibility make the overall management system possible.

Managers must continually adjust the information they need in order to obtain, store, and share with coworkers and even customers. The information they develop and the Internet technologies used to share this information are as important to success as the products they produce. In many service industries, information technology is really part of the product. For example, FedEx has found that its software gives customers faster service and allows customers to do more for themselves. Many other firms are finding that through the use of web sites, the best service is self-service.

The use of web sites is evolving as an important tool to enhance communication and improve productivity for most firms. One company taking a leadership role is Procter & Gamble; P&G is sponsoring its leading distributors' web sites and promoting the coordination of database linkages with customers. In the future, most management systems will be web-based. Enterprisewide connecting of software, computers, and the Internet can coordinate almost everything that relates to how an organization operates. The Internet will empower managers to make decisions and implement business strategy.[1]

Part Four

Creating the Human Resource Advantage

Chapter 10

Motivating the Work Force

Chapter Outline

Introduction

Nature of Human Relations

Historical Perspectives on Employee
Motivation

Theories of Employee Motivation

Strategies for Motivating Employees

Objectives

After reading this chapter, you will be able to:

- Define human relations and determine why its study is important.
- Summarize early studies that laid the groundwork for understanding employee motivation.
- Compare and contrast the human-relations theories of Abraham Maslow and Frederick Herzberg.
- Investigate various theories of motivation, including Theories X, Y, and Z; equity theory; and expectancy theory.
- Describe some of the strategies that managers use to motivate employees.
- Critique a business's program for motivating its sales force.

Massages, Dry Cleaning, Pets, and Concierge Service—Creative Motivation at Work

As research finds that employee attitudes are linked to higher profits, greater productivity, and higher employee loyalty and retention, organizations are scrambling to recruit and retain qualified, happy, and satisfied employees. Some companies are coming up with inventive ways to make life easier and more fun for employees. Eddie Bauer and many Silicon Valley companies offer massages to employees. At least 39 companies, including General Mills, Johnson & Johnson, Intel, and Xerox offer a dry cleaning service. Personal concierge service, which includes services such as sending flowers for employees, is offered by Honda, Starbucks, and Allied Signal.

Autodesk Inc., a US$936 million a year computer software company in California, welcomes employees' pets. On any given day, there are as many as 75 to 100 dogs at work with their owners. Some companies are finding that allowing workers to bring their pets to work on a regular basis relaxes and motivates stressed workers, increases employee productivity, and helps build customer satisfaction. Netscape Communications Corp. has a formal policy that welcomes all pets except cats (due to the number of people allergic to cat dander).[1]

Research In Motion encourages creativity in its casual working environment. Exploring individual horizons and bringing fresh ideas are constantly being encouraged. A full range of medical benefits is offered; group home, auto, and life insurance plans are available, and free financial planning services are provided. But it cannot be overlooked that free beverages are available to all employees, and everyone receives a free BlackBerry wireless handheld Internet access device.[2]

Other strategies being employed by organizations include helping workers develop skills to advance their careers, offering cutting-edge technology and exciting work, making it easier to change jobs within a company, and offering challenging overseas assignments. With a tight labour market and cost pressures, organizations must implement a wider range of creative motivational strategies to remain competitive in an increasingly global marketplace.

Courtesy of AutoDesk, Inc.

Enter the World of Business

INTRODUCTION

Successful programs such as those used at Eddie Bauer, WestJet, Roots, and Netscape teach some important lessons about how to interact with and motivate employees to do their best. Because employees do the actual work of the business and influence whether the firm achieves its objectives, most top managers agree that employees are an organization's most valuable resource. To achieve organizational objectives, employees must have the motivation, ability (appropriate knowledge and skills), and tools (proper training and equipment) to perform their jobs. Ensuring that employees have the appropriate knowledge and skills and the proper training is the subject of Chapter 11; this chapter focuses on employee motivation.

We will examine employees' needs and motivation, managers' views of workers, and several strategies for motivating employees. Managers who understand the needs of their employees can help them reach higher levels of productivity and thus contribute to the achievement of organizational goals.

NATURE OF HUMAN RELATIONS

human relations
the study of the behaviour of individuals and groups in organizational settings

What motivates employees to perform on the job is the focus of **human relations,** the study of the behaviour of individuals and groups in organizational settings. In business, human relations involves motivating employees to achieve organizational objectives efficiently and effectively. The field of human relations has become increasingly important over the years as businesses strive to understand how to boost workplace morale, maximize employees' productivity and creativity, and motivate their ever more diverse employees to be more effective.

motivation
an inner drive that directs a person's behaviour toward goals

Motivation is an inner drive that directs a person's behaviour toward goals. A goal is the satisfaction of some need, and a need is the difference between a desired state and an actual state. Both needs and goals can be motivating. Motivation explains why people behave as they do; similarly, a lack of motivation explains, at times, why people avoid doing what they should do. A person who recognizes or feels a need is motivated to take action to satisfy the need and achieve a goal (Figure 10.1). Consider a person who feels cold. Because of the difference between the actual temperature and the desired temperature, the person recognizes a need. To satisfy the

Figure 10.1

The Motivation Process

need and achieve the goal of being warm, the person may adjust the thermostat, put on a sweater, reach for a blanket, start a fire, or hug a friend. Human relations is concerned with the needs of employees, their goals and how they try to achieve them, and the impact of those needs and goals on job performance.

One prominent aspect of human relations is **morale**—an employee's attitude toward his or her job, employer, and colleagues. High morale contributes to high levels of productivity, high returns to stakeholders, and employee loyalty. Companies with the most satisfied employees have an above average annual return to shareholders. Over 10 years, *Fortune's* 100 Best companies to work for had a 24 percent return to shareholders compared to 15 percent for the Russell 3000, an index of large and small companies comparable to *Fortune's* 100 Best.[3] Mediacorp's *Canada's Top 100 Employers* in 2001 found most of the companies focused on retention and attraction of employees through perks such as personal days, flexible work hours to assist in balancing work and family, and training and development. As can be expected, workplace communication is a high priority as well.[4]

morale
an employee's attitude toward his or her job, employer, and colleagues

Respect, involvement, appreciation, adequate compensation, promotions, a pleasant work environment, and a positive organizational culture are all morale boosters. Many companies offer a diverse array of benefits designed to improve the quality of employees' lives and increase their morale and satisfaction. For example, Rogers Communications Inc. provides a wide range of discounts on Rogers products such as cell phone time, video rentals, Internet service, and Toronto Blue Jays tickets. Intuit Canada Ltd. of Edmonton permits employees to use one of three sleep rooms during the day, all equipped with a bed and alarm clock.[5] Marriott International has found that working fathers feel their work conflicts with developing a close relationship with their children. To improve morale on this issue, Marriott has launched two initiatives to teach fathers how to lead richer lives with their families. "Effective Fathering" is a course developed for front-line employees, and "Daddy Stress/Daddy Success" is a seminar targeted to executives.[6] Conversely, low morale may cause high rates of absenteeism and turnover (when employees quit or are fired and must be replaced by new employees).

The on-site day-care facility at Johnson & Johnson is provided to ease employees' child care concerns, resulting in higher morale and enhanced productivity.

Steve Winter/Black Star

HISTORICAL PERSPECTIVES ON EMPLOYEE MOTIVATION

Throughout the twentieth century, researchers have conducted numerous studies to try to identify ways to motivate workers and increase productivity. From these studies have come theories that have been applied to workers with varying degrees of success. A brief discussion of two of these theories—the classical theory of motivation and the Hawthorne studies—provides a background for understanding the present state of human relations.

Classical Theory of Motivation

The birth of the study of human relations can be traced to time and motion studies conducted at the turn of the last century by Frederick W. Taylor and Frank and

Lillian Gilbreth. Their studies analyzed how workers perform specific work tasks in an effort to improve the employees' productivity. These efforts led to the application of scientific principles to management.

classical theory of motivation

theory suggesting that money is the sole motivator for workers

According to the **classical theory of motivation,** money is the sole motivator for workers. Taylor suggested that workers who were paid more would produce more, an idea that would benefit both companies and workers. To improve productivity, Taylor thought that managers should break down each job into its component tasks (specialization), determine the best way to perform each task, and specify the output to be achieved by a worker performing the task. Taylor also believed that incentives would motivate employees to be more productive. Thus, he suggested that managers link workers' pay directly to their output. He developed the piece-rate system, under which employees were paid a certain amount for each unit they produced; those who exceeded their quota were paid a higher rate per unit for all the units they produced.

We can still see Taylor's ideas in practice today in the use of mathematical models, statistics, and incentives. Moreover, companies are increasingly striving to relate pay to performance at both the hourly and managerial level. For example, at Nucor Corp., a steelmaker in Charlotte, North Carolina, senior officers receive cash bonuses equal to twice their salary, as well as the equivalent of their salary in stock, if the company reaches a maximum target of 22 percent return on stockholders' equity. Production workers generally get about 60 percent of their annual income from performance bonuses based on meeting production quotas. Base pay for production workers is $10–12 an hour, but the production bonuses boost pay to $25 an hour, resulting in highly paid employees and very high productivity.[7]

More and more corporations are tying pay to performance in order to motivate—even up to the CEO level. According to a report in *Business Week*, the 15 top-paid executives in 2000, experienced a 5 percent reduction in their compensation. Much of this had to do with their reluctance to exercise their stock options, which frequently comprise the majority of their remuneration. Their compensation only averaged US$88.7 million in 2000, a drop of US$4.4 million. Some still did well. The co-CEO of financial corporation Citigroup received a total package of US$292.9 million. Cisco's John Chambers came in second at US$157.3 million. Still, the shares these executives receive can be profitable but they are also closely linked to the stock market. Bill Gates is estimated to have lost US$36 billion in 2000. In 2000, John Roth of Nortel earned a total compensation of $70.75 million, and the number two paid executive in Canada, also from Nortel, Clarence Chandran earned $59 million. It is of note that neither of these gentlemen are at Nortel anymore.[8]

Like most managers of the early twentieth century, Taylor believed that satisfactory pay and job security would motivate employees to work hard. However, later studies showed that other factors are also important in motivating workers.

The Hawthorne Studies

Elton Mayo and a team of researchers from Harvard University wanted to determine what physical conditions in the workplace—such as light and noise levels—would stimulate employees to be most productive. From 1924 to 1932, they studied a group of workers at the Hawthorne Works Plant of the Western Electric Company and measured their productivity under various physical conditions.

What the researchers discovered was quite unexpected and very puzzling: Productivity increased regardless of the physical conditions. This phenomenon has

New Digger Construction has been growing significantly in its business of installing water mains, sewers, and roads. Recently it purchased a firm in the lower mainland of BC to complement its operations in Alberta and Ontario.

Some of its most recent jobs have required large crews that warranted the merging of some teams from BC and further east. Normally this would be easy to facilitate but some problems have emerged for Mr. DaSilva, the superintendent on a large project. The British Columbia crew has a large number of South Asian people who eat together and usually speak their native tongue on the job and off. The Ontario crew speaks in Portuguese, which Mr. DaSilva also speaks. They also use Portuguese on and off the job, which causes frustration for the South Asian crew.

To further complicate matters, the Alberta crew is totally English speaking and they feel out of place and at a disadvantage when the other persons use languages they cannot understand.

DaSilva is getting more frustrated with the BC crew, which has refused to change their language habits despite his requests that they use English on the job and when around other members of the company. Most of the Ontario crew has acquiesced, but there is still some resistance to using only English on the job. One of the leaders of the Ontario crew has expressed to DaSilva frustration with many of the practices of the whole operation, and this complicates the matter as the deadline for completion is very tight and profits are also tight in the slowing economy. He has insisted that the requirement of using only English off the job or off company time is unjust.

Consider the following questions:

1. Is DaSilva warranted in requiring that only English be spoken?

2. Is the BC crew defensible in their insistence on using their language on and off the job?

3. What could happen if this matter is not resolved quickly?

4. What basis does DaSilva have to demand the use of English?

5. What are the goals of the company and how does this matter help or hinder the attainment of these goals?

Note: Under safety rules, it is vital when working around heavy equipment that everyone speaks the same language. It is too risky to have a communication gap in such dangerous environments.

Conversely, under human rights legislation and the Constitution, freedom of assembly and speech is guaranteed, but there is a notwithstanding clause that places safety first.

Consider Ethics and Social Responsibility

Language Barriers and Safety

been labelled the Hawthorne effect. When questioned about their behaviour, the employees expressed satisfaction because their coworkers in the experiments were friendly and, more importantly, because their supervisors had asked for their help and cooperation in the study. In other words, they were responding to the attention they received, not the changing physical work conditions. The researchers concluded that social and psychological factors could significantly affect productivity and morale.

The Hawthorne experiments marked the beginning of a concern for human relations in the workplace. They revealed that human factors do influence workers' behaviour and that managers who understand the needs, beliefs, and expectations of people have the greatest success in motivating their workers. Even at colleges and universities, new employees and students are given an orientation program.

Maslow's hierarchy
a theory that arranges the five basic needs of people—physiological, security, social, esteem, and self-actualization—into the order in which people strive to satisfy them

physiological needs
the most basic human needs to be satisfied—water, food, shelter, and clothing

security needs
the need to protect oneself from physical and economic harm

THEORIES OF EMPLOYEE MOTIVATION

The research of Taylor, Mayo, and many others has led to the development of a number of theories that attempt to describe what motivates employees to perform. In this section, we will discuss some of the most important of these theories.

Maslow's Hierarchy of Needs

Psychologist Abraham Maslow theorized that people have five basic needs: physiological, security, social, esteem, and self-actualization. **Maslow's hierarchy** arranges these needs into the order in which people strive to satisfy them (Figure 10.2).[9]

Physiological needs, the most basic and first needs to be satisfied, are the essentials for living—water, food, shelter, and clothing. According to Maslow, humans devote all their efforts to satisfying physiological needs until they are met. Only when these needs are met can people focus their attention on satisfying the next level of needs—security.

Security needs relate to protecting yourself from physical and economic harm. Actions that may be taken to achieve security include reporting a dangerous work-

Figure 10.2

Maslow's Hierarchy of Needs

Source: Adapted from Abraham H. Maslow, "A Theory of Human Motivation," *Psychology Review* 50 (1943), pp. 370–396. American Psychology Association.

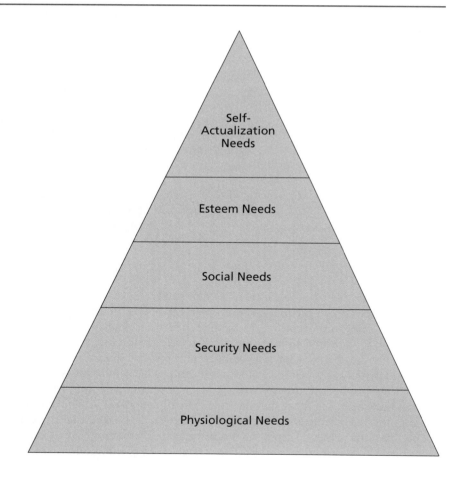

place condition to management, maintaining safety equipment, and purchasing insurance with income protection in the event you become unable to work. Once security needs have been satisfied, people may strive for social goals.

Social needs are the need for love, companionship, and friendship—the desire for acceptance by others. To fulfill social needs, a person may try many things: making friends with a coworker, joining a group, volunteering at a hospital, throwing a party. Once their social needs have been satisfied, people attempt to satisfy their need for esteem.

Esteem needs relate to respect—both self-respect and respect from others. One aspect of esteem needs is competition—the need to feel that you can do something better than anyone else. Competition often motivates people to increase their productivity. Esteem needs are not as easily satisfied as the needs at lower levels in Maslow's hierarchy because they do not always provide tangible evidence of success. However, these needs can be realized through rewards and increased involvement in organizational activities. Until esteem needs are met, people focus their attention on achieving respect. When they feel they have achieved some measure of respect, self-actualization becomes the major goal of life.

Self-actualization needs, at the top of Maslow's hierarchy, mean being the best you can be. Self-actualization involves maximizing your potential. A self-actualized person feels that she or he is living life to its fullest in every way. For John Grisham, self-actualization might mean being praised as the best writer in the world; for actor Leonardo diCaprio, it might mean winning an Oscar.

Maslow's theory maintains that the more basic needs at the bottom of the hierarchy must be satisfied before higher-level goals can be pursued. Thus, people who are hungry and homeless are not concerned with obtaining respect from their colleagues. Only when physiological, security, and social needs have been more or less satisfied do people seek esteem. Maslow's theory also suggests that if a low-level need is suddenly reactivated, the individual will try to satisfy that need rather than higher-level needs. A survey of 6,000 employees at large companies in Canada and the United States in 2001 found that the number one concern of employees was pay, and opportunities for advancement ranked number two. But most age groups ranked work-life balance a close number three. This is a major fallout from the downsizing of the early and mid-1990s, as over 20 percent of those surveyed now work 50 hours or more per week. Employers have to be careful: 58 percent of the respondents admitted that they were either actively looking for work, open to changing jobs, or watching for opportunities.[10] Managers should learn from Maslow's hierarchy that employees will be motivated to contribute to organizational goals only if they are able to first satisfy their physiological, security, and social needs through their work.

Herzberg's Two-Factor Theory

In the 1950s psychologist Frederick Herzberg proposed a theory of motivation that focuses on the job and on the environment where work is done. Herzberg studied various factors relating to the job and their relation to employee motivation and concluded that they can be divided into hygiene factors and motivational factors (Table 10.1).

Hygiene factors, which relate to the work setting and not to the content of the work, include adequate wages, comfortable and safe working conditions, fair company policies, and job security. These factors do not necessarily motivate employees

Abraham Maslow—
Publications Site
www.maslow.com/

social needs
the need for love, companionship, and friendship—the desire for acceptance by others

esteem needs
the need for respect—both self-respect and respect from others

self-actualization needs
the need to be the best one can be; at the top of Maslow's hierarchy

hygiene factors
aspects of Herzberg's theory of motivation that focus on the work setting and not the content of the work; these aspects include adequate wages, comfortable and safe working conditions, fair company policies, and job security

Table 10.1

Herzberg's Hygiene and Motivational Factors

Hygiene Factors	Motivational Factors
Company policies	Achievement
Supervision	Recognition
Working conditions	Work itself
Relationships with peers, supervisors, and subordinates	Responsibility
Salary	Advancement
Security	Personal growth

to excel, but their absence may be a potential source of dissatisfaction and high turnover. Employee safety and comfort are clearly hygiene factors.

Many people feel that a good salary is one of the most important job factors, even more important than job security and the chance to use one's mind and abilities. Salary and security, two of the hygiene factors identified by Herzberg, make it possible for employees to satisfy the physiological and security needs identified by Maslow. However, the presence of hygiene factors is unlikely to motivate employees to work harder.

Motivational factors, which relate to the content of the work itself, include achievement, recognition, involvement, responsibility, and advancement. The absence of motivational factors may not result in dissatisfaction, but their presence is likely to motivate employees to excel. For example, WestJet encourages and empowers flight attendants to keep passengers smiling by telling them jokes, singing safety instructions, and kidding with them during flights. Employees tend to enjoy working for a company that allows them to use their personalities and abilities to create a fun work environment.[11] Many companies are beginning to use self-directed work teams precisely to give employees more responsibility and control and to involve them more in their work, which serves to motivate them to higher levels of productivity and quality. At Playboy Enterprises, Inc., Executive Vice President and Publisher Richard Kinsler says, "I think every problem can be solved if you get three or four of the smartest people on the subject to sit around and strategize."[12]

Herzberg's motivational factors and Maslow's esteem and self-actualization needs are similar. Workers' low-level needs (physiological and security) have largely been satisfied by minimum-wage laws and occupational-safety standards set by various government agencies and are therefore not motivators. Consequently, to improve productivity, management should focus on satisfying workers' higher-level needs (motivational factors) by providing opportunities for achievement, involvement, and advancement and by recognizing good performance.

motivational factors

aspects of Herzberg's theory of motivation that focus on the content of the work itself; these aspects include achievement, recognition, involvement, responsibility, and advancement

WestJet
www.westjet.com/

McGregor's Theory X and Theory Y

In *The Human Side of Enterprise*, Douglas McGregor related Maslow's ideas about personal needs to management. McGregor contrasted two views of management—the traditional view, which he called Theory X, and a humanistic view, which he called Theory Y.

According to McGregor, managers adopting **Theory X** assume that workers generally dislike work and must be forced to do their jobs. They believe that the following statements are true of workers:

1. The average person naturally dislikes work and will avoid it when possible.
2. Most workers must be coerced, controlled, directed, or threatened with punishment to get them to work toward the achievement of organizational objectives.
3. The average worker prefers to be directed and to avoid responsibility, has relatively little ambition, and wants security.[13]

Managers who subscribe to the Theory X view maintain tight control over workers, provide almost constant supervision, try to motivate through fear, and make decisions in an autocratic fashion, eliciting little or no input from their subordinates. The Theory X style of management focuses on physiological and security needs and virtually ignores the higher needs discussed by Maslow.

The Theory X view of management does not take into account people's needs for companionship, esteem, and personal growth, whereas Theory Y, the contrasting view of management, does. Managers subscribing to the **Theory Y** view assume that workers like to work and that under proper conditions employees will seek out responsibility in an attempt to satisfy their social, esteem, and self-actualization needs. McGregor describes the assumptions behind Theory Y in the following way:

1. The expenditure of physical and mental effort in work is as natural as play or rest.
2. People will exercise self-direction and self-control to achieve objectives to which they are committed.
3. People will commit to objectives when they realize that the achievement of those goals will bring them personal reward.
4. The average person will accept and seek responsibility.
5. Imagination, ingenuity, and creativity can help solve organizational problems, but most organizations do not make adequate use of these characteristics in their employees.
6. Organizations today do not make full use of workers' intellectual potential.[14]

Obviously, managers subscribing to the Theory Y philosophy have a management style very different from managers subscribing to the Theory X philosophy. Theory Y managers maintain less control and supervision, do not use fear as the primary motivator, and are more democratic in decision making, allowing subordinates to participate in the process. Theory Y managers address the high-level needs in Maslow's hierarchy as well as physiological and security needs. Today, Theory Y enjoys widespread support and may have displaced Theory X.

Theory Z

Theory Z is a management philosophy that stresses employee participation in all aspects of company decision making. It was first described by William Ouchi in his book *Theory Z—How American Business Can Meet the Japanese Challenge*. Theory Z incorporates many elements associated with the Japanese approach to management,

Theory X
McGregor's traditional view of management whereby it is assumed that workers generally dislike work and must be forced to do their jobs

Theory Y
McGregor's humanistic view of management whereby it is assumed that workers like to work and that under proper conditions employees will seek out responsibility in an attempt to satisfy their social, esteem, and self-actualization needs

Theory Z
a management philosophy that stresses employee participation in all aspects of company decision making

Table 10.2   *Comparison of American, Japanese, and Theory Z Management Styles*

	American	**Japanese**	**Theory Z**
Duration of employment	Relatively short term; workers subject to layoffs when business slows	Lifelong; no layoffs	Long term; layoffs rare
Rate of promotion	Rapid	Slow	Slow
Amount of specialization	Considerable; worker develops expertise in one area only	Minimal; worker develops expertise in all aspects of the organization	Moderate; worker learns all aspects of the organization
Decision making	Individual	Consensual; input from all concerned parties is considered	Consensual; emphasis on quality
Responsibility	Assigned to the individual	Shared by the group	Assigned to the individual
Control	Explicit and formal	Less explicit and less formal	Informal but with explicit performance measures
Concern for workers	Focus is on work only	Focus extends to worker's whole life	Focus includes worker's life and family

Source: Adapted from William Ouchi, *Theory Z—How American Business Can Meet the Japanese Challenge,* p. 58. © 1981 by Addison-Wesley Publishing Company, Inc. Reprinted by permission of Perseus Books Publishers, a member of Perseus Books, L.L.C.

such as trust and intimacy, but Japanese ideas have been adapted for use in North America. In a Theory Z organization, managers and workers share responsibilities; the management style is participative; and employment is long term and often life-long. In a Theory Y organization, managers focus on assumptions about the nature of the worker. The two theories can be seen as complementary. Table 10.2 compares the traditional American management style, the Japanese management style, and Theory Z (the modified Japanese management style).

Variations on Theory Z

Theory Z has been adapted and modified for use in a number of North American companies. One adaptation involves workers in decisions through quality circles. Quality circles (also called quality-assurance teams) are small , usually having five to eight members who discuss ways to reduce waste, eliminate problems, and improve quality, communication, and work satisfaction. Such quality teams are a common technique for harnessing the knowledge and creativity of hourly employees to solve problems in companies. Toyota Motor Manufacturing uses quality circles primarily to provide team members with the secondary benefits of improvements in quality, efficiency, and other aspects of work performance, as well as cost reductions. Currently, Toyota has over 8,000 circles worldwide and claims a total savings of almost US$40 million from quality circle initiatives for a seven-year period.[15]

Even more involved than quality circles are programs that operate under names such as *participative management, employee involvement,* or *self-directed work teams.* Regardless of the term used to describe such programs, they strive to give employees more control over their jobs while making them more responsible for the outcome of their efforts. Such programs often organize employees into work teams of 5 to 15 members who are responsible for producing an entire product item. Team members are cross-trained and can therefore move from job to job within the team. Each team essentially manages itself and is responsible for its quality, scheduling, ordering and use of materials, and problem solving. Many firms have successfully employed work teams to boost morale, productivity, quality, and competitiveness.

Equity Theory

According to **equity theory,** how much people are willing to contribute to an organization depends on their assessment of the fairness, or equity, of the rewards they will receive in exchange. In a fair situation, a person receives rewards proportional to the contribution he or she makes to the organization. However, in practice, equity is a subjective notion. Each worker regularly develops a personal input-output ratio by taking stock of his or her contribution (inputs) to the organization in time, effort, skills, and experience and assessing the rewards (outputs) offered by the organization in pay, benefits, recognition, and promotions. The worker compares his or her ratio to the input-output ratio of some other person—a "comparison other," who may be a coworker, a friend working in another organization, or an "average" of several people working in the organization. If the two ratios are close, the individual will feel that he or she is being treated equitably.

Consider a woman who has a high-school education and earns $25,000 a year. When she compares her input-output ratio to that of a coworker who has a university degree and makes $35,000, she will probably feel that she is being paid fairly. However, if she perceives that her personal input-output ratio is lower than that of the university graduate, she will probably feel that she is being treated unfairly and will be motivated to seek change. Further, if she learns that the coworker who earns $35,000 has only a high-school diploma, she may believe she is being cheated by the organization. To achieve equity, the woman could try to increase her outputs by asking for a raise or promotion. She could also try to have the inputs of the "comparison other" increased or the outputs of the "comparison other" decreased. Failing to achieve equity, the woman may decide to leave the organization.

Because almost all the issues involved in equity theory are subjective, they can be problematic. Managers should try to avoid equity problems by ensuring that rewards are distributed on the basis of performance and that all employees clearly understand the basis for their pay and benefits.

equity theory
an assumption that how much people are willing to contribute to an organization depends on their assessment of the fairness, or equity, of the rewards they will receive in exchange

Expectancy Theory

Psychologist Victor Vroom described **expectancy theory,** which states that motivation depends not only on how much a person wants something but also on the person's perception of how likely he or she is to get it. A person who wants something and has reason to be optimistic will be strongly motivated. For example, say you really want a promotion. And, let's say because you have taken some night classes to improve your skills, and moreover, have just made a large, significant sale, you feel confident that you are qualified and able to handle the new position. Therefore, you are motivated to try to get the promotion. In contrast, if you do not believe you are likely to get what you want, you may not be motivated to try to get it, even though you really want it.

expectancy theory
the assumption that motivation depends not only on how much a person wants something but also on how likely he or she is to get it

Think Globally

Motivating for Global Success

Growth in the chemical industry means expansion into developing countries for the Eastman Chemical Company. Failed overseas employee assignments represent a financial loss to the company and can also prove devastating to the employee—and often, the employee's family. When selecting employees for overseas assignments, Eastman focuses on the employee's family members—their interest in relocation and their adaptability to other cultures—as well as the employee's technical skills and qualifications. Eastman's preparation program is so thorough and effective that 99 percent of participating employees successfully complete their two- to five-year term in a foreign country.

How does Eastman motivate for global success? Potential overseas employees and their families meet with a counsellor to determine the family's cultural adaptivity. Also, Eastman offers cultural orientation for the family, including language training, a house-hunting trip, and counselling to prepare the family for life in a new culture. Financial recognition is offered through the Dual Earnings Family Compensation Plan for those spouses who give up a career to move with an Eastman employee. Employees also can choose not to accept an overseas assignment without risk to their careers with Eastman.

Once a family has relocated overseas, counselling is available locally, and hometown newspapers and company newsletters are sent. Family members also have access to a local contact person to help them adjust to their new surroundings. Employees returning home following an overseas assignment provide information to the human resources management group that helps make assignments more effective for the company and easier for future families.[16]

STRATEGIES FOR MOTIVATING EMPLOYEES

Based on the various theories that attempt to explain what motivates employees, businesses have developed several strategies for motivating their employees and boosting morale and productivity. Some of these techniques include behaviour modification and job design, as well as the already described employee involvement programs and work teams.

Behaviour Modification

behaviour modification

changing behaviour and encouraging appropriate actions by relating the consequences of behaviour to the behaviour itself

B.F. Skinner Foundation
www.bfskinner.org/

Behaviour modification involves changing behaviour and encouraging appropriate actions by relating the consequences of behaviour to the behaviour itself. The concept of behaviour modification was developed by psychologist B.F. Skinner, who showed that there are two types of consequences that can modify behaviour—reward and punishment. Skinner found that behaviour that is rewarded will tend to be repeated, while behaviour that is punished will tend to be eliminated. For example, employees who know that they will receive a bonus, such as an expensive restaurant meal, for making a sale over $2,000 may be more motivated to make sales. Workers who know they will be punished for being tardy are likely to make a greater effort to get to work on time.

However, the two strategies may not be equally effective. Punishing unacceptable behaviour may provide quick results but may lead to undesirable long-term side effects, such as employee dissatisfaction and increased turnover. In general, rewarding appropriate behaviour is a more effective way to modify behaviour. At Eagle Hardware and Garden, associates who complete a work study course and successfully pass a test become "Eagle Experts" and receive an increase in salary and other incentives.[17] At Toyota Motor Manufacturing, recognition includes lapel or hat pins, certificates for merchandise at the company store, opportunities to attend conferences, and payment for eligible suggestions.[18]

Job Design

Herzberg identified the job itself as a motivational factor. Managers have several strategies that they can use to design jobs to help improve employee motivation. These include job rotation, job enlargement, job enrichment, flexible scheduling strategies, and management by objectives.

Job Rotation. **Job rotation** allows employees to move from one job to another in an effort to relieve the boredom that is often associated with job specialization. Businesses often turn to specialization in hopes of increasing productivity, but there is a negative side effect to this type of job design: Employees become bored and dissatisfied, and productivity declines. Job rotation reduces this boredom by allowing workers to undertake a greater variety of tasks and by giving them the opportunity to learn new skills. With job rotation, an employee spends a specified amount of time performing one job and then moves on to another, different one. The worker eventually returns to the initial job and begins the cycle again. Many companies have experimented with job rotation, including Intuit, Inc., maker of Quicken financial software. Each employee of Intuit, including the company's head, rotates into the customer service area so that all employees will know what customers want and stay in touch with what the business does, why, and for whom.[19]

Job rotation is a good idea, but it has one major drawback. Because employees may eventually become bored with all the jobs in the cycle, job rotation does not totally eliminate the problem of boredom. Job rotation is extremely useful, however, in situations where a person is being trained for a position that requires an understanding of various units in an organization. Many executive training programs require trainees to spend time learning a variety of specialized jobs. Job rotation is also used to cross-train today's self-directed work teams.

Job Enlargement. **Job enlargement** adds more tasks to a job instead of treating each task as separate. Like job rotation, job enlargement was developed to overcome the boredom associated with specialization. The rationale behind this strategy is that jobs are more satisfying as the number of tasks performed by an individual increases. Job enlargement strategies have been more successful in increasing job satisfaction than have job rotation strategies. IBM, AT&T, and Maytag are among the many companies that have used job enlargement to motivate employees.

Job Enrichment. **Job enrichment** incorporates motivational factors, such as opportunity for achievement, recognition, responsibility, and advancement, into a job. It gives workers not only more tasks within the job but more control and authority over the job. Job enrichment programs enhance a worker's feeling of responsibility and provide opportunities for growth and advancement when the worker is able to take on the more challenging tasks. AT&T and General Foods use job enrichment to improve the quality of work life for their employees. The potential benefits of job enrichment are great, but it requires careful planning and execution.

job rotation
movement of employees from one job to another in an effort to relieve the boredom often associated with job specialization

job enlargement
the addition of more tasks to a job instead of treating each task as separate

job enrichment
the incorporation of motivational factors, such as opportunity for achievement, recognition, responsibility, and advancement, into a job

Solve the Dilemma

Motivating to Win

St. Lawrence Pharmaceutical has long been recognized for its innovative techniques for motivating its sales force. It features the salesperson who has been the most successful during the previous quarter in the company newsletter, "Hat Trick." The salesperson also receives a hockey jersey, a plaque, and $1,000 worth of St. Lawrence stock. St. Lawrence's "Stanley Cup Club" is for employees who reach or exceed their sales goal, and a "Hart Award," which includes a trip to the Caribbean, is given annually to the top 20 salespeople in terms of goal achievement.

St. Lawrence employs a video conference hook-up between the honoured salesperson and four regional sales managers to capture some of the successful tactics and strategies the winning salesperson uses to succeed. The managers summarize these ideas and pass them along to the salespeople they manage. Sales managers feel strongly that programs such as this are important and that, by sharing strategies and tactics with one another, they can be a successful team.

1. Which motivational theories are in use at St. Lawrence?

2. What is the value of getting employees to compete against a goal instead of against one another?

3. Put yourself in the shoes of one of the four regional sales managers and argue against potential cutbacks to the motivational program.

Flexible Scheduling Strategies. Most North American workers work a traditional 40-hour work week consisting of five 8-hour days with fixed starting and ending times. Facing problems of poor morale and high absenteeism as well as a diverse work force with changing needs, many managers have turned to flexible scheduling strategies such as flextime, compressed work weeks, job sharing, part-time work, and telecommuting. According to a 1996 survey, 24 percent of full-time workers had some form of flexible working arrangement with their employers. The number has almost doubled since 1991, and the numbers are still growing. A Canadian survey showed almost no change in participation in flexible work schedules in 2000. It remained stable at 19 percent having flextime for the past 10 years.

flextime

a program that allows employees to choose their starting and ending times, provided that they are at work during a specified core period

Flextime is a program that allows employees to choose their starting and ending times, as long as they are at work during a specified core period (Figure 10.3). It does not reduce the total number of hours that employees work; instead, it gives employees more flexibility in choosing which hours they work. A firm may specify

Figure 10.3

Flextime, Showing Core and Flexible Hours

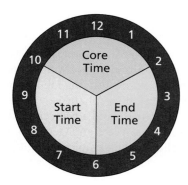

Many firms offer some employees the option of working at home, which may increase employee productivity and reduce costs for the firm.

© 1999 PhotoDisc, Inc.

that employees must be present from 10:00 AM to 3:00 PM. One employee may choose to come in at 7:00 AM and leave at the end of the core time, perhaps to attend classes after work. Another employee, a mother who lives in the suburbs, may come in at 9:00 AM in order to have time to drop off her children at a day-care centre and commute by public transportation to her job.

Family issues are the number one cause of work absences.

Related to flextime are the scheduling strategies of the compressed work week and job sharing. The **compressed work week** is a four-day (or shorter) period in which an employee works 40 hours. Under such a plan, employees typically work 10 hours per day for four days and have a three-day weekend. The compressed work week reduces the company's operating expenses because its actual hours of operation are reduced. It is also sometimes used by parents who want to have more days off to spend with their families.

Job sharing occurs when two people do one job. One person may work from 8:00 AM to 12:30 PM; the second person comes in at 12:30 PM and works until 5:00 PM. Job sharing gives both people the opportunity to work as well as time to fulfill other obligations, such as parenting or school. With job sharing, the company has the benefit of the skills of two people for one job, often at a lower total cost for salaries and benefits than one person working eight hours a day would be paid.

Two other flexible scheduling strategies attaining wider use include allowing full-time workers to work part time for a certain period and allowing workers to work at home either full or part time. Employees at some firms may be permitted to work part time for six months or so in order to care for a new baby or an elderly parent or just to slow down for a little while to "recharge their batteries." By 2005, 37 percent of US workers will be more concerned with caring for a parent than a child, and employees are expected to demand benefits that reflect this major shift.[20] When the employees return to full-time work, they are usually given a position comparable to their original

compressed work week

a four-day (or shorter) period during which an employee works 40 hours

job sharing

performance of one full-time job by two people on part-time hours

Table 10.3

*Facts About
Telecommuting*

Source: Find/SVP, 1997
AT&T Survey of Teleworker
Attitudes and Work Styles,
printed in *The Fort Collins
Coloradoan,* September 21,
1998, p. B2. Reprinted courtesy of *Fort Collins Coloradoan.*

Telecommuter Profile

- There were 11.1 million US telecommuters in 1997.
- Corporate telecommuters work an average of 19.3 hours per week at home.
- Age of telecommuters: 30–49   60%
                                          50 and over   22%
- 74% are married.
- 75% have or have attended classes to obtain a graduate or post-graduate degree.

Personal Life Impact

- 73% report they are more satisfied with their personal and family lives.

Reasons for Increased Satisfaction

- 88% report better relationship with spouse.
- 85% report improved morale.
- 84% report better relationship with children.
- 83% report a better balance between work and personal life.

Career Effects

- 63% report a positive effect on their career.
- 24% have gained greater responsibility.
- 71% are more satisfied with their jobs.

Commitment to Telework

- 36% would either quit or look for another telework job if they could no longer work from home.

full-time position. Other firms are allowing employees to telecommute, or work at home a few days of the week, staying connected via computers, modems, and regular or cellular telephones. Table 10.3 provides more detail on this growing trend. While many employees ask for the option of working at home to ease parenting responsibilities, some have discovered that they are more productive at home without the distractions of the workplace. Others, however, have discovered that they are not suited for working at home. Still, work-at-home programs do help reduce overhead costs for businesses. For example, IBM used to maintain a surplus of office space but has reduced the surplus through employee telecommuting, "hotelling" (being assigned to a desk through a reservation system), and "hot-desking" (several people using the same desk but at different times).[21] Cisco Systems also uses hot-desking, while KPMG Peat Marwick, Ernst & Young, and Andersen Consulting use some version of hotelling.[22] KPMG surveyed over 400 Canadian companies in 1997 and found that 6 percent of employees were telecommuting. Over half of the companies surveyed expect the number to increase. Bell Canada asked 100 of its top customers what benefit they received from the telecommuting and the response was a 15 to 35 percent improvement in productivity. Of course not all jobs can use telecommuting, but the practice is growing.[23]

They share a desk, a telephone, a mailing address, and the single full-time position of coordinator for the Diagnostic Evaluation Center at North Shore Children's Hospital. Margot Kaczynski and Joanne Bartlett each work 20 hours a week, scheduling appointments, processing treatment referrals, and billing insurance companies. Both women want to work, but not full-time. Kaczynski works Monday and Wednesday. Bartlett works Tuesday and Friday, and they split Thursday. The arrangement began when the hospital was downsizing and sought to combine two positions.

The two are typical of most job sharers—they are women in administrative positions who for varying personal reasons do not want full-time work. Job sharing is a small, but important, part of the changes being made in the way people work in corporate North America. Flexibility is the key word and the number one priority for an increasing number of employees who are trying to mesh careers with personal lives. More and more employers are viewing flexibility as a necessity and realizing it can be used as a benefit to attract and retain satisfied employees. Keeping employees happy and loyal to a company can go right to the bottom line. Studies show that employee loyalty correlates to customer loyalty which correlates to greater profits and growth. A firm may actually get greater output from two part-time successful job sharers than one full-time employee. Job sharers are diligent, often focusing intently on the job and maximizing their hours while there.

The arrangement works well for Kaczynski and Bartlett, and their employer, North Shore Children's Hospital, is pleased with the results. Today, employers must not only attract top talent, they must work to retain it. To do that, organizations must create environments that support employees' family and lifestyle issues.[24]

Enhance Productivity

What's Mine Is Yours and What's Yours Is Mine

Companies are turning to flexible work schedules to provide more options to employees who are trying to juggle their work duties with other responsibilities and needs. A Hewitt Associates survey of more than 1,000 major employers found that 73 percent offer flextime, 61 percent permit part-time employment, 32 percent offer job-sharing programs, 24 percent employ compressed work schedules, 20 percent allow employees to work from home or telecommute, at least part-time, and 16 percent offer summer hours.[25] Preliminary results indicate that flexible scheduling plans increase job satisfaction, which, in turn, leads to increases in productivity.

Management by Objectives. **Management by objectives (MBO)** is a process in which a manager and a subordinate conferring together set and agree to goals for the subordinate to achieve. The MBO process has three basic parts (Figure 10.4):

management by objectives (MBO)
a planning process in which a manager and a subordinate confer, set, and agree to goals for the subordinate to achieve

Figure 10.4

Steps in Management by Objectives

Individuals negotiate or are assigned a set of objectives to achieve within a specified period of time.	Individuals are evaluated periodically to see how they are doing.	Individuals are rewarded on the basis of how close they come to achieving their stated goals.

In terms of satisfaction and motivation, where you live can be almost as important as where you work. Obtaining information about various cities can provide fodder for your job hunt and even help you decide to accept or reject a job offer. One source of ratings of cities is the *Places Rated Almanac*, which should be available at your local library. It rates every metropolitan area in the United States and Canada according to quality of life and considers nine factors: cost of living, job outlook, transportation, education, health care, crime, the arts, recreation, and climate. Each city is rated on these factors, and all ratings are combined into one overall evaluation. The top 10 metropolitan areas are:

1. Orange County, CA
2. Seattle—Bellevue—Everett, WA
3. Houston, TX

4. Washington, DC
5. Phoenix—Mesa, AZ
6. Minneapolis—St. Paul, MN
7. Atlanta, GA
8. Tampa—St. Petersburg—Clearwater, FL
9. San Diego, CA
10. Philadelphia, PA[26]

Salary is certainly an important aspect in any job hunt. Various web sites will estimate the salaries necessary to live equivalently in two different cities. One such site is **www2.homefair.com/calc/salcalc.html.** According to this site's calculations, if you currently have a job in Guelph, Ontario, that pays $65,000, you will need a job that pays $84,443 in Calgary in order to maintain your standard of living (calculated on December 19, 2001).

1. Individuals within an organization negotiate with their supervisor a set of objectives to be achieved within a specified period of time—3 months, 6 months, or 12 months.

2. Periodically, the manager conducts performance reviews to determine how well the subordinate is progressing toward the achievement of the goals.

3. At the end of the specified period of time, the subordinate is rewarded on the basis of how close he or she came to achieving the goals.

The rationale behind MBO is that employees who are involved in the goal-setting process will be highly motivated to perform and reach the goals. One major advantage of an MBO program is that it constantly emphasizes what must be done to achieve organizational objectives. A major disadvantage of such a program is that it is time consuming and expensive. For MBO to succeed, objectives must be carefully defined and realistic. Furthermore, managers must be sure that individual objectives are congruent with the broad goals of the organization. At the same time, managers and employees may require changes in the plan due to external factors outside their control, such as a competitor closing down (as Canada 3000 did in November 2001) or a new entry into the market.

Importance of Motivational Strategies

Motivation is more than a tool that managers can use to foster employee loyalty and boost productivity. It is a process that affects all the relationships within an organization and influences many areas such as pay, promotion, job design, training opportunities, and reporting relationships. Employees are motivated by the nature of the relationships they have with their supervisors, by the nature of their jobs, and by characteristics of the organization. Managers can further nurture motivation by being honest, supportive, empathetic, accessible, fair, and open. Motivating employees to increase satisfaction and productivity is an important concern for organizations seeking to remain competitive in the global marketplace.

Review Your Understanding

Define human relations and determine why its study is important.

Human relations is the study of the behaviour of individuals and groups in organizational settings. Its focus is what motivates employees to perform on the job. Human relations is important because businesses need to understand how to motivate their increasingly diverse employees to be more effective, boost workplace morale, and maximize employees' productivity and creativity.

Summarize early studies that laid the groundwork for understanding employee motivation.

Time and motion studies by Frederick Taylor and others helped them analyze how employees perform specific work tasks in an effort to improve their productivity. Taylor and the early practitioners of the classical theory of motivation felt that money and job security were the primary motivators of employees. However, the Hawthorne studies revealed that human factors also influence workers' behaviour.

Compare and contrast the human-relations theories of Abraham Maslow and Frederick Herzberg.

Abraham Maslow defined five basic needs of all people and arranged them in the order in which they must be satisfied: physiological, security, social, esteem, and self-actualization. Frederick Herzberg divided characteristics of the job into hygiene factors and motivational factors. Hygiene factors relate to the work environment and must be present for employees to remain in a job. Motivational factors—recognition, responsibility, and advancement—relate to the work itself. They encourage employees to be productive. Herzberg's hygiene factors can be compared to Maslow's physiological and security needs; motivational factors may include Maslow's social, esteem, and self-actualization needs.

Investigate various theories of motivation, including Theories X, Y, and Z; equity theory; and expectancy theory.

Douglas McGregor contrasted two views of management: Theory X (traditional) suggests workers dislike work, while theory Y (humanistic) suggests that workers not only like work but seek out responsibility to satisfy their higher-order needs. Theory Z stresses employee participation in all aspects of company decision making, often through participative management programs and self-directed work teams. According to equity theory, how much people are willing to contribute to an organization depends on their assessment of the fairness, or equity, of the rewards they will receive in exchange. Expectancy theory states that motivation depends not only on how much a person wants something but also on the person's perception of how likely he or she is to get it.

Describe some of the strategies that managers use to motivate employees.

Strategies for motivating workers include behaviour modification (changing behaviour and encouraging appropriate actions by relating the consequences of behaviour to the behaviour itself) and job design. Among the job design strategies businesses use are job rotation (allowing employees to move from one job to another to try to relieve the boredom associated with job specialization), job enlargement (adding tasks to a job instead of treating each task as a separate job), job enrichment (incorporating motivational factors into a job situation), flexible scheduling strategies (flextime, compressed work weeks, job sharing, part-time work, and telecommuting), and management by objectives (a process in which a manager and a subordinate conferring together set and agree to goals for the subordinate to achieve).

Critique a business's program for motivating its sales force.

Using the information presented in the chapter, you should be able to analyze and defend St. Lawrence Pharmaceutical's motivation program in "Solve the Dilemma," including the motivation theories the firm is applying to boost morale and productivity.

Learn the Terms

behaviour modification 250

classical theory of motivation
    242

compressed work week 253

equity theory 249

esteem needs 245

expectancy theory 249

flextime 252

human relations 240

hygiene factors 245

job enlargement 251

job enrichment 251

job rotation 251

job sharing 253

management by objectives
    (MBO) 255

Maslow's hierarchy 244

morale 241

motivation 240

motivational factors 246

physiological needs 244

security needs 244

self-actualization needs 245

social needs 245

Theory X 247

Theory Y 247

Theory Z 247

Check Your Progress

1. Why do managers need to understand the needs of their employees?
2. Describe the motivation process.
3. What was the goal of the Hawthorne studies? What was the outcome of those studies?
4. Explain Maslow's hierarchy of needs. What does it tell us about employee motivation?
5. What are Herzberg's hygiene and motivational factors? How can managers use them to motivate workers?
6. Contrast the assumptions of Theory X and Theory Y. Why has Theory Y replaced Theory X in management today?
7. What is Theory Z? How can businesses apply Theory Z to the workplace?
8. Identify and describe five job-design strategies.
9. Name and describe some flexible scheduling strategies. How can flexible schedules help motivate workers?
10. Describe the steps of management by objectives (MBO). How can this technique motivate employees?

Get Involved

1. Consider a person who is homeless: How would he or she be motivated and what actions would that person take? Use the motivation process to explain. Which of the needs in Maslow's hierarchy are likely to be most important? Least important?
2. What events and trends in society, technology, and economics do you think will shape management theory in the future?
3. Describe a motivation program for hourly paid restaurant workers, high-paid management consultants, and single-parent office clerical workers. Would the same technique work for all?

Build Your Skills

Motivating

Background: Do you think that, if employers could make work more like play, employees would be as enthusiastic about their jobs as they are about what they do in their leisure time? Let's see where this idea might take us.

Task: After reading the "Characteristics of PLAY," place a √ in column one for those characteristics you have experienced in your leisure time activities. Likewise, check column three for those "Characteristics of WORK" you have experienced in any of the jobs you've held.

√ All That Apply	Characteristics of PLAY	√ All That Apply	Characteristics of WORK
	1. New games can be played on different days		1. Job enrichment, job enlargement, or job rotation.
	2. Flexible duration of play.		2. Job sharing.
	3. Flexible time of when to play.		3. Flextime, telecommuting.
	4. Opportunity to express oneself.		4. Encourage and implement employee suggestions.
	5. Opportunity to use one's talents.		5. Assignment of challenging projects.
	6. Skillful play brings applause, praise, and recognition from spectators.		6. Employee-of-the-month awards, press releases, employee newsletter announcements.
	7. Healthy competition, rivalry, and challenge exist.		7. Production goals with competition to see which team does best.
	8. Opportunity for social interaction.		8. Employee softball or bowling teams.
	9. Mechanisms for scoring one's performance are available (feedback).		9. Profit sharing; peer performance appraisals.
	10. Rules assure basic fairness and justice.		10. Use tactful and consistent discipline.

Discussion Questions

1. What prevents managers from making work more like play?

2. Are these forces real, or imagined?

3. What would be the likely (positive and negative) results of making work more like play?

4. Could others in the organization accept such creative behaviours?

Loyalty in the Workplace

It would seem that people are not sticking to their jobs. Can you blame them? But companies as well as government agencies need young, energetic people to join and stay with the organization.

We see a recent graduate who jumps ship a few months after receiving what many considered a prime position with the largest newspaper in Canada. But he felt he was not beholden to the employer and couldn't pass up a good offer. Is the lack of loyalty a generational factor (young people don't feel obliged to stay in their jobs), or is the lack of loyalty a reflection of cynical workers who have seen organizations let faithful employees go after years of service? Have companies turned off the employees from all the downsizing and cutting in the 1990s in an attempt to return to profitability or reduce the tax burden?

But the next generation is needed badly. Young people entering the work force are creative, knowledgeable, and hence very valuable to the future development and growth of organizations. The Royal Bank has come to realize that the human aspects are critical to staying in a position or with an organization. The loyalty is not to the firm but to the people. In these economic times of constant change, how can employers inspire loyalty in their employees?

Questions

1. In the jobs that you have had, have many people remained with their employer for more than three years? Five years? Ten years?

2. If an employer hires you for a permanent position, what do you owe that employer? Is the individual in the video warranted in changing employers?

3. What does the employer owe employees hired into a permanent position? Should they guarantee jobs for life?

4. Are young people correctly categorized by the immediate need to fulfill the TV remote desires? Do they need instant gratification and hence are not loyal by their own nature and environment?

5. What is your opinion on the level of wages earned by professional athletes, and should they also be required to stay loyal to the team that developed them to the status of high salaries?

6. Considering the wages earned by the executives, does this encourage the loyalty that is needed among the employees?

7. Who is responsible for the career development of the employee?

Source: *Venture*, show number 777, "Loyalty in the Workplace," March 6, 2001, running time 7:20.

Remember to check out our Online Learning Centre at **www.mcgrawhill.ca/college/ferrell**.

Chapter 11

Managing Human Resources

Chapter Outline

Objectives

After reading this chapter, you will be able to:

- Define human resources management and explain its significance.
- Summarize the processes of recruiting and selecting human resources for a company.
- Discuss how workers are trained and their performance appraised.
- Identify the types of turnover companies may experience, and explain why turnover is an important issue.
- Specify the various ways a worker may be compensated.
- Discuss some of the issues associated with unionized employees, including collective bargaining and dispute resolution.
- Describe the importance of diversity in the work force.
- Assess an organization's efforts to reduce its work force size and manage the resulting effects.

"Job Shops" Connect People with Jobs

As a global leader in employment services with revenues of US$8 billion, Swiss-based Adecco connects people to jobs and jobs to people through a network of 3,000 offices in 48 countries. Adecco supplies qualified temporary and full-time personnel to over 65,000 North American businesses.

Job Shop is a colourful kiosk or freestanding booth designed to attract a steady stream of interested people and job seekers. After the successful operation of Job Shop at some 80 locations in Europe, Adecco introduced the innovative, interactive job search kiosk in the US with plans to place them in malls and universities in 33 states. There are also now 101 locations in Canada. Interested parties follow the simple touch-screen guide to submit their qualifications toward new job opportunities. Convenient and easy to use, Job Shop's self-guiding instructions prompt users to enter information such as the type of work desired, schedule and availability, education, experience, salary requirements, and skills, as well as other data. Completed in just a few minutes, the entered information is linked to Adecco's central database for processing. Software screens and matches an applicant's skills and interests to specific jobs available. When a positive match occurs, Adecco professionals contact the applicant to set up an appointment and complete the final steps of screening, testing, and placement. Hailed as a "win/win" proposition, the Job Shop kiosks allow users a choice in pursuing careers—as well as widening the number of qualified candidates that Adecco provides to businesses.

Adecco's Job Shop kiosks, along with the company's web site recruiting programs and screening and testing systems, are part of its strategic use of technology and innovation to better serve job candidates and corporate clients. Debbie Pond-Heide, president of Adecco North America, says, "We're developing technological bridges that connect people to jobs with amazing speed and convenience."[1]

Courtesy of Addecco North America

Enter the World of Business

INTRODUCTION

If a business is to achieve success, it must have sufficient numbers of employees who are qualified to perform the required duties. Thus, managing the quantity (from hiring to firing) and quality (through training, compensating, and so on) of employees is an important business function. Meeting the challenge of managing increasingly diverse human resources effectively can give a company a competitive edge in a cutthroat global marketplace.

This chapter focuses on the quantity and quality of human resources. First we look at how human resources managers plan for, recruit, and select qualified employees. Next we look at training, appraising, and compensating employees, aspects of human resources management designed to retain valued employees. Along the way, we'll also consider the challenges of managing unionized and diverse employees.

THE NATURE OF HUMAN RESOURCES MANAGEMENT

human resources management (HRM)

all the activities involved in determining an organization's human resources needs, as well as acquiring, training, and compensating people to fill those needs

Chapter 1 defined human resources as labour, the physical and mental abilities that people use to produce goods and services. **Human resources management (HRM)** refers to all the activities involved in determining an organization's human resources needs, as well as acquiring, training, and compensating people to fill those needs. Human resources managers are concerned with maximizing the satisfaction of employees and motivating them to meet organizational objectives productively. In some companies, this function is called personnel management.

HRM has increased in importance over the last few decades, in part because managers have developed a better understanding of human relations through the work of Maslow, Herzberg, and others. Moreover, the human resources themselves are changing. Employees today are concerned not only about how much a job pays; they are concerned also with job satisfaction, personal performance, leisure, the environment, and the future. Once dominated by white men, today's work force includes significantly more women, Asian-Canadians, Aboriginals, and other minorities, as well as disabled and older workers. Human resources managers must be aware of these changes and make the best of them to increase the productivity of their employees. Every manager practises some of the functions of human resources management at all times.

PLANNING FOR HUMAN RESOURCES NEEDS

When planning and developing strategies for reaching the organization's overall objectives, a company must consider whether it will have the human resources necessary to carry out its plans. After determining how many employees and what skills are needed to satisfy the overall plans, the human resources department (which may range from the owner in a small business to hundreds of people in a large corporation) ascertains how many employees the company currently has and how many will be retiring or otherwise leaving the organization during the planning period. With this information, the human resources manager can then forecast how many more employees the company will need to hire and what qualifications they must have. HRM planning also requires forecasting the availability of people in the work force who will have the necessary qualifications to meet the organization's future needs. The human resources manager then develops a strategy for satisfying the organization's human resources needs.

Next, managers analyze the jobs within the organization so that they can match the human resources to the available assignments. **Job analysis** determines, through observation and study, pertinent information about a job—the specific tasks that comprise it; the knowledge, skills, and abilities necessary to perform it; and the environment in which it will be performed. Managers use the information obtained through a job analysis to develop job descriptions and job specifications.

A **job description** is a formal, written explanation of a specific job that usually includes job title, tasks to be performed (for instance, waiting on customers), relationship with other jobs, physical and mental skills required (such as lifting heavy boxes or calculating data), duties, responsibilities, and working conditions. A **job specification** describes the qualifications necessary for a specific job, in terms of education (some jobs require a college degree), experience, personal characteristics (newspaper ads frequently request outgoing, hard-working persons), and physical characteristics. Both the job description and job specification are used to develop recruiting materials such as newspaper advertisements.

RECRUITING AND SELECTING NEW EMPLOYEES

After forecasting the firm's human resources needs and comparing them to existing human resources, the human resources manager should have a general idea of how many new employees the firm needs to hire. With the aid of job analyses, management can then recruit and select employees who are qualified to fill specific job openings.

Recruiting

Recruiting means forming a pool of qualified applicants from which management can select employees. There are two sources from which to develop this pool of applicants—internal and external sources.

Internal sources of applicants include the organization's current employees. Many firms have a policy of giving first consideration to their own employees—or promoting from within. The cost of hiring current employees to fill job openings is inexpensive when compared with the cost of hiring from external sources, and it is good for employee morale.

External sources consist of advertisements in newspapers and professional journals, employment agencies, colleges and universities, vocational schools, Internet job boards, recommendations from current employees, competing firms, and unsolicited applications. Using these sources of applicants is generally more expensive than hiring from within, but it may be necessary if there are no current employees who meet the job specifications or there are better-qualified people outside of the organization. Recruiting for entry-level managerial and professional positions is often carried out on college and university campuses. For managerial or professional positions above the entry level, companies sometimes depend on employment agencies or executive search firms, sometimes called *headhunters,* which specialize in luring qualified people away from other companies.

job analysis
the determination, through observation and study, of pertinent information about a job—including specific tasks and necessary abilities, knowledge, and skills

job description
a formal, written explanation of a specific job, usually including job title, tasks, relationship with other jobs, physical and mental skills required, duties, responsibilities, and working conditions

job specification
a description of the qualifications necessary for a specific job, in terms of education, experience, and personal and physical characteristics

recruiting
forming a pool of qualified applicants from which management can select employees

Selection

selection
the process of collecting information about applicants and using that information to make hiring decisions

Monster.ca
www.monster.ca

Workopolis
www.workopolis.ca

Selection is the process of collecting information about applicants and using that information to decide which ones to hire. It includes the application itself, as well as interviewing, testing, and reference checking. This process can be quite lengthy and expensive. At Procter & Gamble, for example, the steps include the application, a problem-solving test, screening and comprehensive interviews, and day visits/site visits.[2] Such rigorous scrutiny is necessary to find those applicants who can do the work expected and fit into the firm's structure and culture. If an organization finds the "right" employees through its recruiting and selection process, it will not have to spend as much money later in recruiting, selecting, and training replacement employees.

The Application. In the first stage of the selection process, the individual fills out an application form and perhaps has a brief interview. The application form asks for the applicant's name, address, telephone number, education, and previous work experience. In addition to identifying obvious qualifications, the application can provide subtle clues about whether a person is appropriate for a particular job. For instance, an applicant who gives unusually creative answers may be perfect for a position at an advertising agency; a person who turns in a sloppy, hurriedly scrawled application probably would not be appropriate for a technical job requiring precise adjustments. The goal of this stage of the selection process is to get acquainted with the applicants and to weed out those who are obviously not qualified for the job. Last year, Salomon Smith Barney, a brokerage firm, received 70 applications for every one it accepted.[3] In addition, applications can be submitted over the Internet at locations such as Monster.ca or Workopolis.ca.

The Interview. The next phase of the selection process involves interviewing applicants. Interviews allow management to obtain detailed information about the applicant's experience and skills, reasons for changing jobs, attitudes toward the job, and an idea of whether the person would fit in with the company. Furthermore, the interviewer can answer the applicant's questions about the requirements for the job, compensation, working conditions, company policies, organizational culture, and so on. A potential employee's questions may be just as revealing as his or her answers. Some companies, including Coopers & Lybrand, are interviewing some job candidates over the Internet. The goal of the online interview is to determine which applicants should be interviewed in person at a later time. Candidates answer detailed questions about their career goals and how they would handle challenging job situations. Questions/answers are assigned points, and a computer scores the responses. Employers then contact the high-scoring applicants to arrange a face-to-face meeting.[4]

Testing. Another step in the selection process is testing. Ability and performance tests are used to determine whether an applicant has the skills necessary for the job. Aptitude, IQ, or personality tests may be used to assess an applicant's potential for a certain kind of work and his or her ability to fit into the organization's culture. One of the most commonly used tests is the Myers-Briggs Type Indicator. The result of the test is 1 of 16 four-letter codes (e.g., ENFJ, ISTP, etc.). The codes are explained in Figure 11.1. Skill tests such as welding, keyboarding, or graphic arts presentations may be used to evaluate the candidate's level of talent and skill. Applicants may also undergo physical examinations to determine their suitability for some jobs, and many companies require applicants to be screened for drug use. Like the application form and the interview, testing serves to eliminate those who do not meet the job specifications.

Figure 11.1

Myers-Briggs Type Indicator Categories

Extroversion/Introversion

Determines the source of mental energy. Extroverts (E) rely on others (peers and supervisors). Introverts (I) rely on themselves.

Sensing/Intuiting

Explains how information is absorbed. Sensing (S) types tend to be literal and methodical. Intuitive (N) types rely on patterns and relationships and are bored by details.

Thinking/Feeling

Refers to how decisions are made. Thinkers (T) are logical and objective. Feelers (F) deal more with emotions and tend to be empathic.

Judging/Perceiving

Refers to how quickly decisions are made. Judging (J) types need closure. Perceivers (P) make decisions slowly.

Source: Christopher Caggiano, "Psycho Path," *Inc.,* July 1998, p. 81. Reprinted with permission of *Inc.* Magazine, Goldhirsh Group, Inc. Reproduced by permission of the publisher via Copyright Clearance Centre, Inc.

Reference Checking. Before making a job offer, the company should always check an applicant's references. Reference checking usually involves verifying educational background and previous work experience. Background checking is important because applicants may misrepresent themselves on their applications or résumés. Consequently, reference checking is a vital, albeit often overlooked, stage in the selection process. Managers charged with hiring should be aware, however, that many organizations will confirm only that an applicant is a former employee, perhaps with beginning and ending work dates, and will not release details about the quality of the employee's work.

Legal Issues in Recruiting and Selecting

Each province and territory as well as the federal government have human rights laws governing individual rights and freedom from discrimination based on race, religion, sexual orientation, age, gender, and so on. These laws extend to the workplace in both the treatment of employees and the hiring procedures. The federal government enacted in 1987 the Employment Equity Act that governs the hiring practices of those organizations under its jurisdiction, such as airlines, shipping companies, telecommunications firms, and banks. The act requires employers with over 100 employees to develop annual plans to include "persons in a designated group who achieve a degree of representation commensurate with their representation in the Canadian workforce and their availability to meet reasonable occupational requirements."

Employment equity programs are the Canadian version of affirmative action programs in the US. These programs are to remedy past discrimination or prevent discrimination in the future. No province at this time requires that organizations under their jurisdiction be required to fulfill these same equity programs, though many public and private organizations do so voluntarily.

employment equity programs

programs developed by employers to undo past employment discrimination or to ensure equal employment opportunity in the future; similar to affirmative action programs in the US

The American affirmative action programs require organizations to employ a proportionate number of women and visible minorities in different job classifications. US laws were revised in 1991 to ensure that the hiring of minorities does not become so focused that organizations overlook hiring the best candidate for the position, which may result in reverse discrimination. Still, solid gains have been made in both the US and Canada, and to a lesser extent the wage gap between genders has been somewhat reduced.

DEVELOPING THE WORK FORCE

orientation
familiarizing newly hired employees with fellow workers, company procedures, and the physical properties of the company

Once the most qualified applicants have been selected and offered positions, and they have accepted their offers, they must be formally introduced to the organization and trained so they can begin to be productive members of the work force. **Orientation** familiarizes the newly hired employees with fellow workers, company procedures, and the physical properties of the company. It generally includes a tour of the building; introductions to supervisors, coworkers, and subordinates; and the distribution of organizational manuals describing the organization's policy on vacations, absenteeism, lunch breaks, company benefits, and so on. Orientation also involves socializing the new employee into the ethics and culture of the new company. Many larger companies now show videotapes of procedures, facilities, and key personnel in the organization to help speed the adjustment process. For example, Howard Schultz, CEO and chairman of Starbucks Coffee Co., greets all new hires (roughly 500 per month) via video. Schultz defines what Starbucks stands for, what it is trying to achieve, and the relevancy of this to the new employee. He believes that valuing employees (or *partners,* as they are called from the very first day) leads to lower turnover.[5]

Training and Development

training
teaching employees to do specific job tasks through either classroom development or on-the-job experience

development
training that augments the skills and knowledge of managers and professionals

Although recruiting and selection are designed to find employees who have the knowledge, skills, and abilities the company needs, new employees still must undergo **training** to learn how to do their specific job tasks. *On-the-job training* allows workers to learn by actually performing the tasks of the job, while *classroom training* teaches employees with lectures, conferences, videotapes, case studies, and, increasingly, web-based training. More than US$55 billion is spent annually in North America on corporate classroom training, including travel costs associated with sending employees to corporate training centres.[6] **Development** is training that augments the skills and knowledge of managers and professionals. Training and development are also used to improve the skills of employees in their present positions and to prepare them for increased responsibility and job promotions. Training is therefore a vital function of human resources management. For example, HSBC Bank of Canada has a well-integrated strategy for training employees. The training is tied in with the strategic vision of the organization and must lead to improved profits and effectiveness, which then leads to more training.

Assessing Performance

Assessing an employee's performance—his or her strengths and weaknesses on the job—is one of the most difficult tasks for managers. However, performance appraisal is crucial because it gives employees feedback on how they are doing and what they need to do to improve their performance. It also provides a basis for determining how to compensate and reward employees, and it generates information about the quality of the firm's selection, training, and development activities.

Performance appraisals may be objective or subjective. An objective assessment is quantifiable. For example, a Westinghouse employee might be judged by how many circuit boards he typically produces in one day or by how many of his boards have defects. A Royal LePage real estate agent might be judged by the number of houses she has shown or the number of sales she has closed. A company can also use tests as an objective method of assessment. Whatever method they use, managers must take into account the work environment when they appraise performance objectively.

When jobs do not lend themselves to objective appraisal, the manager must relate the employee's performance to some other standard. One popular tool used in subjective assessment is the rating scale, which lists various performance factors on which the manager rates the employee.

Many employers offer computer training courses to their employees in a classroom-type setting as depicted in the photo above. These computer training courses can be offered to improve the skills of current employees or to enhance the abilities of new employees.

© 1999 PhotoDisc, Inc.

Whether the assessment is objective or subjective, it is vital that the manager discuss the results with the employee, so that the employee knows how well he or she is doing the job. The results of a performance appraisal become useful only when they are communicated, tactfully, to the employee and presented as a tool to allow the employee to grow and improve in his or her position and beyond. Performance appraisals are also used to determine whether an employee should be promoted, transferred, or terminated from the organization. Most employers conduct the first review within the permitted three-month probationary period for new employees. Generally, employers may terminate an employee within the first three months without cause or severance pay.

Turnover

This section identifies the types of turnover a company may experience and explains why turnover is an important issue. Figure 11.2 shows the annual cost of job turnover in the US when the following factors are considered: lost productivity from a vacancy, search fees, management time devoted to interviewing, and training costs for new employees. In Canada, mostly due to the recession of 1991 and 1992, many employees stayed with their firms much longer than they did during the 1980s. In the 1980s, many jobs lasted 37 months but in 1997 to 1999, most new positions started are expected to last 50 months.[7]

A **promotion** is an advancement to a higher-level job with increased authority, responsibility, and pay. In some companies and most labour unions, seniority—the length of time a person has been with the company or at a particular job classification—is the key issue in determining who should be promoted. Most managers base promotions on seniority only when they have candidates with equal qualifications: Managers prefer to base promotions on merit.

promotion
an advancement to a higher-level job with increased authority, responsibility, and pay

Figure 11.2

*Job Turnover Costs
per Person*

Source: "The Big Picture:
Job-Turnover Tab," *Business
Week*, April 20, 1998, p. 8.

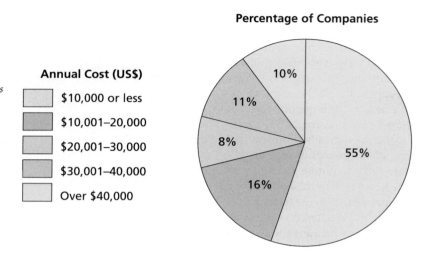

Percentage of Companies

Annual Cost (US$)

- $10,000 or less
- $10,001–20,000
- $20,001–30,000
- $30,001–40,000
- Over $40,000

transfer

a move to another job
within the company at
essentially the same level
and wage

separations

employment changes
involving resignation,
retirement, termination,
or layoff

A **transfer** is a move to another job within the company at essentially the same level and wage. Transfers allow workers to obtain new skills or to find a new position within an organization when their old position has been eliminated because of automation or downsizing.

Separations occur when employees resign, retire, are terminated, or are laid off. Table 11.1 lists rules for peaceful separations from companies. Employees may be terminated, or fired, for poor performance, violation of work rules, absenteeism, and so on. Legislation and court decisions require that companies fire employees fairly, for just cause only. Managers must take care, then, to warn employees when their performance is unacceptable and may lead to dismissal. They should also document all problems and warnings in employees' work records. To avoid the possibility of lawsuits from individuals who may feel they have been fired unfairly, employers should provide clear, business-related reasons for any firing, supported by written documentation if possible. Employee disciplinary procedures should be carefully explained to all employees and should be set forth in employee handbooks.

Many companies have downsized in recent years, laying off tens of thousands of employees in their effort to become more productive and competitive. This hits especially hard on youth (18–24 years) who have a hard time keeping their jobs, and older men (over 50) who have difficulties finding work. Layoffs are sometimes temporary; employees may be brought back when business conditions improve. When layoffs are to be permanent, employers often help employees find other jobs and may extend benefits while the employees search for new employment. Such actions help lessen the trauma of the layoffs.

A well-organized human resources department strives to minimize losses due to separations and transfers because recruiting and training new employees is very expensive. Note that a high turnover rate in a company may signal problems either with the selection and training process or with the compensation program. Table 11.2 lists the top reasons why employees leave based on a poll of executives from 1,000 of the largest companies.

- Leave as soon as practicable after making the decision.

- Prior to leaving, discuss your decision only with those who need to know.

- If asked, be candid about your new job; avoid the appearance of hiding something.

- Prior to leaving, do not disrupt your current employer's business.

- Do not take any documents, computer data, etc. with you.

- Be careful about any paper or electronic trails concerning the process that resulted in your resignation.

- Sign an employment agreement with a new employer only after you have resigned from your current position.

- Do not work for the new employer until after the last day of work at your current job.

- Have the recruiting employer indemnify you regarding judgments, settlements, and lawyers' fees incurred in connection with any litigation initiated by your former employer.

- Specify in a written agreement with your new employer that you will not use or disclose any trade secrets of former employers.

Table 11.1

Rules for Peaceful Separations

Source: Robert Lenzner and Carrie Shook, "Want to Go Peacefully? Some Rules," *Forbes,* February 23, 1998. Reprinted by permission of *Forbes Magazine.* Copyright Forbes Inc., 1998.

COMPENSATING THE WORK FORCE

People don't work for free, and how much they are paid for their work is a complicated issue. Also, designing a fair compensation plan is an important task because pay and benefits represent a substantial portion of an organization's expenses. Wages that are too high may result in the company's products being priced too high, making them uncompetitive in the market. Wages that are too low may damage employee morale and result in costly turnover. Remember that compensation is one of the hygiene factors identified by Herzberg.

Designing a fair compensation plan is a difficult task because it involves evaluating the relative worth of all jobs within the business while allowing for individual efforts. Compensation for a specific job is typically determined through a **wage/salary survey,** which tells the company how much compensation comparable firms are paying for specific jobs that the firms have in common. Compensation for individuals within a specific job category depends on both the compensation for that job

wage/salary survey
a study that tells a company how much compensation comparable firms are paying for specific jobs that the firms have in common

Lack of recognition and praise	34%
Low compensation	29
Limited authority	18
Personality conflicts	8

Table 11.2

Top Reasons Why Employees Leave

Source: "The Power of Recognition," **www.jostens.com/recognition/power/**, August 17, 1998. Copyright Robert Half International, Inc.

and the individual's productivity. Therefore, two employees with identical jobs may not receive exactly the same pay because of individual differences in performance.

Financial Compensation

wages
financial rewards based on the number of hours the employee works or the level of output achieved

Financial compensation falls into two general categories—wages and salaries. **Wages** are financial rewards based on the number of hours the employee works or the level of output achieved. Wages based on the number of hours worked are called time wages. A baker at Tim Hortons, for example, might earn the minimum wage. Time wages are appropriate when employees are continually interrupted and when quality is more important than quantity. Assembly-line workers, clerks, and maintenance personnel are commonly paid on a time-wage basis. The advantage of time wages is the ease of computation. The disadvantage is that time wages provide no incentive to increase productivity. In fact, time wages may encourage employees to do less than a full day's work.

Did you know?

General Motors, the world's #1 auto company, has
• 372,000 employees
• A market value of US$31 billion
Microsoft, the world's #1 software company, has
• 48,030 employees
• A market value of US$319 billion

commission
an incentive system that pays a fixed amount or a percentage of the employee's sales

To overcome these disadvantages, many companies pay on an incentive system, using piece wages or commissions. Piece wages are based on the level of output achieved. A major advantage of piece wages is that they motivate employees to supervise their own activities and to increase output. Skilled craftworkers are often paid on a piece-wage basis. The other incentive system, **commission,** pays a fixed amount or a percentage of the employee's sales. A car salesperson at a Mazda dealership, for example, might receive a specified percentage of the price of each car he or she sells. This method motivates employees to sell as much as they can. Some companies combine payment based on commission with time wages or salaries.

Some companies are launching web sites to put their pay plans online. For example, IBM's site prompts sales representatives to enter some basic information (title, job description, and base salary) and then uses that input to direct employees to a site with their particular incentive plan. There they can determine the impact of their performance on their compensation. They can calculate their compensation based on reaching a percentage of their quota (e.g., 105 percent, 115 percent, or more or less). The site's theme is "Extreme Selling" and it is designed with pictures of bungee jumpers and surfers. The tag line for the site is "How far will you go?" In addition to the benefits of real-time access to customized incentive information and the motivation factor, running a web site cuts costs and saves time for IBM salespeople.[8]

salary
a financial reward calculated on a weekly, monthly, or annual basis

A **salary** is a financial reward calculated on a weekly, monthly, or annual basis. Salaries are associated with white-collar workers such as office personnel, executives, and professional employees. Although a salary provides a stable stream of income, salaried workers may be required to work beyond usual hours without additional financial compensation.

bonuses
monetary rewards offered by companies for exceptional performance as incentives to further increase productivity

In addition to the basic wages or salaries paid to employees, a company may offer **bonuses** for exceptional performance as an incentive to increase productivity further. Many workers receive a bonus at Christmas as a "thank you" for good work and an incentive to continue working hard. KPMG, a large accounting and consulting firm, has recently begun a new compensation plan based on a straight salary plus an incentive-based bonus. The new package replaces KPMG's previous system of paying overtime on an hourly basis for audits and tax assignments.[9]

The proximity of Mexico to the US and Canada and the passage of the North American Free Trade Agreement have made Mexico an increasingly attractive site for foreign investment. However, the closeness of the three countries can be misleading. Canadian and US companies often assume that their human resources management practices can be transported to Mexico as easily as raw materials. In reality, human resources management in Mexico involves unique challenges, especially in the areas of turnover, absenteeism, demographics, employee involvement, and labour unions. The usual tactics for addressing these issues are sometimes unconventional or even not permitted in Canada or the US.

Production worker turnover rates in northern Mexico are high, averaging between 7 and 15 percent per month. One factor is the abundance of potential employers. The number of foreign-owned plants in Mexico that export their finished product has risen by 700 in the last four years, to approximately 2,700. Some managers consider absenteeism a more severe problem than turnover, with the most frequently given reason for absence being family issues. In general, the Mexican culture gives greater value to family than to work.

To combat the excessive levels of turnover and absenteeism, salaries are competitive and financial incentives are frequently offered. For example, some companies offer bonuses to employees who stay 30 days. Another bonus is given after 60 days and then 90 days. Bonuses for attendance are standard, and discount coupons, subsidized transportation to and from work, and subsidized lunches encourage employee loyalty. Nonmonetary benefits help retention rates, too. Parties and picnics are an expected part of the Mexican culture, and it is not uncommon for a job applicant to ask how many parties a company gives each year.

Practices generally viewed as taboo in Canada and the US but frequent in Mexico include the production worker beauty contest, in which employees vote for their plant's most attractive female worker, who then competes against workers from other plants. Gender preference in hiring is legitimate in Mexico, and banners are often seen that say, "Recruiting Female Employees." Because of extensive maternity benefits, however, companies routinely screen job applicants with pregnancy tests. A woman with a positive test may not be hired or may be hired under a short-term contract. This practice is technically illegal in Mexico but is widespread and tolerated.

It is impossible to transfer all human resources management practices from Canada and the US to other areas. Managing cultural diversity in a global environment requires an assessment of specific management challenges and the identification of approaches for meeting such challenges.[10]

Another form of compensation is **profit sharing,** which distributes a percentage of company profits to the employees whose work helped to generate those profits. Some profit-sharing plans involve distributing shares of company stock to employees. Usually referred to as *ESOPs*—employee stock ownership plans—they have been gaining popularity in recent years. One reason for the popularity of ESOPs is the sense of partnership that they create between the organization and employees. Profit sharing can also motivate employees to work hard, because increased productivity

profit sharing
a form of compensation whereby a percentage of company profits is distributed to the employees whose work helped to generate them

Solve the Dilemma

Morale among the Survivors

Medallion Corporation manufactures quality carpeting and linoleum. A recession and subsequent downturn in home sales has sharply cut the company's sales. Medallion found itself in the unenviable position of having to lay off hundreds of employees in the home office (the manufacturing facilities) as well as many salespeople. Employees were called in on Friday afternoon and told about their status in individual meetings with their supervisors. The laid-off employees were given one additional month of work and two weeks severance pay per year of service, along with the opportunity to sign up for classes to help with the transition, including job search tactics and résumé writing.

Several months after the cutbacks, morale was at an all-time low for the company, although productivity had improved. Medallion brought in consultants, who suggested that the leaner, flatter organizational structure would be suitable for more team activities. Medallion therefore set up task forces and teams to deal with employee concerns, but the diversity of the work force led to conflict and misunderstandings among team members. Medallion is evaluating how to proceed with this new team approach.

1. What did Medallion's HRM department do right in dealing with the employees who were laid off?

2. What are some of the potential problems that must be dealt with after an organization experiences a major trauma such as massive layoffs?

3. What can Medallion do to make the team approach work more smoothly? What role do you think diversity training should play?

and sales mean that the profits or the stock dividends will increase. Although many organizations offer employees a stake in the company through stock purchase plans, ESOPs, or stock investments through registered retirement savings plans (RRSPs), employees below senior management levels rarely received stock options, until recently. In a total US work force of approximately 131 million, only about 5 million are eligible to receive stock options. According to studies by management consultants, companies are adopting broad-based stock option plans to build a stronger link between employees' interests and the organization's interests. Hughes Electronic Corp. recently joined the ranks of progressive companies, such as Transalta Utilities, Royal Bank, and BCE, that offer such plans. The "Stock Up on Hughes" program awards a stock option grant to purchase 100 shares of the company's stock at a set price to all eligible Hughes employees, numbering nearly 14,000. Michael T. Smith, chairman and CEO, says, "This program is designed to promote greater employee ownership of the company, which in turn fosters one of the most important elements of Hughes—teamwork and the alignment of interests."[11]

Hughes Electronic Corp.
**www.hughes.com/
home/default.xml**

benefits

nonfinancial forms of compensation provided to employees, such as pension plans, health insurance, paid vacation and holidays, and the like

Benefits

Benefits are nonfinancial forms of compensation provided to employees, such as pension plans for retirement; health, disability, and life insurance; holidays and paid days off for vacation or illness; credit union membership; health programs; child care; elder care; assistance with adoption; and more. In 2000, the average total

It's about relationships

Our benefits solutions start with one simple ingredient – clear dialogue with our customers.

Through dialogue we learn and understand our customers' needs.
And our customers get to know and understand what we can deliver.

It's all about relationships. Relationships built on listening,
understanding each other, and working closely together.

Together we'll find solutions to your benefits needs.
Contact Jeff Kinch, National Marketing, at 1-888-588-5650 or e-mail jeff.kinch@clarica.com

Clarica. Your clear choice for group benefits.

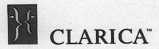

CLARICA™

Investment and insurance solutions - Since 1870

Clarica advertises the customization of benefit packages for its clients.

income for Canadians equalled \$22.65 per hour worked.[12] Table 11.3 lists some of the benefits and work conditions of workers in Canada. Such benefits increase employee security and, to a certain extent, their morale and motivation.

A benefit increasingly offered is the employee assistance program (EAP). Each company's EAP is different, but most offer counselling for and assistance with those

Table 11.3

Benefits and Work Conditions

Source: Statistics Canada, Perspectives on Labour and Income, Catalogue No. 75-001, Winter 1997.

Work Condition/Benefit	Percentage of Union Employees	Percentage of Nonunion Employees
Pension coverage	82.8%	32.9%
Supplemental health plan coverage	83.7	44.4
Dental plan coverage	77.0	41.9
Paid sick leave	77.2	44.7
Paid vacation leave	84.1	65.3
Flextime option	16.7	27.1
Job sharing arrangement	12.1	6.8
Average annual paid vacation leave	20.9 days	15.1 days

employees' personal problems that might hurt their job performance if not addressed. The most common counselling services offered include drug- and alcohol-abuse treatment programs, fitness programs, smoking-cessation clinics, stress-management clinics, financial counselling, family counselling, and career counselling. EAPs help reduce costs associated with poor productivity, absenteeism, and other workplace issues by helping employees deal with personal problems that contribute to these issues. For example, exercise and fitness programs reduce health insurance costs by helping employees stay healthy. Family counselling may help workers trying to cope with a divorce or other personal problems better focus on their jobs. A study that included 90 percent of the *Fortune* 100 indicated that 88 percent of the surveyed employers in the US offer EAPs.[13]

Companies try to provide the benefits they believe their employees want, but diverse people may want different things. Some companies use flexible benefit programs to allow employees to choose the benefits they would like, up to a specified amount. Over the last two decades, the list of fringe benefits has grown dramatically, and new benefits are being added every year.

MANAGING UNIONIZED EMPLOYEES

labour unions

employee organizations formed to deal with employers for achieving better pay, hours, and working conditions

Canadian Auto Workers
www.caw.ca

Employees who are dissatisfied with their working conditions or compensation have to negotiate with management to bring about change. Dealing with management on an individual basis is not always effective, however, so employees may organize themselves into **labour unions** to deal with employers and to achieve better pay, hours, and working conditions. Organized employees are backed by the power of a large group that can hire specialists to represent the entire union in its dealings with management. The Canadian Auto Workers, for example, has considerable power in its negotiations with Ford Motor Company, General Motors, and Daimler Chrysler Corporation.

However, union growth has slowed in recent years, and prospects for growth do not look good. One reason is that most blue-collar workers, the traditional members of unions, have already been organized. Factories have become more automated and need fewer blue-collar workers. Canada is shifting from a manufacturing/resource economy to a service economy, further reducing the demand for blue-collar workers. Moreover, in response to foreign competition, companies are scrambling to find ways to become more productive and cost efficient. Job enrichment programs and participative management have blurred the line between management and workers. Because workers' say in the way plants are run is increasing, their need for union protection is decreasing.

Nonetheless, labour unions have been successful in organizing blue-collar manufacturing, government, and health care workers, as well as smaller percentages of employees in other industries. In fact, about 30 percent of all employed Canadians are represented by a union.[14] Consequently, significant aspects of HRM, particularly compensation, are dictated to a large degree by union contracts at many companies. Therefore, we'll take a brief look at collective bargaining and dispute resolution in this section.

Collective Bargaining

Collective bargaining is the negotiation process through which management and unions reach an agreement about compensation, working hours, and working conditions for the bargaining unit (Figure 11.3). The objective of negotiations is to reach agreement about a **labour contract,** the formal, written document that spells out the relationship between the union and management for a specified period of time, usually two or three years.

In collective bargaining, each side tries to negotiate an agreement that meets its demands; compromise is frequently necessary. Management tries to negotiate a labour contract that permits the company to retain control over things like work schedules; the hiring and firing of workers; production standards; promotions, transfers, and separations; the span of management in each department; and discipline. Unions tend to focus on contract issues such as magnitude of wages; better pay rates for overtime, holidays, and undesirable shifts; scheduling of pay increases; benefits; and job security. These issues will be spelled out in the labour contract, which union members will vote to either accept (and abide by) or reject.

Many labour contracts contain a *cost-of-living escalator clause (COLA),* which calls for automatic wage increases during periods of inflation to protect the "real" income of the employees. During tough economic times, unions may be forced to accept *givebacks*—wage and benefit concessions made to employers to allow them to remain competitive or, in some cases, to survive and continue to provide jobs for union workers.

Resolving Disputes

Sometimes, management and labour simply cannot agree on a contract. Most labour disputes are handled through collective bargaining or through grievance procedures. When these processes break down, however, either side may resort to more drastic measures to achieve its objectives.

Labour Tactics. Picketing is a public protest against management practices and involves union members marching (often waving antimanagement signs and placards) at the employer's plant. Picketing workers hope that their signs will arouse sympathy for their demands from the public and from other unions. Picketing may occur as a protest or in conjunction with a strike.

collective bargaining
the negotiation process through which management and unions reach an agreement about compensation, working hours, and working conditions for the bargaining unit

labour contract
the formal, written document that spells out the relationship between the union and management for a specified period of time—usually two or three years

picketing
a public protest against management practices that involves union members marching and carrying antimanagement signs at the employer's plant

Figure 11.3

The Collective Bargaining Process

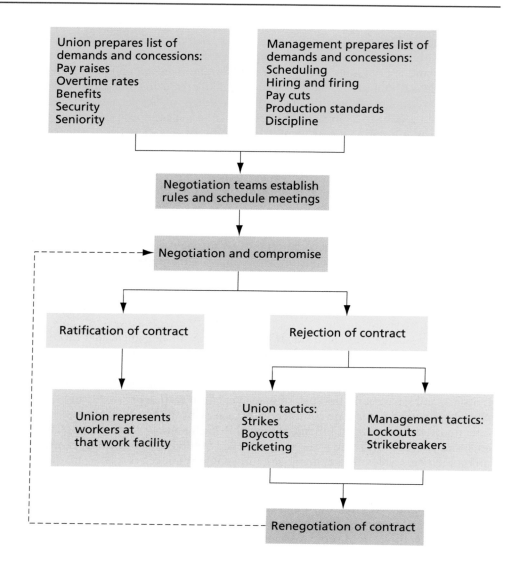

Union prepares list of demands and concessions:
Pay raises
Overtime rates
Benefits
Security
Seniority

Management prepares list of demands and concessions:
Scheduling
Hiring and firing
Pay cuts
Production standards
Discipline

Negotiation teams establish rules and schedule meetings

Negotiation and compromise

Ratification of contract

Rejection of contract

Union represents workers at that work facility

Union tactics:
Strikes
Boycotts
Picketing

Management tactics:
Lockouts
Strikebreakers

Renegotiation of contract

strikes

employee walkouts; one of the most effective weapons labour has

boycott

an attempt to keep people from purchasing the products of a company

    Strikes (employee walkouts) are one of the most effective weapons labour has. By striking, a union makes carrying out the normal operations of a business difficult at best and impossible at worst. Strikes can hurt businesses. For example, an eight-week strike at General Motors resulted in US$2.85 billion in lost profits and an estimated 545,000 units of car and truck production.[15] Strikes receive widespread publicity, but they remain a weapon of last resort. The threat of a strike is often enough to get management to back down. In fact, the number of worker-days actually lost to strikes is less than the amount lost to the common cold.

    A **boycott** is an attempt to keep people from purchasing the products of a company. In a boycott, union members are asked not to do business with the boycotted organization. Some unions may even impose fines on members who ignore the boycott. In order to further gain support for their objectives, a union involved in a boycott may also ask the public—through picketing and advertising—not to purchase the products of the picketed firm.

Management Tactics. Management's version of a strike is the **lockout;** management actually closes a work site so that employees cannot go to work. Lockouts are used, as a general rule, only when a union strike has partially shut down a plant and it seems less expensive for the plant to close completely. In 1999 there were 413 strikes or lockouts in Canada, involving 159,000 workers and resulting in the loss of 2.4 million person-days. This represents two-thirds the number of days and strikes ten years earlier but involves only one-third the number of workers.[16]

Strikebreakers, called "scabs" by striking union members, are people hired by management to replace striking employees. Managers hire strikebreakers to continue operations and reduce the losses associated with strikes—and to show the unions that they will not bow to their demands. Strikebreaking is generally a last-resort measure for management because it does great damage to the relationship between management and labour.

Outside Resolution. Management and union members normally reach mutually agreeable decisions without outside assistance. Sometimes though, even after lengthy negotiations, strikes, lockouts, and other tactics, management and labour still cannot resolve a contract dispute. In such cases, they have three choices: conciliation, mediation, and arbitration. **Conciliation** brings in a neutral third party to keep labour and management talking. The conciliator has no formal power over union representatives or over management. The conciliator's goal is to get both parties to focus on the issues and to prevent negotiations from breaking down. Like conciliation, **mediation** involves bringing in a neutral third party, but the mediator's role is to suggest or propose a solution to the problem. Mediators have no formal power over either labour or management. With **arbitration,** a neutral third party is brought in to settle the dispute, but the arbitrator's solution is legally binding and enforceable. Generally, arbitration takes place on a voluntary basis—management and labour must agree to it, and they usually split the cost (the arbitrator's fee and expenses) between them. Occasionally, management and labour submit to *compulsory arbitration,* in which an outside party (usually the federal government) requests arbitration as a means of eliminating a prolonged strike that threatens to disrupt the economy.

THE IMPORTANCE OF WORK FORCE DIVERSITY

Customers, employees, suppliers—all the participants in the world of business—come in different ages, genders, races, ethnicities, nationalities, and abilities, a truth that business has come to label **diversity.** Understanding this diversity means recognizing and accepting differences as well as valuing the unique perspectives such differences can bring to the workplace.

The Characteristics of Diversity

When managers speak of diverse work forces, they typically mean differences in gender and race. While gender and race are important characteristics of diversity, others are also important. We can divide these differences into primary and secondary

---

lockout
management's version of a strike, wherein a work site is closed so that employees cannot go to work

strikebreakers
people hired by management to replace striking employees; called "scabs" by striking union members

conciliation
a method of outside resolution of labour and management differences in which a third party is brought in to keep the two sides talking

mediation
a method of outside resolution of labour and management differences in which the third party's role is to suggest or propose a solution to the problem

arbitration
settlement of a labour/management dispute by a third party whose solution is legally binding and enforceable

diversity
the participation of different ages, genders, races, ethnicities, nationalities, and abilities in the workplace

characteristics of diversity. In the lower segment of Figure 11.4, age, gender, race, ethnicity, abilities, and sexual orientation represent *primary characteristics* of diversity, which are inborn and cannot be changed. In the upper section of Figure 11.4 are eight *secondary characteristics* of diversity—work background, income, marital status, military experience, religious beliefs, geographic location, parental status, and education—which *can* be changed. We acquire, change, and discard them as we progress through our lives.

Defining characteristics of diversity as either primary or secondary enhances our understanding, but we must remember that each person is defined by the interrelation of all characteristics. In dealing with diversity in the work force, managers must consider the complete person—not one or a few of a person's differences.

Why Is Diversity Important?

As we enter the twenty-first century, the Canadian work force is becoming increasingly diverse. Once dominated by white men, today's work force includes significantly more women, Asian-Canadians, Aboriginals, and other minorities, as well as disabled and older workers. In the 1996 Census, visible minorities represented 11.2 percent of the Canadian population, or 3.2 million people. Chinese, South Asians, and Blacks represented the three largest groups. These numbers exclude Aboriginal Canadians, who represent over 300,000 earners in Canada.[17] These

Figure 11.4

Characteristics of Diversity

Source: Marilyn Loden and Judy B. Rosener, *Workforce America! Managing Employee Diversity as a Vital Resource,* 1991, p. 20. Used with permission. Copyright © 1991 Richard D. Irwin, a Times Mirror Higher Education Group, Inc. company.

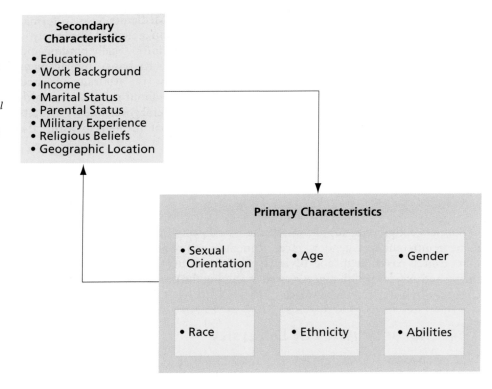

Secondary Characteristics

- Education
- Work Background
- Income
- Marital Status
- Parental Status
- Military Experience
- Religious Beliefs
- Geographic Location

Primary Characteristics

- Sexual Orientation
- Age
- Gender
- Race
- Ethnicity
- Abilities

The Bank of Montreal is a good example of an organization that took the notion of diversity management seriously. Finding that women held 91 percent of the bank's non-management jobs but only 9 percent of the executive positions, the bank made an early attempt to tap the vast potential of its female work force. The bank established a Task Force on the Advancement of Women to identify the constraints facing women who wanted career progress in the bank. Clear goals and action plans were established to eliminate these hurdles. Surveys, focus groups, and intense interviews were carried out to find solutions for faster advancement of women to executive careers.

Apart from the financial benefits it received by tapping a hitherto forgotten resource, the bank also received numerous awards for its success in improving the work climates of women, Aboriginals, and people with disabilities. The Catalyst Award from a New York think-tank, the Distinction Award from the YWCA, and Catalyst: Mercury Awards from the International Communications Academy of Arts and Sciences in New York are particularly noteworthy in this context.

The closing of the gender gap has resulted in finding women in many top-ranking positions in many Canadian companies. The president of GM Canada, the president of Indigo/Chapters/Coles, and the president of Linamar Technologies of Guelph, are all women.

Clearly women can successfully operate large and small businesses to the benefit of the companies, their customers, and the communities in which they operate.[18]

Value Diversity

Her Rise to the Top

groups have traditionally faced discrimination and higher unemployment rates and have been denied opportunities to assume leadership roles in the corporate world. Consequently, more and more companies are trying to improve HRM programs to recruit, develop, and retain more diverse employees to better serve their diverse customers. In a recent study by the Society for Human Resource Management, 75 percent of *Fortune* 500 companies have diversity programs that were developed more than five years ago, and 8 percent are planning to implement diversity programs within the next year. Some firms are providing special programs such as sponsored affinity groups (37 percent), mentoring programs (30 percent), and special career development opportunities (24 percent).[19] Effectively managing diversity in the work force involves cultivating and valuing its benefits and minimizing its problems.

**Explore
Your Career
Options**

*How Much
Does It Pay?*

That's the big question everyone wants to know, whether considering future career options or a specific job in a particular company. While you're not likely to make as much as Eric Lindros or Celine Dion, the potential for big bucks is out there, depending on your choice of career, the organization you ultimately work for, *and* how hard you are willing to work.

Experts suggest that you need to earn four times your age ($140,000/year for a 35-year-old, for example) if you want to be able to own a nice house and car, send your kids to college, stay ahead of inflation, and save for a comfortable retirement. Most people never come close to that yardstick, however. The mean income for a full-time worker who has a Bachelor's degree is $42,054, and it's $25,838 for those with less than a university education.[20]

Clearly, some jobs pay a lot more than others. A CEO of a large corporation can earn millions in salary, benefits, and bonuses; while at the other end of the scale, a preschool teacher might draw just $20,000. Business management, engineers, health professionals, and technology specialists are all hot careers, in terms of both growth potential and pay.

But for many people, money isn't everything. Remember Herzberg's motivation factors? Benefits, job security, desirable working hours, and a satisfying work environment are some of the factors that can help make up for a job that doesn't put you in the same tax bracket as Tom Hanks. The preschool teacher may find moulding young minds for $20,000 just as satisfying as the challenge the millionaire CEO enjoys in running a company. And, with companies increasingly opting for limited pay raises in favour of bonuses tied to performance, people working in even fairly low-paying jobs can find themselves earning good money for hard work. The bottom line is that you have to decide what's important to you and go for it.[21]

The Benefits of Work Force Diversity

There are a number of benefits to fostering and valuing work force diversity, including the following:

1. More productive use of a company's human resources.
2. Reduced conflict among employees of different ethnicities, races, religions, and sexual orientations as they learn to respect each other's differences.
3. More productive working relationships among diverse employees as they learn more about and accept each other.
4. Increased commitment to and sharing of organizational goals among diverse employees at all organizational levels.
5. Increased innovation and creativity as diverse employees bring new, unique perspectives to decision-making and problem-solving tasks.
6. Increased ability to serve the needs of an increasingly diverse customer base.[22]

Companies that do not value their diverse employees are likely to experience greater conflict, as well as prejudice and discrimination. Among individual employees, for example, racial slurs and gestures, sexist comments, and other behaviours by coworkers harm the individuals at whom such behaviour is directed. The victims of such behaviour may feel hurt, depressed, or even threatened and suffer from lowered self-esteem, all of which harm their productivity and morale. In such cases, women and minority employees may simply leave the firm, wasting the time, money, and other resources spent on hiring and training them. When discrimination comes from a supervisor, employees may also fear for their jobs. A discriminatory atmosphere not only can harm productivity and raise turnover, but it may also subject a firm to costly lawsuits and negative publicity.

Astute businesses recognize that they need to modify their human resources management programs to target the needs of *all* their diverse employees as well as the needs of the firm itself. They realize that the benefits of diversity are long term in nature and come only to those organizations willing to make the commitment. Most importantly, as work force diversity becomes a valued organizational asset, companies spend less time managing conflict and more time accomplishing tasks and satisfying customers, which is, after all, the purpose of business.

Review Your Understanding

Define human resources management and explain its significance.

Human resources, or personnel, management refers to all the activities involved in determining an organization's human resources needs and acquiring, training, and compensating people to fill those needs. It is concerned with maximizing the satisfaction of employees and improving their efficiency to meet organizational objectives.

Summarize the processes of recruiting and selecting human resources for a company.

First, the human resources manager must determine the firm's future human resources needs and develop a strategy to meet them. Recruiting is the formation of a pool of qualified applicants from which management will select employees; it takes place both internally and externally. Selection is the process of collecting information about applicants and using that information to decide which ones to hire; it includes the application, interviewing, testing, and reference checking.

Discuss how workers are trained and their performance appraised.

Training teaches employees how to do their specific job tasks; development is training that augments the skills and knowledge of managers and professionals, as well as current employees. Appraising performance involves identifying an employee's strengths and weaknesses on the job. Performance appraisals may be subjective or objective.

Identify the types of turnover companies may experience, and explain why turnover is an important issue.

A promotion is an advancement to a higher-level job with increased authority, responsibility, and pay. A transfer is a move to another job within the company at essentially the same level and wage. Separations occur when employees resign, retire, are terminated, or are laid off. Turnovers due to separation are expensive because of the time, money, and effort required to select, train, and manage new employees.

Specify the various ways a worker may be compensated.

Wages are financial compensation based on the number of hours worked (time wages) or the number of units produced (piece wages). Commissions are a fixed amount or a percentage of a sale paid as compensation. Salaries are compensation calculated on a weekly, monthly, or annual basis, regardless of the number of hours worked or the number of items produced. Bonuses and profit sharing are types of financial incentives. Benefits are nonfinancial forms of compensation, such as vacation, insurance, and sick leave.

Discuss some of the issues associated with unionized employees, including collective bargaining and dispute resolution.

Collective bargaining is the negotiation process through which management and unions reach an agreement on a labour contract—the formal, written document that spells out the relationship written between the union and management. If labour and management cannot agree on a contract, labour union members may picket, strike, or boycott the firm, while management may lock out striking employees, hire strikebreakers, or form employers' associations. In a deadlock, labour disputes may be resolved by a third party—a conciliator, mediator, or arbitrator.

Describe the importance of diversity in the work force.

When companies value and effectively manage their diverse work forces, they experience more productive use of human resources, reduced conflict, better work relationships among workers, increased commitment to and sharing of organizational goals, increased innovation and creativity, and enhanced ability to serve diverse customers.

Assess an organization's efforts to reduce its work force size and manage the resulting effects.

Based on the material in this chapter, you should be able to answer the questions posed in the "Solve the Dilemma" box and evaluate the company's efforts to manage the human consequences of its downsizing.

Learn the Terms

arbitration 279
benefits 274
bonuses 272
boycott 278
collective bargaining 277
commission 272
conciliation 279
development 268
diversity 279
employment equity programs 267

human resources management (HRM) 264
job analysis 265
job description 265
job specification 265
labour contract 277
labour unions 276
lockout 279
mediation 279
orientation 268
picketing 277
profit sharing 273

promotion 269
recruiting 265
salary 272
selection 266
separations 270
strikebreakers 279
strikes 278
training 268
transfer 270
wage/salary survey 271
wages 272

Check Your Progress

1. Distinguish among job analysis, job descriptions, and job specifications. How do they relate to planning in human resources management?
2. What activities are involved in acquiring and maintaining the appropriate level of qualified human resources? Name the stages of the selection process.
3. What are the two types of training programs? Relate training to kinds of jobs.
4. What is the significance of performance appraisal? How do managers appraise employees?
5. Why does turnover occur? List the types of turnover. Why do businesses want to reduce turnover due to separations?

6. Relate wages, salaries, bonuses, and benefits to Herzberg's distinction between hygiene and motivation factors. How does the form of compensation relate to the type of job?
7. What is the role of benefits? Name some examples of benefits.
8. Describe the negotiation process through which management and unions reach an agreement on a contract.
9. Besides collective bargaining and the grievance procedures, what other alternatives are available to labour and management to handle labour disputes?
10. What are the benefits associated with a diverse work force?

Get Involved

1. Although many companies screen applicants for past criminal offences, such screening is somewhat controversial. Find some organizations that screen for prior illegal involvement with children. Debate the pros and cons of these screens.

2. If collective bargaining and the grievance procedures have not been able to settle a current labour dispute, what tactics would you and other employees adopt? Which tactics would be best for which situations? Give examples.

3. Find some examples of companies that value their diverse work forces, perhaps some of the companies mentioned in the chapter. In what ways have these firms derived benefits from promoting cultural diversity? How have they dealt with the problems associated with cultural diversity?

Build Your Skills

Appreciating and Valuing Diversity

Background: Here's a quick self-assessment to get you to think about diversity issues and evaluate the behaviours you exhibit that reflect your level of appreciation of other cultures:

Do you ...	Regularly	Sometimes	Never
1. Make a conscious effort not to think stereotypically?			
2. Listen with interest to the ideas of people who don't think like you do?			
3. Respect other people's opinions, even when you disagree?			
4. Spend time with friends who are not your age, race, gender, or the same economic status and education?			
5. Believe your way is *not* the only way?			
6. Adapt well to change and new situations?			
7. Enjoy travelling, seeing new places, eating different foods, and experiencing other cultures?			
8. Try not to offend or hurt others?			
9. Allow extra time to communicate with someone whose first language is not yours?			
10. Consider the effect of cultural differences on the messages you send and adjust them accordingly?			

Scoring

Number of **Regularly** checks _____ multiplied by 5 = _____
Number of **Sometimes** checks _____ multiplied by 3 = _____
Number of **Never** checks _____ multiplied by 0 = _____
TOTAL _____

Indications from score

40–50   You appear to understand the importance of valuing diversity and exhibit behaviours that support your appreciation of diversity.

26–39   You appear to have a basic understanding of the importance of valuing diversity and exhibit some behaviours that support that understanding.

13–25   You appear to lack a thorough understanding of the importance of valuing diversity and exhibit only some behaviours related to valuing diversity.

0–12   You appear to lack an understanding of valuing diversity and exhibit few, if any, behaviours of an individual who appreciates and values diversity.

Task: In a small group or class discussion, share the results of your assessment. After reading the following list of ways you can increase your knowledge and understanding of other cultures, select one of the items that you have done and share how it helped you learn more about another culture. Finish your discussion by generating your own ideas on other ways you can learn about and understand other cultures and fill in those ideas on the blank lines below.

- Be alert to and take advantage of opportunities to talk to and get to know people from other races and ethnic groups. You can find them in your neighbourhood, in your classes, at your fitness centre, at a concert or sporting event—just about anywhere you go. Take the initiative to strike up a conversation and show a genuine interest in getting to know the other person.

- Select a culture you're interested in and immerse yourself in that culture. Read novels, look at art, take courses, see plays.

- University and college students often have unique opportunities to travel inexpensively to other countries—for example, as a member of a performing arts group, with a humanitarian mission group, or as part of a university or college course studying abroad. Actively seek out travel opportunities that will expose you to as many cultures as possible during your university or college education.

- Study a foreign language.

- Expand your taste buds. The next time you're going to go to a restaurant, instead of choosing that old familiar favourite, use the Yellow Pages to find a restaurant that serves ethnic food you've never tried before.

- Many large metropolitan cities sponsor ethnic festivals, particularly in the summertime, where you can go and take in the sights and sounds of other cultures. Take advantage of these opportunities to have a fun time learning about cultures that are different from yours.

- _____
  _____

- _____
  _____

 **See for Yourself Videocase**   **www.cbc.ca**

International Dining

This short interest video displays the diversity of eating habits and the etiquette involved and required of the employees of an internationally active company or government agency.

There are four different ways identified to eat soup, and there are correct ways to lay your knife, fork, or spoon on your plate when you are finished eating. We don't want to offend anyone, do we? How should a person prepare for a trip to Japan and be ready to dine and entertain international customers? When do you drink the wine, and how do you clink glasses when moving in certain circles? All of these issues are small, one may think, but they can become large and a barrier to doing business when you are the visitor or the host.

Do we as Canadians and North Americans have our particular way of doing something that we would expect others to do, even visitors? What about other employees?

Questions

1. When a person is being considered for a position in a firm or organization, what other skills, talents, and characteristics are included in the assessment?

2. From the perspective of the company, is there an advantage in hiring foreign-born candidates or those from different cultures?

3. When hiring senior personnel, what other attributes are evaluated that are not considered with other jobs. Is this appropriate?

4. Do *you* have the knowledge to do business in the international environment and not offend people by being impolite? Where would you go for training if you do not? (The students in the video are in an MBA program.)

Source: *Venture*, show number 764, "International Dining," November 14, 2000, running time 2:41.

Remember to check out our Online Learning Centre at **www.mcgrawhill.ca/college/ferrell.**

Cyberzone

Creating the HR Advantage through the Internet

The growth and widespread use of the Internet and the World Wide Web have had a strong impact on human resource management. Some of the effects include the ability to immediately access up-to-the-minute information, conduct recruiting, interviewing, and hiring online, and take advantage of web-based training/development and performance appraisals.

Accessing Information

Many managers are tapping into the vast amounts of information available on the web through sites such as that of the Human Resources Professional Association of Ontario (HRPAO). This comprehensive site provides current human resource news, a member directory, and the *HR Professional* magazine, as well as links to other human resource sites.

Online Recruiting/ Interviewing/Hiring

In addition to information gathering on the web, many managers are finding other uses as well. Many firms have built attractive and informative web sites that give job seekers a favourable impression of the company and allow them to view current job opportunities—as well as apply for openings or submit a résumé for potential openings online. Procter & Gamble, for instance, presents its corporate philosophy and general career information, posts job opportunities by location and category, and gives potential employees the opportunity to send a résumé via e-mail. P&G is currently test marketing an online application form. Wal-Mart and Xerox both post job opportunities and have an online form for applicants to complete and submit with just a click.

Many human resource managers responsible for recruiting and hiring are finding that the web attracts a different, special type of individual—one who tends to be savvy, independent, and creative and possesses diverse skills and attitudes. It is estimated that 70 percent of active job seekers are more likely to use the web than traditional job hunting methods.[1] According to the Internet Business Network, more than 1.2 million résumés were processed electronically last year, with the number expected to increase to 2.5 million this year.[2] A recent survey by Management Recruiter International found that nearly 37 percent of the 4,300 executives surveyed recruit online, up from 26.5 percent two years ago.[3] Some employers are finding the web can be less expensive than traditional methods, such as advertising in national newspapers or hiring recruiting firms. The cost of a newspaper ad averages about $128 per résumé received,[4] while registering a company with an online search community site that may yield hundreds of résumés can cost less than $100.[5] Well-known resources for both job seekers and recruiters include Workopolis.ca and Monster.ca. Job seekers can post, update, or delete their résumés for free, search thousands of job listings alphabetically or by location, industry, or keyword. Résumés are posted within 24 hours and remain for up to six months. Employers can post job opportunities and search the résumé listings through paid subscriptions. Some sites allow recruiters to provide employer profiles and post job opportunities. Recruiters surfing the web have found it to be a good hiring tool.

Web-based recruiting and employment sites are "red-hot,"[6] and human resource managers must continue to look to the web for recruiting, hiring, and managing qualified employees who can make an impact on company growth.

Virtual Employees

Another opportunity and challenge for human resource management created by the ever-increasing accessibility and use of the Internet and web is the virtual employee. Many firms have found that virtual employees, sometimes located thousands of kilometres from the company headquarters, help them compete in the global marketplace. Virtual employees are those who communicate with and receive/transmit assignments to and from their employers mainly through e-mail. In many cases, employer and employee never, or rarely, actually meet face-to-face. Businesses using virtual employees with much success include publishing, web mastering, graphic design, architecture, engineering, and photography. One such business is Hammock Publishing, a custom publisher. Rex Hammock says his company couldn't function nearly as well without its virtual staff—many of whom he's never even seen. Hammock Publishing has online relationships with dozens of photographers, writers, and illustrators. The editor and senior editor of one of its publications—the 250,000-circulation *Road King* magazine—communicate daily with Hammock's Nashville-based editorial director from their homes in San Diego and Indianapolis.

Mike Becce, president of MRB Public Relations, a high-tech publicity firm, maintains that "finding really good people is still elusive. Now I see that the key—if you can maintain control over the staff—is not where they live but who has the best qualifica- tions. The virtual office concept certainly makes finding really special people far more possible."[7]

E-mail

The increased usage of e-mail (the average worker receives 30 e-mail messages a day) also impacts human resource management. Liability issues include how long to store e-mail and whether its use should be monitored. Some experts suggest purging e-mail files every 90 days to avoid liability, but others warn that doing so could destroy evidence a company may need in case of a lawsuit.

A survey by the Society of Human Resource Management found that about 20 percent of employers have received complaints about inappropriate e-mail, but only about half of the firms have a policy in place on e-mail usage. Experts suggest mandatory e-mail training for all employees so that inappropriate use is curtailed. About 35 percent of employers currently use surveillance tactics, which include reading employees' e-mail. A message appears on computer screens at Pillsbury reminding employees that they are using company property. At Boeing, workers are encouraged to use restraint when sending messages electronically.[8]

Skilled human resource managers should take advantage of the opportunities afforded by the Internet and the World Wide Web. There are hundreds of sites that can help provide managers with the necessary tools to support good human resource management and foster productive, satisfied employees.

Part Five

Marketing: Developing Relationships

Chapter 12

Customer-Driven Marketing

Chapter Outline

Objectives

After reading this chapter, you will be able to:

- Define marketing and describe the exchange process.
- Specify the functions of marketing.
- Explain the marketing concept and its implications for developing marketing strategies.
- Examine the development of a marketing strategy, including market segmentation and marketing mix.
- Investigate how marketers conduct marketing research and study buying behaviour.
- Summarize the environmental forces that influence marketing decisions.
- Assess a company's marketing plans and propose a solution for resolving its problem.

Putting the Fat Back in

Several years ago, Nabisco introduced Snackwell's, a line of low-fat and fat-free cookies and crackers. At the time, consumers were fat and health conscious, and sales of the snacks soared. Sales peaked, though, at about US$490 million and have since slowed considerably—amid fierce competition from other snack brands and complaints about the taste. For example, the head of nutrition and food studies at New York University commented that "they tasted like sugary straw."

Generally, consumption of healthier foods has slowed over the last couple of years, and only about 11 percent of the cookies consumed in the second half of 1999 were low-fat or fat-free. Consumers still seem concerned about fat content in their food, but now taste is more important.

To reverse the trend of sagging sales, Nabisco changed its strategy to win consumers over to their products with improved taste. To accomplish this, Nabisco put the fat back in—as much as 50 percent more in one product, Snackwell's Zesty Cheese crackers. Cracked Pepper crackers and Wheat crackers went from being fat-free to containing 1.5 grams of fat per serving, an amount that is still about 60 percent less than a regular snack cracker. Chocolate Sandwich cookies have 20 percent more fat. Another Snackwell cookie product now has 4 grams of fat per serving, the most that any Snackwell's product has ever had. A typical regular cookie has from 6 to 8 grams of fat per serving. With the additional fat and sugar in the products, the amount of calories per serving also rose. Only the Devil's Food cookie remains fat-free. All other Snackwell's products are now classified as "reduced fat."

Nabisco's strategy also included discontinuing two products, introducing a new chocolate-covered Mint Creme cookie, redesigning the boxes with bolder lettering and the absence of "low fat," and continuing the pricing strategy of about $2.59 per box. Only time and the Nabisco annual report will show whether the new strategy is enough to counter Snackwell's drag on company profits.[1]

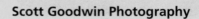

Scott Goodwin Photography

INTRODUCTION

Marketing involves planning and executing the development, pricing, promotion, and distribution of ideas, goods, and services to create exchanges that satisfy individual and organizational goals. These activities ensure that the products consumers want to buy are available at a price they are willing to pay and that consumers are provided with information about product features and availability. Organizations of all sizes and objectives engage in these activities.

During the early growth of North America, most companies focused on producing to fill the demands of growing nations. In the 1920s production started to exceed demand and companies shifted their attention to increasing sales through finding more customers by adding more salespeople to the market. By the 1960s, companies shifted to satisfying the customer's needs as well as the company's goals. Beginning in the 1980s, with increasing global competition, the orientation of companies evolved into continuously researching customer needs and competitors' capacities and sharing the information throughout the organization to create customer value.

In this chapter, we focus on the basic principles of marketing. First we define and examine the nature of marketing. Then we look at how marketers develop marketing strategies to satisfy the needs and wants of their customers. The manipulation of "the Four Ps"—price, product, promotion, and place/distribution—is the major focus of the strategies to reach customers. Next we discuss buying behaviour and how marketers use research to determine what consumers want to buy and why. Finally we explore the impact of the environment on marketing activities.

marketing
a group of activities designed to expedite transactions by creating, distributing, pricing, and promoting goods, services, and ideas

NATURE OF MARKETING

A vital part of any business undertaking, **marketing** is a group of activities designed to expedite transactions by creating, distributing, pricing, and promoting goods, services, and ideas. These activities create value by allowing individuals and organi-

By providing simplicity— something first-time computer buyers value— the iMac computer helped reverse declining sales at Apple Computer.

Courtesy of Apple Computer Company

zations to obtain what they need and want. A business cannot achieve its objectives unless it provides something that customers value. For example, Apple Computer reversed declining sales by introducing the iMac for consumers who were concerned about computers being too complicated and costly. The iMac was designed for the home market, especially first-time computer buyers. Its success was based on simplicity and Internet capabilities.[2] But just creating an innovative product that meets many users' needs isn't sufficient in today's volatile global marketplace. Products must be conveniently available, competitively priced, and uniquely promoted.

Of all the business concepts covered in this text, marketing may be the hardest to master. Businesses try to respond to consumer wants and needs and to anticipate changes in the environment. Unfortunately, it is difficult to understand and predict what consumers want: Motives are often unclear; few principles can be applied consistently; and markets tend to fragment, desiring customized products, new value, or better service.[3]

It is important to note what marketing is not: It is not manipulating consumers to get them to buy products they don't want. It is not just selling and advertising; it is a systematic approach to satisfying consumers. Marketing focuses on the many activities—planning, pricing, promoting, and distributing products—that foster exchanges.

The Exchange Relationship

At the heart of all business is the **exchange,** the act of giving up one thing (money, credit, labour, goods) in return for something else (goods, services, or ideas). Businesses exchange their goods, services, or ideas for money or credit supplied by customers in a voluntary *exchange relationship,* illustrated in Figure 12.1. The buyer must feel good about the purchase, or the exchange will not continue. If your local dry cleaner cleans your nice suit properly, on time, and without damage, you will probably feel good about using its services. But if your suit is damaged or isn't ready on time, you will probably use another dry cleaner next time.

exchange
the act of giving up one thing (money, credit, labour, goods) in return for something else (goods, services, or ideas)

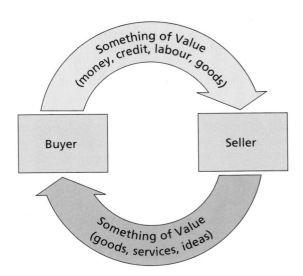

Figure 12.1

The Exchange Process: Giving up One Thing in Return for Another

For an exchange to occur, certain conditions are required. As indicated by the arrows in Figure 12.1, buyers and sellers must be able to communicate about the "something of value" available to each. An exchange does not necessarily take place just because buyers and sellers have something of value to exchange. Each participant must be willing to give up his or her respective "something of value" to receive the "something" held by the other. You are willing to exchange your "something of value"—your money or credit—for compact discs, soft drinks, hockey tickets, or new shoes because you consider those products more valuable or more important than holding on to your cash or credit potential.

When you think of marketing products, you may think of tangible things—cars, stereo systems, or books, for example. What most consumers want, however, is a way to get a job done, solve a problem, or gain some enjoyment. You may purchase a Kenmore vacuum cleaner not because you want a vacuum cleaner but because you want clean carpets. Therefore, the tangible product itself may not be as important as the image or the benefits associated with the product. For example, the major benefit of the Duracell Ultra battery is that it will last up to 50 percent longer than regular alkaline batteries.[4] This intangible "something of value" may be capability gained from using a product or the image evoked by it, such as Tommy Hilfiger jeans.

Marketing Creates Utility

utility
a product's ability to satisfy human needs and wants

The central focus of marketing is to create **utility,** which refers to a product's ability to satisfy human needs and wants. A McDonald's Big Mac, a three-day vacation at Walt Disney World, a computer program—all satisfy needs or wants. Businesses attempt to provide four kinds of utility—place, time, ownership, and form—and three of the four kinds (place utility, time utility, and ownership utility) are created directly by marketing.

place utility
making the product available where the buyer wishes to buy it

Place utility is created by making the product available where the buyer wishes to buy it. Most Canadians do not want to travel to Germany to purchase a Mercedes, to Japan to buy a Sony television, or to Mexico to purchase enchiladas for lunch. Thus, marketers create place utility by making products available at convenient locations.

time utility
making the product available when customers wish to purchase it

Time utility is created by making a product available when customers wish to purchase it. Because some shoppers have time to shop for a new automobile only on Saturdays, auto dealers may miss a sale unless they open for business on Saturdays. Similarly, due to seasonal changes, more convertibles may be desired in April, May, and June and more four-wheel-drive automobiles in December, January, and February.

ownership utility
transference of ownership of a product to the buyer

Ownership utility is created by transferring ownership of a product to the buyer. Regardless of whether a product is a good, a service, or an idea, there is a point when ownership is legally transferred by means of a sales receipt or other formal transaction from one party to another. The transfer of product ownership guarantees the right of the buyer to use that product to satisfy a need.

form utility
utility created through the production process rather than through marketing activities

Form utility is created through the production process rather than through marketing activities. An Acura automobile on display in the dealer's showroom possesses form utility: This product would not be available unless it had gone through a series of production steps, from the manufacture of sheet steel to the final assembly of finished parts. Marketers participate in the creation of form utility by researching what features—air bags, antilock brakes, stereos, and so on—consumers want so that the product is manufactured to satisfy their needs.

A key role of marketers is to create place, time, and ownership utility to ensure that human needs and wants are met. To satisfy customers' needs and wants, marketers must carry out certain functions.

Functions of Marketing

Marketing focuses on a complex set of activities that must be performed to accomplish objectives and generate exchanges. These activities include buying, selling, transporting, storing, grading, financing, marketing research, and risk taking.

Buying. Everyone who shops for products (consumers, stores, businesses, governments) decides whether and what to buy. A marketer must understand buyers' needs and desires to determine what products to make available.

Selling. The exchange process is expedited through selling. Marketers usually view selling as a persuasive activity that is accomplished through promotion (advertising, personal selling, sales promotion, publicity, and packaging.)

Transporting. Transporting is the process of moving products from the seller to the buyer. Marketers focus on transportation costs and services.

Storing. Like transporting, storing is part of the physical distribution of products and includes warehousing goods. Warehouses hold some products for lengthy periods in order to create time utility. Consumers want frozen orange juice year-round, for example, although the production season for oranges is only a few months out of the year. This means that sellers must arrange cold storage for frozen orange juice concentrate all year.

Grading. Grading refers to standardizing products and displaying and labelling them so that consumers clearly understand their nature and quality. Many products, such as meat, steel, and fruit, are graded according to a set of standards that often are established by the government.

Financing. For many products, especially large items such as automobiles, refrigerators, and new homes, the marketer provides credit to expedite the purchase.

Marketing Research. Through research, marketers ascertain the need for new goods and services. By gathering information regularly, marketers can detect new trends and changes in consumer tastes.

Risk Taking. Risk is the chance of loss associated with marketing decisions. Developing a new product creates a chance of loss if consumers do not like it enough to buy it. Spending money to hire a sales force or to conduct marketing research also involves risk. The implication of risk is that most marketing decisions result in either success or failure.

The Marketing Concept

A basic philosophy that guides all marketing activities is the **marketing concept,** the idea that an organization should try to satisfy customers' needs through coordinated activities that also allow it to achieve its own goals. According to the marketing concept, a business must find out what consumers need and want and then develop the good, service, or idea that fulfills their needs or wants. For example, Tim Hortons is

marketing concept
the idea that an organization should try to satisfy customers' needs through coordinated activities that also allow it to achieve its own goals

responding to customers' needs and wants by offering new items such as specialty coffees, bagels, sandwiches, soup, and muffins, and pairing with other stores such as Wendy's. The business must then get the product to the customer. In addition, the business must continually alter, adapt, and develop products to keep pace with changing consumer needs and wants. Each business must determine how best to implement the marketing concept, given its own goals and resources.

Trying to determine customers' true needs is increasingly difficult because no one fully understands what motivates people to buy things. For example, Pacific Sunwear of California claims it stays close to its average 15-year-old customer by not selling clothes, but by selling an image that teenagers call "cool."[5]

Although customer satisfaction is the goal of the marketing concept, a business must also achieve its own objectives, such as boosting productivity, reducing costs, or achieving a percentage of a specific market. If it does not, it will not survive. For example, Sharp Electronics could sell VCRs for $50 and give customers a lifetime guarantee, which would be great for customers but not so great for Sharp. Obviously, the company must strike a balance between achieving organizational objectives and satisfying customer needs and wants.

To implement the marketing concept, a firm must have good information about what consumers want, adopt a consumer orientation, and coordinate its efforts throughout the entire organization; otherwise, it may be awash with goods, services, and ideas that consumers do not want or need. Successfully implementing the marketing concept requires that a business view customer value as the ultimate measure of work performance and improving value, and the rate at which this is done, as the measure of success.[6] Koala Corp. discovered the need for diaper changing stations in public restrooms and designed a plastic, fold-out model that can be found in over 300,000 restaurants, ball parks, retail stores, and gas stations at an average price of US$199.[7] Everyone in the organization who interacts with customers—down to the shipping department and the truck driver—must know what customers want. They are selling ideas, benefits, philosophies, and experiences—not just goods and services.

Someone once said that if you build a better mousetrap, the world will beat a path to your door. Suppose you do build a better mousetrap. What will happen? Actually, consumers are not likely to beat a path to your door because the market is too competitive. A coordinated effort by everyone involved with the mousetrap is needed to sell the product. Your company must reach out to customers and tell them about your mousetrap, especially how your mousetrap works better than those offered by competitors. If you do not make the benefits of your product widely known, in most cases, it will not be successful. For example, Carewell Industries developed SpringClean, a high-tech toothbrush designed to conform to the contours of the user's teeth. However, because Carewell was unable to support its superior product with an adequate advertising and promotion budget, SpringClean failed.[8] You must also find stores willing to sell it to consumers. You must implement the marketing concept to sell your mousetrap.

Orville Wright said that an airplane is "a group of separate parts flying in close formation." This is what most companies are trying to accomplish: They are striving for a team effort to deliver the right good or service to customers. A breakdown at any point in the organization—whether it be in production, purchasing, sales, distribution, or advertising—can result in lost sales, lost revenue, and dissatisfied customers.

Relationship Marketing

Relationship marketing is the process of building intimate customer interactions to maximize customer satisfaction. Most businesses want to develop meaningful, long-term buyer-seller relationships. The goal of relationship marketing is to satisfy customers so well that they become loyal and thus less likely to switch to a competitor. For example, in an effort to provide excellent service, Outback Steak House restaurants give their servers fewer tables than any of their competitors. As a result, customers see their waitperson more often and get what they desire faster. As the customer's confidence in the firm grows, this in turn increases the company's understanding of the customer's needs. Eventually this interaction becomes a strong relationship that allows for cooperative problem solving. The Internet is improving relationship building by using joint communication to solve needs. For example, once someone becomes a customer, the online firm can gain permission to use the Internet to provide future service and information. The customer can use the Internet to ask questions and express needs.[9] Relationship marketing provides a foundation for the entire organization to respond to the customer's next set of problems, sometimes even before the customer becomes aware of these needs.[10] Saturn, for example, provides special seminars and programs to help educate Saturn buyers about how to take care of their vehicles and get the most enjoyment out of them. It even invites all past Saturn buyers to an annual picnic at its Spring Hill, Tennessee, factory. These activities enable Saturn to build a strong relationship with its customers, which hopefully will help it build repeat sales and word-of-mouth advertising.

Saturn Corp.
www.saturnbp.com/

E-Marketing

Electronic marketing, also called e-marketing or e-commerce, consists of the buying and selling of goods and services over the Internet. Fundamentally the basics of marketing do not change on the Internet, but the availability to function 24/7—24 hours a day, 7 days a week—is a significant advantage. At any time, a web site is available to communicate with customers and other interested parties from anywhere in the world. With over 300 million Internet users in 2000, and that number climbing, a company's customer base gets much larger when it goes online. Market research can be conducted by surveying those visiting your site and, at the same time, reaching out with organizational information to many more people in other countries than previously accessible.

The two major categories of e-commerce are business-to-business (B2B) and business-to-consumer (B2C). Much is being made of the B2B sector, as it is proving profitable because the complex information necessary for some transactions can be more easily and more quickly conveyed electronically than via traditional methods. On the other hand, B2C companies, such as Amazon.com, are still struggling. A major reason is that customers are often reluctant to buy products online if they need to see and evaluate those goods. In the travel business, one can book tickets, hotel rooms, and events such as concerts, so many companies must be online in order to keep up with their competitors. A third sector that is growing is the C2C or customer-to-customer segment, which enables consumers to interact. eBay, the Internet auction firm, is proving successful in this area and is generating regular profits as a result of a growing number of consumers interested in buying and selling on the web.

DEVELOPING A MARKETING STRATEGY

To implement the marketing concept, a business needs to develop and maintain a **marketing strategy,** a plan of action for developing, pricing, distributing, and promoting products that meet the needs of specific customers. This definition has two

marketing strategy
a plan of action for developing, pricing, distributing, and promoting products that meet the needs of specific customers

major components: selecting a target market and developing an appropriate marketing mix to satisfy that target market.

Selecting a Target Market

market

a group of people who have a need, purchasing power, and the desire and authority to spend money on goods, services, and ideas

target market

a specific group of consumers on whose needs and wants a company focuses its marketing efforts

A **market** is a group of people who have a need, purchasing power, and the desire and authority to spend money on goods, services, and ideas. A **target market** is a more specific group of consumers on whose needs and wants a company focuses its marketing efforts. For example, an automobile company planning an online advertising campaign for its new sport utility vehicle (SUV) is using studies that show its most likely target market consists of upper-middle-class males in their mid-30s. Fans of rock music and skiing are also likely to be SUV customers. By utilizing an innovative targeting service called TrueSelect, this auto manufacturer is ensuring that its SUV advertising campaign is delivered directly and efficiently to the target audience.[11]

Marketing managers may define a target market as a relatively small number of people, or they may define it as the total market (Figure 12.2). Rolls Royce, for example, targets its products at a small, very exclusive, high-income market—people

Figure 12.2

Target Market Strategies

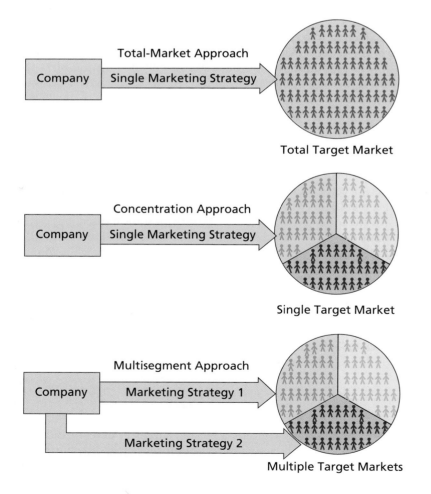

Total-Market Approach

Total Target Market

Concentration Approach

Single Target Market

Multisegment Approach

Multiple Target Markets

who want the ultimate in prestige in an automobile. General Motors, on the other hand, manufactures vehicles ranging from the Geo Metro to Cadillac to GMC trucks in an attempt to appeal to varied tastes, needs, and desires.

Some firms use a **total-market approach,** in which they try to appeal to everyone and assume that all buyers have similar needs and wants. Sellers of salt, sugar, and many agricultural products use a total-market approach because everyone is a potential consumer of these products.

Market Segmentation. Most firms, though, use **market segmentation** and divide the total market into groups of people who have relatively similar product needs. A **market segment** is a collection of individuals, groups, or organizations who share one or more characteristics and thus have relatively similar product needs and desires. Companies use market segmentation to focus their efforts and resources on specific target markets so that they can develop a productive marketing strategy. Two common approaches to segmenting markets are the concentration approach and the multisegment approach.

In the **concentration approach,** a company develops one marketing strategy for a single market segment. The concentration approach allows a firm to specialize, focusing all its efforts on the one market segment. Porsche, for example, focuses all its marketing efforts toward high-income individuals who want to own high-performance sports cars. A firm can generate a large sales volume by penetrating a single market segment deeply. The concentration approach may be especially effective when a firm can identify and develop products for a particular segment ignored by other companies in the industry.

In the **multisegment approach,** the marketer aims its marketing efforts at two or more segments, developing a marketing strategy for each. Many firms use a multisegment approach that includes different advertising messages for different segments. For example, many companies, including AT&T and American Express, are targeting ads and promotions to gay audiences, which represent a potential US$35 billion North American market. AT&T's advertisement depicts several smiling couples—two men, two women, and a man and a woman. The tagline is "Let Your True Voice Be Heard," and the ad includes an endorsement of an AT&T employee group that consists of gay men, bisexuals, and lesbians.[12] Companies also develop product variations to appeal to different market segments. The manufacturer of Raleigh bicycles uses a multisegment approach and has designed separate marketing strategies for racers, tourers, commuters, and children. Because there are so many different kinds of riders, Raleigh builds many different kinds of bicycles. Many other firms also attempt to use a multisegment approach to market segmentation. Colgate has gained the leading share of the toothpaste market with different versions of the Colgate brand of toothpaste, such as baking soda and peroxide and Total, a version that fights diseases such as gingivitis.[13]

Niche marketing is a narrow market segment focus when efforts are on one small, well-defined segment that has a unique, specific set of needs. Breaking from the traditional standardized menu offered in all of its 12,000 US stores, McDonald's is now serving pizza puffs, vegetarian sandwiches, breakfast bagels, and McFlurry ice cream, to meet customer demand in certain regions. But McDonald's continues to use a multisegment approach by developing marketing efforts aimed at seniors and children, as well as at niche markets in certain regions.[14]

For a firm to successfully use a concentration or multisegment approach to market segmentation, several requirements must be met:

1. Consumers' needs for the product must be heterogeneous.
2. The segments must be identifiable and divisible.

total-market approach

an approach whereby a firm tries to appeal to everyone and assumes that all buyers have similar needs

market segmentation

a strategy whereby a firm divides the total market into groups of people who have relatively similar product needs

market segment

a collection of individuals, groups, or organizations who share one or more characteristics and thus have relatively similar product needs and desires

concentration approach

a market segmentation approach whereby a company develops one marketing strategy for a single market segment

multisegment approach

a market segmentation approach whereby the marketer aims its efforts at two or more segments, developing a marketing strategy for each

Value Diversity

Marketing to Ethnic Segments

Increasingly, marketers are targeting ethnic segments of the Canadian market. Traditionally the Quebecois market has been targeted differently from the rest of Canada and treated virtually as its own cultural market and not a subculture of Canada. Its size, main geographic location, purchasing power, and social and political orientation ensure it is treated as its own market separate from the rest of Canada. It is important for marketers to understand the differences of Quebec and their sources. Many studies have demonstrated that due to cultural differences, Quebecers traditionally:

- Accept premium-priced products like gasoline and liquors.
- Exhibit a willingness to pay higher prices for convenience items.
- Use coupons and have a greater desire for premiums than other Canadians.
- Spend more per capita on clothing, tobacco, wine, beer, and personal care items, but they spend less on hard liquor.
- Watch more television.

To market to this culture, the tools and messages used are necessarily different from those directed at other Canadians.

The other ethnic segments of Canada are also of major value to marketers. It is estimated that, annually, minorities in Canada have over $76 billion in spending power. It is no wonder that CHIN television and radio are popular and successful in Toronto and are expanding across Canada. The CFMT television system in Ontario has a Cantonese newscast that boasts a 71 percent reach into the Chinese-Canadian community. It is estimated that with the continued large influx of new Canadians from China, the number of Chinese Canadians will exceed 1 million early in the 21st century. These numbers alone warrant specialized marketing efforts for each significant group.

Toronto's *El Popular* Spanish-language publication is aimed at the 250,000 Spanish-speaking people in the Toronto area and is distributed across Canada. CFMT also broadcasts Armenian, Filipino, Greek, Iranian, Japanese, Korean, Macedonian, Maltese, Polish, Russian, South Asian, and Ukrainian productions. The Aboriginal Media Services of Edmonton sells air time on its radio station and advertising space in its over 60 Aboriginal newspapers.

Canada is a multicultural country, exhibiting diversity and a welcoming environment. For marketers to reach this growing and increasingly affluent market, they will have to advertise and communicate in the languages of their customers. The next time you are downtown in a major Canadian city, look at the banks and frequently you will see signs that read, "Portuguese spoken here" or signs that are written in Chinese. Marketers cannot ignore the growing markets of new Canadians and must reach them on their own terms and language if they want to do business with them.[15]

3. The total market must be divided in a way that allows estimated sales potential, cost, and profits of the segments to be compared.

4. At least one segment must have enough profit potential to justify developing and maintaining a special marketing strategy.

5. The firm must be able to reach the chosen market segment with a particular market strategy.

Bases for Segmenting Markets. Companies segment markets on the basis of several variables:

1. *Demographic*—age, sex, race, ethnicity, income, education, occupation, family size, religion, social class. These characteristics are often closely related to customers' product needs and purchasing behaviour, and they can be readily measured. For example, deodorants are often segmented by sex: Secret and Soft n' Dry for women; Old Spice and Mennen for men.

2. *Geographic*—climate, terrain, natural resources, population density, subcultural values. These influence consumers' needs and product usage. Climate, for example, influences consumers' purchases of clothing, automobiles, heating and air conditioning equipment, and leisure activity equipment.

3. *Psychographic*—personality characteristics, motives, lifestyles. Soft-drink marketers provide their products in several types of packaging, including two-litre bottles and cases of cans, to satisfy different lifestyles and motives.

4. *Behaviouristic*—some characteristic of the consumer's behaviour toward the product. These characteristics commonly involve some aspect of product use. For example, Novartis Seeds, Inc., produces individually customized brochures for over 7,000 farmers based on information provided by independent dealers for each of their customers. Instead of a 30-page catalogue, each customer receives a one-page brochure with only the five or six products he or she needs.[16]

Developing a Marketing Mix

The second step in developing a marketing strategy is to create and maintain a satisfying marketing mix. The **marketing mix** refers to four marketing activities—product, price, distribution, and promotion—that the firm can control to achieve specific goals within a dynamic marketing environment (Figure 12.3). The buyer or the target market is the central focus of all marketing activities.

Product. A product—whether a good, a service, an idea, or some combination—is a complex mix of tangible and intangible attributes that provide satisfaction and benefits. A product has emotional and psychological as well as physical characteristics and

marketing mix
the four marketing activities—product, price, promotion, and distribution—that the firm can control to achieve specific goals within a dynamic marketing environment

Figure 12.3

The Marketing Mix: Product, Price, Promotion, and Distribution

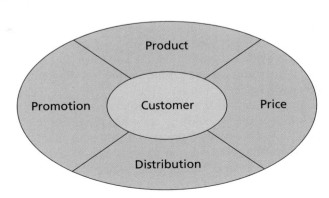

Marketing Environment

Restoration Hardware
www.restoration hardware.com/

price

a value placed on an object exchanged between a buyer and a seller

distribution

making products available to customers in the quantities desired

Grand and Toy
www.grandandtoy.com

includes everything that the buyer receives from an exchange. This definition includes supporting services such as installation, guarantees, product information, and promises of repair.

Products usually have both favourable and unfavourable attributes; therefore, almost every purchase or exchange involves trade-offs as consumers try to maximize their benefits and satisfaction and minimize unfavourable attributes. Restoration Hardware, a chain of home furnishings stores, specializes in nonstandard hardware items and North American-made furniture to compete against hardware retailers such as Home Depot and other giants. The chain sells nostalgic, often high-priced items not found in competitors' stores, including $1,850 Amish cabinets, $20 scissors, and $44 porcupine-shaped bootscrapers. The average Restoration store pays for itself in just under 18 months, and plans call for many more stores.[17]

Products are among a firm's most visible contacts with consumers. If they do not meet consumer needs and expectations, sales will be difficult, and product life spans will be brief. The product is an important variable—often the central focus—of the marketing mix; the other variables (price, promotion, and distribution) must be coordinated with product decisions.

Price. Almost anything can be assessed by a **price,** a value placed on an object exchanged between a buyer and a seller. Although the seller usually establishes the price, it may be negotiated between buyer and seller. The buyer usually exchanges purchasing power—income, credit, wealth—for the satisfaction or utility associated with a product. Because financial price is the measure of value commonly used in an exchange, it quantifies value and is the basis of most market exchanges.

Marketers view price as much more than a way of assessing value, however. It is a key element of the marketing mix because it relates directly to the generation of revenue and profits. Prices can also be changed quickly to stimulate demand or respond to competitors' actions. For example, when Post cereal prices were cut by 20 percent, Kellogg's dropped the price on two-thirds of its cereal products by 19 percent, followed by an 11 percent cut by General Mills.[18] McDonald's, Burger King, and other fast-food chains often use price changes to increase store traffic. For example, 99-cent Whoppers at Burger King and 99-cent Big Macs and Egg McMuffins may be offered for a limited time to increase sales, especially among heavy fast-food users.

Distribution. Distribution is making products available to customers in the quantities desired. Intermediaries, usually wholesalers and retailers, perform many of the activities required to move products efficiently from producers to consumers or industrial buyers. These activities involve transporting, warehousing, materials handling, and inventory control, as well as packaging and communication. Grand and Toy has been providing office supplies since the late 1800s, but now through its web site, customers can order supplies, determine whether certain items are in stock, and confirm when they will receive the order.

Critics who suggest that eliminating wholesalers and other intermediaries would result in lower prices for consumers do not recognize that eliminating intermediaries would not do away with the need for their services. Other institutions would have to perform those services, and consumers would still have to pay for them. In addition, in the absence of wholesalers, all producers would have to deal directly with retailers or customers, keeping voluminous records and hiring people to deal with customers. Home Depot became so concerned about potential web

It takes more
than a hit single to
reach the top.

15% of adult height is added during teen years. So we
give our growing bones lots of calcium by drinking milk. How do
you suppose we reach all those high notes, anyway?

got milk?

BACKSTREET BOYS © 1998 NATIONAL FLUID MILK PROCESSOR PROMOTION BOARD

The Milk Mustache Campaign's strategic approach was to target four audiences: teens; college-age men and women; women age 25–49; and men age 25–34. Ad celebrities were selected based on their appeal to a specific target and their credibility in delivering relevant health messages about milk.

Courtesy of
Bozell/Backstreet Boys
© 1998 National Fluid Milk
Processor Promotion Board

sales by its suppliers, that it wrote to many of them in 1999 advising them that it would view any attempt to sell directly to consumers in a very negative way. The distribution channel is valuable to Home Depot to such an extent that it indirectly threatened to drop suppliers, such as Black and Decker.[19]

Promotion. Promotion is a persuasive form of communication that attempts to expedite a marketing exchange by influencing individuals, groups, and organizations to accept goods, services, and ideas. Promotion includes advertising, personal selling, publicity, and sales promotion, which we will look at more closely in Chapter 13.

promotion
a persuasive form of communication that attempts to expedite a marketing exchange by influencing individuals, groups, and organizations to accept goods, services, and ideas

Figure 12.4

Prime-Time Ad Clutter: Average Number of Prime-Time Advertising Spots on the Top Three US TV Networks.

Source: *USA Today,* September 15, 1998, p. 1D. Copyright 1998, *USA Today.* Reprinted with permission.

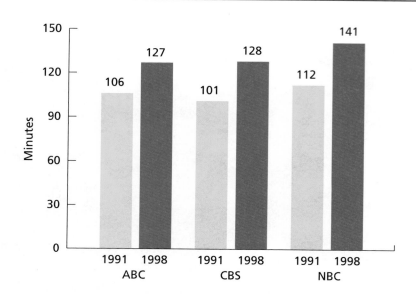

The aim of promotion is to communicate directly or indirectly with individuals, groups, and organizations to facilitate exchanges. When marketers use advertising and other forms of promotion, they must effectively manage their promotional resources and understand product and target-market characteristics to ensure that these promotional activities contribute to the firm's objectives. Figure 12.4 shows the growth in the number of prime-time ads and promotions on the top three US television networks. Zane's Cycles, a bicycle shop with annual sales of US$2.1 million, keeps a database of 19,000 customers with detailed records of every purchase. Each March, the database is searched for those customers who bought bike baby seats three years earlier. Knowing those customers will probably be buying a child's bike soon, a postcard is sent to each customer offering a discount on such a purchase. About 60 percent of those customers return to buy a child's bike from Zane's.[20] More and more companies are setting up home pages on the Internet's World Wide Web to promote themselves and their products. The home page for Betty Crocker, for example, offers recipes, meal planning, the company's history, descriptions for its 200 products, online shopping for complementary items such as dinnerware, linens, and gifts, and the ability to print a shopping list based on recipes chosen or ingredients on hand in the consumer's kitchen. Figure 12.5 shows that many firms expect their biggest marketing spending increase to be on the Internet.

Betty Crocker Homepage
www.bettycrocker.com/

marketing research

a systematic, objective process of getting information about potential customers to guide marketing decisions

marketing information system

a framework for accessing information about customers from sources both inside and outside the organization

MARKETING RESEARCH AND INFORMATION SYSTEMS

Marketing research is a systematic, objective process of getting information about potential customers to guide marketing decisions. This research is vital because the marketing concept cannot be implemented without information about customers.

A **marketing information system** is a framework for accessing information about customers from sources both inside and outside the organization. Inside the organization, there is a continuous flow of information about prices, sales, and expenses. Outside the organization, data are readily available through private or pub-

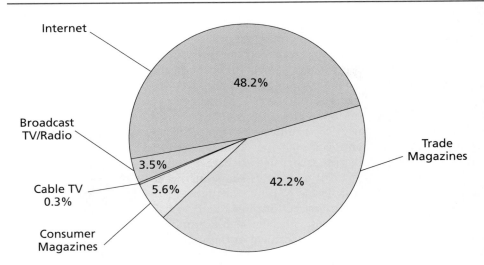

Internet

Broadcast
TV/Radio

48.2%

3.5%

Cable TV
0.3%

5.6%

Consumer
Magazines

42.2%

Trade
Magazines

Figure 12.5

*Increases in Advertising
Spending*

Note: In a survey of 400
manufacturing firms,
almost 50 percent say that
their biggest marketing
spending increase in 1998
will be on the Internet.
Others will be going to
more traditional outlets to
market their products this
year. This shows where
companies will have their
biggest marketing spending
increase in 1998.

Source: Cabners Economics,
*Sales & Marketing Manage-
ment,* April 1998, p. 18.
Reprinted with permission
from *Sales & Marketing
Management,* April 1, 1998.

lic reports and census statistics, as well as from many other sources. Computer networking technology provides a framework for companies to connect to useful databases and customers with instantaneous information about product acceptance,
sales performance, and buying behaviour. This information is important to planning
and marketing strategy development.

Two types of data are usually available to decision makers. **Primary data** are observed, recorded, or collected directly from respondents. If you've ever participated in
a telephone survey about a product, recorded your TV viewing habits for A.C. Nielsen
or Arbitron, or even responded to a political opinion poll, you provided the researcher
with primary data. Primary data must be gathered by researchers who develop a
method to observe phenomena or research respondents. Surveys and focus groups are
costly and time-consuming, with costs for a single focus group running as high as
$20,000. With surveys, respondents are sometimes untruthful in order to avoid seem-
ing foolish or ignorant. New, creative methods for marketing research use passive observation of consumer behaviour and open-ended questioning techniques. Peter
Shamir, vice president of marketing for a company that distributes a thin cracker
called Bible Bread, cruised supermarket cracker aisles and observed unknowing consumers. That research showed that the average consumer takes about 10 seconds to
choose a brand of cracker. Shamir decided that Bible Bread would not be noticed in
big supermarkets and opted to place the crackers in gourmet and specialty stores.
Bible Bread can now be found throughout much of the United States, and revenues
are US$1 million.[21]

Secondary data are compiled inside or outside the organization for some purpose
other than changing the current situation. Marketers typically use information compiled by Statistics Canada and other government agencies, databases created by marketing research firms, as well as sales and other internal reports, to gain information
about customers.

The marketing of products and collecting of data about buying behaviour—
information on what people actually buy and how they buy it—represents marketing research of the future. New information technologies are changing the way
businesses learn about their customers and market their products. Interactive multimedia research, or *virtual testing,* combines sight, sound, and animation to facilitate the testing of concepts as well as packaging and design features for consumer
products. Computerization offers a greater degree of flexibility, shortens the staff

primary data
marketing information
that is observed, recorded,
or collected directly from
respondents

secondary data
information that is
compiled inside or
outside an organization
for some purp3ose other
than changing the
current situation

Before entering an international market, a company should use market research to determine the size of the market, the potential for market growth, and language and cultural issues. Failing to do so may result in costly mistakes. Benchmark Hospitality, Inc., a developer and manager of conference centres, conference hotels, and resorts, made some incorrect assumptions when it entered the market in Thailand. Assuming it should be located in Bangkok, the company spent a tremendous amount of money to locate there. Benchmark later found it could have been just as successful, and with less cost, if it had located outside the city.

There are five steps to conducting international market research: (1) study, (2) size up the market, (3) check assumptions, (4) be creative, and (5) ask the right questions. The first step involves determining market conditions and potential and should include an examination of Industry Canada and External Affairs' country trade reports and databases as well as field research in the intended country. Such study should help in assessing risks and forecasting demand.

The second step involves sizing up the market by using interviews, focus groups, and surveys to determine what customers want, buy, and need. The third step involves investigating assumptions about a country, such as whether it might be too poor to support a particular business. Alphagraphics, a design and printing company, operates in 24 countries, including Honduras and Guatemala, and is researching 10 others, including El Salvador and Panama. Alphagraphics has found Central America to be a very profitable market.

Being creative in research is the fourth step. Shred-It, an industrial shredding company, hires MBA students to do research and provide an understanding of a potential market, with costs running between US$5,000 and US$7,000 per country. Once a market is deemed to have potential, Shred-It hires professional market researchers to continue the process.

The last step involves asking the right questions, either through a firm's own research department or through an international research firm. Concerns to investigate include cultural and language issues, things that might offend local traditions or preferences, market potential, brand loyalty, technology and logistics, and government regulations. If an international research firm is considered, the following questions should be asked before hiring the firm:

1. Do you have people in the country who can do the work?

2. How long have you been doing this kind of work?

3. How many studies have you done in my industry, product area, and this country?

4. How do you supervise and provide quality control?

5. How much will this cost?

Expanding globally may seem like the next step at a firm, but before setting out to enter a country, a well-planned and executed international marketing research campaign is a necessity.[22]

Think Globally

International Marketing Research

time involved in data gathering, and cuts marketing research costs. Hallmark Cards used interactive research to create a virtual shop with 3D shelves and gift wrap samples from which respondents indicated designs they were most likely to buy. The research team found a high correlation between the virtual testing results and actual sales. Using virtual testing, they were able to interview more respondents in more markets, thus getting a more diverse and nationally representative sample. Costs for the research dropped to about US$25,000—a US$15,000 savings over traditional research methods.[23] The evolving development of telecommunications and computer technologies is allowing marketing researchers quick and easy access to a growing number of online services and a vast database of potential respondents.

BUYING BEHAVIOUR

Carrying out the marketing concept is impossible unless marketers know what, where, when, and how consumers buy; marketing research into the factors that influence buying behaviour helps marketers develop effective marketing strategies. **Buying behaviour** refers to the decision processes and actions of people who purchase and use products. It includes the behaviour of both consumers purchasing products for personal or household use as well as organizations buying products for business use. Marketers analyze buying behaviour because a firm's marketing strategy should be guided by an understanding of buyers.

buying behaviour
the decision processes and actions of people who purchase and use products

The Buying-Decision Process

Whether on the Internet or in traditional marketing processes, it is essential to understand the decision process buyers proceed through in their problem-solving efforts. This process is easily broken into six stages:

1. *Need recognition*—the consumer is moved to action by his or her need.
2. *Choice of an involvement level*—the consumer determines the level of energy and time to invest in satisfying the need.
3. *Identification of alternatives*—the consumer collects information about the service, products, and brands.
4. *Evaluation of alternatives*—the consumer weighs the pros and cons of the alternatives.
5. *Purchase and related decisions*—the consumer decides to purchase or not to purchase.
6. *Postpurchase behaviour*—the consumer seeks reassurance that the choice made was the correct one, uses or experiences the purchase, and (the marketer hopes) is satisfied and is prepared to repeat the procedure.

Of course, each individual is different and the complexity varies between consumers and business decisions, especially when considering the values that may be involved. Buying a house is a major decision to a consumer and will require a major investment in time. These six stages may be conscious or not, and they may vary in length of time by person. The consumer can also stop the process at any time. Some stages may even be dropped, but generally this is the complex process most of us follow when making a buying decision. This process leads us to examine both the psychological and social variables affecting buying behaviour.

Psychological Variables of Buying Behaviour

Psychological factors include the following:

- **Perception** is the process by which a person selects, organizes, and interprets information received from his or her senses, as when hearing an advertisement on the radio or touching a product to better understand it.

perception
the process by which a person selects, organizes, and interprets information received from his or her senses

Solve the Dilemma

Will It Go?

Ventura Motors makes mid-sized and luxury automobiles in Canada. Best-selling models include its basic four-door sedans (priced from $15,000 to $20,000) and two-door and four-door luxury automobiles (priced from $40,000 to $55,000). The recent success of two-seat sports cars like the Mazda Miata started the company evaluating the market for a two-seat sports car priced midway between the moderate and luxury market. Research found that there was indeed significant demand and that Ventura needed to act quickly to take advantage of this market opportunity.

Ventura took the platform of the car from a popular model in its moderate line, borrowing the internal design from its luxury line. The car was designed, engineered, and produced in just over two years, but the coordination needed to bring the design together resulted in higher than anticipated costs. The price for this two-seat car, the Olympus, was set at $32,000. Dealers were anxious to take delivery on the car, and salespeople were well trained on techniques to sell this new model.

However, initial sales have been slow, and company executives are surprised and concerned. The Olympus was introduced relatively quickly, made available at all Ventura dealers, priced midway between luxury and moderate models, and advertised heavily since its introduction.

1. What do you think were the main concerns with the Olympus two-door sports coupe? Is there a market for a two-seat, $32,000 sports car when the Miata sells for significantly less?

2. Evaluate the role of the marketing mix in the Olympus introduction.

3. What are some of the marketing strategies auto manufacturers use to stimulate sales of certain makes of automobiles?

---

motivation
an inner drive that directs a person's behaviour toward goals

learning
changes in a person's behaviour based on information and experience

attitude
knowledge and positive or negative feelings about something

personality
the organization of an individual's distinguishing character traits, attitudes, or habits

- **Motivation,** as we said in Chapter 10, is an inner drive that directs a person's behaviour toward goals. A customer's behaviour is influenced by a set of motives rather than by a single motive. A buyer of a home computer, for example, may be motivated by ease of use, ability to communicate with the office, and price.

- **Learning** brings about changes in a person's behaviour based on information and experience. If a person's actions result in a reward, he or she is likely to behave the same way in similar situations. If a person's actions bring about a negative result, however—such as feeling ill after eating at a certain restaurant—he or she will probably not repeat that action.

- **Attitude** is knowledge and positive or negative feelings about something. For example, a person who feels strongly about protecting the environment may refuse to buy products that harm the earth and its inhabitants.

- **Personality** refers to the organization of an individual's distinguishing character traits, attitudes, or habits. Although market research on the relationship between personality and buying behaviour has been inconclusive, some marketers believe that the type of car or clothing a person buys reflects his or her personality.

As you prepare to enter the workplace, you should be aware of how the environment is changing. A major part of your professional development will occur as a result of your ability to respond and adapt to some of these changes. One of the changes that exists today is that we are now living in a service economy. The focus on service means that the jobs available to you will probably require both good product knowledge and an ability to communicate well to customers about how the product can benefit them. Your skills in relating to others are critical to success in your career.

The increased focus on customer service presents opportunities for you in providing superior service to customers. Customer service involves providing what customers need in the best way possible so that they will keep coming back to your company for the products and services they need. Good customer service also helps attract new customers. Typical positions in this area will involve customer service training, customer service management, customer satisfaction, etc. Quality, another major movement, goes hand-in-hand with customer satisfaction. Keeping the company as the number-one choice among customers requires the constant improvement of products and service to ensure that they are of high quality.

To prepare yourself for a career in customer service and customer satisfaction, you may want to major in marketing with a minor in psychology or sociology. Also beneficial will be a class in consumer behaviour, as it will enable you to better understand the purchasers.[24]

Explore Your Career Options

Customer Service in a Service Economy

Social Variables of Buying Behaviour

Social factors include **social roles,** which are a set of expectations for individuals based on some position they occupy. A person may have many roles: mother, wife, student, executive. Each of these roles can influence buying behaviour. Consider the same woman choosing an automobile. Her father advises her to buy a safe car, such as a Volvo. Her teenaged daughter wants her to buy a cool car, such as a Porsche or Miata; her young son wants her to buy a Ford Explorer to take on camping trips. Some of her colleagues at work say she should buy a North American car to help the economy. Thus, in choosing which car to buy, the woman's buying behaviour may be affected by the opinions and experiences of her family and friends and by her roles as mother, daughter, and employee.

Other social factors include reference groups, social classes, and culture.

- **Reference groups** include families, professional groups, civic organizations, and other groups with whom buyers identify and whose values or attitudes they adopt. A person may use a reference group as a point of comparison or a source of information. A person new to a community may ask other group members to recommend a family doctor, for example.

- **Social classes** are determined by ranking people into higher or lower positions of respect. Criteria vary from one society to another. People within a particular social class may develop common patterns of behaviour. People in the upper-middle class, for example, might buy a BMW or a Cadillac as a symbol of their social class.

social roles
a set of expectations for individuals based on some position they occupy

reference groups
groups with whom buyers identify and whose values or attitudes they adopt

social classes
a ranking of people into higher or lower positions of respect

culture
the integrated, accepted pattern of human behaviour, including thought, speech, beliefs, actions, and artifacts

- **Culture** is the integrated, accepted pattern of human behaviour, including thought, speech, beliefs, actions, and artifacts. Culture determines what people wear and eat and where they live and travel. In the multicultural cities of Canada the varieties of cuisine are many to satisfy our diverse cultures.

Understanding Buying Behaviour

Although marketers try to understand buying behaviour, it is extremely difficult to explain exactly why a buyer purchases a particular product. For example, German-based Volkswagen believes that the success of the Beetle is due to the fact that it "draws on people's emotions. It makes them feel warm and optimistic."[25] The tools and techniques for analyzing consumers are not exact. Marketers may not be able to determine accurately what is highly satisfying to buyers, but they know that trying to understand consumer wants and needs is the best way to satisfy them.

THE MARKETING ENVIRONMENT

A number of external forces directly or indirectly influence the development of marketing strategies; the following political, legal, regulatory, social, competitive, economic, and technological forces comprise the marketing environment.

- *Political, legal, and regulatory forces*—laws and regulators' interpretation of laws; law enforcement and regulatory activities; regulatory bodies, legislators and legislation, and political actions of interest groups. Specific laws, for example, require that advertisements be truthful and that all health claims be documented.
- *Social forces*—the public's opinions and attitudes toward issues such as living standards, ethics, the environment, lifestyles, and quality of life. For example, social concerns have led marketers to design and market safer toys for children.
- *Competitive and economic forces*—competitive relationships, unemployment, purchasing power, and general economic conditions (prosperity, recession, depression, recovery, product shortages, and inflation).
- *Technological forces*—computers and other technological advances that improve distribution, promotion, and new-product development. For example, Instant Survey is an Internet service that designs and distributes surveys and then analyzes and delivers results. After a specified number of responses have been collected, Instant Survey automatically compiles survey results and e-mails a report of responses to the firm.[26]

Although the forces in the marketing environment are sometimes called uncontrollables, they are not totally so. A marketing manager can influence some environmental variables. For example, businesses can lobby legislators to dissuade them from passing unfavourable legislation. Figure 12.6 shows the variables in the marketing environment that affect the marketing mix and the buyer.

Figure 12.6

A Marketing Mix and the Marketing Environment

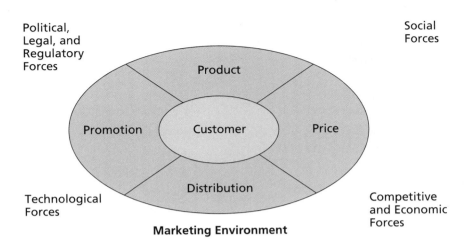

Political, Legal, and Regulatory Forces

Social Forces

Technological Forces

Competitive and Economic Forces

Marketing Environment

Review Your Understanding

Define marketing and describe the exchange process.

Marketing is a group of activities designed to expedite transactions by creating, distributing, pricing, and promoting goods, services, and ideas. Marketing facilitates the exchange, the act of giving up one thing in return for something else. The central focus of marketing is to satisfy needs.

Specify the functions of marketing.

Marketing includes many varied and interrelated activities: buying, selling, transporting, storing, grading, financing, marketing research, and risk taking.

Explain the marketing concept and its implications for developing marketing strategies.

The marketing concept is the idea that an organization should try to satisfy customers' needs through coordinated activities that also allow it to achieve its goals. If a company does not implement the marketing concept, by providing products that consumers need and want while achieving its own objectives, it will not survive.

Examine the development of a marketing strategy, including market segmentation and marketing mix.

A marketing strategy is a plan of action for creating a marketing mix (product, price, distribution, promotion) for a specific target market (a specific group of consumers on whose needs and wants a company focuses its marketing efforts). Some firms use a total-market approach, designating everyone as the target market. Most firms divide the total market into seg-

ments of people who have relatively similar product needs. A company using a concentration approach develops one marketing strategy for a single market segment, whereas a multisegment approach aims marketing efforts at two or more segments, developing a different marketing strategy for each.

Investigate how marketers conduct marketing research and study buying behaviour.

Carrying out the marketing concept is impossible unless marketers know what, where, when, and how consumers buy; marketing research into the factors that influence buying behaviour helps marketers develop effective marketing strategies. Marketing research is a systematic, objective process of getting information about potential customers to guide marketing decisions. Buying behaviour is the decision processes and actions of people who purchase and use products.

Summarize the environmental forces that influence marketing decisions.

There are several forces that influence marketing activities: political, legal, regulatory, social, competitive, economic, and technological.

Assess a company's marketing plans and propose a solution for resolving its problem.

Based on the material in this chapter, you should be able to answer the questions posed in the "Solve the Dilemma" box and help the business understand what went wrong and how to correct it.

Learn the Terms

attitude 310
buying behaviour 309
concentration approach 301
culture 312
distribution 304
exchange 295
form utility 296
learning 310
market 300
market segment 301
market segmentation 301
marketing 294

marketing concept 297
marketing information system
  306
marketing mix 303
marketing research 306
marketing strategy 299
motivation 310
multisegment approach 301
ownership utility 296
perception 309
personality 310
place utility 296

price 304
primary data 307
promotion 305
reference groups 311
secondary data 307
social classes 311
social roles 311
target market 300
time utility 296
total-market approach 301
utility 296

Check Your Progress

1. What is marketing? How does it facilitate exchanges?
2. Name the functions of marketing. How does an organization use marketing activities to achieve its objectives?
3. What is utility? How does marketing create utility?
4. What is the marketing concept? Why is it so important?
5. What is a marketing strategy?
6. What is market segmentation? Describe three target market strategies.
7. List the variables in the marketing mix. How is each used in a marketing strategy?
8. Why are marketing research and information systems important to an organization's planning and development of strategy?
9. Briefly describe the factors that influence buying behaviour. How does understanding buying behaviour help marketers?
10. Discuss the impact of technological forces and political and legal forces on the market.

Get Involved

1. With some or all of your classmates, watch several hours of television, paying close attention to the commercials. Pick three commercials for products with which you are somewhat familiar. Based on the commercials, determine who the target market is. Can you surmise the marketing strategy for each of the three?
2. Discuss the decision process and influences involved in purchasing a personal computer.

Build Your Skills

The Marketing Mix

Background: You've learned the four Ps (variables)—product, promotion, price, and place/distribution—that the marketer can select to achieve specific goals within a dynamic marketing environment. This exercise will give you an opportunity to analyze the marketing strategies of some well-known companies to determine which of the variables received the most emphasis to help the company achieve its goals.

Task: In groups of three to five students, discuss the examples below and decide which of the four Ps received the most emphasis.

A.   Product
B.   Place/Distribution
C.   Promotion
D.   Price

_____ 1.   Starbucks Coffee, with over 2,000 retail stores, began selling bagged premium specialty coffee through an agreement with Kraft Foods to gain access to more than 30,000 supermarkets.[27]

_____ 2.   America Online (AOL) offers 24-hour 9 cents per minute long-distance telephone service for AOL Internet customers who will provide their credit card number and receive bills and information about their account online.

_____ 3.   With 150,000 advance orders, Apple Computer launched the all-new iMac computer with a US$100 million advertising budget to obtain first-time computer buyers who could get Internet access by just plugging in the computer.

_____ 4.   After more than 35 years on the market, WD-40 is in about 80 percent of North American households—more than any other branded product. Although WD-40 is promoted as a product that can stop squeaks, protect metal, loosen rusted parts, and free sticky mechanisms, the WD-40 Company has received letters from customers who have sprayed the product on bait to attract fish, on pets to cure mange, and even on people to cure arthritis. Despite more than 200 proposals to expand the WD-40 product line and ideas to change the packaging and labelling, the company stands firmly behind its one highly successful and respected original product.

_____ 5.   Southwest Airlines makes flying fun. Flight attendants try to entertain passengers and the airline has an impeccable customer service record. Employees play a key role and take classes that emphasize that having fun translates into great customer service.[28]

_____ 6.   Hewlett Packard offered a $100 rebate on a $799 HP LaserJet printer when purchased with an HP LaserJet toner cartridge. To receive the rebate, the buyer had to return a mail-in certificate to certify the purchase. A one-page ad with a coupon was used in *USA Today* stating, "We're taking $100 off the top."[29]

_____ 7.   Denny's, the largest full-service family restaurant chain in the US, serves more than 1 million customers a day. The restaurants offer the Grand Slam Breakfast for $1.99, lunch basket specials for either $2.99, $3.99, or $4.99, and a dinner of prime rib for $5.99.

Firing Your Customers

Have you ever cancelled or missed an appointment and then been charged a fee for the appointment even though you weren't there? It can make you upset, but it is worthwhile to look at the matter from the business's perspective. The video expresses the need for businesses to consider the cost of the customers and the services they demand, and realize that some cost more than the revenue they generate.

What is a firm to do? Fire the customer. The telephone company calculated that 25 to 35 percent of their customers cost them more money than they bring in, and they need to determine who are the good customers and who are the bad customers. Clearnet does data mining to identify the best customers and then gently tries to fire the poor customers. The demographics of the good customers are determined and the marketing efforts are focused on the profitable target market. To discourage unprofitable customers, the company uses many techniques to filter them out. Increasing customer spending and decreasing costs are the two avenues available to the company. Monthly fees are charged that cover the cost of the help lines and discourage those unprepared to pay the monthly charges.

Shoppers are selected by requiring a deposit that the least profitable customers are unwilling or unable to pay. Sometimes dropping certain customers off the mailing list will get the idea across that they are not wanted or that the company ultimately does not care for their business. Clearnet may even buy back a

telephone to eliminate a bad customer and stop the continued losses.

But one must be careful when doing anything like this kind of discouragement effort in Canada. Here in Canada there are only 10 to 12 million households, and any bad publicity or poor word of mouth about the company must be avoided to prevent negative backlash and the loss of current or potential customers. This, however, is not the case south of the border. In the United States you can lose a customer and there are still tens of millions of households or tens of thousands of other businesses to sell to. So a light touch is needed in Canada.

Questions

1. When you go shopping, are there any efforts made to encourage you to spend more? What are they?

2. Have stores or other businesses made subtle efforts to eliminate you or someone you know as a customer? How?

3. Thinking of your family, what marketing efforts have you noticed aimed at you versus your parents? Are they effective?

4. What businesses would be wise to court you and your classmates as customers even if they would lose on your business in the short run?

Source: *Venture*, show number 710, "Firing Your Customer," January 26, 1999, running time 6:56.

Remember to check out our Online Learning Centre at **www.mcgrawhill.ca/college/ferrell.**

Chapter 13

Dimensions of Marketing Strategy

Chapter Outline

Objectives

After reading this chapter, you will be able to:

- Describe the role of product in the marketing mix, including how products are developed, classified, and identified.
- Define price and discuss its importance in the marketing mix, including various pricing strategies a firm might employ.
- Identify factors affecting distribution decisions, such as marketing channels and intensity of market coverage.
- Specify the activities involved in promotion, as well as promotional strategies and promotional positioning.
- Evaluate an organization's marketing strategy plans.

Domino's Delivers

Enter the World of Business

In 1960, Thomas Monaghan paid about $900 for a pizza parlour and turned it into Domino's Pizza, Inc., a 7,000-store company with annual sales of over CDN$5 billion (360 million pizzas a year). Monaghan's strategy for success was simple: Sell only pizza and guarantee delivery in 30 minutes. The delivery guarantee became the company's signature. But after the company was held responsible for a woman's injuries resulting from an accident with a Domino's delivery van, the guarantee was abandoned. To protect its employees, Domino's most important asset, a multimillion-dollar investment in safety and security programs has been made. Applicants must meet safe driving record requirements, and regular checks on employee driving records are made.

For 40 years, Domino's has been committed to delivering quality products and service while offering a total satisfaction guarantee. To maintain its world leadership position in the pizza delivery industry, Domino's gives careful attention to its marketing strategy, making changes in product offerings, pricing, promotions, and distribution, as needed.

Establishing an international presence is an important aspect of Domino's strategy. Domino's operates stores in 64 international markets. Some of these markets (Mexico, Canada, Japan, Australia, the United Kingdom, and Taiwan) have more than 100 stores each. Domino's supports adaptation of operating systems and products to accommodate cultural differences, including delivery vehicles (deliveries in Taiwan are made by motor scooter), store design, and pizza topping selections. Topping selections are the most common adaptation and include pickled ginger in India, squid in Japan, and green peas in Brazil. The dough, sauce, and cheese are consistent worldwide to ensure product integrity.

Adopting an appropriate marketing strategy has allowed Domino's to focus on its core business of pizza delivery, while its continuing commitment to service, quality, and innovation allows it to deliver "a million smiles a day."[1]

Courtesy of Domino's Pizza

INTRODUCTION

As Domino's success illustrates, creating an effective marketing strategy is important. Getting just the right mix of product, price, promotion, and distribution is critical if a business is to satisfy its target customers and achieve its own objectives (implement the marketing concept).

In Chapter 12, we introduced the concept of marketing and the various activities important in developing a marketing strategy. In this chapter, we'll take a closer look at the four dimensions of the marketing mix—product, price, distribution, and promotion—used to develop the marketing strategy. The focus of these marketing mix elements is a marketing strategy that builds customer relationships and satisfaction.

Did you know?

In one year, Domino's used . . .
- 11 million kg of pepperoni
- 66 million kg of mozzarella cheese

THE MARKETING MIX

The key to developing a marketing strategy is maintaining the right marketing mix that satisfies the target market and creates long-term relationships with customers. To develop meaningful customer relationships, marketers have to develop and manage the dimensions of the marketing mix to give their firm an advantage over competitors. Successful companies offer at least one dimension of value that surpasses all competitors in the marketplace in meeting customer expectations.[2] However, this does not mean that a company can ignore the other dimensions of the marketing mix; it must maintain acceptable, and if possible distinguishable, differences in the other dimensions as well.[3]

Wal-Mart, for example, emphasizes price ("Always the low price"). Zellers focuses on "Great Style. Great Savings"—a focus on two dimensions: product and price. Procter & Gamble is well known for its promotion of top consumer brands such as Tide, Cheer, Crest, Ivory, Head & Shoulders, and Folgers. Domino's Pizza is recognized for its superiority in distribution after developing the largest home-delivery pizza company in the world.

PRODUCT STRATEGY

As mentioned previously, the term *product* refers to goods, services, and ideas. Because the product is often the most visible of the marketing mix dimensions, managing product decisions is crucial. In this section, we'll consider product development, classification, mix, life cycle, and identification.

Developing New Products

Each year thousands of products are introduced, but few of them succeed. Thirty-four new food products are launched every day.[4] Currently 25,261 new consumer packaged goods are introduced in one year, but just 6 percent feature innovations in formulation, positioning, packaging, technology, creation of a new market, or merchandising.[5] A firm can take considerable time to get a product ready for the market: It took more than 20 years for the first photocopier. Before introducing a new product, a business must follow a multistep process: idea development, the screening of new ideas, business analysis, product development, test marketing, and commercialization. It may take 3,000 ideas to generate one "commercially successful" new product.

Idea Development. New ideas can come from marketing research, engineers, and outside sources such as advertising agencies and management consultants. IDEO, the world's most influential design firm, creates 90 new products each year.[6] Ideas sometimes come from customers, too. Other sources are brainstorming and intracompany incentives or rewards for good ideas. IDEO has three "brainstorm rooms" in which participants can draw their ideas almost anywhere—on whiteboard-covered walls or butcher paper-covered tables—and a special device photographs every drawing.[7]

IDEO
**www.ideo.com/
ideo.htm**

The Screening of New Ideas. The next step in developing a new product is idea screening. In this phase, a marketing manager should look at the organization's resources and objectives and assess the firm's ability to produce and market the product. Important aspects to be considered at this stage are consumer desires, the competition, technological changes, social trends, and political, economic, and environmental considerations. Basically, there are two reasons new products succeed: They are able to meet a need or solve a problem better than products already available or they add variety to the product selection currently on the market. Schneiders Lunch Mates have been very successful for both reasons. They solve the everyday problem of what to pack in a lunchbox, and they provide a wide variety of deli meats, sandwiches, tacos, and pizza, and a Hershey treat as well. Most new-product ideas are rejected during screening because they seem inappropriate or impractical for the organization.

Business Analysis. Business analysis is a basic assessment of a product's compatibility in the marketplace and its potential profitability. Both the size of the market and competing products are often studied at this point. The most important question relates to market demand: How will the product affect the firm's sales, costs, and profits?

Product Development. If a product survives the first three steps, it is developed into a prototype that should reveal the intangible attributes it possesses as perceived by the consumer. Product development is often expensive, and few product ideas make it to this stage. New product research and development costs vary. Adding a new colour to an existing item may cost as little as $100,000 to $200,000, but launching a completely new product can cost millions of dollars.[8] During product development, various elements of the marketing mix must be developed for testing. Copyrights, tentative advertising copy, packaging, labelling, and descriptions of a target market are integrated to develop an overall marketing strategy.

Test Marketing. **Test marketing** is a trial minilaunch of a product in limited areas that represent the potential market. It allows a complete test of the marketing strategy in a natural environment, giving the organization an opportunity to discover weaknesses and eliminate them before the product is fully launched. For example, after three years in development, including test marketing, Nabisco introduced Teddy Grahams. Within nine months, sales reached US$100 million and continued to climb. However, when Nabisco tried to extend Teddy Grahams into Breakfast Bears Graham Cereal without testing, the results were disastrous. Consumers did not like the taste or consistency, and supermarket managers soon refused to restock the cereal. Testing and retesting new products can be expensive, but they are necessary to avoid product disasters.[9]

test marketing
a trial minilaunch of a product in limited areas that represent the potential market

Commercialization. **Commercialization** is the full introduction of a complete marketing strategy and the launch of the product for commercial success. During commercialization, the firm gears up for full-scale production, distribution, and promotion.

commercialization
the full introduction of a complete marketing strategy and the launch of the product for commercial success

In this ad, Federal Express is announcing its Sunday delivery service, which is an example of a new product.

Courtesy of Federal Express Corporation

Classifying Products

consumer products
products intended for household or family use

Products are usually classified as either consumer products or industrial products. **Consumer products** are for household or family use; they are not intended for any purpose other than daily living. They can be further classified as convenience products, shopping products, and specialty products on the basis of consumers' buying behaviour and intentions.

- *Convenience products,* such as eggs, milk, bread, and newspapers, are bought frequently, without a lengthy search, and often for immediate consumption. Consumers spend virtually no time planning where to purchase these products and usually accept whatever brand is available.

- *Shopping products,* such as furniture, audio equipment, clothing, and sporting goods, are purchased after the consumer has compared competitive products and "shopped around." Price, product features, quality, style, service, and image all influence the decision to buy.

- *Specialty products,* such as ethnic foods, designer clothing and shoes, art, and antiques, require even greater research and shopping effort. Consumers know what they want and go out of their way to find it; they are not willing to accept a substitute.

Industrial products are used directly or indirectly in the operation or manufacturing processes of businesses. They are usually purchased for the operation of an organization or the production of other products; thus, their purchase is tied to specific goals and objectives. They too can be further classified:

- *Raw materials* are natural products taken from the earth, oceans, and recycled solid waste. Iron ore, bauxite, lumber, cotton, and fruits and vegetables are examples.

- *Major equipment* covers large, expensive items used in production. Examples include earth-moving equipment, stamping machines, and robotic equipment used on auto assembly lines.

- *Accessory equipment* includes items used for production, office, or management purposes, which usually do not become part of the final product. Computers, fax machines, calculators, and hand tools are examples.

- *Component parts* are finished items, ready to be assembled into the company's final products. Tires, window glass, batteries, and spark plugs are component parts of automobiles.

- *Processed materials* are things used directly in production or management operations but not readily identifiable as component parts. Varnish, for example, is a processed material for a furniture manufacturer.

- *Supplies* include materials that make production, management, and other operations possible, such as paper, pencils, paint, cleaning supplies, and so on.

- *Industrial services* include financial, legal, marketing research, security, janitorial, and exterminating services. Purchasers decide whether to provide these services internally or to acquire them from an outside supplier.

industrial products
products that are used directly or indirectly in the operation or manufacturing processes of businesses

Product Line and Product Mix

Product relationships within an organization are of key importance. A **product line** is a group of closely related products that are treated as a unit because of similar marketing strategy, production, or end-use considerations. A **product mix** is all the products offered by an organization. For example, Swanson frozen entrees has dozens of line extensions, and Snackwell's cookies and crackers has 105 items.[10]

product line
a group of closely related products that are treated as a unit because of similar marketing strategy, production, or end-use considerations

Product Life Cycle

Like people, products are born, grow, mature, and eventually die. Some products have very long lives. Ivory Soap was introduced in 1879 and is still popular. In contrast, a new computer chip is usually outdated within a year because of technological breakthroughs and rapid changes in the computer industry. There are four stages in the life cycle of a product: introduction, growth, maturity, and decline (Figure 13.1). The stage a product is in helps determine marketing strategy.

In the *introductory stage,* consumer awareness and acceptance of the product are limited, sales are zero, and profits are negative. Profits are negative because the firm has spent money on research, development, and marketing to launch the product. During the introductory stage, marketers focus on making consumers aware of the product and its benefits. A major difficulty is identifying the target markets and developing the appropriate promotional campaign to build their awareness. Sales accelerate as the product enters the growth stage of the life cycle.

product mix
all the products offered by an organization

Figure 13.1

The Life Cycle of a Product

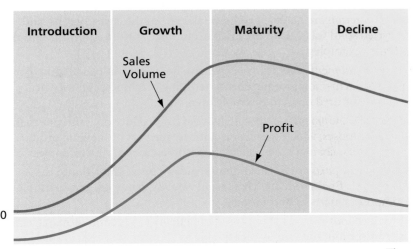

Microsoft
**www.microsoft.com/
ms.htm**

Corel Corporation
www.corel.com/

In the *growth stage,* sales increase rapidly and profits peak, then start to decline. One reason profits start to decline during the growth stage is that new companies enter the market, driving prices down and increasing marketing expenses. During the growth stage, the firm tries to strengthen its position in the market by emphasizing the product's benefits and identifying market segments that want these benefits. A major goal is to obtain the maximum market share and hence, the largest profit. Software companies such as Microsoft compete very strongly with Corel, which markets WordPerfect.

Sales continue to increase at the beginning of the *maturity stage,* but then the sales curve peaks and starts to decline while profits continue to decline. This stage is characterized by severe competition and heavy expenditures. Automobiles are an example of a mature product; intense competition in the auto industry requires Toyota, GM, and other automakers to spend huge sums to make their products stand out in a crowded marketplace. Those companies with the largest share are usually the ones with the lowest cost per unit or have special features or appeal, such as Rolls Royce or Ferrari.

During the *decline stage,* sales continue to fall rapidly. Profits also decline and may even become losses as prices are cut and necessary marketing expenditures are made. As profits drop, firms may eliminate certain models or items. To reduce expenses and squeeze out any remaining profits, marketing expenditures may be cut back, even though such cutbacks accelerate the sales decline. Finally, plans must be made for phasing out the product and introducing new ones to take its place. Frequently, companies may even leave the industry and focus their efforts elsewhere. Other companies merge, as one can see happening in the airline industry during downturns in travel.

Identifying Products

Branding, packaging, and labelling can be used to identify or distinguish one product from others. As a result, they are key marketing activities that help position a product appropriately for its target market.

1. McDonald's		6. Gillette	
2. Coca-Cola		7. Mercedes-Benz	
3. Disney		8. Levi's	
4. Kodak		9. Microsoft	
5. Sony		10. Marlboro	

Table 13.1

Top 10 Worldwide Brands

Source: "The World's Greatest Brands," **www.fastcompany.com/ brandyou**, September 18, 1998. Reprinted with permission of *Fast Company*.

Branding. **Branding** is the process of naming and identifying products. A *brand* is a name, term, symbol, design, or combination that identifies a product and distinguishes it from other products. The top 10 brands in the world based on their influence, extension, appeal, and ability to create consumer loyalty are shown in Table 13.1. The *brand name* is the part of the brand that can be spoken and consists of letters, words, and numbers—such as WD-40 lubricant. A *brand mark* is the part of the brand that is a distinctive design, such as the silver star on the hood of a Mercedes or McDonald's golden arches logo. A **trademark** is a brand that is registered with the Trade Marks Office and is thus legally protected from use by any other firm.

Two major categories of brands are manufacturer brands and private distributor brands. **Manufacturer brands** are brands initiated and owned by the manufacturer to identify products from the point of production to the point of purchase. Kellogg's, Sony, and Texaco are examples. **Private distributor brands,** which may be less expensive than manufacturer brands, are owned and controlled by a wholesaler or retailer, such as Kenmore appliances (Sears), President's Choice (Loblaws), and Life Brand (Shopper's Drug Mart). The names of private brands do not usually identify their manufacturer. Manufacturer brands are fighting hard against private distributor brands.

Another type of brand that has developed is **generic products**—products with no brand name at all. They often come in plain white packages that carry only the generic name of the product—peanut butter, tomato juice, dog food, and so on. They appeal to consumers who may be willing to sacrifice quality or product consistency to get a lower price.

Companies use two basic approaches to branding multiple products. In one, a company gives each product within its complete product mix its own brand name. Warner-Lambert, for example, sells many well-known consumer products—Dentyne, Chiclets, Listerine, Halls, Rolaids, and Trident—each individually branded. This branding policy ensures that the name of one product does not affect the names of others, and different brands can be targeted at different segments of the same market, increasing the company's market share (its percentage of the sales for the total market for a product). Another approach to branding is to develop a family of brands with each of the firm's products carrying the same name or at least part of the name. Gillette, Sara Lee, and IBM use this approach.

Packaging. The **packaging,** or external container that holds and describes the product, influences consumers' attitudes and their buying decisions. It is estimated that consumers' eyes linger only 2.5 seconds on each product on an average shopping trip; therefore, product packaging should be designed to attract and hold consumers' attention. A package can perform several functions including protection, economy, convenience, and promotion.

branding
the process of naming and identifying products

trademark
a brand that is registered with the Trade Marks Office and is thus legally protected from use by any other firm

manufacturer brands
brands initiated and owned by the manufacturer to identify products from the point of production to the point of purchase

private distributor brands
brands, which may cost less than manufacturer brands, that are owned and controlled by a wholesaler or retailer

generic products
products with no brand name that often come in white packages and carry only their generic name

packaging
the external container that holds and describes the product

Strive for Quality

Quality Cyber Service

Quality cyber service, or service provided online, is being increasingly demanded by savvy Internet users. Currently, businesses operating at least partially on the Net handle about 13 percent of their customer inquiries electronically. That number will grow, however, as one-third of online businesses are building sophisticated systems that will automate the buying/selling process. Everything from order taking to customer complaints is being handled online. Sprint Canada long-distance customers can monitor their accounts and pay their bills without cheques, stamps, or envelopes. Customers also can click on an icon and be automatically connected to a service representative. America Online (AOL) offers long-distance service with all communication and account information serviced through the customer's online AOL account.

Using the Internet to provide customer service has benefits for both buyers and sellers. Obviously, buyers can take care of many things, including shopping, paying bills, obtaining account balance information, and getting current investment or finance rates, with just a few clicks of the mouse—all from the convenience of their homes or offices. Sellers can gain cost savings of 30 percent or more while improving service quality at the same time. For example, the electronic account customers at CIBC have instant access to account balances and interest rates. As a result of such online information, these customers place fewer calls to the bank than its regular customers. Sixty-five percent of all bank transactions in Canada are now done electronically.

Some companies are providing a blend of electronic and human help. Automatic reply e-mail systems can answer simple queries, such as current rates, without human help. At Telus Mobility and Nike, Inc., customers are "interviewed" through a series of automatic pop-up online forms to determine the correct response to more complex questions or problems. 1-800-Flowers Inc. and other sites allow users to click on an icon and start an interactive chat with a service representative. At many sites, electronic complaints are routed to a database where they can be studied by companies for recurring problems or repeated requests for features or services.

Firms that are not providing quality customer service on their web sites probably will not have many repeat customers. In "packaging" web sites, companies must offer convenience, reliability, and value that consumers are willing to pay for. Jeff Bezos, CEO of online bookstore Amazon.com, says, "You have to treat every customer as if they can tell thousands of people about the service. Because they can—and they are."[11]

labelling
the presentation of important information on a package

quality
the degree to which a good, service, or idea meets the demands and requirements of customers

Labelling. **Labelling,** the presentation of important information on the package, is closely associated with packaging. The content of labelling, often required by law, may include ingredients or content, nutrition facts (calories, fat, etc.), care instructions, suggestions for use (such as recipes), the manufacturer's address and toll-free number, and other useful information. This information can have a strong impact on sales. The labels of many products, particularly food and drugs, must carry warnings, instructions, certifications, or manufacturers' identifications.

Product Quality. **Quality** reflects the degree to which a good, service, or idea meets the demands and requirements of customers. Quality products are often referred to as reliable, durable, easily maintained, easily used, a good value, or a trusted brand name.

The level of quality is the amount of quality that a product possesses, and the consistency of quality depends on the product maintaining the same level of quality over time.

As global competition intensifies, quality has become a key means for differentiating products or setting them above their competitors in consumers' minds. If a company's product lacks the quality that consumers expect, they will turn to a competitor's product.

Quality of service is difficult to gauge because it depends on customers' perceptions of how well the service meets or exceeds their expectations. In other words, service quality is judged by consumers, not the service providers. A bank may define service quality as employing friendly and knowledgeable employees, but the bank's customers may be more concerned with waiting time, ATM access, security, and statement accuracy. Similarly, an airline traveller considers on-time arrival, on-board food service, and satisfaction with the ticketing and boarding process. Services are becoming a larger part of international competition.

An emerging trend in providing quality service is *e-service*, customized services delivered electronically through the World Wide Web. One example is a credit card called Home Trust Secured Visa Credit Card. Consumers can apply for a Visa credit card online in about 30 seconds by providing their name, address, Social Insurance number, annual income, and a few other details. The Secured Visa web site is integrated with the databases of the major credit bureaus. The e-service provided by the company is a key part of the value provided by this business.[12]

PRICING STRATEGY

Previously, we defined price as the value placed on an object exchanged between a buyer and a seller. Price is probably the most flexible variable in the marketing mix. Although it may take years to develop a product, establish channels of distribution, and design and implement promotion, a product's price may be set and changed in a few minutes. Under certain circumstances, of course, the price may not be so flexible, especially if government regulations prevent dealers from controlling prices.

Pricing Objectives

Pricing objectives specify the role of price in an organization's marketing mix and strategy. They usually are influenced not only by marketing mix decisions but also by finance, accounting, and production factors. Maximizing profits and sales, boosting market share, maintaining the status quo, and survival are four common pricing objectives.

Pricing Strategies

Pricing strategies provide guidelines for achieving the company's pricing objectives and overall marketing strategy. They specify how price will be used as a variable in the marketing mix. Significant pricing strategies relate to the pricing of new products, psychological pricing, and price discounting.

Pricing New Products. Setting the price for a new product is critical: The right price leads to profitability; the wrong price may kill the product. In general, there are two basic strategies to setting the base price for a new product. **Price skimming** is charging the highest possible price that buyers who want the product will pay. This strategy

price skimming
charging the highest possible price that buyers who want the product will pay

penetration price
a low price designed to help a product enter the market and gain market share rapidly

allows the company to generate much-needed revenue to help offset the costs of research and development. Conversely, a **penetration price** is a low price designed to help a product enter the market and gain market share rapidly. Penetration pricing is less flexible than price skimming; it is more difficult to raise a penetration price than to lower a skimming price. Penetration pricing is used most often when marketers suspect that competitors will enter the market shortly after the product has been introduced.

psychological pricing
encouraging purchases based on emotional rather than rational responses to the price

Psychological Pricing. **Psychological pricing** encourages purchases based on emotional rather than rational responses to the price. For example, the assumption behind *even/odd pricing* is that people will buy more of a product for $9.99 than $10 because it seems to be a bargain at the odd price. The assumption behind *symbolic/prestige pricing* is that high prices connote high quality. Thus the prices of certain fragrances are set artificially high to give the impression of superior quality. Some over-the-counter drugs are priced high because consumers associate a drug's price with potency.

discounts
temporary price reductions, often employed to boost sales

Price Discounting. Temporary price reductions, or **discounts,** are often employed to boost sales. Although there are many types, quantity, seasonal, and promotional discounts are among the most widely used. Quantity discounts reflect the economies of purchasing in large volume. Seasonal discounts to buyers who purchase goods or services out of season help even out production capacity. Promotional discounts attempt to improve sales by advertising price reductions on selected products to increase customer interest. Often promotional pricing is geared to increased profits. On the other hand, many companies such as Wal-Mart, Home Depot, and Toys 'R' Us have shunned promotional price discounts and, with everyday low pricing, are focusing more on relationships with customers.

Priceline is an Internet service that allows users to name the price they are willing to pay for airline tickets, and in some areas, hotel rooms and home mortgage rates. In the case of airline tickets, customers must commit to flying at any time of day on any airline. Flights may include connections or stops and cannot be counted toward frequent-flier miles. In just five months, Priceline booked 50,000 tickets valued at US$20 million. Customers who want to make hotel reservations through Priceline must enter the city and part of town in which they want to stay, the desired quality of the hotel (two- to five-star), the price they want to pay, and their credit card number. If the requested criteria are met, the customer is locked into the reservation.[13]

DISTRIBUTION STRATEGY

The best products in the world will not be successful unless companies make them available where and when customers want to buy them. In this section, we will explore dimensions of distribution strategy, including the channels through which products are distributed, the intensity of market coverage, and the physical handling of products during distribution.

Marketing Channels

marketing channel
a group of organizations that moves products from their producer to customers; also channel of distribution

A **marketing channel,** or channel of distribution, is a group of organizations that moves products from their producer to customers. Marketing channels make products available to buyers when and where they desire to purchase them. Organizations that bridge the gap between a product's manufacturer and the ultimate consumer are called *intermediaries*. They create time, place, and ownership utility. Two intermediary organizations are retailers and wholesalers.

Retailers buy products from manufacturers (or other intermediaries) and sell them to consumers for home and household use rather than for resale or for use in producing other products. Toys 'R' Us, for example, buys products from Mattel and other manufacturers and resells them to consumers. Retailing usually occurs in a store, but the Internet, vending machines, mail-order catalogues, and entertainment, such as going to an Edmonton Oilers hockey game, also provide opportunities for retailing. Sales from over 8,000 mail-order catalogues are projected to top US$95 billion in 2000.[14] By bringing together an assortment of products from competing producers, retailers create utility. Retailers arrange for products to be moved from producers to a convenient retail establishment (place utility). They maintain hours of operation for their retail stores to make merchandise available when consumers want it (time utility). They also assume the risk of ownership of inventories (ownership utility). Table 13.2 describes various types of store retailers.

Online shopping is expected to continue to increase rapidly as retailers offer convenience, service, and wide selections.

Bob Schatz/Tony Stone Images

retailers
intermediaries who buy products from manufacturers (or other intermediaries) and sell them to consumers for home and household use rather than for resale or for use in producing other products

Today, there are too many stores competing for too few customers, and, as a result, competition between similar retailers has never been more intense. Further, competition between different types of stores is changing the nature of retailing. Supermarkets compete with specialty food stores, wholesale clubs, and discount stores. Department

Table 13.2 *Types of Store Retailers*

Type of Retailer	Description	Examples
Discount store	Self-service, general merchandise store offering brand name and private name products at low prices	Wal-Mart, Zellers
Department store	Large organization offering wide product mix and organized into separate departments	The Bay, Sears
Supermarket	Self-service store offering complete line of food products and some nonfood products	Loblaw's, Overwaitea, Provigo, Sobey's
Superstore	Giant outlet offering all food and nonfood products found in supermarkets, as well as most routinely purchased products	Maxi Store, Great Canadian Superstore
Warehouse club	Large-scale, members-only establishment combining cash-and-carry wholesaling with discount retailing	Price/Costco
Specialty store	Store offering substantial assortments in a few product lines	Radio Shack, The Limited, The Gap
Off-price store	Store that buys manufacturers' seconds, overruns, returns, and off-season merchandise for resale to consumers at deep discounts	Winners, Army & Navy
Category killers	Very large specialty store concentrating on a single product line and competing on the basis of low prices and product availability	Toys 'R' Us, Home Depot, Pet Smart

Source: Adapted from William M. Pride and O. C. Ferrell, *Marketing: Concepts and Strategies,* 10th ed., p. 346. Copyright © 1997 by Houghton Mifflin Company. Reprinted with permission.

stores compete with nearly every other type of store including specialty stores, off-price chains, category killers, discount stores, and online retailers. Many traditional retailers, such as Wal-Mart, Sears, and the Bay, have created online shopping sites to retain customers and compete with online-only retailers. One of the best-known online only, or cyber, merchants is Amazon.com. Called the "Earth's Biggest Bookstore," Amazon offers over 3 million titles from which to choose, all from the privacy and convenience of the purchaser's home. In many cases, web merchants offer wide selections, ultra-convenience, superior service, knowledge, and the best products. Figure 13.2 shows the results of a survey of web users on the ease of online shopping. With more than one-third of North American adults online and e-commerce projections of US$349 billion in 2002,[15] the Internet presents formidable competition to many traditional retailers that do not have a web presence. More detail on the Internet's effect on marketing strategy and marketing channels can be found in the Cyberzone at the end of Part 5.

wholesalers

intermediaries who buy from producers or from other wholesalers and sell to retailers

Wholesalers are intermediaries who buy from producers or from other wholesalers and sell to retailers. They usually do not sell in significant quantities to ultimate consumers. Wholesalers perform the functions listed in Table 13.3.

Wholesalers are extremely important because of the marketing activities they perform, particularly for consumer products. Although it is true that wholesalers can be eliminated, their functions must be passed on to some other entity, such as the producer, another intermediary, or even the customer. Wholesalers help consumers and retailers by buying in large quantities, then selling to retailers in smaller quantities. By stocking an assortment of products, wholesalers match products to demand.

supply chain management

long-term partnerships among marketing channel members working together to reduce costs, waste, and unnecessary movement in the entire marketing channel in order to satisfy customers

Supply Chain Management. In an effort to improve distribution channel relationships among manufacturers and other channel intermediaries, supply chain management creates alliances between channel members. **Supply chain management** refers to long-term partnerships among marketing channel members working together to reduce costs, waste, and unnecessary movement in the entire marketing channel in order to satisfy customers.[16] It goes beyond traditional channel members (producers, wholesalers, retailers, customers) to include *all* organizations involved in moving products from the producer to the ultimate customer.

Figure 13.2

Is Online Shopping Easy?: Survey of 239 Web Shoppers

Source: *Business Week Bits & Bytes*, **www.business week.com/1998/42/ 63600142.htm**, October 13, 1998.

Extremely difficult

Extremely easy

Somewhat difficult

Somewhat easy

Not particularly easy or difficult

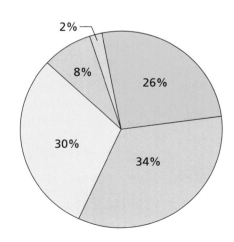

Table 13.3   *Major Wholesaling Functions*

Activity	Description
Wholesale management	Planning, organizing, staffing, and controlling wholesaling operations
Negotiating with suppliers	Serving as the purchasing agent for customers by negotiating supplies
Promotion	Providing a sales force, advertising, sales promotion, and publicity
Warehousing and product handling	Receiving, storing and stockkeeping, order processing, packaging, shipping outgoing orders, and materials handling
Transportation	Arranging and making local and long-distance shipments
Inventory control and data processing	Controlling physical inventory, bookkeeping, recording transactions, keeping records for financial analysis
Security	Safeguarding merchandise
Pricing	Developing prices and providing price quotations
Financing and budgeting	Extending credit, borrowing, making capital investments, and forecasting cash flow
Management and marketing assistance to clients	Supplying information about markets and products and providing advisory services to assist customers in their sales efforts

Source: Adapted from William M. Pride and O. C. Ferrell, *Marketing: Concepts and Strategies,* 10th ed., p. 324. Copyright © 1997 by Houghton Mifflin Company. Reprinted with permission.

The focus shifts from one of selling to the next level in the channel to one of selling products *through* the channel to a satisfied ultimate customer. Information, once provided on a guarded, "as needed" basis, is now open, honest, and ongoing. Perhaps most importantly, the points of contact in the relationship expand from one-on-one at the salesperson–buyer level to multiple interfaces at all levels and in all functional areas of the various organizations.

Channels for Consumer Products. Typical marketing channels for consumer products are shown in Figure 13.3. In Channel A, the product moves from the producer directly to the consumer. Farmers who sell their fruit and vegetables to consumers at roadside stands use a direct-from-producer-to-consumer marketing channel.

In Channel B, the product goes from producer to retailer to consumer. This type of channel is used for products such as college textbooks, automobiles, and appliances. In Channel C, the product is handled by a wholesaler and a retailer before it reaches the consumer. Producer-to-wholesaler-to-retailer-to-consumer marketing channels distribute a wide range of products including refrigerators, televisions, soft drinks, cigarettes, clocks, watches, and office products. In Channel D, the product goes to an agent, a wholesaler, and a retailer before going to the consumer. This long channel of distribution is especially useful for convenience products. Candy and some produce are often sold by agents who bring buyers and sellers together.

Channels for Services. Services are usually distributed through direct marketing channels because they are generally produced *and* consumed simultaneously.

Figure 13.3

Marketing Channels for Consumer Products

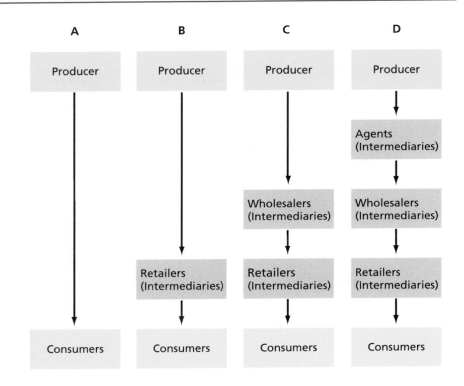

For example, you cannot take a haircut home for later use. Many services require the customer's presence and participation: The sick patient must visit the physician to receive treatment; the child must be at the day-care centre to receive care; the tourist must be present to sightsee and consume tourism services.

Intensity of Market Coverage

A major distribution decision is how widely to distribute a product—that is, how many and what type of outlets should carry it. The intensity of market coverage depends on buyer behaviour, as well as the nature of the target market and the competition. Wholesalers and retailers provide various intensities of market coverage and must be selected carefully to ensure success. Market coverage may be intensive, selective, or exclusive.

Intensive distribution makes a product available in as many outlets as possible. Because availability is important to purchasers of convenience products such as bread, milk, gasoline, soft drinks, and chewing gum, a nearby location with a minimum of time spent searching and waiting in line is most important to the consumer. To saturate markets intensively, wholesalers and many varied retailers try to make the product available at every location where a consumer might desire to purchase it. Frequently, we see confectionary products such as gum, snacks, and chocolate bars at most convenience stores, gas bars, and grocery store check-out lines.

Selective distribution uses only a small number of all available outlets to expose products. It is used most often for products that consumers buy only after shopping

intensive distribution
a form of market coverage whereby a product is made available in as many outlets as possible

selective distribution
a form of market coverage whereby only a small number of all available outlets are used to expose products

and comparing price, quality, and style. Many products sold on a selective basis require salesperson assistance, technical advice, warranties, or repair service to maintain consumer satisfaction. Typical products include automobiles, major appliances, clothes, and furniture.

Exclusive distribution exists when a manufacturer gives an intermediary the sole right to sell a product in a defined geographic territory. Such exclusivity provides an incentive for a dealer to handle a product that has a limited market. Exclusive distribution is the opposite of intensive distribution in that products are purchased and consumed over a long period of time, and service or information is required to develop a satisfactory sales relationship. Products distributed on an exclusive basis include high-quality musical instruments, yachts, airplanes, and high-fashion leather goods.

exclusive distribution
the awarding by a manufacturer to an intermediary of the sole right to sell a product in a defined geographic territory

Physical Distribution

Physical distribution includes all the activities necessary to move products from producers to customers—inventory control, transportation, warehousing, and materials handling. Physical distribution creates time and place utility by making products available when they are wanted, with adequate service and at minimum cost. Both goods and services require physical distribution. Many physical distribution activities are part of logistics, which we discussed in Chapter 9; we'll take a brief look at a few more now.

physical distribution
all the activities necessary to move products from producers to customers—inventory control, transportation, warehousing, and materials handling

Embrace Technology

Truckers' Routes Become Information Superhighways with Computers

Technology has made its way to the trucking industry, cutting costs, reducing delays, increasing shipment reliability, and changing the lives of many long-haul truckers. The long, tedious days of waiting at rest stops, making lonely phone calls home, and using CB radios have been replaced by Internet sites, e-mail, and global positioning systems.

Park 'N View allows truckers to plug into cable, Internet, pay-per-view, and telephone service at 300 truck stops in the US with a $30 monthly subscription card. Global positioning and satellite tracking systems let dispatchers send route changes to a trucker's personal video display and give traffic advice in a matter of seconds. Time spent waiting for load orders and directions has been significantly reduced.

Global positioning satellites also can pinpoint a truck's location to within a 15-metre radius, thus cutting down on the practice by some drivers of being someplace else when they should be on the road. Initial suspicions of such surveillance have been overcome. In an emergency, help is just one push of a button away for the trucker. In addition, by tracking the truck's progress and location, the satellite allows users to send customers updated arrival information.

Systems that monitor engine performance send data to maintenance technicians as trucks make their runs many miles away. A diagnosis of an engine problem is as likely to occur midroute at 100 kph as it is in a maintenance shop.

Instantaneous communication, satellite tracking of a truck's location, and computer analysis of mechanical systems are all turning truckers' routes into "information superhighways."[17]

If this service is not soon expanded into Canada, will a Canadian introduce this service or one similar?

transportation
the shipment of products to buyers

Transportation. **Transportation,** the shipment of products to buyers, creates time and place utility for its products, and thus is a key element in the flow of goods and services from producer to consumer. The major modes of transportation used to move products between cities in Canada are railways, motor vehicles, waterways, pipelines, and airways.

Railroads offer the least expensive transportation for many products. Heavy commodities, foodstuffs, grain, raw materials, and coal are examples of products carried by railroads. Trucks have greater flexibility than railroads because they can reach more locations. Trucks handle freight quickly and economically, offer door-to-door service, and are more flexible in their packaging requirements than are ships or airplanes. Air transport offers speed and a high degree of dependability but is the most expensive means of transportation; shipping is the least expensive and slowest form. Pipelines are used to transport petroleum, natural gas, semiliquid coal, wood chips, and certain chemicals. Many products can be moved most efficiently by using more than one mode of transportation.

Factors affecting the selection of a mode of transportation include cost, capability to handle the product, reliability, and availability, and, as suggested, selecting transportation modes requires trade-offs. Unique characteristics of the product and consumer desires often determine the mode selected.

warehousing
the design and operation of facilities to receive, store, and ship products

Warehousing. **Warehousing** is the design and operation of facilities to receive, store, and ship products. A warehouse facility receives, identifies, sorts, and dispatches goods to storage; stores them; recalls, selects, or picks goods; assembles the shipment; and finally, dispatches the shipment.

Deluxe Chips is one of the leading companies in the salty-snack industry, with almost one-fourth of the $10 billion market. Its Deluxos tortilla chips are the number-one selling brand in North America, and its Ridgerunner potato chip is also a market share leader. Deluxe Chips wants to stay on top of the market by changing marketing strategies to match changing consumer needs and preferences. Promoting specific brands to market segments with the appropriate price and distribution channel is helping Deluxe Chips succeed.

As many middle-aged consumers modify their snacking habits, Deluxe Chips is considering a new product line of light snack foods with less fat and cholesterol and targeted at the 35- to 50-year-old consumer who enjoys snacking but wants to be more health conscious. Marketing research suggests that the product will succeed as long as it tastes good and that consumers may be willing to pay more for it. Large expenditures on advertising may be necessary to overcome the competition. However, it may be possible to analyze customer profiles and retail store characteristics and then match the right product with the right neighbourhood. Store-specific micromarketing would allow Deluxe Chips to spend its promotional dollars more efficiently.

1. Design a marketing strategy for the new product line.

2. Critique your marketing strategy in terms of its strengths and weaknesses.

3. What are your suggestions for implementation of the marketing strategy?

Solve the Dilemma

Better Health with Snacks

Companies often own and operate their own private warehouses that store, handle, and move their own products. They can also rent storage and related physical distribution services from public warehouses. Regardless of whether a private or a public warehouse is used, warehousing is important because it makes products available for shipment to match demand at different geographic locations.

Materials Handling. **Materials handling** is the physical handling and movement of products in warehousing and transportation. Handling processes may vary significantly due to product characteristics. Efficient materials-handling procedures increase a warehouse's useful capacity and improve customer service. Well-coordinated loading and movement systems increase efficiency and reduce costs.

materials handling
the physical handling and movement of products in warehousing and transportation

Importance of Distribution in a Marketing Strategy

Distribution decisions are among the least flexible marketing mix decisions. Products can be changed over time; prices can be changed overnight; and promotion is usually changed regularly. But distribution decisions often commit resources and establish contractual relationships that are difficult if not impossible to change. As a company attempts to expand into new markets, it may require a complete change in distribution. Moreover, if a firm does not manage its marketing channel in the most efficient manner and provide the best service, then a new competitor will evolve to create a more effective distribution system.

PROMOTION STRATEGY

The role of promotion is to communicate with individuals, groups, and organizations to facilitate an exchange directly or indirectly. It encourages marketing exchanges by attempting to persuade individuals, groups, and organizations to accept goods, services, and ideas. Promotion is used not only to sell products but also to influence opinions and attitudes toward an organization, person, or cause. MADD (Mothers Against Drunk Driving), for example, has successfully used promotion to educate people about the costs of drinking and driving. Most people probably equate promotion with advertising, but it also includes personal selling, publicity, and sales promotion. The role that these elements play in a marketing strategy is extremely important.

MADD
www.madd.org/home/

The Promotion Mix

Advertising, personal selling, publicity, and sales promotion are collectively known as the promotion mix because a strong promotion program results from the careful selection and blending of these elements. The process of coordinating the promotion mix elements and synchronizing promotion as a unified effort is called **integrated marketing communications.** When planning promotional activities, an integrated marketing communications approach results in the desired message for customers. Different elements of the promotion mix are coordinated to play their appropriate roles in delivery of the message on a consistent basis.

integrated marketing communications
coordinating the promotion mix elements and synchronizing promotion as a unified effort

Advertising. Perhaps the best-known form of promotion, **advertising** is a paid form of nonpersonal communication transmitted through a mass medium, such as television commercials, magazine advertisements or online ads. Commercials featuring celebrities, customers, or unique creations (the Energizer Bunny, for example)

advertising
a paid form of nonpersonal communication transmitted through a mass medium, such as television commercials or magazine advertisements

serve to grab viewers' attention and pique their interest in a product. Table 13.4 shows the top 10 advertising categories in Canada. Table 13.5 lists the top marketers according to advertising expenditures in both Canada and the United States.

All advertising possesses four basic features:

- A verbal and/or visual message.
- A sponsor who is identified.
- Delivery through at least one medium.
- Payment by the sponsor to the media carrying the message.

Advertising can be intended to encourage direct action by having the consumer use a coupon or call a 1-800 number. Alternatively, the advertising effort may be focused on stimulating the demand for a product or service over a longer period of time by reminding consumers of the company or its offerings, thus building awareness of the firm or brand recognition.

Business-to-business advertising tends to be different from consumer advertising and frequently presents more information to the decision maker in the purchasing role. Still, both types of advertising will try to stimulate either generic demand for items, such as Colombian coffee, or a specific brand, such as BC Hot House tomatoes. This may be done through comparative advertising—actually naming the competitor or its product and presenting the advantages of their own products. Still, in all markets the advertising must be well focused and delivered to the intended target market.

Advertising media are the vehicles or forms of communication used to reach a desired audience. Print media include newspapers, magazines, direct mail, and billboards, and electronic media include television, radio, and cyber ads. Newspapers, television, and direct mail are the most widely used advertising media. Figure 13.4 (on page 338) shows the percentage of adults by age who use four media outlets: newspaper, television, magazine, and online. In the autumn of 2001, Toyota announced a single advertising program of US$160 million, and that was just to

---

Table 13.4

Top 10 Advertising Categories in Canada, 1998

Source: A.C. Nielsen, Markham, Ontario.

Rank	Category	Spending ($ millions)
1	Retail	$953.5
2	Automotive: cars, minivans, trucks, vans, dealer associations	753.8
3	Business equipment and services	521.6
4	Food	395.6
5	Financial and insurance services	388.0
6	Entertainment	314.8
7	Local automotive dealers	266.6
8	Travel and transportation	249.3
9	Restaurants, catering, and nightclubs	199.3
10	Media: TV, radio, out of home, station promo	165.5

Table 13.5

Top 10 Marketers in North America by Country, 1999

Source: "Top 10 marketers by country, North America—June 2000," *Advertising Age*, **http://adageglobal.com/cgi-bin/pages.pl?link=447**, September 4, 2001.

Canada		United States	
Marketer	1999 Advertising Expenditure ($ 000)	Marketer	1999 Advertising Expenditure ($000)
General Motors	$82,881	General Motors	$2,959,979
Sears, Roebuck & Co.	76,067	Procter & Gamble Co.	1,704,178
BCE	67,239	DaimlerChrysler	1,533,447
Govt. of Canada	65,243	Philip Morris Cos.	1,358,388
Procter & Gamble Co.	54,895	Ford Motor Co.	1,272,386
Rogers Communications	47,111	Time Warner	927,440
Hudson's Bay Co.	45,826	Johnson & Johnson	899,025
Viacom	41,085	AT&T Corp.	838,875
Ford Motor Co.	49,941	Walt Disney Co.	782,401
Interbrew	40,566	WorldCom	764,783

support the 2002 Camry model. Ads were developed for television, radio, print, billboards, and many different web sites.[18]

The use of online, or cyber, ads is growing, with over US$1 billion budgeted annually for this media avenue.[19] Online advertising is best for companies whose products or services are purchased mainly online and for those firms whose potential customers are heavy web users. DoubleClick is one of the most established agencies in online advertising. Companies can buy advertising that is targeted to specified sites or sites based on interest. There are 10 interest categories at Double-Click, including business/finance, health, technology, and women/family. Certain categories (e.g., technology) are more expensive than others (e.g., health). Double-Click's network of sites reaches more than 35 million viewers monthly. Online advertising is relatively inexpensive, whereas a one-eighth page, one-time ad in a local newspaper can cost more than $1,000.[20]

Infomercials—large blocks of radio or television air time featuring a celebrity or upbeat host talking about and demonstrating a product—have evolved as an advertising method. Toll-free numbers are usually provided so consumers can conveniently purchase the product. Infomercials usually last 30 minutes and focus on providing potential customers with all the information they will need about a product. Infomercials are about one-fifth the cost of a regular 30-second television commercial.[21] It is estimated that 66 percent of adults have watched part of an infomercial, but only 12 percent have watched one in its entirety.[22]

Personal Selling. **Personal selling** is direct, two-way communication with buyers and potential buyers. For many products—especially large, expensive ones with specialized uses, such as cars, appliances, and houses—interaction between a salesperson and the customer is probably the most important promotional tool.

Personal selling is the most flexible of the promotional methods because it gives marketers the greatest opportunity to communicate specific information that might

personal selling
direct, two-way communication with buyers and potential buyers

Figure 13.4

Media Generation Gap

Source: Pew Research Centre for the People and the Press, *USA Today Snapshots,* September 30, 1998, p. A-1. Copyright 1998, *USA Today.* Reprinted with permission.

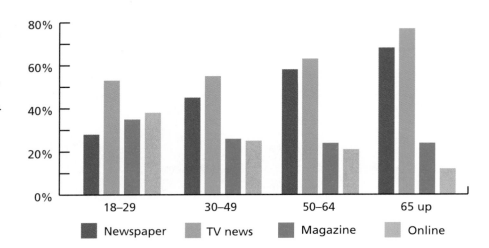

trigger a purchase. Only personal selling can zero in on a prospect and attempt to persuade that person to make a purchase. Although personal selling has a lot of advantages, it is one of the most costly forms of promotion. A sales call on an industrial customer can cost as much as $200 or $300.

There are three distinct categories of salespersons: order takers (e.g., retail sales clerks and route salespeople), creative salespersons (e.g., automobile, furniture, and insurance salespeople), and support salespersons (e.g., customer educators and goodwill builders who usually do not take orders). For most of these salespeople, personal selling is a six-step process:

1. *Prospecting:* Identifying potential buyers of the product.
2. *Approaching:* Using a referral or calling on a customer without prior notice to determine interest in the product.
3. *Presenting:* Getting the prospect's attention with a product demonstration.
4. *Handling objections:* Countering reasons for not buying the product.
5. *Closing:* Asking the prospect to buy the product.
6. *Following up:* Checking customer satisfaction with the purchased product.

publicity

nonpersonal communication transmitted through the mass media but not paid for directly by the firm

Publicity. Publicity is nonpersonal communication transmitted through the mass media but not paid for directly by the firm. A firm does not pay the media cost for publicity and is not identified as the originator of the message; instead, the message is presented in news story form. Obviously, a company can benefit from publicity by releasing to news sources newsworthy messages about the firm and its involvement with the public. Many companies have *public relations* departments to try to gain favourable publicity and minimize negative publicity for the firm.

Although advertising and publicity are both carried by the mass media, they differ in several major ways. Advertising messages tend to be informative, persuasive, or both; publicity is mainly informative. Advertising is often designed to have an immediate impact or to provide specific information to persuade a person to act; publicity describes what a firm is doing, what products it is launching, or other newsworthy information, but seldom calls for action. When advertising is used, the organization must pay for media time and select the media that will best reach target audiences. The mass media willingly carry publicity because they believe it has general public interest. Advertising can be repeated a number of times; most publicity appears in the mass media once and is not repeated.

Advertising, personal selling, and sales promotion are especially useful for influencing an exchange directly. Publicity is extremely important when communication focuses on a company's activities and products and is directed at interest groups, current and potential investors, regulatory agencies, and society in general.

Sales Promotion. **Sales promotion** involves direct inducements offering added value or some other incentive for buyers to enter into an exchange. The major tools of sales promotion are store displays, premiums, trading stamps, samples and demonstrations, coupons, contests and sweepstakes, refunds, and trade shows. Sales promotion stimulates customer purchasing and increases dealer effectiveness in selling products. It is used to enhance and supplement other forms of promotion. Sales promotions are generally easier to measure and less expensive than advertising.

A survey by Target Marketing and Research found that consumers consider sampling to be the best way to evaluate a new product, ranking it ahead of word-of-mouth, coupons, advertising, games, and contests. In fact, 71 percent of those surveyed said they would try a product based on a sample, and if they liked the sample, 7 out of 10 said they would switch brands.[23] Bonne Bell used sampling to support its fragrance line, Bottled Emotion, which contains 10 different scents. Each of the 10 scents represents a different emotion that a teenaged girl is likely to experience, such as "flirty" or "mellow."[24]

The use of online promotion, such as games and sweepstakes, is increasing. An online game offering players a chance to win an all-expense-paid trip to the Caribbean was created for the Arrid XX "Get a Little Closer" advertising campaign. The game attracted more than 30,000 players, and 25 percent of the players purchased Arrid XX during the game.[25] The Million Dollar WebCrawl was designed to persuade people to use America Online's search engine and offered a US$1 million prize. Players had to visit specific web sites and register their e-mail addresses at each one. The sweepstakes attracted more than 350,000 players who made 2.7 million unique web visits.[26]

The most effective and trusted means of promotion is "word of mouth." Satisfied customers are the best ambassadors. This is the most proven method and can be encouraged with customer discounts for referrals. Of course, if a customer is dissatisfied, they can be very destructive to a company's reputation as well.

Promotion Strategies: To Push or to Pull

In developing a promotion mix, organizations must decide whether to fashion a mix that pushes or pulls the product (Figure 13.5). A **push strategy** attempts to motivate intermediaries to push the product down to their customers. When a push strategy is used, the company attempts to motivate wholesalers and retailers to make the product available to their customers. Sales personnel may be used to persuade intermediaries to offer the product, distribute promotional materials, and offer special promotional incentives for those who agree to carry the product. A **pull strategy** uses promotion to create consumer demand for a product

sales promotion
direct inducements offering added value or some other incentive for buyers to enter into an exchange

push strategy
an attempt to motivate intermediaries to push the product down to their customers

pull strategy
the use of promotion to create consumer demand for a product so that consumers exert pressure on marketing channel members to make it available

Figure 13.5   *Push and Pull Strategies*

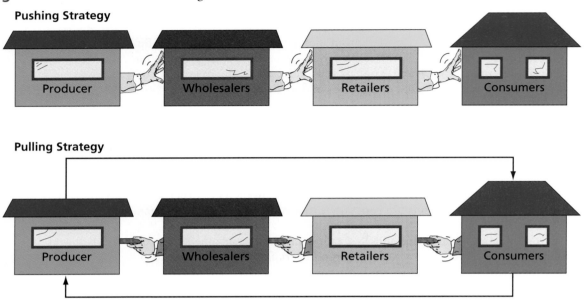

Flow of Communications

so that consumers exert pressure on marketing channel members to make it available.

A company can use either strategy, or it can use a variation or combination of the two. The exclusive use of advertising indicates a pull strategy. Personal selling to marketing channel members indicates a push strategy. The allocation of promotional resources to various marketing mix elements probably determines which strategy a marketer uses.

Objectives of Promotion

The marketing mix a company uses depends on its objectives. It is important to recognize that promotion is only one element of the marketing strategy and must be tied carefully to the goals of the firm, its overall marketing objectives, and the other elements of the marketing strategy. Firms use promotion for many reasons, but typical objectives are to stimulate demand, to stabilize sales, and to inform, remind, and reinforce customers.

Increasing demand for a product is probably the most typical promotional objective. Stimulating demand, often through advertising and sales promotion, is particularly important when a firm is using a pull strategy. Xerox Corporation, for example, is doubling its worldwide advertising spending to more than US$200 million to stimulate the market for its digital products and services.[27]

Another goal of promotion is to stabilize sales by maintaining the status quo—that is, the current sales level of the product. During periods of slack or decreasing sales, contests, prizes, vacations, and other sales promotions are sometimes offered

All organizations need people to perform marketing activities. Whether in manufacturing, financial services, health care, professional services, or nonprofit organizations, companies are constantly seeking individuals who can work to develop new products, use marketing research to stay on top of emerging trends, and, in general, create sales. Broad areas of opportunity in marketing include marketing research, sales, purchasing, advertising, retailing, and direct marketing. Employment of marketing, advertising, and public relations managers is expected to increase faster than average for all occupations through the year 2006. With between one-fourth and one-third of the civilian work force in North America employed in marketing-related jobs, it is clear that marketing offers many diverse career opportunities.

With increasing global and domestic competition and more complex products, students with marketing degrees will find excellent job prospects. Service and high-technology firms, in particular, are experiencing rapid growth and have a high demand for marketers to help develop, distribute, and promote new products. A bachelor's degree is generally necessary, but some higher-level positions require a master's or doctorate degree. Students with a degree or diploma in marketing or advertising can expect to start out earning about $35,000. With experience and education, top-level advertising executives and marketing managers can expect to reach six-figure salaries, depending on the organization and how many people they supervise.[28]

Explore Your Career Options

Diverse Opportunities in Marketing

to customers to maintain sales goals. Advertising is often used to stabilize sales by making customers aware of slack use periods. For example, auto manufacturers often provide rebates, free options, or lower-than-market interest rates to stabilize sales and thereby keep production lines moving during temporary slowdowns. A stable sales pattern allows the firm to run efficiently by maintaining a consistent level of production and storage and utilizing all its functions so that it is ready when sales increase.

An important role of any promotional program is to inform potential buyers about the organization and its products. A major portion of advertising in North America, particularly in daily newspapers, is informational. Providing information about the availability, price, technology, and features of a product is very important in encouraging a buyer to move toward a purchase decision. Nearly all forms of promotion involve an attempt to help consumers learn more about a product and company.

Promotion is also used to remind consumers that an established organization is still around and sells certain products that have uses and benefits. Often advertising reminds customers that they may need to use a product more frequently or in certain situations. Quaker State, for example, has run commercials reminding car owners that they need to change their oil every 5,000 km to ensure proper performance of their cars and promote environmental kindess.

Reinforcement promotion attempts to assure current users of the product that they have made the right choice and tells them how to get the most satisfaction from the product. Also, a company could release publicity statements about a new use for a product through the news media. Additionally, firms can have salespeople communicate with current and potential customers about the proper use and maintenance of a product—all in the hope of developing a repeat customer.

Promotional Positioning

promotional positioning
the use of promotion to create and maintain an image of a product in buyers' minds

Promotional positioning uses promotion to create and maintain an image of a product in buyers' minds. It is a natural result of market segmentation. In both promotional positioning and market segmentation, the firm targets a given product or brand at a portion of the total market. A promotional strategy helps differentiate the product and make it appeal to a particular market segment. For example, to appeal to safety-conscious consumers, Volvo heavily promotes the safety and crashworthiness of Volvo automobiles in its advertising. Mazda relies on nostalgia in its advertising of the Miata sports car to appeal to style- and price-conscious baby boomers who want to relive their youth in a British roadster-type automobile. Promotion can be used to change or reinforce an image. Effective promotion influences customers and persuades them to buy.

Review Your Understanding

Describe the role of product in the marketing mix, including how products are developed, classified, and identified.

Products (goods, services, ideas) are among a firm's most visible contacts with consumers and must meet consumers' needs and expectations to ensure success. New product development is a multistep process: idea development, the screening of new ideas, business analysis, product development, test marketing, and commercialization. Products are usually classified as either consumer or industrial products. Consumer products can be further classified as convenience, shopping, or specialty products. The industrial product classifications are raw materials, major equipment, accessory equipment, component parts, processed materials, supplies, and industrial services. Products also can be classified by the stage of the product life cycle (introduction, growth, maturity, and decline). Identifying products includes branding (the process of naming and identifying products); packaging (the product's container); and labelling (information, such as content and warnings, on the package).

Define price and discuss its importance in the marketing mix, including various pricing strategies a firm might employ.

Price is the value placed on an object exchanged between a buyer and a seller. It is probably the most flexible variable of the marketing mix. Pricing objectives include survival, maximization of profits and sales volume, and maintaining the status quo. When a firm introduces a new product, it may use price skimming or penetration pricing. Psychological pricing and price discounting are other strategies.

Identify factors affecting distribution decisions, such as marketing channels and intensity of market coverage.

Making products available to customers is facilitated by intermediaries who bridge the gap between the producer of the product and its ultimate user. A marketing channel is a group of marketing organizations that direct the flow of products from producers to consumers. Market coverage relates to the number and variety of outlets that make products available to customers; it may be intensive, selective, or exclusive. Physical distribution is all the activities necessary to move products from producers to consumers, including inventory planning and control, transportation, warehousing, and materials handling.

Specify the activities involved in promotion, as well as promotional strategies and promotional positioning.

Promotion encourages marketing exchanges by persuading individuals, groups, and organizations to accept goods, services, and ideas. The promotion mix includes advertising (a paid form of nonpersonal communication transmitted through a mass medium); personal selling (direct, two-way communication with buyers and potential buyers); publicity (nonpersonal communication transmitted through the mass media but not paid for directly by the firm); and sales promotion (direct inducements offering added value or some other incentive for buyers to enter into an exchange). A push strategy attempts to motivate intermediaries to push the product down to their customers, whereas a pull strategy tries to create consumer demand for a product so that consumers exert pressure on marketing channel members to make the product available. Typical promotion objectives are to stimulate demand, stabilize sales, and inform, remind, and reinforce customers. Promotional positioning is the use of promotion to create and maintain in the buyer's mind an image of a product.

Evaluate an organization's marketing strategy plans.

Based on the material in this chapter, you should be able to answer the questions posed in the "Solve the Dilemma" box and evaluate the company's marketing strategy plans, including its target market and marketing mix.

Learn the Terms

advertising 335

branding 325

commercialization 321

consumer products 322

discounts 328

exclusive distribution 333

generic products 325

industrial products 323

integrated marketing
   communications 335

intensive distribution 332

labelling 326

manufacturer brands 325

marketing channel 328

materials handling 335

packaging 325

penetration price 328

personal selling 337

physical distribution 333

price skimming 327

private distributor brands 325

product line 323

product mix 323

promotional positioning 342

psychological pricing 328

publicity 338

pull strategy 339

push strategy 339

quality 326

retailers 329

sales promotion 339

selective distribution 332

supply chain management 330

test marketing 321

trademark 325

transportation 334

warehousing 334

wholesalers 330

Check Your Progress

1. What steps do companies generally take to develop and introduce a new product?
2. What is the product life cycle? How does a product's life-cycle stage affect its marketing strategy? Give an example of a product or service in each stage of the product life cycle.
3. Which marketing mix variable is probably the most flexible? Why?
4. Distinguish between the two ways to set the base price for a new product.
5. What is probably the least flexible marketing mix variable? Why?
6. Describe the typical marketing channels for consumer products.
7. What activities are involved in physical distribution? What functions does a warehouse perform?
8. How do publicity and advertising differ? How are they related?
9. What does the personal selling process involve? Briefly discuss the process.
10. List the circumstances in which the push and pull promotional strategies are used.

Get Involved

1. Pick three products you use every day (either in school, at work, or for pleasure—perhaps one of each). Determine what phase of the product life cycle each is in. Evaluate the marketer's strategy (product, price, promotion, and distribution) for the product and whether it is appropriate for the life-cycle stage.

2. Design a distribution channel for a manufacturer of stuffed toys.

3. Pick a nearby store, and briefly describe the kinds of sales promotion used and their effectiveness.

Build Your Skills

Analyzing Canadian Tire's Marketing Strategy

Background: Canadian Tire Corp. (CTC) is famous for its money and having everything and anything you most likely could need. Based on what is written below and your personal knowledge, you will analyze the marketing strategy of CTC.

Task: Read the paragraphs below and complete the questions that follow.

The Billes brothers with $1,800 in savings founded CTC in 1922. By 1927 they incorporated and despite the depression they continued to grow. In 1934 they opened their first associate store in Hamilton. This new effort has resulted in over 390 Canadian Tire Associate Dealers operating over 430 Associate stores. In the 1950s the company introduced Canadian Tire "money," and the gasoline stations that issue the money encourage the use of the money for purchasing store merchandise. In the 1960s the issuance of the money was extended to the retail environment.

Today nine out of ten Canadians shop at Canadian Tire (CT) at least twice a year, and 40 percent of Canadians shop at CT every week. Eighty-five percent of Canadians live within a 15-minute drive of a CT store. Supported by "A Bike Story" national advertising campaign, CTC demonstrates their unique link with their customers by sending the message of family, work, dreams, and rewards. In 1993 the company stated its mission "To be the first choice for Canadians in Automotive, Sports and Leisure, and Home products, providing total customer value through customer-driven service, focused assortments and competitive operations."

1. In developing a marketing mix, identify in the second column of the table what the current strategy is and then identify any changes you think CTC should consider for carrying it successfully through the next five years.

Marketing Mix Variable	Current Strategy	5-Year Strategy
a. Product		
b. Price		
c. Distribution		
d. Promotion		

2. In December 2001, CTC announced a plan to purchase Mark's Work Wearhouse Ltd. for $119 million. Mark's operates 157 Mark's stores (25 franchise), 144 Work World stores (90 franchise), and 8 Dockers stores across Canada. Their mission is to "grow consistently as a mature and stable enterprise known for being the most customer-sensitive and responsive specialty retail organization…" How does Mark's fit into your strategy above?

 **See for Yourself Videocase**   **www.cbc.ca**

Boom, Bust, and Retail

So who is the darling of retail in Canada? The Salvation Army. They have added or renovated 100 stores recently and sales are growing quickly. One location in Vancouver, in a strong middle-class neighbourhood, is the best store they have on a dollar-per-square-foot basis. Wal-Mart is expected to generate up to 35 percent of the retail market in five years. So what is attracting so many people to Wal-Mart and the Salvation Army thrift stores? Lower prices. What has happened is our disposable income has declined 2 percent in the 1990s versus an increase of 18 percent in the United States. But we all knew that.

Actually the drop in incomes may have been the final nail in the coffin of Eaton's. This lack of income is what scared away Bloomingdale/Macy's from purchasing the upscale retailer and converting it into a Canadian version of the stores in the US at a cost of $380 million. But we do not have as many wealthy people in Canada as in the US. The Bay and Zellers know that. Even Sears, which purchased a few of the old Eaton's stores, now called Eatons, converted some to Sears stores and left only a few in high-end markets as Eatons.

Holt Renfrew, a truly upscale retailer, has even brought out its own house brand of products to offer less expensive products. They need to lower the price points to attract shoppers who are looking for good products but have experienced a drop in their disposable income. Wal-Mart is even facing petitions from small communities requesting that they open stores in areas they are not now serving. All for the sake of lower prices.

Questions

1. Have you or your family experienced a drop in disposable income? Check at home. Does your money go as far as it should?

2. When you shop, do you constantly look for discounts?

3. What efforts have governments made recently to alleviate the drop in incomes? Will these efforts have any impact?

4. What else should or could be done?

Source: *Venture*, show number 714, "Boardrooms," July 13, 1999, running time 8:05.

Remember to check out our Online Learning Centre at **www.mcgrawhill.ca/college/ferrell.**

Cyberzone

Electronic Commerce

The Internet has sparked an era of sweeping change, touching most industries and businesses. In just a few years, the Net has changed from a playground for "techies" into a vast communications and trading centre where more than one-third of North American adults are online.[1] What is e-commerce? How are marketers tapping into this resource to develop relationships and how are they incorporating the web into their marketing strategies? How many companies use the web for e-commerce and what products and services are available for online purchase? What is the potential for online sales and how can marketers be successful with e-commerce? Let's examine these issues briefly.

What Is E-commerce?

Using the Internet to carry out marketing activities (communicating and fostering exchanges and relationships with customers, suppliers, and the public) is called *electronic commerce,* or e-commerce, for short. Such marketing activities include using the Internet for marketing research, for providing price and product information, and for advertising, as well as for online selling.

The Internet provides marketers the opportunity to gather demographic and usage-related data in an effort to better target and understand their customers. Marketers can conduct competitive analyses by visiting competitors' sites to gather information about product offerings, services, prices, etc. Many web sites ask users for information that can be used to build customer profiles or be sold to other companies for their use. Typically requested information includes name, age, and e-mail address. Some web sites offer contests or surveys, sometimes with prizes or premiums for participating, to gain marketing data.

Marketers are not only gaining information from Internet users, they are finding that the Internet community is a lucrative target market, with goods and services sold online doubling in one year to US$5.1 billion.[2]

Incorporating the Web into Marketing Strategy and the Marketing Mix

The phenomenal growth of the Internet and the World Wide Web gives marketers the opportunity to assess target markets and reach potential customers through new and/or existing products, promotion methods, distribution channels, and pricing strategies.

Products

The industry best positioned to take advantage of the Internet is computers, both hardware and software. Computer programs, such as Netscape Navigator and Microsoft's Internet Explorer, have been developed to help consumers use the web. Commercial online services, such as America Online, provide subscribers with access to the Internet and unique content and services. Many telecommunications firms, such as Bell Canada, Sprint, and Rogers, have launched Internet service providers as well. Search engines such as Yahoo, Excite, and Infoseek keep track of and index the information available on the web.

Marketers also have created web sites to increase sales of existing products or services. For example, by accessing the FedEx web site, customers can track shipments, request a pickup or invoice adjustment, or locate the nearest drop-off site. Marketers of consumer food products, including Kraft and Ragu, have created web sites with recipes and tips to help consumers get the most from their products. Many television networks have created web sites to augment their programming and enhance viewer enjoyment.

Promotion

Advertising is probably one of the best ways marketers can take advantage of the web. Thousands of well-known companies, from Wal-Mart to Coca-Cola, have web pages that promote their products, provide company information, list job opportunities, entertain and inform users, and interact with customers. Such information can foster brand identity and loyalty and develop long-term relationships with customers.

Many marketers also advertise their products on the web sites of other organizations through the use of banner ads, keyword ads, button ads, interstitials, or sponsorship ads. For example, every time an Internet user searches Yahoo for the term "laptop," a banner ad for an IBM product appears because the company purchased the rights to that and some 200 other terms on Yahoo.

Distribution

By eliminating intermediaries, salespeople, and sometimes even physical stores, the Net has changed the distribution strategies for many marketers—from travel agents to stockbrokers to retailers. For example, some airlines, such as Air Canada, allow the user to obtain travel information, make reservations, and purchase tickets, thus eliminating the need for a travel agent or airline reservations operator. Online brokerages, such as TD Waterhouse and BMO Nesbitt Burns, allow online customers to buy and sell securities from their home or office without a broker. By offering the online sale of 2,200 toys, ranging from stuffed animals to the latest from Mattel, e-Toys Inc. expects to have revenues of US$10 to US$15 million a year and increase its offering to 4,500 items.[3]

Price

For most marketers, the Internet's effect on pricing strategies relates to consumers having quick access to prices. For example, at Saturn, potential customers can "build" the car of their dreams, find out the price, and get financing options—all without the hassle of actually going to the dealership. Some service organizations, such as Auto-By-Tel, help customers find the best deal on new cars or trucks, negotiate a final price, and contract with member dealers (who pay a fee to participate) who then deliver the vehicle to the nearest dealership. With the exception of books and CDs, however, few online merchants offer radically lower prices in their virtual stores. When shipping and taxes are added into the total price, many items are actually higher.

Who Are the Successful Cybermerchants and Why?

Of the 414,000 commercial web sites available, only about 46 percent are profitable from current sales.[4] The number one online merchant is Dell, with daily online sales of US$5 million and expectations that online sales will account for 50 percent of its revenues in 2000.[5] Among the profitable sites are eBay, the auction service in cyberspace, Eddie Bauer, and Grand and Toy.

Successful "shopkeepers" on the web offer customers a special reason for viewing or "hitting" their sites—either the widest selection, the greatest convenience, top-notch service, the best products, or superior knowledge. Offering over 3 million titles from which to choose, Amazon calls itself the "Earth's Biggest Bookstore." Recreational Equipment's cyberstore receives 35 percent of its online orders between 10 PM and 7 AM, when its regular stores are closed and its mail-order operators are unavailable—thus offering ultraconvenience for customers. One site providing personal service is 1-800-Flowers, which will send e-mail reminders to customers of important dates such as birthdays or anniversaries. Streamline Inc. lets customers order groceries, arrange for dry cleaning pickup, have a hot meal delivered, or have their recyclable trash picked up—all from a single web site. Based on the projections for online sales presented in the exhibit below, many more marketers will be jumping on the cyberspace bandwagon to cash in on the potential. Success will depend on whether or not they can provide what online shoppers are increasingly demanding.

Industry	2001 Sales Estimate ($US)
Financial services	$5 billion
Apparel and footwear	514 million
PC hardware/software	3.8 billion
Entertainment	2.7 billion
Travel	7.4 billion
Books and music	1.1 billion[6]

Part Six

Financing the Enterprise

Chapter 14

Accounting and Financial Statements

Chapter Outline

Objectives

After reading this chapter, you will be able to:

- Define accounting and describe the different uses of accounting information.
- Demonstrate the accounting process.
- Decipher the various components of an income statement in order to evaluate a firm's "bottom line."
- Interpret a company's balance sheet to determine its current financial position.
- Analyze financial statements, using ratio analysis, to evaluate a company's performance.
- Assess a company's financial position using its accounting statements and ratio analysis.

Figure 14.2

The Accounting Equation and Double-Entry Bookkeeping for Anna's Flowers

	Assets			=	Liabilities	+	Owners' Equity
	Cash	Equipment	Inventory		Debts to suppliers	Loans	Equity
Cash invested by Anna	$2,500.00						$2,500.00
Loan from Credit Union	$5,000.00					$5,000.00	
Purchase of furnishings	−$3,000.00	$3,000.00					
Purchase of inventory	−$2,000.00		$2,000.00				
Purchase of roses			$325.00		$325.00		
First month sales	$2,000.00		−$1,500.00				$500.00
Totals	$4,500.00	$3,000.00	$825.00		$325.00	$5,000.00	$3,000.00

$8,325	=	$5,325	+	$3,000
$8,325	=	$8,325		

works through them. Traditionally, all of these steps were performed using paper, pencils, and erasers (lots of erasers!), but today the process is often fully computerized.

Examining Source Documents. Like all good managers, Anna Rodriguez begins the accounting cycle by gathering and examining source documents—cheques, credit-card receipts, sales slips, and other related evidence concerning specific transactions. Each of these documents is then categorized and posted to the appropriate accounts.

Recording Transactions. Next, Anna records each financial transaction in a **journal,** which is basically just a time-ordered list of account transactions. While most businesses keep a general journal in which all transactions are recorded, some also keep specialized journals for specific types of transaction accounts.

Posting Transactions. Anna next transfers the information from her journal into a **general ledger,** a book or computer file with separate sections for each account. This process is known as *posting.* At the end of the accounting period (usually yearly, but occasionally quarterly or monthly), Anna retains a professional accountant to prepare a *trial balance,* a summary of the balances of all the accounts in the general ledger. If, upon totalling, the trial balance doesn't (that is, the accounting equation is not in balance),

journal
a time-ordered list of account transactions

general ledger
a book or computer file with separate sections for each account

The first step of the accounting cycle is to examine source documents. Here a restaurant manager and the chef look over the day's receipts in order to begin recording them in an accounting journal.

Bruce Ayers/Tony Stone Images

Figure 14.3

The Accounting Process for Anna's Flowers

Source documents show that a transaction took place.

The transaction is recorded in the journal.

The transaction is posted to the general ledger under the appropriate account (asset, liability, or some further breakdown of these main accounts).

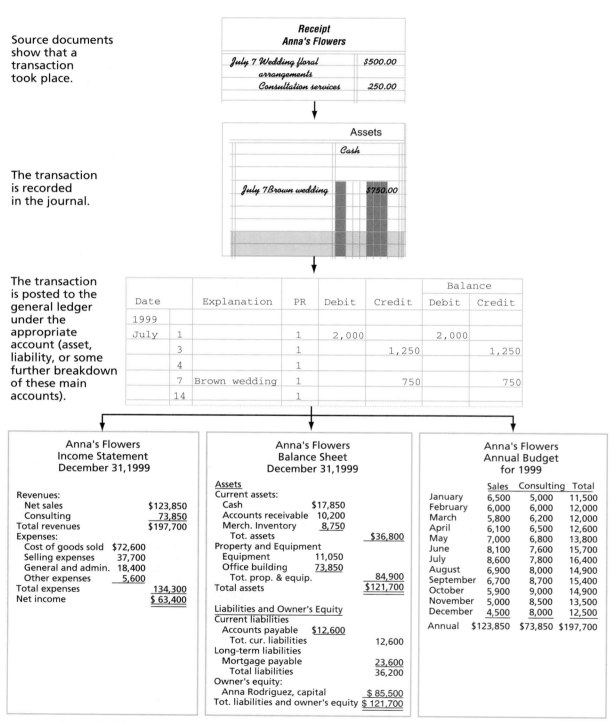

At the end of the accounting period, the ledger is used to prepare the firm's financial statements.

the accountant must look for mistakes (typically an error in one or more of the ledger entries) and correct them. If the trial balance is correct, the accountant can then begin to prepare the financial statements.

Preparing Financial Statements. The information used to calculate the trial balance is also used to prepare the company's financial statements. In the case of public corporations and certain other organizations, a CA must verify that the organization followed acceptable accounting practices in preparing the financial statements. When these statements have been completed, the organization's books are "closed," and the accounting cycle begins anew for the next accounting period.

FINANCIAL STATEMENTS

The end results of the accounting process are a series of financial statements. The income statement and the balance sheet are the two best-known examples of financial statements seen by most laypersons. As previously mentioned, these statements are provided to shareholders and potential investors in a firm's annual report as well as to other relevant outsiders such as creditors, government agencies, and the Canada Customs and Revenue Agency (CCRA).

Unfortunately, for the novice, not all financial statements follow precisely the same format. The fact that different organizations generate income in different ways suggests that when it comes to financial statements, one size definitely does not fit all. Manufacturing firms, service providers, and nonprofit organizations each use a different set of accounting principles or rules upon which the public accounting profession has agreed. As we have already mentioned, these are sometimes referred to as *generally accepted accounting principles (GAAP)*. Moreover, as is the case in many other disciplines, certain concepts have more than one name. For example, *sales* and *revenues* are often interchanged, as are *profits, income,* and *earnings*. Table 14.1 lists a few common equivalent terms that should help you decipher their meaning in accounting statements.

Term	Equivalent Term
Revenues	Sales
Gross profit	Gross income Gross margin
Operating income	Operating profit Earnings before interest and taxes (EBIT) Income before interest and taxes (IBIT)
Income before taxes (IBT)	Earnings before taxes (EBT) Profit before taxes (PBT)
Net income (NI)	Earnings after taxes (EAT) Profit after taxes (PAT)
Income available to common shareholders	Earnings available to common shareholders

Table 14.1

Equivalent Terms in Accounting

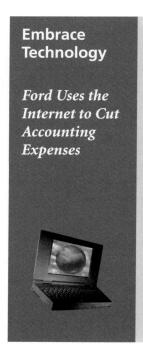
The Income Statement

The question, "What's the bottom line?" derives from the income statement, whose bottom line shows the overall profit or loss of the company after taxes. Thus, the **income statement** is a financial report that shows an organization's profitability over a period of time, be that a month, quarter, or year. By its very design, the income statement offers one of the clearest possible pictures of the company's overall revenues and the costs incurred in generating those revenues. Other names for the income statement include statement of earnings or operating statement. A sample income statement with line-by-line explanations is presented in Figure 14.4, while Figure 14.5 (on page 362) presents the income statement of Mark's Work Wearhouse. The income statement indicates the firm's profitability or income (the bottom line), which is derived by subtracting the firm's expenses from its revenues.

Revenue. **Revenue** is the total amount earned from the sale of goods or services, as well as from other business activities such as the rental of property and investments. Nonbusiness entities typically obtain revenues through donations from individuals and/or grants from governments and private foundations. Mark's Work Wearhouse (Mark's) income statement (see Figure 14.5) shows one main source of income: sales. The total revenues of Mark's were $363,870,000 for the year ending January 27, 2001.

For most manufacturing and retail concerns, the next major item included in the income statement is the **cost of goods sold,** the amount of money the firm spent to buy and/or produce the products it sold during the accounting period. This figure may be calculated as follows:

Cost of goods sold = Beginning inventory + Interim purchases − Ending inventory

income statement
a financial report that shows an organization's profitability over a period of time—month, quarter, or year

revenue
the total amount of money received from the sale of goods or services, as well as from related business activities

cost of goods sold
the amount of money a firm spent to buy or produce the products it sold during the period to which the income statement applies

Figure 14.4

Sample Income Statement

The following exhibit presents an income statement with all the terms defined and explained.

Company Name
for the Year Ended
December 31, 2001

Revenues (sales)	Total dollar amount of products sold (includes income from other business services such as rental-lease income and interest income).
Less: Cost of goods sold	The cost of producing the goods, including the cost of labour and raw materials as well as other expenses associated with production.
Gross profit	The income available after paying all expenses of production.
Less: Selling and administrative expense	The cost of promoting, advertising, and selling products as well as the overhead costs of managing the company. This includes the cost of management and corporate staff.
Less: Depreciation and amortization	This is a noncash expense approximating the decline in the value of plant and equipment. In most accounting statements, depreciation is not separated from selling and administrative expenses. However, financial analysts usually create statements that include this expense.
Income before interest and taxes (operating income or EBIT)	This line represents all income left over after operating expenses have been deducted. This is sometimes referred to as operating income since it represents all income after the expenses of operations have been accounted for. Occasionally, this is referred to as EBIT, or earnings before interest and taxes.
Less: Interest expense	Interest expense arises as a cost of borrowing money. This is a financial expense rather than an operating expense and is listed separately. As the amount of debt and the cost of debt increase, so will the interest expense. This covers the cost of both short-term and long-term borrowing.
Income before taxes (earnings before taxes – EBT)	The firm will pay a tax on this amount. This is what is left of revenues after subtracting all operating costs, depreciation costs, and interest costs.
Less: Taxes	The tax rate is specified in the federal tax legislation.
Net income	This is the amount of income left after taxes. The firm may decide to retain all or a portion of the income for reinvestment in new assets. Whatever it decides not to keep it will usually pay out in dividends to its shareholders.
Less: Preferred dividends	If the company has preferred shareholders, they are first in line for dividends. That is one reason why their stock is called "preferred."
Income to common shareholders	This is the income left for the common shareholders. If the company has a good year, there may be a lot of income available for dividends. If the company has a bad year, income could be negative. The common shareholders are the ultimate owners and risk takers. They have the potential for very high or very poor returns since they get whatever is left after all other expenses.
Earnings per share	Earnings per share is found by taking the income available to the common shareholders and dividing by the number of shares of common stock outstanding. This is income generated by the company for each share of common stock.

Figure 14.5

Consolidated Statements of Earnings and Retained Earnings

Source: Mark's Work Wearhouse, *Annual Report*, 2001.

(thousands except per Common Share amounts)	52 weeks ended January 30, 1999	52 weeks ended January 29, 2000	52 weeks ended January 27, 2001
Corporate and franchise sales (Note 14)	$417,468	$437,670	$487,979
Corporate operations			
Front-line operations (Note 1B)			
Sales	$283,401	$314,547	$363,870
Cost of sales	169,163	186,723	214,361
Gross margin	114,238	127,824	149,509
Front-line expenses			
Personnel, advertising and other	51,869	57,272	67,366
Occupancy	25,868	31,094	35,738
Depreciation and amortization	5,350	6,231	6,664
Interest—short term	2,015	1,610	1,480
	85,102	96,207	111,248
Front-line contribution	29,136	31,617	38,261
Franchise royalties and other (Note 15)	7,016	6,640	6,558
Net front-line contribution before back-line expenses	36,152	38,257	44,819
Back-line operations (Note 1B)			
Back-line expenses			
Personnel, administration and other	15,124	16,590	18,744
Occupancy	998	1,015	1,038
Depreciation and amortization	2,711	3,372	3,624
Software development and maintenance costs	906	1,201	1,238
Computer services	571	687	854
Interest—long term	1,350	2,407	2,498
Franchise bad debt provisions (recoveries)	219	300	(251)
	21,879	25,572	27,745
Earnings before provision for closure of U.S. pilot stores, income taxes and goodwill amortization	14,273	12,685	17,074
Provision for closure of U.S. pilot stores (Note 16)	2,961	—	—
Earnings before income taxes and goodwill amortization	11,312	12,685	17,074
Income Taxes (Notes 1N and 17)			
Current expense	6,566	5,536	8,317
Future expense (benefit)	(1,322)	387	29
	5,244	5,923	8,346
Net earnings before goodwill amortization	6,068	6,762	8,728
Goodwill amortization	316	375	548
Net earnings	5,752	6,387	8,180
Retained earnings at beginning of year	14,858	20,610	26,856
Purchase of capital stock for cancellation (Note 12)	—	(141)	(1,543)
Retained earnings at end of year	$ 20,610	$ 26,856	$ 33,493
Earnings per Common Share			
Before goodwill amortization	22¢	24¢	32¢
Basic	21¢	23¢	30¢
Fully diluted—restated (Note 1K)	20¢	23¢	29¢

Let's say that Anna's Flowers began an accounting period with an inventory of goods for which it paid $5,000. During the period, Anna bought another $4,000 worth of goods, giving the shop a total inventory available for sale of $9,000. If, at the end of the accounting period, Anna's inventory was worth $5,500, the cost of goods sold during the period would have been $3,500 ($5,000 + $4,000 − $5,500 = $3,500). If Anna had total revenues of $10,000 over the same period of time, subtracting the cost of goods sold ($3,500) from the total revenues of $10,000 yields the store's **gross margin** (revenues minus the cost of goods sold required to generate the revenues): $6,500. For Mark's Work Wearhouse, the cost of goods sold was $214,361,000. This allows the reader to determine that on average it cost Mark's 58.9 cents to purchase products for each dollar of sales. Many retailers combine cost of goods sold with other expenses such as selling, general, and administrative expenses on the earnings statement. In so doing they prevent competitors and customers from making a determination of the gross margin earned on sales.

gross margin
revenues minus the cost of goods sold required to generate the revenues

Expenses. **Expenses** are the costs incurred in the day-to-day operations of the organization. Three common expense accounts shown on income statements are (1) selling, general, and administrative expenses, (2) research, development, and engineering expenses, and (3) interest expenses (remember that the costs directly attributable to selling goods or services are included in the cost of goods sold). Selling expenses include advertising and sales salaries. General and administrative expenses include salaries of executives and their staff and the costs of owning and maintaining the general office. Obviously, research and development costs include scientific, engineering, and marketing personnel and the equipment and information used to design and build prototypes and samples. Interest expenses include the direct costs of borrowing money.

expenses
the costs incurred in the day-to-day operations of an organization

   The amount of detail about expenses on income statements varies between organizations. Mark's provides more detail than many (this is referred to as more complete disclosure). Mark's Work Wearhouse has repeatedly received awards for the quality of its annual report. Mark's income statement (Figure 14.5) groups expenses into front-line and back-line operations. The annual report explains the meaning of these terms in Note 1B: "Front-line operations represent those activities where the Company's people come face-to-face with the customers and back-line operations represent activities that support the effective performance of front-line activities."

Net Income. **Net income** (or net earnings) is the total profit (or loss) after all expenses including taxes have been deducted from revenue. Generally, accountants divide profits into individual sections on the earnings statement such as operating income and earnings before interest and taxes. Mark's statements provide added information including the contribution to net income provided by front-line operations. Such disclosures again allow the reader of the financial statements more insight into how Mark's earns its eventual "bottom-line" of just over $8 million.

net income
the total profit (or loss) after all expenses including taxes have been deducted from revenue; also called net earnings

The Balance Sheet

The second basic financial statement is the **balance sheet,** which presents a "snapshot" of an organization's financial position at a given moment. As such, the balance sheet indicates what the organization owns or controls and the various sources of the funds used to pay for these assets, such as bank debt or owners' equity.

   The balance sheet takes its name from its reliance on the accounting equation: Assets *must* equal liabilities plus owners' equity. Figure 14.6 provides a sample balance sheet with line-by-line explanations. Unlike the income statement, the balance

balance sheet
a "snapshot" of an organization's financial position at a given moment

Figure 14.6

Sample Balance Sheet

The following exhibit presents a balance sheet in word form with each item defined or explained.

Typical Company,
December 31, 2001

Assets	This is the major heading for all physical, monetary, or intangible goods that have some dollar value.
Current assets	Assets that are either cash or are expected to be turned into cash within the next 12 months.
Cash	Cash or chequing accounts.
Marketable securities	Short-term investments in securities that can be converted to cash quickly (liquid assets).
Accounts receivable	Cash due from customers in payment for goods received. These arise from sales made on credit.
Inventory	Finished goods ready for sale, goods in the process of being finished, or raw materials used in the production of goods.
Prepaid expense	A future expense item that has already been paid, such as insurance premiums or rent.
Total current assets	The sum of the above accounts.
Fixed assets	Assets that are long term in nature and have a minimum life expectancy that exceeds one year.
Investments	Assets held as investments rather than assets owned for the production process. Most often the assets include small ownership interests in other companies.
Gross property, plant, and equipment	Land, buildings, equipment, and other fixed assets listed at original cost.
Less: Accumulated depreciation	The accumulated expense deductions applied to all plant and equipment over their life. Land may not be depreciated. The total amount represents in general the decline in value as equipment gets older and wears out.
Net property, plant, and equipment	Gross property, plant, and equipment minus the accumulated depreciation. This amount reflects the book value of the fixed assets and not their value if sold.
Other assets	Any other asset that is long term and does not fit into the above categories. It could be patents or trademarks.
Total assets	The sum of all the asset values.

sheet does not represent the result of transactions completed over a specified accounting period. Instead, the balance sheet is, by definition, an accumulation of all financial transactions conducted by an organization since its founding. Following long-established traditions, items on the balance sheet are listed on the basis of their original cost less accumulated depreciation, rather than their present values.

Balance sheets are often presented in two different formats. The traditional balance sheet format placed the organization's assets on the left side and its liabilities and owners' equity on the right. More recently, a vertical format, with assets on top followed by liabilities and owners' equity, has gained wide acceptance. Mark's Work

Figure 14.6

Sample Balance Sheet (continued)

Liabilities and Shareholders' Equity	This is the major heading. Liabilities refer to all indebtedness and loans of both a long-term and short-term nature. Shareholders' equity refers to all money that has been contributed to the company over the life of the firm by the owners.
Current liabilities	Short-term debt expected to be paid off within the next 12 months.
Accounts payable	Money owed to suppliers for goods ordered. Firms usually have between 30 and 90 days to pay this account, depending on industry norms.
Wages payable	Money owed to employees for hours worked or salary. If workers receive paycheques every two weeks, the amount owed should be no more than two weeks' pay.
Taxes payable	Firms are required to pay corporate taxes quarterly. This refers to taxes owed based on earnings estimates for the quarter.
Notes payable	Short-term loans from banks or other lenders.
Other current liabilities	The other short-term debts that do not fit into the above categories.
Total current liabilities	The sum of the above accounts.
Long-term liabilities and equity	All long-term debt and owners' investment.
Long-term debt	Loans of more than one year from banks, pension funds, insurance companies, or other lenders. These loans often take the form of bonds, which are securities that may be bought and sold in bond markets.
Deferred income taxes	This is a liability owed to the government but not due within one year.
Other liabilities	Any other long-term debt that does not fit the above two categories.
Shareholders' equity	The following categories are the owners' investment in the company.
Common stock (100,000 shares @ $1.00 par value)	The tangible evidence of ownership is a security called common stock. In this example there are 100,000 shares held by the owners. The par value is stated value and does not indicate the company's worth.
Capital in excess of par	When shares of stock were sold to the owners, they may have paid more than the par value for each share. If the price paid was $10 per share, the extra $9 per share would show up in this account at 100,000 shares times $9 per share, or $900,000.
Retained earnings	The total amount of earnings the company has made during its life and not paid out to its shareholders. This account represents the owners' reinvestment of earnings into company assets rather than payments of cash dividends. This account does *not* represent cash.
Total shareholders' equity	This is the sum of the above equity accounts representing the owners' total investment in the company.
Total liabilities and shareholders' equity	The total short-term and long-term debt of the company plus the owner's total investment. This combined amount *must* equal total assets.

Wearhouse's balance sheet for 1999, 2000, and 2001 is presented in Figure 14.7. In the sections that follow, we'll briefly describe the basic items found on the balance sheet; we'll take a closer look at a number of these in Chapter 16.

Assets. All asset accounts are listed in descending order of *liquidity*—that is, how quickly each could be turned into cash. Short-term, or current, assets are those that are

Figure 14.7

*Consolidated Balance
Sheets for Mark's Work
Wearhouse*

Source: Mark's Work Wear-
house, *Annual Report,* 2001.

(thousands)	As at January 30, 1999	As at January 29, 2000	As at January 27, 2001
ASSETS			
Current assets			
Cash and cash equivalents (Note 1D)	$ 2,710	$ 1,774	$ 6,993
Accounts receivable (Note 4)	13,364	15,010	13,998
Merchandise inventories	76,982	81,468	84,483
Other current assets (Note 5)	3,304	3,223	4,913
	96,360	101,475	110,387
Other assets (Note 6)	975	1,614	1,056
Capital assets (Note 7)	23,531	25,893	28,148
Future income taxes (Notes 1N & 17)	3,413	3,026	2,997
Goodwill (Note 8)	8,713	11,076	14,472
	$132,992	$143,084	$157,060
LIABILITIES			
Current liabilities			
Accounts payable and accrued liabilities	$ 43,557	$ 45,730	$ 46,131
Income taxes payable	4,976	2,238	6,186
Current portion of long-term debt (Note 10)	7,992	9,328	10,905
	56,525	57,296	63,222
Long-term debt (Note 10)	22,052	23,952	27,016
Deferred gains (Note 7)	1,109	2,265	2,101
	79,686	83,513	92,339
SHAREHOLDERS' EQUITY			
Capital stock (Note 12)	32,696	32,715	31,228
Retained earnings	20,610	26,856	33,493
	53,306	59,571	64,721
	$132,992	$143,084	$157,060

accounts receivable

money owed a company
by its clients or
customers

used or converted into cash within the course of a calendar year. Thus, cash is followed by temporary investments, accounts receivable, and inventory, in that order. **Accounts receivable** refers to money owed the company by its clients or customers. Accounts receivable usually includes an allowance for bad debts that management does not expect to collect. The bad-debts adjustment is normally based on historical collections experience and is deducted from the accounts receivable balance to present a more realistic view of the payments likely to be received in the future. Inventory may be held in the form of raw materials, work-in-progress, or finished goods ready for delivery.

Long-term, or fixed, assets represent a commitment of organizational funds of at least one year. Items classified as fixed include long-term investments, plant and equipment, and intangible assets, such as corporate "goodwill" or reputation.

Liabilities. As seen in the accounting equation, total assets must be financed either through borrowing (liabilities) or through owner investments (owners' equity). Current liabilities include a firm's financial obligations to short-term creditors, which must be repaid within one year, while long-term liabilities have longer repayment terms. **Accounts payable** represents amounts owed to suppliers for goods and services purchased with credit. For example, if you buy gas with a PetroCan credit card, the purchase represents an account payable for you (and an account receivable for PetroCan). Other liabilities include wages earned by employees but not yet paid and taxes owed to the government. Occasionally, these accounts are consolidated into an **accrued expenses** account, representing all unpaid financial obligations incurred by the organization.

Owners' Equity. Owners' equity includes the owners' contributions to the organization along with income earned by the organization and retained to finance continued growth and development. If the organization were to sell off all of its assets and pay off all of its liabilities, any remaining funds would belong to the owners. Not surprisingly, the accounts listed as owners' equity on a balance sheet may differ dramatically from company to company. As mentioned in Chapter 5, corporations sell stock to investors, who become the owners of the firm. Many corporations issue two, three, or even more different classes of common and preferred stock, each with different dividend payments and/or voting rights. Since each type of stock issued represents a different claim on the organization, each must be represented by a separate owners' equity account.

RATIO ANALYSIS: ANALYZING FINANCIAL STATEMENTS

The income statement shows a company's profit or loss, while the balance sheet itemizes the value of its assets, liabilities, and owners' equity. Together, the two statements provide the means to answer two critical questions: (1) How much did the firm make or lose? and (2) How much is the firm presently worth based on historical values found on the balance sheet? **Ratio analysis,** calculations that measure an organization's financial health, brings the complex information from the income statement and balance sheet into sharper focus so that managers, lenders, owners, and other interested parties can measure and compare the organization's productivity, profitability, and financing mix with other similar entities.

A financial analyst performs ratio analysis using information from the income statement and balance sheet.

David R. Frazier/Tony Stone Images

As you know, a ratio is simply one number divided by another, with the result showing the relationship between the two numbers. Financial ratios are used to weigh and evaluate a firm's performance. Interestingly, an absolute value such as earnings of $70,000 or accounts receivable of $200,000 almost never provides as much useful information as a well-constructed ratio. Whether those numbers are good or bad depends on their relation to other numbers. If a company earned $70,000 on $700,000 in sales (a 10 percent return), such an earnings level might be quite satisfactory. The president of a company earning this same $70,000 on sales of $7 million (a 1 percent return), however, should probably start looking for another job!

Looking at ratios in isolation is probably about as useful and exciting as staring at a blank wall. It is the relationship of the calculated ratios to both prior organizational performance and the performance of the organization's "peers," as well as its stated goals, that really matters. Remember, while the profitability, asset utilization, liquidity, debt ratios, and per share data we'll look at here can be very useful, you will never see the forest by looking only at the trees.

accounts payable
the amount a company owes to suppliers for goods and services purchased with credit

accrued expenses
all unpaid financial obligations incurred by an organization

ratio analysis
calculations that measure an organization's financial health

Consider Ethics and Social Responsibility

Charges of Accounting Fraud at Livent Inc.

During the decade of the 1980s, Garth Drabinsky and his partner, Myron Gottlieb, created the Odeon Cineplex movie chain and built it into the second largest in North America, with over 1500 screens throughout Canada and the US. However, as the decade drew to a close, corporate man-oeuvring at the debt-ridden chain forced Drabinsky out, leaving him with only the 2,200-seat Pantages Theatre in Toronto and the Canadian rights to the highly successful *Phantom of the Opera* playing there.

From this base, almost phoenix-like, arose the seemingly highly successful Livent Inc., producer of highly acclaimed musicals including *Kiss of the Spider Woman, Ragtime,* and the revival of *Showboat.* By the late 1990s, like Odeon Cineplex before it, this company also faced financial difficulties. A major cash infusion by US investors brought with it a new management team and a subsequent review of the accounting records. The resulting internal investigation led to allegations that the financial performance of the company had been misstated starting as early as 1990. It is alleged that the income of Livent was overstated through the misuse of accounting procedures. The new management claimed that preproduction costs, properly recorded as expenses, were instead reported as fixed assets. This resulted in reported income and assets owned being overstated. Costs of shows already running were transferred to shows not yet running, again recording expenses as assets.

Livent filed for protection from creditors in the US under Chapter 11 of the US Bankruptcy Code on November 18, 1998, and in Canada under the Companies Creditors Arrangement Act the following day.

On September 29, 1999, the Superior Court of Justice (Ontario) approved Livent Inc.'s request for the appointment of Ernst and Young Inc. as receiver and manager of the property, assets, and undertakings of the company. The members of the board of directors tendered their resignations effective upon the appointment of the receiver. Senior management also announced their departure from the company. This action followed the court-approved sale of Livent's assets to SFX Entertainment Inc. for approximately US$115 million a month earlier. The sale and appointment of a receiver effectively ended the existence of the once crown jewel of Canadian live theatre.

In addition to the allegations of financial statement manipulation, Mr. Drabinsky and Mr. Gottlieb have been accused of operating a kickback scheme allowing them to siphon off almost $7 million of corporate funds for personal use. The US government eventually filed a 16-count indictment against the two on federal fraud conspiracy charges. The US Securities and Exchange Commission also filed accounting and security fraud charges. Shareholders launched several civil suits against the company, former executives, the former board of directors, and the two co-founders.

Much of this matter is still before the courts and it should be noted that Mr. Drabinsky and Mr. Gottlieb deny the claims against them.[2]

profitability ratios
ratios that measure the amount of operating income or net income an organization is able to generate relative to its assets, owners' equity, and sales

Profitability Ratios

Profitability ratios measure how much operating income or net income an organization is able to generate relative to its assets, owners' equity, and sales. The numerator (top number) used in these examples is always the net income after taxes. Common profitability ratios include profit margin, return on assets, and return on equity. The following examples are based on the 2001 income statement and balance sheet for Mark's, as shown in Figures 14.5 and 14.7. Except where specified, all data are expressed in thousands of dollars.

The **profit margin,** computed by dividing net income by sales, shows the overall percentage profits earned by the company. It is based solely upon data obtained from the income statement. The higher the profit margin, the better the cost controls within the company and the higher the return on every dollar of revenue. Mark's profit margin is calculated as follows:

profit margin
net income divided by sales

$$\text{Profit margin} = \frac{\text{Net income}}{\text{Sales}} \qquad \frac{8{,}180}{363{,}870} = 2.3\%$$

Thus, for every $1 in sales, Mark's generated profits of about 2.3 cents.

Return on assets, net income divided by assets, shows how much income the firm produces for every dollar invested in assets. A company with a low return on assets is probably not using its assets very productively—a key managerial failing. By its construction, the return on assets calculation requires data from both the income statement and the balance sheet.

return on assets
net income divided by assets

$$\text{Return on assets} = \frac{\text{Net income}}{\text{Assets}} \qquad \frac{8{,}180}{157{,}060} = 5.2\%$$

In the case of Mark's, every $1 of assets generated a return of 5.2 percent, or profits of 5.2 cents.

Shareholders are always concerned with how much money they will make on their investment, and they frequently use the return on equity ratio as one of their key performance yardsticks. **Return on equity** (also called return on investment [ROI]), calculated by dividing net income by owners' equity, shows how much income is generated by each $1 the owners have invested in the firm. Obviously, a low return on equity means low shareholder returns and may indicate a need for immediate managerial attention. Because some assets may have been financed with debt not contributed by the owners, the value of the owners' equity is usually considerably lower than the total value of the firm's assets. Mark's return on equity is calculated as follows:

return on equity
net income divided by owners' equity; also called return on investment (ROI)

$$\text{Return on equity} = \frac{\text{Net income}}{\text{Equity}} \qquad \frac{8{,}180}{64{,}721} = 12.6\%$$

Asset Utilization Ratios

Asset utilization ratios measure how well a firm uses its assets to generate each $1 of sales. Obviously, companies using their assets more productively will have higher returns on assets than their less efficient competitors. Similarly, managers can use asset utilization ratios to pinpoint areas of inefficiency in their operations. These ratios (receivables turnover, inventory turnover, and total asset turnover) relate balance sheet assets to sales, which are found on the income statement.

asset utilization ratios
ratios that measure how well a firm uses its assets to generate each $1 of sales

The **receivables turnover,** sales divided by accounts receivable, indicates how many times a firm collects its accounts receivable in one year. It also demonstrates how quickly a firm is able to collect payments on its credit sales. Obviously, no payments means no profits. Mark's collected its receivables 26.0 times per year.

receivables turnover
sales divided by accounts receivable

$$\text{Receivable turnover} = \frac{\text{Sales}}{\text{Receivables}} \qquad \frac{363{,}870}{13{,}998} = 26.0\text{X}$$

inventory turnover
sales divided by total inventory

Inventory turnover, sales divided by total inventory, indicates how many times a firm sells and replaces its inventory over the course of a year. A high inventory turnover ratio may indicate great efficiency but may also suggest the possibility of lost sales due to insufficient stock levels. Mark's inventory turnover indicates that it replaced its inventory 4.3 times per year.

$$\text{Inventory turnover} = \frac{\text{Sales}}{\text{Inventory}} \qquad \frac{363,870}{84,483} = 4.3X$$

total asset turnover
sales divided by total assets

Total asset turnover, sales divided by total assets, measures how well an organization uses all of its assets in creating sales. It indicates whether a company is using its assets productively. Mark's generated $2.32 in sales for every $1 in total corporate assets.

$$\text{Total asset turnover} = \frac{\text{Sales}}{\text{Total assets}} \qquad \frac{363,870}{157,060} = 2.32X$$

Liquidity Ratios

liquidity ratios
ratios that measure the speed with which a company can turn its assets into cash to meet short-term debt

Liquidity ratios compare current (short-term) assets to current liabilities to indicate the speed with which a company can turn its assets into cash to meet debts as they fall due. High liquidity ratios may satisfy a creditor's need for safety, but ratios that are too high may indicate that the organization is not using its current assets efficiently. Liquidity ratios are generally best examined in conjunction with asset utilization ratios because high turnover ratios imply that cash is flowing through an organization very quickly—a situation that dramatically reduces the need for the type of reserves measured by liquidity ratios.

current ratio
current assets divided by current liabilities

The **current ratio** is calculated by dividing current assets by current liabilities. Mark's current ratio indicates that for every $1 of current liabilities, the firm had $1.75 of current assets on hand.

$$\text{Current ratio} = \frac{\text{Current assets}}{\text{Current liabilities}} \qquad \frac{110,387}{63,222} = 1.75X$$

quick ratio (acid test)
a stringent measure of liquidity that eliminates inventory

The **quick ratio** (also known as the **acid test**) is a far more stringent measure of liquidity because it eliminates inventory, the least liquid current asset. It measures how well an organization can meet its current obligations without resorting to the sale of its inventory. In 2001, Mark's had $0.41 invested in current assets (after subtracting inventory) for every $1 of current liabilities.

$$\text{Quick ratio} = \frac{\text{Current assets} - \text{Inventory}}{\text{Current liabilities}} \qquad \frac{110,387 - 84,483}{157,060} = 0.41X$$

Debt Utilization Ratios

debt utilization ratios
ratios that measure how much debt an organization is using relative to other sources of capital, such as owners' equity

Debt utilization ratios provide information about how much debt an organization is using relative to other sources of capital, such as owners' equity. Because the use of debt carries an interest charge that must be paid regularly regardless of profitability, debt financing is much riskier than equity. Unforeseen negative events such as recessions affect heavily indebted firms to a far greater extent than those financed exclusively with owners' equity. Because of this and other factors, the managers of most firms tend to keep debt-to-asset levels below 50 percent. However, firms in very stable and/or regulated industries, such as electric utilities, often are able to carry debt ratios well in excess of 50 percent with no ill effects.

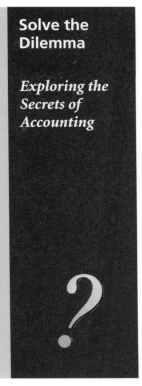

Solve the Dilemma

Exploring the Secrets of Accounting

You have just been promoted from vice president of marketing of BrainDrain Corporation to president and CEO! That's the good news. Unfortunately, while you know marketing like the back of your hand, you know next to nothing about finance. Worse still, the "word on the street" is that BrainDrain is in danger of failure if steps to correct large and continuing financial losses are not taken immediately. Accordingly, you have asked the vice president of finance and accounting for a complete set of accounting statements detailing the financial operations of the company over the past several years.

Recovering from the dual shocks of your promotion and feeling the weight of the firm's complete accounting report for the very first time, you decide to attack the problem systematically and learn the "hidden secrets" of the company, statement by statement. With Mary Pruitt, the firm's trusted senior financial analyst, by your side, you delve into the accounting statements as never before. You resolve to "get to the bottom" of the firm's financial problems and set a new course for the future—a course that will take the firm from insolvency and failure to financial recovery and perpetual prosperity.

1. Describe the two basic accounting statements. What types of information does each provide that can help you evaluate the situation?

2. Which of the financial ratios are likely to prove to be of greatest value in identifying problem areas in the company? Why? Which of your company's financial ratios might you expect to be especially poor?

3. Discuss the limitations of ratio analysis.

The **debt to total assets ratio** indicates how much of the firm is financed by debt and how much by owners' equity.

$$\text{Debt to total assets} = \frac{\text{Total debt}}{\text{Total assets}} \qquad \frac{92,339}{157,060} = 58.8\%$$

Thus, for every $1 of Mark's total assets, 58.8 percent is financed with debt. The remaining 41.2 percent is provided by owners' equity.

The **times interest earned ratio,** operating income divided by interest expense, is a measure of the safety margin a company has with respect to the interest payments it must make to its creditors. It is based on data solely from the income statement. A low times interest earned ratio indicates that even a small decrease in earnings may lead the company into financial straits—or even bankruptcy. Given Mark's income statement, we need to take earnings before income taxes ($17,074 + 548) and add back interest expense ($2,498 + $1,480) and goodwill amortization to get income before interest and taxes.

$$\text{Times interest earned} = \frac{\text{Income before interest and taxes}}{\text{Interest expense}} \qquad \frac{21,052}{3,978} = 5.15\text{X}$$

That means that Mark's earned over 5 times more than it needed to pay its interest expense. A number this high gives Mark's lenders a good level of risk protection. Mark's has safely covered its interest expenses: For every $1 in interest paid by Mark's in the year ending January 27, 2001, the company earned $5.15 of income before interest and taxes.

debt to total assets ratio
a ratio indicating how much of the firm is financed by debt and how much by owners' equity

times interest earned ratio
operating income divided by interest expense

Per Share Data

Investors may use **per share data** to compare the performance of one company with another on an equal, or per share, basis. Generally, the more shares of stock a com-pany issues, the less income is available for each share.

Earnings per share is calculated by dividing net income or profit by the number of shares of stock outstanding. This ratio is important because yearly changes in earnings per share, in combination with other economy-wide factors, determine a company's overall stock price. When earnings go up, so does a company's stock price—and so does the wealth of its shareholders.

$$\text{Earnings per share} = \frac{\text{Net income}}{\text{Number of shares outstanding}}$$

$$\begin{array}{cc} 2000 & 2001 \\ \dfrac{6,387}{27,847} = \$0.23 & \dfrac{8,180}{25,597} = \$0.30 \end{array}$$

Mark's earnings per share increased from 23¢ in 2000 to 30¢ in 2001.

Dividends per share is the actual before-tax cash payment received for each share owned. This ratio, obviously closely related to the earnings per share, is simply another way to analyze the overall return resulting from a shareholder's total investment.

$$\text{Dividends per share} = \frac{\text{Total dividends paid}}{\text{Number of shares outstanding}}$$

Mark's Work Wearhouse paid no dividends during this period. This means that all earnings were reinvested in the business in hopes of generating higher future returns for shareholders. During this period, shareholders' only return on their investment would have to come from increases in the market value of the shares.

Table 14.2

Industry Analysis

Source: Reitmans and La Senza annual reports for year ended December 31, 2000, and Mark's Work Wearhouse annual report for the year ended January 27, 2001.

Ratio	Reitman's	La Senza	Mark's Work Wearhouse
Profit margin	3.9%	4.25%*	2.3%
Return on assets	8.3%*	7.1%	5.2%
Return on equity	10.0%	12.3%	12.6%*
Receivables turnover	202.8X*	78.0X	26.0X
Inventory turnover	13.5X*	8.9X	4.3X
Total asset turnover	2.12X	1.65X	2.32X*
Current ratio	1.73X	2.31X*	1.75X
Quick ratio	0.78X	1.38X*	0.41X
Debt to total assets	17.1%*	42.7%	58.8%
Times interest earned	N/A	5.96X*	5.15X

*Indicates the best ratio for each category.

Industry Analysis

Numbers in a vacuum are not particularly useful for measuring an organization's performance. While comparing a firm's performance to previous years is an excellent gauge of whether corporate operations are improving or deteriorating, another way to analyze a firm is to compare its performance with competitors in its industry. Table 14.2 compares various ratios for Mark's with two competitors in the clothing industry—La Senza (lingerie) and Reitman's (women's wear). Mark's Work Wearhouse lags behind the competitors shown in Table 14.2 in all areas except return on equity and asset turnover. Despite its lower profit margin, Mark's generates a higher return on shareholders' equity by using the assets it has borrowed to acquire to generate sales more efficiently. This leaves more income after the payment of interest to the lenders for the shareholders. This is referred to as the use of leverage.

Perhaps no single area of business study offers better short- and long-term business opportunities than does accounting. Whether employed by private companies, public accounting firms, or government agencies, accountants probably learn and "know the numbers" of their organizations better than any other group of employees. If knowledge is power, then accountants are powerful people. And CAs, CGAs, and CMAs, by virtue of their advanced study and higher prestige, are far and away the most powerful accountants.

Accountants prepare, analyze, and verify financial reports and taxes and monitor the systems that furnish this information to managers in all business, nonprofit, and government organizations. Management accountants are employed by private businesses to prepare, analyze, and interpret the financial information corporate executives need to make sound decisions. Public accountants and private internal auditors, on the other hand, specialize in the verification of corporate and personal financial records and in the preparation of tax filings. Regardless of their actual job descriptions, the increasing computerization of accounting means that accountants are frequently the most computer-literate employees not directly involved with the design and maintenance of an organization's computer systems.

The educational requirements to attain a professional accounting designation have been increasing. Each of the three professional bodies in Canada now require a degree and specify up to 17 courses to be taken within or in addition to the degree as the minimum standard for admission to the professional training programs.

Robert Half International publishes an annual salary guide. The 2001 guide shows the following Canadian salary ranges for careers in accounting:[3]

A/R–A/P	
Supervisor	$38,500 – $55,000
Bookkeeper/ Assistant	$29,750 – $39,000
Accounting Clerk	$26,750 – $35,750
Payroll Manager	$45,250 – $62,750
Payroll Clerk	$28,000 – $36,000
Public Accountant Manager— Large Firm	$71,000 – $98,250
Public Accountant First Year— Large Firm	$33,000 – $38,000

Globeinvestor
www.globeinvestor.com

SEDAR
www.sedar.com

The Globe and Mail's finanacial web site, Globeinvestor, offers a great deal of information on and analysis of publicly listed companies. Company information is accessed using the stock symbol. The site includes a search engine to allow you to look up stock symbols by company name. Company profiles, earning estimates, recent news items, and a variety of links are provided at Globeinvestor. A second site useful in researching corporate financial information is SEDAR's site. This site contains all electronically filed public documents for Canadian companies including corporate annual reports to the shareholders.

Review Your Understanding

Define accounting and describe the different uses of accounting information.

Accounting is the language businesses and other organizations use to record, measure, and interpret financial transactions. Financial statements are used internally to judge and control an organization's performance and to plan and direct its future activities and measure goal attainment. External organizations such as lenders, governments, customers, suppliers, and tax authorities are major consumers of the information generated by the accounting process.

Demonstrate the accounting process.

Assets are an organization's economic resources; liabilities, debts the organization owes to others; owners' equity, the difference between the value of an organization's assets and liabilities. This principle can be expressed as the accounting equation: Assets = Liabilities + Owners' equity. The double-entry bookkeeping system is a system of recording and classifying business transactions in accounts that maintain the balance of the accounting equation. The accounting cycle involves examining source documents, recording transactions in a journal, posting transactions, and preparing financial statements on a continuous basis throughout the life of the organization.

Decipher the various components of an income statement in order to evaluate a firm's "bottom line."

The income statement indicates a company's profitability over a specific period of time. It shows the "bottom line," the total profit (or loss) after all expenses (the costs incurred in the day-to-day operations of the organization) have been deducted from revenue (the total amount of money received from the sale of goods or services and other business activities).

Interpret a company's balance sheet to determine its current financial position.

The balance sheet, which summarizes the firm's assets, liabilities, and owners' equity since its inception, portrays its financial position as of a particular point in time. Major classifications included in the balance sheet are current assets (assets that can be converted to cash within one calendar year), fixed assets (assets of greater than one year's duration), current liabilities (bills owed by the organization within one calendar year), long-term liabilities (bills due more than one year hence), and owners' equity (the net value of the owners' investment).

Analyze financial statements, using ratio analysis, to evaluate a company's performance.

Ratio analysis is a series of calculations that brings the complex information from the income statement and balance sheet into sharper focus so that managers, lenders, owners, and other interested parties can measure and compare the organization's productivity, profitability, and financing mix with other similar entities. Ratios may be classified in terms of profitability (measure dollars of return for each dollar of employed assets), asset utilization (measure how well the organization uses its assets to generate $1 in sales), liquidity (assess organizational risk by comparing current assets to current liabilities), debt utilization (measure how much debt the organization is using relative to other sources of capital), and per share data (compare the performance of one company with another on an equal basis).

Assess a company's financial position using its accounting statements and ratio analysis.

Based on the information presented in the chapter, you should be able to answer the questions posed in the "Solve the Dilemma" box to formulate a plan for determining BrainDrain's bottom line, current worth, and productivity.

Learn the Terms

accounting 352

accounting cycle 356

accounting equation 356

accounts payable 367

accounts receivable 366

accrued expenses 367

asset utilization ratios 369

assets 355

balance sheet 363

budget 353

cash flow 353

certified general accountant (CGA) 352

certified management accountant (CMA) 352

chartered accountant (CA) 352

cost of goods sold 360

current ratio 370

debt to total assets ratio 371

debt utilization ratios 370

dividends per share 372

double-entry bookkeeping 356

earnings per share 372

expenses 363

general ledger 357

gross margin 363

income statement 360

inventory turnover 370

journal 357

liabilities 356

liquidity ratios 370

managerial accounting 353

net income 363

owners' equity 356

per share data 372

private accountants 352

profit margin 369

profitability ratios 368

public accountant 352

quick ratio (acid test) 370

ratio analysis 367

receivables turnover 369

return on assets 369

return on equity 369

revenue 360

times interest earned ratio 371

total asset turnover 370

Check Your Progress

1. Why are accountants so important to a corporation? What function do they perform?
2. Discuss the internal uses of accounting statements.
3. What is a budget?
4. Discuss the external uses of financial statements.
5. Describe the accounting process and cycle.
6. The income statements of all corporations are in the same format. True or false? Discuss.
7. Which accounts appear under "current liabilities"?
8. Together, the income statement and the balance sheet answer two basic questions. What are they?
9. What are the five basic ratio classifications? What ratios are found in each category?
10. Why are debt ratios important in assessing the risk of a firm?

Get Involved

1. Go to the library or the Internet and get the annual report of a company with which you are familiar. Read through the financial statements, then write up an analysis of the firm's performance using ratio analysis. Look at data over several years and analyze whether the firm's performance is changing through time.

2. Form a group of three or four students to perform an industry analysis. Each student should analyze a company in the same industry, and then all of you should compare your results. The following companies would make good group projects:

   Automobiles: DaimlerChrysler, Ford, General Motors

Computers: Apple, IBM, Digital Equipment

Brewing: Big Rock Brewery, Brick Brewing Co., Sleeman Breweries, Molson

Wines: Andre's Wines, Magnotta Winnery, Vincor International

Chemicals: Dupont, Dow Chemical, Monsanto

Department Stores: Hudson's Bay Company, Jean Coutu Group, Sears Canada.

You can determine lists of firms for other industries using the Globeinvestor site. After entering the site, click on "filter" and then on "company financials filter". Remember you can obtain annual reports for Canadian companies at www.sedar.com.

Build Your Skills

Financial Analysis

Background: The income statement for NewNet Productions Ltd., a producer and broadcaster of television shows as well as a distributor of movies both under licence and of its own production, is shown below. NewNet's total assets are $645.7 million, and its equity is $218.5 million.

Consolidated Earnings and Retained Earnings
Year Ended December 2002

(Millions)	2002
Revenue	$294.2
Direct operating expenses	211.8
Gross profit	82.4
Operating expenses	42.2
Operating income	40.2
Interest expense	22.5
Earnings before income taxes	17.7
Income taxes	5.0
Net earnings	12.7
Retained earnings, beginning of year	18.3
Dividends paid	(1.0)
Retained earnings, end of year	30.0

Task: Calculate the following profitability ratios: profit margin, return on assets, and return on equity. Assume that the industry averages for these ratios are as follows: profit margin 5.8 percent, return on assets 4.6 percent, and return on equity 15.3 percent. Evaluate NewNet's profitability relative to the industry averages. Why is this information useful?

 **See for Yourself Videocase**   **www.cbc.ca**

The Auditors

The often-stated purpose of financial accounting is to measure as accurately as possible the periodic net income of a business entity. The CICA in *Terminology for Accountants* defines an audit as "an examination of evidential matter to determine the reliability of a record or assertion or to evaluate the compliance with rules or policies or with conditions of an agreement."[4]

Dr. Rosen points out in the video that alternative ways of recording and reporting accounting information are accepted under GAAP and that these alternatives can lead to the reporting of significantly different profit amounts. In his text *Accounting: A Decision Approach*, Dr. Rosen points out that not all readers of financial reports and audited statements understand them and "tend to believe the figures more than they ought to."[5] He refers to these readers as "naïve investors." He further points out that "sophisticated investors" exercise great care in reading audited financial reports, seeking out other sources of information for comparison purposes to assist them in making informed decisions.

Bob Rutherford of the CICA also states that people may rely more on the auditor's opinion than they should.

Questions

1. Based on your viewing of the video and the definition of an audit above, do you agree that auditors are meeting their responsibilities?

2. Discuss the responsibility of the reader of the financial statements to understand their strengths and limitations.

3. What responsibility to investors should auditors bear for statements that comply with GAAP but lead investors to make costly decisions?

4. Discuss the advantages and disadvantages of focusing on the cash flow generated by a business, rather than accrual-based income measurements, for decision making.

Source: *Venture*, show number 697, "The Auditors," September 29, 1998, running time 9:18.

Remember to check out our Online Learning Centre at **www.mcgrawhill.ca/college/ferrell.**

Chapter 15

Money and the Financial System

Chapter Outline

Introduction

Money in the Financial System

The Canadian Financial System

Challenges and Change in the Banking Industry

Objectives

After reading this chapter, you will be able to:

- Define money, its functions, and its characteristics.
- Describe various types of money.
- Specify how the Bank of Canada manages the money supply and regulates the Canadian banking system.
- Compare and contrast banks, trust companies, and credit unions/caisses populaires.
- Distinguish among nonbanking institutions such as insurance companies, pension funds, mutual funds, and finance companies.
- Investigate the challenges ahead for the banking industry.
- Recommend the most appropriate financial institution for a hypothetical small business.

The Debut of the Euro

Almost a decade after the 1992 Maastricht Summit decision to form the European Monetary Union (EMU), the European currency unit (ECU)—or the euro—is a reality. The 12 nations of the EMU (Germany, France, Italy, Austria, The Netherlands, Spain, Portugal, Finland, Belgium, Ireland, Luxembourg, and Greece) have a common currency.

Introduced for noncash transactions on January 1, 1999, the euro existed as a phantom currency for three years. During this time, American Express, Visa, and MasterCard issued euro-denominated traveller's cheques, but users received cash in the local currency.

On New Year's Day 2002, the years of planning ended with the first transactions using the newly issued 10 billion bank notes and 50 billion coins. The change-over was not without problems, but with patience, perseverance, and good humour, over 300 million people began using the new currency. Italy experienced the slowest introduction with only 10 percent of cash transactions utilizing the euro on January 2nd, while other member countries saw the new currency account for up to 50 percent of cash transactions on the same date. The old local currencies will be gradually withdrawn from circulation by February 28, 2002, and for the first time since the Roman Empire, Europeans will share a common currency.

The monetary union will exert pressure for common monetary policy through the European Central Bank (ECB) and will create more uniform economic policy across the region.

The euro should reduce the cost of doing business in many ways. One very tangible way will be the elimination of exchange rates between these currencies. Companies doing business within these 12 countries will no longer have to hedge against changing currency rates. Before the euro, a German company buying French products would undertake a financial transaction that would protect it against a change in the exchange rates between the German mark and the French franc. If the franc were to increase in value against the mark during the time between order, delivery, and payment, the German firm would end up paying more than expected for the goods. The euro eliminates this risk.

Consumers should see direct benefits as they avoid the expense and inconvenience of exchanging currency at each border crossing. The common currency will facilitate the comparison of prices between member countries, thus encouraging intra-European investment, trade, and travel, each of which should generate economic benefits.[1]

CP Photo Archive. Photograph by Martin Meissner.

INTRODUCTION

finance
the study of money: how it's made, how it's lost, and why

It's true. Money really does make the world go 'round. From Bay Street to Main Street—both overseas and at home—money is the one tool used to measure personal and business income and wealth. Not surprisingly, **finance** is the study of money: how it's made, how it's lost, and why. This chapter introduces you to the role of money and the financial system in the economy. Of course, if you have a chequing account, automobile insurance, a student loan, or a credit card, you already have personal experience with some key players in the financial world.

We begin our discussion with a definition of money and then explore some of the many forms money may take. Next, we examine the roles of the Bank of Canada and other major institutions in the financial system. Finally, we explore the future of the finance industry and some of the changes likely to occur over the course of the next several years.

MONEY IN THE FINANCIAL SYSTEM

money
anything generally accepted in exchange for goods and services

Curt paid Bobby four cigarettes for a small slice of soap. Bobby added the four cigarettes to another six he had been saving and paid Morley 10 cigarettes for an egg. Morley paid seven . . . While fiction as written, this and countless other similar scenes were very real to prisoners of war in World Wars I and II, Korea, and Vietnam. But if cigarettes can be used in place of dollar bills, *then what is money?* Strictly defined, **money** is anything generally accepted in exchange for goods and services. Materials as diverse as salt, cattle, fish, rocks, shells, cloth, as well as precious metals such as gold, silver, and copper have long been used by various cultures as money. While paper money was first used in North America in 1685 (and even earlier in Europe), the concept of *fiat money*—a paper money not readily convertible to a precious metal such as gold—did not gain full acceptance until the Great Depression in the 1930s.

Functions of Money

No matter what a particular society uses for money, it serves three important functions: a medium of exchange, a unit of measurement, and a means of storing purchasing power.

Medium of Exchange. Before fiat money, the trade of goods and services was accomplished through *bartering*—trading one good or service for another of similar value. As any school-age child knows, bartering can become quite inefficient—particularly in the case of complex, three-party transactions involving peanut butter sandwiches, baseball cards, and hair barrettes. There had to be a simpler way, and that was to decide on a single item—money—that can be freely converted to any other good upon agreement between parties.

Unit of Measurement. Money is both the standard for pricing goods and services and the means of buying and selling them. Money allows us to compare the value of goods and services we are considering for purchase. Money also allows us to compare costs, income, and profits over time. Money is used as the measurement unit in accounting, allowing us to plan and make economic decisions.[2]

Means of Storing Purchasing Power for Future Use. With allowance for inflation, money retains its purchasing power. This allows individuals to save for future purchases and to lend these savings to someone else (usually for a fee called *interest*). Money simplifies the formulation of contracts, allowing us to promise to pay a set price at a specified future time.[3]

Characteristics of Money

To be used as a medium of exchange, money must be acceptable, divisible, portable, stable in value, durable, and difficult to counterfeit.

Acceptability. To be effective, money must be readily acceptable for the purchase of goods and services and for the settlement of debts. Acceptability is probably the most important characteristic of money: If people do not trust the value of money, businesses will not accept it as a payment for goods and services, and consumers will have to find some other means of paying for their purchases.

Divisibility. Given the widespread use of quarters, dimes, nickels, and pennies in Canada, it is no surprise that the principle of divisibility is an important one. With barter, the lack of divisibility often makes otherwise preferable trades impossible, as would be an attempt to trade a steer for a loaf of bread. For money to serve effectively as a measure of value, all items must be valued in terms of comparable units— dimes for a piece of bubble gum, quarters for laundry machines, dollars for pop and snack vending machines, and bills (or bills and coins) for everything else.

Portability. Clearly, for money to function as a medium of exchange, it must be easily moved from one location to the next. Large coloured rocks could be used as money, but you couldn't carry them around in your wallet. Paper currency and metal coins, on the other hand, are capable of transferring vast purchasing power into small, easily carried (and hidden!) bundles. US currency is widely accepted throughout Canada. The reverse is not true except in some areas close to the border. US currency is in fact accepted worldwide. More US currency is in circulation outside the US than within. Of the US$450 billion in bills and coins now circulating throughout the world, about two-thirds, or US$300 billion, is abroad.[4]

Stability. Money must be stable and maintain its declared face value. A $10 bill should purchase the same amount of goods or services from one day to the next. The principle of stability allows people who wish to postpone purchases and save their money to do so without fear that it will decline in value. As mentioned earlier, money declines in value during periods of inflation, when economic conditions cause prices to rise. Thus, the same amount of money buys fewer and fewer goods and services. In some countries, particularly in Latin America, people spend their money as fast as they can in order to keep it from losing any more of its value. Instability destroys confidence in a nation's money and its ability to store value and serve as an effective medium of exchange. Ultimately, people faced with spiralling price increases avoid the increasingly worthless paper money at all costs, storing all of their savings in the form of real assets such as gold and land.

Durability. Money must be durable. The crisp new bills you trade at the music store for the hottest new CD will make their way all around town for about 18 months before being replaced. Were the value of an old, faded bill to fall in line with the deterioration of its appearance, the principles of stability and universal acceptability would fail (but, no doubt, fewer bills would pass through the washer!). Although metal coins, due to their much longer useful life, would appear to be an ideal form of money, paper currency is far more portable than metal because of its light weight. Today, coins are used primarily to provide divisibility.

Difficulty to Counterfeit. Finally, to remain stable and enjoy universal acceptance, it almost goes without saying that money must be very difficult to counterfeit—that is, to duplicate illegally. Every country takes steps to make counterfeiting difficult. Most use multicoloured money, and many use specially watermarked papers that are virtually impossible to duplicate. Counterfeit bills represent less than 0.03 percent of the currency in circulation in the US,[5] but it is becoming increasingly easier for counterfeiters to print money with just a modest inkjet printer. In fact, more than 40 percent of the counterfeit money circulated in the United States in 1997 came from inkjet printers. This illegal printing of money is fuelled by hundreds of people—some as young as age 16—who often circulate only small amounts of counterfeit bills.[6] To help thwart the problem of counterfeiting, the Bank of Canada uses a number of security features on the new ten dollar bill:[7]

Serial number	A three-letter prefix followed by a seven-digit number is printed twice on the back of each note.
Colours	Some colours are difficult to reproduce: you may notice a difference in tone when comparing a suspect note with a genuine note.
Fine-line patterns	Observe the sharp, well-defined lines that make up the facial features of the portrait, the circles within the eyes, and the background patterns of the note.
Micro printing	Look for the text TEN 10 DIX printed in clear, small print to the left of the portrait. Notice that the characters in the caption identifying the Library of Parliament become smaller as the text progresses.

Used with the permission of the Bank of Canada.

Fluorescence	A genuine note does not glow under ultraviolet light except for the following features: • The Coat of Arms and the words DIX TEN and BANK OF CANADA BANQUE DU CANADA glow blue over the portrait. • White security fibres, invisible in normal light, glow red; conversely, blue fibres, visible in normal light do not glow.
Hidden numbers	Hold the note at eye level and tilt it at a 45° angle. The number 10 becomes visible.
Raised ink (intaglio)	Run you finger over the words BANQUE DU CANADA—BANK OF CANADA and the large number 10; the ink feels thicker to the touch. You can also feel the raised ink on the portrait and the Coat of Arms.

Iridescent maple leaves	When you tilt the note, the three maple leaves, pale and matte in appearance, change to a reflective gold colour. Note that the edges of the leaves are smooth and well defined.

Types of Money

While paper money and coins are the most visible types of money, the combined value of all of the printed bills and all of the minted coins is actually rather insignificant when compared with the value of money kept in chequing accounts, savings accounts, and other monetary forms.

Chequing Accounts. You probably have a **chequing account** (also called a demand deposit), money stored in an account at a bank or other financial institution that can be withdrawn without advance notice. One way to withdraw funds from your account is by writing a *cheque*, a written order to a bank to pay the indicated individual or business the amount specified on the cheque from money already on deposit. Figure 15.1 explains the significance of the numbers found on a typical Canadian cheque. As legal instruments, cheques serve as a substitute for currency and coins and are preferred for many transactions due to their lower risk of loss. If you lose a $100 bill, anyone who finds or steals it can spend it. If you lose a blank cheque, however, the risk of catastrophic loss is quite low. Not only does your bank have a sample of your signature on file to compare with a suspected forged signature, but you can render the cheque immediately worthless by means of a stop-payment order at your bank.

There are several types of chequing accounts, with different features available for different monthly fee levels or specific minimum account balances. Some chequing

chequing account money stored in an account at a bank or other financial institution that can be withdrawn without advance notice; also called a demand deposit

Figure 15.1

A Cheque

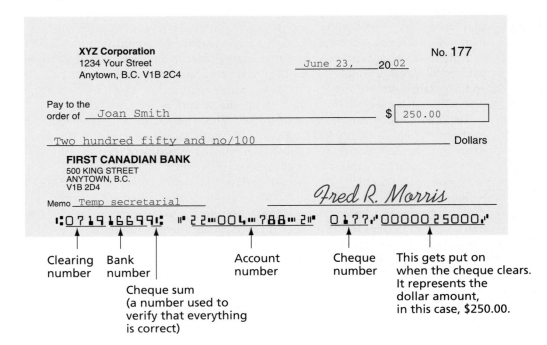

accounts earn interest (a small percentage of the amount deposited in the account that the bank pays to the depositor). One such interest-bearing chequing account is the *NOW (Negotiable Order of Withdrawal) account* offered by most financial institutions. The interest rate paid on such accounts varies with the interest rates available in the economy but is typically quite low (ranging between 2 and 5 percent).

near money

assets that are very easily turned into cash but which cannot be used directly as a medium of exchange like paper money or cheques

savings account

an account with funds that usually cannot be withdrawn without advance notice; also known as a time deposit

guaranteed investment certificate (GIC)

a certificate of deposit with a financial institution, at a fixed rate of interest for a fixed term

credit cards

means of access to preapproved lines of credit granted by a bank or finance company

Near Money. Some assets are called **near money** because they are very easily turned into cash, but they cannot be used directly as a medium of exchange like paper money or cheques. The most common type of near money account, the **savings account** (also known as a time deposit), is an account with funds that usually cannot be withdrawn without advance notice. While seldom enforced, the "fine print" governing most savings accounts prohibits withdrawals without two or three days' notice. Savings accounts are not generally used for transactions or as a medium of exchange, but their funds can be moved to a chequing account or turned into cash. Other examples of near money include money market accounts, certificates of deposit, credit cards, and traveller's cheques.

Guaranteed investment certificates (GICs) are a type of fixed term deposit. A certificate is issued by the financial institution indicating that a stated amount has been deposited for a specified period of time at a stipulated fixed rate of interest. The term of a GIC is generally one to five years. Most financial institutions require a minimum GIC deposit of at least $500. The deposit cannot be withdrawn before maturity except in unusual circumstances. Such withdrawals usually result in loss of interest as a penalty for early withdrawal.

Credit cards, which can access preapproved lines of credit granted by a bank or finance company, are a popular substitute for money because of their convenience, easy access to credit, and acceptance by merchants around the world. Indeed, it is difficult today to find stores (and even some governmental services, such as provincial licence plate branches) that do not accept credit cards. The organization issuing the credit card guarantees payment of a credit charge to merchants and assumes the responsibility for collecting the money from the card owner.

With few exceptions, credit cards allow cardholders great flexibility in paying off their purchases. Some people always pay off their monthly charges as they come due, but many others take advantage of the option of paying a stated minimum monthly amount with interest charges, based on yearly interest rates, added to the balance until it has been paid in full. Average annual fees for the privilege of carrying specific credit cards are an important source of money for issuing banks and can sometimes reach $60 per year, although bank cards are increasingly available with no annual charge.

Two major credit cards—MasterCard and Visa—represent the vast majority of credit cards held in North America. Banks are not the only issuers of credit cards. American Express has long been the dominant card company in the travel and entertainment market, with millions of cards outstanding.

It is estimated that US banks, credit card issuers, and retailers lose up to US$1.5 billion annually to credit card fraud, which includes lost or stolen cards, counterfeit cards, telephone purchases made with someone else's account number, and identity fraud—the most devastating of all credit card frauds. Identity fraud (also known as application or true name fraud) involves the assumption of someone else's identity by a criminal who then charges thousands of dollars in their victim's name.[8]

Major retailers—Sears, The Brick, The Bay, Canadian Tire, and others—offer their own credit cards to encourage consumers to spend money in their stores. Unlike the major credit cards discussed above, these "private label" cards are generally accepted only at stores associated with the issuing company.

A **debit card** looks like a credit card but works like a cheque. The use of a debit card results in a direct, immediate, electronic payment from the cardholder's chequing account to a merchant or other party. While they are convenient to carry and profitable for banks, they lack credit features, offer no purchase "grace period," and provide no hard "paper trail"—all of which have kept debit cards from enjoying much popularity with consumers until recently. However, many financial institutions are encouraging customers to use their debit cards to reduce the number of teller transactions.

Traveller's cheques, money orders, and cashier's cheques are other common forms of near money. Although each is slightly different from the others, they all share a common characteristic: A financial institution, bank, credit company, or neighbourhood post office or postal outlet issues them in exchange for cash and guarantees that the purchased note will be honoured and exchanged for cash when it is presented to the institution making the guarantee.

debit card
a card that looks like a credit card but works like a cheque; using it results in a direct, immediate, electronic payment from the cardholder's chequing account to a merchant or third party

Carrying credit, debit, bank, or ABM cards makes 33 percent of adults more likely to make spontaneous purchases.

THE CANADIAN FINANCIAL SYSTEM

The Bank of Canada

The Bank of Canada was founded in 1934 with the purpose, as stated in the Bank of Canada Act, of regulating, "credit policy and currency in the best interests of the economic life of the nation." In 1938 the Bank of Canada became a Crown corporation. The Minister of Finance now holds all the shares issued by the Bank.

As a Crown corporation, the Bank is the sole issuer of currency and has authority to facilitate management of Canada's financial system. The independence of the Bank allows the separation of the power to spend money, by the federal government, and the Bank's power, through monetary policy, to create money. The distance from the political process allows the Bank to adopt the medium and long-term views necessary for effective monetary policy, rather than the short-term outlook more often adopted by those who must soon seek re-election.

The Bank of Canada is responsible for monetary policy, central banking services, currency, and administration of the public debt.

Monetary Policy. The Bank of Canada seeks to protect the value of Canadian money by keeping inflation low and stable. It does this by controlling the supply of money available in the economy through **monetary policy**.

The currency (bank notes and coins) circulating in the economy is only a small portion of the total money supply. A number of different measures, called money aggregates, are used to measure the money supply. Some of these measures are:

M1   The currency in circulation plus deposits in personal chequing accounts and current accounts at banks.

M2   Includes M1 plus personal savings accounts and other chequing accounts, term deposits, and nonpersonal deposits requiring notice before withdrawal.

On 10 August 1937, Prime Minister William Lyon Mackenzie King and the Bank of Canada's first Governor, Graham Towers, formally laid the cornerstone for the building at 234 Wellington Street, Ottawa.

Courtesy of the Canadian Government Motion Picture Bureau, and the Bank of Canada Archives.

Bank of Canada
www.bank-banque-canada.ca/

monetary policy
a policy that seeks to improve the performance of the economy by regulating money supply and credit

M2[+] Includes M2 plus all deposits at non-bank deposit-taking institutions (e.g., trust companies and credit unions), money-market mutual funds, and individual annuities at life insurance companies.

M2[++] Includes M2[+] plus all types of mutual funds and Canada Savings Bonds.[9]

The Bank of Canada manages the rate of growth of the money supply indirectly through its influence on the target overnight rate, which influences other interest rates and impacts on the level of spending and economic activity in the country.

When interest rates fall, individuals and businesses are apt to increase their money holdings, to borrow more, and to increase spending and investment. When interest rates rise, the reverse is true, as fewer new loans are sought and borrowers attempt to reduce debt to avoid higher costs, resulting in a slowing of the growth of M1 and the other monetary aggregates. The reductions in interest rates by the Bank in late 2001 and early 2002, in response to the terrorist attacks of September 11, 2001, were intended to stimulate growth in the money supply and spur economic activity.

The Bank influences interest rates through its cash management activities with the objective of ensuring that short-term interest rates adjust in line with the goal of non-inflationary growth.

The basic short-run technique is the transfer of Government of Canada deposits with clearing institutions. A draw down on these deposits reduces the money supply, while redeposit has the opposite effect. The bank also uses **open market operations**, purchases or sales, in the securities market to affect the rates for various terms of securities (the rate structure).

open market operations
discretionary Bank of Canada intervention in the domestic securities market

Central Banking Services.
Central banking services include the wide range of policy, regulatory, and operational activities the Bank undertakes in support of monetary policy implementation. The Bank also provides services to the federal government, financial institutions, and the general public.

The Bank offers one-day sale or repurchase transactions (loans) to the market to keep the overnight rate within the one-half of a percentage point target band.

As a result of legislation enacted in 1996, the Bank now has responsibility for overseeing the clearing and settlement systems, including the Automated Clearing Settlement System (ACSS) and the Large Value Transfer System (LVTS).

The Bank acts as the federal government's banker by ensuring sufficient cash in operating accounts, intervening as the agent of the Minister of Finance in foreign exchange markets (to influence the exchange rate by purchasing or selling foreign currency), and managing the government's foreign exchange reserves. The Bank also maintains deposit and safekeeping accounts for Canadian financial institutions and other central banks.[10]

Bank Notes.
The Bank is not only the sole issuer of Canadian bank notes but is also responsible for ensuring their authenticity. The Bank operates to ensure a sufficient supply of currency to meet the needs of the economy.

Administering the Public Debt.
The Bank advises the federal government on borrowing, managing new debt offerings, and servicing outstanding debt. This includes maintaining bondholder records and making payments on the government's behalf for interest and debt redemption.

The Bank also provides operations and systems support for the Canada Investment Savings Agency, administering some 7 million accounts for Canada Savings Bond holders.

Payments System.
The Canadian Payments Association (CPA) was created by an Act of Parliament in 1980 as a not-for-profit organization. The Canadian Payments Act as amended in 2001 expanded the Association's mandate: (i) to establish and operate national systems for the clearing and settlement of payments and other arrangements

for the making or exchange of payments, (ii) to facilitate the interaction of the CPA's systems with others involved in the exchange, clearing, and settlement of payments, and (iii) to facilitate the development of new payment methods and technologies.

The CPA, under the policy objective established in the Act, is to promote the efficiency, safety, and soundness of the clearing and settlement systems.

The CPA is currently administered by an 11-member board of directors. It is expected that a new 16-member board structure will be implemented under the new Canadian Payments Act at the Association's annual meeting in June 2002. The board will be chaired by an officer of the Bank of Canada, three directors are to be appointed by the Minister of Finance, and the remaining 12 are to be elected by CPA members.[11]

Canada's national payments system encompasses the rules and procedures that govern the clearing and exchange of different types of payments including cheques, direct deposits made electronically, withdrawals from banking machines, and debit card transactions.

The CPA operates two major systems, the Automated Clearing Settlement System (ACSS) and the Large Value Transfer System (LVTS). Cheques and electronic deposits are cleared through the ACSS. The LVTS is an electronic wire transfer system that moves irrevocable payments in Canadian dollars quickly and securely in a real-time environment.

The LVTS was introduced by the CPA in 1999 and in March of 2000 was nominated for a Computerworld Smithsonian Award to be presented at a ceremony held in Washington DC on April 3, 2000.

How it works:[12]

Step 1: Payment by one of the many means available—cheque, debit card, direct deposit, and so on.

Step 2: Clearing, the daily process by which CPA members exchange deposited payment items, and then determine the net amounts owed to each other.

Step 3: Settlement, the procedure by which the CPA members use funds on deposit at the Bank of Canada to fulfill their net obligations to all other members.

Canadians can access their deposit accounts from anywhere in the country. The CPA systems are so efficient that many countries are using them as the model to improve their own systems.

Most Canadians receive immediate credit for cheques they deposit at any branch of their financial institution. By contrast, usual practice in many countries is to place a hold on a cheque until the institution can verify the issuer has sufficient funds on deposit to cover the cheque.

Deposit Insurance. Deposits at banks, trust companies, and loan companies are insured by the **Canada Deposit Insurance Corporation**. Funds on deposits with credit unions and caisses populaires are protected by provincial deposit insurance corporations. These insurance funds will be discussed in greater detail in the following section.

Banking Institutions

Banking institutions accept money deposits and make loans to individual consumers and businesses. The most important banking institutions in Canada are the 57 banks, 2,440 credit unions/caisses populaires, and the 25 nonbank trust companies.[13]

Chartered Banks. Canada's **chartered banks** are federally regulated and are chartered under the Bank Act. The Bank Act allows two types of banks: Schedule 1 banks are widely held and no one shareholder is allowed to own more than 10 percent of the bank's shares; and Schedule 2 banks need not be widely held.

Canadian Payments
Association
www.cdnpay.ca/

Canada Deposit
Insurance Corp.
www.cdic.ca/

**Canada Deposit
Insurance
Corporation**
a federal Crown corporation providing deposit insurance for deposits up to $60,000 per deposit at member institutions

chartered bank
a federally regulated financial institution, chartered under the Bank Act

trust company
a corporation that functions as a trustee and usually also provides banking services

Table 15.1 lists the eight Schedule 1 banks and Table 15.2 lists the wide range of services offered to Canadian consumers by Canada's chartered banks.

Trust Companies. Trust companies may be incorporated either federally or provincially and are not governed by the Bank Act. Only trust companies can legally

Table 15.1

Schedule 1 Chartered Banks of Canada

Sources: Based on material from *Report on Business Magazine,* page 111, July 2001; and Canadian Western Bank, Annual Report, 2000.

Schedule 1	Assets ($ millions)
Royal Bank of Canada	$289,742
Canadian Imperial Bank of Commerce	267,702
Toronto Dominion Bank	264,818
The Bank of Nova Scotia	253,171
Bank of Montreal	233,396
National Bank of Canada	75,827
Laurentian Bank of Canada	14,741
Canadian Western Bank	3,191

Table 15.2

What Banks Offer Customers

Source: Based on material from the Canadian Bankers Association, **www.cba.ca**

Automated banking machines	Financial planning	Precious metals
Bill payment	Foreign exchange global trading	Private banking
Canada Savings Bonds	Guaranteed investment certificates	Real-estate services
Cash management services	Information processing	Registered education savings plans
Chequing accounts	Information systems services	Registered retirement income funds
Commercial lending	Insurance	Registered retirement savings plans
Computer banking	International transfers	Safekeeping facilities
Consumer loans	Investment counselling	Safety deposit boxes
Corporate trust services	Letters of credit	Savings accounts
Credit-card plans	Life income funds	Seniors' accounts
Currency exchange	Lines of credit	Special management services
Custodial services	Locked-in retirement accounts	Telephone banking
Debit cards	Managed asset programs	Treasury bills
Derivative securities	Merchant banking	Traveller's cheques
Direct deposit	Money orders	Trustee Services
Discount brokerage	Mortgages	Underwriting
E-commerce solutions	Mutual funds	Venture capital financing
Electronic data interchange	Overdraft protection	Wealth management
Estate management	Portfolio management	Wire transfers
Fiduciary services	Pre-authorized payments	Youth accounts
Financial leasing		

offer trustee services. Whereas the banks have full commercial lending powers, trust companies must have in excess of $25 million regulatory capital and approval of the Office of the Superintendent of Financial Institutions to receive full lending powers.

Credit Unions and Caisses Populaires. Credit unions and **caisses populaires** are regulated by the provincial Minister of Finance, the **Credit Union Central of Canada** and the provincial deposit insurance corporation. Owned by their members, credit unions are typically established to serve a particular group based on geographic location, ethnic background, or employer groups.

There are over 4 million credit union members in Canada, and the credit unions have over $56 billion in assets.[14]

Insurance for Banking Institutions. The Canada Deposit Insurance Corporation (CDIC), established by an act of Parliament in 1967, is a federal Crown corporation. The CDIC has the responsibility to protect the money deposited in financial institutions that are members. Under the terms of the CDIC Act, only banks, trust companies, and loan companies can apply for membership. There are now over 100 member financial institutions.[15]

The maximum protection for each depositor with one member institution is $60,000 including principal and accrued interest. Deposits at different branches of the same institution are not insured separately, although certain classifications of deposits such as RRSPs and RRIFs are covered separately.

Eligible deposits must be in Canadian currency, payable in Canada not later than five years from the date of deposit, and be insurable deposits rather than other types of uninsurable investments.

Although they are not eligible for membership in the CDIC, credit union deposits are similarly protected by one or more organizations in each province. Table 15.3 summarizes the available protection in each province for deposits at credit unions and caisses populaires.

Nonbanking Institutions

Nonbank financial institutions offer some financial services, such as short-term loans or investment products, but do not accept deposits. These include insurance companies, pension funds, mutual funds, brokerage firms, nonfinancial firms, and finance companies.

Insurance Companies. Insurance companies are businesses that protect their clients against financial losses from certain specified risks (death, injury, disability, accident, fire, theft, and natural disasters, for example) in exchange for a fee, called a premium. Because insurance premiums flow in to the companies regularly, but major insurance losses cannot be timed with great accuracy (though expected risks can be assessed with considerable precision), insurance companies generally have large amounts of excess funds. They typically invest these or make long-term loans, particularly to businesses in the form of commercial real estate loans.

Pension Funds. Pension funds are managed investment pools set aside by individuals, corporations, unions, and some nonprofit organizations to provide retirement income for members. One type of pension fund is the *registered retirement savings plan (RRSP),* which is established by individuals to provide for their personal retirement needs. RRSPs can be invested in a variety of financial assets, including

credit union/caisse populaire
a cooperative association that provides members with a full range of banking services and is operated for the benefit of the members

Credit Union Central of Canada
the national trade association and central finance facility for the 2,440 credit unions and affiliated caisses populaires in Canada.

insurance companies
businesses that protect their clients against financial losses from certain specified risks (death, accident, and theft, for example)

pension funds
managed investment pools set aside by individuals, corporations, unions, and some nonprofit organizations to provide retirement income for members

Table 15.3

Credit Union/Caisses Populaires Deposit Protection

Source: **www.cucentral.ca/ Public/whycu/insurance/ content/insurance.htm**

Province	Coverage
Alberta	All deposits including interest. Foreign deposits and deposits with terms exceeding five years are guaranteed.
British Columbia	Deposits and non-equity shares up to a maximum of $100,000 per separate deposit.
Manitoba	All deposits without limit.
New Brunswick	A maximum of $60,000 for insured deposits; separate deposit coverage up to a maximum of $60,000 each for joint deposits, trust deposits, and deposits held in RRSPs and RRIFs.
Newfoundland and Labrador	Insures deposits up to $60,000 (principal and interest) for each account type: demand, joint, RRSP, RIFF, and trust accounts.
Nova Scotia	Deposits to a maximum of $250,000 per individual and each separate RRSP or RRIF and each unique joint or trust account.
Ontario	Each depositor to a maximum of $100,000 for combined principal, interest, and dividends. RRSPs, RRIFs, OHOSP contracts, and each unique joint or trust account are insured separately up to a maximum of $100,000.
Prince Edward Island	Each depositor insured to a maximum of $60,000; separate insurance to a maximum of $60,000 for each unique trust or joint account; RRSPs and RRIFs are fully covered.
Quebec	Deposits covered to a maximum of $60,000.
Saskatchewan	All deposits are fully guaranteed with no limits.

Enhance Productivity

Merger Mania

During the 1990s, commercial banks throughout the world have repeatedly engaged in mergers, making it hard to keep track of the names of the surviving banks.

In Japan the Bank of Tokyo and Mitsubishi united to form the world's largest bank. The Swiss Bank and Union Bank in Switzerland joined to become the second largest. There have also been mergers in Italy, Germany, Saudi Arabia, and The Netherlands. In the US, several mergers have taken place among the larger banks (see Table 15.4).[16]

The merger trend is a response to globalization and increased competition. The infrastructure needed to serve large numbers of customers is more readily financed by larger banks.

The greater the number of customers served by the computer networks, the lower the cost per transaction and the greater the profits for the institution. Banks hoping to compete for the ever-larger deals being completed in the global market require a large capital base. Mergers provide an obvious means of achieving the capital base needed to survive in the increasingly competitive global market.

In Canada, two such mergers were proposed in 1998. The Bank of Montreal and the Royal Bank announced their intention to join together to form the country's largest bank. The TD and CIBC then followed later that same year.

In Canada, such large mergers must meet the approval of the Competition

Bureau. Bank mergers must also receive approval from the Minister of Finance under the Bank Act. The new bank resulting from the merger would then require a new charter under the Bank Act to continue operations.

Neither of the proposed Canadian mergers received the needed government approvals.

The Banking Merger Review Process

The Competition Bureau announced it would apply the same basic rules to bank mergers as to other mergers. Konrad von Finckenstein, Director of the Competition Bureau, indicated two significant decision criteria: (1) individual banks will be limited to no more than 35 percent of the local market, and (2) the four largest banks will be limited to 65 percent of the marketplace.

The procedures adopted by the Competition Bureau for all Schedule 1 bank mergers are:

1. The Bureau will follow its practice of gathering information about proposed bank mergers and in analyzing any possible anticompetitive effects.

2. The Bureau will identify to the merging parties on an ongoing basis any likely anticompetitive issues that may arise.

3. Immediately after having completed its analysis of the merger as proposed, the Director will provide to the parties and to the Minister of Finance, a letter setting out the Director's views on the competitive aspects of the proposed merger. In the event the merger raises competitive concerns, the Director will set out in general terms the sort of measures that have historically been applied to deal with competition concerns.

4. After receiving the letter from the Director and after taking into account any public interest concerns expressed by the Minister of Finance on behalf of the Government of Canada, the parties to the merger would then be in a position to determine if it is appropriate to explore potential remedies with the Bureau in relation to any anticompetitive concerns raised by the Director.

5. In the event the parties subsequently succeed in suggesting competitive remedies acceptable to the Director, such remedies may, if appropriate, still require the approval of the Competition Tribunal; and the resulting merger itself still needs to be

Table 15.4

Bank Mergers

Source: The National Online, "Bank Mergers" **www.tv.cbc.ca/ national/gmnfo/banks/.**

Year	The Mergers	Combined Assets (US $)
1990	ABN and AMRO	$218 billion
1996	Chemical Bank and Chase Manhattan	$297 billion
1996	Mitsubishi Bank and Tokyo Bank	$752 billion
1997	Union Bank of Switzerland and Swiss Bank	$595 billion
1997	NationsBank and Barnett	$310 billion
1998	NationsBank and BankAmerica	$570 billion
1998	Banc One and First Chicago NBD	$240 billion

approved by the Minister of Finance pursuant to the Bank Act.[17]

The proposed mergers of the Royal Bank and the Bank of Montreal would have resulted in combined assets of US$330 billion, and the TD and CIBC's combined assets would have been US$320 billion. This would have left them at less than half the asset values of the world's largest banks, but in the mid range of recently merged US banks.

Bigger is not always better, but many in the banking industry argue that it is necessary. Many consumers, small business owners, and government officials believe the banks must be controlled for the protection and benefit of the economy and society as a whole, not just bank shareholders. Whether the inability to merge will prevent Canadian banks from competing successfully on the world stage or if their smaller size will in the end be found advantageous, cannot yet be determined. Only the passage of time will confirm or deny the correctness of the Competition Bureau's decisions.

shares, bonds, mutual funds, and such low-risk financial "staples" as Canada Savings Bonds. The choice is up to each person and is dictated solely by individual objectives and tolerance for risk. The interest earned by all of these investments may be deferred tax-free until retirement.

Most major corporations provide some kind of pension plan for their employees. Many of these are established with bank trust departments or life insurance companies. Money is deposited in a separate account in the name of each individual employee, and when the employee retires, the total amount in the account can be either withdrawn in one lump sum or taken as monthly cash payments over some defined time period (usually for the remaining life of the retiree).

All employed Canadians contribute to either the Canada Pension Plan or the Quebec Pension Plan through payroll deductions. The funds are managed separately from general tax dollars and the monies generated are used to pay benefits to eligible plan members. The plans offer similar benefits including pensions after age 60, survivor benefits for spouses and dependants, and disability payments.

mutual fund
an investment company that pools individual investor dollars and invests them in large numbers of well-diversified securities

Mutual Funds. A **mutual fund** pools individual investor dollars and invests them in large numbers of well-diversified securities. Individual investors buy shares in a mutual fund in the hope of earning a high rate of return and in much the same way as people buy shares of stock. Because of the large numbers of people investing in any one mutual fund, the funds can afford to invest in hundreds (if not thousands) of securities at any one time, minimizing the risks of any single security that does not do well. Mutual funds provide professional financial management for people who lack the time and/or expertise to invest in particular securities, such as government bonds. While there are no hard and fast rules, investments in one or more mutual funds are one way for people to plan for financial independence at the time of retirement.

A special type of mutual fund called a *money market fund* invests specifically in short-term debt securities issued by governments and large corporations. Although they offer services such as cheque-writing privileges and reinvestment of interest income, money market funds differ from the money market accounts offered by banks primarily in that the former represent a pool of funds, while the latter are basically

Dr. Gregory Hill, a successful optometrist in Calgary, Alberta, has tinkered with various inventions for years. Having finally developed what he believes is his first saleable product (a truly scratch-resistant and lightweight lens), Hill has decided to invest his life savings and open Hill Optometrics to manufacture and market his invention.

Unfortunately, despite possessing true genius in many areas, Hill is uncertain about "the finance side" of business and the various functions of different types of financial institutions in the economy. He is, however, fully aware that he will need financial services such as chequing and savings accounts, various short-term investments that can easily and quickly be converted to cash as needs dictate, and sources of borrowing capacity—should the need for either short- or long-term loans arise. Despite having read mounds of brochures from various local and national financial institutions, Hill is still somewhat unclear about the merits and capabilities of each type of financial institution. He has turned to you, his 11th patient of the day, for help.

1. List the various types of Canadian financial institutions and the primary functions of each.
2. What services of each financial institution is Hill's new company likely to need?
3. Which single financial institution is likely to be best able to meet Hill's small company's needs now? Why?

specialized, individual chequing accounts. Money market funds usually offer slightly higher rates of interest than bank money market accounts.

Brokerage Firms. **Brokerage firms** buy and sell stocks, bonds, and other securities for their customers and provide other financial services. Larger brokerage firms like Merrill Lynch, Scotia Macleod, and CIBC Wood Gundy offer financial services unavailable at their smaller competitors. Merrill Lynch, for example, offers the Merrill Lynch Cash Management Account (CMA), which pays interest on deposits and allows clients to write cheques, borrow money, and withdraw cash much like a bank. The largest of the brokerage firms (including Merrill Lynch) have developed so many specialized services that they may be considered financial networks—organizations capable of offering virtually all of the services traditionally associated with banks.

brokerage firms firms that buy and sell stocks, bonds, and other securities for their customers and provide other financial services

Nonfinancial Firms. Recently, a growing number of nonfinancial firms have moved onto the financial field. These firms include manufacturing organizations, such as General Motors and General Electric, that traditionally confined their financial activities to financing their customers' purchases. GE, in particular, has been so successful in the financial arena that its credit subsidiary now accounts for over 30 percent of the company's revenues and earnings. Not every nonfinancial firm has been successful with its financial ventures, however. Sears, the retail giant, once commanded an imposing financial network composed of real estate (Coldwell Banker), credit card (Discover Card), and brokerage (Dean Witter Reynolds) companies, but losses of hundreds of millions of dollars forced Sears to dismantle its network. The very prestigious brokerage firm Morgan Stanley acquired Dean Witter Discover, thus creating one of the largest investment firms in the US—in a league with Solomon Smith Barney and Merrill Lynch. Perhaps the moral of the story for firms like Sears is "stick to what you know."

electronic funds transfer (EFT)

any movement of funds by means of an electronic terminal, telephone, computer, or magnetic tape

automated banking machine (ABM)

the most familiar form of electronic banking, which dispenses cash, accepts deposits, and allows balance inquiries and cash transfers from one account to another

point-of-sale (POS) systems

systems that allow merchants to withdraw money directly from a customer's bank account the moment a purchase is made

In 2000, Canadians carried out over 1.25 billion ABM transactions.

CP Photo Archive. Photograph by Fred Chartrand.

Electronic Banking

Since the advent of the computer age, a wide range of technological innovations has made it possible to move money all across the world electronically. Such "paperless" transactions have allowed financial institutions to reduce costs in what has been (and what appears to continue to be) a virtual competitive battlefield. **Electronic funds transfer (EFT)** is any movement of funds by means of an electronic terminal, telephone, computer, or magnetic tape. Such transactions order a particular financial institution to subtract money from one account and add it to another. The most commonly used forms of EFT are automated banking machines, point-of-sale systems, and home banking systems.

Automated Banking Machines. Probably the most familiar form of electronic banking is the **automated banking machine (ABM),** which dispenses cash, accepts deposits, and allows balance inquiries and cash transfers from one account to another. ABMs provide 24-hour banking services—both at home (through a local bank) and far away (via worldwide ABM networks such as Interac and Plus). Rapid growth, driven by both strong consumer acceptance and lower transaction costs for banks (about half the cost of teller transactions), has led to the installation of hundreds of thousands of ABMs worldwide.

There are about 50,000 independent automated teller machines (ATMs) across the US that dispense cash at bars, bowling alleys, minimarts, casinos, and discount stores. The largest supplier of these independent machines is CCS Inc., with 4,000 ATMs in 28 states. Seeing possible uses for the machines besides dispensing cash, CCS Inc.'s cofounders, Steven Wright and Jeffrey Jetton, have offered merchants the ability to print store-specific coupons and gift certificates and display on-screen ads. In addition, their machines also offer phone cards and stamps.[18] While these additional services are not yet available in Canada, Canadians remain relatively heavier users of ABMs than Americans, and there are over 21,000 ABMs across Canada.[19]

Point-of-sale Systems. **Point-of-sale (POS) systems** allow merchants to withdraw money directly from a customer's bank account the moment a purchase is made. Many grocery stores and other retailers have a terminal located at the cash register, through which customers slide their debit card (sometimes their ABM card) to pay for their purchases immediately. Of course, the customer must have sufficient cash to cover the transaction. The advantages for merchants and the issuing banks from POS systems are considerable (near immediate access to the funds, a reduction in cheque-processing costs, fewer bad cheques, and reduced store cash holdings).

Home Banking. With the advent of the "information superhighway," the bank of tomorrow is already in some homes today. Using personal computers and telephone lines, consumers and small businesses are now able to make a bewildering array of financial transactions at home 24 hours a day. Functioning much like a vast network of personal ABMs, computer networks such as Bell Sympatico and Rogers@Home allow their subscribers to make sophisticated banking transactions, buy and sell stocks and

Year		Paper	Electronic
2000	Volume	35.04%	64.964%
	Value	85.64%	14.36%
1999	Volume	38.6%	61.4%
	Value	91.0%	9.0%
1998	Volume	43.3%	56.7%
	Value	96.9%	3.1%
1997	Volume	47.5%	52.5%
	Value	97.3%	2.7%
1996	Volume	53.7%	46.3%
	Value	97.4%	2.6%
1995	Volume	61.8%	38.2%
	Value	98.3%	1.7%
1994	Volume	69.4%	30.6%
	Value	98.9%	1.1%
1993	Volume	76.1%	23.9%
	Value	99.0%	1.0%
1992	Volume	80.6%	19.4%
	Value	99.1%	0.9%
1991	Volume	83.7%	16.3%
	Value	99.2%	0.8%
1990	Volume	86.6%	13.4%
	Value	99.4%	0.6%

Table 15.5

Growth in Electronic Banking: Percentage of Paper versus Electronic Items Flowing through the Automated Clearing Settlement System

Source: Based on material from "Growth in Electronic Banking," Communications and Education Division, Canadian Payments Association, **www.cdnpay.ca/eng/pub/acsspercent-e.htm.**

bonds, and purchase products and airline tickets without ever leaving home or speaking to another human being. Most banks allow customers to log directly into their accounts to check balances, transfer money between accounts, view their account statements, and pay many bills via home computer and modem. ING Direct provides banking services to its customers only by phone or internet. Computer and advanced telecommunications technology will literally revolutionize world commerce. Table 15.5 shows the increase in the use of electronic banking over the last decade.

ING Direct
www.ingdirect.ca

CHALLENGES AND CHANGE IN THE BANKING INDUSTRY

Challenges in the Canadian System

Canadian banks face a rapidly changing economic environment with increasing competition from large specialized financial services companies in an increasingly global market.

In response to the changing market, the federal government introduced Bill C-8, its financial sector reform legislation, on February 7, 2001. The bill received royal assent on June 14, 2001.

According to the Canadian Bankers Association, "measures in Bill C-8 offer Canada's financial sector important tools to keep pace with this change in the interest of consumers and of a dynamic industry in the future:

- The expanded range of permitted investments appears to provide more opportunities to bring new products and innovations to Canadians, especially the use of information technology.

- The ability to use holding companies to organize their business activities has the potential to provide bank financial groups with greater flexibility in structuring themselves in line with individual business strategies.

- The increased ownership limits provide new opportunities for banks to forge strategic alliances and partnerships that can benefit retail and business customers.

- Expanding access to the payments system to life insurance companies, securities firms, and money market mutual funds provides an opportunity to increase competition.

- The provision for a merger review process in the policy statement accompanying the legislation provides recognition of mergers as a legitimate business strategy.

- The foreign bank entry provisions provide greater structural choices for foreign banks to help bring increased competition to the marketplace for Canadian consumers."[20]

Whether these newly enacted changes will allow Canadian banks to meet the challenges of the future cannot yet be determined. In assessing the likelihood of success in meeting the global challenges, consider the history of the Canadian system. Canadian banks have suffered a much lower rate of bank failures than other countries. Despite Canadian consumers dissatisfaction with bank service charges, we do have one of the lowest-cost systems in the world. Canadian banks are highly profitable and have grown under the current regulatory system. If the past is a guide to the future, then the continued efforts of the banks and the regulators should allow the continued stability of the system.

Challenges in the US System

In the early 1990s, several large commercial banks were forced to publicly admit that they had made some rather poor loan decisions. Bank failures followed, including that of the Bank of New England, the third-largest bank failure in history. But the vibrant economic growth in the 1990s substantially changed what had been a rather bleak picture for many financial institutions. Better management, combined with better regulation and a robust economy, rescued commercial banks from the fate of the savings and loans associations, which nearly collapsed in the 1980s. Indeed, low inflation rates meant low interest rates on deposits, and high employment led to very low loan default rates. Combined, these factors helped to make the 1990s one of the most profitable decades in the history of the US banking industry. But clearly, many challenges remain and many changes will come.

It is increasingly easy for companies and individuals to buy and sell goods via the Internet and to pay for them without ever writing a cheque. Canadians are served by 57 banks with 8,423 branches. Visiting one of these branches is now only one way that Canadians are doing their banking. More and more, Canadians are carrying out their financial transactions at their own convenience, 24 hours a day and seven days a week, using telephones, ABMs, and computers.

E-commerce has come of age in banking and Canadians are leading the way in its adoption. A March 2000 survey conducted by Strategic Counsel Inc. for the Canadian Bankers Association found:

- 63 percent of Canadians rely on ABMs, the telephone, or a computer to conduct their financial transactions.

- 53 percent expect to increase their use of technology for financial transactions within the next two to three years.

- 46 percent expect to use Internet banking within the next two to three years.

According to the Bank for International Settlements, Canadians use ABMs more than anyone else, averaging 53 transactions per person in 1998. The US is second with 41.4. Canadians are also world leaders in the use of debit cards, with an average of 44.6 transactions per person per year.

To support all of these transactions there are 12,960 debit card terminals for every 1 million Canadians, the highest concentration anywhere.

Self-serve banking using the Internet lets individuals and companies check balances of deposit and loan accounts, transfer funds between accounts and, in some instances, between institutions. Both business and personal loans can be applied for and approved online. Credit card charges can be reviewed and stocks and mutual funds can be traded as well. Bills can be paid without the inconvenience or cost of writing and mailing cheques. The Royal Bank has introduced "Webdocs," the first Internet document delivery service of its kind in Canada. It is no longer necessary to wait for the post office to deliver your bills—they are available anytime on your computer. The current list of "e-presenters" is not long and they are mostly utility companies. If Canadians embrace this latest offering of Internet banking as they have other electronic services, the list will expand rapidly.

That Canadians have accepted the new technology for financial transactions is evidenced by the fact that over 85 percent of all banking transactions in Canada are now done electronically.[21]

Embrace Technology

More than Just Internet Banking

Ever insistent that the one, "best" banking bill is just around the corner, many members of the US Congress are proposing sweeping banking regulation changes that would change the face of the US financial system. Someday, a Citibank customer in New York City may be able to walk into a Citibank branch in Memphis, Tennessee, and make a deposit or withdrawal from his or her account. Expansion of the recent changes in legislation allowing banks to offer specialized investment products may one day make commercial banks and some other financial institutions true "one-stop finance shops," capable of offering everything from deposit services to investment accounts to life and other insurance products to retirement annuities.

Indeed, the recent trend toward ever bigger banks and other financial institutions is not happening by chance alone. Financial services may be an example of a "natural

**Explore
Your Career
Options**

*What Do
Economists Do?*

Economics is the science of money and its interaction within the general economy. Not surprisingly, economists are experts in economics. They study the ways a society uses scarce resources such as land, labour, raw materials, machinery, and money to produce goods and services. Employed by most major companies and virtually all government agencies, economists conduct research, collect and analyze data, monitor economic trends, and develop forecasts concerning a wide range of economic factors and issues. Within private industry, economists are asked to make predictions concerning the likely economic consequences of various government and/or competitor policies, as well as those of the employing firm.

Banks and other financial institutions are major employers of economists. Indeed, the economic forecasts generated by internal economists play a key role in hosts of financial decisions, from those involving changes in loan rates to the likely future direction of the stock and bond markets, to reasoned conjectures about the direction and impact of expected changes in the money supply and/or government tax

policy. While economists can't actually *see* into the future, their estimates about it are frequently so accurate as to suggest otherwise.

Human Resources Development Canada (HRDC) rates the employment outlook for economics graduates as "good," meaning that finding stable work is relatively easy and working conditions are attractive or improving. Salaries vary widely, but HRDC reports average salaries two years after graduation in excess of $31,000 with the top 20 percent of earners averaging over $48,000. Economics graduates follow a variety of career paths, with HRDC reporting the following occupations:[22]

Career	Percentage of Graduates
Auditors, accountants, and investment professionals	21.0%
Managers in financial and business services	13.6%
Finance and insurance administrative occupations	8.0%
Sales, marketing, and advertising managers	7.9%
Policy and program officers, researchers, and consultants	6.4%

oligopoly," meaning that the industry may be best served by a few very large firms rather than a host of smaller ones. As the largest US banks merge into even larger international entities, they will erase the relative competitive advantages now enjoyed by the largest foreign banks. It is by no means implausible that the financial services industry of the year 2020 will be dominated by 10 or so internationally oriented "megabanks." Even with this level of industry concentration, however, advances in technology and the drive toward ever higher levels of customer services and satisfaction will continue. Remember that, after all, the more things change, the more they stay the same.

Rapid advances and innovations in technology are challenging the banking industry and requiring it to change. As we said earlier, more and more banks, both large and small, are offering electronic access to their financial services. ATM technology is rapidly changing, with machines now dispensing more than just cash. Several banks in Europe are testing ATMs that identify users by their irises (a part of the eye). Customers appear to like the "eyedentification" process better than using a card or other form of ID. Citibank is the only US bank using this technology for a pilot program with its employees.[23] Online financial services, ATM technology, and bill presentation are just a few of the areas where rapidly changing technology is causing the banking industry to change as well.

Review Your Understanding

Define money, its functions, and its characteristics.

Money is anything generally accepted as a means of payment for goods and services. Money serves as a medium of exchange, a measure of value, and a store of wealth. To serve effectively in these functions, money must be acceptable, divisible, portable, durable, stable in value, and difficult to counterfeit.

Describe various types of money.

Money may take the form of currency, chequing accounts, or near money. Chequing accounts are funds left in an account in a financial institution that can be withdrawn (usually by writing a cheque) without advance notice. Near money refers to assets that are easily turned into currency but cannot be used directly as a medium of exchange. Examples of near money include savings accounts (funds left in an interest-earning account that usually cannot be withdrawn without advance notice), money market accounts (an interest-bearing chequing account that is invested in short-term debt instruments), credit cards (access to a preapproved line of credit granted by a bank or company), and debit cards (means of instant cash transfers between customer and merchant accounts), as well as traveller's cheques, money orders, and cashier's cheques.

Specify how the Bank of Canada manages the money supply and regulates the Canadian banking system.

The Bank of Canada manages the money supply indirectly through its influence on the target overnight rate. Increases in interest rates reduce the demand for loans and lead to debtors paying down existing debt. This results in slower growth or even a reduction in the money supply.

The Bank can also influence the money supply by increasing or drawing down the federal government's deposits with clearing institutions.

The Bank's other activities include the issuance of Canadian bank notes, provision of banking services for the federal government, and responsibility for the cheque clearing and settlement systems.

Compare and contrast banks, trust companies, and credit unions/caisses populaires.

Chartered banks are federally regulated under the Bank Act. They take and hold deposits in accounts and make loans to individuals and businesses. Trust companies may be incorporated federally or provincially. Trust companies accept and hold deposits in accounts and make loans to individuals but are restricted in commercial lending. Only trust companies can offer trustee services. Credit unions/caisses populaires are provincially regulated cooperatives. Both offer deposit accounts and loan services to their members.

Distinguish among nonbanking institutions such as insurance companies, pension funds, mutual funds, and finance companies.

Insurance companies are businesses that protect their clients against financial losses due to certain circumstances, in exchange for a fee. Pension funds are investments set aside by organizations or individuals to meet retirement needs. Mutual funds pool investors' money and invest in large numbers of different types of securities. Brokerage firms buy and sell stocks and bonds for investors. Finance companies make short-term loans at higher interest rates than do banks.

Investigate the challenges ahead for the banking industry.

Canadian banks face the same globalization challenges as the banks in other countries. This includes increased competition from larger foreign banks both in Canada and abroad. Bill C-8 has been enacted as the federal government's response to the changing global and domestic market. It appears at this time that Canadian banks will have limited ability to increase their capital base through mergers as has been done in other countries.

Recommend the most appropriate financial institution for a hypothetical small business.

Using the information presented in this chapter, you should be able to answer the questions in the "Solve the Dilemma" box and find the best institution for Hill Optometrics.

Learn the Terms

automated banking machine (ABM) 394

brokerage firms 393

Canada Deposit Insurance Corporation (CDIC) 387

chartered bank 387

chequing account 383

credit cards 384

credit union/caisse populaire 389

Credit Union Central of Canada 389

debit card 385

electronic funds transfer (EFT) 394

finance 380

guaranteed investment certificate (GIC) 384

insurance companies 389

monetary policy 385

money 380

mutual fund 392

near money 384

open market operations 386

pension funds 389

point-of-sale (POS) systems 394

savings account 384

trust company 387

Check Your Progress

1. Differentiate between money and near money. Give examples of each.
2. What are the six characteristics of money? Explain how the Canadian dollar has those six characteristics.
3. What is the difference between a credit card and a debit card?
4. Discuss the basic goal of the Bank of Canada's monetary policy.
5. Explain how the Bank of Canada uses open market operations to expand and contract the money supply.
6. Why do credit unions charge lower rates than chartered banks?
7. Why do finance companies charge higher interest rates than chartered banks?
8. How are mutual funds, money market funds, and pension funds similar? How are they different?
9. What are some of the advantages of electronic funds transfer systems?

Get Involved

1. Survey the banks, trust companies, and credit unions in your area and put together a list of interest rates paid and service charges levied on the various types of deposit accounts offered (chequing, savings, and chequing/savings accounts). In which tpe of account and in which institution would you deposit your money? Why? (Hint: You may wish to use the "Shopping for a Bank Account" worksheet available on the Canadian Bankers Association website www.cba.ca to help organize the information you collect.)
2. Survey the same institutions as above, this time inquiring as to the rates asked for each of their various loans. Where would you prefer to obtain a car loan? A mortgage loan? Why?

Build Your Skills

Managing Money

Background: You have just graduated from college and have received an offer for your dream job (annual salary: $35,000). This premium salary is a reward for your hard work, perseverance, and good grades. It is also a reward for the social skills you developed in college doing service work as a tutor for high school students and interacting with the business community through your involvement with the Association of Collegiate Entrepreneurs (ACE). You are engaged and plan to be married this summer. You and your spouse will have a joint income of $60,000, and the two of you are trying to decide the best way to manage your money.

Task: Research available financial service institutions in your area, and answer the following questions.

1. What kinds of institutions and services can you use to help manage your money?

2. Do you want a full service financial organization that can take care of your banking, insurance, and investing needs or do you want to spread your business among individual specialists? Why have you made this choice?

3. What retirement alternatives do you have?

 **See for Yourself Videocase**   **www.cbc.ca**

How the Dutch Do It—The Bank Mergers

The video reviews the impact of bank mergers in a small nation with a similar banking environment to Canada's. Like Canada, The Netherlands had six major banks facing global competition and possible takeover by foreign banks. The bankers put forth the argument that in order to compete in the global market they required a greater capital base, most logically achieved through mergers. Unlike their Canadian counterparts, the Dutch banks were allowed to merge, resulting in three megabanks. Two of these now operate globally, while the third chose not to merge and to focus on domestic business.

Throughout the video, we are presented with a variety of situations that those opposing the Canadian mergers forecast as the results for Canada if the mergers are allowed.

Questions

1. Compare and contrast situation in The Netherlands to that in Canada.

2. Evaluate the mergers in the video under the Canadian government's bank merger criteria.

3. What are the advantages, if any, of the mergers to the banks and to The Netherlands?

4. What has been the effect of the mergers on bank customers?

5. If the same level of merger activity were allowed in Canada, what alternative choices do Canadians have for banking services?

Source: *Venture*, show number 678, "How the Dutch Do It," February 24, 1998, running time 9:18.

Remember to check out our Online Learning Centre at **www.mcgrawhill.ca/college/ferrell.**

Chapter 16

Financial Management and Securities Markets

Chapter Outline

Objectives

After reading this chapter, you will be able to:

- Define current assets and describe some common methods of managing them.
- Identify some sources of short-term financing (current liabilities).
- Summarize the importance of long-term assets and capital budgeting.
- Specify how companies finance their operations and manage fixed assets with long-term liabilities, particularly bonds.
- Discuss how corporations can use equity financing by issuing stock through an investment banker.
- Describe the various securities markets in North America.
- Critique the short-term asset and liabilities position of a small manufacturer and recommend corrective action.

So You Want to Be a Millionaire?—
Start Investing Now

The earlier you start investing, the more money you will have when you retire. If you invest $1,000 when you are 20 years old, it will grow to $117,390 by the time you are 70, assuming a rate of return of 10 percent per year. If you wait until you are 30 years old to invest $1,000, it will grow to only $45,259 by the time you are 70.

Investing $1,000 every year from age 20 to 24 will amount to $489,504 at age 70. However, investing $1,000 every year from age 30 to 34 will only net $188,725. Don't wait until you are 30 years old to start saving and investing. Start today with as little as $50 per month. The mistake most people make is waiting until it is too late to build a big enough nest egg for a comfortable retirement. Everybody has a reason why they can't spare $50 per month or $12.50 per week (less than the price of a medium pizza). To accumulate wealth you have to be disciplined and stick to a saving and investing plan. By starting young, you give your money a chance to compound for longer periods of time. The table below shows how much you will accumulate at various rates of return if you make five consecutive annual investments of $1,000 beginning at either age 20 or age 30.

Age	Years to Maturity	8%	10%	12%
20–24	50–46	$202,245	$489,504	$1,166,802
30–34	40–36	93,678	188,725	375,679

How do you find investments that will be good for the long term? This chapter explains how companies should manage their assets and liabilities and how they should finance their business with long-term debt and equity. By studying the way in which a management team runs a company and by looking at ratios of performance (see Chapter 14), you can begin sorting out successful companies from unsuccessful ones and risky ones from nonrisky ones. By examining a company's marketing strategy and sales growth and comparing the company to others in the industry, you can decide if it is strong or weak relative to its competitors. You can also start by choosing industries that you like or that are expected to perform better than the economy. And, of course, if you prefer, you can choose to invest in a mutual fund where professionals will make these decisions for you.

David Stewart/Tony Stone Images

INTRODUCTION

While it's certainly true that money makes the world go 'round, financial management is the discipline that makes the world turn more smoothly. Indeed, without effective management of assets, liabilities, and owners' equity, all business organizations are doomed to fail—regardless of the quality and innovativeness of their products. Financial management is the field that addresses the issues of obtaining and managing the funds and resources necessary to run a business successfully. It is not limited to business organizations: All organizations, from the corner store to the local non-profit art museum, from giant corporations to county governments, must manage their resources effectively and efficiently if they are to achieve their objectives.

In this chapter, we look at both short- and long-term financial management. First, we discuss the management of short-term assets, which companies use to generate sales and conduct ordinary day-to-day business operations. Next we turn our attention to the management of short-term liabilities, the sources of short-term funds used to finance the business. Then, we discuss the management of long-term assets such as plant and equipment and the long-term liabilities such as stocks and bonds used to finance these important corporate assets. Finally, we look at the securities markets, where stocks and bonds are traded.

MANAGING CURRENT ASSETS AND LIABILITIES

current assets
short-term resources such as cash, investments, accounts receivable, and inventory

current liabilities
short-term debts such as accounts payable, accrued salaries, accrued taxes, and short-term bank loans

working capital management
the managing of short-term assets and liabilities

Managing short-term assets and liabilities involves managing the current assets and liabilities on the balance sheet (discussed in Chapter 14). **Current assets** are short-term resources such as cash, investments, accounts receivable, and inventory. **Current liabilities** are short-term debts such as accounts payable, accrued salaries, accrued taxes, and short-term bank loans. We use the terms *current* and *short term* interchangeably because short-term assets and liabilities are usually replaced by new assets and liabilities within three or four months, and always within a year. Managing short-term assets and liabilities is sometimes called **working capital management** because short-term assets and liabilities continually flow through an organization and are thus said to be "working."

The critical element in working capital management is cash. All inputs, labour and materials, must at some point be paid with cash. Thus managers must ensure that not only is sufficient cash generated in the business to meet these needs but also that it is available at the correct time. Conversely, since cash itself generates no revenue, having excess cash lowers profitability. Thus financial managers must strive for balance, matching the timing and amounts of cash inflow with the cash needs of the business.

Managing Current Assets

The chief goal of financial managers who focus on current assets and liabilities is to maximize the return to the business on cash, temporary investments of idle cash, accounts receivable, and inventory.

Managing Cash. A crucial element facing any financial manager is effectively managing the firm's cash flow. Remember that cash flow is the movement of money through an organization on a daily, weekly, monthly, or yearly basis. Ensuring that sufficient (but not excessive) funds are on hand to meet the company's obligations is one of the single most important facets of financial management.

Idle cash does not make money, and corporate chequing accounts typically do not earn interest. As a result, astute money managers try to keep just enough cash on hand, called **transaction balances,** to pay bills—such as employee wages, supplies, and utilities—as they fall due. To manage the firm's cash and ensure that enough cash flows through the organization quickly and efficiently, companies try to speed up cash collections from customers.

To accelerate the collection of payments from customers, some companies have customers send their payments to a **lockbox,** which is simply an address for receiving payments, instead of directly to the company's main address. The manager of the lockbox, usually a chartered bank, collects payments directly from the lockbox several times a day and deposits them into the company's bank account. The bank can then start clearing the cheques and get the money into the company's chequing account much more quickly than if the payments had been submitted directly to the company. However, there is no free lunch: The costs associated with lockbox systems make them worthwhile only for those companies that receive thousands of cheques from customers each business day.

Large firms with many stores or offices, such as Household International (parent company of the well-known finance company, Household Finance) in the US, frequently use electronic funds transfer to speed up collections. Household Finance's local offices deposit cheques received each business day into their local banks and, at the end of the day, Household's corporate office initiates the transfer of all collected funds to its central bank for overnight investment. This technique is especially attractive for major international companies, which face slow and sometimes uncertain physical delivery of payments and/or less-than-efficient cheque-clearing procedures.

More and more companies are now using electronic funds transfer systems to pay and collect bills online. It is interesting that companies want to collect cash quickly but pay out cash slowly. When companies use electronic funds transfers between buyers and suppliers, the speed of collections and disbursements increases to one day. Only with the use of cheques can companies delay the payment of cash quickly and have a three- or four-day waiting period until the cheque is presented to their bank and the cash leaves their account.

Investing Idle Cash. As companies sell products, they generate cash on a daily basis, and sometimes cash comes in faster than it is needed to pay bills. Organizations often invest this "extra" cash, for periods as short as one day (overnight) or for as long as one year, until it is needed. Such temporary investments of cash are known as **marketable securities.** Examples include Treasury bills, GICs, commercial paper, and Eurodollar loans. Table 16.1 summarizes a number of different marketable securities used by businesses and some sample interest rates on these investments as of March 2002. While all of the listed securities are very low risk, the government securities are the safest.

Many large companies invest idle cash in **Treasury bills (T-bills),** which are short-term debt obligations the federal government sells to raise money. Auctioned biweekly by the Bank of Canada, T-bills carry maturities of between one month to one year. T-bills are generally considered to be the safest of all investments and are called risk free because the federal government will not default on its debt.

One of the most popular short-term investments for the largest business organizations is **commercial paper**—a written promise from one company to another to pay a specific amount of money. Since commercial paper is backed only by the name and reputation of the issuing company, sales of commercial paper are restricted to

transaction balances
cash kept on hand by a firm to pay normal daily expenses, such as employee wages and bills for supplies and utilities

lockbox
an address, usually a chartered bank, at which a company receives payments in order to speed collections from customers

marketable securities
temporary investment of "extra" cash by organizations for up to one year in Treasury bills, GICs, commercial paper, or Eurodollar loans, or shares

Treasury bills (T-bills)
short-term debt obligations issued by the Bank of Canada to raise money for the federal government

commercial paper
a written promise from one company to another to pay a specific amount of money

Table 16.1

Short-Term Investment Possibilities for Idle Cash

Source: www.bankof canada.ca/en/tbill-look. htm; *Toronto Star*, Sunday March 10, 2002, page C2.

Type of Security	Maturity	Issuer of Security	Interest Rate (March 2002)
Treasury bill	1 month	Bank of Canada	1.99%
Treasury bill	3 months	Bank of Canada	2.07
Treasury bill	6 months	Bank of Canada	2.27
Treasury bill	1 year	Bank of Canada	2.88
Government of Canada Bonds	2 years	Government of Canada	3.70
Short-term deposits	30–59 days	Banks, trust, and loan cos.	0.90–1.90
Short-term deposits	60–99 days	Banks, trust, and loan cos.	0.90–1.90
Short-term deposits	90–119 days	Banks, trust, and loan cos.	0.90–1.90
Fixed-term deposits	1 year	Banks, trust, and loan cos.	1.30–2.50
Fixed-term deposits	2 years	Banks, trust, and loan cos.	2.25–3.37

only the largest and most financially stable companies. As commercial paper is frequently bought and sold for durations of as short as one business day, many "players" in the market find themselves buying commercial paper with excess cash on one day and selling it to gain extra money the following day.

Some companies invest idle cash in international markets such as the **Eurodollar market,** a market for trading US dollars in foreign countries. Because the Eurodollar market was originally developed by London banks, any US-dollar-denominated deposit in a non-US bank is called a Eurodollar deposit, regardless of whether the issuing bank is actually located in Europe, South America, or anyplace else. For example, if you travel overseas and deposit US$1,000 in a German bank (where the local currency is the German mark), you will have "created" a Eurodollar deposit in the amount of US$1,000. Since the US dollar is accepted by most countries for international trade, these dollar deposits can be used by international companies to settle their accounts. The market created for trading such investments offers firms with extra dollars a chance to earn a slightly higher rate of return with just a little more risk than they would face by investing in Treasury bills.

Eurodollar market
a market for trading US dollars in foreign countries

Maximizing Accounts Receivable. After cash and marketable securities, the balance sheet lists accounts receivable and inventory. Remember that accounts receivable is money owed to a business by credit customers. For example, if you charge your Sunoco gasoline purchases, until you actually pay for them with cash or a cheque, they represent an account receivable to Sunoco. Many businesses make the vast majority of their sales on credit, so managing accounts receivable is an important task.

Each credit sale represents an account receivable for the company, the terms of which typically require customers to pay the full amount due within 30, 60, or even 90 days from the date of the sale. To encourage quick payment, some businesses offer some of their customers discounts of between 1 to 2 percent if they pay off their balance within a specified period of time (usually between 10 and 30 days). On the other hand, late payment charges of between 1 and 1.5 percent serve to discourage slow payers from sitting on their bills forever. The larger the early payment discount

The Canadian Auto Workers on strike. Strikes can cost manufacturers millions when resulting inventory shortages cause customers to seek other suppliers.

CP Photo Archive. Photograph by Tannis Toohey.

offered, the faster customers will tend to pay their accounts. Unfortunately, while discounts increase cash flow, they also reduce profitability. Finding the right balance between the added advantages of early cash receipt and the disadvantages of reduced profits is no simple matter. Similarly, determining the optimal balance between the higher sales likely to result from extending credit to customers with less than sterling credit ratings and the higher bad-debt losses likely to result from a more lenient credit policy is also challenging. Information on company credit ratings is provided by local credit bureaus, national credit-rating agencies such as Dun and Bradstreet, Dominion Bond Rating Service, and industry trade groups.

Optimizing Inventory. While the inventory that a firm holds is controlled by both production needs and marketing considerations, the financial manager has to coordinate inventory purchases to manage cash flows. The object is to minimize the firm's investment in inventory without experiencing production cutbacks as a result of critical materials shortfalls or lost sales due to insufficient finished goods inventories. Every dollar invested in inventory is a dollar unavailable for investment in some other area of the organization. Optimal inventory levels are determined, in large part, by the method of production. If a firm attempts to produce its goods just in time to meet sales demand, the level of inventory will be relatively low. If, on the other hand, the firm produces materials in a constant, level pattern, inventory increases when sales decrease and decreases when sales increase.

The automobile industry is an excellent example of an industry driven almost solely by inventory levels. Because it is inefficient to continually lay off workers in slow times and call them back in better times, Ford, General Motors, and DaimlerChrysler try to set and stick to quarterly production quotas. Automakers typically try to keep a 60-day supply of unsold cars. During particularly slow periods, however, it is not unusual for inventories to exceed 100 days of sales. When sales of a particular model fall far behind the average and inventories build up, production of that model may be cancelled, as General Motors did with its Chevrolet Caprice Classic. Before eliminating a model outright, however, automakers typically try to "jump-start" sales by offering rebates, special financing incentives, or special lease terms—all of which GM tried without success.

Although less publicized, inventory shortages can be as much of a drag on potential profits as too much inventory. Not having an item on hand may send the customer to a competitor—forever. For example, the low inventory that resulted from the 1998 GM strike cost the company millions of dollars in lost customers and sales. Complex computer inventory models are frequently employed to determine the optimum level of inventory a firm should hold to support a given level of sales. Such models can indicate how and when parts inventories should be ordered so that they are available exactly when required—and not a day before. Developing and maintaining such an intricate production and inventory system is difficult, but it can often prove to be the difference between experiencing average profits and spectacular ones.

Managing Current Liabilities

While having extra cash on hand is a delightful surprise, the opposite situation—a temporary cash shortfall—can be a crisis. The good news is that there are several potential sources of short-term funds. Suppliers often serve as an important source through credit sales practices. Also, banks, finance companies, and other organizations offer short-term funds through loans and other business operations.

Accounts Payable. Remember from Chapter 14 that accounts payable is money an organization owes to suppliers for goods and services. Just as accounts receivable must be actively managed to ensure proper cash collections, so too must accounts payable be managed to make the best use of this important liability.

trade credit
credit extended by suppliers for the purchase of their goods and services

The most widely used source of short-term financing, and therefore the most important account payable, is **trade credit**—credit extended by suppliers for the purchase of their goods and services. While varying in formality, depending on both the organizations involved and the value of the items purchased, most trade credit agreements offer discounts to organizations that pay their bills early. A supplier, for example, may offer trade terms of "1/10 net 30," meaning that the purchasing organization may take a 1 percent discount from the invoice amount if it makes payment by the 10th day after receiving the bill. Otherwise, the entire amount is due within 30 days. For example, pretend that you are the financial manager in charge of payables. You owe Ajax Company $10,000, and it offers trade terms of 2/10 net 30. By paying the amount due within 10 days, you can save 2 percent of $10,000, or $200. Assume you place orders with Ajax once per month and have 12 bills of $10,000 each per year. By taking the discount every time, you will save 12 times $200, or $2,400, per year. Now assume you are the financial manager of Gigantic Corp., and it has monthly payables of $100 million per month. Two percent of $100 million is $2 million per month. Failure to take advantage of such trade discounts can, in many cases, add up to large opportunity losses over the span of a year.

line of credit
an arrangement by which a bank agrees to lend a specified amount of money to an organization upon request

Bank Loans. Virtually all organizations—large and small—obtain short-term funds for operations from banks. In most instances, the credit services granted these firms take the form of a line of credit or fixed dollar loan. A **line of credit** is an arrangement by which a bank agrees to lend a specified amount of money to the organization upon request—provided that the bank has the required funds to make the loan. In general, a business line of credit is very similar to a consumer credit card, with the exception that the preset credit limit can amount to millions of dollars.

Banks make **secured loans**—loans backed by collateral that the bank can claim if the borrowers do not repay the loans—and **unsecured loans**—loans backed only by the borrowers' good reputation and previous credit rating. The *principal* is the amount of money borrowed; *interest* is a percentage of the principal that the bank charges for use of its money. As we mentioned in Chapter 15, banks also pay depositors interest on savings accounts and some chequing accounts. Thus, banks charge borrowers interest for loans and pay interest to depositors for the use of their money.

The **prime rate** is the interest rate banks charge their best customers (usually large corporations) for short-term loans. While, for many years, loans at the prime rate represented funds at the lowest possible cost, the rapid development of the market for commercial paper has dramatically reduced the importance of banks as a source of short-term loans. Today, most "prime" borrowers are actually small- and medium-sized businesses.

The interest rates on commercial loans may be either fixed or variable. A variable, or floating-rate, loan offers an advantage when interest rates are falling but represents a distinct disadvantage when interest rates are rising. By early 1999, interest rates had plummeted, and borrowers were refinancing their loans with low-cost fixed-rate loans.

In the aftermath of the terrorist attacks on September 11, 2001, both the US Federal Reserve and the Bank of Canada followed a policy of lowering their target rates in an effort to inject liquidity into the financial system. This rapid decline of interest rates to the lowest level seen in Canada in over 40 years led to many borrowers seeking to refinance debt with low-cost fixed-rate loans. The savings from such actions can be significant—especially on larger long-term debt, such as home mortgages. The decision to refinance a mortgage is made more complicated by the penalty clauses, which charge up to three months interest for early repayment. Despite these heavy penalties, it was still advantageous for many who had "locked-in" at high rates for long terms to pay the penalty and refinance at the much lower current rates. Individuals and corporations have the same motivation: to minimize their borrowing costs.

Nonbank Liabilities. Banks are not the only source of short-term funds for businesses. Indeed, virtually all financial institutions, from insurance companies to pension funds, from money market funds to finance companies, make short-term loans to many organizations. The largest companies also actively engage in borrowing money from the Eurodollar and commercial paper markets. As noted earlier, both of these funds' sources are typically slightly less expensive than bank loans.

In some instances, businesses actually sell their accounts receivable to a finance company known as a **factor,** which gives the selling organizations cash and assumes responsibility for collecting the accounts. For example, a factor might pay $60,000 for receivables with a total face value of $100,000 (60 percent of the total). The factor profits if it can collect more than what it paid for the accounts. Because the selling organization's customers send their payments to a lockbox, they may have no idea that a factor has bought their receivables.

Additional nonbank liabilities that must be efficiently managed to ensure maximum profitability are taxes owed to the government and wages owed to employees.

secured loans
loans backed by collateral that the bank can claim if the borrowers do not repay them

unsecured loans
loans backed only by the borrowers' good reputation and previous credit rating

prime rate
the interest rate that banks charge their best customers (usually large corporations) for short-term loans

factor
a finance company to whom businesses sell their accounts receivable—usually for a percentage of the total face value

Clearly, businesses are responsible for many different types of taxes, including federal, provincial, and local income taxes, property taxes, mineral rights taxes, unemployment taxes, Employment Insurance premiums, workers' compensation taxes, excise taxes, and even more! While the public tends to think that the only relevant taxes are on income and sales, many industries must pay other taxes that far exceed those levied against their income. Taxes and employees' wages represent debt obligations of the firm, which the financial manager must plan to meet as they fall due.

MANAGING FIXED ASSETS

Up to this point, we have focused on the short-term aspects of financial management. While most business failures are the result of poor short-term planning, successful ventures must also consider the long-term financial consequences of their actions. Managing the long-term assets and liabilities and the owners' equity portion of the balance sheet is important for the long-term health of the business.

long-term (fixed) assets
production facilities (plants), offices, and equipment—all of which are expected to last for many years

Long-term (fixed) assets are expected to last for many years—production facilities (plants), offices, equipment, heavy machinery, furniture, automobiles, etc. In today's fast-paced world, companies need the most technologically advanced, modern facilities and equipment they can afford. The tremendous competition faced by the North American automotive industry in the 1970s and 1980s from producers overseas was due, in large part, to inefficient fixed assets. When General Motors tried to close an outmoded US plant in the late 1990s, the United Automobile Workers Union went on strike. Clearly, balancing the management of long-term assets with employee morale and shareholder returns is not a simple task. After a costly strike, General Motors settled with the union, and financial analysts did not think that General Motors made much headway in getting the union's approval to close old factories.

But modern and high-tech equipment carry high price tags, and the financial arrangements required to support these investments are by no means trivial. Obtaining major long-term financing can be challenging for even the most profitable organizations. For less successful firms, such challenges can prove nearly impossible. We'll take a closer look at long-term financing in a moment, but first let's address some issues associated with fixed assets, including capital budgeting, risk assessment, and the costs of financing fixed assets.

Capital Budgeting and Project Selection

One of the most important jobs performed by the financial manager is to decide what fixed assets, projects, and investments will earn profits for the firm beyond the costs necessary to fund them. The process of analyzing the needs of the business and selecting the assets that will maximize its value is called **capital budgeting,** and the capital budget is the amount of money budgeted for investment in such long-term assets. But capital budgeting does not end with the selection and purchase of a particular piece of land, equipment, or major investment. All assets and projects must be continually reevaluated to ensure their compatibility with the organization's needs. If a particular asset does not live up to expectations, then management must determine why and take necessary corrective action. Mobil Oil sold Montgomery Ward stores (a former subsidiary) because Mobil management determined that retail stores no longer fit into its long-term plans.

capital budgeting
the process of analyzing the needs of the business and selecting the assets that will maximize its value

Figure 16.1

Qualitative Assessment of Capital Budgeting Risk

Highest Risk

Introduce a New Product in Foreign Markets (risk depends on stability of country)

Expand into a New Market

Introduce a New Product in a Familiar Area

Add to a Product Line

Buy New Equipment for an Established Market

Repair Old Machinery

Lowest Risk

Assessing Risk

Every investment carries some risk. Figure 16.1 ranks potential investment projects according to estimated risk. When considering investments overseas, risk assessments must include the political climate and economic stability of a region. The decision to introduce a product or build a manufacturing facility in England would be much less risky than a decision to build one in the Middle East, for example.

Not apparent from Figure 16.1 are the risks associated with time. The longer a project or asset is expected to last, the greater its potential risk because it is hard to predict whether a piece of equipment will wear out or become obsolete in 5 or 10 years. Predicting cash flows one year down the road is difficult, but projecting them over the span of a 10-year project is a gamble.

The level of a project's risk is also affected by the stability and competitive nature of the marketplace and the world economy as a whole. IBM's latest high-technology computer product is far more likely to become obsolete overnight than is a similar $10 million investment in a manufacturing plant. Dramatic changes in the marketplace are not uncommon. Indeed, uncertainty created by the rapid devaluation of Asian currencies in the late 1990s wrecked a host of assumptions in literally hundreds

Glasspray Corporation is a small firm that makes industrial fibreglass spray equipment. Despite its size, the company supplies to a range of firms from small mom-and-pop boatmakers to major industrial giants, both overseas and here at home. Indeed, just about every moulded fibreglass resin product, from bathroom sinks and counters to portable spas and racing yachts, is constructed with the help of one or more of the company's machines.

Despite global acceptance of its products, Glasspray has repeatedly run into trouble with regard to the management of its current assets and liabilities as a result of extremely rapid and consistent increases in year-to-year sales. The firm's president and founder, Stephen T. Rose, recently lamented the sad state of his firm's working capital position: "Our current assets aren't, and our current liabilities are!" Rose shouted in a recent meeting of the firm's top officers, "We can't afford any more increases in sales! We're selling our way into bankruptcy! Frankly, our *working* capital doesn't!"

1. Normally, rapidly increasing sales is a good thing. What seems to be the problem here?
2. List the important components of a firm's working capital. Include both current assets and current liabilities.
3. What are some management techniques applied to current liabilities that Glasspray might use to improve its working capital position?

of projects worldwide. Financial managers must constantly consider such issues when making long-term decisions about the purchase of fixed assets.

Pricing Long-Term Money

The ultimate profitability of any project depends not only on accurate assumptions of how much cash it will generate but also on its financing costs. Because a business must pay interest on money it borrows, the returns from any project must cover not only the costs of operating the project but also the interest expenses for the debt used to finance its construction. Unless an organization can effectively cover all of its costs—both financial and operating—it will eventually fail.

Clearly, only a limited supply of funds is available for investment in any given enterprise. The most efficient and profitable companies can attract the lowest-cost funds because they typically offer reasonable financial returns at very low relative risks. Newer and less prosperous firms must pay higher costs to attract capital because these companies tend to be quite risky. One of the strongest motivations for companies to manage their financial resources wisely is that they will, over time, be able to reduce the costs of their funds and in so doing increase their overall profitability.

In our free-enterprise economy, new firms tend to enter industries that offer the greatest potential rewards for success. However, as more and more companies enter an industry, competition intensifies, eventually driving profits down to average levels. The personal computer industry of the 1980s and early 1990s provides an excellent example of the changes in profitability that typically accompany increasing competition. In the early 1980s, Apple Computer earned very high returns from the sale of its Apple II computer. Soon, new entrants such as IBM and later Compaq entered the personal computer field, and once profitable (but now largely forgotten) Apple competitors such as Osborne and Kaypro fell to the wayside—unable to compete and win in the new environment. Competition intensified with the entrance of mass marketing/manufacturing companies such as Dell, Packard Bell, and Gateway 2000. Prices fell as technology advanced. Weak companies failed, leaving the most efficient producers/marketers scrambling for market share. The expanded market for personal computers dramatically reduced the financial returns generated by each dollar invested in productive assets. The "glory days" of the personal computer industry—the time in which fortunes could be won and lost in the space of an average-sized garage—have long since passed into history. Personal computers are becoming commodity items, and profit margins for companies in this industry are shrinking as the market becomes mature and new PC versions do little to unleash new demand for the product.

FINANCING WITH LONG-TERM LIABILITIES

As we said earlier, long-term assets do not come cheap, and few companies have the cash on hand to open a new store across town, build a new manufacturing facility, research and develop a new life-saving drug, or launch a new product worldwide. To develop such fixed assets, companies need to raise low-cost long-term funds to finance them. Two common choices for raising these funds are attracting new owners (*equity financing*), which we'll look at in a moment, and taking on long-term liabilities (*debt financing*), which we'll look at now.

Long-term liabilities are debts that will be repaid over a number of years, such as long-term bank loans and bond issues. These take many different forms, but in the end, the key word is *debt*. Companies may raise money by borrowing it from banks or other financial institutions in the form of lines of credit, short-term loans, or long-term loans. Many corporations acquire debt by borrowing money from pension funds, mutual funds, or life-insurance funds.

Companies that rely too heavily on debt can get into serious trouble should the economy falter; during these times, they may not earn enough operating income to make the required interest payments (remember the times interest earned ratio in Chapter 14). In severe cases when the problem persists too long, creditors will not restructure loans but will instead sue for the interest and principal owed and force the company into bankruptcy.

long-term liabilities
debts that will be repaid over a number of years, such as long-term loans and bond issues

Bonds: Corporate IOUs

Aside from loans, much long-term debt takes the form of **bonds,** which are debt instruments that larger companies sell to raise long-term funds. In essence, the buyers of bonds (bondholders) loan the issuer of the bonds cash in exchange for regular interest payments until the loan is repaid on or before the specified maturity date. The bond itself is a certificate, much like an IOU, that represents the company's debt to the bondholder. Bonds are issued by a wide variety of entities, including corporations; national, provincial, and local governments; public utilities; and nonprofit corporations. Most bondholders need not hold their bonds until maturity; rather, the existence of active secondary markets of brokers and dealers allows for the quick and efficient transfer of bonds from owner to owner.

The bond contract, or *indenture,* specifies all of the terms of the agreement between the bondholders and the issuing organization. The indenture, which can run more than 100 pages, specifies the basic terms of the bond, such as its face value,

bonds
debt instruments that larger companies sell to raise long-term funds

Table 16.2

A Basic Bond Quote

Source: *The Globe and Mail,* "Money Markets," page B16–17, Wednesday, January 23, 2002.

Issuer (1)	Coupon (2)	Maturity (3)	Price (4)	Yield (%) (5)	Price $ Change (6)
Canada	11.750	Feb 01/03	109.37	2.41	−0.04
Royal Bank	5.400	Apr 07/03	102.99	2.84	−0.034
Suncor	6.700	Aug 22/11	100.88	6.57	−0.05
Domtar	10.000	Apr 15/22	108.58	8.63	−0.05

(1) Issuer—the name or abbreviation of the name of the government or corporation issuing the bond.

(2) Coupon—the annual percentage rate specified on the bond certificate. Domtar's rate is 10%, so a $1,000 bond will receive $100 per year.

(3) Maturity—the bond's maturity date; the date on which the issuer will repay the bondholders the face value of each bond; April 15, 2011 for Domtar.

(4) Price—the closing price. For Domtar, 108.58 = 108.58 percent of the face value or $1,085.58 per bond.

(5) Yield—percentage return from interest, based on the closing price (column 4). If you buy a Domtar bond at today's closing price of 108.85 ($1,085.58) and receive $100 per year, your rate of return to maturity will be 8.63%.

(6) Price $ Change—the change in price from the close of the previous trading day. Domtar's bond price decreased by $0.05.

maturity date, and the annual interest rate. Table 16.2 briefly explains how to determine these and more things about a bond from a bond quote, as it might appear in *The Globe and Mail.* The face value of the bond, its initial sales price, is typically $1,000. After this, however, the price of the bond on the open market will fluctuate along with changes in the economy (particularly, changes in interest rates) and in the creditworthiness of the issuer. Bondholders receive the face value of the bond along with the final interest payment on the maturity date. The annual interest rate (often called the *coupon rate*) is the guaranteed percentage of face value that the company will pay to the bond owner every year. For example, a $1,000 bond with a coupon rate of 7 percent would pay $70 per year in interest. In most cases, bond indentures specify that interest payments be made every six months. In the example above, the $70 annual payment would be divided into two semiannual payments of $35.

In addition to the terms of interest payments and maturity date, the bond indenture typically covers other important areas, such as repayment methods, interest payment dates, procedures to be followed in case the organization fails to make the interest payments, conditions for the early repayment of the bonds, and any conditions requiring the pledging of assets as collateral.

unsecured bonds
debentures, or bonds that are not backed by specific collateral

secured bonds
bonds that are backed by specific collateral that must be forfeited in the event that the issuing firm defaults

Types of Bonds

Not surprisingly, there are a great many different types of bonds. Most are **unsecured bonds,** meaning that they are not backed by specific collateral; such bonds are termed *debentures.* **Secured bonds,** on the other hand, are backed by specific collat-

Many types of organizations need to raise money to run their operations. Companies need money to buy plants and equipment, and provincial and local governments need money for roads, schools, sewers, parks, and other government activities. Even countries need money to run governments and build roads, bridges, hospitals, and other infrastructure projects. One common way for companies and governments to find money is to borrow it. They might be able to borrow it from a bank or an insurance company, or they may sell bonds to many different types of investors. Potential buyers of bonds (lenders) must assess the risk of the entity borrowing the money. The riskier the borrower, the higher the interest rate. It is important to be able to compare the risk of one borrower to another.

Governments almost always borrow at lower interest rates than the companies located within their borders. That is why it is important to know the risk of the country (sometimes called *sovereign risk*) as well as the risk of the company borrowing the money. If the country risk is high, a company within that country will pay higher interest rates than the government when borrowing money.

There are four companies, called credit-rating agencies, that assign risk ratings to the debt of companies and governments. The largest two are Moody's Investor Services and Standard and Poor's. These agencies rate the individual company and government and the specific bond that will be issued to investors. The companies and governments pay these firms a fee for the rating assigned. Sometimes they are not happy because the rating is lower than they think it should be, resulting in a higher, more costly interest rate. Still, obtaining a credit-rating is important, as international investors rarely buy unrated bonds.

In fall 1998, the Peoples Republic of China registered a bond issue with the US Securities and Exchange Commission that was expected to raise US$500 million to US$1 billion in the United States. In December 1998, Moody's Investor Services rated the bonds A3. The 3 following the A indicates that the bond is rated at the lower end of the A range. Moody's ratings between Aaa and Baa are considered investment grade. Bonds with ratings of Ba, B, or Caa and below are sometimes called "junk" bonds and carry higher interest rates. The Chinese Finance Ministry promoted the bonds in New York and Boston, trying to drum up institutional support for the bond issue. Financial analysts expected that the Chinese bonds would carry an interest rate between 2.5 to 2.75 percent higher than US government debt.

Moody's was not as kind in its rating of several state-owned Chinese banks, and it cut the ratings on the State Development Bank of China and the Export-Import Bank of China from A3 to Baa. It also reduced the ratings on the Industrial and Commercial Bank of China, China Construction Bank, and China Merchants Bank.

Think Globally

Rating the Risk of Foreign Bonds

eral that must be forfeited in the event that the issuing firm defaults. Whether secured or unsecured, bonds may be repaid in one lump sum or with many payments spread out over a period of time. **Serial bonds,** which are different from secured bonds, are actually a sequence of small bond issues of progressively longer maturity. The firm pays off each of the serial bonds as they mature. **Floating-rate bonds** do not have fixed interest payments; instead, the interest rate changes with current interest rates otherwise available in the economy.

serial bonds
a sequence of small bond issues of progressively longer maturity

floating-rate bonds
bonds with interest rates that change with current interest rates otherwise available in the economy

junk bonds
a special type of high-interest rate bond that carries higher inherent risks

In recent years, a special type of high-interest rate bond has attracted considerable attention (usually negative) in the financial press. High-interest bonds, or **junk bonds** as they are popularly known, offer relatively high rates of interest because they have higher inherent risks. Historically, junk bonds have been associated with companies in poor financial health and/or start-up firms with limited track records. In the mid-1980s, however, junk bonds became a very attractive method of financing corporate mergers; they remain popular today with many investors as a result of their very high relative interest rates. But higher risks are associated with those higher returns (upwards of 12 percent per year in some cases) and the average investor would be well-advised to heed those famous words: Look before you leap!

FINANCING WITH OWNERS' EQUITY

A second means of long-term financing is through equity. Remember from Chapter 14 that owners' equity refers to the owners' investment in an organization. Sole proprietors and partners own all or a part of their businesses outright, and their equity includes the money and assets they have brought into their ventures. Corporate owners, on the other hand, own stock or shares of their companies, which they hope will provide them with a return on their investment. Shareholders' equity includes common stock, preferred stock, and retained earnings.

Common stock (introduced in Chapter 5) is the single most important source of capital for most new companies. In Canada, new issues of preferred shares are not allowed. Multiple classes of common stock allow shares to be issued having the same characteristics traditionally included in preferred shares. Table 16.3 briefly explains how to gather important information from a stock quote, as it might appear in a financial newspaper or a stock exchange's web site.

Preferred stock was defined in Chapter 5 as corporate ownership that gives the shareholder preference in the distribution of the company's profits but not the voting and control rights accorded to common shareholders. Thus, the primary advantage of owning preferred stock is that it is a safer investment than common stock. The Canadian Business Corporations Act requires that at least one class of common shares be issued.

retained earnings
earnings after expenses and taxes that are reinvested in the assets of the firm and belong to the owners in the form of equity

All businesses exist to earn profits for their owners. Without the possibility of profit, there can be no incentive to risk investors' capital and succeed. When a corporation has profits left over after paying all of its expenses and taxes, it has the choice of retaining all or a portion of its earnings and/or paying them out to its shareholders in the form of dividends. **Retained earnings** are reinvested in the assets of the firm and belong to the owners in the form of equity. Retained earnings are an important source of funds and are, in fact, the only long-term funds that the company can generate internally.

payout ratio
dividends per share divided by earnings per share

When the board of directors distributes some of a corporation's profits to the owners, it issues them as cash dividend payments. But not all firms pay dividends. Many fast-growing firms retain all of their earnings because they can earn high rates of return on the earnings they reinvest. Companies with fewer growth opportunities typically pay out large proportions of their earnings in the form of dividends, thereby allowing their shareholders to reinvest their dividend payments in higher-growth companies. The **payout ratio**—dividends per share divided by earnings per share—expresses the percentage of earnings the company paid out in dividends. Since low dividend payout rates are typically associated with higher growth rates, it

Table 16.3

A Basic Stock Quote

1 365-day high	low	2 Stock	3 Sym	4 Div	5 High	6 Low	7 Close	8 Chg	9 Vol 100s	10 Yld	11 P/e ratio
10.35	1.15	Air Canada	ACA		3.89	3.66	3.68	−0.27	189		
10.90	0.80	Imax	IMX		5.15	4.90	4.90	−0.10	205		
30.81	18.75	Intrawest	ITW	0.16	24.25	23.70	23.85	+0.25	390	0.7	12.1
15.95	9.55	Linamar	LNR	0.16	13.58	13.15	13.30	+0.16	889	1.2	20.1
13.89	5.85	Magna	MIE.A		13.24	12.85	13.00	−0.05	296		72.2
61.10	7.50	Nortel Netwk	NT		12.40	11.45	11.58	−0.32	94,644		
115.00	18.69	Research	RIM		35.90	33.94	34.07	−0.87	7,435		
53.25	41.60	Royal Bank	RY	1.44	50.35	49.56	49.63	−0.66	7,270	2.9	14.0

1. Highest and lowest intra-day price in the past 52 weeks.
2. Abbreviated company name.
3. Ticker symbol assigned to the issue by the exchange.
4. Indicated annual dividend as reported by the exchange.
5. Highest intra-day trading price.
6. Lowest intra-day trading price.
7. The closing price.
8. Number of shares traded in 100s.
9. Change between the closing price and the previous closing stock price.
10. Yield expressed as a percentage, calculated by dividing the dividend by the current market price.
11. Price/earnings ratio; current stock price divided by the company's earnings per share from continuing operations for the latest rolling 12 months.

Source: *The Globe and Mail*, Money Markets, page B16–17, Wednesday, January 23, 2002.

is not clear that stocks paying high dividends will be preferred by investors to those paying little or no dividends. Most large companies pay their shareholders dividends on a quarterly basis.

INVESTMENT BANKING

A company that needs more money to expand or take advantage of opportunities may be able to obtain financing by issuing stock. **Investment banking,** the sale of stocks and bonds for corporations, helps such companies raise funds by matching people and institutions who have money to invest with corporations in need of resources to exploit new opportunities. The first-time sale of stocks and bonds directly to the public is called a *new issue.* Companies that already have stocks or bonds outstanding may

investment banking
the sale of stocks and bonds for corporations

Rogers Cable to Issue $300 Million in Bonds

Rogers Communications Inc.'s cable unit, the largest in Canada, plans to sell its first investment-grade bonds in coming weeks after a November upgrade of its debt rating.

Rogers Cable will sell at least $300 million of five-year bonds to refinance debt due later this year, treasurer Lorraine Daly said. The sale will be the first since Standard & Poor's Corp. raised its rating on the unit's senior secured debt a notch to one level above junk because the parent company eliminated loans between units, making it easier to gauge profits at the cable business.[1]

offer a new issue of stock to raise additional funds for specific projects. When a company offers its stock to the public for the very first time, it is said to be "going public," and the sale is called an *initial public offering.* Many Internet stocks such as Amazon.com, Theglobe.com, Earthlink.com, and eBay have gone public in the last several years by making initial public offerings (IPOs) of their common stock.

primary market
the market where firms raise financial capital

secondary markets
stock exchanges and over-the-counter markets where investors can trade their securities with others

New issues of stocks and bonds are sold directly to the public and to institutions in what is known as the **primary market**—the market where firms raise financial capital. The primary market differs from **secondary markets,** which are stock exchanges and over-the-counter markets where investors can trade their securities with others. Primary market transactions actually raise cash for the issuing corporations, while secondary market transactions do not.

Corporations usually employ an investment banking firm to help sell their securities in the primary market. An investment banker helps firms establish appropriate offering prices for their securities. In addition, the investment banker takes care of the myriad details and securities regulations involved in any sale of securities to the public.

Just as large corporations such as IBM, General Motors, and Microsoft have a client relationship with a law firm and an accounting firm, they also have a client relationship with an investment banking firm. An investment banking firm such as Merrill Lynch, BMO Investorline, or TD Waterhouse can provide advice about financing plans, dividend policy, or stock repurchases, as well as advice on mergers and acquisitions. When Chrysler merged with Daimler Benz, both companies used investment bankers to help them value the transaction. Each firm wanted an outside opinion about what it was worth to the other. Sometimes mergers fall apart because the companies cannot agree on the price each company is worth or the structure of management after the merger. The advising investment banker, working with management, often irons out these details. Of course, investment bankers do not provide these services for free. They usually charge a fee of between 1 and 1.5 percent of the transaction. A $20 billion merger can generate between $200 and $300 million in investment banking fees. The merger mania of the late 1990s allowed top investment bankers to earn huge sums. Unfortunately, this type of fee income is dependent on healthy stock markets, which seem to stimulate the merger fever among corporate executives.

securities markets
the mechanism for buying and selling securities

THE SECURITIES MARKETS

Securities markets provide a mechanism for buying and selling securities. They make it possible for owners to sell their stocks and bonds to other investors. Thus, in the broadest sense, stocks and bonds markets may be thought of as providers of liquidity—the ability to turn security holdings into cash quickly and at minimal expense and effort. Without liquid securities markets, many potential investors would sit on the sidelines rather than invest their hard-earned savings in securities. Indeed, the ability to sell securities at well-established market prices is one of the very pillars of the capitalistic society that has developed over the years in North America.

Unlike the primary market, in which corporations sell stocks directly to the public, secondary markets permit the trading of previously issued securities. There are many different secondary markets for both stocks and bonds. If you want to purchase 100 shares of Du Pont common stock, for example, you must purchase this stock from another investor or institution. It is the active buying and selling by many thousands of investors that establishes the prices of all financial securities. Secondary market trades may take place on organized exchanges or in what is known as the over-the-counter market. Many brokerage houses exist to help investors with financial decisions, and many offer their services through the Internet. One such broker is TD Waterhouse. Its site offers a wealth of information and provides educational material to individual investors. TD Waterhouse received the top ranking in the *Globe and Mail*'s third annual survey of online brokers.[2]

TD Waterhouse
www.tdwaterhouse.com/

The terrorist attacks of September 11, 2001, halted trading on the New York Stock Exchange for six days. Trading resumed on Monday, September 17, and at the market close on Friday, September 21, 10 days after the attacks, the Dow Jones Industrial Average at 8,5235.81 was at its lowest level in almost three years. However, as with previous significant market shocks, including the bombing of Pearl Harbor, the assassination of John F. Kennedy, and the start of the Gulf War, the market rebounded. On December 15, 2001, the Dow Jones was once again above 10,000.

The Toronto Stock Exchange closed early on the day of the terrorist attacks, remained closed the next day, and reopened on September 13, 2001.

Organized Exchanges

Organized exchanges are central locations where investors buy and sell securities. Buyers and sellers are not actually present on the floor of the exchange; instead, they are represented by brokers, who act as agents and buy and sell securities according to investors' wishes. The New York Stock Exchange (NYSE), the largest and most important of all the exchanges in the United States, is located at the corner of Broad and Wall streets in New York City (hence reference to the financial community by the media as "Wall Street"). The American Stock Exchange (AMEX) trades smaller companies than NYSE. Chicago, Boston, Baltimore, Cincinnati, and other cities have regional exchanges.

organized exchanges
central locations where investors buy and sell securities

Incorporated in 1878, the Toronto Stock Exchange (TSE) reached 10th place in dollar value traded at world stock exchanges in 1995. The TSE remains Canada's premier market for senior equities, accounting for over 90 percent of all Canadian equity trading in 2000. Over 40 billion shares were traded that year, with a total value in excess of $944 billion. Junior equities are traded on the Canadian Venture Exchange (CDNX), and the Bourse de Montreal is known as Canada's derivatives exchange.[3]

Toronto Stock Exchange
www.tse.com/

Internationally, the London Stock Exchange, the Paris Bourse, and the Tokyo Stock Exchange are among the many vital organized exchanges that provide venues for trading domestic and international securities.

Did you know?

Online investing (or electronic trading) is projected to reach US$2.2 billion by 2002.

Companies that use the Internet to conduct business do not need to invest money in physical stores or real estate, thereby minimizing their investment in fixed assets. However, they do need sophisticated computer networks and employees with high-tech expertise. There are more companies entering this business every day, and they need money for computer hardware and software, qualified employees, and advertising. Many of these companies offer stock to raise funds for their operation.

There are many publicly traded Internet companies. Companies such as Amazon.com, Theglobe.com, Yahoo, Lycos, America Online, Excite, and others have reached lofty price levels based on great expectations. America Online's 14 million customers make it the dominant player on the Net. It is valued at US$41 billion, which makes it worth more than all but 55 companies in the Standard and Poor's 500 Stock Index. There are rumours that it will be added to the S&P 500 Index when another firm drops out because of a merger.

eBay Inc. operates an online auction site that connects buyers and sellers of items such as computers, stamps and coins, collectibles, and memorabilia. eBay sold 3.5 million shares to the public on September 23, 1998. The investment banking firm of Goldman Sachs priced the new issue at US$18 per share, which was US$4 higher than the original pricing estimate. The stock traded at US$25.25 on its first sale and reached US$52 during the day. Within three weeks the stock price rose to US$80, and the Goldman Sachs analyst who follows Internet companies issued a research report stating that eBay would be US$150 per share in 12 months. Investors didn't wait 12 months to move the price up. By December, the stock had hit a high of US$234 but then dropped to US$175. In late 1998, eBay Inc. was worth US$4.77 billion on estimated revenues of US$43 million and estimated earnings of US$5 million.

There are many more examples of Internet companies that have had similar stock performance. Because Internet-based business is relatively new, valuing the worth of Internet companies is difficult. Only time will tell if the Internet is the place to make millions. Obviously, many investors are betting that it is.[4]

The Over-the-Counter Market

Unlike the organized exchanges, the **over-the-counter (OTC) market** is a network of dealers all over the country linked by computers, telephones, and Teletype machines. It has no central location. In the US many very small new companies are traded on the OTC market, many very large and well-known concerns trade there as well. Indeed, thousands of shares of the stocks of companies such as Apple Computer, Intel, and Microsoft are traded on the OTC market every day. Further, since most corporate bonds and all US securities are traded over the counter, the OTC market regularly accounts for the largest total dollar value of all of the secondary markets.

The Canadian Dealing Network (CDN) was replaced by the Canadian Unlisted Board (CUB) OTC System in late 2000. Most of the stocks quoted on the CDN became listed as Tier 3 of the Canadian Venture Exchange (CDNX) at that time and unquoted shares started trading under CUB. Almost all bonds and debentures and some shares are traded over-the-counter in Canada.

Practically every firm—whether in manufacturing, communications, finance, education, or health care—has one or more financial managers and/or financial analysts. Working under titles such as treasurer, controller, cash manager, or financial analyst, these financial managers and analysts prepare and interpret the financial reports required by organizations seeking to ensure that the resources under their control are optimally employed.

Financial management differs from accounting chiefly by its differential focus. By nature, accounting is based almost exclusively on summaries of past organizational transactions and prior account history. In contrast, financial management, despite its frequent reliance on many accounting statements, primarily looks forward. The question, "Where should we go from here?" could serve as the creed of most financial analysis. Should a new project be implemented? Should a new stock issue be sold? Should dividends be increased? How should the firm invest its excess cash? These and countless other forward-looking questions are ad-

dressed by legions of financial managers and analysts every business day.

The employment outlook for financial managers and analysts is rated by HRDC in *Job Futures 2000* as being good through 2004. This means qualifies individuals should find regular employment with good working conditions with relative ease. The 2001 Robert Half and Accountemps *Salary Guide* supports the outlook listing financial analysts as one of the specialties most in demand. The 2001 *Salary Guide* lists salaries for CFOs and treasurers in large firms from $143,500 to $230,000, while controllers in similar firms earn from $100,500 to $172,000.

Education and experience are major determinants in starting salaries. The Third Annual Business Graduate Salary Survey carried out by the Hay Group and reported in *Business Sense* found average salaries for new MBAs with relevant experience ranged from $51,800 to $65,500, while those without relevant work experience began at salaries of $47,200 to $55,70. Undergraduate business degrees led to average starting salaries of $38,000 to $46,000.[5]

Explore Your Career Options

Financial Management

Measuring Market Performance

Investors, especially professional money managers, want to know how well their investments are performing relative to the market as a whole. Financial managers also need to know how their companies' securities are performing when compared with their competitors'. Thus, performance measures—averages and indexes—are very important to many different people. They not only indicate the performance of a particular securities market but also provide a measure of the overall health of the economy.

Indexes and averages are used to measure stock prices. An *index* compares current stock prices with those in a specified base period, such as 1944, 1967, or 1977. An *average* is the average of certain stock prices. The averages used are usually not simple calculations, however. Some stock market averages (such as the TSE 300) are weighted averages, where the weights employed are the total market values of each stock in the index (in this case 300). The Dow Jones Industrial Average is a price-weighted average. Regardless of how constructed, all market averages of stocks move closely together over time.

Table 16.4

The Stocks in the TSE 35 Index

Abitibi-Consolidated	Canadian Pacific	Placer Dome
Barrick Gold	Canadian Tire Corp.	Research In Motion
Alcan	Dofasco Inc.	Royal Bank of Canada
Bombardier Inc.	Husky Energy	Shaw Communications
BCE Inc.	Magna International	Suncor Energy
Bank of Montreal	Inco Ltd.	TELUS
Bank of Nova Scotia	National Bank of Canada	TransAlta Corp.
Biovail	Nova Chemicals Corp.	Teck Corp.
Celestica	Noranda Inc.	TD Bank
CIBC	Nortel Networks Corp.	Talisman Energy
Canadian National Railway	Nexen	Thomson Corporation
	Petro-Canada	TransCanada Pipleines

Many Canadian investors follow the activity of the Toronto Stock Exchange (TSE) very closely to see whether the stock market has gone up or down. Table 16.4 lists the 35 companies that currently make up the TSE Index. Canadian investors can purchase shares listed on US exchanges as easily as those listed on the TSE. Thus, both the Dow Jones Industrial Average, an index of thirty shares listed on the NYSE, and the TSE 300 are widely reported in Canada and closely followed by Canadian investors.

The numbers listed in an index or average that tracks the performance of a stock market are expressed not as dollars but as a number on a fixed scale. If you know, for example, that the Dow Jones Industrial Average climbed from 860 in August 1982 to over 9,300 in December 1998, you can see clearly that the value of the Dow Jones Average increased more than 10 times in this 16-year period, making it one of the highest rate of return periods in the history of the stock market.

The TSE 300 Composite Index is maintained by a seven-member committee representing Standard and Poor's and the Toronto Stock Exchange. The index comprises over 70 percent of the market capitalization for Canadian-based TSE-listed companies. The size of the TSE 300 and its broad economic sector coverage has made it the most widely followed indicator of Canadian market activity since its inception on January 1, 1977.[6]

The TSE is not linked to the Dow Jones Industrial Average but because of the many interrelationships between Canada and the US, many of the same events affect both markets. Often the direction and even the magnitude of the changes in the two indexes are similar. With Canadian and US interest and inflation rates at their lowest levels in decades, many people think that as long as corporate earnings continue to rise, stock prices will continue to climb. If inflation rises and interest rates go up, and if corporate earnings slow down or decline, the market will most likely be in for a tumble.

The growth of the TSE 300 during the 1980s and 1990s was not quite as strong as that in the US. The TSE 300 more than tripled from 2,321 on May 31, 1984, to 7,665 on April 30, 1998, but had slid to 6,485.9 by the end of that year.[7]

A period of large increases in stock prices is known as a *bull market*, with the bull symbolizing an aggressive charging market and rising stock prices. The bull market of the 1990s was one of the strongest on record, with the Dow Jones rising from 3,300 in April 1992 to over 11,000 in 1999. The TSE 300 during the same period rose from 3,355.5 to 8,413.8 at the end of 1999, and continued on to 11,247.9 on August 31, 2000.[8]

A declining market is known as a *bear market*, with the bear symbolizing sluggish, retreating activity. When stock market prices decline very rapidly, the market is said to crash. The greatest of all crashes occurred on October 19, 1987, when the Dow Jones lost over 508 points, or 23 percent of its value, on a single trading day. The malaise also affected the TSE, which fell 883 points during October of 1987, also a decline of about 23 percent. Less than one year later, however, the US market had recovered all of this loss and more. The TSE 300, on the other hand, did not regain its pre-crash level until July of 1989.

On September 11, 2001, the TSE 300 opened at its high for the day of 7,237.8, and the Dow Jones was at 9,605.5. On September 13, the first day of trading after the terrorist attacks, the TSE 300 was down almost 19 percent to 7102.3. The NYSE did not reopen until September 17 and closed that day down about 7 percent at 8920.7. The indexes continued to fall until September 21. Again the markets recovered, with the Dow Jones making up the loss by October 9 and the TSE 300 by November 13. This proves, yet again, as happened following the Great Crash of October 29, 1929, that although the stock market—and indeed all industry—may stumble, it will eventually return to its long-term pattern of growth.[9]

In order for investors to make sound financial decisions, it is important that they stay in touch with the business news, markets, and indexes. *Profit Magazine, Money Magazine*, and the *Globe and Mail Report on Business Magazine* provide Canadian coverage. *Business Week, Fortune,* and *Money* offer similar information for the US. Many Internet sites, including ProfitMagazine.com, Globeinvestor, and the CNN Finanial News Network, offer this information as well. Many sites such as Globeinvestor and BigCharts.com also offer searchable databases of information by topic, company, and keyword. However investors choose to receive and review business news, doing so is a necessity in today's market.

Globeinvestor
www.globeinvestor.com/

BigCharts.com
www.bigcharts.com/

The New S&P/TSE Composite Index

The Toronto Stock Exchange (TSE) and index manager Standard & Poor's (S&P) on January 17, 2002, announced the first major overhaul of the TSE 300 Composite Index since its introduction in 1977. The index will in the future be called the S&P/TSE Composite Index. Table 16.5 lists the major indices created for the TSE.

Key among the changes announced is a new set of criteria for inclusion and maintenance of the index. There will no longer be a requirement that the index include exactly 300 constituents. The chief determinants of inclusion will be the size and liquidity of the company. Size measurements will be based on two criteria: A company must represent a minimum weight of 0.5 percent of the index, and it must have a minimum trade weighted average price of $1 per share over the past quarter as well as a closing price greater than or equal to $1 at the previous month end.

Three liquidity requirements will have to be met for inclusion:

- Trading volume, value, and transactions of a candidate company for the 12 months immediately preceding its consideration for inclusion in the index must be at least 0.025 percent of the sum of all eligible companies' trading volume, value, or number of transactions, as determined by trading on the TSE.

Table 16.5

*The Major Indices
Created for the TSE*

| TSE 300 Composite Index |
| TSE 300 Capped Composite Index |
| TSE 200 Index |
| TSE 100 Index |
| S&P/TSE 60 Index |
| S&P/TSE 60 Capped Index |
| S&P/TSE Canadian SmallCap Index |
| S&P/TSE Canadian MidCap Index |
| Toronto 35 Index |

- A company must have no more than 25 nontrading days over the past 12 full calendar months.
- The float turnover, calculated by dividing the float shares into the 12-month volume traded, must be equal to 0.25 or greater.[10]

A summary of rules for the inclusion in the index is available at the web sites of both the TSE and S&P.

In order to reduce the impact on the firms being dropped from the index, the changes will be phased in beginning May 1, 2002.

Review Your Understanding

Define current assets and describe some common methods of managing them.

Current assets are short-term resources such as cash, investments, accounts receivable, and inventory, which can be converted to cash within a year. Financial managers focus on minimizing the amount of cash kept on hand and increasing the speed of collections through lockboxes and electronic funds transfer and investing in marketable securities. Marketable securities include Treasury bills, commercial paper, and money market funds. Managing accounts receivable requires judging customer creditworthiness and creating credit terms that encourage prompt payment. Inventory management focuses on determining optimum inventory levels that minimize the cost of storing and ordering inventory without sacrificing too many lost sales due to stockouts.

Identify some sources of short-term financing (current liabilities).

Current liabilities are short-term debt obligations that must be repaid within one year, such as accounts payable, taxes payable, and notes (loans) payable. Trade credit is extended by suppliers for the purchase of their goods and services. A line of credit is an arrangement by which a bank agrees to lend a specified amount of money to a business whenever the business needs it. Secured loans are backed by collateral; unsecured loans are backed only by the borrower's good reputation.

Summarize the importance of long-term assets and capital budgeting.

Long-term, or fixed, assets are expected to last for many years, such as production facilities (plants), offices, and equipment. Businesses need modern, up-to-date equipment to succeed in today's competitive environment. Capital budgeting is the process of analyzing company needs and selecting the assets that will maximize its value; a capital budget is the amount of money budgeted for the purchase of fixed assets. Every investment in fixed assets carries some risk.

Specify how companies finance their operations and manage fixed assets with long-term liabilities, particularly bonds.

Two common choices for financing are equity financing (attracting new owners) and debt financing (taking on long-term liabilities). Long-term liabilities are debts that will be repaid over a number of years, such as long-term bank loans and bond issues. A bond is a long-term debt security that an organization sells to raise money. The bond indenture specifies the provisions of the bond contract—maturity date, coupon rate, repayment methods, and others.

Discuss how corporations can use equity financing by issuing stock through an investment banker.

Owners' equity represents what owners have contributed to the company and includes common shares, preferred shares, and retained earnings (profits that have been reinvested in the assets of the firm).

To finance operations, companies can issue new common and preferred shares through an investment banker that sells shares and bonds for corporations.

Describe the various securities markets in North America.

Securities markets provide the mechanism for buying and selling stocks and bonds. Primary markets allow companies to raise capital by selling new stock directly to investors through investment bankers. Secondary markets allow the buyers of previously issued shares of stock to sell them to other owners. The major Canadian secondary market is the Toronto Stock Exchange. The major US secondary markets are the New York Stock Exchange, the American Stock Exchange, and the over-the-counter market. Investors measure stock market performance by watching stock market averages and indexes such as the Dow Jones Industrial Average, the Standard and Poor's (S&P) Composite Index, and the TSE 300.

Critique the short-term asset and liabilities position of a small manufacturer and recommend corrective action.

Using the information presented in this chapter, you should be able to "Solve the Dilemma" presented by the current bleak working capital situation of Glasspray Corporation.

Learn the Terms

bonds 413

capital budgeting 410

commercial paper 405

current assets 404

current liabilities 404

Eurodollar market 406

factor 409

floating-rate bonds 415

investment banking 417

junk bonds 416

line of credit 408

lockbox 405

long-term (fixed) assets 410

long-term liabilities 413

marketable securities 405

organized exchanges 419

over-the-counter (OTC) market 420

payout ratio 416

primary market 418

prime rate 409

retained earnings 416

secondary markets 418

secured bonds 414

secured loans 409

securities markets 418

serial bonds 415

trade credit 408

transaction balances 405

Treasury bills (T-bills) 405

unsecured bonds 414

unsecured loans 409

working capital management 404

Check Your Progress

1. Define working capital management.
2. How can a company speed up cash flow? Why should it?
3. Describe the various types of marketable securities.
4. What does it mean to have a line of credit at a bank?
5. What are fixed assets? Why is assessing risk important in capital budgeting?
6. How can a company finance fixed assets?
7. What is a bond and what do companies do with them?
8. How can companies use equity to finance their operations and long-term growth?
9. What are the functions of securities markets?
10. Define bull and bear markets.

Get Involved

1. Using your local newspaper or the *National Post,* find the current rates of interest on the following marketable securities. If you were a financial manager for a large corporation, which would you invest extra cash in? Which would you invest in if you worked for a small business?
   a. Three-month T-bills
   b. Six-month T-bills
   c. Guaranteed investment certificates
   d. Commercial paper
   e. Eurodollar deposits
   f. Money market deposits
2. Select five of the stocks from Table 16.4. Look up their earnings, dividends, and prices for the past five years. What kind of picture is presented by this information? Which stocks would you like to have owned over this past period? Do you think the next five years will present a similar picture?

Build Your Skills

Choosing among Projects

Background: As the senior executive in charge of exploration for High Octane Oil Co., you are constantly looking for projects that will add to the company's profitability—without increasing the company's risk. High Octane Oil is an international oil company with operations in Latin America, the Middle East, Canada, the US, and Mexico. The company is one of the world's leading experts in deep-water exploration and drilling. High Octane currently produces 50 percent of its oil in the US, 25 percent in the Middle East, 5 percent in Canada, 10 percent in Latin America, and 10 percent in Mexico. You are considering six projects from around the world.

Project 1—Your deep-water drilling platform in the Gulf of Mexico is producing at maximum capacity from the Valdez oil field, and High Octane's geological engineers think there is a high probability that there is oil in the Sanchez field, which is adjacent to Valdez. They recommend drilling a new series of wells. Once commercial quantities of oil have been discovered, it will take two more years to build the collection platform and pipelines. It will be four years before the discovered oil gets to the refineries.

Project 2—The Brazilian government has invited you to drill on some unexplored tracts in the middle of the central jungle region. There are roads to within 50 miles of the tract and British Petroleum has found oil 800 kilometres away from this tract. It would take about three years to develop this property and several more years to build pipelines and pumping stations to carry the oil to the refineries. The Brazilian government wants 20 percent of all production as its fee for giving High Octane Oil Co. the drilling rights or a $500 million up-front fee and 5 percent of the output.

Project 3—Your fields in Saudi Arabia have been producing oil for 50 years. Several wells are old, and the pressure has diminished. Your engineers are sure that if you were to initiate high-pressure secondary recovery procedures, you would increase the output of these existing wells by 20 percent. High-pressure recovery methods pump water at high pressure into the underground limestone formations to enhance the movement of petroleum toward the surface.

Project 4—Your largest oil fields in Alaska have been producing from only 50 percent of the known deposits. Your geological engineers estimate that you could open up 10 percent of the remaining fields every two years and offset your current declining production from existing wells. The pipeline capacity is available and, while you can only drill during six months of the year, the fields could be producing oil in three years.

Project 5—Some of High Octane's west Texas oil fields produce in shallow stripper wells of 600- to 1,200-metre depths. Stripper wells produce anywhere from 10 to 2,000 barrels per day and can last for six months or 40 years. Generally, once you find a shallow deposit, there is an 80 percent chance that offset wells will find more oil. Because these wells are shallow, they can be drilled quickly at a low cost. High Octane's engineers estimate that in your largest tract, which is closest to the company's Houston refinery, you could increase production by 30 percent for the next 10 years by increasing the density of the wells per square kilometre.

Project 6—The government of a republic in the former Soviet Union has invited you to drill for oil in Siberia. Russian geologists think that this oil field might be the largest in the world, but there have been no wells drilled and no infrastructure exists to carry oil if it should be found. The republic has no money to help you build the infrastructure but if you find oil, it will let you keep the first five years' production before taking its 25 percent share. Knowing that oil fields do not start producing at full capacity for many years after initial production, your engineers are not sure that your portion the first five years of production will pay for the infrastructure they must build to get the oil to market. The republic also has been known to have a rather unstable government, and the last international oil company that began this project left the country when a new government demanded a higher than originally agreed-upon percentage of the expected output. If this field is in fact the largest in the world, High Octane's supply of oil would be insured well into the twenty-first century.

Task:

1. Working in groups, rank the six projects from lowest risk to highest risk.

2. Given the information provided, do the best you can to rank the projects from lowest cost to highest cost.

3. What political considerations might affect your project choice?

4. If you could choose one project, which would it be and why?

5. If you could choose three projects, which ones would you choose? In making this decision, consider which projects might be highly correlated to High Octane Oil's existing production and which ones might diversify the company's production on a geographical basis.

The Canadian Youth Business Foundation

The video introduces seven young entrepreneurs from across Canada. Although each is from a different region and has a different business idea, they shared the need for initial financing. Like most young entrepreneurs, they found the commercial lenders unwilling to provide the needed capital and turned to the Canadian Youth Business Foundation (CYBF) for a loan to start their businesses.

In a manner similar to the SEED Loan Fund introduced in Chapter 1, the CYBF provides financing for new small businesses for a clearly defined group of borrowers who are unlikely to obtain financing from traditional commercial sources. Also like the SEED Loan Fund, the CYBF becomes more involved with their clients than do commercial lenders, providing mentoring and guidance to help ensure business success. As a result, the businesses supported by the CYBF have a success rate of 80 percent, much higher than the norm. Additional information about the CYBF is available at www.cybf.ca.

Questions

1. What are the stated criteria for funding by the CYBF?

2. The entrepreneurs interviewed point out several advantages and disadvantages of self-employment. What are they?

3. Why might commercial lenders be willing to lend to these entrepreneurs after they have had financing from the CYBF, when they would not do so initially?

Source: *Venture*, show number 747, "Canadian Youth Business Foundation," April 11, 2000, running time 7:04.

Remember to check out our Online Learning Centre at **www.mcgrawhill.ca/college/ferrell.**

Cyberzone

Financing the Enterprise

The Internet contains a vast amount of information useful in the areas of finance, banking, and the economy. On the Yahoo Business and Economy site, you can find business libraries as well as information on hundreds of thousands of companies, economic indicators, economics, finance and investment, the international economy, and many other areas of value. It is easy to research a particular company, an entire industry, or even the economy. Many financial decision makers rely, at least partially, on the Internet as an important tool for gathering and sharing information. Much of the information is free and is provided by the Canadian federal and provincial governments, the US government, businesses, organizations, and trade and professional associations in both Canada and the US.

The Bank of Canada is responsible for regulation of the banking system and the implementation of monetary policy for Canada. The Bank produces a number of general publications and research papers available in print and on the Bank's web site. General publications include:

- *The Annual Report*, published every January, reviews the past year's activities and indicates what the Bank sees as significant for the future.

- *The Monetary Policy Report*, published in May and November with updates in February and August, provides a detailed summary of the Bank's policies and strategies, and a look at the current economic conditions and the outlook for inflation.

- *The Bank of Canada Review*, published quarterly, combines economic commentary with feature articles and statistics.

The US Federal Reserve Board is responsible for the regulation of the banking system and the implementation of monetary policy for the United States. The Federal Reserve System includes 12 regional Federal Reserve banks, each with its own research staff. Each Federal Reserve Bank publishes a monthly economic report for its region called the "beige book." Corporations, bankers, and financial analysts are all interested in the economic strength of each of the 12 regions, and they use the information provided in the beige book to make decisions about their businesses. Each Federal Reserve Bank has its own web site that can be reached directly or through the Federal Reserve Board of Governors web site.

We also know that the banking industry and their customers are increasingly using the Internet. Canadian banks provide web-based banking, allowing their clients to transfer funds between accounts and in some cases between institutions, pay bills, apply for and receive loans deposited to their accounts, and effectively carry out almost all banking needs, except the receipt of cash, on the Internet. Banks through their affiliates such as BMO InvestorLine and TD Waterhouse offer online trading of mutual funds, equities, options, and fixed income securities, and provide investor information such as stock quotes and market news.

The corporate and investing communities have a multitude of uses for the financial and economic data available on the Internet. Corporations, as well as individual investors, may need such data to make decisions, forecast expected demand and supply for the next quarter and beyond, and measure the strength of the economy. There are many government-operated web sites in both Canada and the US that provide information on the economy and business matters, including Human Resource Development Canada and Industry Canada. The federal government's Business Gateway site provides extensive information with links to other useful sites. The US Commerce Department provides information on the US economy, which is also important for consideration by Canadian investors.

In addition to information on the economy, corporations and investors need financial data from companies. Companies want to see the financial statements of their competitors, and investors want to be able to compare the financial statements of all the publicly traded companies in the same industry in order to determine which company or companies might make good investments. The Canadian Securities Administrators provide easy access to public securities filings through the System for Electronic Document Analysis and Retrieval (SEDAR). The web site provides interim financial reports, annual reports, company profiles, press releases, and other required filings of interest and importance to shareholders for both listed companies and mutual funds. The US Securities and Exchange Commission requires all companies to file quarterly financial statements covering the balance sheet, the income statement, and the statement of cash flows. Additionally an annual statement called the 10K is required, as well as reports on change in ownership, bankruptcy, and other matters of significance.

Online investing is another exciting use of the Internet in the financial area. Canadians are increasingly using the Internet for stock trading. Forrester Research reported that online brokerage accounts totalled $1.5 million in 1996, rose to $5.4 million by 1999, and are forecasted to reach $20.4 million in 2003. Registration for online trading among Canadians with an account at a discount broker increased from 47 percent to 63 percent in 2001.[1] Discount brokerage firms, such as Charles Schwab, offer traditional methods of buying and selling stock but charge lower fees to trade on the Internet. Firms that specialize in Internet trading, such as E*Trade, charge fees as low as $8 per trade. Low-cost Internet trading has given investors many more options than they previously had. Some industry analysts estimate that large retail brokers like Merrill Lynch eventually will be forced to offer their clients Internet trading at reduced cost. However, traditional retail brokerage firms have an edge over Internet brokers in providing service. Firms such as Morgan Stanley Dean Witter and Paine Weber provide research to their customers and advise them on what to buy and sell. Internet traders must rely on their own research to make decisions.

Technology has brought an amazing amount of financial information to our fingertips, and it is clear that the future will bring even more. The transformation to electronic commerce, banking, and stock trading has begun. The major benefits of the Internet include cost reduction to the companies providing service, convenience and time savings for the user, and improvements in the speed and amount of information that is available. However, problems may occur with increased use of the Internet. Most importantly, users must determine the reliability and usefulness of the information they find.

Appendix A

The Business Plan

A key element of business success is a *business plan,* a written statement of the rationale for the enterprise and a step-by-step explanation of how it will achieve its goals. A business plan is a blueprint, or written document, that structures all of a firm's activities, including the implementation and control of those activities. It should explain the purpose of the company, evaluate its competition, estimate income and expenses, and indicate a strategy for acquiring sufficient funds to keep the firm going. It should also be formally prepared and contain a detailed statement of how the firm will carry out its strategy. However, a business plan should act as a reference guide, not a shackle that limits the firm's flexibility and decision making.

Developing a business plan is important for both brand new and existing businesses. For a start-up firm, the business plan provides a street map to help it fulfill the entrepreneur's vision. For existing businesses, it is an excellent way for a company to renew its commitment to existing goals and evaluate their merits. Regardless of whether the business plan is for a new or already-existing firm, it should include an executive summary, situation analysis, SWOT (strengths, weaknesses, opportunities, and threats) analysis, business resources, business strategy, financial projections and budgets, and controls and evaluation (Table A.1).

Table A.1

The Components of a Business Plan

I. Executive Summary

II. Situation Analysis

   A. Competitive forces

   B. Economic forces

   C. Legal and regulatory forces

   D. Technological forces

   E. Sociocultural forces

III. SWOT Analysis

   A. Strengths

   B. Weaknesses

   C. Opportunities

   D. Threats

IV. Business Resources

   A. Financial

   B. Human

   C. Experience and expertise

V. Business Strategy

   A. Objectives

   B. Key strategy for using capabilities and resources

VI. Financial Projections and Budgets

VII. Controls and Evaluation

   A. Performance standards and financial controls

   B. Monitoring procedures

   C. Performance analysis

EXECUTIVE SUMMARY

The executive summary is simply a brief synopsis of the overall business plan. It generally consists of an introduction, highlights of the major aspects of the plan, and implementation considerations. It does not provide detailed information. Rather, the summary should be short and interesting, and it should give the reader an idea of what is contained in the business plan. It is essentially an overview of the plan so that readers can quickly identify the key issues or concerns related to their role in the planning process.

SITUATION ANALYSIS

The situation analysis examines the difference between the business's current performance and past-stated objectives. In a brand-new firm, it assesses where the entrepreneur is now in his or her development. The situation analysis may also summarize how the current business situation came to be, using data obtained from both the firm's external and internal environment. Depending on the situation, details on the composition of the target market, current marketing objectives and strategies, business trends, and sales and profit history may also be included. The situation analysis enables the entrepreneur either to evaluate the business's current mission or, in instances where a clear vision is nonexistent, to facilitate the articulation of its mission. This situation analysis should include a careful evaluation of the firm's current objectives and performance, as well as specify how performance is to be measured.

A good situation analysis provides input for the next step in the business plan, the SWOT analysis. It is the situation analysis that identifies the issues, concerns, or variables analyzed in the SWOT analysis.

SWOT ANALYSIS

The SWOT (strengths, weaknesses, opportunities, and threats) analysis section of the business plan identifies and articulates all the organization's competitive advantages/strengths as well as its weaknesses in order to develop strategies for capitalizing on the strengths and minimizing the weaknesses. Obviously, if the business is to be successful, its strengths should outweigh its weaknesses. A SWOT analysis also includes a clear assessment of existing and future opportunities and discusses ways of exploiting them. Finally, it examines the threats facing the firm and ranks them in order of their impact on the business.

In analyzing strengths and weaknesses, opportunities and threats, the business plan must address both internal and external elements. Internally, the firm must look at the strengths and weaknesses of its major functional areas—management, operations, finance, and marketing; it must also look at the opportunities and threats related to specific elements in the external environment of the business—the economic, political, legal and regulatory, competitive, technological, and social and cultural factors. The business plan should also include predictions about the future directions of those forces and their possible impact on the implementation of the business plan. Because of the dynamic nature of these factors, managers should periodically review and modify this section of the plan to allow for changes.

The SWOT analysis has gained widespread acceptance because it provides a simple framework for evaluating a company's strategic position. When analyzing the strengths and weaknesses in terms of specific target markets, both quantitative and qualitative variables identified in the situation analysis should be considered. The firm must focus on those strengths and opportunities that will yield competitive advantage as well as those threats and weaknesses that will erode it. Thus, it is a good idea for the planner to rank the factors under each category according to their impact on the execution of the businesses strategy.

Strengths and Weaknesses

Strengths and weaknesses exist inside the firm or in key relationships between the firm and its suppliers, resellers, and customers. Strengths include any competitive advantage or other distinctive competencies (things that the firm does better than any others) that a company can employ in the marketplace. Strengths exist relative to competitors, such as cheaper access to capital, good relations with vendors and customers, a unique product, or an advantageous location. Thus, strengths specified in a firm's business plan will be specific to that firm and not shared by its competitors. If all of a business's competitors have low production costs, then low cost is not a strength for that business, unless its costs are even lower. A company's distinctive competency can play a key role in positioning it and its products in the minds of customers and so forms a unique strength.

Weaknesses are constraints that limit certain options in the business strategy. A poor image of the firm's products in the minds of consumers is an example of a weakness. It is also true that some weaknesses are less important than others. For example, having higher costs than competitors may not be an issue if cost is not the basis for competition in the industry. The planner must therefore determine which weaknesses have the greatest effect on the firm's competitive position and thus require immediate attention.

In developing a business strategy, a business needs to both capitalize on its skills and talents and ensure that its strategies emphasize these. In order to identify strengths and weaknesses, it is important to have data about current market/product positions, including past performance and expected performance in the next planning period, which should be expressed in the situation analysis.

Opportunities and Threats

The second part of the SWOT analysis addresses external opportunities and threats present in the firm's operating environment. These opportunities and threats exist largely independent of the firm and its operations.

An opportunity is a favourable set of conditions, which limit barriers or provide rewards, that the firm can exploit with a high probability of success. Examples of opportunities include an unmet product need (assuming the firm has the capability to meet that need); a new, lower-cost source of a vital raw material; new technology; or new legislation that opens up a product market or restricts competitors' access to a market. This section of the business plan should place the most attractive opportunities having the greatest potential for success at the head of the list, while those that are less attractive or have a smaller potential for success should receive less emphasis.

Threats relate to barriers or conditions that may prevent the organization from achieving its objectives, ultimately leading to a loss of competitive advantage. Examples include the direct actions of competitors (such as the introduction of a new product or product innovation), adverse governmental legislation, loss of access to cheap capital or other resources, or an economic downturn. This phase of the business plan orders priorities for action in light of the strengths and weaknesses of the firm in dealing with a particular set of external circumstances.

The analysis of the threats and opportunities cannot be completed without the previously mentioned assessment of legal, political, regulatory, technological, competitive, social, and economic factors that will affect the firm's internal strengths and weaknesses. It is also necessary to make predictions about the future. While environmental factors may threaten a firm's ability to achieve its objectives, they may also provide opportunities.

BUSINESS RESOURCES

A company's human and financial resources, as well as its experiences and expertise, are major considerations in developing a business plan. The business plan should therefore both outline the human, financial, and physical resources available for accomplishing goals and describe resource constraints that may affect implementation of the plan. This section also describes any distinctive competencies that may give the firm an edge, and it takes into account strengths and weaknesses that may influence the firm's ability to achieve implementation.

Financial resources include all funds available to carry out the plan. It is necessary to detail what funds the firm has at hand and what can be accessed through other sources, such as loans, lines of credit, or additional equity arrangements (such as a venture partner or a public stock offering). Human resources refer to the people that the business has ready to commit to the execution of the plan as well as the quality of that labour force. Physical resources include such things as property, facilities, and equipment required to execute the strategy. This category includes the raw materials available as well as retail outlets and office space. These financial, human, and physical resources comprise the tangible aspects of the firm's resources.

Experience and expertise are intangible aspects, but they are just as crucial to success as the tangible ones. Experience refers to any competence the firm may have developed over time as a result of carrying out activities related to future ones envisioned in the plan. For instance, the firm may have experience marketing home electronics, which may be transferable to marketing computers for home use. Or, the firm may just be further along on the experience curve than its competitors. Expertise is related to experience and includes any proprietary knowledge that the firm may possess, such as patents. Other areas of expertise that represent vital resources include superior knowledge of the market and industry, management wisdom, and competence or scientific knowledge embodied in research and development personnel.

BUSINESS STRATEGY

This section of the business plan spells out the business's objectives and its strategy for achieving them.

Objectives

After taking an inventory of the business's resources and conducting a SWOT analysis, the planner should develop concrete, specific objectives. For example, the plan might specify the firm's objective to become the leader, in terms of market share or sales, in a particular industry, segment, or niche. Or the objective might be to achieve a high return on investment and thus focus on profitability. While a company can have multiple objectives, each should be stated explicitly, in quantifiable terms if possible. For instance, an objective of being the leader in sales should state the level of sales desired and in what time period. A profitability objective should state what return on investment is targeted and within what time period. These objectives will therefore serve as goals to be achieved by the firm and as yardsticks against which to measure its progress. Because most firms have a number of objectives, they should be ranked in order of importance.

Strategy

Once the objectives have been expressed, the business plan should spell out the strategy (or strategies) the firm will use to achieve those objectives. The strategies should be clearly stated in order to guide development of the specific programs and activities that will be used to execute them. For example, if the firm's primary objective is to accumulate market share, it may adopt the strategy of being the lowest-cost producer. Therefore, the implications of being the lowest-cost producer should be specifically stated in the plan. If the major objective is to achieve high returns on investment, the chosen strategy may be a focus strategy, combining a low-cost orientation with some focus on a particular market niche. This strategy would then have to identify the targeted niche, the desired cost levels, and so on, in order to allow formulation of programs and their implementation.

FINANCIAL PROJECTIONS AND BUDGETS

Financial projections and budgets delineate costs and estimates of sales and revenues. This section outlines the returns expected from implementing the business plan. It should estimate the costs of implementing the plan and weigh those costs against the expected revenues. It should also include a budget to allocate resources in order to achieve business objectives. These financial projections and budgets should be sufficiently detailed to identify the source and projected use of funds, broken down according to each activity in the plan. For instance, if employees need additional training, what will it cost and where will the funds come from? How much will be used in advertising? In reality, budgetary considerations play a key role in the identification of alternative strategies, as well as in the development of plans for those strategies that are identified as most promising.

The financial realities of the organization must be monitored at all times. For example, proposing to expand into new geographic areas or to alter products without specifying the extent and source of the financial resources needed to do so is a waste of time, energy, and opportunity. Even if the funds are available, the expansion must be a "good value" and provide an acceptable return on investment to be part of the final plan.

CONTROLS AND EVALUATION

This section of the business plan details how the results of the plan will be calculated. It should specify what measures of performance will be used to assess the current achievements and identify internal performance data and external-environmental relationships for diagnosis and evaluation. Next, a schedule should be developed for comparing and monitoring the results achieved with the objectives set forth in the business plan. Finally, the plan may offer guidelines outlining who is responsible for monitoring the program and taking remedial action.

In order for controls to be implemented, the firm must utilize information from the SWOT analysis, look ahead, and determine what will affect the implementation of the business plan during the upcoming planning period. This should create the database for monitoring and evaluating performance and taking corrective action.

I. EXECUTIVE SUMMARY
The executive summary is a synopsis of the overall business plan. It is best written after the entire business plan has been completed.

_____

_____

_____

_____

_____

II. SITUATION ANALYSIS
The situation analysis examines the difference between the business's current performance and past-stated objectives.

A. Competitive Forces
Who are our major competitors as of today? What are their strengths and weaknesses?

_____

_____

_____

Who are likely to be our major competitors in the future?

_____

_____

_____

(Repeat analysis to examine economic, political, legal and regulatory, technological, and sociocultural forces.)

III. SWOT ANALYSIS
The SWOT analysis identifies and describes the organization's strengths and weaknesses and the opportunities and threats it faces in order to develop strategies for capitalizing on the strengths and opportunities and minimizing the weaknesses and threats.

A. Strengths
Strength 1: _____

How does this strength affect the operations of the company?

_____

_____

_____

How does this strength assist the company in meeting its objectives?

_____

_____

_____

(Repeat this process for all of the strengths that can be identified.)

B. Weaknesses

Weakness 1: _____

How does this weakness affect the operations of the company?

_____

_____

_____

How does this weakness reduce the company's ability to meet its objectives?

_____

_____

_____

(Repeat this process for all of the weaknesses that can be identified.)

C. Opportunities

Opportunity 1: _____

How is this opportunity related to current or future company operations?

_____

_____

_____

What actions must the company take in order to take advantage of this opportunity?

_____

_____

_____

(Repeat this process for all of the opportunities that can be identified.)

D. Threats

Threat 1: _____

How is this threat related to current or future company operations?

_____

_____

_____

What actions must the company take to reduce or eliminate this threat?

_____

_____

_____

(Repeat this process for all of the threats that can be identified.)

IV. BUSINESS RESOURCES

This section outlines the human, financial, and physical resources available for accomplishing goals and describes resource constraints that may affect implementation.

A. Financial Resources

What financial resources are available for accomplishing company goals?

_____

_____

_____

B. Human Resources
Does the company have the personnel needed to implement the goals?

_____

_____

_____

C. Experience and Expertise
Do employees have the experience and expertise needed to successfully achieve stated goals? Will employees require additional training? How will this training be funded?

_____

_____

_____

V. BUSINESS STRATEGY
This section spells out the business's objectives and its strategy for achieving them.

A. Objectives
Objective 1: _____
What is the specific and measurable outcome and time frame for completing this objective?

_____

_____

How does this objective take advantage of a strength or opportunity?

_____

_____

(Repeat this process for all of the objectives specified.)

B. Strategy for Using Capabilities and Resources
How can the company's strengths be matched to its opportunities to create capabilities?

_____

_____

How can the company convert its weaknesses into strengths?

_____

_____

How can the company convert its threats into opportunities?

_____

_____

VI. FINANCIAL PROJECTIONS AND BUDGETS
Financial projections and budgets delineate costs and estimates of sales and revenues, so this section outlines the returns expected through implementation of the plan and weighs the costs incurred against the expected revenues.

Attach financial projections to this worksheet and develop alternative scenarios.

_____
_____
_____
_____
_____
_____

VII. CONTROLS AND EVALUATION
This section details how the outcomes of the plan will be monitored and measured.

A. Performance Standards and Financial Controls

Activity 1/Budget: _____

Performance Standard: _____

Possible Corrective Action: _____

(Repeat this process for all of the performance measures.)

B. Monitoring Procedures
How will all of the activities be monitored in order to ensure success?

_____
_____
_____

What will be the schedule of the monitoring of activities (i.e., will the monitoring be done weekly, monthly, quarterly, etc.?)?

_____
_____
_____

C. Performance Analysis
Currently, how is the company performing in terms of sales volume, market share, and profitability?

_____
_____
_____

How does the company's current performance compare to other firms in the industry?

_____
_____
_____

If the company's performance is declining, are its objectives inconsistent with changes in the external environment?

_____
_____
_____

Is the performance of the industry as a whole improving?

_____
_____
_____

Appendix B

Personal Career Plan

The tools and techniques used in creating a business plan are just as useful in designing a plan to help sell yourself to potential employers. The outline in this appendix is designed to assist you in writing a personalized plan that will help you achieve your career goals. While this outline follows the same general format found in Appendix A, it has been adapted to be more relevant to career planning. Answering the questions presented in this outline will enable you to:

1. Organize and structure the data and information you collect about job prospects, the overall job market, and your competition.

2. Use this information to better understand your own personal strengths and weaknesses, as well as recognize the opportunities and threats that exist in your career development.

3. Develop goals and objectives that will capitalize on your strengths.

4. Develop a personalized strategy that will give you a competitive advantage.

5. Outline a plan for implementing your personalized strategy.

As you work through the following outline, it is very important that you be honest with yourself. If you do not possess a strength in a given area, it is important to recognize that fact. Similarly, do not overlook your weaknesses. The viability of your SWOT analysis and your strategy depend on how well you have identified all of the relevant issues in an honest manner.

I. Summary
If you choose to write a summary, do so after you have written the entire plan. It should provide a brief overview of the strategy for your career. State your career objectives and what means you will use to achieve those objectives.

II. Situation Analysis
A. The External Environment
1. Competition
   a) Who are your major competitors? What are their characteristics (number and growth in the number of graduates, skills, target employers)? Competitors to consider include peers at the same university or college or in the same degree field, peers at different

universities or colleges or in different degree fields, and graduates of trade, technical, or community colleges.

b)   What are the key strengths and weaknesses of the total pool of potential employees (or recent university or college graduates)?

c)   What are other university and college graduates doing in terms of developing skills, networking, showing a willingness to relocate, and promoting themselves to potential employers?

d)   What are the current trends in terms of work experience versus getting an advanced degree?

e)   Is your competitive set likely to change in the future? If so, how? Who are these new competitors likely to be?

2.   **Economic conditions**

a)   What are the general economic conditions of the country, region, province, and local area in which you live or in which you want to relocate?

b)   Overall, are potential employers optimistic or pessimistic about the economy?

c)   What is the overall outlook for major job/career categories? Where do potential employers seem to be placing their recruitment and hiring emphasis?

d)   What is the trend in terms of starting salaries for major job/career categories?

3.   **Political trends**

a)   Have recent elections changed the political landscape so that certain industries or companies are now more or less attractive as potential employers?

4.   **Legal and regulatory factors**

a)   What changes in international, federal, provincial, or local laws and regulations are being proposed that would affect your job/career prospects?

b)   Have recent court decisions made it easier or harder for you to find employment?

c)   Have global trade agreements changed in any way that makes certain industries or companies more or less attractive as potential employers?

5.   **Changes in technology**

a)   What impact has changing technology had on potential employers in terms of their need for employees?

b)   What technological changes will affect the way you will have to work and compete for employment in the future?

c)   What technological changes will affect the way you market your skills and abilities to potential employers?

d)   How do technological advances threaten to make your skills and abilities obsolete?

6.   **Cultural trends**

a)   How are society's demographics and values changing? What effect will these changes have on your:

(1)   Skills and abilities:

(2)   Career/lifestyle choices:

(3)   Ability to market yourself:

    (4)   Willingness to relocate:

    (5)   Required minimum salary:

   b) What problems or opportunities are being created by changes in the cultural diversity of the labour pool and the requirements of potential employers?

   c) What is the general attitude of society regarding the particular skills, abilities, and talents that you possess and the career/lifestyle choices that you have made?

B. **The Employer Environment**

1. **Who are your potential employers?**

   a) Identifying characteristics: industry, products, size, growth, profitability, hiring practices, union/nonunion, employee needs, etc.

   b) Geographic characteristics: home office, local offices, global sites, expansion, etc.

   c) Organizational culture: mission statement, values, priorities, employee training, etc.

   d) In each organization, who is responsible for recruiting and selecting new employees?

2. **What do your potential employers look for in new employees?**

   a) What are the basic or specific skills and abilities that employers are looking for in new employees?

   b) What are the basic or specific needs that are fulfilled by the skills and abilities that you *currently* possess and that other potential employees currently possess?

   c) How well do your skills and abilities (and those of your competitors) currently meet the needs of potential employers?

   d) How are the needs of potential employers expected to change in the future?

3. **What are the recent hiring practices of your potential employers?**

   a) How many employees are being hired? What combination of skills and abilities do these new hires possess?

   b) Is the growth or decline in hiring related to the recent expansion or downsizing of markets and/or territories? Changes in technology?

   c) Are there major hiring differences between large and small companies? If so, why?

4. **Where and how do your potential employers recruit new employees?**

   a) Where do employers make contact with potential employees?

      (1)   College and university placement offices:

      (2)   Job/career fairs:

      (3)   Co-op and internship programs:

      (4)   Headhunting firms:

      (5)   Unsolicited applications:

      (6)   The Internet:

   b) Do potential employers place a premium on experience or are they willing to hire new graduates without experience?

5. **When do your potential employers recruit new employees?**

   a) Does recruiting follow a seasonal pattern or do employers recruit new employees on an ongoing basis?

C. **Personal Assessment**
1. **Review of personal goals, objectives, and performance**
   a) What are your personal goals and objectives in terms of employment, career, lifestyle, geographic preferences, etc.?
   b) Are your personal goals and objectives consistent with the realities of the labour market? Why or why not?
   c) Are your personal goals and objectives consistent with recent changes in the external or employer environments? Why or why not?
   d) How are your current strategies for success working in areas such as course performance, internships, networking, job leads, career development, interviewing skills, etc.?
   e) How does your current performance compare to that of your peers (competitors)? Are they performing well in terms of course performance, internships, co-op placements, networking, job leads, career development, interviewing skills, etc.?
   f) If your performance is declining, what is the most likely cause?
   g) If your performance is improving, what actions can you take to ensure that your performance continues in this direction?
2. **Inventory of personal skills and resources**
   a) What do you consider to be your marketable skills? This list should be as comprehensive as possible and include areas such as interpersonal skills, organizational skills, technological skills, communication skills (oral and written), networking/team-building skills, etc.
   b) Considering the current and future needs of your potential employers, what important skills are you lacking?
   c) Other than personal skills, what do you consider to be your other career-enhancing resources? This list should be as comprehensive as possible and include areas such as financial resources (to pay for additional training, if necessary), personal contacts or "connections" with individuals who can assist your career development, specific degrees or certificates you hold, and intangible resources (family name, prestige of your educational institution, etc.).
   d) Considering the current and future needs of your potential employers, what important resources are you lacking?

III. **SWOT Analysis (your personal strengths and weaknesses and the opportunities and threats that may impact your career)**
A. **Personal Strengths**
1. Three key strengths
   a) Strength 1:
   b) Strength 2:
   c) Strength 3:
2. How do these strengths allow you to meet the needs of your potential employers?
3. How do these strengths compare to those of your peers/competitors? Do these strengths give you an advantage relative to your peers/competitors?

B. **Personal Weaknesses**
1. Three key weaknesses
    a) Weakness 1:
    b) Weakness 2:
    c) Weakness 3:
2. How do these weaknesses cause you to fall short of meeting the needs of your potential employers?
3. How do these weaknesses compare to those of your peers/competitors? Do these weaknesses put you at a disadvantage relative to your peers/competitors?

C. **Career Opportunities**
1. Three key career opportunities
    a) Opportunity 1:
    b) Opportunity 2:
    c) Opportunity 3:
2. How are these opportunities related to serving the needs of your potential employers?
3. What actions must be taken to capitalize on these opportunities in the short term? In the long term?

D. **Career Threats**
1. Three key career threats
    a) Threat 1:
    b) Threat 2:
    c) Threat 3:
2. How are these threats related to serving the needs of your potential employers?
3. What actions must be taken to prevent these threats from limiting your capabilities in the short term? In the long term?

E. **The SWOT Matrix**

F. **Matching, Converting, Minimizing, and Avoiding Strategies**
1. How can you match your strengths to your opportunities to better serve the needs of your potential employers?
2. How can you convert your weaknesses into strengths?
3. How can you convert your threats into opportunities?
4. How can you minimize or avoid those weaknesses and threats that cannot be converted successfully?

IV. **Resources**
A. **Financial**
1. Do you have the financial resources necessary to undertake and successfully complete this plan (i.e., preparation/duplication/mailing of a résumé; interviewing costs, including proper attire; etc.)?

B. **Human**
1. Is the industry in which you are interested currently hiring? Are companies in your area currently hiring?

C. **Experience and Expertise**
1. Do you have experience from either part-time or summer employment that could prove useful in your current plan?
2. Do you have the required expertise or skills to qualify for a job in your desired field? If not, do you have the resources to obtain them?

V. **Strategies**
   A. **Objective(s)**
      1. Potential employer A:
         a) Descriptive characteristics:
         b) Geographic locations:
         c) Culture/values/mission:
         d) Basic employee needs:
         e) Recruiting/hiring practices:
         f) Employee training/compensation practices:
         g) Justification for selection:
      2. Potential employer B:
         a) Descriptive characteristics:
         b) Geographic locations:
         c) Culture/values/mission:
         d) Basic employee needs:
         e) Recruiting/hiring practices:
         f) Employee training/compensation practices:
         g) Justification for selection:
   B. **Strategy(ies) for Using Capabilities and Resources**
      1. Strategy A (to meet the needs of potential employer A)
         a) Personal skills, abilities, and resources
            (1) Description of your skills and abilities:
            (2) Specific employer needs that your skills/abilities can fulfill:
            (3) Differentiation relative to peers/competitors (why should *you* be hired?):
            (4) Additional resources that you have to offer:
            (5) Needed or expected starting salary:
            (6) Expected employee benefits:
            (7) Additional employer-paid training that you require:
            (8) Willingness to relocate:
            (9) Geographic areas to target:
            (10) Corporate divisions or offices to target:
            (11) Summary of overall strategy:
            (12) Tactics for standing out among the crowd of potential employees:
            (13) Point of contact with potential employer:
            (14) Specific elements
                 (a) Résumé:
                 (b) Internships/co-op placements:
                 (c) Placement offices:
                 (d) Job fairs:
                 (e) Personal contacts:
                 (f) Unsolicited:
            (15) Specific objectives and budget:
      2. Strategy B (to meet the needs of potential employer B)
         a) Personal skills, abilities, and resources
            (1) Description of your skills and abilities:
            (2) Specific employer needs that your skills/abilities can fulfill:
            (3) Differentiation relative to peers/competitors (why should *you* be hired?):

        (4)   Additional resources that you have to offer:
        (5)   Needed or expected starting salary:
        (6)   Expected employee benefits:
        (7)   Additional employer-paid training that you require:
        (8)   Willingness to relocate:
        (9)   Geographic areas to target:
        (10)   Corporate divisions or offices to target:
        (11)   Summary of overall strategy:
        (12)   Tactics for standing out among the crowd of potential employees:
        (13)   Point of contact with potential employer:
        (14)   Specific elements
            (a)   Résumé:
            (b)   Internships/co-op placements:
            (c)   Placement offices:
            (d)   Job fairs:
            (e)   Personal contacts:
            (f)   Unsolicited:
        (15)   Specific objectives and budget:

  C. **Strategy Summary**
      1. How does strategy A (B) give you a competitive advantage in serving the needs of potential employer A (B)?
      2. Is this competitive advantage sustainable? Why or why not?

VI. **Financial Projections and Budgets**
  A. Do you have a clear idea of your budgetary requirements (e.g., housing, furnishings, clothing, transportation, food, other living expenses)?
  B. Will the expected salaries/benefits from potential employers meet these requirements? If not, do you have an alternative plan (i.e., a different job choice, a second job, requesting a higher salary)?

VII. **Controls and Evaluation**
  A. **Performance Standards**
      1. What do you have to offer?
          Corrective actions that can be taken if your skills, abilities, and resources do not match the needs of potential employers:
      2. Are you worth it?
          Corrective actions that can be taken if potential employers do not think your skills/abilities are worth your asking price:
      3. Where do you want to go?
          Corrective actions that can be taken if potential employers do not offer you a position in a preferred geographic location:
      4. How will you stand out among the crowd?
          Corrective actions that can be taken if your message is not being heard by potential employers or is not reaching the right people:
  B. **Monitoring Procedures**
      1. What types and levels of formal control mechanisms are in place to ensure the proper implementation of your plan?
         a) Are your potential employers hiring?
         b) Do you need additional training/education?
         c) Have you allocated sufficient time to your career development?

        d)   Are your investments in career development adequate?
            (1)   Training/education:
            (2)   Networking/making contacts:
            (3)   Wardrobe/clothing:
            (4)   Development of interviewing skills:
        e)   Have you done your homework on potential employers?
        f)   Have you been involved in an internship or co-op program?
        g)   Have you attended job/career fairs?
        h)   Are you using the resources of your placement centre?
        i)   Are you committed to your career development?

C. **Performance Analysis**
    1. Number/quality/potential of all job contacts made:
    2. Number of job/career fairs attended and quality of the job leads generated:
    3. Number of résumés distributed:
        a)   Number of potential employers who responded:
        b)   Number of negative responses:
    4. Number of personal interviews:
    5. Number/quality of job offers:

Endnotes

Chapter 1

1. **www.jnj.com/who_is_jnj/enviro_package.html**, November 30, 1998.
2. Canadian Tire, *Annual Report to Shareholders*, 2000.
3. "Hourly Workers and Their Supervisors Say Management Flunks When It Comes to Knowing How to Keep Them," *PR Newswire*, December 3, 1998.
4. "Reversing the Decline in Corporate Loyalty Leads to Higher Profits, More Secure Jobs," *PR Newswire*, December 1, 1998.
5. "Johnson & Johnson to Realign Its Global Manufacturing Network and Take After Tax Charge of $800 Million against 4th Quarter Earnings," *PR Newswire*, December 3, 1998.
6. Vanessa Richardson, "A Computer That Cooks Popcorn," *Money.com*, Fall 1998, p. 14.
7. "Burger King Corporation's Tie-In," *PR Newswire*.
8. Anne Linsmayer, "Smothered by Money," *Forbes*, November 30, 1998, p. 138.
9. **www.tbs-sct.gv.ca.report/crown/00/cc-sc/e.html**.
10. Leyla Kokmen, "'PC' Stands for Plunging Cost," *The Denver Post*, November 2, 1998, p. E1.
11. Doug Levy, "Compaq Heats up Direct-sale Competition," *USA Today*, November 12, 1998, p. 6B.
12. Robert D. Hof, Ellen Neuborne, and Heather Green, "Amazon.com: The Wild World of E-commerce," *Business Week*, December 14, 1998, pp. 106–119.
13. Frank Bilovsky, "E-tailing Picking up Steam," *Fort Collins Coloradoan*, December 7, 1998, p. B3.
14. *Profit Magazine*, May 2001, p. 18.
15. Lorrie Grant, "They Still Cheer at Company Meetings," *USA Today*, November 6, 1998, pp. 1B, 2B.
16. Maggie Jones, "25 Hottest Careers for Women," *Working Women*, July 1995, pp. 31–33; and Thomas A. Stewart, "Planning a Career in a World without Managers," *Fortune*, March 20, 1995, pp. 72–80; and "Reversing the Decline in Corporate Loyalty," *PR Newswire*.

Chapter 2

1. Seth Lubove, "Fixing the Product," *Forbes*, November 2, 1998, p. 224, and **www.pplsi.com/**, December 2, 1998.
2. "Pepsico Claims Coke Unfair, Sues," *The Commercial Appeal*, May 5, 1998, p. B4.
3. "AT&T Settles Lawsuit against Reseller Accused of Slamming," *Business Wire*, May 26, 1998.
4. Marcia Stepanek, "2000 Reasons to Celebrate," *Business Week*, November 9, 1998, p. 54.
5. Sylvie Cote and Marc Pistorio, "Resolving Disputes," *CMA Management*, October 2001, pp. 18–19.
6. "Merrill Lynch Settles Gender Discrimination Lawsuit," *PR Newswire*, May 4, 1998.
7. Manitoba Public Insurance Website, **www.mpi.mb.ca/english/claims/insfraud.html**, November 16, 2001.
8. Harvey S. Perlman, *Interference with Contract and Other Economic Expectancies . . .*, 49 University of Chicago Law Review 61 (1982), **www.fplc.edu/TFIELD/plfip/plfip3.htm**, November 18, 1998.
9. Michael White, "US Firms May Have Bought Drug Money," *Associated Press Newswire*, May 29, 1998.
10. Tim W. Ferguson, "Shutter Bugs," *Forbes*, November 2, 1998, p. 88.
11. Youssef M. Ibrahim, "As Trademarks Multiply, Infringement Does, Too," *The New York Times*, November 12, 1998.
12. The Institute of Law Clerks of Ontario, **www.ilco.on.ca**, November 15, 2001; and the Ministry of Training, Colleges and Universities, **www.edu.gov.on.ca/eng/general/college/progstan/humserv/lawclerk.html**, November 15, 2001.
13. Suzanne Perry, "EU Acts to Boost Confidence in Electronic Commerce," *Reuter's Newswire*, November 18, 1998.
14. "How the New Law Will Cramp Sales Styles," *Business Week*, November 2, 1998.
15. William T. Neese and Charles R. McManis, "Summary Brief: Law, Ethics, and the Internet: How Recent Federal Trademark Law Prohibits a Remedy against 'Cyber-Squatters,'" *Proceedings from the Society of Marketing Advances*, November 4–7, 1998.

Chapter 3

1. "About Starbucks," **www.occ.com/starbucks/about**, April 23, 1998; "Starbucks Corporation," **www.hoovers.com**, April 23, 1998; "Starbucks: Making Values Pay," reprinted from Howard Schultz and Dori Jones Yang, "Pour Your Heart into It," *Fortune*, September 29, 1997, pp. 261–272; and "Starbucks Pays Premium Price to Benefit Workers," *Business Ethics* 12 (March/April 1998), p. 9.

2. "Honda's Bribery Suit Settlement Gets Final Approval," *Bloomberg Newswire*, October 9, 1998.

3. "Ethics Poll Answers: The Company Made Me Do It," *St. Petersburg Times*, August 26, 1996, p. 14.

4. Ethics Essential in New Directions, Canadian Centre for Philanthropy, **www.ccp.ca/imagine/publications/new_directions/issues3/ethics.html**.

5. "US Lawsuit Says Tobacco Firms Target Blacks, Inquiry Reports," *Bloomberg Newswire* from the *Philadelphia Enquirer*, October 22, 1998, p. A1.

6. Lorrie Grant, "Originals Increasingly Taking Knockoffs to Court," *USA Today*, October 26, 1998, p. 6B.

7. Richard Behar, "Why Subway Is the Biggest Problem in Franchising," *Fortune*, March 16, 1998, and "Subway Sandwich Shops, Inc.," **www.hoover.com**, April 12, 1998.

8. "What Would You Do If Your Employer's Behavior Went against Your Ethical Standards?" Lutheran Brotherhood Reports: Ethics in the Workplace (Twelfth in a Series), *PR Newswire*, October 6, 1998.

9. Ted Bridis, "More Details Emerge in Suit against Microsoft," *The Denver Post*, September 12, 1998, p. 3B.

10. *USA Today*, October 19, 1998, p. D1.

11. Nanci Hellmich, "For the Big Drug Firms, Market Is Ripe for Expansion," *USA Today*, October 14, 1998, p. D1.

12. Mark Maremont, "Eyeway Robbery," *Business Week*, February 27, 1995, p. 48.

13. Alex Markels, "Employers Sabotage Office Computer Games," *The Wall Street Journal*, February 6, 1995, p. B1.

14. Thomas M. Jones, "Ethical Decision Making by Individuals in Organizations: An Issue-Contingent Model," *Academy of Management Review* 2 (April 1991), p. 371–373.

15. Sir Adrian Cadbury, "Ethical Managers Make Their Own Rules," *Harvard Business Review* 65 (September–October 1987), p. 72.

16. "NLC Names Corporate Names in Sweatshop Reports," *Business Ethics*, January/February, 1998, p. 9.

17. Rebecca Goodell, "Ethics in American Business: Policies, Programs and Perceptions" (Washington, DC: Ethics Resource Center, Inc., 1994), p. 22.

18. Taking Action on Business Ethics, **www2.conferenceboard.ca/ccbc/knowledge-areas/ethics/ethics.htm**.

19. O.C. Ferrell, John Fraedrich, and Linda Ferrell, *Business Ethics: Ethical Decision Making and Cases*, 4th edition (Boston: Houghton Mifflin Company, 2000).

20. Archie B. Carroll, "The Pyramid of Corporate Social Responsibility: Toward the Moral Management of Organizational Stakeholders," *Business Horizons* 34 (July/August 1991), p. 42.

21. "Reebok Achieves Milestones in Improving Factory Workplace Conditions," *Business Wire*, October 8, 1998.

22. 1994 Cone/Roper as reported in Susan Gaines, "Good Guys Finish First," *Business Ethics* 9 (March/April 1995), p. 13.

23. Paula Rogowski, "The Nitty Gritty of Social Screening," *Business Ethics*, July/August 1998, p. 20.

24. Dewanna Lofton, "Nike Unveils New Wear, Social Plans," *The Commercial Appeal*, September 24, 1998, p. B4.

25. Ferrell, Fraedrich, and Ferrell, *Business Ethics*.

26. "Ben & Jerry's Settles Fraud Suit," *Business Ethics*, July/August 1998, p. 10.

27. Patricia Sellers, "First: Sunbeam's Investors Draw Their Knives—Exit for Chainsaw?" *Fortune*, June 8, 1998, pp. 30–31; Martha Brannigan and Ellen Joan Pollock, "Dunlap Offers Tears and a Defense," *The Wall Street Journal*, July 9, 1998, p. B1; "Sunbeam to Restate Financial Results," *PR Newswire*, September 13, 1998; The Alexander Law Firm, **defrauded.com/sunbeam/shtml**, September 13, 1998; Albert J. Dunlap and Bob Aldeman, "How I Save Bad Companies and Make Good Companies Great," *Mean Business*, rev. ed. (New York: Simon and Schuster Inc., 1997); and John A. Byrne, "How Al Dunlap Self-Destructed," *Business Week*, July 6, 1998, pp. 58–65.

28. Liz Butler and Dave Wise, "Home Depot Day of Action," Home Depot press release, October 12, 1998.

29. "Six Arrested for Disrupting NY Macy's Fur Salon," *Reuters Newswire*, October 12, 1998.

30. "Oregon Salmon Stream Gets $250 Million Protection," *Reuters Newswire*, October 17, 1998.

31. "Shell Aims to Cut Emissions of 'Greenhouse Gases' 10% by 2002," *Bloomberg Newswire*, October 16, 1998.

32. *USA Today Snapshots*, **www.usatoday.com**.

33. Susan Gaines, "Holding out Halos," *Business Ethics* 8 (March/April 1994), p. 21; Judith Kamm, "Ethics Officers: Corporate America's Newest Profession," *Ethics, Easier Said Than Done*, Summer 1993, Josephson Institute, 38; and Robert Levering and Milton Moskowitz, *The 100 Best Companies to Work for in America* (New York: The Penguin Group, 1994), p. 123.

34. "Worth Noting," *Business Ethics*, July/August 1998, p. 9.

35. "Microsoft Kicks off Annual Employee Giving Campaign," *PR Newswire*, September 18, 1998.

36. "The Minute Maid Company Produces 2,000 Cases of Hi-C Fruit Juice for Second Harvest," *PR Newswire*, June 2, 1998.

37. "Northwest Passengers Donate More than 13 Million Worldperk Miles to AirCares Charity Partners," *PR Newswire*, May 6, 1998.

38. **www.conferenceboard.ca/press/2000/BusEdAwards.htm**.

39. **www.conferenceboard.ca/press/2000/Mentoring.htm**.

40. Permission granted by the author of *Gray Matters,* George Sammet, Jr., Vice President, Office of Corporate Ethics, Lockheed Martin Corporation, Orlando, Florida, to use these portions of *Gray Matters: The Ethics Game* © 1992. If you would like more information about the complete game, call 1-800-3ETHICS.

Chapter 4

1. Neil Weinberg, "Bull in a Stationery Shop," *Forbes,* August 24, 1998, pp. 90–91.

2. Viceroy Homes Website, **www.viceroy.com/finance/**, November 20, 2001.

3. O.C. Ferrell, Michael D. Hartline, George H. Lucas, Jr., and David Luck, *Marketing Strategy* (Ft. Worth: Dryden, 1999), p. 176.

4. Karen Pennar, "Two Steps Forward, One Step Back," *Business Week,* August 31, 1998, p. 116.

5. Michelle Wirth Fellman, "Colgate-Palmolive's Mark Leads Company to Global Excellence," *Marketing News,* March 30, 1998, p. E2.

6. Pennar, "Two Steps Forward."

7. Vera Gibbons, "Face-Off: Eastman Kodak," *Smart Money,* October 1997, p. 42.

8. "Software Piracy Flourishing," *USA Today Snapshots,* August 13, 1998, p. B1.

9. Stan Crock, "Sanctions against Cuba: The Beginning of the End?" *Business Week,* August 3, 1998, p. 45.

10. "Burger King Corporation Announces the Opening of the Company's 10,000th Restaurant," *PR Newswire,* November 6, 1998.

11. Shelly Reese, "Culture Shock," *Marketing Tools,* May 1998.

12. Ibid.

13. Louise Lee, "Ad Agencies in Asia Hit a Nerve, Showing Men Doing Housework," *Wall Street Journal Interactive Edition,* **www.interactive.wsj.com**, August 14, 1998.

14. "China Soon the Largest Mobile Telephone Market?" *CNN Interactive,* **www.cnn.com/TECH/science/**, August 16, 1998.

15. Douglas Harbrecht, Owen Ullmon, Bill Javetski, and Geri Smith, "Finally, GATT May Fly," *Business Week,* December 20, 1993, pp. 36–37.

16. "Farmers Blockade Canadian Goods," *Inbound Logistics,* October 1998, p. 16.

17. "Six Candidate Nations Begin EU Membership Talks," *CNN World News, CNN Interactive,* **www.cnn.com**, March 31, 1998.

18. "Countdown to the Euro," *Merrill Lynch Insights & Strategies* 3, no. 4 (1998), p. 2.

19. Maricris G. Briones, "The Euro Starts Here," *Marketing News,* July 20, 1998, pp. 1, 39.

20. Mark Memmott, "US: Japan Must Ease Import Rules," *USA Today,* February 20, 1998, p. B1.

21. Martha T. Moore, "Latest Japan–US Rift," *USA Today,* November 6, 1995, p. B1.

22. Dexter Roberts, "Now, It's Reform or Bust," *Business Week,* April 6, 1998, p. 54.

23. Louis Kraar, "The Risks Are Rising in China," *Fortune,* March 6, 1995, p. 179.

24. Louis Kraar, "Asia's Rising Export Powers," *Fortune,* Special Pacific Rim 1989 Issue, pp. 43–50.

25. **www.imf.org**, November 4, 1998.

26. Dean Foust, "What the IMF Needs Is a Good Alarm System," *Business Week,* February 20, 1995, p. 55.

27. Linda Grant, "Stirring It Up at Campbell," *Fortune,* May 13, 1996.

28. "Airlines Create 'Oneworld'," CNNFN, **cnnfn.com/**, September 21, 1998.

29. "Major Firms Spend Big Bucks in Asia," *The Commercial Appeal,* November 1, 1998.

30. Debbie Jones, "Home Depot and Emerson Tool Company: Building an Everlasting Partnership," **www.homedepot.com/press/ridgid.htm**, October 28, 1998.

31. Gene Koprowski, "Click Clique Marketing," *Marketing Tools,* May 1998, and "Internet Global Village," *USA Today Snapshots,* October 24, 1998, p. A1.

32. Philip R. Cateora, *International Marketing,* 8th ed. (Homewood, IL: Richard D. Irwin, 1993), pp. 25–26; *Global Exchanges,* T. Bettina Cornwell, ed. (Boston: Allyn and Bacon, 1993), pp. 61–63; "NAFTA: Exports, Jobs, Wages, and Investment," *Business America,* October 18, 1993, p. 3; and *VGM's Handbook of Business & Management Careers,* Annette Selden, ed. (Lincolnwood, IL: VGM Career Horizons, 1993), pp. 43–44.

33. "Campbell Soup Consolidates Advertising into Two Global Agencies," *PR Newswire,* November 9, 1998.

34. Campbell's Soup 1997 Annual Report.

35. Joseph Albright and Marcia Kunstel, "Schlotzsky's First China Opening Less than Red Hot," *The Austin American-Statesman,* **www.austin360.com**, May 27, 1998.

36. "Lucent Technologies Establishes Global Design Center in China for 5ESS AnyMedia Switch Software Development," *Business Wire,* November 9, 1998.

Chapter 5

1. Kylo-Patrick Hart, "Step 4: Decide Your Legal Structure," *Entrepreneur* Magazine's Small Business Square, **www.entrepreneurmag.com/startups/start_smart4.hts**, September 1, 1998.

2. Kara Kuryllowicz, "Learning the Ropes," *Profit Magazine,* October 2001, Vol. 20, No. 6, pp. 42–45.

3. Patrick McMahon, "Nordstrom Undergoes Store, Corporate Face Lift," *USA Today,* September 21, 1998, p. 11B.

4. Robert Schwab, "Horizon Organic Dairy Rides Boom in Sales of Natural Foods," *Denver Post,* October 10, 1998, p. 1C.

5. Paul Cox, "Technology: Web Wise," *The Wall Street Journal Interactive Edition,* September 28, 1998, **interactive.wsj.com/articles/SB906560452148333500.htm**.

6. Jeremy Quittner, "Why Paul Orfalea Didn't Franchise Kinko's," *Business Week Online,* September 23, 1998; "Kinko's Aims to Be More than Copycat," abstracted from *Globe & Mail,* June 29, 1998; "For the Officeless, a Place to Call Home," abstracted from the *New York Times,* July 6, 1998; "Europe Gets Kinko's Business Services," abstracted from *Newsbytes News Network,* February 11, 1998 (all abstracts viewed on CareerMosaic Company Backgrounder on September 28, 1998); and Kinko's home page, **www.kinkos.com**, September 28, 1998.

7. Anna Muoio, "Is Bigger Better?" *Fast Company,* September 1998, p. 79.

8. Manuel Schiffres, "Merger Math," *Kiplinger's Personal Finance Magazine,* September 1998, p. 70.

9. Ibid.

10. Emily Nelson and Alejandro Bodipo-Memba, "Claire's Stores Moves in on Rival: Will It Eventually Buy Gadzooks?" *The Wall Street Journal Interactive Edition,* September 17, 1998, **interactive.wsj.com/articles/SB905990224571147000.htm**.

11. Gordon Fairclough, "AMP Chief Promises Incentive to Avoid Hostile Takeover Bid," *The Wall Street Journal Interactive Edition,* September 11, 1998, **interactive.wsj.com/articles/SB905473075691575000.htm**.

12. Statistics Canada, Yearbooks 1948–1949, 1962, 1972, 1990, and 1997.

13. Mo Krochmal, "Merger Mania Hits Silicon Valley Net Agencies," **www.techweb.com/wire/story/TWB19980624S0010**, August 26, 1998.

14. Ken Miller, "How the Merger Boom Will End," *Fortune,* October 27, 1997, **www.pathfinder.com/fortune/1997/971027/fro.html**, August 23, 1998.

Chapter 6

1. *Small Business Job Creation, 1993,* Canadian Federation of Independent Business.

2. *Small Business Canada Magazine,* January 1999.

3. "Moving Forward: Small Business Is the Key to Economic Recovery," CFIB, October 29, 2000.

4. The Educated Entrepreneur, **www.educatedentrepreneur.com**.

5. Steve Hamm, "Jim Clark Is Off and Running Again," *Business Week,* October 12, 1998, pp. 64–65.

6. *Small Business Job Creation, 1993,* Canadian Federation of Independent Business.

7. *Small Business Quarterly,* June 2, 2001.

8. Guy Gellatly, "Differences in Innovator and Non-innovator Profits: Small Establishments in Business Services," Statistics Canada.

9. Made in Canada—Canadian Inventors and Inventions, **www.inventors.about.com**.

10. Dennis Berman, "Entrepreneur Profiles: This Woman Thrives in the Toxic-Waste World," *Business Week Online,* January 20, 1998, **www.businessweek.com/smallbiz/news/date/9801/e980120a.htm**, August 21, 1998.

11. About Tim Hortons, **www.timhortons.com/english/english.html**.

12. The Inside Edge, Summer 2001, Conference Board of Canada.

13. "Exploring by Small Firms," SBA Office of Advocacy, April 1998, **www.sbaonline.sba.gov/advo/stats/exp_rpt.html**, October 12, 1998.

14. The Conference Board of Canada Small Business Primer 98, **cfib.ca/research/reports/primer98_e.asp**.

15. Sara Terry, "Genius at Work," *Fast Company,* September 1998, pp. 171–181.

16. Statistics Canada, *The Daily,* **www.statcan.ca/Daily/English/010117/010117a.htm**.

17. **www.nqi.ca/english/cae_announcement_2001.htm**.

18. **www.dell.com/corporate/access/factpak/index.htm**, October 1998.

19. **www.cweya.com/Steinhauer.pdf**.

20. "Where Technology Can Take Your Business," Special Advertising Supplement, *Inc.,* October 1998, p. 8.

21. Barbara Hetzer, "Find a Niche—and Start Scratching," *Business Week Online,* September 25, 1998, **www.businessweek.com/smallbiz/news/columns/98-37/e3595056.htm**.

22. Jerry Langdon, "Small Businesses Shun Technology," *USA Today,* September 21, 1998, p. 9B.

23. CFIB Research, Banking on Small Business, Results of CFIB Banking Survey, March 2001.

24. "How Can Somebody Not Be Optimistic," *Business Week/Reinvesting America 1992,* Special issue, p. 185; and Mark Memmott, "Cutbacks Create Fierce Undertow," *USA Today,* October 20, 1993, p. B1.

25. Gifford Pinchott III, *Intrapreneuring* (New York: Harper & Row, 1985), p. 34.

26. Adapted from Carol Kinsey Goman, *Creativity in Business: A Practical Guide for Creative Thinking,* Crisp Publications, Inc., 1989, p. 5–6. © Crisp Publications, Inc., 1200 Hamilton Court, Menlo Park, CA 94025.

Chapter 7

1. Global Business Forum, **www.alberta-canada.com/aeda/ bio_bouchard.html**.

2. CAAWS at Chatelaine Women of Influence series, **www.caaws.ca/ Leadership/wom_influen2.htm**.

3. Patricia Sellers, "The 50 Most Powerful Women in American Business," *Fortune,* October 12, 1998.

4. "Another Star Is Born: A Summary of How Mercedes-Benz US International Began," *PR Newswire,* **www.prnewswire.com**, September 30, 1998.

5. O.C. Ferrell, Michael D. Hartline, George H. Lucas, Jr., and David Luck, *Marketing Strategy* (Fort Worth: The Dryden Press, 1999), pp. 81, 83.

6. "Gillette Sees Oral Care Sales Doubling," *Reuters Newswire,* October 28, 1998.

7. Tara Parker-Pope, "P&G, in Effort to Give Sales a Boost, Plans to Revamp Corporate Structure," *Wall Street Journal Interactive Edition,* September 2, 1998.

8. Ibid.

9. "Pizza Hut Pulling out of Moscow," *Associated Press,* October 25, 1998.

10. Lawrence L. Knutson, "Fisher Price Recalls Toy Cars," *Associated Press Newswire,* October 23, 1998.

11. "Death Toll in Nigeria Oil Pipeline Fire Now 500," *Reuters Newswire,* October 19, 1998.

12. Parker-Pope, "P&G, in Effort to Give Sales a Boost."

13. "Drake Beam Marin Finds Companies Fixated on Maximizing Workforce ROI," *PR Newswire,* October 13, 1998.

14. **www.magnaint.com**.

15. Fabrice Taylor, The Story Behind Nortel's Fall," *Globe & Mail,* November 17, 2001, p. B1.

16. "An Audience with Innovation," **www.virgin.com_diary**, October 1998.

17. "Runaway CEO Pay," **www.paywatch.org/problem/index.html**, August 13, 1998.

18. "CEOs Push Management Diversity," *Wall Street Journal,* HR Briefs, **public.wsj.com/careers/resources/documents/ 19980127-kennedy.htm**, September 13, 1998.

19. Tara Parker-Pope, "P&G Makes Pitch to Keep Women, and So Far the Strategy Is Working," *Wall Street Journal Interactive Edition,* September 9, 1998.

20. "Leading vs. Managing—They're Two Different Animals," **www.onlinewbc.org/docs/manage/leading.html**, October 19, 1998.

21. "Key Traits of Successful Leaders," **www.onlinewbc.org/docs/ manage/traits.html**, October 19, 1998.

22. Elizabeth Weil, "Every Leader Tells a Story," *Fast Company,* June/July 1998, p. 40.

23. Brent Schlender, "The Three Faces of Steve," *Fortune,* November 9, 1998, pp. 96–104.

24. Chad Kaydo, "Riding High," *Sales & Marketing Management,* July 1998, pp. 64–66.

25. Cathy Olofson, "The Ritz Puts on Stand-up Meetings," *Fast Company,* September 1998, p. 62; John Grossman, "We've Got to Start Meeting Like This," *Inc.,* April 1998, pp. 70–74; and "Important Structures of Successful Meetings," **www.onlinewbc/ org/docs/manage/meetings.html**, October 19, 1998.

26. Dyan Machan, "There's Something about Henry," *Forbes,* October 5, 1998.

27. Parker-Pope, "P & G, in Effort to Give Sales a Boost."

28. TD Economics, "The Shape of Things to Come," **www.td.com/ economics**.

29. *You and the Job Market,* Queen's Printer for Ontario, 2001.

30. "The Fogelman News: Student Edition," Special Issues/Career Week, 1995; "Managing Your Career, The College Edition of the National Business Employment Weekly," *The Wall Street Journal,* Spring 1994; US Department of Labor, Bureau of Labor Statistics, *Occupational Outlook Handbook,* 1994–1995 ed., Bulletin 2450, May 1994.

31. John P. Kotter, "What Effective General Managers Really Do," *Harvard Business Review* 60 (November–December 1982), p. 160.

32. Machan, "There's Something about Henry."

33. **www.globetechnology.com/robmag/robmagjune_ol.html**.

34. NRG Group Inc., Third Quarter Results, released October 31, 2000.

Chapter 8

1. John Byrne, "The Corporation of the Future," *Business Week,* August 31, 1998, pp. 102–104, and Matt Goldberg, "Cisco's Most Important Meal of the Day," *Fast Company* 13, p. 56.

2. Adam Smith, *Wealth of Nations* (New York: Modern Library, 1937; originally published in 1776).

3. Jon R. Katzenbach and Douglas K. Smith, "The Discipline of Teams," *Harvard Business Review* 71 (March/April 1993), pp. 111–120.

4. Ibid.

5. **www.rim.net**, December 2001.

6. "Deloitte & Touche Recognized as One of Working Mother's '100 Best Companies for Working Mothers' for Fifth Consecutive Year," *PR Newswire,* September 14, 1998.

7. Ed Brown, "War Games to Make You Better at Business," *Fortune,* September 28, 1998.

8. Peter Carbonara, "Mervyn's Calls in the SWAT Team," *Fast Company,* April/May 1998, p. 54.

9. Richard S. Wellins, William C. Byham, and Jeanne M. Wilson, *Empowered Teams: Creating Self-Directed Work Groups That Improve Quality, Productivity, and Participation* (San Francisco: Jossey-Bass Publishers, 1991), p. 5.

10. Susan Lee and Ashlea Ebeling, "Can You Top This for Cost-efficient Management?" *Forbes*, April 20, 1998, pp. 207–212.

11. Louis Uchitelle, "Layoffs Hit Lowest Rate this Decade," *The Commercial Appeal*, August 22, 1998, p. B3.

12. Stephanie Armour, "Gillette Plans to Eliminate 4,700 Workers," *USA Today*, September 29, 1998, p. B1.

13. Adapted from Robert Gatewood, Robert Taylor, and O.C. Ferrell, *Management: Comprehension, Analysis, and Application* (Homewood, IL: Austen Press, 1995), pp. 361, 365–366.

14. Stephanie Armour, "Failure to Communicate Costly for Companies," *USA Today*, September 30, 1998, p. B1.

15. Ibid.

16. Robert Bryce, "At BSG, There's Only One Speed-Faster," *Fast Company* **www.fastcompany.com/online/02/bsgsec.html**, September 18, 1998, and James Wetherbe, *The World on Time*,

(Santa Monica, CA: Knowledge Exchange, 1996), pp. 20–21 and 133–135.

17. James Champy, "Wasteful Meetings," *Forbes*, November 2, 1998, p. 173.

18. Jackson and Stafford, "Workers Learn a Lot in Informal Talk," pp. B1, B2.

19. Ibid.

20. Ibid.

21. Gatewood, Taylor, and Ferrell, *Management*.

22. Peter Verburg, "Prepare for Takeoff," *Canadian Business*, December 25, 2001.

23. Michael D. Maginn, *Effective Teamwork, 1994*, p. 10. Copyright © 1994 Richard D. Irwin, a Times Mirror Higher Education Group, Inc., company.

Chapter 9

1. Lee B. Weaver, "Schlitterbahn," *American-Statesman*, August 13, 1998, and Leslie J. Nicholson, "Roller Coaster Lessons," *The Philadelphia Inquirer*, June 1, 1998.

2. "Smart Cars: Technology for the New Millennium," *Business Week*, Special Advertising Section, November 23, 1998.

3. Doug Levy, "Compaq Heats up Direct Sale Competition," *USA Today*, November 12, 1998, p. 6B.

4. Leonard L. Berry, *Discovering the Soul of Service* (New York: The Free Press, 1999), pp. 86–96.

5. Mike Snider, "Latest 'Thin' TVs Are a Huge Lure," *Fort Collins Coloradoan*, October 17, 1998, p. B2.

6. Amy Barrett and Gail DeGeorge, "Home Improvement at Black & Decker," *Business Week*, May 11, 1998, p. 56.

7. Earle Eldridge, "Low Cost Drives Modular Vehicle Assembly," *USA Today*, September 21, 1998, p. 3B.

8. Jeffrey Leib, "Canmaking's on the Ball," *The Denver Post*, October 19, 1998, p. 1E.

9. "Another Star Is Born: A Summary of How Mercedes-Benz US International Began," *PR Newswire*, September 30, 1998.

10. "Smart Cars," *Business Week*.

11. "Who Is AeroHydro?" **www.aerohydro.com/company.htm**, November 10, 1998.

12. "Adept Technology Selected by Technistar for World Class Bakery Production Flexible Automation System," **www.adept.com/PR46_797.html**, February 3, 1998.

13. Mary Powers, "Robotics Give Surgeons Extra Set of Arms," *The Commercial Appeal*, October 11, 1998, p. A1.

14. Andy Reinhardt, "Log on, Link up, Save Big," *Business Week*, June 22, 1998, p. 132.

15. Michael Miley, "Year of the Tiger," *Profit Magazine*, November 1998, pp. 118, 120.

16. Eldridge, "Low Cost Drives Modular Vehicle Assembly."

17. Lorraine Woellert, " 'OK, Think—Where Is That Wrench?' " *Business Week*, November 16, 1998, p. 8.

18. "Telxon Wireless Mobile Computers Help Chrysler Monitor Quality Control," *PR Newswire*, August 6, 1998.

19. Steven Butler, "Green Machine," *Fast Company* 3, p. 112, **www.fastcompany.com/online/03/gunterp.html**, September 18, 1998.

20. T.E. Benson, "Quality Goes International," *Industry Week*, August 19, 1991, pp. 54–57; A.F. Borthick and H.P. Roth, "Will Europeans Buy Your Company's Products?" *Business Credit*, November/December 1992, pp. 23–24; S.J. Harrison and R. Stupak, "Total Quality Management: The Organizational Equivalent of Truth in Public Administration Theory and Practice," *Public Administration Quarterly* 6 (1992), pp. 416–429; C.W.L. Hart and P.E. Morrison, "Students Aren't Learning Quality Principles in Business Schools," *Quality Progress*, January 1992, pp. 25–27; and D. Marquardt, "Vision 2000: The Strategy for the ISO 9000 Series Standards in the 90's," *Quality Progress*, May 1991, pp. 25–31.

21. "Menlo Logistics Receives ISO Certification with NCR," *Business Wire*, October 7, 1998.

22. "Rainier Sets Industry Precedent with ISO 9002 Certification," *PR Newswire*, August 18, 1998.

23. James Wetherbe, "Principles of Cycle Time Reduction," *Cycle Time Research*, 1995, p. iv.

24. Stan Davis and Christopher Meyer, *Blur: The Speed of Change in the Connected Economy* (Reading, MA: Addison-Wesley, 1998), p. 5.

Chapter 10

1. Max Jarman, "Pets Help Reduce Office Stress (at Netscape, No Cats, Please)," *The Commercial Appeal*, September 6, 1998, p. H2; "Employee Attitudes Linked to Higher Profits, Greater Productivity and Higher Employee Retention," *Business Wire*, July 27, 1998; Aaron Bernstein, "We Want You to Stay. Really," *Business Week*, June 22, 1998, pp. 67–72; and

Anne Fisher, "You Inc.: 100 Best Companies to Work for in America," *Fortune*, January 12, 1998.

2. **www.rim.net/careers/work/index.shtml**.

3. Dan Lockhart and Jeff Ellis, "Happy Workers, High Returns? It's More Complex," *Marketing News*, May 25, 1998, p. 9.

4. D'Arcy Jenish and Berton Woodward, "Canada's Top 100 Employers," *Maclean's*, November 5, 2001.

5. Ibid.

6. Mark Todd, "Marriott Makes Room for Daddies," *Fast Company*, June/July 1998, p. 62.

7. Karen Jacobs, "Pay for Performance Has Dedicated Admirers," *The Wall Street Journal Interactive Edition*, June 11, 1998.

8. **www.top1000.globeinvestor.com/ceo/index.html**.

9. Abraham Maslow, *Motivation and Personality* (New York: Harper & Row, 1954).

10. D'Arcy Jenish and Berton Woodward, "Canada's Top 100 Employers," *Maclean's*, November 5, 2001.

11. Peter Verburg, "Prepare for Takeoff," *Canadian Business*, December 25, 2001.

12. Michele Marchetti, "Master Motivators," *Sales and Marketing Management*, April 1998, p. 40.

13. Douglas McGregor, *The Human Side of Enterprise* (New York: McGraw-Hill, 1960), pp. 33–34.

14. McGregor, *The Human Side of Enterprise*, pp. 47–48.

15. "TMMK Yearly Savings from Quality Circle Activity," **www.qualitycircles.com/Geninfo/Info1.html**, August 13, 1998.

16. "Going Global, Eastman Chemical Company's Expatriate Program," **www.hemnet.com/body_globalissues.htm**, September 1, 1998.

17. **www.eaglehardware.com/annual.htm**, August 17, 1998.

18. "TMMK Yearly Savings."

19. Joan B. Michelson, "Employees Are Firm's Greatest Marketing Force," *Marketing News*, May 25, 1998, p. 4.

20. "Who Needs You Most?" *Business Week*, June 22, 1998, p. 8.

21. Melanie Warner, "Working at Home—The Right Way to Be a Star in Your Bunny Slippers," *Fortune*, March 3, 1997.

22. Leigh Gallagher, "Death to the Cubicle!" *Forbes*, September 7, 1998, p. 54.

23. Steven McShane, *Canadian Organizational Behaviour*, 4th ed. (McGraw-Hill Ryerson, 2001).

24. Michael Cohen, "Share and Share Alike...," *Boston Business Journal*, July 13, 1998.

25. Hewitt Newstand press release, "Hewitt Study Shows Increase in Work and Family Benefits," July 22, 1998.

26. David Savagean and Geoffrey Loftus, *Places Rated Almanac* (Macmillan, 1997).

Chapter 11

1. "Global Employment Services Leader Adecco Introduces Innovative Job Search Kiosks to Washington State," Business Wire, August 12, 1998, from AOL search on August 19, 1998.

2. **www.pg.com/careers/us/faq/htm**, August 17, 1998.

3. Adele Malpass, "Ready for that Job on the Street?" *Business Week*, March 16, 1998, p. 118.

4. Catherine Siskos, "Need a Job? Be a Cybercruit," *Kiplinger's*, August 1998, p. 18.

5. Stephanie Gruner, "Lasting Impressions," *Inc.*, July 1998, p. 126.

6. Business Wire search, August 4, 1998.

7. Statistics Canada, *The Daily*, Wednesday, April 14, 2001.

8. Michele Marchetti, "Helping Reps Count Every Penny," *Sales and Marketing Management*, July 1998, p. 77.

9. "KPMG Peat Marwick LLP: The Importance of Being Ernst," WFP Insider Preview, **www.wetfeet.com/webc/wetfeet/c116.html?sid52PG4v@NJi**, August 19, 1998.

10. Lisa H. Pelled, "So Close and Yet So Far: Human Resource Management in Northern Mexico," *Marshall*, Spring 1998, pp. 35–39.

11. "Hughes Offers Broad-based Stock Option Plan," Business Wire search, August 6, 1998.

12. Statistics Canada, **www.estat.statcan.ca/cgi**.

13. "Hewitt Study Shows Increase in Work and Family Benefits," Hewitt Newstand press release, July 22, 1998.

14. Herman Schwind, Hari Das, and Terry Wagar, *Canadian Human Resource Management: A Strategic Approach*, 6th ed. (McGraw-Hill Ryerson, 2001).

15. Sara Nathan, "GM Strike Impact," *USA Today*, August 17, 1998, p. 1B.

16. Statistics Canada, Perspectives on Labour and Income, Catalogue No. 75-001.

17. Statistics Canada, *The Daily*, **www.statcan.ca/Daily/English/980512/d_980512.htm**, August 23, 2001.

18. Michelle Martinez, "Equality Effort Sharpens Bank's Edge," *HR Magazine*, January 1995, pp. 38–43.

19. "SHRM Survey Explores the Best in Diversity Practices: *Fortune* 500 Firms Outpace the Competition with Greater Commitment to Diversity," PR Newswire, August 25, 1998, **www.hemnet.com/body_news_div.htm**.

20. Statistics Canada, *The Daily*, **www.statcan.ca/Daily/english/980512/d_980512.htm**, August 23, 2001.

21. "Earnings by Educational Attainment and Sex, 1996," US Bureau of the Census, **www.infoplease.com/ipa/A0104685.shtml**, August 24, 1998.

22. Taylor H. Cox, Jr., "The Multicultural Organization," *Academy of Management Executives* 5 (May 1991), p. 34–47; Marilyn Loden and Judy B. Rosener, *Workforce America! Managing Employee Diversity as a Vital Resource* (Homewood, IL: Business One Irwin, 1991).

Chapter 12

1. Constance L. Hays, "Fickle Finger of Fat," *Continental,* August 1998, pp. 61–63.

2. Catalina Ortiz, "Macintosh Faithful Welcome Futuristic New iMac," *Marketing News,* September 14, 1998, p. 12.

3. "Winning Ideas in Marketing," *Fortune,* May 15, 1995, p. 201.

4. William C. Symonds, "Duracell's Bunny Buster," *Business Week,* March 2, 1998, p. 42.

5. Kelly Barron, "Cool It," *Forbes,* November 2, 1998, p. 218.

6. Michael Treacy and Fred Wiersema, *The Discipline of Market Leaders* (Reading, MA: Addison Wesley Publishing Co., 1995), p. 176.

7. Christopher Palmeri, "Beyond the Bathroom," *Forbes,* November 2, 1998, p. 210.

8. Robert M. McMath, "Flaunt What You've Got," *American Demographics,* July 1998, **www.marketingtools.com/publications/ad/98_ad/9807_ad/ad98079.htm**, October 13, 1998.

9. William C. Taylor, "Permission Marketing," *Fast Company,* April–May 1998, p. 202.

10. Treacy and Wiersema, *The Discipline of Market Leaders,* p. 135.

11. "MatchLogic Introduces Intelligent Targeting Service," *Business Wire,* October 7, 1998.

12. Laura Koss-Feder, "Out and About," *Marketing News,* May 25, 1998, pp. 1, 20.

13. Linda Grant, "Outmarketing P&G," *Fortune,* January 12, 1998, pp. 150–152.

14. Cliff Edwards, "2 All-beef Patties, etc. Lack Bite in Burger Wars Now?" *The Commercial Appeal,* September 10, 1998, pp. B4, B8.

15. Montrose Sommers and James Barnes, *Fundamentals of Marketing,* 9th Canadian edition (McGraw-Hill Ryerson, 2001), p. 164–167.

16. Chad Kaydo, "Planting the Seeds of Marketing Success," *Sales & Marketing Management,* August 1998, p. 73.

17. Ann Marsh, "Not Your Dad's Hardware Store," *Forbes,* January 26, 1998, p. 45.

18. Carleen Hawn, "General Mills Tests the Limits," *Forbes,* April 6, 1998, **www.forbes.com/forbes/98/0406/610704a.htm**, September 28, 1998.

19. Jim Carroll, "Futures: When Old Partners Become Competitors," *Marketing Magazine,* November 22, 1999.

20. Kaydo, "Planting the Seeds of Marketing Success."

21. Joshua Macht, "The New Market Research," *Inc. Online,* July 1998, p. 86.

22. Lambeth Hochwald, "Are You Smart Enough to Sell Globally?" *Sales & Marketing Management,* July 1998, pp. 52–56.

23. Paula Kephart, "Virtual Testing," *Marketing Tools,* June 1998.

24. Donna J. Yena, *Career Directions,* 2nd ed. (Richard D. Irwin, Inc., 1993).

25. Bill Meyers, "Nostalgia Lines Beetle Shell," *USA Today,* October 19, 1998, p. 10B.

26. Tim Riester, "A Few Well-Placed Questions," *Inc. Online,* Technology Issue no. 3, 1998, p. 108.

27. Gary Strauss, "Starbucks Coffee Headed for Store Shelves," *USA Today,* September 29, 1998, p. 1B.

28. Chad Kaydo, "Riding High," *Sales & Marketing Management,* July 1998, pp. 66–68.

29. *USA Today,* October 21, 1998, p. 7B.

Chapter 13

1. **www.dominos.com**, October 13, 1998.

2. Michael Treacy and Fred Wiersema, *The Discipline of Market Leaders* (Reading, MA: Addison-Wesley Publishing Co., 1995), p. 20.

3. Treacy and Wiersema, *The Discipline of Market Leaders,* p. 21.

4. Marcia Mogelonsky, "Product Overload?" *American Demographics,* August 1998.

5. Nancy Ten Kate, "New and Improved," *American Demographics,* March 1998, **www.demographics.com/publications/ad/98_ad/9803_ad/ad980310.htm**, September 3, 1998.

6. Tia O'Brien, "Benchmark: Encourage Wild Ideas," **www.fastcompany.com/online/02/ideosec.html**, September 18, 1998.

7. Ibid.

8. Mogelonsky, "Product Overload?"

9. Robert McMath, "To Test or Not to Test," *American Demographics,* June 1998, **www.marketingtools.com/publications/ad/98_ad/9806_ad/ad980630.htm**, September 3, 1998.

10. Robert M. McMath, "Don't Bite Off More Than You Can Chew," *American Demographics,* March 1998, **www.marketingtools.com/publications/ad/98_ad/9803_ad/ad980332.htm**, September 3, 1998.

11. Peter Burrows, "Instant Info Is Not Enough," *Business Week,* June 22, 1998, p. 144, and Thomas A. Stewart, "Packaging What You Know," *Fortune,* November 9, 1998, pp. 253–254.

12. Stewart Alsop, "The Dawn of E-Service," *Fortune,* November 9, 1998, p. 243.

13. "Web Site Lets You Set the Price," **www.usatoday.com/life/cyber/tech/ctd480.htm**, September 22, 1998.

14. Roy Furchgott, "Have I Got a Catalog for You," **www.businessweek.com/smallbiz/news/columns/98-06/e3564033.htm**, September 15, 1998.

15. Peter Coy, "You Ain't Seen Nothin' Yet," *Business Week,* June 22, 1998, p. 130.

16. O.C. Ferrell, Michael D. Hartline, George Lucas, and David Luck, *Marketing Strategy* (Fort Worth: The Dryden Press, 1999), p. 103.

17. Justin Bachman, "Computers Turn Truckers' Routes into Information Superhighways," *The Commercial Appeal*, August 26, 1998, pp. B4, B8.
18. Steve Erwin, "Taking Aim at the Big Three," *The Record*, August 28, 2001, p. C6.
19. Dennis Berman, "Can Cyber-Ads Work for Your Company?" *Business Week Online*, September 24, 1998, **www.businessweek.com/smallbiz/news/date/9809/e980924.htm**, September 28, 1998.
20. Ibid.
21. "Infomercials," **www.cftech.com/BrainBank/MARKETING/Infomercial.html**, October 13, 1998.

22. "Success of Infomercials," *USA Today Snapshots*, **www.usatoday.com/snapshot/life/lsnap054.htm**, October 1, 1998.
23. Alison Wellner, "Try It—You'll Like It!" *American Demographics*, August 1998.
24. Ibid.
25. William C. Taylor, "Permission Marketing," *Fast Company*, April–May 1998, p. 208.
26. Ibid.
27. "Xerox to Double '99 Ad Budget...," *Business Wire*, October 7, 1998.
28. The Bureau of Labor Statistics 1998–99 Occupational Outlook Handbook, **www.stats.bls.gov/oco/ocos020.htm#_outlook**, October 15, 1998.

Chapter 14

1. Fara Warner, "Ford Uses Internet to Slash the Costs of Ordinary Tasks," *The Wall Street Journal*, October 13, 1998.
2. **www.infoculture.cbc.ca/archives/theatre/theatre_08111998_liventimplodes.html**; **www.infoculture.cbc.ca/archives/theatre/theatre_01271999_drabinsky.html**; **www.infoculture.cbc.ca/archives/theatre/theatre_08301999_liventdies.html**; **www.infoculture.cbc.ca/archives/theatre/theatre_01131999_livent.html**; and **www.infoculture.cbc.ca/archives/special_coverage/special_coverage_drabinsky_e.htm**.
3. Robert Half, 2001 Accountemps Salary Guide.
4. *Terminology for Accountants*, 4th ed., Canadian Institute of Chartered Accountants.
5. L.S. Rosen, *Accounting: A Decision Approach* (Prentice Hall Canada, 1986).

Chapter 15

1. *Globe and Mail*, "How Many francs for that crisp euro?" January 3, 2002, p. A16; *Globe and Mail*, "ECB declares euro launch a big success?" January 4, 2002, p. B6; *Globe and Mail*, "Adieu franc, ciao lira, hello Europe" January 5, 2002, p. A11; and *Globe and Mail*, "Euro's smooth launch belies rough policy road ahead" January 8, 2002, p. B13.
2. The Bank of Canada, **www.bankofcanada.ca**.
3. Ibid.
4. Christian Caryl, "They Love Our Money," *U.S. News Online*, April 27, 1998.
5. **www.treas.gov/press/releases/pr2462.htm**, December, 8, 1998.
6. Michael James, "Computers Aid Modern-Day Counterfeiting," *The Commercial Appeal*, July 11, 1998, p. A7.
7. The Bank of Canada, **www.bankofcanada.ca**.
8. "Whether at the Mall or Snuggled in for a Winter's Nap, Powerful Software Protects Your Identity; Identity Fraud Fastest Growing Credit Card Crime," *PR Newswire*, December 8, 1998.
9. **www.bankofcanada.ca/en/backgrounders/bg-m2.htm**.
10. **www.bankofcanada.ca/en/bserv.htm**.
11. **www.cdnpay.ca/eng/pub/Intro.to.CPA.ENG.htm**.
12. Ibid.
13. **www.cba.ca**, October 1, 2001.
14. **www.cucentral.ca**.
15. **www.cdic.ca/?id=100**.
16. **www.tv.cbc.ca/national/pgminfo/banks/mergerworld.html**.
17. Annex 1: Banking Merger Review Process, **strategis.ic.gc.ca/SSG/ct01287e.html**.
18. Carleen Hawn, "The Soul of a New Machine," *Forbes*, April 20, 1998, pp. 74–76.
19. **www.interac.org/**.
20. **www.cba.ca/eng/CBA_on_the_Issues/Reports/billc8.cfm**.
21. Canadian Bank Facts, **www.cba.ca**.
22. **www.jobfutures.ca/jobfutures/fos/U820.html**.
23. Melissa Wahl, "Electronic Commerce on Display at Bankers' Conference," **www.chicagotribune.com/business/chicagoinsider/article/0,1051, ART-19716,00.html**, December 6, 1998.

Chapter 16

1. "Rogers cable to issue $300 million in bonds" *Toronto Star*, January 22, 2002, p. C6.
2. *Globe and Mail*, September 1, 2001. p. B9.
3. TSE History, **www.tse.com**.

4. Jeffrey M. Laderman and Geoffrey Smith, "Internet Stocks," *Business Week,* December 14, 1998, pp. 120–122.

5. *Business Sense,* Volume 3, November 2001, p. 18.

6. Standard and Poor at **www.spglobal.com**.

7. **www.neatideas.com/data/data/tse300**.

8. Ibid.

9. Yahoo Finance Historical Quotes, **chart.yahoo.com/d?s=^tse**.

10. Toronto Stock Exchange, **www.tse.com/**.

Did You Know Source

p. 50: KPMG, **www.kpmg.ca**.

p. 119: Joseph Nathan Kane, *Famous First Facts*, 4th edition (New York: The H. W. Wilson Company, 1981), p. 202.

p. 199: "Message Mania," **www.usatoday.com/snapshot/money/msnap016.htm**, March 31, 1999.

p. 218: **www.hersheys.com/totally/product/kisses/**, April 1, 1999.

p. 253: "Why Workers Don't Show Up," *Business Week*, November 16, 1998, p. 8.

p. 272: **www.gm.com/flash_homepage** and **www.microsoft.com/ms.htm**.

p. 304: **www.cocacola.com/co/faqs.html#general** and **www.cocacola.com/gateway.html**. Coca-Cola is a registered trademark of the Coca-Cola Company. Reprinted with permission.

p. 320: "Corporate Profile: 1997 Product Usage Facts," **www.dominos.com/info/97usage.html**, October 14, 1998. Copyright DPI.

p. 353: Robert Half International Hot Jobs Report, 1999 Salary Guide.

p. 384: International Mass Retail Association. Reprinted with permission.

p. 419: **www.usatoday.com/snapshot/moey/msnap019.htm**. Copyright 1999 USA Today, a division of Gannett Company, Inc.

Cyberzone

Part One

1. Cindy Hall and Sam Ward, "What Boss Is Doing on Web," *USA Today Snapshots,* November 2, 1998, p. B1.

2. Adapted from William Pride and O. C. Ferrell, *Marketing: Concepts and Strategies* (Boston: Houghton Mifflin, 2000).

3. Hall and Ward, "What Boss Is Doing on Web."

Part Two

1. James Penhune, "A Quiet Revolution," *Buyers Guide,* Fall 1998, p. 13.

2. GD Sourcing Statistics Pack, **www.gdsourcing.com/StatsPack**.

Part Three

1. Polly Labarre, "Unit of One," *Fast Company,* January 1999, pp. 73–81. Scott Kirsner, "Great Ideas, Fast Growth, No Paper," *Fortune,* December 14, 1998, p. 58. Eryn Brown, "VF Corp. Changes Its Underwear," *Fortune,* December 7, 1998, pp. 115–118.

Part Four

1. "Firms Respond to Jump in Web Job Seekers," HR Briefs, August 10–16, 1998, *The Wall Street Journal* (Careers On-line), **www.public.wsj.com/careers/resources/documents/19980811-kennedy.htm**, September 13, 1998.

2. Judith N. Mottl, "Employers Head to the Web," *Internet Week,* August 10, 1998.

3. Ibid.

4. Ibid.

5. Rivka Tadjer, "Surfing the Web Can Pay Off for Employers," *The Wall Street Journal Interactive Edition,* September 11, 1998.

6. Mottl, "Employers Head to the Web."

7. Rivka Tadjer, "Virtual Employees Are a Mixed Blessing," *The Wall Street Journal Interactive Edition,* September 11, 1998.

8. Stephanie Armour, "E-mail Delivers Legal, Privacy Issues," *USA Today,* November 12, 1998, p. 3B.

Part Five

1. Elizabeth Weise, "America's On Line: 70.5 Million Adults," *USA Today,* August 25, 1998, p. 1D.

2. Robert D. Hof, Gary McWilliams, and Gabrielle Saveri, "The 'Click Here' Economy," *Business Week,* June 22, 1998, p. 122.

3. Heather Green and Seanna Browder, "Cyberspace Winners: How They Did It," *Business Week,* June 22, 1998, p. 160.

4. Green and Browder, "Cyberspace Winners," pp. 154, 156.

5. Ibid., p. 158.

6. Hof, McWilliams, Saveri, "The 'Click Here' Economy," p. 124.

Part Six

1. NFO CF Group News Release, December 19, 2001.

Glossary

A

absolute advantage a monopoly that exists when a country is the only source of an item, the only producer of an item, or the most efficient producer of an item

accountability the principle that employees who accept an assignment and the authority to carry it out are answerable to a superior for the outcome

accounting the recording, measurement, and interpretation of financial information

accounting cycle the four-step procedure of an accounting system: examining source documents, recording transactions in an accounting journal, posting recorded transactions, and preparing financial statements

accounting equation assets equal liabilities plus owners' equity

accounts payable the amount a company owes to suppliers for goods and services purchased with credit

accounts receivable money owed a company by its clients or customers

accrued expenses all unpaid financial obligations incurred by an organization

acquisition the purchase of one company by another, usually by buying its stock

administrative managers those who manage an entire business or a major segment of a business; they are not specialists but coordinate the activities of specialized managers

advertising a paid form of nonpersonal communication transmitted through a mass medium, such as television commercials or magazine advertisements

agency a common business relationship created when one person acts on behalf of another and under that person's control

agent acts on behalf of the principal to accomplish the task

analytical skills the ability to identify relevant issues, recognize their importance, understand the relationships between them, and perceive the underlying causes of a situation

arbitration settlement of a labour/management dispute by a third party whose solution is legally binding and enforceable

asset utilization ratios ratios that measure how well a firm uses its assets to generate each $1 of sales

assets a firm's economic resources, or items of value that it owns, such as cash, inventory, land, equipment, buildings, and other tangible and intangible things

attitude knowledge and positive or negative feelings about something

automated banking machine (ABM) the most familiar form of electronic banking, which dispenses cash, accepts deposits, and allows balance inquiries and cash transfers from one account to another

B

balance of payments the difference between the flow of money into and out of a country

balance of trade the difference in value between a nation's exports and its imports

balance sheet a "snapshot" of an organization's financial position at a given moment

bankruptcy legal insolvency

behaviour modification changing behaviour and encouraging appropriate actions by relating the consequences of behaviour to the behaviour itself

benefits nonfinancial forms of compensation provided to employees, such as pension plans, health insurance, paid vacation and holidays, and the like

board of directors a group of individuals, elected by the shareholders to oversee the general operation of the corporation, who set the corporation's long-range objectives

bonds debt instruments that larger companies sell to raise long-term funds

459

bonuses monetary rewards offered by companies for exceptional performance as incentives to further increase productivity

boycott an attempt to keep people from purchasing the products of a company

branding the process of naming and identifying products

breach of contract the failure or refusal of a party to a contract to live up to his or her promises

bribes payments, gifts, or special favours intended to influence the outcome of a decision

brokerage firms firms that buy and sell stocks, bonds, and other securities for their customers and provide other financial services

budget an internal financial plan that forecasts expenses and income over a set period of time

budget deficit the condition in which a nation spends more than it takes in from taxes

business individuals or organizations who try to earn a profit by providing products that satisfy people's needs

business ethics principles and standards that determine acceptable conduct in business

business law the rules and regulations that govern the conduct of business

business plan a precise statement of the rationale for a business and a step-by-step explanation of how it will achieve its goals

buying behaviour the decision processes and actions of people who purchase and use products

C

Canada Deposit Insurance Corporation a federal Crown corporation providing deposit insurance for deposits up to $60,000 per deposit at member institutions

capacity the maximum load that an organizational unit can carry or operate

capital budgeting the process of analyzing the needs of the business and selecting the assets that will maximize its value

capitalism, or free enterprise an economic system in which individuals own and operate the majority of businesses that provide goods and services

cartel a group of firms or nations that agrees to act as a monopoly and not compete with each other, in order to generate a competitive advantage in world markets

cash flow the movement of money through an organization over a daily, weekly, monthly, or yearly basis

centralized organization a structure in which authority is concentrated at the top, and very little decision-making authority is delegated to lower levels

certificate of incorporation a legal document that the province or federal government issues to a company based on information the company provides in the articles of incorporation

certified general accountant (CGA) a professional accountant who has completed all CGA courses and satisfied all other requirements for membership in the Certified General Accountants Association of Canada

certified management accountant (CMA) a professional accountant who has completed the Society of Management Accountants' professional program and satisfied all other requirements for admission to the Society of Management Accountants

chartered accountant (CA) a professional accountant who has passed the CICA Uniform Final Exams of the Institute of Chartered Accountants and satisfied all the other requirements for membership in the CICA

chartered bank a federally regulated financial institution chartered under the Bank Act

chequing account money stored in an account at a bank or other financial institution that can be withdrawn without advance notice; also called a demand deposit

classical theory of motivation theory suggesting that money is the sole motivator for workers

codes of ethics formalized rules and standards that describe what a company expects of its employees

collective bargaining the negotiation process through which management and unions reach an agreement about compensation, working hours, and working conditions for the bargaining unit

commercial paper a written promise from one company to another to pay a specific amount of money

commercialization the full introduction of a complete marketing strategy and the launch of the product for commercial success

commission an incentive system that pays a fixed amount or a percentage of the employee's sales

committee a permanent, formal group that performs a specific task

communism first described by Karl Marx as a society in which the people, without regard to class, own all the nation's resources

common stock stock whose owners have voting rights in the corporation, yet do not receive preferential treatment regarding dividends

comparative advantage the basis of most international trade, when a country specializes in products that it can supply more efficiently or at a lower cost than it can produce other items

competition the rivalry among businesses for consumers' dollars

compressed work week a four-day (or shorter) period during which an employee works 40 hours

computer-assisted design (CAD) the design of components, products, and processes on computers instead of on paper

computer-assisted manufacturing (CAM) manufacturing that employs specialized computer systems to actually guide and control the transformation processes

computer-integrated manufacturing (CIM) a complete system that designs products, manages machines and materials, and controls the operations function

concentration approach a market segmentation approach whereby a company develops one marketing strategy for a single market segment

conceptual skills the ability to think in abstract terms and to see how parts fit together to form the whole

conciliation a method of outside resolution of labour and management differences in which a third party is brought in to keep the two sides talking

consumer products products intended for household or family use

consumerism the activities that independent individuals, groups, and organizations undertake to protect their rights as consumers

continuous manufacturing organizations companies that use continuously running assembly lines, creating products with many similar characteristics

contract manufacturing the hiring of a foreign company to produce a specified volume of the initiating company's product to specification; the final product carries the domestic firm's name

contract a mutual agreement between two or more parties that can be enforced in a court if one party chooses not to comply with the terms

controlling the process of evaluating and correcting activities to keep the organization on course

cooperative (or co-op) an organization composed of individuals or small businesses that have banded together to reap the benefits of belonging to a larger organization

corporation a legal entity, created by the state, whose assets and liabilities are separate from its owners

cost of goods sold the amount of money a firm spent to buy or produce the products it sold during the period to which the income statement applies

countertrade agreements foreign trade agreements that involve bartering products for other products instead of for currency

court of appeal a court that deals solely with appeals relating to the interpretation of law

court of original jurisdiction a court that determines the facts of a case, decides which laws pertain, and applies these laws to resolve the dispute

credit cards means of access to preapproved lines of credit granted by a bank or company

credit union/caisse populaire a cooperative association that provides members with a full range of banking services and is operated for the benefit of the members

Credit Union Central of Canada the national trade association and central finance facility for the 2,440 credit unions and affiliated caisses populaires in Canada

crisis management or contingency planning an element in planning that deals with potential disasters such as product tampering, oil spills, fire, earthquake, computer virus, or airplane crash

Crown corporations corporations owned and operated by the federal, provincial, or local government

culture the integrated, accepted pattern of human behaviour, including thought, speech, beliefs, actions, and artifacts

current assets short-term resources such as cash, investments, accounts receivable, and inventory

current liabilities short-term debts such as accounts payable, accrued salaries, accrued taxes, and short-term bank loans

current ratio current assets divided by current liabilities

customer departmentalization the arrangement of jobs around the needs of various types of customers, such as commercial banking versus consumer banking services

customization making products to meet a particular customer's needs or wants

D

debit card a card that looks like a credit card but works like a cheque; using it results in a direct, immediate, electronic payment from the cardholder's chequing account to a merchant or third party

debt to total assets ratio a ratio indicating how much of the firm is financed by debt and how much by owners' equity

debt utilization ratios ratios that measure how much debt an organization is using relative to other sources of capital, such as owners' equity

deceit a tort that arises where a party suffers damage by acting upon a false representation made by a party with the intention of deceiving the other

decentralized organization an organization in which decision-making authority is delegated as far down the chain of command as possible

delegation of authority giving employees not only tasks, but also the power to make commitments, use resources, and take whatever actions are necessary to carry out those tasks

demand the number of goods and services that consumers are willing to buy at different prices at a specific time

departmentalization the grouping of jobs into working units usually called departments, units, groups, or divisions

depression a condition of the economy in which unemployment is very high, consumer spending is low, and business output is sharply reduced

development training that augments the skills and knowledge of managers and professionals

direct investment the ownership of overseas facilities

directing motivating and leading employees to achieve organizational objectives

discounts temporary price reductions, often employed to boost sales

distribution making products available to customers in the quantities desired

diversity the participation of different ages, genders, races, ethnicities, nationalities, and abilities in the workplace

dividends profits of a corporation that are distributed in the form of cash payments to shareholders

dividends per share the actual cash received for each share owned

double-entry bookkeeping a system of recording and classifying business transactions that maintains the balance of the accounting equation

downsizing the elimination of significant numbers of employees from an organization in order to reduce costs

dumping the act of a country or business selling products at less than what it costs to produce them

E

earnings per share net income or profit divided by the number of stock shares outstanding

economic contraction a slowdown of the economy characterized by a decline in spending and during which businesses cut back on production and lay off workers

economic expansion the situation that occurs when an economy is growing and people are spending more money; their purchases stimulate the production of goods and services, which in turn stimulates employment

economic order quantity (EOQ) model a model that identifies the optimum number of items to order to minimize the costs of managing (ordering, storing, and using) them

economic system a description of how a particular society distributes its resources to produce goods and services

economics the study of how resources are distributed for the production of goods and services within a social system

electronic funds transfer (EFT) any movement of funds by means of an electronic terminal, telephone, computer, or magnetic tape

employment equity programs programs developed by employers to undo past employment discrimination or to ensure equal employment opportunity in the future; similar to affirmative action programs in the US

embargo a prohibition on trade in a particular product

enterprise resource planning (ERP) the integration of all departments and functions of a company into one computer system

entrepreneur an individual who risks his or her wealth, time, and effort to develop for profit an innovative product or way of doing something

entrepreneurship the process of creating and managing a business to achieve desired objectives

equilibrium price the price at which the number of products that businesses are willing to supply equals the amount of products that consumers are willing to buy at a specific point in time

equity theory an assumption that how much people are willing to contribute to an organization depends on their assessment of the fairness, or equity, of the rewards they will receive in exchange

esteem needs the need for respect—both self-respect and respect from others

ethical issue an identifiable problem, situation, or opportunity that requires a person to choose from among several actions that may be evaluated as right or wrong, ethical or unethical

Eurodollar market a market for trading US dollars in foreign countries

European Union (EU) a union of European nations established in 1958 to promote trade among its members; one of the largest single markets today

exchange the act of giving up one thing (money, credit, labour, goods) in return for something else (goods, services, or ideas)

exchange controls regulations that restrict the amount of currency that can be bought or sold

exchange rate the ratio at which one nation's currency can be exchanged for another nation's currency or for gold

exclusive distribution the awarding by a manufacturer to an intermediary of the sole right to sell a product in a defined geographic territory

expectancy theory the assumption that motivation depends not only on how much a person wants something but also on how likely he or she is to get it

expenses the costs incurred in the day-to-day operations of an organization

exporting the sale of goods and services to foreign markets

F

factor a finance company to whom businesses sell their accounts receivable—usually for a percentage of the total face value

finance the study of money: how it's made, how it's lost, and why

financial managers those who deal with an organization's financial resources

financial resources the funds used to acquire the natural and human resources needed to provide products; also called capital

first-line managers those who supervise both workers and the daily operations of an organization

fixed-position layout a layout that brings all resources required to create the product to a central location

flexible manufacturing the direction of machinery by computers to adapt to different versions of similar operations

flextime a program that allows employees to choose their starting and ending times, provided that they are at work during a specified core period

floating-rate bonds bonds with interest rates that change with current interest rates otherwise available in the economy

form utility utility created through the production process rather than through marketing activities

franchise a licence to sell another's products or to use another's name in business, or both

franchisee the purchaser of a franchise

franchisor the company that sells a franchise

franchising a form of licensing in which a company—the franchisor—agrees to provide a franchisee a name, logo, methods of operation, advertising, products, and other elements associated with a franchisor's business, in return for a financial commitment and the agreement to conduct business in accordance with the franchisor's standard of operations

fraudulent misrepresentation a false statement of fact by a person who knows, or should know, that it is false, and is made with the intention of deceiving the other

free-market system pure capitalism, in which all economic decisions are made without government intervention

functional departmentalization the grouping of jobs that perform similar functional activities, such as finance, manufacturing, marketing, and human resources

G

General Agreement on Tariffs and Trade (GATT) a trade agreement, originally signed by 23 nations in 1947, that provides a forum for tariff negotiations and a place where international trade problems can be discussed and resolved

general ledger a book or computer file with separate sections for each account

general partnership a partnership that involves a complete sharing in both the management and the liability of the business

generic products products with no brand name that often come in white packages and carry only their generic name

geographical departmentalization the grouping of jobs according to geographic location, such as province, region, country, or continent

global strategy (globalization) a strategy that involves standardizing products (and, as much as possible, their promotion and distribution) for the whole world, as if it were a single entity

grapevine an informal channel of communication, separate from management's formal, official communication channels

gross domestic product (GDP) the sum of all goods and services produced in a country during a year

gross margin revenues minus the cost of goods sold required to generate the revenues

guaranteed investment certificate (GIC) a certificate of deposit with a financial institution, at a fixed rate of interest for a fixed term

group two or more individuals who communicate with one another, share a common identity, and have a common goal

H

holding company a corporation that controls one or more other corporations through ownership of their common stock

human relations skills the ability to deal with people, both inside and outside the organization

human relations the study of the behaviour of individuals and groups in organizational settings

human resources the physical and mental abilities that people use to produce goods and services; also called labour

human resources management (HRM) all the activities involved in determining an organization's human resources needs, as well as acquiring, training, and compensating people to fill those needs

human resources managers those who handle the staffing function and deal with employees in a formalized manner

hygiene factors aspects of Herzberg's theory of motivation that focus on the work setting and not the content of the work; these aspects include adequate wages, comfortable and safe working conditions, fair company policies, and job security

I

import tariff a tax levied by a nation on goods imported into the country

importing the purchase of goods and services from foreign sources

income statement a financial report that shows an organization's profitability over a period of time—month, quarter, or year

industrial products products that are used directly or indirectly in the operation or manufacturing processes of businesses

inflation a condition characterized by a continuing rise in prices

infrastructure the physical facilities that support a country's economic activities, such as railroads, highways, ports, airfields, utilities and power plants, schools, hospitals, communication systems, and commercial distribution systems

inputs the resources—such as labour, money, materials, and energy—that are converted into outputs

insolvency the inability to pay debts as they become due under the normal course of business

insurance companies businesses that protect their clients against financial losses from certain specified risks (death, accident, and theft, for example)

intangible component that part of the product lacking physical existence; often a service component or contractual obligation such as a warranty

integrated marketing communications coordinating the promotion mix elements and synchronizing promotion as a unified effort

intellectual property property that is generated by a person's creative activities

intensive distribution a form of market coverage whereby a product is made available in as many outlets as possible

intermittent organizations organizations that deal with products of a lesser magnitude than do project organizations; their products are not necessarily unique but possess a significant number of differences

international business the buying, selling, and trading of goods and services across national boundaries

International Monetary Fund (IMF) organization established in 1947 to promote trade among member nations by eliminating trade barriers and fostering financial cooperation

intrapreneurs individuals in large firms who take responsibility for the development of innovations within the organizations

inventory all raw materials, components, completed or partially completed products, and pieces of equipment a firm uses

inventory control the process of determining how many supplies and goods are needed and keeping track of quantities on hand, where each item is, and who is responsible for it

inventory turnover sales divided by total inventory

investment banking the sale of stocks and bonds for corporations

ISO 9000 a series of quality assurance standards designed by the International Organization for Standardization (ISO) to ensure consistent product quality under many conditions

J

job analysis the determination, through observation and study, of pertinent information about a job—including specific tasks and necessary abilities, knowledge, and skills

job description a formal, written explanation of a specific job, usually including job title, tasks, relationship with other jobs, physical and mental skills required, duties, responsibilities, and working conditions

job enlargement the addition of more tasks to a job instead of treating each task as separate

job enrichment the incorporation of motivational factors, such as opportunity for achievement, recognition, responsibility, and advancement, into a job

job rotation movement of employees from one job to another in an effort to relieve the boredom often associated with job specialization

job sharing performance of one full-time job by two people on part-time hours

job specification a description of the qualifications necessary for a specific job, in terms of education, experience, and personal and physical characteristics

joint venture a partnership established for a specific project or for a limited time; the sharing of the costs and operation of a business between a foreign company and a local partner

journal a time-ordered list of account transactions

junk bonds a special type of high-interest-rate bond that carries higher inherent risks

jurisdiction the legal power of a court, through a judge, to interpret and apply the law and make a binding decision in a particular case

just-in-time (JIT) inventory management a technique using smaller quantities of materials that arrive "just in time" for use in the transformation process and therefore require less storage space and other inventory management expense

L

labelling the presentation of important information on a package

labour contract the formal, written document that spells out the relationship between the union and management for a specified period of time—usually two or three years

labour unions employee organizations formed to deal with employers for achieving better pay, hours, and working conditions

lawsuits dispute resolution procedures in which one individual or organization takes another to court

leadership the ability to influence employees to work toward organizational goals

learning changes in a person's behaviour based on information and experience

leveraged buyout (LBO) a purchase in which a group of investors borrows money from banks and other institutions to acquire a company (or a division of one), using the assets of the purchased company to guarantee repayment of the loan

liabilities debts that a firm owes to others

licensing a trade agreement in which one company—the licensor—allows another company—the licensee—to use its company name, products, patents, brands, trademarks, raw materials, and/or production processes in exchange for a fee or royalty

limited partnership a business organization that has at least one general partner, who assumes unlimited liability, and at least one limited partner, whose liability is limited to his or her investment in the business

line of credit an arrangement by which a bank agrees to lend a specified amount of money to an organization upon request

line structure the simplest organizational structure in which direct lines of authority extend from the top manager to the lowest level of the organization

line-and-staff structure a structure having a traditional line relationship between superiors and subordinates and also specialized managers—called staff managers—who are available to assist line managers

liquidity ratios ratios that measure the speed with which a company can turn its assets into cash to meet short-term debt

lockbox an address, usually a chartered bank, at which a company receives payments in order to speed collections from customers

lockout management's version of a strike, wherein a work site is closed so that employees cannot go to work

logistics all activities involved in obtaining and managing raw materials and component parts, managing finished products, packaging them, and getting them to customers

long-term (fixed) assets production facilities (plants), offices, and equipment—all of which are expected to last for many years

long-term liabilities debts that will be repaid over a number of years, such as long-term loans and bond issues

M

management a process designed to achieve an organization's objectives by using its resources effectively and efficiently in a changing environment

management by objectives (MBO) a planning process in which a manager and a subordinate confer, set, and agree to goals for the subordinate to achieve

managerial accounting the internal use of accounting statements by managers in planning and directing the organization's activities

managers those individuals in organizations who make decisions about the use of resources and who are concerned with planning, organizing, leading, and controlling the organization's activities to reach its objectives

manufacturer brands brands initiated and owned by the manufacturer to identify products from the point of production to the point of purchase

manufacturing the activities and processes used in making tangible products; also called production

market a group of people who have a need, purchasing power, and the desire and authority to spend money on goods, services, and ideas

market segment a collection of individuals, groups, or organizations who share one or more characteristics and thus have relatively similar product needs and desires

market segmentation a strategy whereby a firm divides the total market into groups of people who have relatively similar product needs

marketable securities temporary investment of "extra" cash by organizations for up to one year in Treasury bills, GICs, commercial paper, or Eurodollar loans or shares

marketing a group of activities designed to expedite transactions by creating, distributing, pricing, and promoting goods, services, and ideas

marketing channel a group of organizations that moves products from their producer to customers; also channel of distribution

marketing concept the idea that an organization should try to satisfy customers' needs through coordinated activities that also allow it to achieve its own goals

marketing information system a framework for accessing information about customers from sources both inside and outside the organization

marketing managers those who are responsible for planning, pricing, and promoting products and making them available to customers

marketing mix the four marketing activities—product, price, promotion, and distribution—that the firm can control to achieve specific goals within a dynamic marketing environment

marketing research a systematic, objective process of getting information about potential customers to guide marketing decisions

marketing strategy a plan of action for developing, pricing, distributing, and promoting products that meet the needs of specific customers

Maslow's hierarchy a theory that arranges the five basic needs of people—physiological, security, social, esteem, and self-actualization—into the order in which people strive to satisfy them

material-requirements planning (MRP) a planning system that schedules the precise quantity of materials needed to make the product

materials handling the physical handling and movement of products in warehousing and transportation

matrix structure a structure that sets up teams from different departments, thereby creating two or more intersecting lines of authority; also called a project-management structure

mediation a form of negotiation to resolve a dispute by bringing in one or more third-party mediators to help reach a settlement; a method of outside resolution of labour and management differences in which the third party's role is to suggest or propose a solution to the problem

merger the combination of two companies (usually corporations) to form a new company

middle managers those members of an organization responsible for the tactical planning that implements the general guidelines established by top management

mission the statement of an organization's fundamental purpose and basic philosophy

mixed economies economies made up of elements from more than one economic system

modular design the creation of an item in self-contained units, or modules, that can be combined or interchanged to create different products

monetary policy a policy that seeks to improve the performance of the economy by regulating money supply and credit

money anything generally accepted in exchange for goods and services

money market accounts accounts that offer higher interest rates than standard bank rates but with greater restrictions

monopolistic competition the market structure that exists when there are fewer businesses than in a pure-competition environment and the differences among the goods they sell are small

monopoly the market structure that exists when there is only one business providing a product in a given market

morale an employee's attitude toward his or her job, employer, and colleagues

motivation an inner drive that directs a person's behaviour toward goals

motivational factors aspects of Herzberg's theory of motivation that focus on the content of the work itself; these aspects include achievement, recognition, involvement, responsibility, and advancement

multidivisional structure a structure that organizes departments into larger groups called divisions

multinational corporation (MNC) a corporation that operates on a worldwide scale, without significant ties to any one nation or region

multinational strategy a plan, used by international companies, that involves customizing products, promotion, and distribution according to cultural, technological, regional, and national differences

multisegment approach a market segmentation approach whereby the marketer aims its efforts at two or more segments, developing a marketing strategy for each

mutual fund an investment company that pools individual investor dollars and invests them in large numbers of well-diversified securities

N

natural resources land, forests, minerals, water, and other things that are not made by people

near money assets that are very easily turned into cash but which cannot be used directly as a medium of exchange like paper money or cheques

net income the total profit (or loss) after all expenses including taxes have been deducted from revenue; also called net earnings

networking the building of relationships and sharing of information with colleagues who can help managers achieve the items on their agendas

nonprofit corporations corporations that focus on providing a service rather than earning a profit but are not owned by a government entity

nonprofit organizations organizations that may provide goods or services but do not have the fundamental purpose of earning profits

North American Free Trade Agreement (NAFTA) agreement that eliminates most tariffs and trade restrictions on agricultural and manufactured products to encourage trade among Canada, the US, and Mexico

O

oligopoly the market structure that exists when there are very few businesses selling a product

open market operations discretionary Bank of Canada intervention in the domestic securities market

operational plans very short-term plans that specify what actions individuals, work groups, or departments need to accomplish in order to achieve the tactical plan and ultimately the strategic plan

operations the activities and processes used in making both tangible and intangible products

operations management (OM) the development and administration of the activities involved in transforming resources into goods and services

organizational chart a visual display of the organizational structure, lines of authority (chain of command), staff relationships, permanent committee arrangements, and lines of communication

organizational culture the firm's shared values, beliefs, traditions, philosophies, rules, and heroes

organizational layers the levels of management in an organization

organized exchanges central locations where investors buy and sell securities

organizing the structuring of resources and activities to accomplish objectives in an efficient and effective manner

orientation familiarizing newly hired employees with fellow workers, company procedures, and the physical properties of the company

outputs the goods, services, and ideas that result from the conversion of inputs

over-the-counter (OTC) market a network of dealers all over the country linked by computers, telephones, and Teletype machines

owners' equity equals assets minus liabilities and reflects historical values

ownership utility transference of ownership of a product to the buyer

P

packaging the external container that holds and describes the product

partnership an association of two or more persons who carry on as co-owners of a business for profit

partnership agreements legal documents that set forth the basic agreement between partners

payout ratio dividends per share divided by earnings per share

penetration price a low price designed to help a product enter the market and gain market share rapidly

pension funds managed investment pools set aside by individuals, corporations, unions, and some nonprofit organizations to provide retirement income for members

per share data data used by investors to compare the performance of one company with another on an equal, per share basis

perception the process by which a person selects, organizes, and interprets information received from his or her senses

personal property all property other than real property

personal selling direct, two-way communication with buyers and potential buyers

personality the organization of an individual's distinguishing character traits, attitudes, or habits

physical distribution all the activities necessary to move products from producers to customers—inventory control, transportation, warehousing, and material handling

physiological needs the most basic human needs to be satisfied—water, food, shelter, and clothing

picketing a public protest against management practices that involves union members marching and carrying anti-management signs at the employer's plant

place utility making the product available where the buyer wishes to buy it

plagiarism the act of taking someone else's work and presenting it as your own without mentioning the source

planning the process of determining the organization's objectives and deciding how to accomplish them; the first function of management

point-of-sale (POS) systems systems that allow merchants to withdraw money directly from a customer's bank account the moment a purchase is made

preferred stock a special type of stock whose owners, though not generally having a say in running the company, have a claim to profits before other shareholders do

price a value placed on an object exchanged between a buyer and a seller

price skimming charging the highest possible price that buyers who want the product will pay

primary data marketing information that is observed, recorded, or collected directly from respondents

primary market the market where firms raise financial capital

prime rate the interest rate that commercial banks charge their best customers (usually large corporations) for short-term loans

principal in an agency relationship, the party who wishes to have a specific task accomplished

private accountants accountants employed by large corporations, government agencies, and other organizations to prepare and analyze their financial statements

private corporation a corporation owned by just one or a few people who are closely involved in managing the business

private distributor brands brands, which may cost less than manufacturer brands, that are owned and controlled by a wholesaler or retailer

process layout a layout that organizes the transformation process into departments that group related processes

product a good or service with tangible and intangible characteristics that provide satisfaction and benefits

product departmentalization the organization of jobs in relation to the products of the firm

product-development teams a specific type of project team formed to devise, design, and implement a new product

product layout a layout requiring that production be broken down into relatively simple tasks assigned to workers, who are usually positioned along an assembly line

product liability businesses' legal responsibility for any negligence in the design, production, sale, and consumption of products

product line a group of closely related products that are treated as a unit because of similar marketing strategy, production, or end-use considerations

product mix all the products offered by an organization

production the activities and processes used in making tangible products; also called manufacturing

production and operations managers those who develop and administer the activities involved in transforming resources into goods, services, and ideas ready for the marketplace

profit the difference between what it costs to make and sell a product and what a customer pays for it

profit margin net income divided by sales

profit sharing a form of compensation whereby a percentage of company profits is distributed to the employees whose work helped to generate them

profitability ratios ratios that measure the amount of operating income or net income an organization is able to generate relative to its assets, owners' equity, and sales

project organization a company using a fixed-position layout because it is typically involved in large, complex projects such as construction or exploration

project teams groups similar to task forces which normally run their operation and have total control of a specific work project

promotion a persuasive form of communication that attempts to expedite a marketing exchange by influencing individuals, groups, and organizations to accept goods, services, and ideas; an advancement to a higher-level job with increased authority, responsibility, and pay

promotional positioning the use of promotion to create and maintain an image of a product in buyers' minds

psychological pricing encouraging purchases based on emotional rather than rational responses to the price

public accountant an independent professional who provides accounting services ranging from the preparation and filing of individual tax returns to complex audits of corporate financial records

public corporation a corporation whose stock anyone may buy, sell, or trade

publicity nonpersonal communication transmitted through the mass media but not paid for directly by the firm

pull strategy the use of promotion to create consumer demand for a product so that consumers exert pressure on marketing channel members to make it available

purchasing the buying of all the materials needed by the organization; also called procurement

pure competition the market structure that exists when there are many small businesses selling one standardized product

push strategy an attempt to motivate intermediaries to push the product down to their customers

Q

quality the degree to which a good, service, or idea meets the demands and requirements of customers

quality control the processes an organization uses to maintain its established quality standards

quality-assurance teams (or quality circles) small groups of workers brought together from throughout the organization to solve specific quality, productivity, or service problems

quick ratio (acid test) a stringent measure of liquidity that eliminates inventory

quota a restriction on the number of units of a particular product that can be imported into a country

R

ratio analysis calculations that measure an organization's financial health

real property real estate and everything permanently attached to it

receivables turnover sales divided by accounts receivable

recession a decline in production, employment, and income

recruiting forming a pool of qualified applicants from which management can select employees

reference groups groups with whom buyers identify and whose values or attitudes they adopt

responsibility the obligation, placed on employees through delegation, to perform assigned tasks satisfactorily and be held accountable for the proper execution of work

retailers intermediaries who buy products from manufacturers (or other intermediaries) and sell them to consumers for home and household use rather than for resale or for use in producing other products

retained earnings earnings after expenses and taxes that are reinvested in the assets of the firm and belong to the owners in the form of equity

return on assets net income divided by assets

return on equity net income divided by owners' equity; also called return on investment (ROI)

revenue the total amount of money received from the sale of goods or services, as well as from related business activities

routing the sequence of operations through which the product must pass

S

salary a financial reward calculated on a weekly, monthly, or annual basis

sales promotion direct inducements offering added value or some other incentive for buyers to enter into an exchange

savings account an account with funds that usually cannot be withdrawn without advance notice; also known as a time deposit

scheduling the assignment of required tasks that is given to departments or even specific machines, workers, or teams

secondary data information that is compiled inside or outside an organization for some purpose other than changing the current situation

secondary markets stock exchanges and over-the-counter markets where investors can trade their securities with others

secured bonds bonds that are backed by specific collateral that must be forfeited in the event that the issuing firm defaults

secured loans loans backed by collateral that the bank can claim if the borrowers do not repay them

securities markets the mechanism for buying and selling securities (stocks and bonds) for both corporations and governments

security needs the need to protect oneself from physical and economic harm

selection the process of collecting information about applicants and using that information to make hiring decisions

selective distribution a form of market coverage whereby only a small number of all available outlets are used to expose products

self-actualization needs the need to be the best one can be; at the top of Maslow's hierarchy

self-directed work team (SDWT) a group of employees responsible for an entire work process or segment that delivers a product to an internal or external customer

separations employment changes involving resignation, retirement, termination, or layoff

serial bonds a sequence of small bond issues of progressively longer maturity

small business any independently owned and operated business that is not dominant in its competitive area and does not employ more than 500 people

social classes a ranking of people into higher or lower positions of respect

social needs the need for love, companionship, and friendship—the desire for acceptance by others

social roles a set of expectations for individuals based on some position they occupy

socialism an economic system in which the government owns and operates basic industries but individuals own most businesses

sole proprietorships businesses owned and operated by one individual; the most common form of business organization in Canada

span of management the number of subordinates who report to a particular manager

specialization the division of labour into small, specific tasks and the assignment of employees to do a single task

staffing the hiring of people to carry out the work of the organization

standardization the making of identical, interchangeable components or products

statistical process control a system in which management collects and analyzes information about the production process to pinpoint quality problems in the production system

stock shares of a corporation that may be bought or sold

strategic alliance a partnership formed to create competitive advantage on a worldwide basis

strategic plans those plans that establish the long-range objectives and overall strategy or course of action by which a firm fulfills its mission

strikebreakers people hired by management to replace striking employees; called "scabs" by striking union members

strikes employee walkouts; one of the most effective weapons labour has

structure the arrangement or relationship of positions within an organization

subsidiary corporation a corporation the majority of whose stock is owned by another corporation (known as the parent company)

supply the number of products—goods and services—that businesses are willing to sell at different prices at a specific time

supply chain management long-term partnerships among marketing channel members working together to reduce costs, waste, and unnecessary movement in the entire marketing channel in order to satisfy customers

T

tactical plans short-range plans designed to implement the activities and objectives specified in the strategic plan

tangible component that part of the product having physical existence; it can be felt

target market a specific group of consumers on whose needs and wants a company focuses its marketing efforts

task force a temporary group of employees responsible for bringing about a particular change

team a small group whose members have complementary skills; a common purpose, goals, and approach; and hold themselves mutually accountable

technical expertise the specialized knowledge and training needed to perform jobs that are related to particular areas of management

test marketing a trial minilaunch of a product in limited areas that represent the potential market

Theory X McGregor's traditional view of management whereby it is assumed that workers generally dislike work and must be forced to do their jobs

Theory Y McGregor's humanistic view of management whereby it is assumed that workers like to work and that under proper conditions employees will seek out responsibility in an attempt to satisfy their social, esteem, and self-actualization needs

Theory Z a management philosophy that stresses employee participation in all aspects of company decision making

time utility making the product available when customers wish to purchase it

times interest earned ratio operating income divided by interest expense

top managers the president and other top executives of a business, such as the chief executive officer (CEO), chief financial officer (CFO), and chief operations officer (COO), who have overall responsibility for the organization

tort a private or civil wrong other than breach of contract

total asset turnover sales divided by total assets

total-market approach an approach whereby a firm tries to appeal to everyone and assumes that all buyers have similar needs

total quality management (TQM) philosophy and set of principles that provide a foundation for the continuous improvement of an enterprise

trademark a brand that is registered with the Trade Marks Office and is thus legally protected from use by any other firm

trade surplus a nation's positive balance of trade, which exists when that country imports less than it exports

trading company a firm that buys goods in one country and sells them to buyers in another country

training teaching employees to do specific job tasks through either classroom development or on-the-job experience

transaction balances cash kept on hand by a firm to pay normal daily expenses, such as employee wages and bills for supplies and utilities

transfer a move to another job within the company at essentially the same level and wage

transportation the shipment of products to buyers

Treasury bills (T-bills) short-term debt obligations issued by the Bank of Canada to raise money for the federal government

trust company a corporation that functions as a trustee and usually also provides banking services

U

undercapitalization the lack of funds to operate a business normally

unemployment the condition in which a percentage of the population wants to work but is unable to find jobs

unsecured bonds debentures, or bonds, that are not backed by specific collateral

unsecured loans loans backed only by the borrowers' good reputation and previous credit rating

utility a product's ability to satisfy human needs and wants

V

venture capitalists persons or organizations that agree to provide some funds for a new business in exchange for an ownership interest or stock

W

wage/salary survey a study that tells a company how much compensation comparable firms are paying for specific jobs that the firms have in common

wages financial rewards based on the number of hours the employee works or the level of output achieved

warehousing the design and operation of facilities to receive, store, and ship products

whistleblowing the act of an employee exposing an employer's wrongdoing to outsiders, such as the media or government regulatory agencies

wholesalers intermediaries who buy from producers or from other wholesalers and sell to retailers

working capital management the managing of short-term assets and liabilities

World Bank an organization established by the industrialized nations in 1946 to loan money to underdeveloped and developing countries; formally known as the International Bank for Reconstruction and Development

World Trade Organization (WTO) international organization that deals with the global rules of trade between nations

Name Index

Subject Index

477

URL Index